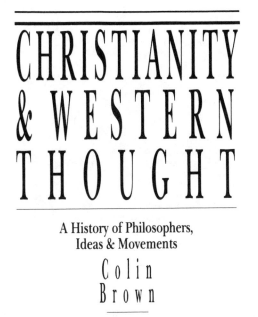

CHRISTIANITY & WESTERN THOUGHT

A History of Philosophers,
Ideas & Movements

Colin
Brown

VOLUME 1

FROM THE ANCIENT WORLD TO THE AGE OF ENLIGHTENMENT

INTERVARSITY PRESS
DOWNERS GROVE, ILLINOIS 60515

InterVarsity Press is the book-publishing division of InterVarsity Christian Fellowship, a student movement active on campus at hundreds of universities, colleges and schools of nursing. For information about local and regional activities, write Public Relations Dept., InterVarsity Christian Fellowship, 6400 Schroeder Rd., P.O. Box 7895, Madison, WI 53707-7895.

Distributed in Canada through InterVarsity Press, 860 Denison St., Unit 3, Markham, Ontario L3R 4H1, Canada.

ISBN 0-8308-1752-2

Printed in the United States of America ∞

Library of Congress Cataloging-in-Publication Data

Brown, Colin, 1932-
    Christianity and western thought Vol. 1/Colin Brown.
       p.   cm.
    Includes bibliographical references.
    ISBN 0-8308-1752-2
    1. Christianity—Philosophy.   2. Faith and reason—History of doctrines.   3. Philosophy—History.   I. Title.
    BR100.B6483   1990   *89-48564*
                                                          CIP

16   15   14   13   12   11   10   9   8   7

09   08   07   06   05

Introduction

"What is real?" "What is true?" "How do we know?" Time and again people have found these questions harder to answer than they are to ask. In one of his more whimsical moments C. S. Lewis imagined a modern materialist at the end of the world. He envisaged a scene like that described in Revelation with the heavens rolled up, the great white throne appearing and the materialist himself going through the sensations of being hurled into the Lake of Fire. The materialist, Lewis suggested, would regard the whole experience as an illusion, preferring rather to seek explanations in psychoanalysis and cerebral pathology. For seeing is not believing, and complex questions cannot be settled simply by appealing to experience. Lewis went on to argue: "Experience by itself proves nothing. If a man doubts whether he is dreaming or waking, no experiment can solve his doubt, since every experiment may itself be part of the dream. Experience proves this, or that, or nothing, according to the preconceptions we bring to it."[1]

Whether we fully agree with Lewis or not, there can be no doubt that what we see is always filtered through the twin lenses of our experience and our understanding. This applies to the things of everyday life. I can recognize a rose bush because I have seen other rose bushes. I know that the thin metal object in my pocket is the ignition key of my car because I have seen it and used it before. It fits into the pattern of my experience and understanding. We apply the same kind of procedure to the deeper, more complex questions of life. We judge that this action is right and that action is wrong in the light of our scheme of moral values. We decide for or against such notions as free will and life after death not because of a single item of evidence or a simple experiment that we can perform. Any new item has to be assessed in relation to the fabric of beliefs and values that each of us has been weaving from birth.

If we are inclined to use fancy, quasi-technical language to describe all this, we might talk about how people's perceptions are affected by their *Weltanschauung*. But this is only a more obscure way of saying in German what the words "world view" say in English. More recently, it has become fashionable to talk of paradigms and paradigm shifts. The latter term was given currency by philosopher of science Thomas S. Kuhn in his description of what happens in a scientific revolution. Kuhn rejects the idea of scientific neutrality. Instead, he argues that "an apparently arbitrary element, compounded of personal and historical accident, is always a formative ingredient of the beliefs espoused by a given scientific community at a given time.[2] The beliefs of the community in question constitute the paradigm which defines the legitimate problems and methods of a research field for succeeding generations of practitioners.[3]

In ancient times people came to think that the world was made up of the four elements of earth, air, fire and water. This way of thinking provided the paradigm for thinking about the physical world. Another paradigm was supplied by the view that the course of human destiny was in the hands of the gods. In time scientific thinking came to be dominated by Aristotelian physics. In the Age of Enlightenment this gave way to Newtonian physics, which in modern times was further modified by Einstein's relativity. Kuhn argues that in any given era the practitioners of science operate within the accepted paradigms. But every now and again the paradigm proves to be inadequate to cope with the new understanding of reality. It is then that a paradigm shift comes about in order to accommodate the new approach.

This book is about the changes in preconceptions, world views and paradigms that have affected the ways in which people have thought about religion in general and Christianity in particular in the Western world. Although it is written from the standpoint of someone who is deeply committed to the Christian faith, this book is not an essay in apologetics. Its aim is not to present a defense of Christianity against all comers. Rather, it is a historical sketch, written to help students—and anyone else who might be interested—to get a better grasp of the love-hate relationship between philosophy and faith that has gone on for close on two thousand years. This is not to say that I have deliberately suppressed my own views. I have regularly chanced my arm and entered the fray of debate by way of offering comments on the strengths and weaknesses of different views. However, I have not attempted to present my own brand of philosophy. Still less have I sought to force what I see into some kind of pattern of development. I have just called 'em as I see 'em. Readers will judge for themselves whether I have called 'em right.

Twenty years ago I wrote a book entitled *Philosophy and the Christian Faith: A Historical Sketch from the Middle Ages to the Present Day.* It was written with the fire and passion of youth—or at least the fire and passion of an aspiring scholar in his thirties writing his second book. Since then the book has gone through more than a dozen printings in America and Britain. It has been translated into Chinese and Portuguese; and an Indonesian translation is underway. Numerous people have told me that this was the book that helped them get through philosophy at college, university or seminary. To be told this is both encouraging and humbling. In the meantime InterVarsity Press invited me to undertake a revision to make the book more useful for the present generation. As I worked on the revision, I could not suppress the growing feeling that tinkering about with the original book would ruin whatever was good in it. If I did anything at all, I needed to write a completely new book. There is much in *Philosophy and the Christian Faith* that I still stand by. There are many passages which—try as I may—I cannot improve upon. For all that, I feel a growing kinship with Saint Augustine who toward the end of his career wrote his *Retractations*. I have therefore written what is virtually a new book on the same basic theme.

In the past two decades I have been reading and rereading both primary sources and some of the massive flood of secondary literature which has poured from the academic presses on both sides of the Atlantic. I must confess that when I wrote *Philosophy and the Christian Faith* I had never heard of Pyrrhonism. If I had paid more attention to the texts of Pascal, Hume and their contemporaries, I might have known better.

But I did not. My ignorance may perhaps be partially excused by the paucity of references to Pyrrhonism in the standard histories, textbooks, and reference works. Even *The Encyclopedia of Philosophy* lacks an article on Pyrrhonism, though this deficiency is later remedied by the article on Skepticism. I now see that Pyrrhonism was not only a significant movement in its own right but a key to understanding the minds of Descartes and Pascal and the direction taken by European thought in the seventeenth century. The positions adopted by Descartes and Pascal cannot be properly appreciated unless we see them as responses to Pyrrhonian skepticism. Accordingly, I have included in this new book a section devoted to Pyrrhonian skepticism. This in turn has drastically affected my account of Continental rationalism and other philosophical movements.

I have made countless changes in my exposition and assessment of numerous thinkers and movements. I have introduced many matters which are absent from my earlier book. As someone who has not only changed his country of residence but also his nationality between writing the two books, I have also changed some of my perspectives. In a small way this is reflected by paying more attention to philosophy on the American side of the Atlantic. But the biggest change of all is the inclusion of a discussion of philosophy in the ancient world, the early centuries of the Christian church and in the Middle Ages.

Philosophy and the Christian Faith began with a cursory account of medieval philosophy, which amounted to miscellaneous thoughts chiefly on Anselm's ontological argument, Aquinas's five ways and the doctrine of analogy. The previous history of philosophy was passed over in a scant five pages. These handicaps placed serious limitations on the usefulness of the work as a textbook, not only on account of the missing subject-matter, but also on account of the foreshortened, limited perspective and its failure to see important connections between later philosophy and earlier philosophy.

Perhaps this shortsightedness may be put down to the facts that *Philosophy and the Christian Faith* was a product of the 1960s, and that its author was a child of the age of linguistic analysis. That era was already passing, but its children were still being taught that the main problems of philosophy were reducible to the problems of the meaningfulness of language. So far as the history of philosophy was concerned, modern philosophy (i.e., the only worthwhile philosophy) began with Descartes. Descartes himself—so the story went—mistakenly thought that philosophy should be founded on the specious certitude proferred by the notorious *cogito ergo sum*. Prior to the twentieth century, seven philosophers were deemed worthy of serious attention in the philosophy curriculum: three Continental rationalists (Descartes, Spinoza and Leibniz) and three British empiricists (Locke, Berkeley and Hume), followed by Kant (the one to whom all roads led). Each of these—so the tradition went—demonstrated the egregious mistakes of his predecessor. The prize for smartness was usually awarded to the skeptical Hume. Then came Kant's elaborate but vain attempt to salvage what he could from the ravages of Hume. Such was the standard tale. But philosophy in the 1980s is in a different world from that of a mere twenty years ago. All the classical questions are being examined with renewed vigor. Nothing falls under the taboo of the analytical philosopher. There is an astonishing amount of interest in both the major and the minor thinkers of all ages. Inevitably, the map of the landscape has changed.

I have chosen to call this book *Christianity and Western Thought*. The title carries with it the risk of appearing to offer more than I actually give. However, my subtitle makes it clear that my central interest lies in the interaction of philosophy with Christian faith. I have opted for the broader title, partly because I wish to include certain topics which lie outside the strict confines of philosophy, and partly because philosophy itself has always been influenced by matters which lie outside it.

Although I would have liked to have written a single-volume work for the non-specialist student and general reader, these remain my target readers. However, I am deeply committed to the importance of quoting sources and giving references. This has a double value. On the one hand, it forces the writer to stick to what someone has said rather than give the writer's version. On the other hand, it enables readers to check out for themselves and follow through the ideas that are presented to them. Inevitably this has meant a bigger book. The additional material and the extensive endnotes have turned the idea of a single-volume work into an impossible dream. But truth to tell, my original book *Philosophy and the Christian Faith* was not really a single-volume history of philosophy. By beginning as it did with its cursory account of medieval thought, it was really the second volume of a two-volume history, the first volume of which was never written.

The present volume is intended to give a basic, introductory account of Christianity and Western thought from the ancient world to the Age of Enlightenment. In other words, it covers the vast period from pre-Socratic philosophy in the sixth century B.C. to the close of the eighteenth century A.D. A second volume will deal with philosophy in the nineteenth and twentieth centuries. It is obvious that the two volumes are not evenly balanced, and that no attempt has been made in this present first volume to give equal space to everyone. The divisions of the two books and the choice of topics within the books are alike determined by the arbitrary, but only possible, criterion of what seems to be important. There is a sense in which the end of the eighteenth century marks the big divide in history. Up to the middle of the eighteenth century religious belief and metaphysical commitments provided the dominant paradigms for Western thought. From the middle of the eighteenth century secularism makes increasing claims to provide the paradigms for thought and both private and public behavior. In the nineteenth and twentieth centuries the streams of secular paradigms have become a flood. The flood has also brought forth Christian responses. However, this must remain the theme for the next volume.

Histories of ideas tend to be written from a male point of view, and the contribution of women can be easily overlooked. To help remedy this defect, I have inserted at the end of the book a retrospective survey entitled "A Note on the Role of Women in the History of Western Thought."

This book is written by a non-specialist for non-specialists. Doubtless a trained, professional philosopher would have handled things differently. My own professional training and expertise, such as they are, lie in the area of theology. However, I have several excuses to plead for writing this book. The first is that most professional philosophers appear to be uninterested in writing a historical survey of this kind. I marvel at their expertise in handling logical problems and in writing for each other. But by and large they are specialists who fulfill their vocation within their area of specialization. More positively, however, as a theologian I am convinced that good theology cannot be done without an awareness of the philosophical dimensions of theological questions. The questions that confront us today cannot be understood without an understanding of the philosophical background of the past and the philosophical horizons of the present. I am therefore content to remain an amateur among the professionals. Not every jogger aspires to be an Olympic athlete. But you do not have to be an Olympic athlete to get some benefit out of jogging. It is the same with philosophy. You do not have to be a professional to get benefit from reading philosophy.

There is one other major difference between the present book and *Philosophy and the Christian Faith*. The latter gave references in the form of footnotes at the bottom of the page. The present book uses endnotes. The inconvenience of having to turn to the back of the book for a reference is outweighed by a double advantage. On the one hand, the reader who is not interested in the details of the argumentation can read through the book without distraction. On the other hand, the endnotes have given the writer the freedom to give information without having to worry about cluttering up the main text with technical data. I have used the endnotes not only to give references, but also to give bibliographical information. Readers who desire such information will find it in the appropriate endnote, relating to the beginning of the discussion of the writer or topic in question. Because this book is intended to be a basic introduction, I have confined the bibliographical information to books published in English. Readers who want information about journal articles and works in foreign languages will find them in the sources referred to. I have generally avoided giving references in the endnotes to dictionary and encyclopedia articles and discussions in standard histories. However, information about standard histories and reference works is given in the note on books which I have appended to this book.

It remains for me to express my warm gratitude and deep appreciation to many people who have helped me with this book. James Hoover, the academic editor of InterVarsity Press, is ultimately responsible for its origin. Several years ago, it was he who suggested revising and updating *Philosophy and the Christian Faith*. I thank him and the staff of InterVarsity Press in the United States for their patience and encouragement as they have witnessed and taken part in a modest revision that became the creation of a completely new book. I wish to thank Janet Gathright of the Word Processing Department of Fuller Theological Seminary for processing my original typescript, and Sandy Bennett and David Sielaff who worked on the numerous revisions. I wish to pay tribute to the staff of the McAlister Library of Fuller Theological Seminary; without their help and the library's resources, the writing of this book would not have been possible.

Dr. L. Russ Bush of Southeastern Baptist Theological Seminary made numerous helpful suggestions for improving this volume and also its sequel. I am especially grateful to the readers of the first draft of my text who drew my attention to many specific points where changes needed to be made: Professor Arthur F. Holmes of Wheaton College; Dr. Kelly James Clark of Gordon College; and Dr. Peter Hicks in England. Needless to say, the responsibility for the remaining faults and idiosyncracies remains mine alone.

My greatest debt of gratitude is to my wife, Olive, for her selfless help and loving critical comments at every stage of this work. Though I did not know it at the time, she was among those students who used *Philosophy and the Christian Faith* to get through her philosophy exams at university. It is to her that I dedicate this book.

Center for Advanced Theological Studies, School of Theology
Fuller Theological Seminary
Pasadena, California

PART I
PHILOSOPHY
IN THE ANCIENT WORLD

1. SOCRATES AND PRE-SOCRATIC PHILOSOPHY

In the ancient world people were doing philosophy long before anyone thought up the word.[1] But, according to the first great historian of philosophy, Diogenes Laertius, it was the Greeks who began it all. In *Lives and Opinions of Eminent Philosophers* he noted the belief that philosophy had its beginnings among the barbarians. He mentioned the magi of the Persians, the Chaldaeans of Mesopotamia, the gymnosophists among the Indians, the druids of the Celts and Gauls, and the priests and prophets of the Egyptians. But for Diogenes Laertius, it was with the Greeks that philosophy began. He identified Musaeus as "the first to compose a genealogy of the gods and to construct a sphere." Musaeus believed that "all things proceed from unity and are resolved into unity." However, the first man to use the term *philosophy* and to call himself a *philosopher* was Pythagoras,[2] the thinker and mathematician who lived in the sixth century B.C.

To Pythagoras the term *philosopher* was evidently a term of modesty. It is made up of two Greek words. The *phil-* part of the word means "love." The Greek words *sophia* and *sophos* mean "wisdom" and "wise" respectively.[3] Pythagoras declared that no one was wise except God. He himself disclaimed the title of being "wise" and preferred to be known as a "philosopher" or "lover of wisdom." The subject that we today call *philosophy* was the study of wisdom. Sometimes it was called simply *wisdom*. Its early practitioners were known as *wise men, sages (sophoi)* or *sophists (sophistoi).*[4]

Diogenes Laertius went on to observe that philosophers could be divided into two classes: dogmatists and skeptics. The dogmatists were "all those who make assertions about things assuming that they can be known." The skeptics included "all who suspend their judgment on the ground that things are unknowable."[5] Diogenes Laertius may well have been a skeptic himself. He lived in the third century A.D. and so was separated by centuries from many of the thinkers he was writing about. He freely used traditions and material from earlier writers. Nevertheless, his work provides important testimony to ways of thinking in the ancient world.

Today a dividing line is often drawn between pre-Socratic philosophy and the classical philosophy which came later. The line is marked by the life and thought of Socrates who lived in the fifth century B.C. Although he left behind him no philosophical treatises, Socrates exerted an enormous influence on Plato and his generation. Although some may regret it,[6] philosophy was never quite the same after Socrates.

The Milesian School

No complete work by any pre-Socratic philosopher has survived.[7] Some thinkers, including Socrates himself, did not write books at all. The views of others we know only from fragments or accounts given in later writers. The earliest proper philosophy had its beginnings in the commercial centers of Ionia on the coast of Asia Minor in the sixth century B.C. The region gave its name to the Ionian School, also called the Milesian School after the city of Miletus. From Miletus came Thales, Anaximander and Anaximenes.

All three thinkers sought to understand the nature of reality. In their different ways each of them was concerned to discover what it is that underlies everything. What is the world really made of? Thales replied that the world was really made of water.[8] To our ears the answer sounds strange. But Thales had his reasons for saying this. The land which is surrounded by the sea appears to rest on water. Plants, animals and human beings need water in order to survive. Nutriment requires moisture in order to be consumed and assimilated. Moreover, the semen of living creatures is moist. By reflecting on what he observed, Thales came to the conclusion that water was the first principle of things. The importance of Thales lies not so much in his conclusions as in the kind of questions that he asked and his motive for asking them. In the words of a modern historian of science, "If he had championed the cause of treacle as the sole element, he would still have been rightly honored as the father of speculative science."[9]

Thales is important in at least two other ways. He believed that the soul was the "motive force" of the body.[10] In teaching this he belongs to the long line of Greek thinkers who drew a sharp distinction between soul and body as two separate entities. Thales also taught that "all things are full of gods."[11] From our distance in time it is tempting to dismiss this pronouncement as an example of a crude, outworn belief in polytheism. But perhaps we need to be reminded that when sophisticated Greek thinkers used the word *theos,* they did not necessarily mean an individual "god" or deity as in the Judeo-Christian tradition.[12] The word *theos* could also suggest a power that is more than human, a force that is not subject to death, a reality which was there before we were born and which will continue after we are gone. On this reckoning the soul was also divine, since it was a power or force which moved and transcended the body. The goal of classical Greek philosophy was to discover the nature of the forces which governed the world and human life.

Anaximander was a younger friend of Thales. In some ways his view of reality was very modern. He believed that the world was cylindrical like a drum, but not resting on water—as Thales believed, for Thales' view raised the question of what the water rested on, and so on. Anaximander believed that the earth rested on nothing. It was suspended in a spherical universe, equidistant from all other points, held in a kind of tension which prevented it from falling in any one direction.

Anaximander taught a theory of evolution well over two thousand years before Charles Darwin. He saw the world as the product of a conflict between qualities which were always in mutual opposition. Four of them were primary: hot and cold, wet and dry. The perpetual conflict between these opposites is seen in the changing seasons. It may also be seen every time that the sun's heat dries up water and water quenches fire. The process has a cyclical character to it. Thales had traced things from a single first principle, but Anaximander rejected this. If water were such a principle, there could be no heat or fire. For fire does not come from water, but destroys it. Anaximander imagined an original state of formless matter which gradually evolved into the universe as we know it. Things came into being through a process of separating out. Living things originated from a primeval slime. Although different early writers gave different accounts of Anaximander's teaching, he seems to have believed that human beings originally came from fishlike creatures.

The third member of the Milesian school, Anaximenes, taught an alternative view of primary substance. He returned to the idea that everything derives from a single substance, but suggested that the substance was air. Anaximenes' doctrine was taken a step further in the fifth century B.C. by Diogenes of Apollonia, who believed that the air inside both human and animal bodies constitutes their souls. "Mankind and the other animals live on air, by breathing; and it is to them both soul and mind."[13]

The Pythagoreans

In his account of the history of Greek philosophy Diogenes Laertius noted two original schools.[14] One was the Ionian or Milesian school. The other was the Italian school under the sixth-century teacher Pythagoras, who worked for most of his life in southern Italy where he had fled as a refugee. Whereas the Ionians were motivated by scientific curiosity, the Pythagoreans were a religious brotherhood. By the time of Plato, Pythagoras had already become a figure of legendary proportions. He came to assume a semi-divine stature. It is not easy to discover what Pythagoras exactly taught, not least because his followers came to regard it as a pious duty to ascribe new doctrines in the school to the founder himself.

In Pythagorean teaching religion and philosophy merge into each other in ways which anticipate Plato but which are radically different from Christianity. The Pythagoreans believed that the soul was by nature immortal. Souls existed not only in human beings but also in animals. Through a series of incarnations in animal and human bodies, souls were purified by the wheel of existence. This doctrine of the transmigration of souls was also bound up with a view of the kinship of all life. The aim in life was to become pure by removing the taint of the body and rejoining the universal spirit. In this process, it was important not to injure other souls or become further tainted. For this reason the Pythagoreans enjoined various taboos. The eating of animal flesh was prohibited, lest one eat the flesh inhabited by a kindred soul. Also prohibited was the eating of beans. Among the reasons put forward for this prohibition was the belief that beans resembled genital organs, the gates of Hades and the form of the universe.[15]

Pythagoreanism was a form of pantheism. The universe was a single whole which displayed order, fitness and beauty. Just as the universe was a *kosmos,* so each person was a *kosmos* in miniature. Pythagorean interest in the orderliness of the *kosmos* was bound up with a deep interest in mathematics and music. Pythagoras may well have discovered the theorem in geometry which bears his name. He is reputed to have made the discovery that the chief musical intervals are capable of being expressed in mathematical ratios. In Pythagorean thought mathematics came to be seen not only as the key for understanding nature; it also provided the impetus for directing the soul to eternal reality. Mathematical knowledge was not simply a tool for research; it was a quasi-religious means of initiation into the mystery of being. Whereas things in the world come and go, numbers appear to have a constancy which is beyond change. The Pythagorean view of the importance of mathematics was endorsed by Plato, who observed that the study of arithmetic "strongly directs the soul upward and compels it to discourse about pure numbers, never acquiescing if anyone proffers to it in the discussion numbers attached to visible and tangible bodies."[16] Likewise, geometry was for Plato "the knowledge of the eternally existent."[17]

Heraclitus

If Plato took over some of the beliefs and doctrines of the Pythagoreans, he was also open to the ideas of others. Among them was the arch-opponent of Pythagoras, Heraclitus of Ephesus. Heraclitus lived sometime during the sixth and fifth centuries B.C. Little is known about his life. Scholars dispute whether he actually wrote a book. What we know of his thought is gleaned from the study of fragments which propound ideas in the form of enigmatic oracles. His teaching earned him the nicknames of "The Obscure One" and "The Riddler."

Heraclitus scoffed at the Pythagorean ideal of a peaceful harmonious world. "War," he said, "is father of all and king of all, and some he reveals as gods, others as men, some he makes slaves, others free."[18] The

pronouncement both evokes and contradicts the titles that Homer ascribed to Zeus, the king of the gods. The supreme deity is not Zeus, but
conflict. To Heraclitus everything that happens comes about through
strife. Reality is in a constant state of flux. The point is vividly illustrated
by his famous remark "You cannot step into the same river twice."[19] But
the primary symbol for reality was fire which is constantly changing,
and thrives by consuming and destroying. The *kosmos*, or world-order,
is the same for all, both gods and humans. It is "an ever-living fire which
is kindled in measures and extinguished in measures."[20] The divine fire
is also the logos, the word or reason, which governs everything. It is to
this divine fire that the fire in the virtuous human soul eventually returns.

Parmenides

While to Heraclitus reality was characterized by change, to Parmenides
reality consisted of a single unchanging substance. Parmenides of Elea
lived in the fifth century B.C. His approach to doing philosophy marks
a break with his predecessors. Parmenides expressed his ideas in a poem
of which more has been preserved than any other pre-Socratic philosophical writing. The poem was in two parts, the "Way of Truth" and the
"Way of Seeming." In the "Way of Truth" Parmenides reflects on the
meaning of existence. To say that something "is" is to say that it exists.
He claimed that "what is not" is unthinkable and unknowable. Change
involves passage from "what is" into "what is not."[21] But the notion of
"what is not" is unintelligible. Therefore, movement is impossible.
Things only appear to move and change, but this is due to the decep-
tiveness of our senses.

According to one of the leading contemporary authorities on Greek
philosophy, W. K. C. Guthrie, the significance of Parmenides lies in the
fact that "he started the Greeks on the path of abstract thought." He set
the mind working "without reference to external facts," exalting its results above those of sense-perception. "In this the Greeks were apt pupils, so much so that according to some their genius for abstract thought
and for neglecting the world of external fact set European science on
the wrong track for a thousand years or so."[22] This verdict may seem
somewhat harsh in view of the contribution to scientific thought made

by the atomists, by Aristotle and, to a lesser extent, by the Epicureans, but it is not without some truth.

Parmenides figures in the rather obscure dialogue by Plato which bears his name as a title.[23] He appears to raise serious questions about the teaching of the young Socrates who ends by acquiescing in the teaching of his famous opponent. In the *Sophist* Plato raises serious objections to Parmenides' method of argument and the fallacy of assuming that a person must be saying something, even though he may actually be saying nothing.[24] Nevertheless, Plato's thought was much indebted to Parmenides. The debt was twofold. On the one hand, there was the metaphysical idea of immutable or changeless being. On the other hand, there was the epistemological view that true knowledge comes about through the mind's contact with this reality. What we perceive with our senses is the transitory world, but true knowledge is the mind's grasp of that which lies behind the world and which does not change. This view of reality and knowledge is summed up in Plato's *Timaeus,* where Timaeus insists on making a fundamental distinction by asking:

> What is that which always is and has no becoming, and what is that which is always becoming and never is? That which is apprehended by intelligence and reason is always in the same state, but that which is conceived by opinion with the help of sensation and without reason is always in a process of becoming and perishing and never really is.[25]

Not every Greek philosopher drew this conclusion. The pluralists argued that the world consists in a plurality of existents. Among them was Empedocles, who appeared to have combined the roles of physician, wonder-worker, philosopher and Pythagorean mystic. He devoutly believed in the transmigration of souls and in the power of his knowledge to control nature. Empedocles believed that there were ultimately four elements. Sometimes he called them by divine names, and sometimes he used alternative terms, but essentially the four elements were fire, water, earth and air.[26] Although this doctrine was questioned by the atomists,[27] it continued to hold sway well into the Middle Ages and beyond.

The Atomists

The atomism of Leucippus of Miletus and his younger contemporary, Democritus of Abdera, who both lived in the fifth century B.C., was an attempt to reconcile Parmenides' thesis that matter is unchangeable with the evidence of sense experience. Leucippus was the originator of the theory, but it was Democritus who developed it. Democritus agreed with Parmenides that *qualitative* change was unintelligible and impossible. But it was different with *quantitative* change. Democritus believed that the physical world was made up of innumerable indivisible, unchanging entities or atoms. (The word *atom* comes from the Greek *atomos*, which means "indivisible.") The properties of objects derived from the arrangement of their atomic constituents, and change was due to the rearrangement of their configuration. The atoms themselves possessed shape and solidity, but not properties like warmth, color and smell.

Later Greek atomists modified the theory in two ways. Some allowed for qualitative differences between atoms. Others, including Aristotle, held that even the atoms could be further divided, though it was agreed that there had to be some limit to divisibility. Despite the attractiveness of atomism in the hindsight of modern knowledge, atomism failed to supplant its rival theories about the physical world. This was in part due to the influence of Plato and Aristotle, and, more importantly, in part due to the fact that Democritus's followers failed to develop his insights. The Greek philosopher Epicurus and his popularizer, the Latin poet Lucretius, took over his scheme of thought more or less as he left it.

Socrates and the Sophists

To many people the views of Parmenides strained belief beyond endurable limits. But the teaching of his opponents was scarcely more acceptable. Many people wanted something more practical, and this need was met by the Sophists. The Sophists of the fifth century were itinerant teachers of practical wisdom who imparted their knowledge for an appropriate fee. They were concerned with what worked, whether it happened to be the winning of arguments or making things. A key topic was *aretē*, a word which is commonly translated as "virtue." But virtue in this case meant first and foremost "skill." The Sophist Hippias provided a walking advertisement for his craft by turning up at the Olympic Games wearing nothing which he had not made himself, right down to the ring on his finger.[28] If the Sophists had lived in the twentieth century, they would have been the authors of best-selling books and videos on how to succeed in business, make money, lose weight and keep fit. On a more serious level was the social-contract theory of Protagoras.[29] He argued that societies came into being on account of the need of people to protect themselves against wild creatures and also in order to advance their standard of living. Laws and conventions were needed for the mutual benefit of the members of a society. Otherwise anarchy would prevail. In order to avoid this, laws were devised in which the strong pledge themselves not to attack the weak. But the laws could be changed when people thought fit. Protagoras's position was summed up as follows:

> I hold that whatever practices seem right and laudable to any particular state are so, for that state, so long as it holds by them. Only, when the practices are, in any particular case, unsound for them, the wise man substitutes others that are and appear sound. On the same principle the Sophist, since he can in the same manner guide his pupils in the way that they should go, is wise and worth a considerable fee to them when their education is completed.[30]

Today Protagoras is remembered for his dictum "Man is the measure of all things."[31] It was evidently intended to be a sheer statement of fact. It certainly appears to fit Protagoras's views on laws and society. But the words contain more than a hint of relativism and skepticism. They not only imply that human beings must use their minds to determine truth and decide issues. They also suggest that what may be true or valuable for someone under one set of circumstances may not be so for someone else under different circumstances. When pressed further, this line of thought leads to the conclusion that right and wrong are just names which can be manipulated according to one's purpose. It was this kind of thinking that earned the Sophists the reputation for being cynical pragmatists. It was this outlook which Socrates sought to combat as being both morally harmful and thoroughly wrongheaded.

Socrates (c. 470-399 B.C.) was born in Athens where he spent most of his life. His life, like that of his fellow countrymen, was overshadowed by the Peloponnesian War (431-404 B.C.) which ended in victory for Sparta and disaster for Athens. Although he served in the army, Socrates remained on the fringe of political life. In old age he was accused of introducing strange gods and of corrupting youth. He was sentenced by the Athenian Assembly to die by drinking hemlock. Refusing to compromise his views and rejecting the possibility of escape, Socrates drank the hemlock thirty days after his condemnation.[32]

Socrates himself wrote no books.[33] What we know of his teaching is derived mainly from the numerous dialogues of Plato in which Socrates is a prominent figure. It is a matter of academic debate how much the ideas put forward in Plato's dialogues are those of Socrates himself or whether they are more the work of Plato. It is widely thought that Socrates' influence on Plato was at its strongest in Plato's earlier writings. Socrates' mother was a midwife, and Socrates saw his role as a teacher as being like that of a midwife.[34] He disclaimed having any sort of wisdom himself, and repudiated the idea of having intellectual offspring of his own. His task was to assist at the birth of wisdom in his partners through dialogue. The wisdom itself came from heaven.

Socrates' role in teaching was to enable people to discover wisdom by themselves from within. To this end he employed dialectic. The Greek word *dialektikē* means discussion by question and answer. Socrates went about his work doing just that. By relentless questioning of ideas he sought to distinguish truth from mere opinion and faulty thinking. The dialogue form in which Plato presented his teaching was the appropriate medium for his philosophy. Truth was not something that could be learned by knowing the right techniques. The learner had to see it for himself. It was apprehended through a process of learning and inquiry. Once the learner had grasped it, the teacher ceased to be important. Last but not least is the spirit in which the dialogue is conducted. The Sophists practiced eristic, polemical disputation with a view to winning the debate. Socrates could be tough in his comments and questions, but his goal and his method was the disinterested pursuit of truth in which he and his partners in dialogue joined.

2. PLATO'S VISION OF REALITY

P*lato (c. 427-347 B.C.)*[1] *was born into a leading Athenian family some four* years after the outbreak of the Peloponnesian War. It is open to question whether Plato was actually a pupil of Socrates, but there can be no doubt about the high esteem in which Plato held him or about the impact of Socrates' death on his mind. As the war went on Plato witnessed a succession of changes of government in Athens, and came to be disillusioned with the ineffectiveness of democracy and the tyranny of oligarchy. Plato paid several visits to Italy and Sicily, where he got to know members of the Pythagorean school. As a result of his experiences, Plato came to the conclusion that the constitution of all existing states was bad and that their institutions were all but past remedy.[2] The only hope lay in developing a "correct philosophy" and in creating a new society governed by philosopher-rulers who appreciated philosophy. It was to be an ordered, educated society in which the citizens fulfilled functions according to their natural aptitudes. At some time in the 380s Plato founded his famous Academy which was the forerunner of the modern university. Plato's best-known work, the *Republic,* paints a picture of a utopian society and the education of its rulers in accordance with Plato's vision of reality.

The State
Like all of his other major writings, except his letters and *Laws* (which appears to have been conceived in the form of a series of addresses), the *Republic* was written as a dialogue. It begins with a discussion of justice, in which the ideas of the Sophists are rejected. Justice is not a

matter of gaining personal advantage but of doing what is right. For example, in medicine the just physician is not the one who pockets the largest fee for the least work, but the one who applies his skills to curing his patient.[3] In a society each member has work to do. Justice lies in fully discharging that vocation.

In many ways Plato's theories about education, personality and the welfare state anticipated and inspired a good deal of modern thinking. Plato's division of education into the three stages of primary, secondary and higher education corresponds to general Western practice today. His views on state control, including the regulation of property and the family,[4] anticipated socialism. A line may be drawn from Plato's ideal society to the Marxist totalitarian state controlled by those who ostensibly know best.[5] But to appreciate Plato's position, we must remember that, like the attractions of Marxism for many people today, it grew out of disillusionment with existing forms of government. Plato himself was of aristocratic descent. But his bitter experience of the government of Athens under oligarchy, tyranny and democracy forced on him the conclusion that all existing forms of government were evil.

As the Peloponnesian War dragged on, it became increasingly apparent that the democracies of Athens lacked truly capable and responsible leaders, and those in charge were all too easily swayed by the desire to please the populace. The last straw was the treatment meted out to Socrates by the Athenian democracy. Plato saw three main elements in human psychological make-up. There was reason, the faculty which calculates and decides; desire or appetite, which has to do with the instincts; and ambition. In every human being all three are normally present, but in each person one of these elements predominates. Corresponding to these elements, Plato saw three main classes in society. In the ideal just state the peoples' roles would correspond to what kind of people they were. The bulk of society would constitute the third class which was made up of farmers, manufacturers and traders. Above them was the class of auxiliaries who function like a police force or army, enforcing the decisions of the rulers. The highest class of all were the rulers who had been trained in mathematics and philosophy and who would have preferred to spend their days on these pursuits but for their sense of obligation to the state which prompted them to accept the role of rulers.

Theory of Forms

Plato believed that the philosopher-rulers would acquire wisdom through study, especially of the higher subjects like mathematics and philosophy. He believed that most human beings were preoccupied with material things. What they needed was to have their thoughts turned to the immaterial reality behind the world, and thus be weaned away from the objects of their lower passions. To Plato truth had an objective reality which was grounded in the nature of things. The world was more than a world of appearances. Behind each particular thing is the idea or form of the thing. Moreover, the ideas or forms are all ultimately related to the Form of the Good. The Form of the Good is like the sun which not only gives visibility to objects but sustains them and causes living things to grow, without itself being part of the earthly process. The Good is not only the source of the intelligibility of the objects of knowledge, but also of their existence and reality.[6]

Plato divided our ideas and beliefs about the world into two main categories which were each subdivided into two more categories.[7] The two main categories were knowledge and belief. Plato's use of these terms was almost exactly the opposite to that of our modern, secular, materialistic society. When Plato spoke of belief, it had to do with our ideas of the material world. When he spoke of knowledge, it had to do with the immaterial reality behind the material world. Belief covered the two subcategories of opinions or beliefs about physical things and illusions or mistaken ideas about such things. Knowledge, on the other hand, covered the two subcategories of mathematical reasoning and intelligence or understanding of the Forms. It was the latter which was the highest form of knowledge.

Plato compared the human condition to a cave in which the prisoners could see only the shadows of objects cast in the light of a fire.[8] The prisoners in the cave mistook the shadows for reality. But if some of the prisoners were released, they would see that the shadows were not real objects and that the shadows were not the whole of reality. As their eyes gradually grew accustomed to the outside world, they might even be able to look directly at the sun and see it as the sustainer of everything. But if the escaped prisoners were to return to the cave and tell their former companions what reality was like, the others would think them mad and try to kill them.

This last point was evidently an allusion to the fate of Socrates. In the famous story about the cave Socrates is made to present the account as a vision of reality. It is not demonstratively proved but told as a picture to help the reader understand.

> And if you assume the ascent and the contemplation of the things above is the soul's ascension to the intelligible region, you will not miss my surmise, since that is what you desire to hear. But God knows whether it is true. But, at any rate, my dream as it appears to me is that in the region of the known the last thing to be seen and hardly seen is the idea of good, and that when seen it must needs point us to the conclusion that this is indeed the cause for all things of all that is right and beautiful, giving birth in the visible world to light, and the author of light and itself in the intelligible world being the authentic source of truth and reason, and that anyone who is to act wisely in private or public must have caught sight of this.[9]

The Soul and Immortality

True wisdom and wise action required not only an understanding of the nature of the world in relation to the Forms. It also required an understanding of the soul. Plato believed that the soul was an immaterial entity which in some ways was like the Forms. In the dialogue entitled *Meno* an uneducated slave boy is brought in, and in response to Socrates' questions shows himself capable of doing geometrical theorems. Where did the boy get his knowledge? The answer lies in Plato's doctrine of recollection. The boy already had it in his soul. He simply needed to be reminded of it by being asked the right questions. From this Socrates concludes that "if the truth about reality is always in our soul, the soul must be immortal, and one must take courage and try to discover—that is, to recollect—what one doesn't happen to know, or, more correctly, remember, at the moment."[10] The same applies to virtue. It cannot be taught or acquired by techniques, as the Sophists argued. It is in the soul already.

In the dialogue entitled *Phaedo* Plato gives an account of Socrates' beliefs about the immortality of the soul, which explains why Socrates did not fear death. The soul is not perishable like the body. Just as day follows night and the seasons follow each other, so life follows death. When death comes, the immortal part of a person retires to another existence.[11] If death were a release from everything, it would be a boon to the wicked. But the wicked have no escape. The only way of escape for the soul is by becoming "as good and wise as it possibly can."[12] Those who are good find ultimate release from the body in a higher existence. Those who have not been particularly good or bad undergo further purification. The wicked are cast into the torments of Tartarus.

The tenth and final book of the *Republic* closes with an even more elaborate account of the fate of the soul at death. Socrates tells the story of Er, a soldier killed in battle who returned to life and told of what he had seen.[13] His tale appears to draw on the Pythagorean doctrine of the transmigration of souls and the imagery of Orphism, the Greek mystic religion of purification and reincarnation. Souls are successively reincarnated in the bodies of humans, animals and even birds, until they are purified. The very wicked, however, are tormented eternally in Tartarus. The fact that human beings do not appear to remember their previous existences is simply explained by their being compelled to drink from the River of Forgetfulness. The foolish drink more than their measure! But all fall asleep and are wafted away to be born again in another form.

Plato and Religion
Platonism in one form or another exerted great influence on Western thought. Here we have been able to do no more than touch on a few of the ideas that appear in a few of Plato's many writings. We may, however, pause to ask whether—as many people down the ages have maintained—Plato offers some kind of philosophical underpinning for Christian faith. After all, his doctrine of the Forms and especially his view of the Form of the Good clearly reject a skeptical and materialistic view of reality. The Form of the Good might even be identified with God. Moreover, Plato clearly taught a doctrine of life after death which was linked with rewards and punishments.

But having said this, it is also clear that there are major differences between Plato's teaching and the Judeo-Christian tradition of the biblical writings. Perhaps the nearest that they come to each other is in their use of narrative, dialogue and story in order to communicate moral and religious truth. But Plato makes no claims of divine revelation. The truths that he finds are truths which come from within the human soul by recollection and rational reflection.

Plato's doctrine of Forms presents several problems. In Christian thought God is not a Form or Idea which is somehow related to all other Forms or Ideas in the world. Even in Plato's writings there are a number of unanswered questions. In the *Timaeus* Plato speaks of God as the Demiurge (artisan or craftsman) who makes the world according to the model of the Forms.[14] But it is unclear whether in Plato's thought God was ultimately the creator of the Forms or whether the Forms already existed, or indeed whether all of this was not just a highly figurative way of speaking.

Plato's *Timaeus* also mentions a world-soul which the demiurge or creator put into the world. Plato argued that intelligence could not be present in anything which was "devoid of soul."

> For which reason, when he was framing the universe, he [the demiurge] put intelligence in soul, and soul in body, that he might be the creator of a work which was by nature fairest and best. On this wise, using the language of probability, we may say that the world came into being—a living creature truly endowed with soul and intelligence by the providence of God.[15]

It is far from clear how all this relates to the rest of Plato's thought, not least because there is a lack of agreement among scholars as to where to place the *Timaeus* in relation to Plato's other writings. Some experts think that it is late and represents Plato's final thoughts, while others place it somewhere in the middle of Plato's writings. In this case it might not be Plato's last word on the subject. Perhaps this is to be found in the *Laws*, in which he gives a form of the cosmological argument.[16] Plato's concern here is to refute atheism. But this belongs to a wider concern which is to establish that the principles of justice are not simply the inventions of the politicians, but are there by nature and are therefore binding upon all human beings. Plato argues that no one ever broke laws intentionally, unless they believed that the gods do not exist, or that they are not concerned with human affairs, or that the gods are easily appeased by prayers and sacrifice. The whole argument turns on the existence of the gods, which Plato seeks to prove by showing that there must exist a soul which is the cause of all motion, including those souls that human beings call gods. As the argument reaches its climax, Plato asks rhetorically:

> Of all the planets, of the moon, of years and months and all seasons, what other story shall we have to tell than just this same, that since soul, or souls, and those souls good with perfect goodness, have proved to be the causes of all, these souls we hold to be gods, whether they direct the universe by inhabiting bodies, like animated beings, or whatever the manner of their action? Will any man who shares this belief bear to hear it said that all things are not "full of gods?"[17]

The question receives the reply: "No man, sir, can be so much beside himself." Thus Plato's form of the cosmological argument is used in the service of vindicating polytheism. This still leaves open the question of how all this relates to the doctrine of the Forms.

Although the doctrine of the Forms is widely held to be a major characteristic of Plato's thought, the doctrine occupies a relatively small place in the corpus of Plato's works and is absent altogether from some of them. In the *Sophist* and *Parmenides* it is handled critically. In the latter work the old philosopher Parmenides takes the young Socrates to task for his sloppy thinking, using arguments similar to those that Aristotle used against Plato. Is there a Form corresponding to each individual thing in the world? If so, it would require a separate world of concept-objects. What about largeness and smallness? Are they Forms? Are there such things as Forms of hair and mud? Socrates is pressed to admit that "we do not possess the forms themselves, nor can they exist in our world. . . . So beauty itself or goodness itself and all the things we take as forms in themselves are unknowable to us."[18]

Further differences between Plato and Christian thought emerge when we compare their differing attitudes to human nature and ethics.[19] As Arthur F. Holmes puts it, "In his *Republic* Plato assumes that those who know what is good will love and desire it. But he also recognizes that moral virtue is of itself a prerequisite to knowing the good. So I must both know the good in order to desire virtue, and be virtuous in order to know the good. In order to break into this vicious circle Plato proposes to organize society in such a way that those who do not know the good will be ruled by those who do. But the question remains, why *ought* those who know the good do it? They may *want* to, but *ought* they? Whence comes the obligation?"[20]

We might also ask about those who are ruled and who may lack the rulers' perception of the good. Does Plato's philosophy have anything to tell them other than that they should obey those who know better? There appears to be other unresolved tensions in Plato's thought. Right living is somehow bound up with service to the gods. But it is not clear how the gods relate to goodness. In *Euthyphro* Socrates declares that "apparently the holy is that which the gods love."[21] However, it is not clear whether something is right because the gods command it, or whether they command it because it is right.

In the *Laws*, which Plato wrote toward the end of his life, the issue remains unresolved. As we have just seen, Plato recognized that there were atheists in his day. There were also those who believed that the gods were indifferent to human conduct, or that they could be lightly placated by prayer or sacrifice. Although Plato recognized the strength of the atheist's arguments, he was convinced that the atheist could not be a good citizen and warned against the impiety of unbelief.[22] Religious piety and morality somehow go together. But within Plato's polytheistic framework of thought, it remains unclear not only how the two are related in practice, but also how they are related theoretically. The Christian can point out that morality is grounded in the righteous character of God, the Creator and Redeemer. In the Judaeo-Christian tradition, human beings are to be holy because God is holy (Lev 11:44-45; 19:2; Eph 1:3-5; 1 Pet 1:16). But no clear answer as to how morality and religion are related can be given by a philosophy which tries to combine enlightenment with polytheism.

Plato's doctrine of the soul also has its difficulties. It poses, rather than settles, the question of how we should think of human nature.[23] The idea of reincarnation is a theory for which there is next to no evidential support. It founders on the fact that there is no solid, reliable testimony to experience of previous existences in the form of memories, comparable with memories of our earlier life.[24] The doctrine of recollection in Plato's *Meno* is patently fallacious, for the ability to work out geometrical theorems under the direction of a teacher does not indicate knowledge that only an eternal soul could have acquired. All that it requires is a certain degree of intelligence and the guidance of a teacher who knows the right questions to ask. Plato's view of human improvement through education and salvation through personal goodness is a world apart from the Christian message of redemption by a loving, personal God.

3. ARISTOTLE AND THE PHYSICAL WORLD

Greek thought reached its climax with Aristotle (384-322 B.C.), whose writings brought a new depth and profundity to the study of logic, psychology, natural history, physics, metaphysics and ethics.[1] Aristotle was the son of Nicomachus, court physician to the king of Macedonia. In about 367 B.C. Aristotle entered Plato's Academy in Athens, where he remained until Plato's death in 347. The headship of the Academy did not, however, pass to Aristotle, but to Plato's nephew and heir, Speusippus. No doubt the event was a factor in Aristotle's decision to leave Athens. In 342 B.C. Philip II of Macedon made Aristotle the tutor of his thirteen-year-old son, the future Alexander the Great. Aristotle's supervision of Alexander's education lasted some three years. In 355 B.C. Aristotle opened the Lyceum, which became a rival to the Academy and attracted some of the latter's most distinguished members. Whereas the Academy had stressed mathematics, the Lyceum laid emphasis on biology and scientific research. Aristotle sought to build up a major library. Instruction was given in a covered portico (*peripatos*). Aristotle's habit of pacing up and down while teaching gave rise to the term *peripatetic*, which came to be used to denote Aristotle's followers. On the death of Alexander the Great in 323 B.C. there was a resurgence of anti-Macedonian feeling in Athens. Aristotle withdrew with some of his followers to Chalcis, where he died the following year at the age of sixty-two.

In his earlier years Aristotle followed Plato in casting his books in dialogue form. But apart from a few fragments that have been preserved by later writers, the dialogues have been lost. The treatises that have been preserved are essentially textbooks based on Aristotle's own notes or memoranda prepared for his students. Twentieth-century students of Aristotle have keenly debated the question of whether a pattern of development can be discerned in his thought. Werner Jaeger saw a gradual development which began with an enthusiastic endorsement of Plato and ended with the abandonment of Platonic metaphysics. However, different dating of certain books and different interpretations of key passages have led others to disagree with this view. It now seems clear that Aristotle became increasingly critical of Plato. He rejected outright some of Plato's views. Aristotle's own philosophy was an attempt to formulate more satisfactory and systematic views of physical and metaphysical reality.

In his treatise on *Topics* Aristotle divided knowledge into three divisions: theoretical, practical and productive.[2] Although Aristotle changed his mind from time to time as to which precise subjects should fit into which division, his classification of subjects has continued to influence thought down to the present. The theoretical division includes logic, metaphysics and mathematics. Included in the practical division are such scientific subjects that could be studied for the sake of practical action and also ethics. The productive division included rhetoric and poetry. In other words, it included what today would be called literature. We shall not attempt to review here the whole range of Aristotle's thought in its divisions. Instead, we shall simply note a number of points that bear on our central theme.

Logic

Aristotle's work on logic laid the foundation of all later work on the subject. The term *logic* comes from the Greek word *logos*. Its meaning includes "reason," "speech," "discourse" and "word." In a broad sense logic is the study of the structure of reasoning and argument. However, Aristotle's preferred name for the subject was not "logic" but "analytics." He regarded it as a preliminary study to all branches of knowledge, calling it an instrument *(organon)* of study. The term *Organon* was later applied to the collection of Aristotle's logical treatises which included his *Categories, On Interpretation, Prior Analytics, Posterior Analytics, Topics,* and *On Sophistical Refutations.* At the heart of Aristotle's work on logic was his study of syllogisms. Syllogisms are usually thought of as a three-step to have arranged the order of Aristotle's works, and placed the *Metaphysics* after the *Physics (meta ta physika)*. The Greek word *meta* has a variety of meanings which include both "after" and "beyond." Already in early times two rival explanations were put forward for the term. One was that metaphysics was a subject which was to be studied *after* physics. The other was that metaphysics was the study of those things which lie *beyond* the physical realm. To explore the range of Aristotle's thought on the subject is impossible here. But three topics call for attention: potentiality and actuality, the notion of causes and the idea of the Prime Mover.

Aristotle's understanding of *potentiality* and *actuality*[5] made a significant advance on previous Greek ideas about the nature of things. *Actuality* (Greek: *energeia*) is a mode of being in which something can bring about other things or be brought about by them. *Potentiality* (Greek: *dynamis*) is the power to effect change or be changed. The point can be put like this: If we think of a tree growing in a forest, the sum total of its material exists in the mode of a tree. But its wood has the potentiality to be made into a house or furniture. When this happens, the tree has ceased to be a tree and taken on other modes of being. But potentially the house and the furniture are also firewood which could be turned and transformed into heat. The same could be said of anything in the world, including living creatures and human beings. A child is potentially an adult and a parent. The actual parent is no longer a child, but is potentially a grandparent, and so on.

Three observations may be made at this point. The first is that a thing, an animal or a person cannot be potential and actual in the same respect at the same time. The tree is either a living tree or timber, but not both simultaneously. The child is either a child or an adult, or something in between, but not all at once. The second observation is to point out that in order to bring about a change from potentiality to actuality there has to be some outside agent or agents. Trees do not become timber, houses and furniture on their own. Children do not grow up to become adults without the nurture and care of others and the life support provided by their environment. The third observation is simply to say that the changes that we have noted do not necessarily take place. Whether a tree ends up as part of a house, a piece of furniture, paper pulp or remains in the forest until it dies and decays, depends on a whole range of factors, often beyond all human prediction. On the other hand, nothing in this world is immune from change of one kind or another. Things are in constant transition from potentiality to actuality and from actuality to potentiality.

Book 1 of Aristotle's *Metaphysics* contains a critique of previous Greek philosophers down to Plato. The latter's doctrine of Forms may have been an improvement on previous notions, but it raised more problems for Aristotle than it solved.[6] Was there a corresponding Form for each actual entity or perhaps even more than one Form for each entity? Does each human being have a Form and a separate Form for each organ? Do the Forms exist apart from entities? If so, how do they relate to entities? How do numbers relate to Forms? Instead of a theory of Forms on Platonic lines, Aristotle put forward a theory of causes. Aristotle argued that, when we look at something, we can think of it in terms of different kinds of causes. Aristotle identified four types of causes.[7] These were clearly not all of the same kind, as can be seen from Aristotle's own examples. We shall call them here by the terms which were given to them later.

The first type of cause is the *material cause*. It consists of the matter from which something is made—for example, the bronze of a statue or the silver of a saucer. The second type of cause is the *formal cause,* which is the form or pattern which the thing takes. It is the shape of the statue or the saucer. The third type of cause is known as the *efficient cause.* It designates the agent which initiates the change, the maker of the thing made and the producer of the changing. In the case of a statue the efficient cause is the sculptor who made it. In the case of the birth of a child the parents constitute the efficient cause. The fourth type of cause is the *final cause,* the end or purpose for which one does something. At this point Aristotle anticipated the modern fitness movement by talking about health. Health may be said to be the final cause of walking, for people walk in order to become healthy. Thus the desired goal may be said to be the cause of an action. Diet, exercise and medicine, on the other hand, may all serve as efficient causes which promote health.

The Unmoved Mover

Aristotle's views of potentiality, actuality and causation led him to his doctrine of the Prime, or Unmoved, Mover.[8] For something to change from a state of potentiality to a state of actuality there has to be an agent or agents of change. Nothing that we see or know of this world is its own cause. There has to be a cause or causes which set any given change in motion. But how were the myriads of causes that we can think of, and the many more that we cannot think of, set in motion? Aristotle's answer is that the whole process would not start or come into being without a Prime, or Unmoved, Mover that is ultimately the source of all causation and movement. Such a Prime Mover must be different from all other types of causes. For all other causes have prior causes. Even the heavens require something which moves them. "And since that which is moved and moves is intermediate, there is a mover which moves without being moved, being eternal, substance, and actuality."[9]

Aristotle's argument is an early form of the cosmological argument which argues for the existence of God as the cause of the cosmos. We shall look at the argument several times in the course of our survey. Instead of examining its strengths and weaknesses at this point, it might be helpful to make four observations.

The first observation concerns Aristotle's method of approach. Aristotle's basic method of approach is to make observations and to work backwards by means of rational reflection. He is concerned with the nature of substances. By thinking critically about experience, he arrives at conclusions about what lies behind experience. In so doing the method of approach is like what was said earlier about Aristotle's view of the syllogism. Beginning with what can be observed, Aristotle deduces a conclusion about something which cannot be directly observed. He believes that the causes of different things bear analogy to each other, and that the Unmoved Mover bears some analogy to the causes that we infer from our ordinary experience of cause and effect.

The second observation is to note that the argument posits the existence of the Unmoved Mover as the presupposition of causation and movement. The Unmoved Mover is not seen directly. He is invoked as the necessary ground of all finite or contingent causes.

The third observation is to note that Aristotle's argument involves both causation and contingency. Contingency denotes the property of not having to exist. It characterizes all finite beings. Aristotle's Unmoved Mover is a being that *has to* exist. Otherwise, all the secondary or intermediate causes would not have come into existence.

The fourth observation is to note that Aristotle's Unmoved Mover is not, as is sometimes imagined, a static being. The Unmoved Mover is not moved by any cause external to himself. But this is not the same as saying that the Unmoved Mover is motionless. Rather, the Unmoved Mover is a different kind of entity from the kinds of causes and agents that we find in the world which are themselves *caused causes*. The Unmoved Mover is an uncaused cause. He may be said to be pure actuality. He is not potential but actual. He is the ground of change, without being changed himself or undergoing change in the process. Or in Aristotle's words, "There is a mover which moves without being moved, being eternal, substance, and actuality."[10] The point has bearing on discussions of the immutability of God. This idea does not mean, as some people have imagined it to mean, that God exists in some kind of eternally frozen immobility. Rather, it means that God's being is unique in that he is eternally alive and active, but without being subject to the changes of growth and diminution that belong to all finite agents and causes.

However, when all this has been said, a number of questions still remain. What sort of God did Aristotle believe in? Is Aristotle's Unmoved Mover personal in any sense? How does the Unmoved Mover relate to the world? As Aristotle describes God at the end of his *Physics*, "the first mover causes a motion that is eternal and causes it during an infinite time. It is clear, therefore, that is indivisible and is without parts and without magnitude."[11] The Unmoved Mover is not like the Demiurge of Plato's *Timaeus*, who is a craftsman who produces his crafted objects in time. The Unmoved Mover transcends the world and is a being of a different order from any other being. To this extent, at least, Aristotle's God is more compatible with the biblical notions of God than is Plato's God.

Elsewhere, Aristotle seems to suggest that divine activity consists in thought and contemplation. In the *Metaphysics* Aristotle represents the Unmoved Mover as the *final cause* (but not apparently the *efficient cause*) not only of the eternal heavens but of all things.

There is then, something which is always moved with an unceasing motion, which is motion in a circle; and this is plain not in theory only but in fact. Therefore the first heavens must be eternal. There is therefore also something which moves them. And since that which is moved and moves is intermediate, there is a mover which moves without being moved, being eternal, substance, and actuality. And the object of desire and the object of thought move in this way; they move without being moved. The primary object of desire and of thought are the same. For the apparent good is the object of appetite, and the real good is the primary object of wish. But desire is consequent on opinion rather than opinion on desire; for thinking is the starting point.[12] This passage seems to make the Unmoved Mover the goal toward which all things are drawn. As such, the Unmoved Mover is their cause. It is a thought which invites comparison with the biblical idea of God as the goal of all things. But in biblical thought, God is the origin as well as the goal, the Alpha and the Omega, the beginning and the end (Rom 11:36; Rev 1:6, 21:6, 22:13).

Aristotle goes on to describe the Unmoved Mover as "a first principle,"[13] which, because it thinks, has life.

And thought thinks itself because it shares the nature of the object of thought; for it becomes an object of thought in coming into contact with and thinking its objects, so that thought and object of thought are the same. For that which is *capable* of receiving the object of thought, is thought. And it is *active* when it *possesses* this object. Therefore the latter rather than the former is the divine element which thought seems to contain, and the act of contemplation is what is most pleasant and best. If, then, God is always in that good state in which we sometimes are, this compels our wonder; and if in a better this compels it yet more. And God *is* in a better state. And life also belongs to God; for the actuality of thought is life, and God is that actuality; and God's essential actuality is life most good and eternal. We say therefore that God is a living being, eternal, most good, so that life and duration continuous and eternal being belong to God; for this *is* God.[14]

Aristotle's view again invites comparison with the biblical view of creation by the Word of God, which in the New Testament is expressed christologically. The divine Word which brought the cosmos into being is the same divine Word which was made flesh in the person of Jesus Christ, the redeemer of creation, whom God the Father has made Lord of all (Gen 1:3-26; Ps 33:6; Jn 1:1-14; Rom 14:10-12; 1 Cor 15:20-28; Phil 2:5-11; Col 1:15-20; Heb 1:1-4).

In the *Nicomachean Ethics* Aristotle develops the theme of divine activity as consisting in contemplation in a passage which extols contemplation as the highest form of activity. Human nature is not self-sufficient for this activity; it needs other things. But with the gods, it is different. They are self-sufficient. This leads Aristotle to the thought that the contemplative person is dearest to the gods.

> For if the gods have any care for human affairs, as they are thought to have, it would be reasonable both that they delight in that which was best and most akin to them (i.e. the intellect) and that they should reward those who love and honour this most, as caring for the things that are dear to them and acting both rightly and nobly. And that all these attributes belong most of all to the wise man is manifest. He, therefore, is the dearest to the gods. And he who is that will presumably be also the happiest; so that in this way the wise man will more than any other be happy.[15]

It is clear that there are here marked differences from the Judeo-Christian conception of God. The latter is strictly monotheistic, whereas Aristotle can speak both of the Unmoved Mover and also of the gods. Although the wisdom literature of the Bible can praise the wise person, wisdom there is more than the contemplative life. It consists in meditating on the Word of the Lord and in walking in his ways.[16] If the idea of a unique personal Creator who is both the agent and goal of creation is lacking in Aristotle, there are nevertheless aspects of his thought which are compatible with Christian thought and capable of adaptation, as Thomas Aquinas was to show centuries later. Not the least of these is Aristotle's method of reflecting on questions posed by our experience of the world, and his notion of the Unmoved Mover as a being of a different order from other beings, the self-sufficient, living source of all life and energy.

Aristotle's approach to theological questions was Platonic in the broad sense of insisting that the material world that we apprehend with our senses depends upon a different kind of reality which exists independently of it. But Aristotle's explanation of that reality was very different from Plato's. In the course of time both Plato and Aristotle were to find

followers in the Christian church who made use of their ideas in order
to provide a philosophical framework for expressing their faith.

Human Nature and Ethics

Aristotle's view of human nature had some things in common with Plato's, but there were important differences. Like Plato, he disapproved of
the Sophists. But the Form of the Good seemed to Aristotle to be an
empty metaphor. Nor did he share Plato's view of the transmigration of
souls. To Aristotle the soul *(psyche)* "is in some sense the principle of all
animal life."[17] He even took the view that every living thing had some
kind of a soul *(psyche)*. What distinguishes the human soul from all other
kinds of souls is its rational capacity.[18] Humanity is both a rational animal and a political animal.[19] This means more than just that human
beings live together like bees and other gregarious creatures. "It is a
characteristic of man that he alone has any sense of good and evil, of
just and unjust, and the like, and the association of living beings who
have this sense makes a family and a state."[20]

Aristotle's ethical teaching appears in three treatises, the *Nicomachean
Ethics*, the *Eudemian Ethics* and the *Magna Moralia.*[21] The word *ethics*
transliterates the Greek work *ēthika*. In modern usage ethics have to do
with the standards which regulate behavior. But Aristotle's understanding of ethics had more to do with habit and character. He was concerned
with *aretē* and *eudaimonia*. The former term often has the sense of
"virtue," and the latter of "happiness." But in Aristotle's ethics *aretē* has
more the sense of "excellence." It is something which characterizes both
passions and actions.[22] Just as we can ask what makes an excellent axe
or an excellent argument, we can also ask what makes human excellence. Aristotle replied in terms of *eudaimonia*. This was not happiness
in the sense of the satisfaction of physical needs and desires, but the
actualization of what human beings are capable of. The highest activity
lies in contemplation, but not at the expense of health and material
needs. The wise person is "dearest to the gods."[23] For if the gods care
about human affairs, as they are thought to do, they will care most for
those who care for the same things as they do. And those who are
dearest to the gods will presumably be the happiest.

In order to prepare for the happy life of excellence, human beings need training in the development of habits in a society governed under the right laws. They need to act rationally and live according to the mean. Wisdom and virtue lie in the avoidance of extremes.[24] Bravery lies between cowardice and foolhardiness. Temperance avoids the excesses of profligacy and asceticism. In saying this, Aristotle was not so much providing procedures for making moral decisions, but was making what might be called meta-ethical statements about the form of moral concepts. Virtue lies in between opposite extremes. Aristotle's teaching laid the basis for what came to be known as the doctrine of the Golden Mean.[25]

In contrast with much modern thinking which focuses on the subjective individual, and which fails to see any overall structure and purpose in the world, Aristotle was concerned with the discovery of objective truth and purpose. His starting point was the conviction that "every art and every inquiry, and similarly every action and choice, is thought to aim at some good; and for this reason the good has rightly been declared to be that at which all things aim."[26] To Aristotle virtue was not something that could be separated from character. "Moral excellence," he observed "comes about as a result of habit."[27] By the word *habit* Aristotle meant an inward characteristic or ability. This observation led Aristotle to make a complex analysis of the relationship between human action and character formation. Moreover, action and character could not be separated from life in the context of society.

In the Middle Ages Aristotle provided conceptual tools for Thomas Aquinas in the development of his ethical thinking in the second part of his *Summa Theologiae*. In recent years it has provided impetus to Christian ethicists like Stanley Hauerwas[28] and Alasdair MacIntyre[29] in their endeavors to present a rational and coherent account of ethics for the present age, which faces the confusion and lack of character of liberal individualism.[30]

4. EPICUREANS, STOICS, SKEPTICS AND CYNICS

T*he golden age of Plato and Aristotle was followed by the age of Hellenistic* philosophy. The word *Hellenism* is connected with the Greek word for a Greek, *Hellēn*. Originally the word *Hellēnismos* denoted the dominance of the "common Greek" language. But later on Hellenism came to denote the period in which Greek power and culture dominated the Eastern Mediterranean world. Some writers have attempted to give chronological precision to the Hellenistic age by dating it from 323 B.C., the year of the death of Alexander the Great, to 30 B.C., when the Romans overthrew the last Greek empire. But ages cannot be dated with absolute precision. The period was in the making before Alexander's death. His expeditions to the East were already extending Greek influence. Nor did that influence suddenly terminate with the ascendency of the Romans. Hellenism in general was a complex phenomenon in which Greek power and culture infiltrated the East, but in turn was influenced by the East. Part of this phenomenon was the interaction of Greek and Jewish culture and religion which provided the milieu for the rise of Christianity. In the realm of philosophy the age was characterized by the emergence of new schools of thought. Athens remained the center of Greek philosophy. The Aristotelian tradition was continued by the Peripatetics. But onto the scene came the rival schools of Epicureans, Stoics and Skeptics.[1]

Epicureanism
Epicureanism is the philosophy associated with Epicurus (c. 341-270 B.C.). However, his teaching has survived only in fragments and letters. From the days of Epicurus himself down to modern times, Epicureanism

has been alternately admired and despised. When the disciples of Epicurus preached their message to Rome, around 170 B.C., the ruling
aristocracy, whose power was founded on authority and tradition, had
them expelled as dangerous subversives. However, a century later when
Greek culture had penetrated Roman society more deeply, Epicureanism
won more converts. Among them was the poet Lucretius (99/94-55/51
B.C.) whose great poem *On the Nature of Things* presented a major exposition of Epicurean doctrine. Classical Epicureanism survived into the
third century of the Christian era,[2] but was revived in more modern
times. In the Renaissance Lucretius was rediscovered as a poet. In the
seventeenth century the rationalist scientist and priest, Pierre Gassendi,
put forward an atomistic theory of the universe based on the Epicurean
model which he derived from his study of classical Epicurean texts. In
the eighteenth century materialistically inclined thinkers—among them
David Hume and Thomas Jefferson—made professions of Epicureanism. In many respects the empiricism of modern times may be seen as
a linear descendent of classical Epicureanism.

The age which saw the birth of Epicureanism and Stoicism was an age
of uncertainty and unrest. The democratic ideals of the city-state had lost
their appeal amid the political power struggles and the economic crises
of the times. The great minds of the previous century—Plato and Aristotle—seemed to have no message for the disillusioned and the skeptical. The temples and the deities remained, but people were beginning
to question them. It was in such an age that the Epicureans and Stoics
presented their competing world views as answers to the questions that
were troubling the hearts and minds of the thoughtful.

In a sense, Epicurus was the forerunner of the modern empiricist. He
taught that all our knowledge derives from the sensations we receive
from the use of our senses. Repeated sensations give rise to general
concepts which enable us to make judgments. Using Epicurus's own
example, we are able to recognize a horse, a cow or a man because our
present perceptions fit the previous perceptions which we associate with
these words.[3] Whether a judgment is correct or not must be confirmed
by evidence in the light of closer inspection.

Epicurus went on to say that the world is made up of indivisible elements which move about in a void. These atoms are infinite in number,

and are in continual motion. Sometimes they swerve at random. This guarantees a certain indeterminacy and freedom to human action. The atoms collide and form objects. Our world is one of an infinite number of worlds, some of which resemble our world and some of which do not. Particular objects and our world itself change and perish. But the atoms are indestructible and do not change. They continue to exist in different configurations.[4]

As Epicurus pondered the subject of nature, he came to accept a doctrine of the survival of the fittest. He rejected the idea of destiny and divine providence. Epicurus allowed that the gods exist, but insisted that popular conceptions of the gods were mistaken.[5] For one thing, there were not as many gods as people believed. For another thing, the gods do not interfere in the affairs of the world. There is no such thing as an afterlife. Death is simply the end of human life, and with it the end of our experience of good and evil.[6] For with the death of the body, our senses also die. And so we lose our capacity to feel pleasure and pain. Death, therefore, is not to be feared as an evil.

Few people today study the thoughts of Epicurus, but his name survives in the term *epicure*. It is a term which conjures up the image of persons who pride themselves on their good taste, especially in matters of food and wine. It suggests someone who elevates material pleasure in personal consumption to a fine art. Although one can draw a line of descent from the modern idea of an epicure back to Epicurus himself, the modern image of the epicure is not exactly what Epicurus himself had in mind. Admittedly he viewed the world as essentially material. He regarded pleasure as "our first and kindred good,"[7] and saw pain as an evil. In making decisions, the one should be measured against the other. But Epicurus recognized that bread and water could sometimes give more pleasure than the most expensive food. Real pleasure was "the absence of pain in the body and of trouble in the soul."[8] Indulgence in either sex or gourmet food could cause both of these. The greatest good was therefore prudence, for from it sprang all the other virtues. The prudent person was capable of enjoying the pleasures of the mind and dismissing the dark thoughts of fate, chance and the fear of death, which afflict the rest of humanity.

The school of Epicurus was as much a commune as an academy.

Epicurus himself was a kind of secular evangelist who preached a gospel of nature. He presided over his community, which included both men and women. The sect practiced a certain austerity, though it was not immune from charges of indulging in orgies and sexual license. The Epicurean communities offered their members an escape from ordinary society and an alternative lifestyle, guided by the teachings of their master. Epicurus rejected some of the traditional ideas of education. He warned against assuming heavy responsibilities like marriage and having children. It is better to be independent, he said, and enjoy the security of a quiet life withdrawn from the multitude.

Stoicism

A major rival to Epicureanism was Stoicism, which was a dominant philosophical force for five hundred years.[9] Whereas Epicureanism won a following among the elite and cultured, Stoicism had a much broader appeal. Stoicism began in Greece but was eventually embraced by some of the best Roman minds. It spans a time frame from the third century B.C. to the second century A.D. Stoicism got its name from the *poikilē stoa*, the Painted Porch, in Athens where Zeno of Citium began to teach round about 300 B.C.[10] The place was actually a colonnade containing paintings or frescoes, and was more or less the equivalent of the National Gallery of ancient Athens. Zeno attracted a considerable following. In due course all kinds of honors were showered on him. Not the least of these were a golden crown and a bronze statue. The term *Stoic* eventually replaced the earlier term *Zenonian* as a title for Zeno's followers.

Stoicism went through three main phases. The term *Early Stoa* is given to Zeno and his immediate successors, Cleanthes and Chrysippus, and other followers down to Antipater who died in 129 B.C. Only fragments of their writings remain, though Diogenes Laertius gives an extensive account of them in Book 7 of his *Lives of Eminent Philosophers*. Zeno appears to have stressed the need for strength of character in personal ethics and politics. Cleanthes was a poet and religious visionary. He was the author of the celebrated "Hymn to Zeus,"[11] which depicts human beings as the children of Zeus, the universal Word or *logos* which sustains all things. Chrysippus was responsible for turning Stoicism into a system. It was said of him that "if the gods took to dialectic, they would adopt no other system than that of Chrysippus."[12] However, his reputation was tarnished by the story of his being somewhat unsteady on his legs at wine parties. On a happier note it was said that "but for Chrysippus, there would have been no Stoa." Diogenes Laertius gave him the following obituary:

> Chrysippus turned giddy after gulping down a draught of Bacchus; he spared not the Stoa nor his country nor his own life, but fared straight to the house of Hades.[13]

The Middle Stoa flourished in the second and first centuries B.C. Its most distinguished members were Paenetius of Rhodes and his pupil Posidonius of Apamea. Under Paenetius it began to win a following among Roman intellectuals. Among them was Scipio. Posidonius developed a golden age theory of history and theorized about cosmology.

The Late Stoa belongs to the Roman world of the Christian era. Its three greatest representatives were Seneca, Epictetus and the emperor Marcus Aurelius. Seneca (c. 4 B.C.-A.D. 65) was an orator and tragedian. With Seneca the diatribe acquired renewed popularity as a vehicle for expressing ideas and teaching. The term comes from the Greek *diatribē*, meaning discourse or short ethical treatise. It had been developed by Zeno and Cleanthes, and became a characteristic vehicle for Stoic and Cynic teaching. Seneca served as tutor, political adviser and minister to Nero. A man of the world, some people found it difficult to reconcile his practices with the moral teaching of his treatises. Seneca found it increasingly difficult to condone the crimes of Nero and retired from public life. Eventually he was obliged to relinquish his vast wealth to the emperor. He devoted his last years to the study of philosophy and the company of friends. In A.D. 65 he was forced to commit suicide on account of alleged conspiracy against the emperor. Jerome and Augustine both mention correspondence between Seneca and the apostle Paul, but the letters that have been preserved are apocryphal and spurious.[14] There is also the wider question of whether Paul's writings made use of the literary technique of the Stoic diatribe, which we shall explore in the next chapter.

Epictetus (c. 50-c. 138) was a freed slave of a member of Nero's bodyguard. He remained in Rome until A.D. 90, when the emperor Domitian expelled philosophers from the city. His teaching is preserved in the *Discourses* taken down by his pupil Arrianus, who also compiled Epictetus's *Enchiridion* or *Manual*. Like Seneca, he was chiefly concerned with ethical matters. He believed in innate moral predispositions which could either be left to decay or actualized by education.

The last of the great Stoics was Marcus Aurelius (121-180), who became emperor in 161. He was the author of a series of *Meditations* which he wrote in Greek on the marshes by the Danube while struggling against the barbarians. He had a profound distrust of logic and cosmology. Like earlier Stoics, Marcus Aurelius distinguished between the body, the soul or life and the mind *(nous)*.[15] He agreed with Epictetus in saying that the mind was the spark of divinity in everyone. God was thus in everyone. However, the *nous* will perish in the conflagration which brings the cosmos to an end. In his moral teaching he stressed inward self-control and useful citizenship. Life should be faced rationally with Stoic calm, regardless of whether there is a purposeful providence or chaos.

> Either there is a fatal necessity and invincible order, or a kind Providence, or a confusion without a purpose and without a director. If then there is an invincible necessity, why dost thou resist? But if there is a Providence which allows itself to be propitiated, make thyself worthy of the help of the divinity. But if there is a confusion without a governor, be content that in such a tempest thou hast in thyself a certain ruling intelligence. And even if the tempest carry thee away, let it carry away the poor flesh, the poor breath, everything else; for the intelligence at least it will not carry away.[16]

Marcus Aurelius was widely regarded as a great emperor. But it was the values that he himself prized that caused him to despise the Christian church. His reign witnessed persecutions in different parts of the Roman Empire, and a number of writers addressed apologies to him.

Today the word *Stoic* suggests people who do not set their hopes too high or allow their fears to overwhelm them. To face life stoically is to make oneself as immune as possible to joy and distress. It is to embrace the outlook recommended by Marcus Aurelius in his *Meditations*. But historical Stoicism was more than that. It embraced a range of ideas not only in the field of ethics, but also in logic and physics. From the standpoint of religion, the most significant aspect of Stoicism is what has been called "a 'mundanization' or materialization of the divine, or, on the contrary, a divinization or spiritualization of matter."[17] Zeno and his followers taught that

> there are two principles in the universe, the active principle and the passive. The passive principle, then, is a substance without quality, i.e. matter, whereas the active is the reason [or *logos*] inherent in this substance, that is, God. For he is everlasting and is the artificer of each several thing throughout the whole extent of matter.[18]

Zeno could also say that "God is one and the same with Reason, Fate and Zeus; he is also called by many other names."[19] The term *kosmos* could likewise mean God himself, the orderly arrangement of the heavenly bodies, or the sum total of God and the universe together.[20] The Stoics had various arguments for the existence of God. But perhaps the most basic one was the belief that people everywhere have a sense of God's existence. As Cicero summed it up in his treatise *On the Nature of the Gods:* "The main issue is agreed among all men of all nations, inasmuch as all have engraved in their minds an innate belief that the gods exist."[21]

Although classical Stoicism came to an end with Marcus Aurelius, its ideas continued to make themselves felt in the sixteenth century and beyond. The New Testament presents the apostle Paul drawing on and responding to Stoic teaching (as we shall see in the next chapter). Echoes of Stoic teaching can be found in such an unlikely pair as Calvin and Spinoza. Calvin could speak like Cicero of a sense of God engraved on the hearts of men. Spinoza's idea of the single reality of God or nature is a restatement of the Stoic view of reality. But these are questions that we shall have to look at more closely later on.

Skepticism

The first skeptics were not called skeptics. They were called Pyrrhoneans after the name of their master, Pyrrho of Elis (c. 360-c. 270 B.C.).[22] The Greek word *skeptikos* originally meant an "inquirer." But from the time of Pyrrho it acquired the overtone of casting doubt on the claims of people to know facts and of questioning whether facts are knowable at all. Pyrrho himself left behind no writings. What is known about him and his ideas is gleaned chiefly from the writings of Diogenes Laertius and Sextus Empiricus, both of whom lived in the second or third centuries of the Christian era. Sextus Empiricus was certainly a skeptic, and Diogenes Laertius may well have been one too. The early skeptics believed in what they called *epochē*, which meant suspension of judgment about things which were not evident. One early skeptic pushed this suspension of judgment to its logical conclusion, when he challenged the propriety of calling the movement by the name of Pyrrhonism. After all, no one could be sure what Pyrrho himself intended, and without knowing that the skeptics could not call themselves Pyrrhonists.[23] However, it was agreed that one could call oneself a Pyrrhonean if one's lifestyle resembled Pyrrho's.

The stories told about Pyrrho suggest that he tried to avoid all theories about the nature of reality or even thinking about the future. For theorizing only led to frustration, and wondering about what might happen simply made one worry. Pyrrho's goal, like that of his followers down to Sextus Empiricus, was to attain *ataraxia*, the state of being unperturbed. The story is told about Pyrrho that he was once on a ship in a storm. The other passengers became unnerved, but Pyrrho "kept calm and confident, pointing to a little pig in the ship that went on eating, and telling them that such was the unperturbed state *[ataraxia]* in which the wise man should keep himself."[24]

It fell to Pyrrho's successors to codify the teaching of skepticism. In the meantime the Academy at Athens went the way of skepticism. Following the death of Plato there was a backlash against Platonism. In the third century B.C. Arcesilaus inaugurated what came to be known as the Middle Academy. Its skeptical approach lasted for two centuries. Arcesilaus himself urged a return to Socrates. Instead of imparting knowledge and accepting the dogmas of the philosophical schools, one should follow Socrates and devote one's energies to the refutation of erroneous thinking. The Middle Academy gave way to the even more skeptical New Academy. A major object of attack was Stoicism. In particular, the Academicians attacked such matters as our criteria for knowing, dogmatic ideas about the nature of the universe, belief in fate and beliefs about the nature of the gods.

Round about 80 B.C. the Academy reverted to dogmatism. But soon

afterwards a skeptical school was founded at Alexandria which revived
Pyrrhonism. In the course of time this school forged links with the
empirical school of medicine. The empirical school of medicine laid
stress on observing symptoms, describing syndromes, and noting connections between them. This was in contrast with the theoretical or
logical school of medicine, which went in for elaborate theorizing about
the hidden causes of disease. The greatest representative of the alliance
between the skeptical school of philosophy and the empirical school of
medicine was the man who came to be thought of as the codifier of
Greek skepticism, Sextus Empiricus.

Sextus Empiricus lived in the last half of the second century and the
first quarter of the third century of the Christian era. He knew Athens,
Rome and Alexandria, but no one today knows exactly where he taught.
Two of his major works have survived. Together they constitute the only
complete, firsthand account of classical skepticism. His *Outlines of Pyrrhonism* appear to contain introductory lectures which define the key terms
of skepticism and attack the dogmas of Stoicism. *Against the Dogmatists*
uses skeptical techniques to refute philosophers and scientists. In logic
Sextus Empiricus tried to show that syllogisms were really vicious circles,
since the truth of the conclusion was already contained in the major
premise.[25] His own general position was equally opposed to the dogmatism of the Stoics and the hardline skepticism of the Academy. He took
the view that in the light of conflicting arguments the proper course of
action was to suspend judgment. A case in point is that of the existence
or non-existence of the gods. "For different people have differing and
discordant notions about them, with the result that it is possible neither
to believe all of them, as they are conflicting, nor to believe some of
them, on account of their being of equal force."[26]

The skepticism that Sextus Empiricus advocated belonged to what
might be called the soft variety. It did not extend to everything. Suspension of judgment *(epochē)* applied only to claims about reality behind
phenomena. It was a means to attaining the state of being unperturbed,
ataraxia. Even the arguments of the skeptic laid no claim to absolute
validity. Sextus Empiricus thought of them as a kind of mental laxative.

In regard to all the Sceptic formulae it must be understood in advance
that we make no assertions to the effect that they are absolutely true.

We even say that they can be used to cancel themselves, since they are included in those things to which they refer, just as purgative medicines not only remove the humours from the body but expel themselves together with the humours. Also, we do not pretend that in setting up these formulae we are revealing the real nature of the things for which they are used. On the contrary, we use them indifferently and (if you will) loosely.[27]

Sextus Empiricus was well aware of the problems that he would create for himself if skepticism were pushed to its limits. The only outcome would be a mental paralysis, brought about by doubt about everything. Instead of producing a state of unperturbedness, it could result in inner turmoil and panic caused by mental and moral inertia. Sextus Empiricus was the last major skeptic of the ancient world. The above quotation highlights the uses and limitations of skepticism. Critical scrutiny of claims and counterclaims is useful. But to take refuge in the existence of conflicting opinions on any matter is to confuse the problem with the solution. The pursuit of knowledge requires careful examination of conflicting views and the evaluation of them. The soft type of skepticism advocated by Sextus Empiricus was skeptical about metaphysical questions but shrank from consistent application of skeptical techniques to more mundane questions. It has commended itself to thinkers over and over again. But it has never succeeded in carrying complete conviction. For the cut-off point at which one stopped being skeptical had an air of being arbitrary. Moreover, to live on a diet of skepticism is like living on a diet of laxatives.

Skepticism was still sufficiently important in Augustine's day for the saint to write a refutation in the form of his treatise *Against the Academicians.* Interest in skepticism and the thought of Sextus Empiricus resurfaced in the sixteenth century, and played a major part in shaping the course of European philosophy. But of this we shall have more to say in a later chapter.

Cynics

Among the contemporaries of the Stoics and the skeptics were the Cynics. The Cynics never really amounted to an organized school, but they form part of the world of ancient philosophy and the background of the

New Testament. Their history goes back to the colorful figure of Diogenes of Sinope (c. 400-325 B.C.), whose outrageous behavior earned him the nickname *kyon* or "dog." The term *Cynic* is formed from the adjective *kynikos* or "dog-like." The story is told of how he once heard Plato conversing about the Forms, using words like "tablehood" and "cuphood." Diogenes commented: "Table and cup I see; but your tablehood and cuphood, Plato, I can nowise see." To this Plato replied: "That's readily accounted for, for you have the eyes to see the visible table and cup; but not the understanding by which the ideal tablehood and cuphood are discerned." To Plato, Diogenes was a "Socrates gone mad."[28]

Numerous epigrams were attributed to Diogenes. The love of money was "the mother-city of all evils."[29] Good men were "the images of the gods, and love the business of the idle."[30] There was a touch of the actor in him. He lit a lamp in broad daylight, and as he went about he said, "I am looking for a man."[31] Greed, pretentiousness and folly were constant targets of his wit. His underlying message was that happiness is to be found by satisfying one's natural needs in the simplest, cheapest and most basic ways. The result was a philosophy of life which combined self-sufficiency with shamelessness. Conventions which he deemed unnatural could be flouted. He could praise the value of having laws, but saw nothing wrong in having a community of wives, or for that matter, a community of sons.[32]

The Cynics flourished in the third century B.C. and helped to shape Stoic thought.[33] In the writings of Epictetus, Diogenes is no longer the showman and master of repartee, but an ennobled detached ascetical teacher. For a time the Cynics faded out, but the movement saw a revival in the first century A.D. Cynicism was a movement of extremes. On the one hand, there were the wandering preachers of simplicity who went about Greece with stick and knapsack proclaiming that one could live happily in the midst of turmoil by renouncing possessions and keeping aloof from social entanglements. On the other hand, there were the somewhat disreputable Cynic beggar-philosophers who became familiar figures in Rome and the Orient, and who survive in literature into the sixth century.[34]

5. FROM GREEKS
TO GOSPEL

How *does all this tie in with Christian faith and practice? Not all that long* ago it was fashionable to draw sharp lines between Greek philosophy and Jewish and Christian ways of thinking. Greeks were said to believe in the immortality of the soul; Christians believed in the resurrection of the body. Greeks were said to think abstractly; biblical writers were said to think concretely. Greeks were thought to share a cyclical view of time; the Jews had a linear view. The grammar of the Greek and Hebrew languages was said to have played a basic part in shaping the ways that Greeks and Jews thought about things. But from what we have seen here in this quick sketch of Greek thinkers, it is clear that the Greeks did not think alike.

It is now evident from linguistic studies that the argument about different grammatical patterns shaping different outlooks is grossly exaggerated.[1] It is also clear from the study of Jewish history in the centuries preceding the birth of Jesus that Judaism was far more pervasively influenced by Hellenism than had been acknowledged.[2] But the question remains: How does New Testament Christianity relate to Greek philosophy? To answer this question adequately is a major field of study in itself. Scholars spend their lives exploring the many facets of the New Testament in the light of the culture, ideas, and history of the ancient world. Such an undertaking lies outside the scope of this book.[3] However, we can pinpoint some key issues. But before we do so, it will be helpful to take note of a Jewish writer who was a contemporary of Jesus and Paul and who drew extensively on Greek thought to interpret the Jewish faith—Philo of Alexandria.

Philo of Alexandria

It has been said that "the history of Christian philosophy begins not with a Christian but with a Jew, Philo of Alexandria, elder contemporary of St. Paul."[4] To this could be added the further paradox that nowhere in his voluminous writings does Philo mention Christianity. Very little is actually known about Philo's life (c. 20 B.C.—c. A.D. 50).[5] He appears to have belonged to a wealthy, aristocratic Jewish family. He acted as a customs agent, collecting dues on all goods imported into Egypt from the East. He seems to have been given Roman citizenship. He once headed a delegation to the Roman emperor to seek redress for wrongs inflicted on the Jews. He also made a visit to the Jerusalem temple. But beyond such bare facts his life is shrouded in obscurity. On the other hand, he left behind him over thirty books which show what could happen when Greek philosophy came into contact with Jewish tradition.

Philo has been variously seen as a great thinker, a rigid proponent of Jewish orthodoxy, and as a simple-minded exegete of the Jewish Scriptures who was dazzled by the glitter of Greek philosophy and culture. Certainly he was not an original philosopher, but the gaps in his education are now seen to lie more in his lack of Jewish training than in his philosophical reading.[6] Although his writings were cast largely in the form of biblical interpretation, Philo seems to have relied almost exclusively on Greek translations of the Bible, being apparently unable to consult the Hebrew original. Philo wrote as a Jew in a Gentile world. He was thoroughly conversant with Greek literature and the prevailing philosophies of his day—Platonism, Stoicism and Neopythagoreanism. Perhaps he may be best described as a Jew who was deeply committed to the institutions of Judaism, and who wrote "to deliver his Jewish compatriots from an oppressive sense of inferiority that came from living in the shadow of a pervasive, powerful and alluring hellenistic culture." Turning the tables, he sought to show that "Judaism was superior to Hellenism—that Plato took his great insights from Moses and that the Hebrew Scriptures were both compatible with and superior to Hellenism."[7]

Philo's name is linked with allegorical interpretation of Scripture, which was widely followed in the Christian church down to the present day. Basically this was an attempt to discern deeper truths and spiritual

implications behind the more obvious sense of the text. But the method
itself was much older than Philo. It was already used in the sixth century
B.C. by Theagenes of Rhegium to explain Homer. It was employed by
the Cynics and Stoics to demythologize the gods. The method can be
seen in Cicero's account of how the Stoics explained the gods as natural
forces.

This subject was handled by Zeno and was later explained more fully
by Cleanthes and Chrysippus. For example, an ancient belief pre-
vailed throughout Greece that Caelus was mutilated by his son Saturn,
and Saturn himself thrown into bondage by his son Jove: now these
immoral fables enshrined a decidedly clever scientific theory. Their
meaning was that the highest element of celestial ether or fire, which
by itself generates all things, is devoid of that bodily part which requires union with another for the work of procreation.[8]

Philo adapted the technique of allegorical interpretation to explain the
Jewish Scriptures. His exegetical writings are divided into three main
categories.[9] The first consists of *Questions and Answers to Genesis and Exodus* in which a brief literary answer is followed by lengthy allegorical
explanation. The second category deals with the *Allegory of the Law*, and
consists of treatises giving detailed exposition of Scripture. The third
deals with broad themes under the general title of *Exposition of the Law.*

Here we can give only one out of countless examples of Philo's allegorical method. Psalm 46:4 speaks of "a river whose streams make glad
the city of God." Now Philo knew full well that no river runs through
Jerusalem. He, therefore, argued that the passage must be taken allegorically to "show something different from the obvious." The river refers
to "the impetuous rush of the divine word," which gladdens the whole
universe.[10] Philo's language combines the Old Testament idea of the
Word of the Lord with the Stoic concept of the Logos in an interpretation which sees a philosophical and mystical meaning in the psalm.

Elsewhere Philo could speak of "the saintly company of the Pythagoreans" and "the sacred authority of Plato."[11] His account of creation
pictured God fashioning the world in accordance with ideas which had
"no other location than the Divine Reason, which was the Author of this
ordered frame."[12] Whether Philo believed in creation from nothing or
creation from some form of primary matter is open to question. So too

is the question of whether the world had a beginning or whether it was eternal. On the other hand, there can be no doubt that Philo's thought was a conscious synthesis which drew on a wide range of Greek ideas in order to interpret the teaching of the Jewish Scriptures. In the judgment of a leading modern authority on Philo, David Winston, "In Philo's philosophy, the Logos is the Divine Mind, the Idea of Ideas, the first-begotten Son of the Uncreated Father, eldest and chief of the angels, the man or shadow of God, or even the second God, the pattern of all creation and the archetype of human reason. The Logos is God immanent, holding together and administering the entire chain of creation . . . , and man's mind is but a tiny fragment of this all-pervading Logos."[13]

The chief followers of Philo were not Jews but Christian intellectuals of the second and third centuries. Perhaps one reason for this was the extent of Hellenistic influence on Philo's mind in an age when the catastrophes which befell Judaism caused Jews to turn back to their Jewish roots and specifically Jewish traditions. The Jews followed the rabbinic interpretation of Scripture as set out in the Mishnah and later the Talmud. As a consequence, Philo seems to stand closer to the Christian philosophical theologians of Alexandria, Clement and Origen than he does to either the rabbinic tradition or the apostle Paul.

The Apostle Paul and Ancient Philosophy

When we turn to the New Testament, we find only one reference to the word *philosophy* and just one reference to "philosophers." The latter comes in Acts 17:18, which mentions the apostle Paul's meeting with some Epicurean and Stoic philosophers at Athens. To some it seemed that Paul was preaching foreign divinities because he preached Jesus and the resurrection. The encounter leads to Paul's Areopagus address. What is striking about this address is the fact that Paul assumes a point of contact. There is no need for him to attempt to demonstrate the existence of God. That point is not an issue. The Athenians are in every way "very religious" (Acts 17:22). It is the character and actions of God, on the one hand, and the appropriate human response, on the other hand, that are the key questions. But here too there is a point of contact. For Paul goes on to give two quotations from Greek authors in support of his contention that God is not far from each one of us. "For 'In him we live and move and have our being'; as even some of your own poets have said, 'For we are indeed his offspring' " (Acts 17:28 RSV).

The whole passage has been the subject of much discussion.[14] The Areopagus address may well follow the pattern of the rhetorical model of the day. But our special interest here lies in this: Paul bases his argument on the fact that Greek thinkers have genuine insights into the existence and character of God. The quotations from Greek authors, when placed in their context, address God as Zeus, the principal deity as understood in the Stoic tradition.[15] As such, he is the father of human-kind and the source of all life. God is, therefore, not to be thought of as a finite being that dwells in a shrine. The deity should not be thought of as an image. But this is as far as natural knowledge goes. It is supplemented by the gospel of Christ, which calls all people everywhere to repent because God "has fixed a day on which he will judge the world in righteousness by a man whom he has appointed, and of this he has given assurance to all men by raising him from the dead" (Acts 17:31 RSV). Mention of the resurrection had a triple effect. It caused some to mock, others to want to hear more at a later date, and some to believe.

It has been argued that Paul's strategy at Athens was a mistaken failure in view of the modest handful of converts he left behind. Certainly there was no major church in Athens comparable with the other churches that Paul founded in the course of his missionary journeys. The absence of such a church is seen by some as proof of the failure that results from deploying philosophical arguments instead of preaching the gospel. Others have seen this presumed comparative failure as tacit testimony to the weakness of natural theology as compared with the power evangelism associated with the signs and wonders which accompanied the apostolic preaching of the gospel.

But both these conclusions are premature and false. Closer examination of Paul's earlier missionary strategy in the churches of Asia Minor and Greece shows that his success was frequently mixed and that Paul did not found a major church everywhere that he preached. In and of itself public response to an idea is not a measure of its truth and validity. However, it is worthwhile to reflect further on Paul's argument in its historical context. For Paul had already used a similar argument at Lystra, and he went on to repeat it in his letter to the Romans.

At Lystra the preaching of Paul and Barnabas led to a remarkable incident in which a lame man was enabled to walk (Acts 14:8-20). The citizens of Lystra greeted the event as an act of divine intervention, believing that the gods had come down to earth in the persons of Paul and Barnabas. They hailed Barnabas as Zeus, the chief god and guardian of human beings and also the god of weather, presumably because Barnabas remained silent. As Paul was doing most of the talking, they hailed him as Hermes, the messenger of the gods, on the assumption that he was acting as spokesman for Barnabas. The priest of Zeus, whose temple lay outside the city, even wanted to offer sacrifice to them. But Paul and Barnabas tore their garments and rushed among the people crying:

> Men, why are you doing this? We also are men, of like nature with you, and bring you good news, that you should turn from these vain things to a living God who made the heaven and the earth and the sea and all that is in them. In past generations he allowed all the nations to walk in their own ways; yet he did not leave himself without witness, for he did good and gave you from heaven rains and fruitful seasons, satisfying your hearts with food and gladness. (Acts 14:15-17 RSV)

Luke, the author of the Acts of the Apostles, notes that with these words, they scarcely restrained the populace from offering sacrifice to them. However, there was a sudden reversal of fortune. Hostile Jews came along from Antioch and Iconium and urged the people to turn against Paul, who was stoned and dragged from the city in the belief that he was dead.

Two things stand out from this episode. The first is Paul's contention that nature bears witness to the goodness and greatness of God. Nature herself bears ample testimony to the fact that the Creator should not be confused with the creature. But this leads us to the other thing that stands out, the power of preconceptions and world views over the way people perceive things. This power is so great that it can distort not only the way people think about nature at large but about the ways people see particular events. It was evident to those present that a remarkable healing had taken place through the agency of Paul. But the citizens of

Lystra saw the event in the light of their world view with its beliefs in the ancient deities of Greece. The protestations of Paul and Barnabas had a temporary restraining effect. But all this was swept away with the arrival of hostile Jews from Antioch and Iconium who succeeded in defaming the character of the apostle. It was not that the basic fact of the healing had changed; it was the way that this fact was interpreted in the light of the preconceptions that were brought to bear on it. First, there were the preconceptions which led the citizens of Lystra to treat Paul and Barnabas as gods in human form. Then there was Paul's interpretation which countered this view. Finally, there were the representations of Paul's Jewish opponents which produced a complete reversal of the original interpretation. From being venerated as a god Paul was treated as a evildoer worthy of death.

The teaching attributed to the apostle Paul on these two occasions described in Acts 14 and 17 was evidently adapted to gentile audiences. When Paul preached to Jewish audiences, he emphasized themes which addressed the Jewish religious situation.[16] Nevertheless, this appeal to revelation in nature and a natural awareness of God is not isolated and unique. It could well be that Paul's experience of preaching in Greece, particularly at Lystra and Athens, underlies his teaching in his letter to the Romans. This letter was evidently written from nearby Corinth, either immediately after he had moved on from Athens or more likely during his last stay there.[17] At any rate Paul sets out the same basic argument in the opening chapters of Romans that we have already noted in his preaching at Lystra and Athens. Paul uses it as testimony to the goodness and greatness of God and as the foundation of his argument that human beings are accountable to God. But as in the preaching described in the Acts of the Apostles, this knowledge of God through nature is supplemented by the gospel.

In Romans 1:19-20 Paul writes: "What can be known about God is plain to them, because God has shown it to them. Ever since the creation of the world his invisible nature, namely, his eternal power and deity, has been clearly perceived in the things that have been made. So they are without excuse" (RSV). Here too Paul is not arguing that God exists; he is arguing about the notions of God that we should have and the kind of response that we should make in view of human experience in the world. The Creator should not be confused with the creature. The one who is mighty enough to bring all things into being should not be reduced to the level of the creature. But this is just what human beings have done in their folly, and the present plight of humankind is the result of human failure to respond to God.

In Acts Paul drew on Greek authors in support of his argument. In Romans 1 he draws on the Wisdom of Solomon 13, which likewise speaks of the inexcusable human folly in failing to respond to the works of God in creation. Here and elsewhere Paul can draw on both Old Testament teaching and outside thought, including Stoic ideas,[18] in order to make his point. But whenever Paul does this, he is not simply embracing Greek philosophy. He can draw on Philo and Hellenistic Jewish thought, and he uses the language of Stoicism. He can acknowledge that Stoics and others have genuine insights and correct ideas. But his message tells of something that cannot be found in philosophy, the gospel of Jesus Christ.[19] Moreover, philosophical ideas need to be corrected in the light of the truth that Paul found in Christ.

How does all this tie in with the apparent denigration of philosophy in Colossians 2:8, which is the only place in the New Testament where the word *philosophy* is actually mentioned? Here the readers are warned: "See to it that no one makes a prey of you by philosophy and empty deceit, according to human tradition, according to the elemental spirits of the universe, and not according to Christ" (RSV). Scholars see in this admonition a warning against a variety of possible philosophies, ranging from the pursuit of wisdom, through sundry Jewish sects, to incipient gnosticism, and the worship of the elements of earth, fire, water and air.[20] On the other hand, it is possible that there is an element of irony here. The following verses do not explicitly address philosophical questions. Instead, they talk about matters like circumcision, food, feasts, the sabbath and angel worship. All these were matters of importance to Jews, but which Paul now sees to be made obsolete and irrelevant by Christ's death. They are, in fact, a form of bondage from which Christ has made the believer free. It may be, therefore, that Paul is ironically calling these practices "philosophy and empty deceit, according to human tradition." To put trust in such things is like trusting some empty alien philosophy which is the product of human tradition.

Before we leave these brief comments on the apostle Paul and ancient philosophy, it is important to note the change of approach that has taken place in the interpretation of Paul. In the earlier part of the present century Paul was repeatedly represented as a kind of Platonist. Typical of this view was George Holley Gilbert's claim that:

In his view of man's constitution the apostle stands with the Greek philosophers rather than with the Hebrew Scriptures. With Plato he thinks of a human being as consisting of an outer man and an inner man (2 Cor. 4:16), and with Greek philosophy in general he thinks of the body as the prison of the spirit (Rom. 7:24; 8:23). With the Orphic faith he holds the doctrine of original sin and locates the evil principle in the "flesh," where it has been enthroned since the hour of Adam's transgression (Rom. 5:12). The dual aspect of this thought comes to its classic expression in Rom. 7:15-18.[21]

In response to these claims, two comments are in order. On the one hand, close examination of what Paul actually wrote shows that this claim cannot be substantiated. Modern biblical exegetes see Paul's understanding of human nature as diametrically opposite to the Platonic Greek dichotomy of body and soul.[22] On the other hand, recent research into the life and thought of the apostle Paul has increasingly stressed Paul's thoroughly Jewish character.[23] Paul's understanding of human nature is to be seen in the light of the Old Testament Scriptures. If Paul could on occasion use the language of Greek philosophy, it was the language of Stoicism, rather than that of Platonism. But in such cases Paul's purpose was not to teach philosophy, but to communicate the gospel in the language of the contemporary world of his day. The message itself was a reinterpretation of the Hebrew Scriptures in the light of the life, death and resurrection of Jesus Christ.

The Gospel of John

Another major battleground is the Gospel of John, and nowhere is the fighting more fierce than the conflict over the interpretation of the so-called prologue to the Gospel (Jn 1:1-18). John's Gospel opens with the declaration: "In the beginning was the Word [logos], and the Word was with God, and the Word was God" (Jn 1:1 RSV).[24] It goes on to say that all things were made by the Word, and that this Word became flesh. The influential American philosopher John Herman Randall, Jr., saw in John's Gospel Paul's basic concern with redemption. But he saw John's interests as "much more intellectual and philosophical" than Paul's. John was consciously attempting to appeal to the Hellenistic mind in his attempt to explain redemption to the Greek world. "In his Prologue about the word, the *Logos,*" Randall observed, "he is adopting Philo Judaeus' earlier Platonization of the Hebraic tradition."[25]

Whether John was trying to be more intellectual and philosophical than Paul is open to question. This way of putting it appears to identify being intellectual with a certain style of philosophizing. It also overlooks John's Jewishness and closeness to Jesus' life and times.[26] Moreover, it is apt to distort the perspective of John's prologue by directing attention to Philo's idea of the divine Logos and away from the parallels between John and the Old Testament.

The prologue to John deliberately echoes the opening of the Book of Genesis with its account of creation by the word of God. It is possible that John was using language which had meaning to readers who were attuned to Stoicism and Philo. If so, we have here another example of the kind of thing that Paul was doing. It is to take language and ideas which are valid for the hearer as a means for communication. The Hellenistic Jew and the Stoic understood creation by the divine *logos.* But John uses the idea to communicate something more. The *logos* which was there in the beginning, which created all things, and which enlightens everyone, became flesh and dwelt among us (Jn 1:14).[27]

The Letter to the Hebrews

Another book which has been the subject of much controversy is the letter to the Hebrews. A number of scholars believe that they have detected in it evidence of Platonism and of Philo's exegetical style. This has prompted the suggestion that the author was a converted Philonist. The letter reflects on Jewish history, the priesthood, and the sacrifical ritual associated with the tabernacle and later the temple in Jerusalem. In particular, it focuses on the annual Day of Atonement ritual, in which the high priest offered sacrifice and entered the Holy of Holies. The letter argues that the entire ritual cult was really a foreshadowing of Christ, who by his death made atonement, and then entered the Father's presence as our true high priest. Typical statements include the following:

Thus it was necessary for the copies of the heavenly things to be purified with these rites, but the heavenly things themselves with better sacrifices than these. For Christ has entered, not into a sanctuary made with hands, a copy of the true one, but into heaven itself, now to appear in the presence of God on our behalf. (Heb 9:23-24 RSV)

For since the law has but a shadow of the good things to come instead of the true form of these realities, it can never, by the same sacrifices which are continually offered year after year, make perfect those who draw near. (Heb 10:1 RSV)

Despite the plausibility of the claim that Hebrews was a product of Platonism and Philonism, an emerging consensus of scholars sees the claim as too simplistic. F. F. Bruce acknowledges that "it is natural to recognize the influence of Platonic idealism in our author's thought and language, mediated through Philo and Alexandrian culture in general; and such influence need not be ruled out."[28] But Bruce goes on to point out that the idea of the earthly sanctuary as a copy of God's dwelling place goes back far beyond Plato. Moreover, the author does not use allegory in the same way as Philo. Philo treated Old Testament characters, institutions and events as allegories setting forth eternal principles of ethics and metaphysics, whereas the author of Hebrews treats them as historical foreshadowings of the fulfillment which has taken place in history.[29] More recently, Harold W. Attridge has observed:

The extreme and simplistic positions positing a direct and exclusive dependence of Hebrews on either Philo or the Essenes have been easily refuted. Hebrews does not display the same elaborate allegorical exegetical techniques as Philo. Neither does the text, despite its rhetorical deployment of commonplace philosophical categories, display the same, more or less consistent philosophical interpretation of Jewish traditions as does Philo. Furthermore, the seriousness that Hebrews accords to the eschatological expectation clearly separates him from the Alexandrian. At the same time . . . there are undeniable parallels that suggest that Philo and our author are indebted to similar traditions of Greek-speaking and -thinking Judaism. . . . there is no single strand of Judaism that provides a clear and simple matrix within which to understand the thought of our author and his text.[30]

Retrospect

When Christianity came into the world, it did not invent a new language to be spoken only by Christians. The first disciples and converts from Judaism spoke Aramaic like their fellow Jews. As Christianity spread in the gentile world, the followers of Jesus spoke Greek, the common language of the Eastern Mediterranean lands. Sometimes they used new words, and sometimes they used old words with new meanings. But they did not invent whole new languages. They used and adapted what they found. The same was true of culture and philosophy. The early church responded to, used and adapted what it found.

The two dominant philosophies of the first century A.D. were Epicureanism and Stoicism. Later centuries were to see revivals of other styles of doing philosophy, especially Platonism and Aristotelianism, but for the moment other ways of thinking got more attention. But even when we speak of Epicureanism and Stoicism, or any other sorts of -ism, things are apt not to be quite so clear-cut as a label might suggest. For every -ism has a history, and most of them draw on other -isms for ideas and inspiration. Here, as everywhere else when we come to assess ideas, the important point is not to identify the idea as coming from this or that -ism, but to ask whether it is true and useful, and to ask what counts to make it true and useful. Of course, it is helpful to know where an idea comes from. If we know where an idea comes from, we can understand and assess it better. But what counts in the end is truth.

Our quick look at the encounter of philosophy and the Christian faith in the New Testament shows something that we shall see repeated over and over in the course of the succeeding centuries. It is the love/hate relationship that exists between philosophy and faith. The New Testament church never turned to philosophy for a foundation for its faith. It did not try to prove the existence of God by a series of philosophical arguments and then build an edifice of theology on the philosophical foundation. It did not turn to philosophy to give its beliefs academic sanction and an aura of intellectual respectability. It certainly did not attempt to convert the faith and practice of Christianity into a philosophical system. When it encountered philosophies with fundamentally different outlooks from its own, the church was not afraid to challenge them. On the other hand, Paul and others were not afraid to acknowledge the philosophical insights of pagan thinkers. Nor did they disdain to use the language of philosophy in order to communicate their message.

If we look in the Acts of the Apostles at the account of Paul's preaching at Athens and at his argument in the first chapter of Paul's letter to the Romans, the apostle does not seem to fit very well into the rival schools of modern apologists and their ways of thinking. The foundationalist tries to lay a philosophical foundation for faith by demonstrating certain basic truths, such as the existence of God. The presuppositionalist rejects this approach in favor of trying to show that the presuppositions of his opponents are invalid and that his own are preferable. But Paul followed neither tack. Instead, he acknowledged that people are aware of the existence of God and that there are genuine insights outside the faith that he preached. On the other hand, there are also a great many confused and even perverse ideas. He urged his audience to use their reason to reflect on why these ideas were wrong. Only when he had done this did Paul proceed to tell his audience about something that philosophy on its own could never tell them—the gospel of Jesus Christ.

To Paul rational thinking was important. Without it the unbeliever and the believer alike could bring disaster upon themselves. Philosophy could be used, but not as a substitute for faith and discipleship. To Paul and other New Testament writers philosophy was what it was to many other great Christians in later ages—a good servant but a bad master.

PART II
FROM CHURCH FATHERS
TO MEDIEVAL SCHOLASTICS

6. PHILOSOPHY AND
THE CHURCH FATHERS

T *he period from the church fathers to the medieval scholastics spans fourteen* centuries. It begins in an age when the Christian church was a minority sect. At his trial before the Jewish Sanhedrin in Jerusalem, Jesus of Nazareth had been condemned for blasphemy. To the Jewish community the followers of Jesus were dangerous upstarts who were desecrating the Law and the sacred traditions. To the educated Roman politician the church was a disreputable sect which constituted a threat to law and order. In the circumstances it is not surprising that the Christian church found itself frequently scorned and repeatedly outlawed and persecuted during the first three centuries. But gradually the church won recognition and respect.[1] It moved from the status of being barely tolerated to one in which it became the dominant religion in Western Europe. All kinds of factors were at work in this process. Not the least of them was the ability of the church's teachers to present their faith in forms which met the challenges of their day.

The Mystery Religions and Gnosticism
The world of the early centuries of the Christian era resembled the modern world in one respect at least: it was a world full of different religions and philosophies which competed for the hearts and minds of men and women. These included the mystery religions which offered ritual, purification, religious experiences and initiation into the divine mysteries.[2] The evidence for the mystery religions is largely fragmentary. Much of it consists in brief references and allusions in ancient authors— many of whom were bound to secrecy or loathed the subject that they

were treating—inscriptions, and sundry art works. The mystery cults took many different forms. But running through them was a common dread of evil and a desire to be set free. Salvation meant escape from destiny, release from corruption, and renewal of life. To do this, the initiate participated in the secret rites of the cult, with a view to entering into mystical communion with a deity and receiving immortality. Mystery cult myths included the death and restoration to life of the savior-god, who became the Lord of his devotees.

In addition to the mystery cults there was Gnosticism, whose formidable challenge to the church provoked weighty replies from church fathers like Irenaeus, Hippolytus, Tertullian, Clement and Epiphanius.[3] At one time Gnosticism was thought to be an acute form of the secularization of Christianity through the church's contact with the Hellenistic world.[4] But continued research on the basis of various discoveries, especially at Nag Hammadi in Egypt in the 1940s, has transformed the picture.

Gnostic teaching has to be reconstructed from numerous sources. Among them are the various replies to gnostic teachers by early church fathers. Another source is the so-called *Hermetica,* a collection of Greek and Latin religious and philosophical writings, attributed to Hermes Trismegistus, Hermes the Thrice-Greatest, a name given to the Egyptian god Thoth, who was believed to be the father and protector of knowledge. These writings date from the middle of the first to the end of the third centuries of the Christian era. They are thus generally much later than the New Testament, though some scholars think that they preserve ideas that were current in New Testament times.

The writings contain a mixture of Platonic, Stoic, Neo-Pythagorean and Eastern religious elements in the form of Platonic dialogues. Their aim was to impart deification through secret knowledge. In most of them Hermes himself, or a similar divine figure, communicates this knowledge to a disciple. The first and most important of the essays, the *Poimandres,* contains visions of the origin of the universe, an account of the archetypal man and the present state of humanity, and the way of salvation. Leaving behind everything mortal and corruptible, the soul passes through seven spheres. It finally enters into God himself, and so becomes divine. The disciple is then charged to preach the beauty and piety of knowledge. It would seem that Hermetic philosophers were engaged in an evangelistic enterprise which rivalled that of the Christian church.

The library of Coptic writings, discovered at Nag Hammadi, belonged to a sect which turned Christianity into a form of Gnosticism. Most of the forty-five separate writings have some Christian element in them. In some cases it is quite strong. Among the texts is the non-Christian *Eugnostos the Blessed* and a gnostic Christianized version of the same writing entitled *The Sophia of Jesus Christ*. *The Gospel of Thomas* is not a Gospel like the New Testament Gospels, but a collection of sayings attributed to Jesus. The collection drew heavily on the Gospel tradition. But it includes new sayings which have a definite gnostic flavor, and other sayings have been edited with a gnostic slant. *The Gospel of Truth* is not a Gospel like Matthew, Mark, Luke and John, which tell about the life, teaching, death and resurrection of Jesus. It is a homily which reinterprets Jesus in terms of a gnostic scheme of thought.

The other principal sources of knowledge of Gnosticism are the Mandaic writings, the chief of which is the *Ginza* or "Treasure." The Mandeans descended from a community east of the Jordan in the first or second centuries, and survive today in Iraq and Iran. Their surviving writings date from the seventh and eighth centuries, and have affinities with Manichaean dualism. They represent an oriental development of Gnosticism.

The term *Gnosticism* is connected with the Greek word *gnōsis*, meaning "knowledge" or "insight." A leading contemporary authority, Kurt Rudolph, describes Gnosticism as "a dualistic religion, consisting of several schools and movements, which took up a definitely negative attitude toward the world and the society of the time, and proclaimed a deliverance ('redemption') of man precisely from the constraints of earthly existence through 'insight' into his essential relationship, whether as 'soul' or 'spirit,'—a relationship temporarily obscured—with a supramundane realm of freedom and of rest."[5] Gnosticism has certain affinities with earlier Greek thought, but the dualism of the spiritual and the material is pushed in Gnosticism to the point of hostility to the world. In the twentieth century Rudolf Bultmann has argued that Gnosticism played a major part in shaping New Testament Christianity. But it now appears that Bultmann's position was anachronistic, and that key ideas which he believed Christianity drew from Gnosticism, were in fact derived by Gnosticism from Christianity.[6] To quote Kurt Rudolph once more, "The gnostic movement was originally a non-Christian phenomenon which was gradually enriched with Christian concepts until it made its appearance as independent Christian gnosis."[7]

The main impact of Gnosticism on the church was to provoke the church fathers to develop orthodox Christian teaching in order to refute what had become a rival heresy. Whereas the Gnostics traced human ills to the material character of the world, the church fathers stressed the goodness of creation. Whereas the Gnostics speculated about series of emanating deities and attributed the world's existence to the activity of an evil lesser deity, the fathers taught that it was the same good God who was both the creator and redeemer. Redemption was not a form of spiritual illumination which enabled the spiritual person to escape from the thrall of the material world with the help of a redeemer who only appeared to be human. The church fathers insisted that the root cause of human ills was sin, and that redemption was made possible only by God himself becoming a real human being, dying a real death and rising again from the dead.

Platonism, Neoplatonism and Their Rivals
While Gnosticism was trying to take over the church, the traditional philosophies of Greece and Rome continued to compete for attention. In the world of the early church, popular philosophy was regarded as a "way of life." Sometimes it had a religious tinge. The modern historian Robert L. Wilken describes how "adherents often came to resemble doctrinaire proponents of inherited views rather than inquiring philosophers. In some cases, members of a particular school exhibited an almost religious veneration of the founder, celebrating his memory with a festival that included religious sacrifices, a banquet, and readings from his works."[8] The scene described by Wilken pictures philosophers behaving like hucksters and traveling evangelists, addressing crowds on street corners and in the marketplace. They would offer advice on how to live one's life and deal with personal problems. Appealing less to logic and argument, the popular philosopher would direct his hearer's attention

to the wondrous accomplishments of the school's founder and the high esteem in which the school was held.

The scene was captured by the second-century satirist Lucian in his dialogue *Philosophies for Sale.*[9] The action takes place in a slave market in the Eastern Mediterranean. In the opening scene Zeus gives the order for benches to be arranged for the prospective buyers, and tells an attendant to "bring on the philosophies and put them in line; but first groom them up, so that they will look well and will attract as many as possible." The word that Lucian uses for "philosophies" here is *bious,* literally "lives," that is, ways of life. Lucian proceeds to poke fun at a Pythagorean, a Cynic, a Democritean, a Heraclitean, a Platonist, a Stoic and a Skeptic, who are in turn paraded before the buyers and questioned about what they can do for their owners.

When it comes to the turn of the Skeptic, the buyer asks why he is carrying a pair of scales. The Skeptic replies: "I weigh arguments in them and make them balance one another, and when I see they are precisely alike and equal in weight, then, ah! then I do not know which is the true."[10] Is there anything else that the Skeptic can do fairly well? He replies that he can do everything except catch a runaway slave. Why cannot he do that? "Because, my dear sir, I am unable to apprehend anything." While Lucian lampooned the philosophical schools, his contemporary, the physician and philosopher Galen (c. 129-c. 199) gave more sober but scarcely less critical assessment.

> People admire this or that particular physician or philosopher without proper study of their subject and without a training in scientific demonstration, with the help of which they would be able to distinguish between true and false arguments: some do this because their fathers, others because their teachers, others because their friends were either empirics or dogmatics or methodics, or simply because a representative of a particular school was admired in their native city. The same applies to the philosophical schools: different people have for different reasons become Platonists, Aristotelians, Stoics or Epicureans.[11]

Galen himself had studied Stoicism, Platonism, Aristotelianism, and Epicureanism. While learning from all of them, he refused to become an adherent of any. A prolific writer who rose to eminence in his native Pergamum and later in Rome, his medical works continued to dominate

Western medicine until the Renaissance. Unlike earlier observers, Galen did not regard Christianity as an alien cult or superstitious sect. He treated both Judaism and Christianity as philosophical schools on the same footing as Greek philosophy.[12] He was the first pagan of whom we know who had anything good to say about Christianity. Galen could even praise Christians for their moral lives, self-control and their pursuit of justice which had reached a pitch "not inferior to that of genuine philosophers." Nevertheless, he faulted the followers of Moses and Christ for teaching their pupils "to accept everything on faith." He further complained that most people were "unable to follow any demonstrative argument," but needed parables about rewards and punishments in a future life.[13]

In the meantime the Platonic tradition survived in cities where higher education was given, especially in Alexandria on the Nile Delta in Egypt. The form of Platonism which flourished between 80 B.C. and A.D. 220 is known as Middle Platonism.[14] This was the Platonism which influenced the Christian philosophical theologians of Alexandria, Clement and Origen. It was also the philosophy of one of Christianity's sharpest critics, the philosopher Celsus.

About the year 170 Celsus composed a treatise with the Greek title *Alethes Logos*. The title has been translated as *The True Word* and also *True Doctrine*. The different translations bring out different shades of meaning of the word *Logos*. The book was evidently influential, for some eighty years later the Christian theologian Origen felt that it was important enough to merit a line-by-line refutation. Celsus's work has not survived, but his argument can be reconstructed from quotations to which Origen replies in his book *Against Celsus*.[15]

Origen initially depicted Celsus as an Epicurean, but the picture of Celsus the Epicurean is gradually replaced by that of Celsus the Platonist. In Graeco-Roman society to call someone an Epicurean was like calling someone a Communist in the McCarthy era of American politics. It carried with it the impression of an atheist who was undermining society.[16] For his part, Celsus evidently knew Christianity first-hand and subjected it to a wide-ranging critique. He saw the church as a kind of counterculture which threatened the foundations of society. The Christian movement had transgressed the law of Judaism, the tradition from which it sprang, and was threatening to destroy Hellenistic culture. For Celsus "true doctrine" was the same as the ancient doctrine of such sages and "divinely inspired men" as Plato.[17]

Celsus's work may have been designed to reply to Christian writers like Justin Martyr. The latter had argued that the divine *Logos* which had inspired the Old Testament prophets and illuminated the great philosophers had been made flesh in the person of Christ. Celsus sought to counter this by arguing that "there is an ancient doctrine *[logos]* which has existed from the beginning, which has always been maintained by the wisest nations and cities and wise men."[18] Celsus respected the Jews for their form of this doctrine in their religion and culture. For that matter, he could tolerate a wide variety of beliefs and practices, so long as they were traditional.[19] What he could not stand was a religion which made unique claims about the Logos becoming flesh and being revered as Lord above the Roman emperor. For then there would be nothing to prevent the emperor from being "abandoned, alone and deserted,"[20] and the order of the Roman world would be replaced by chaos. What really offended Celsus about Christianity were its unique claims for Jesus and its recognition of an authority above that of the state.

We shall turn to Christian attitudes to philosophy shortly. But before we do, we need to note a new philosophical synthesis which took over the earlier forms of classical philosophy. In the course of the third century of the Christian era, Middle Platonism was superseded by the philosophy that is now known as Neoplatonism. It was a form of Platonism developed by Plotinus which also embraced elements of Aristotelianism, Pythagoreanism, and Stoicism, and combined them into a religious philosophical system.[21] In its early phases it was centered at Alexandria in Egypt, which had long since displaced Athens as the intellectual center of the Roman world. It soon spread to Rome, and by the fifth century it had got a firm footing in Athens.

Plotinus (205-270) was born in Upper Egypt. He studied philosophy under Ammonius Saccas under whom Origen also studied. Eventually Plotinus made his way to Rome, where he opened a school of philosophy and began to write. His writings were posthumously edited by his disciple Porphyry, who arranged them into six groups of nine, and who also wrote a *Life* of Plotinus in which he explained his method of editing.

Plotinus's works are known as the *Enneads,* which comes from a Greek word meaning "group of nine." Plotinus himself seems to have been fairly informal in his teaching. The arrangement of the *Enneads* into arbitrary divisions was the work of Porphyry.

For Plotinus reality was essentially spiritual. What in our common sense approach to life we call matter was to Plotinus something like the thoughts of the mind. Plotinus distinguished three hypostases or forms of reality: the Soul, Intelligence and the One. Sometimes Plotinus spoke of souls as individual entities which could become embodied. At other times he could speak as if all souls form only one Soul. Plotinus's notion of intelligence corresponds to Plato's realm of Ideas or Forms. But he saw the Ideas as the Ideas of God, and insisted that such thoughts do not exist outside the intelligence. The highest form of reality was the One, which was absolutely above everything.

Plotinus's doctrine of the One involves several ideas which are important for later thought. The things that we know in everyday life all have different parts. But because the One is one, it does not have different parts. It cannot be resolved into several constituents. The One is utterly self-sufficient. It is not defective in any way, or dependent on anything else in order to exist. Because the One transcends everything, the One cannot accurately be described. Plotinus, therefore, uses what may be called a negative theology. All language is inadequate to describe the reality that transcends language. In trying to speak about the One, we must speak *as if* our language were accurate, but we must realize that it is not. We should not even speak of the One as Good. "It is the Good in a different sense, transcending all other goods."[22]

Two other ideas are bound up with Plotinus's view of the One. The first is his mysticism, which involves a leap that enables the soul to be blissfully one with the One.[23] The second is Plotinus's view of evil.[24] In one respect it was similar to the view of Augustine who was in fact influenced by Neoplatonism, but in another respect it verged on Gnosticism. Insofar as Plotinus thought of evil as non-being—meaning something which is not created but is an absence of the good—his thought was akin to Augustine's. But insofar as matter represented the end of the creative process and has no good in it, Plotinus's thought appears to come close to Gnosticism.

Neoplatonism presented the ancient world with a rival interpretation of reality to that of Christianity. The fact in itself is significant. Earlier critics of the church could dismiss the Christian faith as a dangerous superstition. Neoplatonism was an attempt to revive and restate classical philosophy as a viable alternative to the Christian faith. Under Iamblichus (c. 250-c. 325), Neoplatonism received further systematic elaboration. An element of ritual magic became a feature. But Iamblichus' teacher, Porphyry, was not content with merely developing an alternative philosophy. He launched the most formidable intellectual onslaught on the Christian faith to date. Several generations of Christian writers down to Augustine found it necessary to respond to Porphyry.

Porphyry (c. 233-c. 305)[25] was born and raised in the city of Tyre on the Eastern Mediterranean. As a young man, he made his way down the coast to Caesarea in order to hear Origen, the leading Christian intellectual of the first three centuries. The experience proved to be disappointing. He complained that:

> Origen, a Greek educated in Greek learning, drove headlong towards barbarian recklessness; and making straight for this he hawked himself and his literary skill about; and while his manner of life was Christian and contrary to the law, in his opinions about material things and the Deity he played the Greek, and introduced Greek ideas into foreign fables. For he was always consorting with Plato, and was conversant with the writings of . . . the distinguished men among the Pythagoreans; and he used also the books of Chaeremon the Stoic and Cornutus, from whom he learnt the figurative interpretation, as employed in the Greek mysteries, and applied it to the Jewish writings.[26]

Porphyry then went to Athens and later to Rome, where he met Plotinus and embraced his teaching. Shortly before the latter's death he went to Sicily, where he wrote many of his philosophical works. Toward the end of his life he returned to Rome, where he taught with much success and had Iamblichus among his pupils.

Porphyry's attack on Christianity was two-pronged. One prong took the form of a massive critique of the way in which Christian teachers like Origen interpreted the Hebrew Scriptures. This critique appeared in the fifteen books of his treatise *Against the Christians*. The work is now lost, but numerous fragments of it have survived in various places. The other prong of the attack was Porphyry's *Philosophy from Oracles,* a work written in three books. It was not a treatment of Christianity as such, but a restatement of traditional pagan religion and belief in one high God. Prophyry's strategy was, in the words of Robert L. Wilken, "to sever the link between Christianity and Hellenism by showing that Christians had abandoned worship of this God in favor of the worship of Christ."[27] It was a strategy which Augustine felt it necessary to counter a full century after Porphyry's death. Augustine regarded Porphyry as "the most learned of philosophers." Nevertheless, Porphyry's argument was specious.[28]

Despite its initial hostility to Christianity, Neoplatonism seemed to some later Christian thinkers to offer a basis and a framework for formulating Christian teaching. By the middle of the fifth century there were two main schools of Neoplatonism. The one at Alexandria became Christian, while the one at Athens was pagan. Neoplatonism continued into the thirteenth century as a dominant philosophical system in Europe. Its downfall came about partly through the revival of interest in Aristotle. But its influence continued to be felt long afterwards.

Two Christian Approaches to Philosophy

In view of all the conflicting ideas which they found around them, it is not surprising that Christian intellectuals found themselves in two opposing camps.[29] There were those who endorsed philosophy and made use of it, and there were those who said that it was of the devil and were utterly opposed to it. An important factor which helped to decide which camp one was in was the role that philosophy played in one's spiritual pilgrimage.

Justin Martyr (died c. 165) had turned to philosophy in his search for God.[30] He first tried a Stoic teacher, but got little help. He then turned to a Peripatetic, but the latter asked for a fee, and Justin concluded that the man was not a philosopher at all. A Pythagorean teacher insisted that he must first study music, astronomy and geometry. Justin then found a Platonist who led him to an overpowering perception of immaterial things. But Platonism could not take him further than that. Finally, he met an old man who introduced Justin to the Scriptures, and who told him that only prayer could open the way to God. Justin came to see the Christian faith as "the only reliable and profitable philosophy."[31] From that point onwards Justin began to teach that Christianity was the culmination of all true philosophies. He continued to wear the *pallium*, the philosopher's cloak, and argued that Greek philosophy was a preparation of the pagan world for the coming of Christ. It was the divine Word or *logos* which had enlightened thinkers like Socrates to see the errors of paganism. Those in the pagan world who lived according to the divine *logos* within them were unconscious Christians.[32]

Justin's idea of the *logos* provided him with the conceptual tools for seeking to understand the divinity of Christ. How could Jesus be both God and man? How could God remain God and also be personally present in Jesus? Justin replied that when we utter a word *(logos)* and so give expression to our mind, the word is in a sense separate from us. But at the same time it remains our word without diminishing the power of thought within us.[33] Justin used this idea as a kind of model for understanding how the divine reason or word which created all things (Gen 1; Jn 1) and which is present in human rational thought could be present in Jesus Christ. His point is summed up in a passage in which he defends Christians against the charge of atheism in view of their rejection of the deities of the ancient world. Justin writes: "For not only among the Greeks did reason *[logos]* prevail to condemn these things through Socrates, but also among the barbarians were they condemned by reason [or the Word, *logos*] himself, who took shape and became man, and was called Jesus Christ."[34]

The *logos* doctrine of Justin and the Apologists played a significant part in the thinking of the early church about the identity of Jesus and the formulation of the doctrines of the Trinity and the Incarnation. With Justin the doctrine was firmly anchored in biblical teaching. It was not something to be detached from the Scripture and the faith of the church. Nor was it to be pressed beyond its limitations. If, as Justin believed, the divine reason is thought of as being active wherever it is present, and not separated from God, Justin's idea is helpful. As such, Justin's use of philosophical reflection is an example of the endeavor to understand on the basis of faith which characterizes the best of early church and medieval thought. If, however, an idea is detached from its context and made the basis of speculation, the result can have the opposite effect. This happened in the case of the Arians who, following Origen, believed that the Word or reason is somehow separate from God, and is thus a creature or created thing. For them the Word incarnate was a creature of some kind and Christ could not be worshipped as God incarnate.

The Alexandrian theologians Clement (c. 150-c. 215) and Origen (c. 185-c. 254) went even further in their respect for philosophy. Clement's *Stromateis* set out to prove that Christian gnosis is superior to other forms of gnosis. In the course of his discussion Clement tried to show that Greek philosophy had borrowed extensively from the philosophy expounded by the Old Testament prophets. Both Clement and Origen drew on Philo's allegorical method of interpreting Scripture.[35] Their intention was not to turn the Christian faith into a form of contemporary philosophy but to show the true meaning of the text. Origen argued that just as human beings have body, soul and spirit, so does Scripture. Corresponding to the body was the literal meaning of the passage. Corresponding to the spirit was its moral meaning. But highest of all was the spiritual significance. Thus on the literal level, the story of the healing of the two blind men at Jericho (Mt 20:29-34) was an account of their healing. On the moral level it meant that our eyes must be opened by the Word of God and that we must come out of our Jericho. On the spiritual level the story taught that the two beggars are Israel and Judah, and that Jericho is the world.[36]

Origen's view of God, the Incarnation and salvation was a *tour de force* in its combination of Middle Platonism and the teaching of the Christian church.[37] But it proved disastrous for the church. Origen's insistence that the Father alone was divine, in the strict sense of the term, prepared the ground for the Arian controversy in the fourth century. His account of the Incarnation united the Platonic idea of pre-existent souls with biblical teaching about the Fall and the Incarnation. Like Plato, Origen believed in the pre-existence of the soul. All souls except one fell and became united with human bodies in the form of sinful men and women. But one soul did not fall. This was the soul of Jesus, which was united with the divine Logos in perfect love. When that soul became incarnate, the result was Jesus Christ. Like Plato, Origen believed in successive purifications after the present life. It led him to his doctrine of the universal salvation of all, including Satan. Origen's teaching was an attempt to present Christian belief using the philosophical tools of his day. But instead of solving problems, it gave rise to a series of controversies which resulted in his condemnation as a heretic in the sixth century.

By contrast with the Greek fathers that we have been looking at, the Latin writer Tertullian (c. 155-c. 220) held a downright hostile attitude toward philosophy. The doctrines of humankind were "the doctrines of demons." In a passage which became a battle-cry for later denunciations of philosophy, Tertullian asked:

> What indeed has Athens to do with Jerusalem? What concord is there between the Academy and the Church? What between heretics and Christians? Our instruction comes from "the porch of Solomon," who had himself taught that the Lord should be sought with "simplicity of heart." Away with all attempts to produce a mottled Christianity of Stoic, Platonic, and dialectic composition! We want no curious disputation after possessing Christ Jesus, no inquisition after enjoying the gospel! With our faith, we desire no further belief.[38]

If, however, we look behind Tertullian's rhetoric, three facts stand out. The first is the fact that Tertullian sees philosophy as an amalgam of rival world views, which are based on premises which are very different from the biblical revelation. In the passage which follows the above quotation Tertullian observes that the opinion that the soul dies comes from the Epicureans, the idea that matter is equal to God comes from Zeno, while the denial of the resurrection of the body is taken from sundry philosophical schools. If given the choice between philosophy and faith, Tertullian chooses faith without a moment's hesitation. The second fact that stands out is Tertullian's conviction that "heresies are themselves instigated by philosophy." In particular, he blames Valentinian Gnosticism on Plato and Aristotle. He thinks that Paul's warning against philosophy in Colossians 2:8 sprang from Paul's contact with philosophers at Athens.

But there is a third fact which stands out from a wider perusal of Tertullian's writings. It is his own tacit use of philosophical ideas, in particular Stoic ideas, when it comes to formulating Christian teaching.[39] On occasion Tertullian could grudgingly admit that philosophers had sometimes said the same thing as Christians. But where similarities existed, he resorted to the strategy of saying that pagan thinkers stole such ideas from the Old Testament. Seneca was quite often on the side of truth, but generally philosophers were mistaken and wrong.[40] A modern authority on Tertullian sees him as a Christian sophist, a master of the Cynic diatribe and rhetoric, who showed "that a Christian can take his pagan intellectual inheritance with him into his new faith."[41]

Tertullian's exposition of the Trinity combined biblical teaching with secular thinking. Like Plato's Form of the Good and Aristotle's Prime Mover, Tertullian's God stands above all change. For Tertullian the impassibility of God—i.e., the view that God cannot suffer—was a cardinal doctrine.[42] He could allow that Jesus suffered as a man, but God the Father was above all change and suffering. The divine element in Jesus did not suffer. It was only his human nature that suffered. By way of illustration Tertullian gave an example from what today would be called ecology. If a river is polluted, the pollution affects the river from the point of pollution onwards. But the spring above the pollution remains pure. So it was the divinity which remained untouched by the human sufferings of Jesus.

It is to Tertullian that the Western church owes some of its basic theological vocabulary. Tertullian restated in Latin the *logos* doctrine of Justin and the Greek Apologists. But in doing so he gave theology a new precision. He was the first to use the terms *persona* ("person") and *trinitas* ("trinity").[43] He also gave theological currency to the word *substantia* ("substance"), a term which in Stoic thought denoted a highly rarified species of matter.[44] Tertullian could say that the Son was "of one substance with the Father," and that the Son and the Spirit were "consorts of the Father's substance."[45] He could also say that the Son was composed of two "substances," that is, the divine and the human.[46]

In using terms like these, Tertullian was both solving and creating a problem. The terms themselves were not biblical. They were drawn from the secular world, where they could be used in philosophical contexts with somewhat different meanings. Tertullian used the terms in order to express his understanding of the truth of the Christian faith. They translated into the language of his day the implicit significance of statements that are to be found in various parts of Scripture. This act of translation meant synthesizing the ideas of different texts and expressing them by means of terms which came from elsewhere. The justification for this procedure lay in the fact that the texts themselves both demanded interpretation and also contained the materials which warranted it. By this means Tertullian reached his understanding of the divinity of Christ and the Trinity. It thus solved the problem of how to think about these questions. But in so doing it raised the question of whether it was legitimate to go beyond the language of the Bible to express biblical truth. It raised the further questions of whether Tertullian's answers were the correct ones, and of what constituted legitimate justification for embarking on the enterprise of formulating Christian teaching.

For over two hundred years after Tertullian's death, the church found itself locked in a series of combats over the formulation of Christian belief. The strife gave rise to the great ecumenical councils which defined Christian belief about the divinity and humanity of Christ. In the end the church followed the same path as Tertullian. The Council of Nicea (325) affirmed belief that Christ was "consubstantial" with the Father with regard to his divinity. This decision was ratified and amplified by the Council of Chalcedon (451), which went on to assert that the Son was also consubstantial with us with regard to his humanity. To explore these issues further would take us away from our main theme, but one observation may be made. Tertullian did not invent the problem. It was already there. It arises as soon as anyone asks what they should think about Jesus. To give an answer at all we have to engage in the enterprise of translation. And that in turn raises philosophical questions.

Augustine
Augustine (354-430) was one of the great thinkers of all time.[47] He was also one of the most personal thinkers. Augustine does not fit into the philosophical mold which tries to keep the personal life of the thinker as detached as possible from his thoughts. In Augustine's case, life and thought, and philosophy and theology are inseparably intertwined. For this reason we shall approach his thought through an account of his life.

Augustine was born in North Africa in the country which is now Algeria. His mother was a Christian but his father was a pagan. In his

youth he rejected Christianity. Through reading Cicero, he felt led to
seek wisdom. His spiritual pilgrimage took him by a long, circuitous route
before he finally became a Christian. His problems were both intellectual and personal. On the intellectual level, he could not see how the
existence of evil could be reconciled with the good God proclaimed by
the church and the Scriptures. For a time Augustine embraced the dualistic teaching of the Manichees, which claimed that there were two
ultimate principles. One of these was responsible for good and the soul,
and one was the source of evil, including matter and the body. On a
personal level, Augustine was dominated by sexual and other passions
which he found impossible to overcome. At the time Manichaeism
seemed to offer a convenient explanation, by allowing him to claim that
it was not he who was responsible for his sin, but something else in
him.[48]

For a time Augustine taught in Carthage, but then moved to Rome and
Milan, where he became a professor of rhetoric (384). By this time he
was beginning to lose faith in Manichaeism. He was impressed by the
skepticism of the Academy.[49] But he also came across "certain books of
the Platonists" which Marius Victorinus had translated into Latin.[50] The
books probably included Plotinus's *Enneads*. Victorinus, who has long
been neglected, played a significant part in the history of Western
thought. He wrote a number of treatises and was responsible for translating Neoplatonic writings and some of Aristotle into Latin. He thereby
mediated Greek thought into Latin. In later life Victorinus himself became a Christian. His theological writings paved the way for the adaptation of Neoplatonism to Christian thinking.

Victorinus deeply impressed Augustine both for his Neoplatonism and
his Christian faith. Neoplatonism convinced Augustine of two things.[51]
First, it convinced him that there could be and was in fact a spiritual
reality. Secondly, it convinced him that the existence of evil could be
reconciled with the doctrine of creation. Augustine came to see that evil
was not a positive, created, actual thing. It was a *privation* or lack. By this
he did not mean to say that evil was all in the mind or just an illusion.
It had a reality. But it was not a created thing. Blindness, for example,
is not an illusion. It is a terrible affliction. But it is not something that
God created as such. Blindness is the *lack* of sight. Moral evil is certainly

real. But it is not a created entity. It comes about through the way people choose and act. It involves an absence of the right in the human will. In putting forward this view of evil, Augustine was not attempting to set out a comprehensive account of evil. What he was doing was to provide a more realistic and convincing account than that of the Manichees. It was an account which held human beings responsible for their own actions. It was an explanation which showed how the existence of moral and physical evil in the world is compatible with belief in a good Creator.[52]

Neoplatonism was not the end of Augustine's pilgrimage. It was more like a stepping stone to faith. For Neoplatonism did not solve Augustine's personal moral problems. His conversion to Christianity came about through the preaching of Ambrose of Milan, his own study of the New Testament, and through reading about the conversion of Victorinus and the life of Anthony of Egypt. For a time he continued in turmoil, deeply impressed by the intellectual truth of Christianity, attracted by the Christian lifestyle, but reluctant to give up his own questionable way of life. In his *Confessions* Augustine described how, at the height of his inner turmoil, he overheard a child repeat the words: "Take up and read. Take up and read." He opened the writings of the apostle Paul by chance at Romans 13:13-14: "Let us behave decently, . . . not in sexual immorality and debauchery, not in dissension and jealousy. Rather, clothe yourselves with the Lord Jesus Christ, and do not think about how to gratify the desires of the sinful nature" (NIV). He felt no need to read further "for instantly at the end of this sentence, by a light as it were of serenity infused into my heart, all the darkness of doubt vanished away."[53]

Augustine was baptized by Ambrose at Easter in 387. He returned to Africa the following year. He was ordained priest in 391, and became a bishop four years later. He succeeded to the see of Hippo in 396. He died while the Vandals were besieging the city. Augustine's years as bishop of Hippo were tremendously fruitful. His writings laid the foundation not only for later Western theology but also for a good deal of later philosophy. Augustine's *Confessions*, which were written between 397 and 401, created a new literary genre. They were not simply a chronicle of events, but an epoch-making work of psychological and spiritual self-analysis. Augustine's numerous writings against the Manichaeans, including his three books *On Free Will* (388-95), set out a doctrine of creation, evil and the human will which was a superior alternative to the type of thinking that had attracted so many to Gnosticism and Manichaean dualism. Augustine's response to the Donatist schism in the church set the pattern for the Western doctrine of the church. His writings on the subject of Pelagianism clarified, as no one before him and few after him, the crucial issues in the question of grace and free will.[54] His many theological writings included his major work *On the Trinity* (399-419), which presented better models for thinking about the Trinity than those of the Greek fathers. Augustine's book *On the City of God* (413-416) was a reply to those who blamed the church for the declining fortunes of the Roman Empire at the hands of the barbarians. It gave both a panoramic view of history and a theology of history in terms of the basic conflict between the divine society and the earthly society.

It has often been said that both Catholicism and Protestantism can be traced back to Augustine. Certainly the Catholic stress on the church and the Protestant emphasis on free grace can be found in him. But, as with all generalizations, oversimplification can bring with it distortion. It would be absurd to assume from this that the Catholic church had no conception of grace and Protestantism had no concern for the church. What cannot be denied is the enormous influence that Augustine had on later thought. Nor was this influence limited to strictly theological issues. Augustine put forward a theory of time which Bertrand Russell pronounced superior to earlier views and much better than the subjective theory of Kant.[55] Augustine's account of how we learn language provided Wittgenstein with the starting point for his *Philosophical Investigations*.[56] In answering skepticism Augustine put forward an argument which anticipated Descartes's *cogito ergo sum* without falling into the pitfalls commonly associated with the argument.[57]

With regard to faith, reason and the existence of God, Augustine developed the position commonly associated with Anselm's formula *credo ut intelligam*—"I believe that I may understand." To put the point this way is to risk sounding anachronistic. For Anselm was really echoing Augustine on this matter, as he did on sundry other matters, including the celebrated ontological argument for the existence of God.[58] Augustine believed that faith and reason belong together, and that both play their part in acquiring knowledge. As he put it at the end of one of his sermons: *Intellige, ut credas, verbum meum; crede, ut intelligas, verbum Dei*— "Understand, so that you may believe my word; believe, so that you may understand the word of God."[59]

Augustine explained the point more fully in a letter in which he observed that reason is a God-given faculty. It is reason which distinguishes human beings from animals. Augustine urged that "we must refuse so to believe as not to receive or seek a reason for our belief, since we could not believe at all if we did not have rational souls." He went on to say that there are some things which bear on our salvation which are for the present beyond the grasp of reason. In such cases it is *reasonable* to let faith precede reason. Referring to prophetic utterance in Isaiah 7:9, Augustine observed:

> Therefore the Prophet said with reason: "If you will not believe, you will not understand"; thereby he undoubtedly made a distinction between these two things and advised us to believe first so as to be able to understand whatever we believe. It is, then, a reasonable requirement that faith precede reason, for, if this requirement is not reasonable, then it is contrary to reason, which God forbid. But if it is reasonable that faith precede a certain great reason which cannot yet be grasped, there is no doubt that, however slight the reason which proves this, it does precede faith.[60]

For Augustine, knowledge of God is a basic, intuitive perception. But this knowledge is compatible with experience, and it is confirmed by rational reflection on the nature of things. The God who speaks through his Word is also the God to whom creation testifies. For creaturely finitude attests the existence of the Creator.[61] Human finite existence cries out for God; it requires an explanation which is ultimately theological.

In an Easter sermon Augustine depicted the philosophical quest. Ultimately this quest is a quest for beatifying truth—the truth which makes human life truly blessed. The desire for truth is more than an expression of intellectual curiosity, though sometimes it might not rise above that level. Deep down, human beings are driven by the search for a reality beyond the material world which satisfies the needs of the whole person. But here again human sinfulness often holds people back and causes them to seek satisfaction in things which do not ultimately satisfy. Reflection on beautiful things in the world prompts the question "Who made these beautiful things unless it be the unchanging Beauty?" Reflection on human nature as body and soul has brought philosophers "to the knowledge of God through the things which He has made."[62]

However, philosophy which does not glorify God is vain. Philosophy needs a reality beyond itself, and philosophical notions about the body and soul need to be corrected in the light of the gospel of the resurrection. Augustine believed that philosophical reflection may correct mistaken notions, lead to a grasp of truth and serve to clarify belief. But philosophy is not a substitute for faith, and rational reflection is not a substitute for the beatific vision of God. For it is the apprehension of God as love which transforms human life and alone satisfies our deepest needs.

Like all philosophers, Augustine was a child of his age. He used the conceptual apparatus of his age. In particular he was deeply influenced by Platonism and Neoplatonism. But Augustine was never simply a Platonist. Centuries later, Thomas Aquinas observed that "Augustine, who was steeped in the doctrines of the Platonists, whenever he found anything in their statements consistent with the Faith he accepted it, but amended what he found hostile."[63] Augustine's view of the soul stands in the Platonic tradition, but he repudiated the doctrines of pre-existence and transmigration, and his psychological analysis goes deeper than anything in Platonism. Augustine's view of transcendent spiritual reality might also be said to have affinities with Plato, but Augustine's approach was not an attempt to erect an edifice of Christian theology on either Platonic or Neoplatonic foundations. Very few of his writings were philosophical in the strict sense of the term. Philosophical ideas were at best ways of seeking to express the truth of Augustine's spiritual vision of reality.

Augustine recognized that "all that are called philosophers are not lovers of the true wisdom." For true wisdom was the love of God. "Now if God be wisdom, as truth and Scripture testify, then a true philosopher is a lover of God."[64] Such a view could be held only by someone who was convinced that a view of reality that was not related to God was incomplete and defective. It was a view which corresponded to Augustine's view of human existence. As Augustine put it at the beginning of his *Confessions,* "Thou madest us for Thyself, and our heart is restless, until it repose in Thee."[65] As human creatures we come from God, and to God all life is directed. For Augustine and for Christian medieval thought after him, this conviction was basic.

Postscript

Robert L. Wilken, the astute observer of paganism and Christianity in the Roman world, has noted that since the Age of Enlightenment it has been fashionable to set Christianity in opposition to classical antiquity. But, as Wilken goes on to point out, there is something strange about attacking Christianity because it was supposed to have supplanted reason by faith. To Wilken, the best refutation of this view is the ongoing dialogue between pagans and Christians. In the early days Christianity was regarded as a superstition and form of atheism, in view of its rejection of pagan religion. But once the Christian apologists got going, the pagan and the Christian intellectual found themselves playing on the same turf. Both of them appealed to reason and used reason in order to defend their world views, which were ultimately religious. Wilken comments: "No one can read Celsus's *True Doctrine* and Origen's *Contra Celsum* and come away with the impression that Celsus, a pagan philosopher, appealed to reason and argument, whereas Origen based his case on faith and authority. One of the things pagans resented most was that Christian thinkers had adopted Greek ideas and methods of thinking to expound Christian teaching. Porphyry said Origen 'played the Greek,' and Celsus complained that Christians had adopted the technique of allegory, an achievement of Greek reason, to interpret the Hebrew and Christian Scriptures. Indeed, one might legitimately argue that the debate between paganism and Christianity in antiquity was at bottom a conflict between two *religious* visions."[67] If pagan philosophy was ultimately religious, Christian thinking had become increasingly philosophical. Philosophy was like language. It was the medium of thought. It provided the means to friends and foes alike to express their thoughts and work out their implications. Christianity was always more than a philosophy. But from now on, philosophy in one form or another was here to stay as a means for exploring the meaning and truth of the Christian faith.

7. EARLY MEDIEVAL PHILOSOPHY

T*he period that we shall be looking at in the next two chapters ends with the* fifteenth century.[1] It takes us to the close of the Middle Ages and the end of Scholasticism. By this time Christianity had long been established as the majority religion in Europe, though politically it was being threatened by Islam, and intellectually it was being challenged by both Islamic and Jewish philosophers. We shall look at this challenge and the way that Christian thinkers responded to it in due course. But before we begin this part of our survey, it is worthwhile to comment on the terms *Middle Ages* and *Scholasticism*.

The Changing World of Christendom

The term *Middle Ages* covers the period from the time of Augustine in the fifth century down to the end of the fifteenth century. It is arguable whether Augustine himself should be regarded as the last of the early church fathers or the first medieval thinker. It is not a question that I shall attempt to answer here. What is perhaps more important is that Augustine was already witnessing the breakup of the Roman Empire, though he did not live long enough to see the fall of the Western Empire in 476. It was a time of transition both politically and intellectually. In the latter respect Augustine himself was a major catalyst of change. The notion of a *Middle Age (medium aevum)* is already found toward the close of the period itself. It occurs in the writings of the Italian humanist historian Flavio Biondo (1392-1463) and was in established use shortly after his death. Flavio Biondo used the term to describe the thousand-year period between the end of the ancient world (which he dated from the sack of Rome in 410) and the Italian Renaissance. At one time the Middle Ages were seen as an age of stagnation which held up all real progress until it was superseded by the Renaissance and the Reformation. Today they are widely regarded as one of the most fertile periods in human history which left a rich heritage and also set the agenda for later ages to work through.

The term *Scholasticism* is often treated as a rough equivalent for medieval thought. Strictly speaking, however, Scholasticism denotes the educational tradition of the Medieval Schools.[2] In a broad sense it is used of the medieval approach which combines philosophical and theological speculation in order to attain deeper understanding of Christian doctrine. The foundations were laid by Augustine and Boethius. In a sense it was Augustine who set the agenda for Scholasticism by his insistence on the need for dialectics in the study of Christian doctrine. For Augustine "belief is nothing else than to think with assent." Augustine would have nothing to do with the kind of piety which divorces faith from reason. On the other hand, he believed that it was equally wrong to start with ourselves and then supplement our thinking by referring to God. In order to know God, we must reflect on what God gives us. The way we know an object is determined by the nature of the object. The way we know God is determined by God's own nature. To know the living God we need to respond in faith and by using our reason. Augustine himself summed it up like this:

> It is necessary that everything which is believed should be believed after thought has preceded; although even belief itself is nothing else than to think with assent. For it is not everyone who thinks that believes, since many think in order that they may not believe; but everyone who believes, thinks,—both thinks in believing, and believes in thinking.[3]

In taking this position Augustine was laying down the basis for Anselm's formula *credo ut intelligam*—"I believe in order that I may understand."[4] Or to put it the other way around, Anselm's famous formula was essentially a restatement of the Augustinian position.[5] A further step toward the development of Scholasticism was taken by Boethius and his successors who developed the notion of the Seven Liberal Arts as the basis for secular and sacred learning. The Liberal Arts came to be divided into two groups. The *Trivium* consisted of the three basic arts of grammar, rhetoric and dialectic. The *Quadrivium* consisted of music, arithmetic, geometry and astronomy. This choice of subjects for study has clear affinities with pre-Christian philosophy. No doubt it contributed to greater philosophical precision. But its neglect of the natural sciences also contributed to the lack of progress in certain obvious fields.

The developed Scholasticism of the eleventh and twelfth centuries asserted both the right and the duty of reason to inquire into revealed truths. It was not that reason and philosophy provided an independent foundation for establishing such truths as God has made known. Rather, to understand what God has communicated about himself was a way of glorifying God. A feature of developed Scholasticism was the technique of the *Quaestio* or question. The method was to take a question and look at its different sides in the light of various authorities and what previous thinkers had said. The question was analyzed and answered by means of philosophical reflection on the received truths of the faith. The method had a certain rigor which is sometimes lacking in other methods of discussion. It required objections to be stated and answered.

In the early Middle Ages the centers of learning had been the monastic and cathedral schools. The latter half of the twelfth century saw the emergence from these of what came to be called universities. The universities were religious and Christian in origin.[6] Initially a key factor was the assertion of the right of Christian clerical scholars to regulate curriculum and educational conditions and to license teachers independently of secular and local authorities. The Italian universities were soon followed by the creation of the Universities of Paris and Oxford early in the thirteenth century. To this era belongs a renewed interest in the writings of Aristotle, whose thought radically affected the way people like Thomas Aquinas set about doing theology. Two types of instruction emerged in the universities. One was the lecture, which originally was not simply an instructional discourse delivered before a class. The lecture involved a preliminary reading of a prescribed text with explication of obscure passages. Perhaps more important was the *Quaestio*, or disputation, in which problems were debated in set form by students and master before being resolved by the master. The universities sponsored public disputations on certain feast days. In addition there were open disputations, known as *Quodlibital* disputations—from the Latin *quodlibet,* meaning "whatever"—in which scholars disputed whatever burning issue of the day presented itself. The emergence of the universities inaugurated a new era.

Alongside the ecclesiastical authorities they gained growing prestige as arbitrators of the truth. Initially the universities belonged to the church and served the church. Philosophy served theology, which was the queen of the sciences. Scholars were monks and friars who professed the Christian faith and owed allegiance to the church. But with the creation of the universities an unconscious step was taken in a process which over the centuries led to the separation of faith and knowledge. With the secularization of the modern university, faith became the province of the church and knowledge the province of the university.

Boethius and the Era of Transition

The decline and fall of the Roman Empire brought with it a decline in classical culture. The single empire that at one time stretched from Britain to North Africa and from Spain to the Holy Land was split into unconnected states. With the political split came a cultural and intellectual fragmentation. But the so-called Dark Ages from the fifth to the eleventh centuries were not an era of total darkness. The intellectual traditions of the past were kept alive in the monasteries of Europe, which became centers of a new culture and learning.

A figure who forms a bridge between the classical past and the Middle Ages was the Roman philosopher-statesman Boethius (c. 480-524).[7] Boethius was a high-ranking official under Theodoric, king of the Ostrogoths in Italy. In his early years he was sent to Athens, where he came into contact with Aristotelianism, Neoplatonism and Stoicism. On returning he rose to the position of friend and advisor to the king. In the midst of his political commitments Boethius found time to translate some of Aristotle's works on logic into Latin, as well as works by other thinkers in the Aristotelian tradition. He also wrote philosophical commentaries, a treatise *On the Holy Trinity* and one on Christology, which he entitled *Book against Eutyches and Nestorius.* At the height of his career he fell foul of Theodoric, who himself was an Arian. He was accused of treason and perhaps was suspected of practicing astrology. While in prison Boethius wrote his most famous work, *On the Consolation of Philosophy*. He was eventually beheaded.

We have already noted the fact that the medieval educational concept of the *Quadrivium* was indebted to the educational theories of Boethius. Boethius is now recognized as a great student of logic. But his writings present a number of enigmas. Among them are questions concerning the authenticity of his different works. Another is the question of whether some of his works were lost for a time and rediscovered later on in the Middle Ages. But perhaps the most intriguing question of all is why Boethius makes no explicit reference to Christianity in his great work, *On the Consolation of Philosophy*. The work was popular among the learned in succeeding centuries. It was translated into Anglo-Saxon by King Alfred. It describes how the soul attains the knowledge of the vision of God through philosophy.

On the Consolation of Philosophy gives a picture of Boethius in prison. Filled with self-pity, Boethius is visited in his cell by the personification of philosophy. Having given Boethius the opportunity to show his innocence, she reproves him for blaming fortune for taking away the gifts she gave. For the material gifts in life cannot be enjoyed for long or without alloy. The wise person will not value them highly. Philosophy then argues that, in their search for the partial and imperfect goods of this world, human beings are really searching for the highest Good, though they are misled by their ignorance. The highest Good is to be identified with God.

Toward the end of the book, Philosophy discusses fate, providence and divine foreknowledge. As in Aristotelianism and Neoplatonism, the universe is seen as a nexus of cause and effect. Chance events are really the coincidence of previously unconnected causes and effects. Fate is the chain of cause and effect. But fate is under the control of divine providence which arranges everything for the best. With regard to divine foreknowledge, Boethius saw God as existing outside the process of time. Therefore, things which appear to us as past, present, and future, are known to God at once, as if it were an event taking place in the present.

Some scholars think that Boethius lost faith in religion and turned to Platonic philosophy for consolation, perhaps in the absence of support from the church in his hour of need. On the other hand, the work does not advocate a return to paganism. The work shows numerous parallels with Augustine's approach to philosophy. Perhaps the most apt judgment is that of Henry Chadwick who observes that "the *Consolation* is a work written by a Platonist who is also a Christian, but is not a Christian work."[8]

The ideas of Boethius commanded the attention of major medieval thinkers, including Aquinas. His influence on the eleventh and twelfth centuries was second only to that of Augustine. But his appeal did not endure. His style of thinking held no appeal for post-Reformation rationalists and empiricists, and from a Christian standpoint his thought could not be compared with that of Augustine for devotional richness and theological insight.

Pseudo-Dionysius

A sixth-century contemporary of Boethius was the writer known today as Pseudo-Dionysius.[9] To the medievals he was thought to have been Dionysius the Areopagite who became a disciple of the apostle Paul (Acts 17:34). He is now known to have belonged to the Byzantine world, and probably lived in Syria. Among his works that have survived are treatises on *Mystical Theology, Celestial Hierarchy, Ecclesiastical Hierarchy* and *Divine Names.* His letters set out a system which combines theology with Neoplatonism.

As with Augustine, God is the center of all speculation. But the method of approach of Pseudo-Dionysius was both positive and negative. The positive method is termed *cataphatic*—in Greek, *kataphatikē,* meaning affirmative or positive. God, as the efficient cause of everything, is the highest thing that can be known. To that extent one can attribute to God all the perfections known through the study of his creatures. But God is transcendent, and therefore the higher one goes, the more one must use the negative method, which goes under the term *apophatic method*—in Greek, *apophatikē,* meaning negative. Using the positive method, God may be called goodness, being, light or unity. But because God is not a being with physical attributes, like the beings that are in the world, the negative method must take over. From this point of view, God should be called non-being. The highest knowledge of God is a mystic ignorance. Pseudo-Dionysius paved the way for numerous medieval successors to draw up elaborate hierarchical tables of reality. His thought influenced the West through the translation by John Scotus Erigena (c. 810-c. 877). His mysticism inspired many others to attempt to describe the soul's mystical ascent to God.

Realism and Nominalism

In the meantime, the problems and world views inherited from classical Greek philosophy continued to exercise the philosophically minded. John Philoponus (c. 475-c. 565)[10] attacked the view of the Aristotelians that the world was eternal. But the question which provoked the longest debate in the Middle Ages was the question of universals.[11] The question goes back at least as far as Plato's theory of Forms. It has to do with the relationship between the abstract and general concepts that we have in our minds and particular things. What, for example, is the relationship between the idea of a pine tree and a particular pine tree growing in a forest? Two extreme viewpoints emerged. The realists followed Plato in insisting that universals were things or realities—in Latin, *res*—with a real existence apart from the individuals or particulars in which they are embodied. An extreme form of realism flourished from the ninth to the twelfth centuries. Among its proponents were John Scotus Erigena, Anselm and William of Champeaux. The opposite extreme was nominalism which replied that universals were just names—in Latin, *nomina*. They have no objective existence apart from that fabricated in the mind. The individual is the only existing substance. Nominalism reached its climax with William of Occam in the fourteenth century and Gabriel Biel in the fifteenth. In their hands nominalism removed religion almost entirely from the area of reason and made it a matter of faith beyond the comprehension of reason.

The two extremes of realism and nominalism proved unsatisfactory. Realism in its most rigorous form posited two separate realities—the abstract world of universals and the concrete world of particular objects. But the nominalist alternative, which denied common characteristics apart from their existence in our thought, was, if anything, even worse. Between the two extremes a more moderate form of nominalism was proposed by Peter Abelard (1079-1142) who, though critical of the idea of the separate existence of universals, nevertheless believed that resemblances among particular things justified the use of universals for establishing knowledge.[12] Thomas Aquinas and Duns Scotus favored a moderate realism which rejected the view that universals exist apart from individual entities in favor of the view that they do indeed exist, but only in actual entities.

Islamic and Jewish Philosophy

The Christian church was not the sole heir of the legacy of classical philosophy. Both Islamic and Jewish thought was affected by the study of ancient philosophy. The results were important in their own right, but in turn they also provided a fresh stimulus to Christian thinkers to respond to the challenge of Greek thought translated into the sphere of Islamic and Jewish thinking.

Islam came into contact with Greek philosophy as the Islamic conquest of Europe spread.[13] Many of the conquered people were Hellenistic in culture. At first elements of popular philosophy were absorbed. But by the eighth century many Islamic scholars were engaged in translating Greek texts into Arabic. The prime motive was an interest in Greek medical writings which was prompted by the concern of the Islamic rulers for their health. But in the course of time the major works of Aristotle were also translated.

The Greek work which made the greatest impact on early Islamic thinking was the so-called *Theology of Aristotle*. Despite its title, it was more Neoplatonic than Aristotelian. The founder of Islamic philosophy was al-Fārābī (870-950). He is said to have been the author of more than a hundred works, most of which have perished, though some survive in Latin translation. He wrote commentaries on Aristotle, but he was also deeply influenced by Plato's *Republic*. His major surviving work is a commentary on the *Philosophy of Plato and Aristotle*.[14]

From the standpoint of the Christian West the two most important Islamic philosophers were Ibn Sīnā and Ibn Rushd. Ibn Sīnā (980-1037) or Avicenna, as he was known in the West, made substantial contributions to both medicine and philosophy. He related how he read Aristotle's *Metaphysics* forty times without comprehending it, until he came across a commentary by al-Fārābī. His own philosophy drew on Aristotelianism and Neoplatonism, which he used to interpret the Islamic understanding of God. Following Aristotle, he taught that God was a single necessary being on whom the world depended. But in Neoplatonic fashion, he maintained that there was a hierarchy of emanations from God. Of these the most important is the "active intellect" which he thought of as an entity in a Platonic world of ideas. The "passive intellect" is the individual human mind which acquires ideas by contact with the "active intellect."

Ibn Rushd (1126-98) or Averroës, as he was known in the West, was born into a Mohammedan family in Córdoba, Spain. He served both as judge and as physician to the caliph, who was the head of state. His commentaries on Aristotle earned him the title of "The Commentator." He venerated Aristotle as the greatest genius of all time. But like other Arabic philosophers, his own thought showed traces of Neoplatonism. Like Aristotle, he saw God as the Prime Mover. But God was entirely separated from the world and exercised no providential guiding influence. Between God and human beings are a series of intelligences. Among his other doctrines were the eternity of matter and monophysism, the view that all human beings participate in one single intellect. He rejected personal immortality. While retaining a literal interpretation of the Qu'rān for ordinary people, his own interpretation was allegorical. In the century after his death the theories of Averroës attracted the attention of leading Christian scholars. Albertus Magnus wrote an attack on his view of the intellect, as did Thomas Aquinas. The study of Aristotle had become part of the curriculum in the University of Paris, but the leading interpreters of Aristotle were the Islamic philosophers. The work of Albertus Magnus and Thomas Aquinas on the subject of the intellect appeared too late to deter Siger of Brabant and others from embracing a mixture of Christian and Averroist ideas. In 1270 Stephen Tempier, the bishop of Paris, issued a condemnation of Averroism in thirteen propositions. Among the condemned propositions were: "That the intellect of all men is one and numerically the same" (# 1); "That the world is eternal" (# 5); and "That God cannot grant immortality or incorruptibility to a corruptible or mortal thing" (# 13).[15]

Within Judaism two philosophical trends may be noted: the Cabala and the adaptation of Judaism to Greek philosophy.[16] The Cabala, or perhaps more accurately Kabbalah, gets its name from the Hebrew word for "tradition." It was a Jewish form of mysticism, whose roots reached back into Persian thought, Neoplatonism, Neopythagoreanism and Gnosticism, not to mention some Christian influence and borrowings from Islam. God in his essence is unknowable. Between him and the world is a series of emanations. Because all substance emanates from God, the Kabbalah was pantheistic. The emanations served as an itinerary to the mind of God. The Kabbalah combined speculation with Jewish piety. Among the chief works of the movement are the *Book of the Pious (Sefer Hasidim)* and the *Book of Splendor (Sefer Ha-Zohar)*. The Jewish pietistic movement of modern times known as Hasidism has its roots in the Kabbalah.

The Jewish medieval assimilation of Greek philosophy took place chiefly in Spain under Arab rule. The Jewish philosophers were indebted to their Islamic counterparts. But there was one major difference. Whereas the Islamic thinkers were interested in the whole range of philosophy, Jewish philosophers were concerned above all with the philosophy of religion. Their most famous representative was Moses ben Maimon (1135-1204), who was called Maimonides by Latin authors and Rambam among Jewish writers—from the consonants formed from the initial letters of Rabbi Moses ben Maimon.[17] Maimonides was born in Córdoba, the son of a distinguished scholar. Religious persecution at the hands of an extreme Muslim sect caused the family to flee to North Africa. Eventually the family settled in Egypt, where Maimonides became a court physician and leader of the Jewish community. The scope of Maimonides' writings ranged from commentaries on the Mishnah in Arabic and Hebrew, a treatise on logic, and several works on medicine, to theological writings. His chief work was his *Guide to the Perplexed* (1190).

The perplexed in question were Jews who did not question the existence of God, but thought about him in anthropomorphic ways. Drawing especially on Aristotle, Maimonides produced a synthesis of Jewish faith and the findings of reason. The book falls into three main parts. The first part deals with the idea of God; the second with his existence, the creation of the world in time and prophecy; and the third with the problem of evil, the end of the world, providence and divine knowledge. Maimonides developed four main arguments for the existence of God.[18] The first two argued for the existence of a Prime Mover. A third argument is a form of the cosmological argument, arguing from the existence of things to a necessary being as their cause. The fourth argument turns on the Aristotelian distinction between potentiality and actuality, arguing for the existence of a being who is wholly actual and who constantly causes the transition from potentiality to actuality. Although Maimonides believed that God's existence could be proved, it did not follow from this that we could have any positive knowledge of God's essence. We can attain to God only by recognizing what God is not. *The Guide to the Perplexed* was written in Arabic, but was translated into Hebrew during Maimonides' lifetime. A Latin version followed within ten years of his death. His thought was thus available to the Christian theologians of the West. His synthesis of Jewish biblical teaching and Aristotle served as a model and guide for Thomas Aquinas, whose own arguments for the existence of God—the so-called Five Ways—followed Maimonides, even sometimes using the same wording,[19] though with much greater brevity.

Anselm and Early Medieval Philosophy

If we retrace our steps and go back to the eleventh century, we come across a thinker whose argument for the existence of God is generally considered fallacious but nevertheless continues to fascinate philosophers down to the present time. The ontological argument was propounded by Anselm, though he himself did not call it by that name.[20] Anselm (c. 1033-1109) was an Italian by birth. His coming to Britain as archbishop of Canterbury was one of the byproducts of the Norman Conquest of Britain. He had succeeded Lanfranc as Abbot of Bec in Normandy, when Lanfranc became archbishop of Canterbury, and on Lanfranc's death he succeeded to the archbishopric. Anselm is recognized as one of the truly great occupants of the see of Canterbury. He was also the greatest Christian thinker between Augustine and Thomas Aquinas. His writings range from treatises on logic to an explanation of the divine inner logic of the atonement in *Cur deus homo.*[21] On his deathbed he expressed the hope that he might live long enough to settle the question of the origin of the human soul, for he feared that no one would be able to solve it after his death.[22] It was a hope that was denied him. He died peacefully in faith on Palm Sunday as the Gospel story of Christ's passion was being read to him.

Anselm stood in the tradition of Augustine and Platonic realism. Like other medieval thinkers he drew no sharp distinction between philosophy and theology. For him theology was the enterprise of exploring the divine logic behind created reality and the acts of God. He did so from the standpoint of the Christian faith. His method of approach was not to look around for evidence from which he could draw inferences, but to seek to penetrate the divine logic which underpinned the Christian church's view of things.

In his first systematic treatise, written at the age of thirty-one, the *Monologion*, Anselm put forward a series of arguments for the existence of God. Starting from the fact that beings exist, Anselm explored the idea of the hierarchy of being and deduced the existence of a highest, necessary being.[23] But the famous ontological argument first appears in the brief *Proslogion*, where it is stated four times in chapters two, three and four. Whether the different forms of the argument are all the same and contain the same flaws is a matter of keen debate among philosophers. In the past it had been assumed that the form of the argument in chapter two was the basic form. Moreover, the context of the argument—which is actually a prayer—was largely ignored. The upshot was that the argument was taken to be an attempt to deduce the existence of God from the abstract notion of God. In what follows I will attempt to state Anselm's argument in its first form. I will then look at some of the ways that this argument has been understood. Finally, I will attempt to set it in the wider context of Anselm's thought, and make some observations of my own.

Unlike a good deal of philosophy both before and after Anselm, Anselm's argument is set in the context of prayer. In fact, there are two prayers. First, there is the prayer in chapter one which provides the overarching context for the whole work. Anselm cries to God: "Let me find You in loving You; let me love You in finding You." He goes on to say that he is not seeking to comprehend God in his sublimity, for his intellect is not equal to the task. But he yearns to understand some measure of God's truth, which his heart believes and loves. "For I do not seek to understand in order to believe but I believe in order to understand [*credo ut intelligam*]. For I believe even this: that I shall not understand unless I believe."[24] In other words, Anselm's position is not one of doubt or agnostic neutrality. He is rather following in the footsteps of Augustine in seeking to understand the truth of what he believes in.

The ontological argument itself is introduced by a second prayer: "Therefore, Lord, Giver of understanding to faith, grant me to understand—to the degree You deem best—that You exist, as we believe, and that You are what we believe You to be." This prayer leads immediately to a confession of faith which contains a definition—or, perhaps more accurately, a designation—of God: "Indeed, we believe You to be something than which nothing greater can be thought." It is upon this designation of God that the whole argument turns. At this point Anselm recalls the statements of Psalms 14:1 and 53:1 that the fool has said in his heart that there is no God. How is it logically possible for the fool to say this? Anselm's argument seeks to give an answer.

As Anselm states it in chapter two of the *Proslogion,* there are three basic steps in the argument. In step one Anselm observes that the fool surely understands what he hears. In step two Anselm draws a distinction between understanding a notion in the mind and understanding that the notion actually exists. By way of illustration Anselm gives the example of a painter who has an image in his mind of a picture he is about to paint. After he has painted the picture, the painter not only has the image in his mind, but he also knows that the image exists in reality in the painting. Even the fool who says in his heart that there is no God must at least have the notion in his mind and understanding. In step three Anselm contrasts the notion in the mind with the notion that exists in reality. If "that than which a greater cannot be thought existed only in the understanding, then that than which a greater *cannot* be thought would be that than which a greater *can* be thought!" But this is surely impossible. For to exist in reality is greater than to exist merely in the understanding. "Hence, without doubt, something than which a greater cannot be thought exists both in the understanding and in reality."

With this sudden conclusion the modern reader is apt to be left feeling that he has been listening to a fast-talking automobile salesman. From Anselm's day right down to the present many a reader has had the same gut-level feeling that something was wrong somewhere. Is there some sleight of hand which prevents the reader from seeing the fatal flaw? Anselm's contemporary, a monk named Gaunilo of the convent of Marmoutier near Tours in France, thought that he had detected the flaw and wrote a reply *On Behalf of the Fool.* In it Gaunilo said that he could imagine a perfect Lost Island, but that does not mean to say that such an island actually exists. Anselm wrote a reply to Gaunilo which simply brushed the objection aside. Perfect islands are not perfect in the same sense that God is perfect. Anselm's argument applies only to God. A perfect island is not that than which nothing greater can be thought, and therefore the argument cannot apply to the island. It applies only to God.[25]

From that day to this philosophers have been divided about the merits of Anselm's argument. Some, like Descartes[26] and Leibniz,[27] have restated it and adapted it to suit their own philosophies. Others, like Thomas Aquinas[28] and Kant,[29] have dismissed it as fallacious. While the argument continues to fascinate thinkers, most philosophers today reject the argument on three main counts. The first count has to do with the nature of definitions, the second with existence, and the third with the nature of necessity.

First of all, many philosophers would agree with Gaunilo and Kant in saying that definitions do not tell anything about reality, unless they are confirmed by observation. Merely to define something does not mean to say that it exists. Nor does the definition of something as *existing* entail its existence. As Kant remarked, to define something as existing is just like a merchant adding a series of noughts to the figures on his balance sheet. No matter how many noughts he might add, his balance remains the same unless there is some reality which corresponds to the figures. This reality cannot be discovered merely on the basis of definition.

This leads us to the second line of objection. The argument appears to treat existence as if it were a quality or predicate. But existence is not one quality which an object may or may not have alongside others, and yet still continue to be there. The point is brought out by G. E. Moore's celebrated comparison of the two sentences: "Some tame tigers don't growl" and "Some tame tigers don't exist."[30] The latter sentence is nonsense. But in order to make its point, the ontological argument appears to treat existence as a quality which makes the actual existing "that than which nothing greater can be thought" greater than the mere idea of "that than which nothing greater can be thought."

The third line of objection has to do with the nature of necessity. The argument presents God as the one being who necessarily exists. However, it has been objected that necessity is a logical concept and does not apply to beings, hence all existing entities exist contingently. If this is so, the argument is actually a disproof of the existence of God.[31]

If the ontological argument has produced a harvest of objectors, it has also produced not a few defenders. The defenders tend to argue that the standard objections may well be true in themselves, but they miss the target because Anselm's argument was different from what the objectors supposed it to be. Charles Hartshorne, for example, has revived the argument and deployed it in support of process theology.[32] In his view God is unsurpassable by anything else, but God is continually surpassing himself. Hartshorne's argument is certainly astute. However, few philosophers have found it convincing. It prompted E. L. Mascall to say, "There is indeed something paradoxical in the assertion that, while almost everyone since Anselm has radically misunderstood the nature of Anselm's argument, Anselm himself radically misunderstood the nature of God."[33]

Another scholar who thinks that Anselm's argument has been misunderstood is Karl Barth, whose book *Anselm: Fides Quaerens Intellectum* (1931; Eng. tr. 1960) is a line-by-line exposition of the Latin text of the argument. Barth's title, which means "Faith Seeking Understanding," is taken from a title which Anselm himself toyed with before finally settling on *Proslogion*. Barth rejected the picture of Anselm as a rationalist philosopher engaged in a natural theology which sought to prove the existence of God by reason alone. He drew attention to the context of prayer in Anselm's work, the importance of *credo ut intelligam,* and the fact that the objection to God's existence was taken from the Psalms. Moreover, Barth drew attention to the forms of the argument in chapters three and four of the *Proslogion.*

How is it, then, that the fool can say in his heart that there is no God? Barth's answer was to say that Anselm's definition of God was based on the faith of the church. It was not an abstract piece of rationalism but a description of the church's faith in the God who has revealed himself. What the fool is denying is not the living God who is known to faith and who necessarily exists, but his own notion of God. In other words, Anselm's argument is a medieval anticipation of the twin Barthian themes of the necessity of God's self-revelation and the barrenness of natural theology. What the fool "can prove is this and only this, that he does not know him whose Existence he denies. And it is not his denial, but his not knowing, that constitutes his folly."[34] Anselm never set out to provide a proof of God outside the church's faith. "God gave himself as the object of his knowledge and God illumined him that he might know him as object. Apart from this event there is no proof of the existence, that is of the reality of God."[35]

Barth's interpretation has the appearance of being a *tour de force,* which most subsequent writers comment on but which few accept. To most of them it seems to be a case of the Barthianization of history, a process by which history is rewritten on Barthian lines. Its strength lies in its acknowledgment of the role of faith in Anselm's philosophical theology. Its weakness lies in the way that it makes Anselm a Barthian before Barth. It presents Anselm as a fideist who rejects all attempts to prove the rationality of faith in favor of reliance upon biblical revelation. In fact, however, Anselm was not attempting to expound biblical teaching about revelation so much as to show the rationality of belief in God.

Several modern philosophers have questioned whether Anselm is really guilty of the fallacies entailed by the standard objections.[36] Others have argued that even if the first form of the argument is fallacious, the remaining forms are not open to these objections. Thus, Norman Malcolm has argued that the arguments in *Proslogion* chapter three and the *Reply* chapter one show that God's existence is *necessary existence.*[37] In an article which examines the historical objections to Anselm's argument, Malcolm contends:

> What Anselm has proved is that the notion of contingent existence or contingent nonexistence cannot have any application to God. His existence must either be logically necessary or logically impossible. The only intelligible way of rejecting Anselm's claim that God's existence is necessary is to maintain that the concept of God, as a being greater than which cannot be conceived, is self-contradictory or nonsensical. Supposing that this is false, Anselm is right to deduce God's necessary existence from his characterization of Him as a being a greater than which cannot be conceived.[38]

In short, the argument is about whether God's existence is impossible or necessary. Malcolm clarifies his point by contending:

> *Necessary existence* is a property of God in the same sense that *necessary omnipotence* and *necessary omniscience* are His properties. And we are not to think that "God necessarily exists" means that it follows necessarily from something that God exists *contingently*. The a priori proposition "God necessarily exists" entails the proposition "God exists," if and only if the latter also is understood as an a priori proposition: in which case the two propositions are equivalent. In this sense Anselm's proof is a proof of God's existence.[39]

Although Malcolm thinks that the argument as such is valid, he does not regard it as an argument which would convert someone into a believer. The only effect that it would have on Anselm's "fool" would be to compel him to recognize that he could no longer meaningfully say or think "there is no God."[40] Without a deeper inclination to believe, he would still remain an atheist. The refinements of Malcolm's reinterpretation of Anselm's argument have been widely applauded, but they have failed to find general acceptance. To Alvin Plantinga the argument is still flawed.

> It is a necessary truth that if God exists, then there is a being who neither comes into nor goes out of existence and who is in no way dependent upon anything else. But from this it does not follow, contrary to Malcolm's argument, that the proposition *There is a being who neither comes into nor goes out of existence and who depends upon nothing* is necessary; nor does it follow that *God exists* is necessary. Malcolm's reconstruction of the ontological argument therefore fails.[41]

Anselm's argument makes most sense in the context of a realist philosophy which posits the reality of universals in a way similar to the way Plato treated the reality of the Forms and the Form of the Good. Thus the argument may be seen as an attempt to distinguish God's being which necessarily exists from other notions, including false notions of God. God is not a particular created entity like an island, or even a universal, but a reality beyond our conception. In a sense Anselm may be answering the Neoplatonic agnosticism which says that we can say nothing positive about God. Strictly speaking, Anselm does not define God, for he knows that God is beyond all human comprehension. His designation of God as "something than which nothing greater can be thought" is open-ended. It is like saying "x stands for God." But the x in question is not an empty term. This x is differentiated from all other entities by being unsurpassable. It is a different sort of entity from the rest on account of its greatness and necessary existence. Anselm's argument was not a piece of natural theology designed as a knock-down proof of God's existence, and drawn from an abstract idea of God. As such it is not convincing. But as one recent commentator has put it, "Anselm is no philosophical magician pulling a real rabbit out of a conceptual hat. Reality is in a sense there from the beginning."[42] Anselm's vision of God is that of supreme reality to start with. His argument is an exploration of what is entailed by the believer's awareness of God. It is an argument which continues to exercise some of the best philosophical minds of our own day.

8. AQUINAS AND LATER MEDIEVAL PHILOSOPHY

B*y common consent the greatest philosophical theologian of the Middle Ages* was Thomas Aquinas. He is also perhaps the most misunderstood, especially by evangelical Protestants. Aquinas has been compared with a lake into which many streams have flowed and from which many have drawn, but which was not a spring.[1] Others have laid at his door the responsibility for the fateful separation of philosophy from revelation, which allowed philosophy "to take wings, as it were, and fly off wherever it wished, without relationship to the Scriptures."[2] Both views are misleading. The former hardly does justice to the creativity with which Aquinas met the intellectual challenges of his day. The latter misrepresents the function of philosophy, as Thomas saw it. Thomas himself warned against two opposing errors. On the one hand, there is the error of thinking that philosophy provides some kind of autonomous vantage point from which people can get at ultimate truth apart from revelation. On the other hand, there is the error of falling into the opposite trap of denying that non-Christians have genuine insights or knowledge. "The study of philosophy," Aquinas observed, "is not done in order to know what men have thought, but rather to know how truth herself stands."[3]

Aquinas and His Age

Thomas Aquinas (1225-74)[4] was born in his family's castle at Roccasecca in southern Italy. He was the youngest son of a feudal noble family that was in decline. At the age of five he became an oblate in the Benedictine monastery at Monte Casino. This meant that he was offered to God by his parents for the monastic life. It was not that he became a monk as a child. Rather, it ensured his education in the monastery with a view to entering the religious life at the age of discretion. Doubtless, his family had in mind the possibility of him becoming the future abbot of Monte Casino. However, political rivalries made the monastery unsafe, and Thomas was sent at the age of fourteen to study at the new University of Naples. Here he embarked on the study of the *trivium*, and probably began to read Aristotle together with the commentaries of Avicenna. It was at this time that Thomas decided to join the Dominican Order of Preachers, which like the Franciscans stressed poverty and obedience but unlike them stressed the importance of intellectual life. Initially, his family was opposed to the move and forcibly retained him in the family castle for a year. Eventually, the family relented, and Thomas became a Dominican friar.

For a time Thomas studied in Paris and then in Cologne with Albertus Magnus, where he deepened his knowledge of Aristotle. In 1252 he returned to Paris, where he began his teaching career as a professor at the Dominican Convent of St.-Jacques. Paris was now the theological and philosophical center of Europe. The university had grown out of the cathedral school of Notre Dame and the theological schools of the monasteries of St. Victor and Mont Ste. Geneviève. Thomas was required to lecture on Scripture and the *Sentences* of Peter Lombard, a standard compilation of Christian doctrine which contained a wealth of quotations from the church fathers.[5] But increasingly Thomas was drawn into the critical debates of his day. By this time Plato was known only through the imperfect translations of the *Timaeus*, the *Phaedo* and the *Meno*, though Neoplatonism was much better known. As we have already seen, Islamic and Jewish thinkers were much better acquainted with Aristotle, and for nearly two centuries they had been wrestling with questions posed by Aristotelianism to religious faith. For Aquinas and his Christian contemporaries the issue was doubly acute. On the one hand, there were the questions posed by Aristotle's way of thinking. On the other hand, there were the answers already given by Islamic and Jewish thinkers which were hardly acceptable to a Christian thinker. Aquinas decided to face the problem head-on. He made his own study of Aristotle, on whom he wrote extensively. He also made his own study of non-Christian thinkers. He subjected all ideas to rigorous scrutiny, giving due recognition to the truth of ideas, wherever they came from, but giving his own evaluation of every issue, point by point.

The years 1259 to 1268 saw Thomas back in his native Italy, where he taught in a number of Dominican houses. It was in this period that he completed his *Summa Contra Gentiles* and began his greatest work, the *Summa Theologiae*. The word *summa* means a "compend" or "handbook." Prior to Thomas, a summa was a collection of "sentences" which aimed at presenting the truths of Christian doctrine. It contained the testimonies of the church fathers and other ancient writers. But in the course of time the *summa* evolved into a literary work which set out concisely a given field of knowledge, which organized the objects of this field in a synthetic way, and which as such could be used for teaching students.[6] The *Summa Contra Gentiles* was a Christian apologetic, designed for the cross-cultural situation posed by the presence of Islam in Europe, and especially in Spain. The *Summa Theologiae* is Thomas's statement of Christian doctrine in the light of Scripture, the interpretations of the church fathers and ancient and modern philosophy.

In 1269 Thomas was sent back to Paris where he was caught up in the controversies posed by Aristotelianism. At one end of the spectrum was the rector of the faculty of arts, Siger of Brabant, who was an Averroist. At the other end was the bishop of Paris, Stephen Tempier, who issued a condemnation of Siger, and who eventually also posthumously condemned Thomas himself in 1277.[7] Thomas returned to Italy in 1273, where he continued to teach, to work on the *Summa Theologiae,* and to write commentaries on Aristotle and on Scripture. Suddenly in December 1273 Thomas ceased to write. He told a friend that he could not go on because "all that I have written seems like straw to me." Whether Thomas had suffered a brain hemorrhage or had experienced a mystical vision—or both—is a question discussed by scholars.[8] The following year, at the age of forty-nine, Thomas died on his way to attend the Council of Lyons.

The teaching of Thomas was a matter of rivalry between the Franciscan and Dominican orders. For a time the Franciscans forbade their members to read Thomas, but the Dominicans embraced it as the official teaching of their order. The condemnations of Thomas were soon reversed, and in 1323 he was made a saint. In the course of time Thomas came to be hailed as the Common Doctor (or teacher) of the Catholic Church and as the Angelic Doctor. In an effort to stem the rising tide of liberalism and secularism Pope Leo XIII published in 1879 an encyclical letter, *Aeterni Patris,* asserting the permanent value of his teachings, and urging Catholic philosophers to draw their inspiration from it. Not all have done so. The fortunes of Thomism have waxed and waned over the years. In the 1960s they were at a fairly low ebb, and Pope Paul VI used the occasion of the new edition of the *Summa Theologiae* to say that Thomas's teaching "is a treasure belonging not only to the Dominican Order but to the whole Church, and indeed the whole world; it is not merely medieval but valid for all times, not least of all for our own."[9]

In all, Thomas produced about a hundred different writings. His work ranged from philosophical commentaries to hymns. He was helped by secretaries who took down his dictation. Even so, his accomplishment is phenomenal, especially in view of his travels, which he was obliged to make on foot as the regulations of the Dominican Order required. In a survey like the present one it is impossible to examine the whole range of Thomas's thought. At the risk of making an invidious choice, we shall focus on just two of the many issues that Thomas treated: the five ways, or proofs of the existence of God, and his doctrine of analogy. The five ways themselves occupy little space in relation to the *Summa Theologiae* as a whole. But they became very important in later Thomist thought, and they are widely regarded as a major but succinct statement of arguments for the existence of God. The doctrine of analogy focuses on the crucial question of what kind of meaning words have when we apply them to God.

Before we examine these two questions, it may be useful to make some comments on Thomas's method of procedure in the *Summa Theologiae.* The *Summa Theologiae* is divided into three main parts. The first part deals with God and the going out of all things from him. The second part deals with the return of all things to God as their home. The uncompleted third part deals with Christ and the sacraments. This division is further complicated by the fact that the second part is subdivided into the first part of the second (psychology, morality, law, sin and grace) and the second part of the second (virtues, vices, gifts of the Spirit, the Christian life, contemplation, action and perfection). The whole work is divided into questions, which are in turn subdivided into articles.

Each article has the same basic form, which the reader needs to keep in mind in order to see what Thomas is doing. The article has three main parts. The first part of the article states the problem in the form of one or more objections to the position that Thomas himself is going to take. The objections are introduced by the words *Videtur quod,* or "It seems that. . . ." Here Aquinas states briefly the problems posed for the Christian view of things. The next section is introduced by the words *Sed Contra,* or "But on the other hand." Here Thomas quotes a passage from Scripture or some statement from an authority which he himself accepts but which is apparently at odds with the objections and difficulties already noted. This is followed by the third part of the article, which is introduced by the word *Responsio,* or "Reply." It is in this part of the article that Thomas gives his own view of the question. He first states his general view of the way the issue may be resolved and then he turns to the specific objections and difficulties which he noted at the outset and states how he resolves them.

Thomas's way of proceeding does not exactly make for light bedtime reading. But it has a rigor and succinctness which few have emulated. As its title indicates, the *Summa Theologiae* is a work of theology. Philosophy certainly enters into it. Aristotle is referred to not by name but simply as "the philosopher." But in all this, Thomas does not see philosophy as an alternative track to theology which enables him to prove rationally and intellectually items of faith which ordinary people have to accept simply by faith. Rather, it is a tool for clarifying issues. Despite its size, the *Summa Theologiae* was not a definitive system in which theological truth was set in concrete for all generations. It was more a series of exercises in thinking aloud on current questions. It took into account different views, both ancient and modern, and resolved questions by showing how they could be analyzed and answered.

The Five Ways

The five ways of Aquinas occupy less than three pages of printed text, but like Anselm's equally brief ontological argument they have generated endless discussion.[10] They appear in the *Responsio* of the *Summa Theologiae* 1, Q 2. art. 3. Thomas has already rejected the ontological argument on the grounds that God's existence is not self-evident.[11] God's existence, Thomas argues, is self-evident to God himself but not to us. For we do not see God directly, as God sees himself. What we in this life see is not God himself but his effects. Aquinas sees this to be Paul's meaning in Romans 1:20 where Paul says that the hidden things of God can be clearly understood from the things that he has made. Therefore, we have to start with the effects in order to form some idea of their cause.

This leads to the question in article 3 of whether God exists. Thomas begins by noting two objections which have a definitely modern ring to them. The first is bound up with the existence of evil. If God is infinite, how can evil exist? But evil does exist, therefore God does not. The second objection is bound up with our view of causes. If natural causes can be found for natural effects, and human action can be explained in terms of reasoning and the will, what need is there to look for further explanations? There is therefore no need to suppose that a God exists. God would seem to be a superfluous hypothesis. This brings Thomas to the *Sed Contra*. The book of Exodus represents God as saying "I AM WHO I AM" (Ex 3:14). This in turn leads to the *Responsio* which states that "there are five ways in which one can prove that there is a God." The five ways themselves clearly draw on Aristotle's view of causation, actuality and potentiality.[12]

The first way is based on motion or change. It is clear that many things around us are in process of change. Such change is never purely spontaneous. It is always the result of outside factors. A piece of wood would not burn if it were not caused to ignite by something else. The piece of wood itself is potentially fire. But it must be actually wood and potentially fire or actually fire and no longer wood. The same thing cannot be actually *x* and potentially *x* at exactly the same time. In order to bring about the change, there has to be an agent of change. The world is a series of such changes brought about by agents of change. But one has to posit a first agent of change. For otherwise the whole process of change would never start. "Hence one is bound to arrive at some first cause of change not itself being changed by anything, and this is what everybody understands by God."

The second way has a similar form, and the question has been asked whether the second way is not simply a restatement of the first way, which uses the idea of efficient causes instead of motion or change. In a series of efficient causes, one has to posit a first cause which is not antecedently caused by any other cause outside itself. Otherwise, the process of causation would never start. This leads Thomas to the similarly worded conclusion: "One is therefore forced to suppose some first cause, to which everyone gives the name 'God.' "

The third way explores the notion of contingent being. None of the things that we observe in the world last forever. They spring up and die away. None of them is necessary in the sense that they must eternally exist. But if all being is contingent, we have a problem. "If nothing was in being nothing could be brought into being, and nothing would be in being now, which contradicts observation." As in the two previous ways, Thomas sees a problem in the idea of an infinite regress. To put it in modern language, it is like a series of dominoes falling. Each one that is knocked over is itself knocked over by another domino. The dominoes have been so set up that, when the first domino falls, it knocks over the next domino, and so on. The line of dominoes may be long, and the pattern of their arrangement intricate. The whole process is triggered off by the fall of the first domino. But the first domino will not fall, unless there be some agent *outside* the series of falling dominoes to knock it over. Otherwise, the process of knocking over would never start. Moreover, this first agent has to be of a different kind and outside the series. In order to explain contingent being, one has to posit a necessary being. Thomas concludes, "One is forced therefore to suppose something which must be, and owes this to no other thing than itself; indeed it is the cause that other things must be."

The fourth way is based on gradation and has a ring of Aristotelian-Platonic metaphysics about it. The argument assumes that there must be an exemplary cause for all gradation. Thus, there must be something that is hottest which is the exemplification and cause of all hot things. The name that is given to the exemplary cause of all gradation is God. Broadly speaking, the first four ways are forms of the cosmological argument which posits an ultimate cause for the universe.

The fifth way is a form of the teleological argument which, as the Greek word *telos*, "goal" or "purpose," suggests, looks at evidence of purpose in the world.[13] Thomas begins by noting that there is evidence of order in nature. This is so even in inanimate objects and living things that lack intelligence. There is a certain constancy in nature which is too frequent to attribute to accident. Things which lack awareness do not tend toward a goal unless they are directed by an agent "with awareness and understanding." If we were to see an arrow flying through the air toward a target, we would assume an archer, even if we could not see him. Aquinas concluded that "everything in nature, therefore, is directed to its goal by someone with understanding, and this we call 'God.' "

With this Thomas returns to the two original objections which introduced the argument. In reply to the objection that evil is incompatible with the existence of an infinite God, Thomas observes that it is a mark of God's limitless goodness that he can permit evils to exist and draw good out of them. In response to the idea that God is an unnecessary hypothesis, Thomas pointed out that, while finite causes explain finite effects, they themselves require explanation in terms of an ultimate cause which brought them into being.

Estimates of the value of the five ways vary wildly. At one end of the scale, there are those who say that when they are properly understood and carefully restated, the five ways provide a rational foundation for Christian belief in God.[14] At the other end of the scale, there are those who think that they are so full of flaws that they are worthless. One thing that is clear is the fact that the arguments were not particularly original. In form at least they add little to what Aristotle, the Islamic philosophers and Maimonides had to say on the subject.[15] This fact has even prompted the suggestion that Thomas himself had no great enthusiasm for the arguments, but was merely summarizing current opinions without seriously committing himself to any of them.[16]

If we treat the arguments as proofs of the truth of the Christian understanding of God, a number of major cracks in the arguments can easily be spotted. First of all, there is the problem of demonstrating that the first cause is the same as the Prime Mover and the Great Designer, and that all of them are one and the same as the God of Christian faith. Logically, we are not entitled to attribute to a cause any capacities other than those necessary to produce the effect in question.[17] That is, when we try, as the arguments do, to get at the causes simply by looking at the effects, we cannot say that the different effects must have been produced

by the same cause. If for the purposes of argument we grant the existence of a first cause, the proof does not entitle us to say that he, she
or it is the same as the designer. The maker and the designer are not
necessarily identical. Nor do the arguments themselves furnish this missing link of proof, unless (as some people suspect) they are really disguised forms of the same argument. But in that case we have not five
different proofs, but only one.

The irony is that the more "proofs" we have of this kind, the more
the difficulty is intensified. It reaches its climax when we try to identify
the different gods of the different arguments with the Trinitarian God
of the Christian faith. As David Hume put it later on, "A great number
of men join in building a house or ship, in rearing a city, in framing a
commonwealth: Why may not several Deities combine in contriving and
framing a world?"[18] We seem to be left with what has been called a
celestial *Council of Five*. But is Thomas really guilty of sloppy thinking
which he tries to cover up by the ambiguity of the word *god*, which he
introduces in the punch line of each of the five ways? How does all this
square with the fact that Thomas himself acknowledged that the Trinity[19]
and creation[20] were both doctrines of faith rather than reason?

The argument about design raises a number of issues. For one thing,
no human being is able, merely from looking at the world, to say what
the goal or purpose of the world is as a whole. To do this we would have
to put ourselves in the place of God.[21] Christians believe that they know
something of the purposes of God, but they do so on the basis of their
understanding of revelation. The question of design is further complicated by the issue of evolution, which we shall look at more closely in
volume two of this work. For the moment, however, one or two brief
observations may be made.

Thomas is not claiming to know by rational reflection what is the
overall goal of the universe. He is merely observing that things in our
experience appear to obey natural laws. There seem to be no exceptions.
If we introduce the question of evolution, we are at once confronted by
a paradox. To many thinkers today, evolution seems to have destroyed
forever the idea of an overall purpose in the universe. And yet science
itself operates with the assumption that the world exhibits structures that
are amenable to rational inspection. As philosopher of science Stanley

L. Jaki has eloquently put it, "Water molecules, so many marvels of exact rationality, are never seen by the naked eye. They hide their marvels in the apparent irrationality of muddy puddles, torrential rains, and stormy oceans, so many symbols of the flood of errors by which man can be overwhelmed."[22] To Jaki, despite the many pointers to chaos, waste, and suffering, there are also "pointers of purpose." However, evidences of nature's rationality "can be secured only if one is receptive to them, an attitude that takes one beyond what is simply revealed to the senses." In his own way, Thomas Aquinas was making a similar point. He maintained that, even if the world had its origin in what the ancients called "primary matter,"[23] there were certain pointers of order in things which "lack awareness" which pointed to an intelligence outside them.

What then was Thomas trying to do? Was he trying to lay a foundation for Christian theology by what he called "natural reason"? Was Aquinas, the classical foundationalist who saw Christian truth like a two-story building, laying the foundations by reason and completing the rest of the building by faith from materials supplied by revelation? If this is so, the result is very unsatisfactory, for the foundations will not bear the weight of the building. Faith and reason so conceived do not fit very well together. Moreover, this view of Thomas does not fit too well with his own stress on revelation and faith which comes out over and over again in the *Summa Theologiae*. Nor, for that matter, does such a view of the five ways fit too well with the appeal in the *Sed Contra* to Exodus 3:14, which represents God as saying, "I AM WHO I AM."

It has been observed that the word *God* at the end of each of the five ways is not a proper name. It is not as if Thomas, by metaphysical sleight of hand, was trying to convert it into the proper name of the Christian God. It is at most a minimal designation for the being presupposed by the phenomena examined in the argument. Such a being is not actually seen directly as one phenomenon among the many observable phenomena. But then, neither do Christian believers claim to observe God directly as one phenomenon among the many other phenomena in the world. E. L. Mascall has observed that the five ways are not to be seen as five different arguments but "as five different ways of exhibiting the radically un-self-sufficient character of finite beings and so of leading us to see them as dependent on a transcendent self-sufficient creative

Cause."[24] Reason reflecting on the structure of finite being points us in the direction of such a Cause. But closer knowledge of this Cause comes through faith. The self-sufficient creative Cause that is adequate to answering the un-self-sufficiency of finite beings is the God of the Christian faith. The being that we call God and who is worshipped in the Christian church is the mysterious reality who is adequate to answer the problems of finite existence exhibited by the five ways.

If this interpretation is correct, Thomas Aquinas was more of a presuppositionalist than he has normally been credited with being. He was also engaging in what Paul Tillich has called *correlation*. He was relating philosophy and theology, and reason and faith in such a way as to give rational philosophical reflection a legitimate role in analyzing questions, while at the same time recognizing that the answer to those questions lies outside the realm of philosophy and reason. He did not imagine that either philosophy or theology could or should eliminate the mystery of God's being. No human being sees God directly. Our knowledge of God is always indirect and imperfect. For this reason Thomas could say that "we cannot grasp what God is, but only what He is not and how other things are related to Him."[25] This did not mean that Thomas was at heart an agnostic. It meant rather that our apprehension of God is always mediated through a medium which itself is *not* God. In other words the divine mystery is apprehended through the created order. And with this we come to Aquinas's doctrine of analogy.

Analogy

Aquinas's teaching on the subject of analogy is a theory about the meaning of words when we apply them to God.[26] It is especially relevant today in the light of the fierce debate on the meaning and nature of language—particularly religious, metaphysical and moral language—which dominated philosophical discussion in the mid-twentieth century. It was the common complaint of agnostic philosophers that, because they could not read into religious statements the same testable meanings that they found in secular language, religious utterances were either meaningless or disguised pieces of wishful thinking. But it should also be seriously noted that the subject of analogy is also relevant in the light of complaints that biblical and theological language is riddled by male sexism, and that God is commonly assumed to be a male.

We shall look at the question of religious language more closely in volume two. In the meantime it is worth noting that the problem of speaking meaningfully about God had already had a long history before Aquinas. Thomas's response to it bore in mind what Neoplatonist, Islamic and Jewish thinkers had had to say on the subject. Thomas's view steered a middle course between a Neoplatonism which held that we can say nothing positive about God at all because God is so utterly different from creatures, and a simplistic literalism which naively supposed that religious language meant exactly the same when applied to God as it does when applied to human beings. Thomas's doctrine of analogy was never intended to be a complete account of religious language. It was more a series of observations about the meaning of words, when we apply them to God.

The Neoplatonists had followed what was known as the *Via Negativa,* or "negative way," which insisted that God was *not* like a human being or, for that matter, like anything in the world. Thomas agreed with this up to a point. Our human language needs to be purged of wrong ideas. If we speak of the wrath of God, it does not mean that God is spiteful and perpetually bad tempered. But when pushed to its logical conclusion, the negative way ended up with saying nothing at all about God. For, if God is utterly different, there is nothing more to be said. Thomas believed that the *Via Negativa* must be complemented by the *Via Positiva* ("positive way") or *Via Affirmativa* ("way of affirmation"), which meant that some things could be said positively about God. But in so doing he recognized that when we use bodily words for God (e.g., the hand of God, the eyes of the Lord, or God speaking), such language is metaphorical, because God does not have a body.[27] Thus, when one of the prophets says "Thus, says the Lord . . . ," the statement does not mean that God has a tongue, teeth, lips and vocal cords, which are prerequisites for human speech.

Thomas noted that words are often used in a *univocal* and in an *equivocal* sense. But neither option was open to Christians when they want to speak about God. In the case of *univocal* words, the words have the same form and meaning whenever they are used. If words used for God were *univocal,* these words would mean exactly the same when we use them about God as when we use them in ordinary contexts. If, for example, we think of John the Baptist's description of Jesus as "the Lamb of God" (John 1:29), we are not intended to think that Jesus was literally a four-legged, woolly animal. When Christians call God their Father, they do not mean to say that he is a human being, existing in time and space, who has brought children into the world by natural procreation. On the other hand, Christians do not think that their language is *equivocal*. In that case, their words would mean something on the human level, but something entirely different on the religious level.

If words about God belonged to the former category, we should be reducing God to the level of an object or being, existing in time and space. If they belong to the latter category, religious language would be meaningless. For what we might say on the human level, the divine reality would be utterly different from the sense of our words as we understand them. Aquinas believed that users of religious language need not be impaled on either of the horns of this dilemma, even though we cannot avoid using human language in speaking about God. He suggested:

> Some words are used neither univocally nor purely equivocally of God and creatures, but analogically, for we cannot speak of God at all except in the language we use of creatures, and so whatever is said both of God and creatures is said in virtue of the order that creatures have to God as to their source and cause in which all the perfections of things pre-exist transcendentally.[28]

Thomas further distinguished two types of analogy. In the first, a word could be used for two things, because each of them is related to a third thing. For example, we can use the word *healthy* of both a diet and of someone's complexion because both are related to human health. The first (the diet) is the cause and the second (the complexion) is the sign of health. In the second type of analogy, the same word is used for two things because of a relation between them. The word *healthy* can be used for both a diet and a person because the diet is the cause of that health in the person.

In the hands of Aquinas the doctrine of analogy is both a warning about the limitations of language and assurance that, despite the limitations, language is still meaningful. It clearly means that terms used in analogy have to be balanced against each other. The use of male language about God does not mean that God is literally a male. If God can be called "our Father" in the Lord's Prayer, he can also be described in female language in the parable of the lost coin (Lk 15:8-10), the mother hen and her brood (Mt 23:37), and the figure of God's wisdom (Prov 8). On a literal level the images conveyed by different analogies cannot be reconciled together in a single picture. We cannot form a single composite picture of Christ as the Lamb of God, the light of the world, the bread of life, the vine and the shepherd. For no human being can be these literally and simultaneously. But analogy points us to an apprehension of divine reality which is beyond our comprehension. The doctrine of analogy has been vigorously debated. Some philosophers have objected that analogy involves us in an infinite regress. In order to explain the point of an analogy we have to use further analogies which themselves require explanation by means of still more analogies. Thus, we never get to the plain, bare meaning. But this kind of objection is an objection to pretty well all language. Moreover, in the case of God it involves a demand which cannot be met—at least in this life. We do not encounter the pure presence of God in this world. God's presence is always mediated by words, people, situations and forms of worship, and Aquinas's teaching gives due recognition to this fact.

It is not as if we can stop the world and get off, so that we can look at our language and compare it with God, and see if the language is appropriate. Such a process is conceivably possible. It has been given the name *eschatological verification*.[29] A more simple way of describing it would be to call it dying and entering into the presence of God. But such a step is irrevocable, and is not an option open to the philosopher of language who wishes to report back on his findings. At best the claim that religious language may be open to eschatological verification is an attempt to identify conditions under which such language might be verified. As such it fends off the positivistic claim that religious language is in principle unverifiable, and is thus factually meaningless. However, to talk about eschatological verification does not help us very much in explaining how religious language relates to what it purports to describe. But to say this is not to concede that the doctrine of analogy is in the end meaningless. For it is the common experience of believers down the ages that religious language, though not literal, is a medium through which they apprehend the transcendent God.

It has sometimes been suggested that the doctrine of analogy implies an analogy of being, *analogia entis*, between God and creatures. By assuming that God and creatures both share common characteristics of being, it has been argued that the Creator was thereby reduced to being just a scaled-up creature. To some this has suggested that the doctrine of analogy could be used as a basis for human speculation which resulted in humans making God in their own image. But such thoughts were far removed from the mind of Aquinas. He was adamant that "the resemblance of creatures to God is an imperfect one . . . for they do not even share a common genus."[30] His doctrine of analogy was not based on a speculative metaphysic of being but on the doctrine of creation. The God who made the world made it in such a way as to permit "the invisible things of God" to be "made known by those things that are made."[31]

The doctrine of analogy is by no means a complete account of religious language. In Thomas's hands it was not the elaborate ontology of being that it became in later thinkers. It was a semantic theory which suggested kinds of meaning that words might have when applied to God. Without such a theory it is difficult to see how talk about God could have any meaning.

If it is a mark of a great thinker that his ideas continue to stimulate later generations, then Aquinas belongs to the great thinkers of the world. In the past twenty-five years evangelical scholars have embarked on a process of rediscovering Thomas Aquinas. This is not to say that they have bought into his theology uncritically. But they have begun to understand him better and see how some of his ideas and ways of approaching questions may help us today. When Aquinas spoke of nature and grace, he was not attempting to create two separate, autonomous realms. The realm of nature was itself the work of grace in creation. But to appreciate this, one needs to see creation from the standpoint of revelation. The *Summa Theologiae* has to be read as a compend of theology—not as a compend of philosophy. Rational reflection on the world serves Thomas as a preamble to faith. It does not function as the philosophical foundation for the theological building.

Nor is philosophy a substitute. As we leave this brief and very selective account of Aquinas, perhaps we should let him have the last word on the subject of philosophy and faith.

> Christian theology issues from the light of faith, philosophy from the natural light of reason. Philosophical truths cannot be opposed to the truth of faith, they fall short indeed, yet they also admit common analogies; and some moreover are foreshadowings, for nature is the preface to grace.[32]

> And it is well to take warning here, to forestall rash attempts at demonstration by arguments that are not cogent, and so provide unbelievers with the occasion for laughing at us and thinking that these are our reasons for believing the things of faith.[33]

Alternatives to Thomism

If we step back and look at the broad sweep of intellectual development, we can see Aquinas as a Christian thinker who stood in the empirical tradition in philosophy. It is a tradition which reached back to Aristotle and stretched forward to the empiricism of the seventeenth and eighteenth centuries and modern science. This tradition stressed the importance of observation in acquiring knowledge. Reason by itself cannot lead us to know reality. It has to have something to work on. That something is provided by our senses. In taking this stand, Thomas Aquinas was adopting a very different approach from Anselm and also from his contemporary, Bonaventure (1221-74).[34] The latter was a Franciscan theologian who taught at Paris before being made cardinal bishop of Albano shortly before his death. Bonaventure had little sympathy with Aristotelianism, and was much less open than Thomas to the new ways of thinking. He put a higher premium on the ability of reason than did Thomas. Bonaventure could even argue that reason could demonstrate that the world was created in time. On the other hand, Bonaventure had a mystical approach to divine knowledge. Whereas Aquinas taught that our knowledge of God is mediated via the created order and our words for God are analogical in character, Bonaventure laid emphasis on mystical illumination which God sheds on faithful believers. By contrast with this illumination, all human wisdom is folly.

Arabic philosophers were interested in medicine and mathematics, and Thomas's Aristotelianism was certainly open to the encouragement of science. But it was in Britain that scholars began to push further Aristotle's interest in natural science. At Oxford, in addition to the traditional disciplines of philosophy and theology, languages, mathematics and the natural sciences were studied. A key figure in this development was Thomas's older contemporary Robert Grosseteste (c. 1175-1253).[35] Grosseteste had taught at Oxford before becoming bishop of Lincoln, which was then the largest diocese in England. As a bishop, he was committed to church reform. He witnessed the confirmation of the Magna Carta in 1236. He also translated Aristotle and performed scientific experiments, though his views on nature were more like those of Augustine and the Arabic Neoplatonists than those of Aristotle.

Another leading thinker of the thirteenth century was the Franciscan Roger Bacon (c. 1214-92),[36] who found himself the frequent object of suspicion and persecution by his superiors. His ideas were condemned by Bishop Tempier of Paris. According to some sources, he was even thrown into prison for his views. In the course of his stormy career he was credited with inventing a rudimentary telescope, gunpowder and the thermometer. Bacon recognized three modes of knowledge: authority, reason and experience. Both authority and reason needed the confirmation of experience. The latter was twofold: external and internal. The external experience of our senses was needed to confirm scientific ideas. But the highest experience of all was internal experience which leads to mystical knowledge of God. To Bacon, philosophy and science were important but subordinate disciplines. Their function was to explain the truth of God revealed in sacred Scripture.

Scotus, Occam and Biel

One of the greatest intellects of the later Middle Ages was John Duns Scotus (c. 1266-1308).[37] As his name suggests, he was born in Scotland, where he entered a Franciscan convent. He taught at Cambridge, Oxford and Paris, and died prematurely in Paris where he had been transferred to teach. In later ages he was known as the *Subtle Doctor*. His family name was Duns, but on account of his subtle teaching it became a term of ridicule in the form of *dunce*. However, there was nothing dullwitted or stupid about Duns Scotus, as anyone who has ever attempted to study his extensive writings will quickly find out. Nevertheless, they present a paradox, or perhaps a series of paradoxes. On the one hand, Scotus makes heavy intellectual demands on his readers. On the other hand, he downplays the intellect. Of all the discussions of the existence of God by medieval theologians, that of Duns Scotus is the most elaborate.[38] Nevertheless, Scotus insisted that love and the will held prior place over the intellect. He also insisted on our human need of revelation in addition to our natural knowledge.[39]

Scotus had a genius for speculation, but he considered speculation merely a means to an end. He could say that "thinking of God matters little, if he be not loved in contemplation." Like Thomas, he could appeal to Aristotle as the philosopher. But he could also appeal to "our philosopher, Paul" who taught that love, when directed to God, makes human beings truly wise.[40] Nevertheless, the writings of Scotus vividly illustrate a widening gulf between philosophy and theology in later medieval thought. Scotus thought of himself primarily as a theologian of the church. His ultimate goal was theological in character. Nevertheless, there appears in his writings a separation between the philosophical and the theological. In Thomas Aquinas the two are intertwined. In Scotus theology is increasingly reduced to what is given us to believe by supernatural means in revelation. The domain of philosophy, on the other hand, is whatever comes within the scope of natural reason.

This process of separation was carried even further by William of Occam (c. 1300-c. 1349)[41] and his German disciple, Gabriel Biel (c. 1420-95).[42] Occam and Biel were leading figures in a new school of thought which came to be known as the *via moderna* ("modern way"). The term implies a deliberate contrast with the *via antiqua* ("old way"), which was used to denote the teaching of Albertus Magnus, Aquinas and Scotus. The *via moderna* represented a continuation of the nominalist tradition, though perhaps the term *nominalist* is misleading. For it suggests a single school of thought, preoccupied with denying the universals. In point of fact, the term *nominalism* embraces a number of schools of thought, though it is perhaps best reserved for thinkers of the twelfth century. Occam himself was not generally regarded as a nominalist by his contemporaries, though his followers were dubbed nominalists by their opponents.

Frederick Copleston suggests that a better name for them would be *terminists*.[43] For while they were critical of realism, the logicians of the new movement were more concerned with the logical status and function of terms. "The nominalist spirit, if one may so speak," adds Copleston, "was inclined to analysis rather than to synthesis, and to criticism rather than to speculation." Moreover, the new movement was not, as it has been represented in the past, a bankrupt form of extreme scholasticism. It is important as a theological movement in its own right and as a forerunner of the Reformation.[44]

William of Occam was probably born in the village of Ockham near London. He became a Franciscan at an early age and studied at Oxford. He was prevented from receiving his license to teach through charges of heresy brought against him by the chancellor of the University of Oxford. Occam was summoned in 1324 to the papal court at Avignon to defend himself. During his stay there, he became embroiled in a controversy between the pope and the Franciscan order concerning the Franciscan view of the life of poverty. He concluded that the pope was contradicting the Gospels, and therefore was not a true pope. In 1328 he fled to Pisa, where the emperor, an opponent of the pope, was residing. Excommunicated after leaving Avignon, Occam stayed at the imperial court, enjoying the emperor's protection. Occam died in Munich, perhaps of the Black Death. Occam's voluminous writings fall into two well-defined groups. Prior to his flight from Avignon, he devoted himself to theological and philosophical works. After the flight, Occam turned to polemical defenses of the Franciscan order and of the emperor, and condemnations of the pope for heresy and abuse of spiritual power.

To Occam the realist view that universals are real things, and not just names, was "the worst error of philosophy."[45] Most philosophers of the thirteenth and fourteenth centuries had been won over by Aristotle's arguments against Plato, and held a moderate realism which, in Occam's words, maintained that "the nature, which is somehow universal—at least potentially and incompletely—really exists in the individual." To Occam this was still unsatisfactory. He taught that universals had no reality in things, or even in the mind of God. They were simply abstractions of the human mind, which enabled human beings to identify and classify things. Science was not the science of things, but the science of signs and symbols which are called universals.

Occam has often been pictured as pushing nominalism to the verge of skepticism. However, in her recent magisterial study of his thought, Marilyn McCord Adams has portrayed him as a Franciscan Aristotelian, who was much more conservative in both philosophy and theology than is commonly supposed.[46] As others before him had done, Occam drew a distinction between the knowledge possessed by the blessed in heaven who see God and that possessed by the pilgrim believer on earth who lacks such vision. For the pilgrim believer there are truths which are naturally knowable (e.g., God exists) and truths which are supernaturally knowable (e.g., God is three in one and God is incarnate). In emphasizing this distinction, Occam was drawing a line between natural and revealed philosophy more clearly than his predecessors had done. At the same time he was also contributing to the separation of philosophy from theology.

Gabriel Biel was one of the most important theologians of the late Middle Ages. After lengthy study in the arts faculty at Heidelberg, he studied theology at Erfurt, a center of the *via moderna* which favored Occam to the exclusion of Thomas and Scotus, and at Cologne, where Thomas Aquinas and Albertus Magnus remained the honored scholars. Biel thus was fully conversant with both the *via moderna* and the *via antiqua*. In later life, although he remained a dedicated Occamist, he criticized narrow rivalry between the schools and drew on the teaching of Scotus and Thomas. In the middle part of his life he served as cathedral preacher and vicar in the Rhineland city of Mainz. He later went to Württemberg to assist with the establishment of new houses of the Brethren of the Common Life. In 1484 he was appointed to the theological faculty of the newly founded University of Tübingen, where he served both as a professor and as the university's rector. At one stage Biel was seen as the embodiment of the disintegration of late medieval thought, the man whose misrepresentation of Catholic teaching misled Luther and his followers. More recent research has presented a different picture. Biel has emerged as a teacher who links medieval theology with post-Reformation Catholicism. Moreover, whereas Occam devoted his considerable mental powers to theoretical questions in theology, Biel explored the pastoral applications of Occamism.

Outside the world of philosophy, Occam's name lives on in the term *Occam's Razor*. It is preserved in the Latin formula *entia non multiplicanda praeter necessitatem*. It means that "entities are not to be multiplied beyond necessity." As such, it is a principle of economy which has applications in science, philosophy, theology and elsewhere. Although the basic idea is there, this particular form of words is unfortunately not to be found in the works of Occam that have survived. Moreover, Occam did not invent the idea. It can be found in Scotus and others, and may be traced back to Aristotle.[47] As the Middle Ages gave way to the Renaissance and the Reformation, Occam's Razor proved to be an idea whose time had come. Whether the growing separation of philosophy and theology was a good idea depends on one's viewpoint. To some the separation of philosophy and theology marks the beginning of modern secularism. To others it marks the end of an unfortunate confusion and the beginning of the possibility of allowing philosophy and theology to have their proper functions. What is beyond doubt is the fact that the debates of the fourteenth century set something in motion the after-effects of which are still being felt today.

PART III
FROM THE REFORMATION
TO THE AGE OF ENLIGHTENMENT

9. PHILOSOPHY AND THE REFORMERS

T*he period from the Reformation to the Age of Enlightenment spans three* hundred years. Looking back on these years, it is now clear that the sixteenth, seventeenth and eighteenth centuries were the cradle of modern thought. Roman Catholicism took its decisive shape from the Middle Ages. Protestant theology took its form from the Reformation in the sixteenth century, and the modern secular outlook from the rational, Enlightenment philosophies of the seventeenth and eighteenth centuries.

This is not to say that the eighteenth century contributed nothing to Christian theology, or that later secular thought appeared like a bolt from the blue. The Evangelical Revival, led by men like John Wesley (1703-91) and George Whitefield (1714-70), brought new life to the churches and gave to many a sense of God in their personal experience. But like the Puritan movement a century earlier, the revival was essentially a continuation of the Reformation. On the other hand, there were active rationalists in the Reformation Era, like Faustus Socinus (1539-1604), who rejected the doctrine of the Trinity in favor of Unitarianism and condemned the doctrine of atonement as immoral and irrational. The Reformation itself owed not a little to that rebirth of secular learning and quest for knowledge which blossomed in the fourteenth century and which is known as the Renaissance.

Renaissance and Reformation
The idea of a rebirth of literature and the arts originated in the fourteenth century. Eventually the French word *renaissance* became the ac-

cepted designation for the cultural movement that began in Italy and spread to the rest of Europe in the fifteenth and sixteenth centuries. The term carries with it an implied negative verdict on the Middle Ages, which were seen by Renaissance writers as a kind of interlude between the glories of the classical past and the renewed appreciation of them in their own age.[1] One of the features which marked off the Renaissance from the Middle Ages was a rebirth of interest in the philosophy of Greece and Rome. Works which had been neglected for centuries were made accessible to a wider public by the invention of printing. Among the most important, from a philosophical point of view, were Lucretius's *On the Nature of Things* and Cicero's *On the Nature of the Gods.*

The main philosophical stream during the Renaissance continued to be Aristotelianism. But in the field of science, Aristotelianism began to be challenged though not replaced. Interestingly enough, when Francis Bacon became dissatisfied with Aristotelian science and looked for new ways of exploring nature, he did not altogether abandon Aristotle. He turned instead to the rhetorical method derived from Aristotle in order to question nature. However, in Italy Platonism began to take a new lease on life after centuries of comparative neglect, during which it was known chiefly through Aristotle's critique of it. Major factors in this revival were Marsilio Ficino's translations of Plato into Latin, and the academy he founded on the model of Plato's academy. Neoplatonism also enjoyed renewed interest, partly due to the fact that Ficino's translations of Plato also included translations of Proclus and Porphyry. Florentine Platonism gave new impetus to natural religion.

A number of Renaissance writers tried to gloss over the differences between Plato and Aristotle, claiming that there were no essential differences between them. Though few thinkers professed Stoicism, Stoic ideas were well known through new editions of Cicero, Seneca and Greek commentators on Aristotle. Medieval writers had followed the church fathers in repudiating Epicurus as an atheist. Anyone who believed that the soul perished at death was apt to be described as an Epicurean. Renaissance writers adopted a more friendly view of Epicureanism, due in part to the appeal of Lucretius's poem. But it was not until Gassendi in the seventeenth century that Epicurus's theory of atoms was taken seriously.[2] Perhaps even more significant in the long run than the renewed interest in Stoicism and Epicureanism was the rediscovery of classical skepticism. We shall look at this in the next chapter.

Alongside the interest in classical thought went an interest in the occult. Strange as it may seem to the modern mind, the Renaissance was perhaps more receptive to the occult than were the Middle Ages, especially to writings purporting to contain ancient wisdom. The Hermetic literature attributed to Hermes Trismegistus[3] enjoyed great prestige.

In one sense the Reformation was an outgrowth of the Renaissance.[4] The critical study of ancient texts helped to facilitate the study of the Scriptures and the church fathers. The printing presses which produced classical literature were also used to print Bibles and theological works. But in another sense the spirit of the Reformation was more akin to that of the Middle Ages, though it was characterized by a different focus of interest. Medieval thought had viewed all life in relation to God. But the intense debates caused by the Reformers' understanding of justification by faith shifted the focus away from metaphysical analysis and speculation and onto personal experience and the role of Scripture in the believer's knowledge of God.

Luther's colleague, Philip Melanchthon, put the point graphically in his *Loci Communes* (1521), the first textbook of Reformation theology. Melanchthon complained at the way that previous theologians had philosophized too much, preferring to pile up opinions rather than set forth the meaning of Scripture. He asked rhetorically whether Paul had philosophized about such matters as the mystery of the Trinity and the mode of the Incarnation. To Melanchthon there were two issues at stake. One had to do with matters beyond human understanding; the other had to do with practical importance.

> Just as some [doctrines] are altogether incomprehensible, so there are others which Christ has willed the universal body of Christians to know with the greatest certainty. We do better to adore the mysteries of Deity than to investigate them. . . . But as for the one who is ignorant of other fundamentals, namely "The Power of Sin," "The Law," and "Grace," I do not see how I can call him a Christian. For from these Christ is known, since to know Christ is to know his benefits, and not as *they* teach, to reflect upon his natures and the mode of his incarnation.[5]

In point of fact, Melanchthon's denigration of scholastic concerns came back to haunt him. For within a generation the Lutherans were bitterly arguing among themselves and with other varieties of Reformers about the very issues that Melanchthon had judged obscure and irrelevant. There was something inevitable about this, for sooner or later, practical matters raise theoretical questions. Nevertheless, the theoretical questions raised by Reformed teaching did not displace the renewed awareness of the personal reality of God which lay at the heart not only of the Reformation, the Puritan movement and the Evangelical Revival, but also of Catholic spirituality. The theological and philosophical conflicts of this period grew out of the fundamental practical question of the relationship of human beings to God.

The Agenda of the Reformation

The first major figure of the continental Reformation was Martin Luther (1483-1546).[6] For most of his life he was a professor of theology at Wittenberg, a university which by sixteenth-century standards ranked as rather upstart and second-rate compared with the venerable universities founded in the Middle Ages. In his student days Luther had abandoned the study of law to seek peace with God by entering an Augustinian order of monks. He found it, but not in the way he had expected. The traditional ways of the church—the sacramental system, the penitential discipline and the study of medieval Scholasticism—only made God seem more remote and hostile.

The turning point came through the advice of his superior to study and teach the Scriptures. Through them, Luther encountered God not as an alien but as a friend, not as judge but as a Savior who forgave those who turned to him in simple faith. This new insight found expression in the doctrine of justification by faith which became the keystone of the Reformation. It featured prominently in the Confession of Augsburg (Art. 4, 1530), which became the classic statement of the Lutheran position:

> Men cannot be justified in God's sight by their own strength, merits or works; on the contrary, they are justified freely on account of Christ through faith, when they believe that they are received into grace and that their sins are remitted on account of Christ who by his own death

made satisfaction for our sins. This faith God imputes for righteousness in his own sight. Rom. 3 and 4.[7]

The rediscovery of justification by faith marked the beginning of the continental Reformation. For Luther it meant that everything must be looked at afresh in the light of the Word of God in Scripture. It meant not only changes in his private life and devotions; it meant the reformation of the life, thought and worship of the whole church. At first Luther cherished the fond hope that the authorities would prove sympathetic. But his appeals for reform and protests against indulgences and other abuses in his *Ninety-five Theses* of 1517 and other works only served to entrench them in their positions. His writings were condemned, and he himself was excommunicated and even placed under the imperial ban. Yet despite enormous opposition the Reformation cause went from strength to strength.

Without Luther the Reformation would have taken a different course, but it would have happened all the same. Elsewhere, persons of independent minds and working independently of Luther felt the same call from God to seek reformation in the light of the Word of God. Like Luther, they were often accused of being upstarts and innovators. But also like him, their consciences were captive to the Word of God.

In Switzerland the Reformation was led by Zwingli (1484-1531) at Zurich and Calvin (1509-64) at Geneva. Both had come from backgrounds colored by Renaissance humanism, but both became convinced that humanism alone was not enough. Like Luther, they were scholars. But again like him, they found themselves compelled by events to be practical. One of the most striking things about the teaching of all the leading Reformers was its broad unanimity. There were differences of emphasis, especially on the Lord's Supper, but they were united in taking the Word of God in Scripture as their primary datum for thinking about God. There was, however, one way in which Calvin differed from Luther and Zwingli. The writings of the latter were largely occasional, dashed off to meet the needs of the moment. Calvin also turned his hand to this important but ephemeral kind of work. But he also tried to summarize Reformed teaching in his *Institutes of the Christian Religion*. It began life as a small handbook, but over the years successive editions greatly increased its size. The final Latin edition of 1559 was still no rival in bulk to the *Summa Theologiae* of Aquinas. But its influence over succeeding generations was scarcely less; and, like the *Summa,* it continues to be translated and reprinted today.[8]

Whereas on the Continent the Reformation was first doctrinal and then political, in England it was the reverse. The occasion was Henry VIII's desire to divorce Catherine of Aragon which finally drove him to take the affair out of the hands of the pope and into his own. But the cause of the religious reformation was the same as on the Continent. So long as Henry VIII remained on the throne, the official religion of England was virtually Catholicism without the pope. But all the time such men as Cranmer, Ridley and Latimer felt the call to reform life and thought in the light of the Word of God. For each of these three their faith brought them martyrdom. It fell to their successors to establish the Protestant faith in England.

The approach of the Reformers can be studied in summary form in the Thirty-nine Articles of the Church of England (1571)[9] which may readily be compared with other sixteenth-century confessions of faith.[10] In the next century the classic statement of Protestant faith was the Westminster Confession (1646), which became the normative statement of Presbyterian teaching. Whereas the latter differed from the Anglicans on matters of church government, their approach to truth was basically the same.[11] This also applies to the Evangelicals of the eighteenth century, many of whom (including the original Methodists) were Anglicans. What they sought was not a new approach to truth, but a fresh application of the truth they already had in Scripture to contemporary life. All this may seem to be a far cry from contemporary, or for that matter from classical, philosophy. Is there any connection at all? And if so, what?

Luther and "the Devil's Whore"

Luther's last sermon at Wittenberg has gone down in history as a classic invective against reason, "the Devil's Whore."[12] But it is by no means an isolated attack on philosophy. Those who have taken the trouble to comb through the indices of Luther's collected works have experienced little difficulty in finding references to Aristotle as a "destroyer of pious doctrine," a "mere Sophist and quibbler," an "inventor of fables," "the stinking philosopher," a "billy-goat" and a "blind pagan."[13] The list could

easily be extended. This sort of thing has earned for Luther the reputation of being an irresponsible irrationalist. It has also contributed to
the widespread impression that philosophy and biblical theology have
nothing to do with each other.

But this is only half the picture. In a less heated moment Luther
reflected: "When I was a monk they used to despise the Bible. Nobody
understood the Psalter. They used to believe that the Epistle to the
Romans contained some controversies about matters of Paul's day and
was of no use for our age. Scotus, Thomas, Aristotle were the ones to
read."[14] Circumstances change, and the academic world has its fashions
like anyone else. We might substitute for the names of Scotus, Thomas
and Aristotle those of Sartre, Heidegger and Wittgenstein. But the situation Luther is describing is not all that far removed from that in the
Western universities today. Philosophy has seemed to make the Bible
irrelevant, and reason has taken over the place of revelation.

For a man of Luther's temperament, living in that age and under such
pressures, it is not surprising that he expressed himself in the way he
did. But as modern research has shown, Luther was not condemning
reason as such. He himself employed it with great effect. The real target
of his attacks was the abuse of reason, situations where philosophy had
crowded out the truth of the Christian faith. Reason had its legitimate
place in science and everyday affairs. It had its true function in grasping
and evaluating what was set before it. But it was not the sole criterion
of truth.

For Luther there were three lights which illuminated human existence.[15] There was the light of nature where reason and common sense
sufficed to solve many of the questions of everyday life. There was the
light of grace by which the revelation in Scripture gave humanity knowledge of God which was otherwise unattainable. And there was the light
of glory which belonged to the future. For there were many questions
which Scripture left unresolved. There were apparent contradictions,
like the sovereignty of God and the responsibility of man for his actions,
to which both Scripture and Christian experience testified but which
neither Scripture nor reason resolved. Luther believed that the right
approach was not to let these antinomies cancel each other out, but to
hold both in tension and leave it to the light of glory to resolve them.

In the meantime God had revealed all that people needed—or could bear—to know of themselves in Christ. "It is perilous," Luther said:

to wish to investigate and apprehend the naked divinity by human reason without Christ the mediator, as the sophists and monks have done and taught others to do. . . . There has been given to us the Word incarnate, that is placed in the manger and hung on the wood of the Cross. This Word is the Wisdom and Son of the Father, and He has declared unto us what is the will of the Father toward us. He that leaves this Son, to follow his own thoughts and speculations, is overwhelmed by the majesty of God.[16]

What Luther is talking about here is the distinction between what he called the *theology of the cross* and the *theology of glory*. The theology of glory meant to attempt to know God as he is in himself by speculation or by mystical contemplation. Luther flatly rejected such an approach. God has revealed himself in Christ and his cross. Therefore, the only way open to human beings who wish to seek God is to seek him in the way that God has lovingly dealt with human beings, by sending his Son Jesus Christ to live among them and die for them. The only true theology for Luther is therefore the theology of the cross. It was a theology that was based on the Bible and which tried to avoid philosophical speculation. Nevertheless, it did not altogether succeed in avoiding philosophical questions.

One of the questions that Luther's theology raises is the question of how good Luther's knowledge of philosophy was. Luther bitterly attacked Thomas Aquinas. But did he really know Aquinas, or was his knowledge largely secondhand? The answer seems to be that Luther regularly lumped Thomist teaching on grace with Scotist and Occamist views, and that he read Thomas through the eyes of others, especially those of Gabriel Biel.[17] Moreover, late medieval knowledge of Aquinas seems to have been based more on his commentaries than on the *Summa*. Even so, the question remains whether Luther's theology would have been different if he had possessed a firsthand knowledge of Thomas. The answer remains doubtful. In general, however, the attitude of the Reformers to Aquinas was not uniformly negative. Martin Bucer, Peter Martyr Vermigli and Jerome Zanchi remained Thomists after their conversion to the Protestant cause. Melanchthon read Thomas with profit while writing his lectures on John. Recently, attention has been drawn to the similarities between Calvin and Aquinas.[18]

Another question that Luther's theology raises for us is that of how far Luther's interpretation of Scripture was influenced—consciously or unconsciously—by philosophical ideas. As a student, Luther had been schooled in the allegorical method of interpretation, which as we saw earlier had its roots in ancient philosophy.[19] By Luther's day the method had been elaborated into a fourfold method of interpreting Scripture, which students memorized by means of a Latin verse. The literal sense tells what happened. The allegorical sense tells what the Christian must believe. The tropological or moral sense gives the moral application of the passage. The anagogical sense speaks of things to come. Luther came to reject this way of understanding the meaning of Scripture. In his *Lectures on Galatians* (1535) he noted that according to this method, Jerusalem in Galatians 4:26 "literally signified the city of that name; tropologically, a pure conscience; allegorically, the church militant; and anagogically, our heavenly fatherland or the church triumphant."[20] But he went on to dismiss this approach, complaining that such foolish fables "tore Scripture apart into many meanings" and robbed people of sure instruction. Nevertheless, when we look at the way Luther himself expounded Scripture and saw Christ in all kinds of places in the Old Testament, we cannot help wondering if in his hands the allegorical method survived under another name.[21] Despite the enormous number of studies on Luther, the full account of his relationship with philosophy has yet to be given.

Calvin and Classical Philosophy

Although philosophy recedes into the background in the writings of the Reformers, it certainly did not disappear. Scholars continued to ponder the writings of Aristotle and weigh his merits against those of Plato and other writers of antiquity.[22] Aristotelian philosophy continued to feature in the curricula of the European universities. The age of the Renaissance and the Reformation witnessed a decline in medieval Scholasticism and a renewed interest in the writers of antiquity and the early Christian era. This phenomenon left its mark on the mind of Calvin. A glance at the index of the 1559 version of the *Institutes* reveals a handful of references to Bonaventure, Scotus, Biel and Occam, but rather more to Aristotle, Plato and Cicero. Aquinas and Peter Lombard figure more prominently. But Augustine vastly outnumbers them all. Luther was wrestling with the problems inherited from the medieval church. Calvin was doing this too, but he was also seeking to state the Christian faith in the wider context of a culture which maintained a continuity with the world of classical antiquity.

Calvin's approach was less colorful but more systematic than Luther's. In essentials it was, however, the same. Calvin spoke of a *twofold knowledge* of God.[23] On the one hand, there is an awareness of God which is shared by human beings in general. This is not a matter of Scholastic proofs that can be followed by those who have the necessary philosophical background. It is a profound inner awareness of God, which Calvin described as "a sense of deity" or "a sense of divinity."[24] It may not be well defined or easy to pin down. Nevertheless, it is there. Furthermore, the glory of the created order reflects God's own glory.[25] But in spite of all this, human beings are so far gone in sin that their spiritual sense has become blunted.[26] This knowledge is at best a knowledge of the Creator, though on account of sin it does not amount to very much. On the other hand, God has revealed himself through Scripture not only as the Creator but as the Redeemer in Christ.[27] In Scripture God has spoken and revealed himself in a way which is significant for all ages. To Calvin Scripture not only provided information which could not be found elsewhere, but also was like spectacles which put things into focus.[28] The value and use of spectacles can best be appreciated by using them. So it is with Scripture. Its value emerges in the light of its capacity to convey knowledge of God and to see ourselves in his sight.

For Calvin the Bible was the Word of God, and therefore all our thinking about God must be based on the Bible. Calvin could even say that "we owe to Scripture the same reverence that we owe God; because it has proceeded from him alone, and has nothing belonging to man mixed with it."[29] On the face of it, it would look as if Calvin's theology sought to be an expression of biblical theology, restated in systematic form for the sixteenth century. Nevertheless, it raises a number of philosophical questions. For one thing, there is his claim that human beings in general have "a sense of deity." Some readers may find it puzzling that, when Calvin talked about this, he did not bring forward any biblical argument for it, whereas on other matters he habitually did. On the other hand, it could be argued that if people really have a sense of deity, scriptural proof is simply not needed. If they have got it, they have got it! In point of fact, Calvin's argument is in part an echo of a widely held view in the ancient world. As a sheer matter of fact, people believed in God. Calvin observed, "Yet there is, as the eminent pagan says, no nation so barbarous, no people so savage, that they have not a deep-seated conviction that there is a God." The "eminent pagan" that Calvin referred to was Cicero, who made this observation in his book *On the Nature of the Gods* as he discussed the views of Epicurus.[30] But for Calvin such bare knowledge of God is not enough if it does not lead to fear and reverence, and teach people to seek God and acknowledge him as the source of all good.

Modern research into Calvin's writings shows that he had an extensive knowledge of classical philosophy.[31] He could frequently criticize philosophers for falling short of true insight and for preferring intellectual argument to repentance, faith and worship. But he could also condemn as "superstitious" those "who do not venture to borrow anything from heathen authors. All truth is from God; and consequently, if wicked men have said anything that is true and just, we ought not to reject it; for it has come from God."[32] Calvin himself made extensive use of Aristotelian ideas, not least in his doctrine of election and predestination.[33] A case in point is Calvin's explanation of predestination in Ephesians 1:5, in which he drew on Aristotle's fourfold notion of causation. Calvin wrote: "Three causes of our salvation are mentioned in this clause, and a fourth is shortly afterwards added. The efficient cause is the good pleasure of the will of God; the material cause is Christ; and the final cause is the praise of his grace."[34] The remaining fourth cause is detected by Calvin in Ephesians 1:8, where he identified the "formal cause" with "the preaching of the Gospel, by which the goodness of God flows out to us. For by faith is communicated to us Christ, through whom we come to God, and through whom we enjoy the benefit of adoption."[35]

What is interesting in this passage from the standpoint of philosophy is the fact that Calvin adopts without question Aristotelian categories in order to express his understanding of biblical teaching. Moreover, he used the term "Sophists," taken from ancient Greek philosophy, to designate adversaries who have taken a different view.[36] On the subject of philosophy in general Calvin was eclectic. He could use Aristotelian ways of thinking, when they seemed appropriate. He could also endorse the insights of Epicurus, Plato, the Stoics and Cicero, when he found them to be true.[37] On other issues Calvin was in basic agreement with Thomas Aquinas.[38] However, in all this, Calvin did not seek to lay a single rational or empirical foundation for his thought in the manner of later foundationalism. Rather, he acknowledged truth where he found it, giving reasons why he believed it to be truth. On the other hand, he believed that the greatest insights of the philosophers fell far short of the truth revealed in Scripture. Even so there remains the tantalizing but important question of whether Calvin's theology was influenced, consciously or unconsciously, by philosophical ideas. Calvin believed that his teaching on divine sovereignty, election and the predestination of the elect to salvation and the wicked to damnation was lifted straight from the Bible. But could it be that his notions of sovereignty, election and causation were influenced by unconscious models, philosophical ideas and sixteenth-century ways of thinking about the physical world, so that the outcome was not purely and simply biblical theology? Despite all the work done so far on Calvin's thought, still more research needs to be done on Calvin and philosophy.

Retrospect and Prospect
In one sense the Reformation belongs to the world of the late Middle Ages. In another sense, it marks the beginnings of modern thinking in religion. The practices and beliefs that the Reformers were protesting against were practices and beliefs that the sixteenth century had inherited from the Medieval church. To that extent the agenda of the Reformation was set by the Middle Ages. Moreover, from what we have seen of Luther his approach to the interpretation of Scripture did not represent a complete break with medieval methods. It was more a modification of the allegorical methods of the past than an anticipation of historical, philological and critical methods of later times.

It is arguable that the thought-world of the German Reformation was more medieval than modern, despite the Lutheran repudiation of Scholasticism. If we were to explore Luther's sacramental teaching, as set out, for example, in his *Babylonish Captivity of the Church* (1520), and pursue the bitter sacramental controversies of the age, we would find a repudiation of medieval teaching and an attempt to return to Scripture. But the problems discussed and the ground rules of the discussion were shaped by the teaching handed down by the Middle Ages.

Calvin presents a contrasting picture. We have seen that he too inherited Aristotelian ways of thinking, and we have noted recent research which suggests that he had more in common with Thomas Aquinas than had previously been imagined. But Calvin was also conversant with the ancient philosophy that had come to the fore in the culture of the Renaissance. Though Luther was not ignorant of the classical culture discovered by the Renaissance and took a view of it similar to Calvin's,[39] the world in which Calvin moved was penetrated more deeply by the Renaissance than was Luther's. In both Luther and Calvin, familiarity with ancient philosophy is perhaps most evident in those places which are concerned with the vindication of basic religious beliefs in the face of skepticism.

Reformation theology could draw on ancient philosophy and acknowledge its insights without embracing it *in toto* or endorsing any one particular philosophy. In the sixteenth century the cultures of the Renaissance and the Reformation shared a common milieu and overlapping interests. It was an age in which science and learning still came under the aegis of the church. Such early great pioneers of science as Copernicus and Galileo were Catholic. Modern science had begun prior to the Reformation. But the Reformation also contributed indirectly to the growth of science in that Reformed teaching on creation enabled the natural order to be seen in its own right as God's creation and not simply as material for metaphysical speculation.[40]

Despite the deep and bitter tensions between Catholicism and Protestantism, these two forms of Christianity shared the common belief which viewed all life in relation to the God of the Christian revelation. But even at the height of the Reformation signs began to appear which threatened this world view. Copernicus's heliocentric account of the universe was taken by Catholics and Protestants alike as a threat to the biblical account of creation—with the earth and human beings as the pinnacle of everything. In due course, it was realized that this problem was more imagined than real, and that it had arisen through misconceptions about the implications of creation. But it was not science which in the end posed the biggest challenge to the Christian world view. It was the philosophical interpretations of the world which had their roots in the ancient pagan philosophy rediscovered in the Renaissance.

The main stream of Protestant and Catholic thought reached back through the Middle Ages and the early church to the Scriptures of the Old and New Testaments. But alongside this there emerged rival world views which drew on ancient pagan philosophy and encouraged the growing secularization of thought which culminated in the Age of Enlightenment in the eighteenth century. This thought was not entirely irreligious. But such religion as it had tended to bear increasingly less resemblance to Catholic and Protestant Christianity.

Karl Barth has drawn attention to the way this process has worked out in the two classic revolutionary documents of the eighteenth century, the Declaration of Independence of the United States of America of July 1776 and the Statement of Human and Civil Rights ratified by the French National Assembly in August 1789.[41] Both retain a veneer of religion, but in many places it is worn so thin as to be almost non-existent. The French one speaks of the Supreme Being in its preamble, and the American one makes passing acknowledgment of the Creator. But neither has much time for God. Both are concerned with humanity and with what seems to be so obviously right in itself. The rights they assert are believed to be natural. The French were concerned with freedom, property, security and the right to protect oneself from violence; the Americans with life, liberty and the pursuit of happiness. There is no question of obligations toward God, except in the most general terms. Law is the expression not of the mind of God but of the will of the people. Governments derive their authority not from the Almighty but from the consent of the governed. The happiness that the framers of the Declaration of Independence had in mind was not the beatitude described in the Sermon on the Mount, but the kind of happiness envisaged in the Greek philosophers' vision of the good life.

In so far as there is religion here at all, as Barth remarks, it is Calvinism and Catholicism respectively gone to seed. To modern secular eyes this is not a bad thing. What has happened is that humanity has become more rational. People have thrown off outmoded beliefs. They have rejected, if not God, then at least the ritual and paraphernalia of the churches. It is all part and parcel of humanity's coming of age and living a life of its own. The seeds of this secularization are to be found in the Renaissance. In the chapters that follow we shall trace the course of their growth.

10. OLD QUESTIONS AND NEW CRISES

I*n this chapter we shall look at two lines of development which affected both* Catholic and Protestant thought. They both reach back into antiquity, and bring to bear the thought of the past to current questions of the day. But they do so in different ways.

At the risk of oversimplification, it may be said that the first line of thought introduces us to theologians who were wrestling with questions which were internal to the Christian faith. Here we shall look briefly at Molina, Suárez, Bãnez and Arminius. At issue was the question of how to reconcile their understanding of the sovereignty of God with human freedom, responsibility and God's saving grace. As such, these questions were questions of Christian belief within the wider context of the Christian belief system. The issue had become acute under pressure from the Renaissance understanding of human freedom. But the questions themselves and the handling of them belong to a tradition which went back through the Middle Ages to the age of the early church.

The thinkers concerned with the second line of development—those linked in one way or another with Pyrrhonian skepticism—were raising fundamental questions about the validity of the Christian belief system itself. In the first instance, the issue was one of vindicating the rival truth claims of Protestantism and Catholicism. But soon the question was broadened into whether any system of thought could be validated. The impetus for this line of thinking came not from the Middle Ages, but from the Renaissance rediscovery of ancient, pagan skepticism.

Molina, Suárez, Bañez and Arminius

The questions of God's omnipotence and omniscience have exercised great minds down the ages. In point of fact, they form two sets of separate, but related, questions. One set of questions concerns God's power, and the other set concerns God's knowledge. Both vitally affect how we think of the sovereignty of God, and of God's relationship with the world and human beings.

It might seem obvious to say that God is omnipotent and omniscient, in order to mark God off from other beings. But if we say that God is all-powerful, what does this do to human freedom? If God is the sovereign Creator and Ruler of the universe, does it mean that he causes everything both good and evil—whether it be something small and beautiful like the fluttering of a butterfly's wings or something unthinkably horrendous like the Holocaust? Is everything preprogrammed? Do human beings have any choice in how they act? Is human freedom of action merely an illusion?

Similar problems arise when we say that God is omniscient. If God knows everything, does he know events because he causes them to happen? If so, we would seem to have a divine determinism on our hands. Or does God know things only when they happen? If so, it would seem that we have reduced God to being in the role of a spectator who is not in control of events.

These kinds of questions have had a long history. Among the highlights in the great conflicts of the past over God's sovereignty are Augustine's controversy with the Pelagians,[1] Luther's conflict with Erasmus over the bondage of the will,[2] and Calvin's battles over the question of predestination and providence.[3] The controversy flared up again in a sixteenth-century Catholic dispute between religious orders, which in time spread over into Protestant theology.

In the Catholic Church both the Dominican Order and the Society of Jesus looked to Thomas Aquinas as their "Doctor," and still regarded Aristotle as the Philosopher. Even before the Reformation, a revival of Thomism was led by the Dominican theologian Cajetan, with his commentary on the *Summa Theologiae*. Cajetan himself was the first teacher to take the *Summa* as a theological textbook instead of the *Sentences* of Peter Lombard.[4]

On the subject of predestination, Aquinas himself was solidly Augustinian. He took Augustine's opinion that "predestination is a prevision of God's benefits" as a fixed point for his conclusion: "Foreknowledge is not in the things foreknown, but in the foreknower. Neither, then, is predestination in the predestined, but in the one who predestines."[5] Whereas Cajetan and the Dominicans tended to be conservative in their handling of Aquinas, there were others, especially the Jesuits, who felt no such constraint, especially where their understanding of the nature of divine sovereignty was concerned.

Under pressure from the Renaissance desire to give greater recognition to the role of human autonomy and achievement, theologians of the Jesuit Order felt constrained to develop a modified Thomism. They sought to avoid a divine determinism in which all events were fatalistically predetermined by God, and allow for a certain human freedom and autonomy. At the same time, they did not wish to abandon God's sovereignty or rule out divine predestination.

The new approach was developed by the Spanish Jesuit Luis de Molina (1535-1600), who devoted years to the writing of his *Concordia liberi arbitrii cum gratiae donis, divina praescientia, providentia, praedestinatione et reprobatione [The Concord of the Free will with the Gifts of Grace, Divine Foreknowledge, Providence, Predestination, and Reprobation]* (1588). Molina concluded that the grace of God becomes efficacious when the human will freely cooperates with it. At the same time he believed that God's providence governs not only things in general but also particular things.

In order to reconcile his view of human freedom with God's providence and foreknowledge, Molina introduced the notion of *scientia media* ("middle knowledge").[6] The term was coined to designate God's knowledge of *futuribilia,* knowledge of things which do not yet exist but which would exist if certain conditions were realized. Such things are intermediate between mere possibilities and actual future events. The kind of knowledge that God has of such events stands in between God's "natural knowledge" (God's knowledge of all possible worlds) and his "free knowledge" (God's knowledge of the actual world).

Molina's theory held that God knows infallibly how any human will would react in every conceivable set of circumstances. This knowledge forms the basis of the divine ordering of all things. Middle knowledge has been compared with a dress rehearsal in which people rehearse various parts before they actually play them.[7] In such a rehearsal, given the appropriate circumstances, a Peter might deny Jesus, or a Judas might betray him. Because God knows what they would do of their own free will under the circumstances, he chooses to effect what he foresaw.

Molinism was further developed by the Spanish Jesuit Francisco de Suárez (1548-1617),[8] who introduced the idea of Congruism. According to Suárez, God does not (as in Thomism) cause human free acts.[9] In virtue of his *scientia media*, God brings about the salvation of the elect by giving them grace which, by his foreknowledge, he foresees that they will put to good use. Such grace is congruous with, or suited to, the circumstances of the case and obtains the free consent of the elect. In working out his position, Suárez adopted a style of writing which had more in common with the Renaissance than traditional Scholasticism. But the problem and the proposed solution were, despite their novelty, essentially a continuation of medieval Scholastic thought.

The leading adversary of Molinism was the Spanish Dominican Domingo Bañez (1528-1604), who was a strict Thomist. He accused Molina of making the power of divine grace subordinate to the human will. In his opinion, Molina's *scientia media* was a mere term which had no corresponding reality. Bañez maintained that God knows the future, including conditional future free acts, in virtue of his divine decrees, which predetermine all events. He insisted on beginning with metaphysical principles. As the first cause and Prime Mover, God must be the cause of all human acts. Bañez sought to safeguard the reality of human freedom by insisting that God moves every finite being in a manner appropriate to its nature. God moves non-free agents to act necessarily and free agents to act freely, whenever they act as free agents.

By the end of the sixteenth century the dispute between the Dominicans and the Jesuits had become acrimonious. Putting it at its mildest, the Bannezians accused the Molinists of teaching a faulty metaphysics, which subordinated God's grace to the human will, and whose novel doctrine of *scientia media* was an empty term. The Molinists conceded that the notion was hypothetical, but preferred the hypothesis to a view which appeared to eliminate free choice and make God responsible for sin. The controversy became so acute that Pope Clement VIII set up a special Congregation in Rome to examine the disputed issues. The *Congregatio de auxilliis* sat between 1598 and 1607. The outcome was a decision to permit both viewpoints, and in fact the two positions have coexisted in a kind of cold war down to the present. But in order to dampen the hostility, the Dominicans were forbidden to call the Jesuits Pelagians, and the Jesuits were ordered not to call the Dominicans Calvinists.[10]

In the meantime, the same basic dispute was being acted out in the Reformed Church. It focused on the teaching of the Dutch theologian Jacobus Arminius (1560-1609).[11] Arminius was a widely travelled scholar, having studied at Marburg, Leiden, Geneva, Basel, Padua and Rome, before receiving a call in 1587 to ministry in Amsterdam. In 1603 he was appointed to the vacant chair of theology at Leiden, where he was opposed by the strict Calvinist Franciscus Gomarus (1563-1641). Arminius's earlier studies on Paul's letter to the Romans had led to accusations of Pelagianism. To renewed charges of Pelagianism were added further charges of Socinianism. However, Arminius managed to clear himself, though for the rest of his life he was embroiled in controversy.

Arminius sought unsuccessfully to obtain revision of the two chief documents of the Dutch Calvinistic Church, the Belgic Confession and the Heidelberg Catechism. After his death, the Arminian position was set out in a brief document entitled Arminian Articles or Remonstrance (1610).[12] Against the rigorous, deterministic logic of strict Calvinism, the Remonstrance proposed a modified Calvinism. In place of double predestination, the Remonstrance made belief in Christ the decisive factor in salvation (Art. 1). Appealing to John 3:16 and 1 John 2:2, it taught universal atonement and redemption which, however, required appropriation by faith to be effective (Art. 2). Human beings do not have saving grace in themselves; they need to be born again in Christ, through the Spirit, and be renewed in order to understand, think and will what is good (Art. 3). Human beings need "prevenient or assisting, awakening, following and cooperative grace," but grace is "not irresistible" (Art. 4). Divine grace is sufficient to prevent Satan or any power from plucking the believer out of Christ's hand (Jn 10:28), but it is nevertheless possible for someone to forsake the faith and turn back to the world (Art. 5).

The initial opposition to Arminianism was led by Gomarus. The situation was further complicated by accusations against the Arminians that they were a pro-Spanish party. In 1618-1619 the Synod of Dort (Dordrecht) was convened to resolve the theological issue. Although the synod was primarily an assembly of Dutch theologians, it was attended by a number of foreign delegates from different Reformed churches. The outcome was a foregone conclusion. Two hundred Arminian clerics were deprived. The great Arminian scholar Hugo Grotius was sentenced by the States General to life imprisonment (though his wife contrived his escape in a box of books, and he settled in Paris). J. van Oldenbarneveldt was less fortunate, and was beheaded on a false charge of treason.

From a theological viewpoint the teaching of the Synod of Dort was of lasting significance. The Belgic Confession and Heidelberg Catechism were reaffirmed, and the Canons of Dort laid down under five "heads of doctrine" the position of orthodox Calvinism which has endured to the present.[13] The first head of doctrine dealt with predestination, teaching unconditional election (there are no grounds in us—not even our faith—to cause election) and double predestination (insisting that the "decree of reprobation" which determines the damnation of the wicked does not make God responsible for their sin). The second head dealt with atonement and redemption, insisting that because redemption is effectual, atonement must be limited. Christ died only for the elect. The third and fourth heads were linked together, teaching total depravity (sin extends to all human acts and affections) and irresistible grace (God is the sole author of salvation, producing "both the will to believe and the act of believing also"). The fifth head taught the doctrine of the perseverance of the saints (those who are truly regenerate will persevere, because God is faithful). The argument of the Canons of Dort was set out in much more detail than the Remonstrance, and each point was supported by appeals to Scripture.

The questions that we have been looking at in this chapter continue to be burning issues among philosophers and theologians. Process philosophers like Charles Hartshorne see notions like omnipotence and omniscience as major theological mistakes, and put forward process philosophy as a better alternative to traditional theism. But critics of process thought see process thought itself as fatally flawed, and have presented vindications of traditional ways of viewing the divine attributes.[14] A number of scholars, including contemporary evangelical philosophers, find the idea of middle knowledge to be a viable notion for today.[15] But as the twentieth-century Dominican philosopher R. Garrigou-Lagrange observed, Molina's theory of middle knowledge contains an internal contradiction. Garrigou-Lagrange endorsed the traditional objection of the Thomists that:

> the middle knowledge conceived to safeguard the freedom of the human will, virtually implies a denial of it. How can God see in a cause, which by its nature is undetermined as to whether it will act or not, that it will *de facto* act? The supercomprehensive knowledge of a cause cannot enable anyone to see in it a determination which is not there. And if, in reply, we are told that this determination is known through the circumstances in which the free will would be placed, the theory ends fatally in Determinism, which is the denial of free will. The foreseeing of the circumstances may enable one, indeed, to form conjectures, but not to have an infallible knowledge of the conditionally free acts of the future.[16]

If the Molinist "middle knowledge" theory fails to escape determinism, so does the Augustinian orthodoxy of Geneva and Rome. At least, that is the view of J. R. Lucas, who traces modern determinism back to Augustine. Lucas's own solution lies in the radical suggestion that God (in his omnipotence) has deliberately limited his omnipotence in order to permit human freedom. Similarly, he has limited his *infallible* knowledge in order to let human beings be independent of him. God still knows what is going on, but it is by means of *fallible* knowledge. "Fallible foreknowledge is enough to enable God not to live only from day to day, but to foresee the likely course of events and to take such actions, consistent with human freedom, as will work out for the best in the context of those decisions men are likely to take."[17] To the traditional theist, this view sounds all too much like a deistic restatement of Pelagianism. A more attractive proposal is that of Peter Geach who sees his view as compatible with that of Aquinas, but incompatible with the determinism later propounded by Jonathan Edwards. Like Aquinas, Geach suggests that God knows the future by *controlling* it. However, God controls it, not by predetermined divine decree, but by his actual involvement in the world. God acts like a supreme chess player who is able to produce his desired outcome, regardless of the moves made by the other players. Geach writes:

> God is the supreme Grand Master who has everything under his control. Some of the players are consciously helping his plan, others are trying to hinder it; whatever the finite players do, God's plan will be executed; though various lines of God's play will answer to various moves of the finite players. God cannot be surprised or thwarted or cheated or disappointed. God, like some grand master of chess, can carry out his plan even if he has announced it beforehand. "On that square," says the Grand Master, "I will promote my pawn to Queen and deliver checkmate to my adversary": and it is even so. No line of play that finite players may think of can force God to improvise: his knowledge of the game already embraces all the possible variant lines, theirs does not.[18]

On the theological front, the questions raised by Molina and Arminius continue to divide Christians as they have done ever since the seventeenth century.[19] The Presbyterian tradition has followed the teaching of Dort, while the Methodist tradition has embraced Arminianism. To explore the issues would take us beyond the scope of this book. But as we leave this debate, one cannot help wondering whether the protagonists on both sides have not fueled the fires of controversy by reading their systems into Scripture, and by thinking of God's action in history in terms of physical force rather than the power of love.[20]

Pyrrhonian Skepticism

In many ways Reformed theology and sixteenth-century rationalism seem to be worlds apart. They appear to be absorbed by completely different issues. And yet there are certain links which until fairly recently have been overlooked. The Reformation was not simply a reformation of practices in the church. It inaugurated an intellectual crisis which shook Christendom to its foundations, for the theology of the Reformers implied a thoroughgoing reappraisal of the questions of authority, the sources of knowledge and methods of thinking. The clarion call of *sola Scriptura*—"by Scripture alone"—was not exactly new. It had been used in the Middle Ages and by theologians and reformers ever since to assert the authority of Scripture over councils, popes and church fathers. But the Reformers' appeal to Scripture raised the question of knowledge in theology to a new pitch of intensity. The theological debates concerning authority and the source of our knowledge of God coincided with a revival of interest in ancient Greek skepticism and the publication of classic texts on the subject. Already in the 1520s in his debate with Luther on the question of free will, Erasmus protested that the issue was so obscure that he would prefer to avoid assertions and take refuge in the opinion of the skeptics wherever Scripture and the decrees of the church permitted. To this Luther replied:

> Permit us to be assertors, to be devoted to assertions and delight in them, while you stick to your Skeptics and Academics till Christ calls you too. The Holy Spirit is no Skeptic, and it is not doubts or mere opinions that he has written on our hearts, but assertions more sure and certain than life itself and all experience.[21]

For those who shared Luther's experience of the Spirit this reply was unanswerable. Yet there were Catholics who preferred to remain agnostic on controversial matters and to take refuge with Erasmus in the teaching of the church as the divinely appointed guardian of theological truth. To them Luther's appeal to the Holy Spirit was a dubious and dangerous form of subjectivism. So too was Calvin's claim that "the highest proof of Scripture derives in general from the fact that God in person speaks in it."[22] Was not this a circular argument?

My own reply to this question would be to counter it by making three observations. First, there is nothing intrinsically absurd or self-contradictory about such a claim. Secondly, in the very nature of the case the situation could not be otherwise. For in the last analysis only God can attest to God. To claim that Scripture contains a lot of true facts about history or geography does not amount to a demonstration that it is the Word of God. It only proves that (like other books) it contains reliable information about things and people. But this falls far short of the claim that it is the Word of God. Thirdly, if however men and women experience what they can only describe as God speaking to them through Scripture and if this brings light and meaning to their lives, then we may have a circle of truth, but this is very different from a subjective circular argument which confuses premises with conclusions. As Karl Barth put it in our own time:

The doctrine of Holy Scripture in the Evangelical Church is that this logical circle is the circle of self-asserting, self-attesting truth into which it is equally impossible to enter as it is to emerge from it: the circle of our freedom which as such is also the circle of our captivity.[23] The appeal to Scripture was perhaps the most fundamental issue which precipitated the intellectual crisis of the Reformation. To those who thought like Calvin, the Word of God in Scripture was basic to their thinking, beliefs and the conduct of their lives. But many who remained Catholic felt unsure about this and preferred to stay with the old ways. The situation was intensified by the renewal of interest in ancient skepticism by Renaissance thinkers in the sixteenth century and the application of skeptical ideas to the theological battles of the day.[24] There were three main sources of access to ancient skepticism: Diogenes Laertius's *Lives of Eminent Philosophers,* the writings of Cicero, and those of Sextus Empiricus. Until the middle of the sixteenth century, Sextus Empiricus had remained in obscurity. By the end of the seventeenth century he was hailed as the founder of modern philosophy, which was dated from the rediscovery of his thought.[25]

The new skepticism came to be known as Pyrrhonism on account of Sextus Empiricus's discussion of the ideas of the first Greek skeptic, Pyrrho, in his book *Outlines of Pyrrhonism.* The Pyrrhonists took over from Sextus Empiricus a skepticism about the reliability of the senses and the inability of reason to discover ultimate truth. Armed with arguments that they found in his writings, they proceeded to assail claims to knowledge made by Scholastics, Platonists, Renaissance naturalists, Aristotelian scientists and Calvinists. If the senses were unreliable, then so too was Aristotelian science. If reason and experience were unreliable, there were only two options in religion: utter skepticism or fideism. According to the former, nothing could be known with certainty, though it was permissible to conform with the conventions of both church and state for the sake of public order. According to the latter, ideas which could not be established by reason and experience could nevertheless be accepted by faith. With this in mind, some Pyrrhonists called themselves "Christian skeptics."

Pyrrhonism provided an arsenal of weapons for religious apologists. In the hands of Catholic apologists like Gentian Hervet, Jean Gontery and François Veron (who taught philosophy and theology at the Jesuit College de la Flèche while Descartes was a student there), the so-called New Pyrrhonism became a "new engine of war" forged for the destruction of Calvinism. But Protestant apologists soon found that the same weapons could be turned against Catholicism. Among them were David-Renaud Bouillier, Jean La Placette and the Anglican divine and erstwhile Catholic convert, William Chillingworth.[26] They showed that the claim of the Catholic church to be the guardian of theological truth was itself highly vulnerable in view of the fact that it rested ultimately on the Catholic Church's own word.

The leading Pyrrhonist of the sixteenth century was the French nobleman Michel de la Montaigne (1533-92). In childhood he had been taught by a German tutor who knew no French, so that he might learn Latin as his mother-tongue. In later life he had slogans and phrases from Sextus Empiricus carved into the woodwork of his study so that he could brood upon them. He adopted the motto *Que sçais-Je?*—"What do I know?" Montaigne came to believe that no certainty could be reached by rational means. He claimed that wisdom never benefited anyone and that the natives of Brazil (at that time recently discovered) were nature's noblemen who "spent their life in admirable simplicity and ignorance, without letters, without law, without king, without religion of any kind."[27] He argued that the Christian message was about the cultivation of ignorance in order to believe by faith alone.[28] In support of this extreme form of fideism Montaigne appealed to Paul's teaching on God's destruction of the wisdom of the wise (1 Cor 1:19). Whether this was the point that Paul had in mind in writing to the Corinthians is quite a different matter.[29] The text served Montaigne's purpose at the time of writing. Whether Montaigne's argument was a defense of Christianity or a cynical attack in disguise is also another matter.[30] It is a point that students of his writings have debated from his own day down to the present.

In the seventeenth century the true heir to Pyrrhonism was the skeptical professor of philosophy and history at Rotterdam, Pierre Bayle (1647-1706). Nominally he remained a member of the French Protestant church, and on his death he professed to die "as a Christian philosopher." However, his antagonism of the church cost him his professorial chair in 1693. His relentless arguments proved to be "the Arsenal of the

Enlightenment" in the eighteenth century. Bayle's most famous work was his *Historical and Critical Dictionary* (1695-97; 2nd enlarged edition 1702).[31] It was a kind of *Who's Who* of people and movements from Abimelech and King David in the Old Testament down to his own contemporary, Spinoza. He also included articles on such diverse topics as Japan and Jupiter. The latter, he observed, was "the greatest of all the gods of paganism. . . . There is no crime that he did not commit." The concise, elegantly written articles were furnished with a series of notes in which Bayle took the opportunity to ponder on the significance of points that he had raised and drew skeptical lessons from them.

In the meantime a more moderate Pyrrhonism was advocated by two leading French intellectuals, Marin Mersenne (1588-1648) and Pierre Gassendi (1592-1655). Both were clerics. Gassendi was a professor of philosophy at Aix, but became a professor of mathematics in Paris in 1645. In his earlier work he claimed that knowledge of the real nature of things was impossible. Later he changed to a more moderate skepticism. He conceded that we could not know what things are in themselves. But even the skeptics had to concede that we know something about appearances, and interpretations of appearances could be tested by seeking to verify predictions. Gassendi's own view of the universe was a form of atomism based on the Epicurean model.

Gassendi's close friend, Marin Mersenne, was also a lifelong friend of Descartes, with whom he had been a pupil at La Flèche. Theoretically, he was a Pyrrhonist, but he shrank from the application of rigorous skepticism to practice. He conceded that we cannot prove that there was nothing certain in physics, and that even some of the most common effects, like the cause of light, could not be explained. The truths of mathematics were only conditional. If there were such entities as triangles, the truth of certain theorems necessarily followed. But only on that condition. Nevertheless, scientific achievement did not depend upon some unshakable system of metaphysics. Science was not necessarily a true and absolute picture of the real world. It was a means of organizing and using knowledge. Hence science could be detached from metaphysics without loss.

It was thus that Pyrrhonian skepticism set the agenda for rationalism with its quest to show the underlying rationality of the universe. But it

also set the agenda for empiricism, which was an attempt to correct
rationalism and give better answers to the questions posed by the problem of knowledge. Deism was in part an answer to Pyrrhonism and in
part an alternative to orthodox Christianity. It purported to present a
reasonable account of religion based on rational ideas and free from
superstition. The thought of Pascal was a Christian alternative form of
orthodoxy which sought to give due place to the separate disciplines of
science and faith. But to appreciate the seventeenth-century scene we
need to look at the scientific revolution that was taking place and the
views of the philosophers who were engaged in it.

11. THE AGE OF
RATIONALISM

In *everyday language rationalism has come to mean the attempt to judge* everything in the light of reason. Bound up with this is the assumption that, when this is done, reason will have completely disposed of the supernatural, and that we will be left with nothing but nature and hard facts. But in the technical, philosophical sense of the term, rationalism denotes a more particular and certainly less atheistic approach. The rationalists of the seventeenth and eighteenth centuries differed widely among themselves in the way they worked out their different systems. But common to all was a belief in the rationality of the universe and the power of reason to grasp it. Behind all the complex machinery of nature there was a rational mind, and this could be known by the right use of reason. Given the right premises, it was possible to lay bare the underlying structure of reality, provided that one made the correct logical connections.

Rationalist philosophy came into being in response to several factors. Essentially, it was an attempt to develop a way of doing philosophy that would be adequate to the modern world of the seventeenth century. As such, it was partially a response to the Pyrrhonian skepticism, which we noted in the last chapter. Pyrrhonian skepticism raised questions not only about the validity of religious beliefs; it also raised doubts about the results and foundations of the scientific revolution that had been gathering momentum since the Renaissance. Rationalist philosophy sought to meet the challenge of skepticism by providing an account of reality, which would show the universe to be a rational whole, accessible to rational thought. It was a philosophy which embraced both the world of the scientist and that of the religious believer as it endeavored to bring the two into relationship with each other and at the same time place scientific thought and religious belief on a rational basis.

If we compare the ethos of rationalism with that of the Protestant and Catholic religious worlds of the Reformation and post-Reformation eras, the difference is striking. Protestant and Catholic theologians might be bitterly opposed to each other, but they shared a common concern for reaching a correct understanding of righteousness, faith, salvation, the church, the interpretation of the Scriptures and authority in religion. As the seventeenth century dawned, the question of free will, human responsibility and God's sovereignty was becoming increasingly acute for Catholic and Protestant theologians alike. But the minds of the rationalist philosophers were focused on different questions. It was not that they had no place for God in their schemes of thought. Rather, the burning issue for them was to discover the right way to think about the world and God under the impact of scientific knowledge and scientific ways of thinking and the challenge of Pyrrhonian skepticism.

It would be a mistake to think of rationalism as something totally new. Some of the ideas and arguments that it drew on had a long history, reaching back through the Middle Ages to the early church and ancient philosophy. But these ideas and arguments were put to new use in the interests of working out a philosophy that would embrace the needs of science. The leading rationalist thinkers were deeply interested in science, especially the field of mathematics to which Descartes and Leibniz made notable contributions. The rationalists were impressed by the role of mathematics in science and by the rational structure of the world revealed by science. The procedures of mathematics, and especially of geometry, seemed therefore to be appropriate in the realm of philosophy not least when thinking about God. The idea of God figured in all the great rationalist philosophies—but in different ways, ranging from the deistically inclined Catholicism of Descartes through the rational pantheism of Spinoza to the mechanistic Protestantism of Leibniz and Wolff. Before we turn to the rationalists themselves, we need to look briefly at the changing world of science.

Galileo and the Copernican Revolution

Today it is all too commonly assumed that everyone prior to Copernicus believed that the earth was flat, and that when Christopher Columbus made his famous voyage across the Atlantic Ocean, there was thought to be a real danger of his sailing over the edge. In point of fact, medieval scholars widely held that the earth was a sphere. They combined the biblical story of creation with Aristotle's view that the heavens were a series of perfect spheres with the earth as the center. This traditional view derived from the theories of the Alexandrian astronomer Ptolemy in the second century of the Christian era. Drawing on Plato and Aristotle, Ptolemy explained the apparent motion of the sun, moon and planets on the assumption that the earth was stationary. The medieval view was given poetical expression by Dante (1265-1321), whose *Divine Comedy* located hell inside the earth which lay in the center of the spheres.

The medieval scheme was challenged by the father of modern astronomy, the Pole Nicholas Copernicus (1473-1543).[1] Copernicus had pursued his studies at Cracow, Bologna and Rome, before settling in Prussia, where he became a canon of the church. Copernicus rejected the Ptolemaic system in favor of the startling view that the center of the planetary system was the sun. He argued that it was improbable that a large body like the sun should move around a small body like the earth. His account offered a better explanation of the variation of the seasons, the equinoxes, and the motion of the planets. Copernicus's brief outline of his theory, the *Commentariolus* (1531), won the approval of Pope Clement VII. However, his major treatise, *Concerning the Revolutions of the Celestial Orbs,* was not published until the year of his death. By then he was unable to prevent the inclusion of a preface by the Protestant theologian Osiander, warning readers that they should treat the author's conclusions as hypothetical. The authorities of the Catholic Church became increasingly alarmed, and in 1616—over seventy years after its author's death—Copernicus's work was placed on the index of prohibited books, where it remained until 1757.

Copernicus's work was taken up by the German astronomer Kepler and the Italian astronomer, physicist and mathematician Galileo. Johannes Kepler (1571-1630) became acquainted with Copernican theory at the University of Tübingen. In 1601 he became court astronomer in Prague, where he developed his account of the laws of planetary motion under the influence of Neoplatonism. Despite his recognition of the authority of Scripture, Kepler's understanding of the world was at heart pantheistic (although at the time the term had not yet been coined). He viewed the world-order as the expression of the being of God, particularly in the relations between the sun (the image of the Father) and the planets.

The outlook of Galileo Galilei (1564-1642) was more orthodox, even though eventually he was pronounced a heretic.[2] Galileo was born at Pisa. Poverty prevented him from completing his degree at the University of Pisa, but after a period of private study he was appointed professor of mathematics there in 1589. In 1592 he assumed the chair of mathematics at Padua, where he remained for eighteen years. Here he discovered the law of free-falling bodies, but his attention was drawn away from mechanics by the discovery of the telescope in Holland. Galileo made his own improved telescope and in 1610 published *The Starry Messenger*, which described the mountainous character of the moon, the existence of countless stars, and the four satellites of Jupiter. Shortly afterwards he received an appointment to the Duke of Tuscany.

Galileo's *Discourse on Bodies in Water* (1612) rejected the Aristotelian theory of elements. His *Letter on Sunspots* (1613) aroused theological opposition by its support of Copernicus and its assertion of the motion of the earth and the stability of the sun. In reply to his critics, Galileo insisted that interpretations of the Bible should not be allowed to prejudge scientific observation. Nevertheless, he saw no fundamental contradiction between science and faith. In a letter to Fr. Benedetto Castelli dated December 21, 1613, Galileo observed: "Holy Scripture and nature equally proceed from the divine Word, the first as dictated by the Holy Spirit, the second as the very faithful executor of God's commands."[3]

In 1616 the Copernican theory was condemned at Rome, and Galileo was forbidden to teach it. For several years Galileo refrained from publishing. However, in 1623 he published *The Assayer*, where he attacked current Aristotelian thinking and set out a theory of atoms which was inspired in part by reading Lucretius's poem *On the Nature of Things*. The following year, 1624, Galileo received permission in Rome to write on the Copernican and Ptolomaic systems, on the condition that he did so impartially. The result was Galileo's controversial *Dialogue Concerning the*

Two Chief World Systems which finally appeared in 1632 after prolonged difficulties in obtaining the necessary license for publication. Galileo was summoned to Rome the following year, forced to recant under threat of torture and condemned to prison on suspicion of heresy. After some months he was released and allowed to return to Florence, where he continued his scientific observations under house arrest. His work on physics, *Two New Sciences,* was smuggled to Holland, where it was printed in 1638. The official condemnation of Galileo has remained until modern times.[4]

Galileo's trial is widely seen as a landmark attempt of the church to control science. As such, Galileo's opponents are represented as reactionaries resisting the evidence of empirical science in the interests of a world view based on a combination of a literal interpretation of Scripture and an obsolete understanding of science. However, the traditional view of Galileo's trial has recently been challenged by Pietro Redondi, who has discovered documentary evidence which suggests that the charge of Copernicanism was really a cover-up for an even more serious charge of heresy concerning the Eucharist. According to Redondi, Galileo's theory of atoms posed an even greater threat to Catholic theology in that it undermined the doctrine of transubstantiation.

The doctrine was an attempt to explain how Christ could be present in the celebration of the Mass. Drawing on Aristotle's theory of substance, it held that the substance of bread and wine in the Eucharist are changed through the act of consecration into the body and blood of Christ, though the "accidents" (i.e., outward appearance and characteristics) of bread and wine remain. The doctrine had been repudiated by the Protestant Reformers, but was reaffirmed in the Council of Trent in 1551, and was central to Catholic theology and piety.[5]

Although Galileo created no new philosophical system, his influence on philosophy was marked, not least in his separation of science from philosophy, his rejection of authority as a criterion for scientific truth, his stress on empirical observation, and his skepticism concerning received opinions. Galileo's criticisms of Aristotle were more symbolic than substantial. Aristotelianism was the accepted philosophy of his opponents. Whilst rejecting some of Aristotle's scientific views, Galileo regularly boasted that he was a better Aristotelian than his opponents, and he drew heavily on Aristotelian arguments in the *Dialogue* in order to support Copernican theory.[6]

Galileo's advocacy of Copernican theory introduced one of the great paradigm shifts in the history of thought. The world lost its place as the center of the universe. Copernicus's theory not only inaugurated a change in the way people thought about the relationship of the earth to the sun; it also involved a change in the way people thought about the relationship of science to philosophy and theology. The revolutionary change came about not simply because the Copernican theory fitted the facts, whereas the Ptolemaic theory did not (for both theories maintained some inconsistency with observations). Nor was it that the Copernican view was more simple, more probable, or even more capable of predicting individual novel facts than its rival. In and of itself the Copernican view does not seem to be indebted to the Renaissance, the Reformation, or to the Counter-Reformation. It would seem that, in the end, the theory triumphed because of its greater predictive power and fruitfulness for further discovery.[7] In this respect not least, the theory pointed the way to the future.

Descartes

The first of the great rationalist philosophers was the French mathematician and scientist René Descartes (1596-1650).[8] His dates make him a contemporary of Charles I and Oliver Cromwell, of Kepler, Galileo and Harvey. Descartes received his education not at a university but at the Jesuit College of La Flèche in Anjou. But this proved no detriment, for he was given a better grounding in mathematics than he could have otherwise got at most universities at the time. Seeking leisure to pursue his studies, Descartes found it for a time by embarking upon a military career. He saw service in Holland, Germany, Bohemia and Hungary. Eventually he retired to Holland, a country which in the seventeenth century afforded refuge for a number of thinkers whose thoughts would have led them into trouble elsewhere. He lived in Holland for twenty years. But in 1649 he went to Sweden at the request of Queen Christina who (as Bertrand Russell has remarked[9]) thought that, as sovereign, she had the right to waste the time of great men. The queen could only spare the hour of five in the morning for her daily lessons, and this, coupled with the rigors of the Scandinavian winter, cut short the philosopher's life.

Descartes seems to have made a sustained effort to keep up the appearances of a gentlemanly amateur. He is said to have worked short hours and read little. He tried his hand at various sciences, including medicine. But his main contributions were made in the fields of geometry and philosophy. In the former he invented co-ordinate geometry. In the latter he pioneered rationalism, and in the minds of many people his name is indissolubly linked with Cartesian doubt and Cartesian dualism. While in Holland, Descartes wrote a major treatise, *The World,* but withheld publication after the condemnation of Galileo in 1633. However, some of its key ideas were stated in his *Principles of Philosophy* (1644), including the view for which Galileo had been condemned: the earth's rotation around the sun. Descartes was the author of a series of *Rules for the Direction of the Mind* (1628) and a treatise on *The Passions of the Soul* (1649). But he is best remembered for his *Discourse on Method* (1637) and his *Meditations on First Philosophy* (1641).

In the *Discourse* Descartes recorded his intellectual testimony. Chronologically, it began a few months after the conclusion of the Synod of Dort, but the problems that Descartes was wrestling with were vastly different from those which had occupied the best theological minds of Dutch Calvinism. Descartes recalled how in the winter of 1619/20 he entered a stove[10] and spent the day in meditation. It is tempting to say that when he entered, his philosophy was half-baked, and that when he emerged, its basic form was set. As a first principle he resolved "never to accept anything as true if I did not have evident knowledge of its truth: that is, carefully to avoid precipitate conclusions and preconceptions, and to include nothing more in my judgments than what presented itself to my mind so clearly and distinctly that I had no occasion to doubt it." His second rule was to divide each difficulty into as many parts as possible. Thirdly, he sought to proceed in an orderly manner, beginning with the simplest and advancing to the most complex. Finally, he sought to make enumerations so complete and reviews so comprehensive, that he could be sure of leaving nothing out. Descartes's ideal and method was modelled on mathematics, as he went on to explain:

Those long chains composed of very simple and easy reasonings,

which geometers customarily use to arrive at their most difficult dem-
onstrations, had given me occasion to suppose that all things which
can fall under human knowledge are interconnected in the same way.
And I thought that, provided we refrain from accepting anything as
true which is not, and always keep to the order required for deducing
one thing from another, there can be nothing too remote to be
reached in the end or too well hidden to be discovered.[11]

To Descartes the process of reconstructing his philosophy was like rebuilding a house.[12] It was not enough to tear down the old building, or
even to get together an architect and the materials. One needed somewhere to live, while the house was being built. Descartes solved the
problem of what to do while rebuilding his philosophical house by deciding to accept the laws and customs of his country and the religion he
had been brought up in. He would be decisive in action even under
pressure of doubt until a clearer way presented itself. He would seek to
master himself rather than his fortune and change his desires rather
than the order of the world. Finally, he would seek the occupation best
suited to him. In other words, for nine years Descartes solved the problem practically by carrying on as before. It was not until he went to
Holland in 1629 that he found the peace and tranquility that enabled
him to devote himself "solely to the search for truth."

There were three major steps in the reconstruction of Descartes's
philosophical edifice. The first step was to discover a *first principle* for his
philosophy. He began with the resolve to "reject as if absolutely false
everything in which I could imagine the least doubt, in order to see if
I was left believing anything that was entirely indubitable." After all,
geometricians sometimes committed logical fallacies. In dreams people
experience things as if they were real. Could everything be just an illusion? At this point Descartes was struck by a thought.

But immediately I noticed that while I am trying thus to think everything false, it was necessary that I, who was thinking this, was something. And observing that this truth *"I am thinking, therefore I exist"* was
so firm and sure that all the most extravagant suppositions of the
sceptics were incapable of shaking it, I decided that I could accept it
without scruple as the first principle of the philosophy I was seeking.[13]

Thus the famous *cogito, ergo sum* ("I am thinking, therefore I am") became the first principle of Cartesian philosophy. Descartes went on to observe that there was nothing in that proposition to assure him that he was speaking the truth except that he saw "very clearly that in order to think it is necessary to exist." This led him to "take it as a general rule that the things we conceive very clearly and very distinctly are all true." The only problem here lay in recognizing which things were conceived very clearly. Again there was the problem of doubt. Descartes needed further reason for the veracity of human perception. He found it by taking the second major step, which was to establish rationally the existence of God as the perfect being.

In taking this step, Descartes recognized the conditional character of geometry. However, he insisted that the existence of God as the perfect being was not like a deduction from a hypothetical premise.

> For example, I saw clearly that the three angles of any given triangle must equal two right angles; yet for all that, I saw nothing which assured me that there existed any triangle in the world. Whereas when I looked again at the idea I had of a perfect being, I found that this included existence in the same way as—or even more evidently than—the idea of a triangle includes the equality of its three angles to two right angles, or the idea of a sphere includes the equidistance of all the points on the surface from the centre. Thus I concluded that it is at least as certain as any geometrical proof that God, who is this perfect being, is or exists.[14]

Descartes's third major step was to recognize that the rule that "everything we conceive very clearly and very distinctly is true is assured only for the reasons that God is or exists, that he is a perfect being, and that everything in us comes from him."[15]

Descartes could describe God as a *substance*. By this he meant a reality which subsists by itself. Strictly speaking, God was the only substance that fitted this description.[16] But created substances also exist in view of the "concurrence of God." Each substance has a principal attribute. That of the mind is thought, while that of the body is extension in space.[17] In the last analysis there were for Descartes two kinds of reality: the mental and the material. The mental included the mind or soul and its thoughts (including God's mind and thoughts). The material was the sphere of physical existence. On account of these two types of reality Descartes's thought is often described as dualistic. Descartes himself was well aware of the enormous problems raised by dualism. How is the mental related to the physical? How is the mind related to the body?

Descartes responded to these problems by insisting that there are in us "certain primitive notions" like existence, number, duration, which apply to everything we can conceive. With regard to the body we have the notion of extension and the consequent notions of shape and movement. With regard to the soul we have the notion of consciousness. "Finally, as regards the soul and body together, we have merely the notion of their union; and on this there depend our notions of the soul's power to move the body, and of the body's power to act on the soul and cause sensations and emotions."[18] Descartes put forward the further suggestion that the soul was located in the pineal gland in the brain. The soul thus received the perceptions of the senses via the brain. "And conversely, the mechanism of our body is so constructed that simply by this gland's being moved in any way by the soul or by any other cause, it drives the surrounding spirits towards the pore of the brain, which direct them through the nerves to the muscles; and in this way the gland makes the spirits move the limbs."[19] Although this part of Descartes's view is no longer taken seriously, Descartes's approach to the body/mind question continues to find repercussions today. Gilbert Ryle dismissed the Cartesian understanding of the soul and derided it as "a ghost in a machine." To Ryle the notion of the soul or mind was as redundant as that of presuming that a machine needs some kind of a spirit to keep it in operation. However, other thinkers have not been so reductionistic and have refused to reduce the human mind to the operations of the physical brain.[20]

Descartes is widely regarded as the founder of modern philosophy. At the same time it is recognized that he owes much to the past, and his thought forms a bridge between the pre-scientific world and the modern age. Descartes's body-soul dualism sounds like an echo of the body-soul dualism of Plato and early Christian thinking. His main argument for the existence of God was a restatement of Anselm's ontological argument. Even the celebrated *cogito ergo sum* was not new. It had been put forward in different forms by Augustine. Perhaps Descartes had come across it during his days at La Flèche, and it had lodged unconsciously in his mind until he lighted on it as the first principle of his philosophy. Years later his attention was drawn to Augustine's use of the idea, whereupon Descartes checked the reference in a library but insisted that his use of it was different from Augustine's. Whereas Augustine used it in developing his doctrine of the Trinity, Descartes protested that his own use was "to establish that this conscious I is an immaterial substance with no corporeal element."[21]

From Descartes's own day the *cogito ergo sum* has been argued over by philosophers. It figured in the series of *Objections and Replies* occasioned by Descartes's *Meditations*. For example, the British philosopher Thomas Hobbes objected that one might just as well say "I am walking, therefore I exist."[22] In modern times Hobbes's objection has been echoed by Bertrand Russell, who pointed out that if Descartes had really wanted to start with *doubt*, his initial premise should have been "There are doubts." Descartes was not entitled to infer from this the existence of a personal self, an "I" with all the qualities that we take for granted in everyday life.[23] To Hobbes and Russell the latter were smuggled into the argument unnoticed. Other philosophers have objected that the argument was a disguised tautology, merely repeating the same premise in different words. As A. J. Ayer observed, "If I start with the fact that I am doubting, I can validly draw the conclusion that I think and that I exist. That is to say, if there is such a person as myself, then there is such a person as myself, and if I think, I think."[24]

There remains, however, the possibility that the *cogito ergo sum* is neither a dubious syllogism nor a disguised tautology but the expression of an unshakable basic conviction, possessed by Descartes and human beings in general. For Descartes it was a given fact of existence that we have the incorrigible intuition of ourselves as thinking persons. It may also be that his use of the ontological argument was not the deduction of the existence of God from the hypothetical notion of God but the expression of a basic perception of a God whose existence he could not doubt. If this is so, Descartes's perception of God is much closer to Calvin's than is often imagined. Admittedly, Descartes's God is a "philosophical God." Yet even here we must ask with Alexandre Koyré, "What else can a philosopher's God possibly be?" In a philosophical interpretation of reality—as distinct from preaching or the believer's daily walk with

God—the concept of God must be treated philosophically. Even so, Descartes's God is not a pale lifeless abstraction. As Koyré observes, "He is even the Christian God, as nobody can doubt who has read the texts Descartes left us."[25]

In one of his more whimsical moments Archbishop William Temple was once tempted to ask himself which was the most disastrous moment in European history. The answer he came up with was the day Descartes shut himself up in his stove.[26] In saying this, Temple was not so much thinking about Descartes's view of God but about the trend he set in European thinking. It epitomized a shift of concern. It symbolized a retreat into the individual self-consciousness as the one sure starting point of philosophy. As a matter of fact, Temple went on to lump Luther together with Descartes as the religious counterpart to the latter's philosophical individualism. But neither judgment was historically accurate. When Luther was confronted by the ecclesiastical authorities, he took his stand, not on his individual, private conscience, but upon the Word of God to which his conscience was captive. Luther's authority was outside himself.

Likewise Descartes was not the founder of rugged philosophical individualism. In a sense he was not even the founder of Cartesian doubt. When Descartes resolved to doubt everything that he could legitimately doubt, he was not the original pioneer of elevating doubt into a methodological principle. Rather, he was accepting the premises of the Pyrrhonian skeptics who had already done this and was answering them with their own weapon. He was, in fact, arguing that there were a number of things that could not be doubted. Among them was the fact of the existence of the doubter. Another indubitable fact was the existence of a perfect and veracious God.

To some of Descartes's contemporaries this reply looked like dogmatism. To others, who felt uncomfortable with the idea of such basic perceptions, it looked like a form of skepticism dressed up as a positive answer. On this view, Descartes could be described as a skeptic in spite of himself.[27] What is clear is that the questions that Descartes touched on were questions which set the agenda not only for continental rationalism and British empiricism but for Western philosophy in general down to the present day.

Spinoza

Baruch (or Benedictus de, to use the Latinized form of his name which he later assumed) Spinoza (1632-77)[28] was born in Amsterdam of Jewish parents. Some years before his birth the Netherlands had proclaimed freedom of thought and in so doing had become a haven for all those who sought refuge from persecution or who had found that they could not get their books printed anywhere else. Although brought up as a Jew, Spinoza's free thought resulted in his expulsion from the synagogue in 1656. By expelling the young Spinoza for his unorthodox ideas, the Jewish authorities were in fact absolving themselves from responsibility for views that were no less repugnant to the Christian civil authorities. Spinoza spent much of his life in seclusion, apart from a small circle of friends, his letter writing and occasional contact with some of the great thinkers of his day. He earned his living by grinding and polishing lenses. His premature death from consumption was aggravated by the dust from the grinding. In 1673 he was offered a chair of philosophy at Heidelberg. However, he declined, fearing that teaching would interfere with his research and that his unorthodox views might result in his freedom being curtailed.[29]

Spinoza admired Descartes, but thought that his views needed correction. In 1663 he published an exposition of the French philosopher under the title *Parts I and II of Descartes's Principles of Philosophy, Demonstrated in the Geometric Manner*. It was the only book published during his lifetime that bore his name on the title page. It was followed in 1670 by a treatise on politics and religion, *Tractatus Theologico-Politicus*, which among other things pioneered biblical criticism.[30] But his chief work was published posthumously in a collection of his writings—*Ethics, Demonstrated in Geometrical Order and Divided into Five Parts*. This too was written in Latin and was set out in quasi-geometrical form with definitions, axioms, propositions and proofs (to which Q.E.D. was duly appended). It began with a lengthy discussion of the nature and existence of God, and concluded with the claim that the knowledge and love of God is the greatest human good.

Spinoza has been variously described as a hideous atheist and as God-intoxicated.[31] In fact, he was (to use a term later coined by the British Deist John Toland) a pantheist. But Spinoza was not the kind of pantheist of the romantic, poetical imagination. His was a rational pantheism, soberly worked out from premises akin to those of Descartes. Like the latter, he began with clear and distinct ideas, notions which he thought to be self-evidently true. Their truth could be seen merely by stating them properly. Unlike Descartes, he did not treat the *cogito ergo sum* as a basic intuition which could serve as a first principle of philosophy. He began rather with a notion of substance, taken over from Descartes, which he defined as "what is in itself and is conceived through itself, i.e., that whose concept does not require the concept of another thing, from which it must be formed."[32] He treated this idea as self-evidently true. "If someone were to say that he had a clear and distinct, i.e., true, idea of a substance, and nevertheless doubted whether such a substance existed, that would indeed be the same as if he were to say that he had a true idea, and nevertheless doubted whether it was false (as is evident to anyone who is sufficiently attentive)."[33] From here Spinoza went on to argue that there was only one substance,[34] and that "whatever is, is in God, and nothing can be or be conceived without God."[35]

Taken at face value, this statement like numerous others in Spinoza's writings could be understood in a Christian theistic sense. But one does not have to probe very deeply in order to discover that he did not think of God as a personal being who exists over and above the world and on whom the world depends for its existence. Spinoza thought of God as *deus sive natura*—"God or nature." Since God was infinite, no other substance could exist outside God. "God is the immanent, not the transitive, cause of things."[36] Whether we say God or nature, we are really talking about the same thing. To speak of God draws attention to the ground or cause of reality; to speak of nature points to the outward effect of that cause.

Spinoza's teaching was worked out in considerable detail. In the course of his discussion he argued for determinism[37] and denied that God could love human beings in a personal way.[38] Religion was the *intellectual love of God*. This too was given a pantheistic interpretation. "The Mind's intellectual Love of God is the very Love of God by which God loves himself, not insofar as he is infinite, but insofar as he can be explained by the human Mind's essence, considered under the species of eternity, i.e., the Mind's intellectual Love of God is part of the infinite Love by which God loves himself."[39]

Spinoza's philosophy has been described as both skeptical and anti-skeptical.[40] It was anti-skeptical in the sense that it purported to offer a rational metaphysics which could be seen to be true by anyone with the necessary rational capacities and patience to follow the deductive reasoning. It gave a place to God but at the price of questioning the validity of religion as practiced in both Judaism and Christianity. The locus of truth was not religion itself but reason. However, the other side of this anti-skepticism was profound skepticism about the truth and importance of biblical religion. Spinoza recognized the place of the latter in history, but rejected its foundational importance. "The sphere of reason is . . . truth and wisdom; the sphere of theology is piety and obedience."[41]

This stance enabled Spinoza to adopt a critical approach to prophecy, the authorship of Scripture and its authority in the *Tractatus Theologico-Politicus*. He rejected the traditional Christian appeal to fulfilled prophecy and miracles as objective divine attestation of revelation.[42] To Spinoza "the universal laws of science" were the decrees of God which followed from "the necessity and perfection of the Divine nature." Hence, any event which contradicted the laws of science was *ipso facto* a contradiction of the divine decree and God's own perfection. To claim an event as a miracle was tantamount to claiming that God had acted against his own nature. Thus, miracles were by definition impossible. Spinoza did not go so far as to deny the historicity of all biblical miracles. Rather, he insisted that when an alleged miracle occurred, there must be a rational and natural explanation. In speaking of natural laws as divine decrees, Spinoza was echoing the language of the Calvinistic divines at the Synod of Dort. His deterministic view of reality also had something in common with high Calvinism. But although he spoke of God, Spinoza had something very different in mind from the Calvinistic theologians.

Some scholars have seen in Spinoza's philosophy links with the Jewish Kabbalah of the Middle Ages, but others stress the profound difference in temper and outlook between Spinoza and earlier Jewish philosophy.[43] Whereas earlier Jewish philosophers sought to interpret the Jewish tradition by means of different philosophical schemes, Spinoza sought to judge biblical religion in the light of his rational metaphysics. Reality was a rational system which was open to a rational explanation. In so doing, it proferred an alternative view of God. God was no longer the personal, transcendent Creator of the universe. God was the name given to the immanent rationality which was the ground of all things and which manifested itself in all things. However, Spinoza's system raised the perennial problems that all pantheistic schemes raise. If all reality is the manifestation of God, then evil must also be a manifestation of God. This applies to both physical evils like natural disasters and moral evils running the whole range of evil from petty theft to genocide. Good and evil are alike expressions of the divine nature. The idea of free will is likewise illusory, for in a pantheistic system all human actions are ultimately divine actions. No room is left for human autonomy of any kind. Nor is any place left for human autonomy in the process of acquiring knowledge, for the human mind is part of the Divine Mind which thinks its thoughts through human minds. This conclusion would seem to be required in pantheism, despite the apparent absurdity of different human minds thinking contradictory thoughts on the same subject and attributing the whole process to the Divine Mind thinking out its ideas through them.

Spinoza's views found little following in his own day. But in the Age of Enlightenment he attracted a growing number of supporters. Toward the end of his life Lessing professed to be a Spinozist. In the Age of Romanticism Schleiermacher spoke of "the holy, rejected Spinoza" who was pervaded by "the high World-Spirit." Later still D. F. Strauss remarked that if the key themes of the first part of Schleiermacher's *Christian Faith* were translated into Latin, they would turn out to be formulations of Spinoza.[44] In due course Spinoza found admirers among the English Romantic poets. But no Spinozist school ever emerged. In a sense Spinoza marked a parting of the ways. To some his philosophy opened up the possibility of an atheistic rationalism. To others it was a philosophy which required modification in the direction of Idealism. To Hegel Spinozism was an important stepping stone toward his own form of Absolute Idealism.[45] But to others it marked a dead end. It failed to do justice to the living reality of religion, and the attempt to give an account of reality by means of deductions from allegedly self-evident definitions was nothing more than a case of building abstraction upon abstraction.

Leibniz

Descartes was a Roman Catholic, and Spinoza a free-thinking Jew. An eminent Protestant thinker who was indebted to both but critical of both was Gottfried Wilhelm Leibniz (1646-1716).[46] Leibniz was a universal genius. He combined the career of mathematician, logician and philosopher with that of international diplomat. He invented a calculating machine (which earned him membership of the Royal Society in England). He was a member of the Paris Academy, and the Prussian Academy was largely his creation. He corresponded with and met many of the most eminent thinkers in Europe. His schemes included a plan for reuniting the Christian churches. His thought encompassed a theory designed to give an account of the presence of Christ in the Lord's Supper. He even composed a *Discourse on the Natural Theology of the Chinese.* From the standpoint of theology, however, his most important works were his *Theodicy: Essays on the Goodness of God, the Freedom of Man, and the Origin of Evil* (1710) and his *Monadology* (written in 1714 and published in 1721). The latter was a brief outline of his views on the nature of reality. Leibniz discovered the differential and integral calculus. However, his final years were clouded with controversy over whether he or Sir Isaac Newton should be credited with this achievement. He died in obscurity.

It has been said that the role played in Descartes's philosophy by the veracity of God is played in Leibniz's thought by the intelligibility of the universe.[47] For Spinoza God was the name for the underlying essence of things. But with Leibniz we come back to a theism which combines conviction about the essential rationality of existence with belief in the transcendence of God. Indeed, it is the God who is worshiped in the Christian religion who is the Creator of the universe and thus the ground of rationality. Science is grounded ultimately in theology, for scientific explanation is possible only because of the order imposed on the universe by God. Leibniz observed that human reasoning was founded on "two great principles."

The first is the principle of *contradiction,* by virtue of which we consider as false what implies a contradiction and as true what is the opposite of the contradictory or false.

The second is the principle of *sufficient reason,* by virtue of which we hold that no fact can be true or existing and no statement truthful without a sufficient reason for its being so and not different; albeit these reasons most frequently must remain unknown to us.[48] Leibniz went on to draw a further distinction between two kinds of truth. It was a distinction that was to play an important role in subsequent philosophy.

> There are also two kinds of *truths:* those of *reason,* which are necessary and of which the opposite is impossible, and those of *fact,* which are contingent and of which the opposite is possible. When a truth is necessary, the reasons for it can be found through analysis, that is, by resolving it into simpler ideas and truths until one comes to primitives.[49]

Leibniz maintained that mathematics exemplified the analytical method. However, a sufficient reason had to be found also for *contingent truths* or *truths of fact.* Ultimately the sufficient reason must lie outside the succession or series of contingent particulars.

> Consequently, the ultimate reason for all things must subsist in a necessary substance, in which all particular changes may exist only virtually as in its source: this substance is what we call *God.*[50]

In his numerous writings restatements of the ontological, teleological, and cosmological arguments may be found.[51] His arguments converge in a view of God as the necessary being who is the sufficient reason for the existence of all contingent beings. Leibniz's later thought made use of the idea of the *monad* which he defines as "a simple substance, which enters into the composites."[52] God himself was the original monad or "simple substance, of which all the created or derivative monads are products, born, so to speak, every moment by continual fulgurations from the divinity, and limited by the capacities of creatures, to which limitation is essential."[53] Leibniz envisaged a perfect harmony between the causes in nature and God's ultimate purposes. God was both "the architect of the machine of the universe" and "the monarch of the divine city of the spirits."[54] The processes of nature serve the purposes of grace. "Thus sin must entail punishment according to the order of nature and as the very result of the mechanical structure of the universe; and, analogously, good actions will attract their rewards through machine-like corporeal processes. Of course, these results cannot be and ought not always to be obtained as an immediate consequence."[55]

This vision of the world as a rationally ordered machine which brings about moral results was anticipated many years earlier in Leibniz's *Theodicy*. Here Leibniz argued that God had weighed up all possible systems for the world and had chosen the best.[56] Leibniz did not wish to deny the existence of evil. He certainly did not wish to blame God for all the evil in the world. Physical ills were the result of the physical characteristics of the world we live in. Moral evil is the result of the misuse of human freedom. God is able to bring greater good out of evil. However, before God decreed anything he considered all the possible consequences. He envisaged the Fall and also redemption through Christ. "God grants his sanction to this sequence only after having entered into all its detail, and thus pronounces nothing final as to those who shall be saved or damned without having pondered upon everything and compared it with other possible sequences. Thus God's pronouncement concerns the whole sequence at the same time; he simply decrees its existence."[57]

In this way Leibniz endeavored to preserve an orthodox Christian view of God and the world in the tradition of Augustine. He sought to maintain human freedom by saying that human freedom was genuine and that God had decreed it. At the same time he preserved the Reformed/Augustinian emphasis on God's sovereignty by saying that God anticipated everything and decreed what he anticipated. It was as if God possessed a supercomputer which printed out an unlimited series of programs, and God chose the best. Another way of looking at it is to see it like alternative scripts for a play in which the characters exercise their freedom, but when the author finally decides on which plot to keep, the actions of the characters are fixed forever. Leibniz's view was certainly an alternative to that of Spinoza. It combined rationalism with Christian orthodoxy. But in the end it was scarcely less deterministic. It leaves us admiring the brilliance of Leibniz and at the same time wondering at the adequacy of the rationalism of his day to accomplish what he wanted it to do.

In the next century the idea of the world as the best of all possible worlds was held up for ridicule by Voltaire in his novel *Candide*. The hair-raising adventures of *Candide* and his companions at the hands of unscrupulous enemies (both professed Christians and infidels) were designed to show the vacuity of the notion. Leibniz's ideas received more sympathetic treatment from Christian Wolff (1679-1754),[58] the rationalist philosopher of the German Enlightenment. Wolff had corresponded with Leibniz during the last twelve years of the latter's life. Although he rejected Leibniz's doctrine of monads, he drew heavily on both Leibniz and Descartes. Wolff sought to present a synthesis of human knowledge. The entire enterprise was to be organized in a formal plan, controlled by the deductive methods of rationalism. In his heyday Wolff enjoyed enormous prestige in Germany. There were also Wolffians in France and elsewhere. But even before his death his influence was beginning to be undermined by those who favored the ideas of the French Enlightenment and Newtonian natural philosophy. It fell to Kant to administer the *coup de grace* to German rationalism in the Wolffian style. But before we turn to Kant we need to consider the competing philosophies of a number of thinkers. As we shall see, some of them were passionate believers, while others were bitterly hostile to traditional Christianity.

Pascal

It may seem odd to include Pascal in a chapter on rationalism, but there is at least one good reason for doing so. Not only was Pascal a contemporary of the great rationalists, he also shared their scientific interests. Moreover, his approach to reason and philosophy serves to bring out the differences between rationalism and the kind of Augustinian thinking that Pascal presented.

Blaise Pascal (1623-62)[59] was a junior contemporary of Descartes and a slightly senior contemporary of Spinoza. Before he was twenty he had invented a calculating machine to assist his father in his post as Commissioner of Taxes in Upper Normandy. He thus pioneered the modern calculator. Pascal also made major contributions to geometry, probability, number theory and the philosophy of mathematics. His physical experiments demonstrated the existence of the vacuum and successfully challenged the idea that nature always abhors a vacuum. Pascal's scientific work helped to banish the occult from science and to establish the mechanistic view of the physical world. At the same time Pascal's growing commitment to the Christian faith led him to develop an alternative approach to Pyrrhonian skepticism and to philosophical rationalism.

In his younger days Pascal had led a worldly life. But in 1646 he came into contact with Jansenism, a Catholic movement with a strong Augustinian emphasis on humankind's need of divine grace. Jansenism was bitterly opposed by the Jesuits, and was condemned by the Sorbonne in 1649 and by Pope Innocent X in 1653. In 1654 Pascal had a conversion experience which he described on a piece of parchment that was sown into his clothing as a perpetual reminder. It contained the following words:

Fire

"God of Abraham, God of Isaac, God of Jacob," not of philosophers and scholars.
Certainty, certainty, heartfelt, joy, peace.
God of Jesus Christ.
God of Jesus Christ.
My God and your God.
"Thy God shall be my God."
The world forgotten, and everything except God.
He can only be found by the ways taught in the Gospels . . . .

Let me not be cut off from him for ever! "And this is life eternal, that they may know thee, the only true God, and Jesus Christ whom thou hast sent." Jesus Christ. Jesus Christ. . . .[60]

Pascal was increasingly drawn into the Port-Royal circle in Paris, which was the center of French Jansenism. His sister had earlier become a nun there. Pascal's *Provincial Letters* (1656-57) were a brilliant defense of Jansenism and an attack on current Jesuit theories about grace and moral theology. In 1656 Pascal began collecting material for what he intended to be an *Apology for the Christian Religion,* putting down his thoughts on scraps of paper. His premature death at the age of thirty-nine prevented the work from becoming anything more than a series of disconnected thoughts. Nevertheless, these thoughts—or *Pensées* (as they are termed in French)—remain one of the great classics of Christian meditation and apologetics.

Pascal's *Pensées* present an alternative to Pyrrhonian skepticism which doubts everything and philosophical rationalism which tends to relegate God to a term of philosophical explanation. At the same time they give a profound analysis of the human condition. Pascal looked deep into the human heart and challenged his readers to consider their real situation. He saw the boredom and anxiety pervading human life. "Man finds nothing so intolerable as to be in a state of complete rest, without passions, without occupation, without diversion, without effort. Then he faces his nullity, loneliness, inadequacy, dependence, helplessness, emptiness. And at once there wells up from the depths of his soul boredom, gloom, depression, chagrin, resentment, despair."[61] Sport, entertainment, fashion, art and society are so often pursued not because of the pleasure they bring, but to take our minds off ourselves.[62]

Pascal had little use for the hypothetical God of philosophical argument. Among the sayings attributed to Pascal, one went so far as to say: "I cannot forgive Descartes: in his whole philosophy he would like to do without God; but he could not help allowing him a flick of the fingers to set the world in motion; after that he had no more use for God."[63] To Pascal the standard proofs of the existence of God were at best questionable and at worst irrelevant.

> The metaphysical proofs for the existence of God are so remote from human reasoning and so involved that they make little impact, and, even if they did help some people, it would only be for the moment during which they watched the demonstration, because an hour later they would be afraid they had made a mistake.
>
> *What they gained by curiosity they lost through pride* [Augustine, *Sermons*, 141].
>
> That is the result of knowing God without Christ, in other words communicating without a mediator with a God known without a mediator.
>
> Whereas those who have known God through a mediator know their own wretchedness.[64]

If rationalist philosophy could not answer the deepest human needs, neither could Pyrrhonian skepticism. On the one hand, consistent skepticism was impossible. On the other hand, reason needed a foundation outside itself. It was impossible to prove beyond doubt that one was awake, for when one dreams, one dreams that one is awake. "There is no certainty, apart from faith, as to whether man was created by a good God, an evil demon, or just by chance, and so it is a matter of doubt, depending on our origin, whether these innate principles are true, false or uncertain."[65] The arguments of the rationalists were vulnerable to the skeptics, but consistent skepticism is impossible to carry through and it is also impossible to live by.

What then is man to do in this state of affairs? Is he to doubt everything, to doubt whether he is awake, whether he is being pinched or burned? Is he to doubt whether he is doubting, to doubt whether he exists?

No one can go that far, and I maintain that a perfectly genuine skeptic has never existed. Nature backs up helpless reason and stops it going so wildly astray.[66]

Pascal's answer to this dilemma was to insist that one should live by faith, and make faith the basis not only of the spiritual life but of science and philosophy. Knowledge for Pascal is not simply a matter of drawing rational inferences.

The heart has its reasons of which reason knows nothing: we know this in countless ways.

I say that it is natural for the heart to love the universal being or itself, according to its allegiance, and it hardens itself against either as it chooses. You have rejected one and kept the other. Is it reason that makes you love yourself?

It is the heart which perceives God and not the reason. That is what faith is: God perceived by the heart, not by the reason.[67]

In taking up this position Pascal realized that he was not immune from the questioning of the Pyrrhonian skeptics. But skepticism was itself vulnerable for reasons already noted. The alternative, therefore, was to face the challenge of Pascal's famous "Wager."[68] In it Pascal confronted his readers with the fact that they had to take a risk. They were in fact risking their lives and the possibility of eternal salvation. On the other hand, there was no evading the risk and the choice. For life is relentlessly moving on, and the decision not to make a choice is itself an act of making a choice.

In addition to the philosophical questions addressed by the *Pensées*,

Pascal devoted a good deal of his work to theological questions. He found a place for discussion of prophecy and miracles in Scripture. His argument followed traditional apologetic lines in appealing to fulfilled prophecy and miracles as grounds for believing in Christ. However, he recognized that they were not proofs which would convince the unbeliever of the truth of the Christian faith. Prophecy and miracles did not provide hard, factual foundation for establishing the truth of the Christian belief-system. Rather, they function *within* the belief-system to indicate the identity of Jesus as Messiah.[69]

Sometimes Pascal's teaching is classified as a kind of voluntarism, the implication being that he sets greater store by the will than by the intellect. It has even been represented as a kind of self-inflicted brainwashing, in which the will to believe is allowed to banish all intellectual considerations. But this is a caricature. It neglects to mention that the idea of the wager was addressed to the sporting men of the day, reminding them of a game played at infinitely greater odds. It does not take into account the attention and energy that Pascal devoted to analyzing the scope and limitations of reason, showing that skepticism could not be lived by and that rationalism was not an adequate answer. At the same time he realized, "What a long way it is between knowing God and loving him!"[70] The challenge presented by Pascal was a challenge to question the fashionable philosophies of his day in the name of the God of the Bible. His alternative to Pyrrhonian skepticism and dogmatic rationalism was not only a tenable philosophy on the intellectual level; it also spoke to the human condition at its deepest psychological level.

12. RATIONAL RELIGION AND THE ERA OF DEISM

P*yrrhonian skepticism and philosophical rationalism were like stones dropped* into a pond which sent out ever-widening ripples. The ripple-effect continued throughout the seventeenth and eighteenth centuries. It produced two kinds of response. On the one hand, there was the response which carried further the effects of skepticism. On the other hand, there was the response which attempted to refine in different ways the rationalists' attempt to give a coherent account of the real nature of things. In the following chapters we shall see both tendencies at work. At the same time the lines between skepticism and whatever was advocated in opposition to it became more and more entangled. For one person's dogmatism was another's skepticism. Different thinkers chose to be skeptical about different things. The practice of skepticism went hand-in-hand with a quest for certainty, even if it was only a certainty that one's opponents were wrong. Nowhere was this more true than in the realm of religion.

The seventeenth and eighteenth centuries witnessed many bitter theological battles. Sometimes they were acrimonious, as in the Arminian controversy within Calvinism and the conflicts surrounding Puritanism in Britain. Sometimes they were bloody in the most literal sense of the term. On the continent of Europe Protestants fought Catholics in the Thirty Years' War (1618-48). In Britain Protestants fought Protestants in the Civil War which led to the beheading of Charles I (1649) and the establishment of the short-lived Commonwealth under Oliver Cromwell. In all the theological and political turmoil it is not surprising that fanatics and zealots arose on every side and that others sought refuge in the avoidance of extremes. The politics of the seventeenth and eighteenth centuries gave added impetus to the drive toward skepticism and to the quest for certainty in the realms of philosophy and religion.

Hobbes

A combination of skepticism and rationalism in religion found expression in the thought of the English thinker Thomas Hobbes (1588-1679).[1] Hobbes was born in the Elizabethan Age, apparently prematurely as the Spanish Armada approached the English coast. In later life he remarked, "Fear was my twin." His father was a profligate country parson who deserted his family and disappeared after a brawl outside the church door.

An uncle enabled Hobbes to be educated at Magdalen College, Oxford, at a time when the college was under Puritan administration. Here he distinguished himself at Latin and Greek. As a young man, Hobbes became secretary to Sir Francis Bacon. In 1634, on one of his trips to the Continent, he met Galileo in Florence. Hobbes began to contrast the scientific methods of Galileo and the Padua School (of which Galileo had been a member) with the older medieval views which were still being taught at Oxford.

Hobbes lived through the English Civil War, the Puritan Commonwealth under Oliver Cromwell, and the Restoration of the Stuart monarchy and the Anglican Church under King Charles II. For a time Hobbes had been Charles's tutor in France during his exile there. On an earlier visit to France in 1640 Hobbes had lived in a convent presided over by Mersenne. At Mersenne's suggestion, he submitted to Descartes a series of objections to the latter's *Meditations.* From that point onwards relations between Descartes and Hobbes went downhill.[2]

Hobbes was a prolific author. The philosophy that he wanted to write had three parts. The first part would deal with matter, the second with human nature, and the third with society. In the event, however, the third part came to be written first in the form of the *Leviathan,* which Hobbes wrote during the turbulent times of the English Civil War. The other parts of Hobbes's philosophy are contained in various other writings. Today Hobbes is remembered chiefly as a political theorist on account of the *Leviathan, or the Matter, Form and Power of a Commonwealth,*

Ecclesiastical and Civil (1651). In it Hobbes depicted human life in its natural state as "solitary, poor, nasty, brutish, and short."[3] In order to alleviate the human condition, Hobbes argued for the absolute sovereignty of the political state and the need for conformity in religion. The book's title was taken from the creature mentioned in the Old Testament. Hobbes applied it to the state, which he described as a kind of "artificial man," brought into being for the defense and protection of citizens.[4] Hobbes rejected the idea of the divine right of kings to rule (which Charles I had vainly appealed to in his conflict with Parliament). In its place Hobbes proposed a theory of natural law as the basis of all laws, a representative theory of government and the absolute authority of the state to which all citizens were bound by a form of social contract. Hobbes believed that civil war could be averted permanently only if a new view of government, based on a scientific study of humankind, could be worked out.

Hobbes was fascinated with the idea he found in Greek thought that everything is in motion. It was reinforced by the vision that he caught from Galileo of a universe in perpetual motion. What Galileo had done by way of explaining the movement of physical bodies, Hobbes sought to do in his explanation of human nature. Human beings, like physical objects, were governed by the laws of nature. To Hobbes, "*A law of nature, lex naturalis,* is a precept, or general rule, found out by reason, by which a man is forbidden to do that which is destructive of his life, or taketh away the means of preserving the same, and to omit that by which he thinketh it may be best preserved."[5]

Such a view of law is very different from the older prescriptive view of moral law, which set out what ought to be done, either because it was God's will or because there was some intrinsic ethical obligation. Although it was presented as an attempt to treat the study of human behavior on the model of the natural sciences, Hobbes's view of natural law in the realm of ethics was not based on observation and controlled experiment. Rather, it was a construct that Hobbes placed on his pessimistic and materialistic view of human nature.

Hobbes's definition assigns an absolute value to the self-preservation of the individual, and treats the *prescription* for self-preservation as a *description* of the causes which govern human conduct. Hobbes went on to describe the human condition as one of "war of every one against every one." In the circumstances, it was mutually advantageous *"to seek peace and follow it,"* which was "the first and fundamental law of nature." Hence followed the second natural law: *"that a man be willing, when others are so too, as far forth as for peace and defence of himself he shall think it necessary, to lay down this right to all things; and be contented with so much liberty against other men as he would allow other men against himself."*[6]

Although Hobbes's writings contain references to God and religion, the system of philosophy that he preached was the forerunner of modern materialism. The universe, as he saw it, "that is, the whole mass of all things that are, is corporeal, that is to say, body . . . and consequently every part of the universe is body, and that which is not body is no part of the universe: and because the universe is all, that which is no part of it is nothing, and consequently nowhere."[7]

To Hobbes, therefore, it made no sense to talk about the soul as some kind of separate entity. Human beings were just living bodies, and death was simply the cessation of bodily functions.[8] In Hobbes's mechanistic scheme of things, free will was defined so as to make it compatible with determinism.[9] The final chapters of *Leviathan* contain a discussion of religion under the overall heading "Of the Kingdom of Darkness." Here Hobbes anticipated twentieth-century criticism of religious language in his attempt to show that certain beliefs were not unscriptural or even false (as other contemporaries might have done), but were incoherent and absurd.[10]

Although attempts have been made to present Hobbes as a believer of sorts,[11] and it certainly cannot be denied that in his scheme of things Hobbes left a place for religion, it is equally clear that religion was not central in Hobbes's thinking. Nor did it occupy a place of honor. The kind of philosophy that Hobbes advocated was an attempt to work out a world view and a prescription for human conduct and public life in secular terms. Hobbes himself saw it as a version of rationalism in which geometry was seen as a model for reasoning, conducive to the discovery of "general, eternal, and immutable truth."[12] He excluded from philosophy all appeals to experience (for experience had no part in "original knowledge") and to supernatural revelation (for knowledge alleged to be attained by such means was not acquired by reasoning). On the subject of miracles, Hobbes's somewhat veiled discussion implies that, where a miraculous event had actually happened, there must be a rational explanation.[13] In the end, religion was a matter of private belief and public conformity to whatever was authorized by the state.

> A private man has always the liberty, because thought is free, to believe or not believe in his heart those acts that have been given out for miracles, according as he shall see what benefit can accrue, by men's belief, to those who pretend or countenance them, and thereby conjecture whether they be miracles or lies. But when it comes to confession of that faith, the private reason must submit to the public; that is to say, to God's lieutenant.[14]

What Hobbes said here about belief in miracles in particular applied to religious belief in general. In an age of passionate religious convictions and bloody religious wars, it is not surprising that Hobbes found himself in conflict on all sides. His *magnum opus* was published in the early years of Cromwell's dictatorship, and although its author managed to make peace with the government, it was at the price of retiring to private life. In both France and England he was suspected of atheism: in France, because of his criticism of the Catholic Church; in England, because of his materialism. When the Stuart monarchy replaced Puritan rule, Hobbes gained the royal favor of his former pupil King Charles II, but he continued to alienate public opinion. His relationships with the scientific community of the newly founded Royal Society were strained on account of his contempt for their inductive methods of research and the scholars' rejection of Hobbes's mathematical theories. The upshot was that Hobbes was excluded from the Royal Society.

The Great Plague of 1665 and the Great Fire of London the following year were seen by some as acts of divine judgment on a country which tolerated Hobbes's secularism. The *Leviathan* narrowly escaped suppression by Act of Parliament, and Hobbes never received permission again to publish anything to do with religion and ethics. His later Latin works were brought out in Amsterdam, and many of his writings only appeared posthumously. Hobbes lived to the age of ninety-one. But his thinly veiled secularism did not die with him. It was only one—albeit the most blatant to date—of the many versions of secularism that were to appear in the years to come.

The Cambridge Platonists

Continental rationalism and aversion to theological extremism gave rise to that form of rational religion known as Cambridge Platonism.[15] However, unlike Hobbes's thought, Cambridge Platonism was an attempt to express a temperate form of Christianity. Indeed, it was partly an attempt to answer Hobbes by using reason to defend orthodoxy. The founder of the movement was Benjamin Whichcote (1609-83), the Provost of King's College and the eloquent Sunday-afternoon lecturer at Holy Trinity Church. Other members included Nathanael Culverwel (1618-51), John Smith (1616-52), Ralph Cudworth (1617-88) and Henry More (1614-87). At the time Cambridge University was a citadel of Puritanism. The Cambridge Platonists came from this background, but rejected the theology of high Calvinism, especially the doctrine of predestination. Their thinking was influenced not only by Dutch Arminianism[16] but by rationalist philosophy. They were impressed by Descartes, but raised questions about his separation of the material from the spiritual and his tendency toward mechanism. But Spinoza was seen as an atheist and materialist. If anything, Hobbes was even worse, for the thrust of his thought was directed against theism, and his occasional professions of belief were nothing but calculated hypocrisy.

The term *Cambridge Platonists* is not strictly exact. They were steeped in classical learning and drew heavily on Plato's dialogues for their views on the role of ideas, the nature of the soul, the place of reason and moral concepts. But they also drew on other classical sources, and quoted Plotinus even more often than Plato.[17] They saw Plotinus as carrying forward Plato's teaching, which to them was very relevant to the issues of their own day. An anonymous contemporary observer noted their intention of bringing the church back to "her old loving nurse, the Platonic philosophy."[18] In this they saw themselves as carrying on the tradition of the Alexandrian church fathers.

Materialism and atheism were synonymous to the Cambridge Platonists. The root error, Cudworth observed, lay in the fact that it dethroned mind as the originating principle behind all things and replaced it with arbitrary chance or unthinking matter.[19] Reason, on the other hand, was the answer both to materialistic atheism and to religious fanaticism. As Benjamin Whichcote said, "To go against reason is to go against God; it

is the selfsame thing to do that which the reason of the case doth require
and that which God himself doth appoint. Reason is the divine governor
of man's life; it is the very voice of God."[20] To Culverwel the human
understanding was "the candle of the Lord." By it human beings discover:

First, that all the moral law is founded in natural, and common light
of reason; secondly, that there's nothing in the mysteries of the Gospel contrary to the light of reason, nothing repugnant to this light, that
shines from "the candle of the Lord."[21]

Such optimistic sentiments were not shared by the Calvinists. As events
turned out, the Calvinists felt that their suspicions were amply justified
in view of the use made of this argument by the Deists.

English Deism

In his celebrated *Dictionary of the English Language* (1755), Dr. Samuel
Johnson defined Deism as "the opinion of those that only acknowledge
one God, without the reception of any revealed religion."[22] The term
(which comes from the Latin *deus*, "god") has been traced back to the
sixteenth century in connection with an unidentified group who professed belief in God but rejected Christ and his teaching. Among those
who professed such beliefs was the erstwhile convert to Judaism, Uriel
da Costa, who is sometimes regarded as a precursor of Spinoza. However, Deism in the strict sense of the term applies to a small number of
writers, most of whom are generally regarded as scholars of the second,
if not the third, rank, who lived in the seventeenth and early eighteenth
centuries. Their influence was out of all proportion to their numbers.
They may rightly be seen as the pioneers of biblical criticism[23] and the
initiators of the quest of the historical Jesus.[24] Their arguments against
miracles anticipated David Hume's famous argument[25] and adumbrated
the secular interpretation of religious history of Edward Gibbon and his
successors. The outlook of such founding fathers of the American constitution as Benjamin Franklin and Thomas Jefferson was at heart Deistic. In Europe Deism reached full flower in the French and German
Enlightenment.

The man who is generally credited with being "the father of English
Deism" was Lord Edward Herbert of Cherbury (1583-1648).[26] Lord Herbert served for a time as English ambassador in Paris, where he became

personally acquainted with the "new Pyrrhonians" and the attempts of
the rationalists to counteract them.[27] In 1624 Lord Herbert published in
Latin his treatise *On Truth, as it is Distinguished from Revelation, the Probable, the Possible, and the False*.[28] It was in part a reply to Pyrrhonian
skepticism and in part an alternative to Protestantism and Catholicism.
Like the rationalists, Lord Herbert believed in innate ideas. He maintained that common to all religions were five such innate principles or
common notions which did not depend on any special revelation: the
existence of God; that God should be worshipped; that virtue is the chief
element of worship; that repentance is a duty and that there will be
rewards and punishments after this life. The book was well received,
though before long Gassendi criticized its indefensible dogmatism whilst
Descartes attacked it for its inadequate dogmatism. Later still John Locke
denounced Lord Herbert's argument as being vague and failing to satisfy
Lord Herbert's own criteria for what actually constituted a common
notion. In language which echoed the vocabulary of Calvin (albeit in a
hostile way), Locke complained: "It will scarce seem possible that God
should engrave principles in men's minds, in words of uncertain signi-
fication, such as *virtues* and *sins*, which, amongst different men, stand for
different things."[29]

In the meantime Lord Herbert published an enlarged edition of his
book (1645) which included an explicit attack on revealed religion. The
rational, generally acknowledged common notions were not simply central truths of institutional religion. They now served as a kind of launch-
ing-pad to attacking religion based on revelation. He urged that all religion should be investigated historically and be tested by the common
notions. He criticized bibliolatry, and denounced the idea of an infallible church. The attack on revealed religion in the name of reason,
morality and historical truth was the central theme of Deism.

Lord Herbert found few followers during his lifetime, but he had a
posthumous disciple in the person of Charles Blount (1654-93). Some of
his writings were little more than restatements of the thoughts of Lord
Herbert and Thomas Hobbes. The tract generally attributed to Blount,
Miracles No Violations of the Laws of Nature (1693), was virtually a paraphrase of Spinoza's argument in the *Tractatus*. But in one important
respect Blount mounted a new type of attack on Christianity. Drawing

on his classical learning, he used the literature of pagan antiquity, especially of the post-Christian era, in an attempt to undermine Christian claims to uniqueness. In 1680, he published *The Two First Books of Philostratus Concerning the Life of Apollonius of Tyana, written originally in Greek, with philological notes on each chapter.* The significance of this lay in the fact that Apollonius was a reputed holy man and miracle worker who lived roughly at the same time as Jesus.

From this point onward the figure of Apollonius has repeatedly been brought forward either as an example of a holy man whose deeds seem to diminish the uniqueness of Jesus or as evidence of ancient hagiography said to exemplify tendencies at work in the New Testament. In the background is the hint of guilt by association. If Apollonius was a sham, then perhaps Jesus was too. Philostratus's work was written early in the third century A.D. at the request of the empress Julia Domna. There is reason to think that the work itself was originally intended to be anti-Christian propaganda, drawing on the stock-in-trade of historical romances of the time.[30] In which case there is no real parallel at all. But this has not deterred liberal and radical theologians down to the present day from trying to make capital out of Apollonius of Tyana.

The year following Blount's death an event occurred which was to have far-reaching consequences for freedom of thought in Britain. In 1694 the Licensing Act was allowed to lapse. Although stringent libel laws remained—including the blasphemy laws which continued to be applied—the event heralded a new era of free speech which was marked by hundreds of books and pamphlets dealing with matters of religion. In Germany it took another hundred years before such freedom of expression was permitted. The first major Deistic work which availed itself of the new freedom was John Toland's *Christianity Not Mysterious, Showing that there is Nothing in the Gospel Contrary to Reason, nor above it; And that No Christian Doctrine can properly be Call'd a Mystery* (1696).[31] Toland (1670-1722) depicted Jesus as a preacher of a simple, moral religion. The so-called mysteries of Christianity were ascribed to the fateful intrusion of pagan ideas and priestcraft. In a succession of writings Toland amplified and modified his views, eventually combining them into a form of pantheism (a term which owes its currency to Toland).

While Toland's Deism was evolving in the direction of pantheism, Anthony Collins (1676-1729) was preparing to mount an attack on the foundations of traditional Christian apologetics. Collins was a younger friend of John Locke and was named trustee in Locke's will. Whereas Locke (as we shall see in the next chapter) used his empiricism to develop the traditional argument that miracles and fulfilled prophecy functioned as divine accreditation of revelation, Collins attacked the credibility of this argument.[32] Already in his *Discourse of Free Thinking* (1713) Collins argued that people have a moral obligation to think about religious questions. He sought to meet this obligation in his *Discourse on the Grounds and Reasons of the Christian Religion* (1724) and its sequel, *The Scheme of Literal Prophecy Consider'd* (1727). Collins argued that a number of key prophecies like Isaiah 7:14 (cf. Mt 1:23) and Hosea 11:1 (cf. Mt 2:15) were not originally predictions of Jesus as the Messiah. They had a fulfillment within the lifetime of the prophets who made them. Therefore, they could not be used as supernatural predictions of Jesus. The Christian use of such prophecies, Collins argued, was based on rabbinic methods of allegorical interpretation. Christianity was based on allegory, rather than on solid history. What Collins overlooked was the possibility that prophecy in the Gospels might be neither simply literal and predictive nor allegorical but typological.[33]

Having dealt with prophecy, Collins then announced his intention of turning to the question of miracles, thus completing the work of undermining the other pillar of the traditional apologetic argument that prophecy and miracles served as supernatural proof of Christian truthclaims. However, it fell to the erratic Cambridge scholar Thomas Woolston (1670-1727) to undertake the completion of the second half of Collins's plan.

Woolston approached the task with a history of controversy behind him. He had already been deprived of his college fellowship, and an attempt had been made to prosecute him for his heterodox writings. Woolston's stormy career reached its climax with the publication of a series of six *Discourses on the Miracles of our Saviour* (1727-29). Each of the pamphlets was dedicated to a bishop of the Church of England. Woolston argued that the miracles could not be treated as historical events, but were allegories comparable with the allegories detected by Collins in the New Testament use of prophecy. He compared the star of Bethlehem with a will-o'-the-wisp. He complained that if Apollonius of Tyana had performed a miracle of turning water into wine, people would have reproached his memory with it. If the healing miracles were at all genuine, there must be a natural explanation. But Woolston's harshest criticism was reserved for the accounts of Jesus' resurrection, which he denounced as a romance which put him in mind of Robinson Crusoe. It was the most manifest, barefaced, most self-evident imposture "ever put upon the world." Woolston's explanation was that the disciples stole the body of Jesus, having bribed the soldiers guarding the tomb. It was not the resurrection but belief in it that was the true miracle.

Among the later Deists were Peter Annet, who wrote a series of pamphlets defending Woolston's point of view, Thomas Chubb and Thomas Morgan. However, Deism received its most authoritative statement from the pen of Matthew Tindal (1655-1733). This Oxford scholar was already past seventy when he published the work which became known as "the Bible of Deism," *Christianity as Old as the Creation; or, the Gospel a Republication of the Religion of Nature* (1730). It was not without significance that the title was drawn from a sermon of the renowned orthodox bishop Thomas Sherlock. Similar statements abounded in the utterances of the learned divines of the day. But whereas Sherlock and his colleagues proceeded to draw inferences akin to those of Locke, Tindal inverted the argument. The gospel, he insisted, must not be made to teach anything beyond the grasp of reason and nature. Since orthodox Christianity and rational religion are not coextensive, Tindal proposed to jettison certain expendable doctrines of the former. High on the list were those of the Fall and original guilt, and the atonement. True religion consisted of moderation and of acting according to one's nature.

Replies to Deism

Unlike many armchair philosophers, Woolston became a martyr for his views. In 1729 he was tried for blasphemy by the Lord Chief Justice and sentenced to a year's imprisonment and a fine of £100. Unable to pay the fine, he spent the remainder of his days serving his sentence. Despite the efforts of orthodox churchmembers like Samuel Clarke to procure his release, he remained under a form of house arrest at the time of his death. A less savage, but more effective, reply came from Thomas Sherlock (1678-1761), bishop of Bangor (and later of Salisbury and London). Sherlock was one of the bishops to whom Woolston had dedicated his *Discourses*. Sherlock had already published his sermons replying to Collins under the title of *The Use and Intent of Prophecy* (1725). In his next major work he showed himself to be a kind of eighteenth-century C. S. Lewis. His *Tryal of the Witnesses of the Resurrection* (1729) went through many editions both in England and on the continent of Europe.

The book reopened Woolston's case in the form of a private discussion of gentlemen of the Inns of Court. But this time it is the witnesses of the resurrection that were put in the dock. The testimony, the motives and the plausibility of the actions of the participants were subjected to close questioning. The conclusion was drawn that, whatever else they were, the disciples were sincere in their testimony. But was such testimony credible? In the case of a unique historical event it was impossible to go back in time. The only evidence was whatever happened to remain.

At this point Sherlock introduced an argument earlier put forward by John Locke.[34] He recognized that when we try to judge the credibility of a piece of testimony, we have to ask whether it is feasible. We try to answer the question by asking whether it *could* happen, in other words whether it fits our understanding of the laws of nature and of the way things work. But in his summing up, the judge in Sherlock's book ruled that in this case it was not enough to appeal to "the settled course of nature." For our knowledge of nature is limited. If people living in the eighteenth century had lived all their lives in a tropical climate, they would have said that no one could walk on water. But anyone living in Northern Europe knew full well that water freezes, and if the ice is thick enough it is possible to walk on it. In the ordinary course of human experience, the dead do not come to life again. But this did not rule out the possibility of resurrection, since from our limited human perspective we just do not know what God could do. We may be right to say from our experience that resurrection is highly unlikely. But logically we are not entitled to say that it is impossible.[35] In Sherlock's *Tryal of the Witnesses* the jury duly acquitted the apostles of giving false evidence.

Another work which belongs to the era of Deism is Handel's *Messiah* (1741). Handel composed the music to words based on Scripture texts, generally thought to have been selected by Charles Jennens. In its conception the work was innovative and yet at the same time deeply traditional. Handel had already set sacred themes to music, as had Bach and many other composers. The novelty lay in presenting the life and death of Christ as an oratorio, performed in music halls and secular buildings by professional singers as an entertainment. In London the work had to be advertised simply as *A Sacred Oratorio*. An anonymous writer in *The Gospel Magazine* expressed his sense of incongruity at the prospect of a performance at the Theatre Royal Covent Garden of the life and death of Jesus set to music for public entertainment with "orange wenches and whores ready as usual."[36] It was partly due to the good offices of Bishop Sherlock that the work was performed at all in London.

And yet the music and development of the theme of the Messiah was a profound reaffirmation of the Christian message in an intellectual and cultural climate which was emerging from the Deistic controversy and which was about to witness the evangelical revival. As in traditional apologetics the first part of the work begins with prophecy of the coming of Christ. But as the work progresses it becomes less and less an account of Christ's life and becomes a soul-stirring meditation on Christ's redemptive work and eternal hope.[37] Like the evangelical preaching of John Wesley and his contemporaries, Handel's *Messiah* answers skepticism with a reaffirmation of belief by addressing the heart.[38]

On an intellectual level there were numerous responses to Deism, but the most enduring reply of all was Joseph Butler's *The Analogy of Religion, Natural and Revealed, to the Constitution and Course of Nature* (1736).[39] The work was written while Butler (1692-1752) was the vicar of a country parish in northern England. Later on he became bishop of Bristol, dean of St. Paul's Cathedral in London and bishop of Durham. In his lifetime he came to be regarded as the greatest thinker in the church; modern assessments have not overthrown that verdict. Butler refrained from dealing with his adversaries by name, but his philosophy was a response to the naturalism and skepticism in British thinking from Hobbes to Toland. The latter called him "the judicious Mr. Butler." Whereas the Deists had drawn a sharp distinction between natural and revealed religion, using the former to criticize the latter, Butler argued that there was an *analogy* between the two.

Today Butler's style and language sounds quaint, but his ideas are anything but quaint. In a number of ways he anticipated modern thinking. Butler drew attention to the role of probability in thought. He acknowledged that probable evidence only enables us to form approximate ideas. To an infinite intelligence everything would be certain. But human beings do not possess infinite intelligence. Therefore, for them "probability is the very guide to life."[40] In saying this Butler recognized that human conclusions are at best interpretations, made by beings of limited intelligence on the basis of a limited selection of evidence, which is in turn interpreted in the light of an unknown number of hypotheses, most of which they have never examined personally. In other words, he was saying that all facts are theory laden.[41] But this point applies to the skeptic no less than to the believer. Moreover, the Deists' arguments against Christianity could equally well be leveled against natural religion.

Although Butler alluded to proofs for the existence of God, his case was built on a form of presuppositionalism. He argued that the presupposition of "an intelligent Author and Governor of nature" was the necessary condition of belief in the rationality of the universe and in the genuine objectivity of moral values.[42] Moreover, the Christian scheme of things was not incompatible with the obvious physical and moral facts of the world. Indeed, Christianity was able to account for the phenomena that natural religion sought to account for. But it also did more, in making human beings aware of realities which could not be discovered by reason alone.[43]

Butler's approach to apologetics could be described as holistic. It was an approach comparable with his picture of the network of scientific theories which together seek to give an account of the physical world. The account does not stand or fall by the discovery of a single decisive fact, but by the feasibility of the overall comprehensive picture.

Turning to the subject of miracles, Butler did not attempt to examine specific cases as Woolston had done. Instead, he reflected on the underlying philosophical issue of their probability. He observed that while scientific laws contain an element of predictability, there is a presumption of millions to one against most common facts. For example, we can predict in general that tomorrow objects that are heavier than air will fall to the ground because of the law of gravity. On the other hand, I cannot predict with anything like the same degree of certainty what I shall do tomorrow. The chances that I will drink this particular cup of coffee at breakfast rather than later are incalculable from even a moderately remote distance in time. Butler suggested that if there was a presumption against even ordinary particular events happening, the presumption against miracles happening was no greater. It was unreasonable to reject miracles before even examining the evidence for them. Moreover, if religion is able to suggest how miracles might fit into the overall pattern of God's purposes, there is even greater reason to give credence to them.

Critics of Butler's argument have claimed that Butler was confusing two types of events. They have pointed out that there is a difference between the normal range of experience which determines what kinds of events are probable and improbable, on the one hand, and claims about what is unique and without parallel in our experience, on the other hand. But Butler's defenders have replied that this was the point that Butler was making. Normal experience (which itself is incapable of making exact predictions of specific events) should not be appealed to in order to determine the possibility of reported events that are outside its range, especially in cases where our overall world view is able to give feasibility to the event in question.

As a scholar and thinker, Bishop Butler was treated with great respect in his own day. He hovered in the background of Hume's writings on religion, serving as a model for the figure of Cleanthes in Hume's *Dialogues Concerning Natural Religion.*[44] His thought also figured in Hume's *Natural History of Religion,* a work which knocked a final coffin nail into English Deism, with its reminder that savages were not enlightened Deists. But to many people today Butler is remembered most for his painful encounter with John Wesley, whom he forbade to preach in his diocese. The bishop saw Wesley as an enthusiast. He sent him away on the grounds that pretending to have extraordinary revelations and gifts of the Holy Spirit was "a very horrid thing." But Wesley stayed, claiming that his business on earth was to do what good he could wherever he could; and at that time he thought that he could do most good in the bishop's diocese.[45] Perhaps the two were talking at cross purposes. There are indications that the bishop's personal faith was nearer to Wesley's than this encounter suggests,[46] and certainly Wesley did not overlook the importance of scholarship in the service of the gospel.[47] But clearly Wesley and Butler had different vocations. In his youth Butler had confessed to Dr. Samuel Clarke: "I design the search for truth as the business of my life." He was, in the words of Ian T. Ramsey, "a proper prelate for the age of reason; for he laboured to establish the conviction of the reasonableness of Christianity."[48]

Repercussions

The English Deists were never more than a handful of individual writers who were united by their hostile attacks on institutional Christianity in the name of natural, reasonable religion. By the 1750s they were virtually an extinct breed. Their ideas, however, took root in fields far and wide. The most pervasive of all was the idea that the supernatural cannot be admitted as a factor in history. This idea lay behind the Deists' attacks on prophecy and miracles in the New Testament. It gave impetus to the belief that the real, historical Jesus was radically different from the Christ depicted in the pages of the New Testament. It was a thought which (as we shall see in our final chapter) helped to launch the so-called quest of the historical Jesus.

In the meantime, nearer home, an Anglican scholar by the name of Conyers Middleton published a book on early church history. He entitled it *A Free Inquiry into the Miraculous Powers which are Supposed to have Subsisted in the Christian Church, from the Earliest Ages through Several Successive Centuries* (1748).[49] It was a detailed study which worked its way through Christian writers from the close of the New Testament period down to the fifth century. He noted that in case after case Christian writers of repute did not claim to have performed miracles themselves. Often it was a case of knowing someone who knew someone else who testified to a miracle. Middleton made fun of miracles stories connected with the bones and relics of the saints which wrought greater wonders than the saints themselves during their lifetime. But underlying everything was the concerted attempt to replace supernatural explanations by natural explanations. It may have been something of an exaggeration when David Hume remarked that all England was in a ferment on account of the book. But at any rate John Wesley felt that Middleton had contrived to "overthrow the whole Christian system," for the main arguments that Middleton had deployed against the church fathers could well have been turned against the New Testament.[50]

Scarcely more than a quarter of a century after Middleton's work there appeared the first of six volumes of Edward Gibbon's *History of the Decline and Fall of the Roman Empire* (1776-88). It was a work written in much the same spirit as Middleton's *Free Inquiry*, Hume's essay "Of Miracles" and the Deists' critique of the supernatural. There was, however, one important difference. Gibbon did not attack the miraculous element in Christianity directly. Instead, he chose to mock it with elegant irony in passages like the following:

> The supernatural gifts, which even in this life were ascribed to the Christians above the rest of mankind, must have conduced to their own comfort, and very frequently to the conviction of infidels. Besides the occasional prodigies, which might sometimes be effected by the immediate interposition of the Deity when he suspended the laws of nature in the service of religion, the Christian church, from the time of the apostles and their first disciples, has claimed an uninterrupted succession of miraculous powers, the gift of tongues, of vision, and of prophesy, the power of expelling daemons, of healing the sick, and of raising the dead. The knowledge of foreign languages was frequently communicated to the contemporaries of Irenaeus, though himself was left to struggle with the difficulties of a barbarous dialect, whilst he preached the gospel to the natives of Gaul.[51]

Underlying this whole approach to history were three basic assumptions. First was the assumption that sacred history must be treated no differently from secular history. The same criteria and methods must be used for both. Second is the assumption that there must be an analogy between the types of events which happen now and the types of events which happened in the past. Our understanding of the way in which things happen now is the measure of how things happened in the past. Moreover, what does not fit our understanding may safely be discarded as myth, falsehood or pious fabrication. Third is the assumption that history consists of a network of homogeneous events which may be described in terms of finite causes and effects. They became part and parcel of the way of doing secular history and also biblical studies in later ages.[52] They came to the fore in the era of Deism.

The impact of Deism on thought in America and Europe was deeper and broader than anything experienced in Britain. In America Deism achieved status and influence thanks partly to the reputation and vigor of its advocates and partly to the appeal of its political implications. The Deistic repudiation of institutional religion chimed in with the philosophy of those leaders of the revolution who sought to separate church and state by establishing the Constitution of the United States on rational, secular principles. In Europe leading thinkers of the Enlightenment, like Voltaire in France and Reimarus in Germany, were well acquainted with the writings of the English Deists.[53] English Deism gave renewed vigor to the skepticism which dated back to the sixteenth century. When looked at more closely, the religion of the Enlightenment was none other than Deism in slightly different dress. But these are issues which we shall deal with in our final chapters.

13. THE RISE OF
BRITISH EMPIRICISM

I*n philosophy the term* empiricism *stands above all for a British movement* which emerged in the seventeenth and eighteenth centuries which challenged the rationalism of Descartes and his successors on the continent of Europe. It is linked with the names of three thinkers, an Englishman, an Irishman and a Scotsman: Locke, Berkeley and Hume.[1] There are a number of oddities and ironies in the situation. None of the three were professional philosophers. Locke had a medical degree, though he did not practice medicine as a profession. He spent much of his time in diplomatic and public service. Berkeley was a bishop of the Anglican Church. Hume twice failed in bids to obtain chairs of philosophy in Scotland. He held a variety of positions, but in his lifetime he owed his fame and fortune to his now-no-longer-read *History of England.*

Another irony of the situation is the fact that the term *empiricism,* as a description of the style of doing philosophy associated with Locke, Berkeley and Hume, did not become current until after their time. Initially, it carried with it negative overtones, associated with the empirical school of medicine in the ancient world. The empirics confined themselves to observation and remedies which worked. They were skeptical of general, theoretical explanations. With the revival of interest in the writings of Sextus Empiricus in the sixteenth century, the term was linked with skepticism. The Greek word *empeiria* means "experience" and the adjective *empeiros* means "skilled." But by the sixteenth century "empirical" was already being contrasted with "scientific," and it degenerated into a term of abuse as an alternative to charlatan or quack.

In the narrower, philosophical sense of the term (as a style of doing philosophy from Locke onwards), empiricism has a negative and a positive side. Negatively, empiricism rejects the rationalist view that the mind is furnished with a range of ideas and perceptions which owe nothing to experience. The positive side to this is the doctrine that all knowledge depends upon experience which comes to us via the senses. Statements (apart from those of logic) can be known to be true only from experience.

The Empirical Tradition

In a broader sense, empiricism was part of a tradition which went back for centuries. Kant regarded Aristotle as "the chief of the *empiricists,*" and saw Locke as a latter-day follower of Aristotle.[2] What they had in common was the attempt to derive "all concepts and principles from experience." However, Kant found fault in them for trying to go beyond experience, bounded by time and space, by attempting to prove such metaphysical ideas as the existence of God and the immortality of the soul. Kant found Epicurus more consistent, insofar as he did not attempt to draw inferences beyond the limits of experience.

In the sense that Thomas Aquinas rejected the rational deductive approach of Anselm in favor of an Aristotelian emphasis on reflection on the basis of observation, Aquinas could be said to have had an empirical approach. However, empiricism in the seventeenth and eighteenth centuries was more closely related to the rise of science in England with its stress on observation, experiment and inductive reasoning.[3] This approach was pioneered by Francis Bacon (1561-1626), the essayist, orator, lawyer and amateur philosopher-scientist. In the course of his colorful career Bacon rose to the position of Lord Chancellor only to fall in disgrace amid charges of corruption. Alexander Pope described him as "the brightest, wisest, meanest of mankind."[4] Bacon died in the depths of winter following a chill caught as a result of an experiment. He had the idea that flesh might be preserved through preserving it in snow just as well as by the then customary method of preserving it in salt. He obtained a hen which he proceeded to stuff with snow. But the experiment brought on the fatal chill.

The episode characterizes his approach to knowledge as set out in works like the *Novum Organum* (1620), a title which recalls Aristotle's

Organon. Bacon tried to improve existing notions of scientific method. He argued that induction was not simply a matter of enumeration. Syllogistic logic was not a means of empirical discovery. It served rather as an aid to show what could be deduced from what was already known. Bacon stressed the need to check generalizations by looking for "negative instances." He believed that scientific laws were established on the basis of observation, but went beyond Aristotle in his insistence on the need to test conclusions by examining possible counter-instances. In so doing, he recognized that the laws of nature could never be conclusively verifiable, for perfect induction is possible only in cases where complete access is possible to a limited subject. On the other hand, Bacon appreciated the importance of testing conclusions by trying to falsify them by means of conducting experiments to show that they were wrong. Bacon also discussed what he called the "idols of the mind" which were persistent beliefs and opinions which stood in the way of knowledge.

Bacon brought prestige to the study of the natural world, and began a process which was continued by King Charles II's patronage of the Royal Society of London for the Improvement of Natural Knowledge.[5] In its early years many of the leading figures in the Royal Society were also prominent clergy of the Church of England. Among the leading lay scientists were Sir Isaac Newton, who served as president from 1703 until his death in 1727 and Robert Boyle (1627-92), whose memory is preserved in the immortal phrase "the father of chemistry and son of the Earl of Cork." Boyle's book *The Sceptical Chemist* (1661) divorced chemistry from alchemy by repudiating the still prevalent Greek view of the four elements. Boyle insisted that the nature of material substances must be based on experimental evidence. His view was summed up in the motto of the Royal Society, *Nullius in Verba,* which conveys the idea of being bound to nothing by mere authority.[6] Boyle was also a student of Scripture and a devout believer. In his will he left the sum of £50 a year for a series of lectures against unbelievers to be delivered in a London church—the "Boyle lectures."

Sir Isaac Newton (1642-1727)[7] was a slightly junior contemporary and friend of John Locke. Isaac Newton was educated at Grantham Grammar School, where he followed in the footsteps of Henry More, the Cambridge Platonist and inveterate opponent of Hobbes's materialism. More spent most of his career as a Fellow of Christ's College, Cambridge. In 1661 Newton entered nearby Trinity College, where he was elected a Fellow in 1667. In his student notebooks Newton referred to "the excellent Dr. More." More was, in fact, one of the first Englishmen to appreciate Descartes. He was also, like Cudworth, an early member of the Royal Society.

Although the Cambridge Platonists believed in the rational structure of the world, they were generally ill-equipped in mathematics and lacked the scientific competence to develop a scientific case for their theism. It was otherwise with Isaac Barrow, the Greek scholar and Lucasian Professor of Mathematics at Cambridge, and his pupil at Trinity College, Isaac Newton. Barrow, who had strong affinities with the Cambridge Platonists, had made Trinity College the center of mathematics at Cambridge. In 1669 Barrow resigned his chair in favor of his pupil, Newton. As an ordained clergyman, Barrow felt the call to devote himself to the ministry of the gospel. He went on to become a famous preacher, and eventually became Master of Trinity College. In the meantime, Newton began to emerge as the leading scientist of the age. In 1694 he moved to London, and was appointed Master of the Mint in 1699. He was knighted by Queen Anne in 1705. He had been a member of the Royal Society since 1672, and was its president until his death in 1727.

Newton's scientific achievements include the formulation of the laws of motion and gravitation, the discovery (apparently coincidentally with Leibniz) of differential calculus, and the first correct analysis of white light. Newton's laws of motion helped to establish the mechanical view of the universe which dominated physics down to modern times. Newton's *Philosophiae Naturalis Principia Mathematica* (1687) gave an account not only of the motion of bodies on the earth but throughout the universe. Newton's views raised big questions for theology. Where did God fit into this mechanistic world? Newton himself believed that his theory of universal gravitation supported belief in a deity, whom he described in the preface to his *Principia Mathematica* as "the most perfect mechanic of all." Newton believed that time and space had an absolute fixed character.[8] Thus whatever happens in space and time is determined by the characteristics of space and time. But Newton rejected the idea that the world was the body of God or a way of thinking about God (in the manner of Spinoza). Newton thought of infinite space as the divine sensorium in which God perceives his creatures.[9]

Newton's view of the laws of nature pointed him to the divine lawgiver. He supposed that such irregularities that could not be explained in terms of laws were due to the direct intervention of God. Newton's views of God's relationship with the world brought him into conflict with Leibniz. The latter complained that Newton's view was like a watch which needed to be wound up, cleaned and repaired every so often. He felt that such a view reflected badly on a God who lacked the foresight to make it a perpetual motion. Leibniz himself preferred to think of "the same force and vigor" always remaining in the world, passing perpetually from one part to another in accordance with the laws of nature and "the beautiful pre-established order." To Newton's defender, the Anglican divine Samuel Clarke, this view smacked of materialism and fate. It seemed to exclude God's providential care and concern which—far from being a diminution—was "the true glory of his workmanship."[10]

Sir Isaac Newton was deeply interested in theological questions. Newton's *Observations upon the Prophecies of Daniel, and the Apocalypse of St. John* were published posthumously in 1733. Other theological writings were not published until modern times.[11]

Newton's private papers reveal a mind of considerable theological learning. Newton had a high regard for the Bible, but questioned some points of the church's creeds. He believed "that religion and philosophy are to be preserved distinct. We are not to introduce divine revelations into philosophy nor philosophical opinions into religion." "What cannot be understood," he remarked, "is no object of belief."[12]

Newton's scientific work posed major questions for philosophy. What sort of philosophy was appropriate for the science of the eighteenth century? Descartes's thought provided a stimulus, but Newton found in him much to criticize. He saw his own method as empirical and inductive. The British empirical philosophers took up the task of working out the philosophical implications of Newtonian science. The common agenda was dictated by the question of knowledge. But the answers they gave were wildly contradictory. This was true not only in the seventeenth and eighteenth centuries but also of nineteenth-century thinkers like

J. S. Mill, and twentieth-century followers of the empiricist tradition like
Bertrand Russell and the Logical Positivists. The first major philosopher
to undertake this task was John Locke.

Locke

John Locke (1632-1704)[13] was the son of a small country land-owner and
lawyer. He went up to Oxford when Puritanism was in its heyday and
the university was under the vice-chancellorship of the great John Owen.
Among other things Locke studied medicine and was eventually awarded
an M.D. John Locke was also a semi-public figure. But in the last years
of the Stuart monarchy he found it prudent to live in Holland, and did
not return until after the Glorious Revolution of 1688. While in Holland
he enjoyed the company of Dutch Arminian theologians, and had the
time and leisure to complete his major philosophical treatise, *An Essay
Concerning Human Understanding* (1690), and his first *Letter on Toleration*
(1689). Locke subsequently published further letters on the same subject,
and treatises on education and civil government. *The Reasonableness of
Christianity* (1695) was followed by the posthumous *Paraphrase and Notes
on the Epistles of St. Paul* (1705-7) and *A Discourse of Miracles* (1706). In his
later years Locke served as a Commissioner of Trade in London, living
with the Masham family in Essex. He was a member of the Anglican
Church. On his deathbed Lady Masham (the daughter of Ralph Cudworth, the Cambridge Platonist) read psalms to him.

Locke was the most brilliant creative thinker of his age. His thought
embraced the new science, political theory and Christian theology in a
creative synthesis which re-examined the philosophical basis of thought
in these areas. His solutions to contemporary questions sought to reaf-
firm Christian thinking, while addressing the political and scientific revolutions of the seventeenth century.

Locke's *Two Treatises of Government* (1690) justified the revolution of
1688 which deposed King James II and brought William of Orange to
the English throne. Locke was nineteen years old when Hobbes's *Leviathan* was published. His *Two Treatises of Government* were not directed
against Hobbes, but against Hobbes's contemporary, Sir Robert Filmer,
who shared some of the latter's absolutist views on government.[14] Sir
Robert, who died a prisoner in 1653 during the the English Civil War,

had been an ardent defender of the divine right of kings. His *Patriarcha; or the Natural Power of Kings* had been composed in the 1630s and circulated privately in manuscript form. Its publication in 1680 kept alive his views, and prompted Locke's response.

Sir Robert insisted that it was unnatural for the people to govern or choose governors. He ridiculed the idea of a society based on a social contract, and rhetorically asked how an assembly convened for the purpose of making a universal contract could make a valid vote. What about the rights of women, servants, children, the sick and those who were either absent or not granted a vote? Sir Robert's alternative view purported to represent the teaching of Scripture. Every individual, he argued, is bound to obey absolutely a country's established political authority, because that authority enjoys by divine decree the powers conferred upon Adam at creation. Sir Robert also believed that society was hierarchically ordered, with males superior to females. Property and political power were distributed in accordance with the patriarchal decrees of the Old Testament, and belonged absolutely to the person who inherited them.

Locke's *Two Treatises of Government* rejected the absolutist views of Hobbes and Filmer in favor of a democratic view of government. He vindicated the overthrow of the Stuart kings by appealing both to natural law and to the teaching of Scripture. Filmer's argument was nothing but an argument for slavery, and his reasoning was a mere "rope of sand." Locke dismissed as "glib nonsense" the idea of the hereditary kingship of Adam and its imagined descent to modern rulers.

Locke pointed out that not even Adam had absolute rights. In any case, no existing ruler (least of all the English kings) could trace his claims to sovereignty back to Adam. In place of this view Locke put forward his theory of the social contract. In order to preserve the rights and order mandated by the law of nature, civil governments were instituted in accordance with an implied social contract. The contract is not between the ruler and the ruled but between all free persons. Its purpose is to preserve the lives, freedom and property of all, as they belong to all under natural law. If persons, such as monarchs, try to get absolute power, they put themselves in a state of war with the people. If no redress can be found, the people may resort to revolt. The aim of such a revolution is not to return to the state of nature, but to establish a new and just government.

In the course of time Filmer's *Patriarcha* and Locke's reply to it in his *First Treatise* ceased to be read, except by historians. But Locke's *Second Treatise,* which set out his political theory, became one of the seminal works which shaped the course of history. In Britain it helped to establish the constitutional monarchy which has been the keystone of British government from Locke's day to the present. In America and France it played a significant part in the political thinking behind the great revolutions of the eighteenth century. Its ideas were formative in the minds of many who attended the Constitutional Convention of 1787, and who took part in the framing of the American Constitution.

In his student days the brand of philosophy taught at Oxford was scholastic Aristotelianism. To Locke it seemed to be confused by obscure terms and useless questions, and had little to do with the discovery of truth. The reading of Descartes was like a breath of fresh air. With the rationalists Locke could insist that "reason must be our last judge and guide in everything."[15] Locke valued the importance of "clear and distinct ideas."[16] Like the Cambridge Platonists, Locke regarded reason as "the candle of the Lord."[17] But, although human beings are endowed with reason, Locke rejected the rationalist idea that the mind had stamped on it from birth certain primary, self-evident notions.[18] He likewise repudiated the idea, found in Cicero by Calvin and his followers, that human beings have a sense of the deity inscribed on their hearts.[19] Instead, Locke pictured the mind as a blank which received all its impressions from outside. In his characteristic seventeenth-century rhetoric Locke propounded his thesis that experience is the source of all knowledge. Or, to be more precise, all ideas come from sensation or reflection on sensation.

> Let us then suppose the mind to be, as we say, white paper, void of all characters, without any ideas; how comes it to be furnished? Whence comes it by that vast store, which the busy and boundless fancy of man has painted on it with an almost endless variety? Whence has it all the materials of reason and knowledge? To this I answer, in one word, from EXPERIENCE; in that all our knowledge is founded, and from that it ultimately derives itself. Our observation,

employed either about external sensible objects, or about the internal operations of our minds, perceived and reflected on by ourselves, is that which supplies our understandings with all the materials of thinking. These two are the fountains of knowledge, from whence all the ideas we have, or can naturally have, do spring.[20]

In other words, what we know is either *ideas* (impressions in the mind derived from sense-experience of "yellow, white, heat, cold, soft, hard, bitter, sweet, and all those which we call sensible qualities"[21]) or the mind's own *reflections* on them.[22] From this Locke drew the conclusions that the human mind "hath no other immediate object but its own *ideas*, which it alone does and can contemplate,"[23] and that "knowledge is the perception of the agreement or disagreement of two ideas."[24]

In arguing this, Locke was advancing what is sometimes called the representative theory of knowledge. The mind itself has no direct knowledge of the outside world, for it is never able to by-pass the senses, upon which it gets to work. The senses represent the world outside us to the mind, and the mind provides an interpretation. In propounding this theory of knowledge Locke set the agenda for generations to come. Later philosophers would question Locke's use of the word *idea*. The term had a long and venerable use dating back to Plato's and classical philosophy. But Locke's use was poles apart from Plato's. Whereas Plato saw Ideas or Forms as the eternal models or archetypes of things in the world, to Locke ideas were sense data occasioned by experience. Locke's theory pointed critics like Hume and Kant in the direction of skepticism. But to Locke himself this theory of knowledge was part of a larger structure which linked everyday knowledge with scientific knowledge and the knowledge of God.

Locke distinguished faith from reason. He defined the latter as:

the discovery of the certainty or probability of such propositions or truths, which the mind arrives at by deduction made from such ideas, which it has got by the use of its natural faculties, viz. by sensation or reflection. *Faith,* on the other side, is the assent to any proposition not thus made out by the deductions of reason, but upon the credit of the proposer, as coming from God, in some extraordinary way of communication. This way of discovering truths to men we call *revelation.*[25]

A page or two previously Locke had laid down the further distinction between that which was according to reason, that which was above and that which was contrary to reason.

> 1. *According to reason,* are such propositions whose truth we can discover, by examining and tracing those *ideas* we have from *sensation* and *reflection;* and by natural deduction find to be true or probable.
>
> 2. *Above reason,* are such propositions whose truth or probability we cannot by reason derive from those principles.
>
> 3. *Contrary to reason,* are such propositions as are inconsistent with, or irreconcilable to, our clear and distinct *ideas.* Thus the existence of one God is according to reason; the existence of more than one God contrary to reason; the resurrection of the dead, above reason.[26]

Thinkers may disagree as to what should be put into these three pigeon-holes. I myself would want to qualify further what I mean by reason and being reasonable. An idea is reasonable if we can demonstrate it logically beforehand. An idea may also be called reasonable if it is warranted by experience. It may be that it contains implications which have not been fathomed or that we are incapable of examining at the moment. Nevertheless, if observation and experience warrant the conclusion, the idea may be said to be reasonable. It is in this sense Locke held that the existence of God is according to reason. But there are many aspects of the Christian faith which, as Locke points out, are above reason. Locke's method was to accept such items on the basis of authority which he had established by reason.

> Reason is natural *revelation,* whereby the eternal Father of light, the Fountain of all knowledge, communicates to mankind that portion of truth which he has laid within the reach of their natural faculties; *Revelation* is natural *reason* enlarged by a new set of discoveries communicated by God immediately, which *reason* vouches the truth of, by the testimony and proofs it gives that they come from God.[27]

What Locke was doing here was to combine the traditional apologetic approach, which stressed fulfilled prophecy and miracles as divine attestation of Christian truth claims, with his empirical approach to knowledge. The argument is summed up in the *Discourse of Miracles:* "Where the miracle is admitted, the doctrine cannot be rejected; it comes with the assurance of a divine attestation to him that allows the miracle, and he cannot question its truth."[28] In taking up this position Locke was adopting a form of foundationalism which argued that there had to be a rational foundation for belief. Acceptance of divine revelation was rational because there were rational grounds for believing that the revelation (understood in terms of unverifiable propositions) had come from God. If we cannot verify the propositions themselves because they are *above reason,* we can at least verify the credentials of their source. It was therefore important to Locke to be able to identify divinely wrought miracles as historical events. Accordingly, he defined a miracle as "a sensible operation, which, being above the comprehension of the spectator, and in his opinion contrary to the established course of nature, is taken by him to be divine."[29]

Locke was well aware of the problems that belief in miracles raised for the educated mind in the world of Newtonian physics. His definition of a miracle involves an element of inference. The spectator does not actually see God act directly as the cause of the miracle. What is seen is one state of affairs before the miracle and another after it. The spectator observes effects and infers a divine cause. Locke's position allowed for mistakes and differences of interpretation. Locke recognized that one person might regard an event as miraculous, while another saw the same event as an ordinary occurrence. He was also aware of the counter-argument that raised doubts about Christian truth-claims associated with miracles by drawing attention to miracles in other religions.

Locke's response to all this was to point out that in some religions, like Islam, truth-claims were not linked with miracles, while in polytheistic religions truth-claims were not a burning issue. In the case of Jesus' miracles it was not any single miracle that provided conclusive evidence. It was rather the cumulative effect of them. Moreover, miracles should not be treated as isolated events designed to impress by their sheer stupendous character.

For this reason Locke further qualified his definition of a miracle by making three further stipulations.[30] (1) No mission supported by a miracle which detracts from the honor of God or is "inconsistent with natural religion and the rules of morality" can be regarded as divine. (2) God cannot be expected to perform miracles in order to attest something trivial or inform people about things which can be discovered by the use of their natural faculties. (3) Genuine miracles are not trivial events, but are events which exhibit the over-ruling power of God in connection with the revelation of "supernatural truths relative to the glory of God, and some great concern of men."

Examination of Locke's position shows that Locke recognized the importance of contexts. He did not value miracles for their abnormality but for their supernatural character which was congruent with what could be known about God from other sources. The miracle thus has to be *feasible* as an act of God. It also had to be feasible—even if incomprehensible—as a physical act. A miracle could be contrary to experience, but our limited experience can only help to determine the degree of probability within the context of that experience. The point is illustrated by Locke's story of the King of Siam and the Dutch ambassador.[31] The ambassador told the king that in his country people could walk on water. Even an elephant could do so. The king replied: "Hitherto I have believed the strange things you have told me, because I look upon you as a sober fair man; but now I am sure you lie." What the king could not appreciate, because he had no experience of it, was the fact that in European winters water can freeze and become ice. If reports of miracles are judged solely by normal experience of the non-miraculous, one would have to say that they are so improbable that the report is more likely to be mistaken than that the event in question actually happened. But if miracles belong to a wider context which enables the accounts of them to be seen as manifestations of God's power and grace, the dynamics of the argument are significantly changed. They remain incomprehensible, but they become feasible within the wider context.

The argument from miracles figures again in *The Reasonableness of Christianity, as Delivered in the Scriptures*, where Locke saw Jesus' miracles as a fulfillment of messianic expectation (John 7:31).[32] Here it is set in the context of Locke's apologetic for what today might be called the Christian world view. Locke's work is a theological rationale for the Christian belief in the restoration of humankind from its fallen condition by Jesus Christ. God has dealt with human beings "as a compassionate and tender Father." He has given them "reason and with it a law, that could not be otherwise than what reason should dictate." But considering the frailty of human beings, God "promised a deliverer, whom in his good time he sent; and then declared to all mankind, that whoever would believe in him to be the Saviour promised, and take him now raised from the dead, and constituted Lord and Judge of all men, to be their King and Ruler, should be saved."[33]

The Christian faith was not just an intellectual system for Locke. It was a source of hope, renewal and meaning in life. Nevertheless, it was related to a connected system of beliefs which, as a system, were reasonable and could readily be grasped by anyone. The Christian church was not a kind of "Academy or Lycaeum" which admitted only those capable of following abstruse arguments. The truth of the gospel was "plain and intelligible," capable of being grasped by "the bulk of mankind," including the illiterate laborer and humble plowman. In addition, for Locke miracles were not the foundation of belief in God. They had a part to play in establishing the truth-claims of special revelation.

In the last chapter we saw how the Deists attacked those claims. We shall presently see how David Hume carried on this assault. In both cases the issue at stake was not simply the theoretical possibility of miracles. Underlying all the arguments was the deeper question of the truth of Christianity as a whole. On this issue Locke himself stood at the parting of the ways. Locke was an advocate of rational religion. He had developed an empirical case for the rationality of the belief system of the Christian religion which was in tune with the scientific, empirical attitude of the age. At the same time he maintained his connection with the Anglican Church. Nevertheless, some of his readers, like the country parson John Edwards and the Bishop of Worcester Edward Stillingfleet, detected in Locke's writings a position which came suspiciously close to Unitarianism. Locke evidently believed in God, but what sort of a God did he really believe in? Different readers gave different answers. Some thought that his approach supported belief in the deity of Christ and the divine Trinity, while others concluded that his views fell short of these beliefs. In the years that followed his death Locke's writings provided a legacy of ammunition for both believers and skeptics.

Berkeley

The truth of Christian beliefs and the nature of reality were questions

which received novel and ingenious answers from George Berkeley
(1685-1753).[34] Berkeley was born in Ireland and entered Trinity College,
Dublin when he was fifteen. By 1707 he had become a fellow of the
college, where he lectured intermittently on Greek, Hebrew and divinity.
As a student, Berkeley had studied Locke and the French philosopher-
theologian, Nicholas Malebranche. The latter had developed his own
form of Cartesian philosophy which proved to be both a rival and a
stimulus to the philosophies developed by Locke, Berkeley and the next
generation of British thinkers.[35]

Most of Berkeley's philosophical writing was done in his twenties
during the tenure of his fellowship at Trinity College. His *Essay towards
a New Theory of Vision* (1709) was a discussion of how we perceive objects.
It was shortly followed by *A Treatise concerning the Principles of Human
Knowledge* (1710) and *Three Dialogues between Hylas and Philonous* (1713).
The latter, which was intended as a semi-popular version of the *Principles*, revived the classical dialogue form of Platonic philosophy. The
names of the central characters were also evocative of the world of
ancient Greece. Philonous (as its Greek derivation suggests) is the "lover
of mind," while Hylas is the materialist. Some twenty years later, while
the Deistic controversy was at its height, Berkeley published yet another
dialogue in the classical mold as a reply to skepticism, *Alciphron, or the
Minute Philosopher* (1732).

In the meantime, Berkeley's career had taken several turns. In 1724
he had become Dean of Derry. It was a position he continued to occupy
for ten years, though he never actually took up residence there. In the
1720s Berkeley was preoccupied with a project to found a missionary
college in Bermuda. He sailed to Newport, Rhode Island, with a collection of books intended for the college library. However, he never set foot
on Bermuda. Government funds he had counted on never materialized.
He did, however, make contact with the American philosopher Samuel
Johnson, who taught at Yale and who became the first president of
King's College (later renamed Columbia University). While on Rhode
Island, Berkeley wrote his *Alciphron.*

When the failure of the missionary project became evident, Berkeley
donated his collection of books to Yale College and sailed back across
the Atlantic. In 1734 he became Bishop of Cloyne, where he devoted his

energies to the work of the church and the alleviation of the economic plight of the people. In his later years he earned a reputation as advocate of the virtues of tar-water as a remedy for a wide range of ills from indigestion to smallpox.

Berkeley's philosophical reputation rests upon his unique form of empiricism. It was inspired by Newton and Locke (both of whom Berkeley greatly admired), but at the same time was critical of them. Berkeley's criticism is already hinted at in the full title which he gave to his major work on the theory of knowledge. He called it A *Treatise concerning the Principles of Human Knowledge, Wherein the chief causes of error and difficulty in the Sciences, with the grounds of Scepticism, Atheism, and Irreligion, are inquired into.*

The root error which Berkeley detected in the scientific thought of his day concerned *matter.* The Newtonian world depicted space and time as the containers of material objects. To Berkeley, the Newtonian account was unsatisfactory. It seemed to lend support to the idea of the independent existence of corporeal matter, which Berkeley perceived to be "the main pillar and support of *scepticism,* so likewise upon the same foundation have been raised all the impious schemes of *atheism* and irreligion."[36]

Moreover, Locke's account of knowledge failed to redress the situation. According to Locke's representative theory of perception, material objects are perceived mediately by means of ideas. The mind does not perceive the material object directly, but only through the medium of the ideas formed by the senses and reflection on them. To Berkeley, this presented a problem. If we know only our *ideas,* we can never be sure whether any of them are really like the material qualities of objects, since we can never compare the ideas with them.[37] Indeed, how is it possible to answer skepticism on such a view?[38] In any case, Locke's position failed to deal adequately with the nature of matter. Berkeley thought that a better explanation was called for. Locke was like a man trying to see things through a mist.[39] He had failed to explain the nature of the reality perceived by our senses. In fact, Locke had failed to do justice to common sense. According to Berkeley, common sense told people that neither ideas nor objects had any existence apart from minds which perceive them.[40]

If Berkeley was opposed to Locke's form of empiricism, he was even more opposed to rationalist metaphysics. In his notebooks Berkeley wrote a memorandum to himself: "To be eternally banishing Metaphisics &c & recalling Men to Common Sense."[41] Over and over again Berkeley's starting point is his analysis of the act of perception. The *Dialogue between Hylas and Philonous* concludes with Philonous pointing to a fountain rising into the air and falling down in accordance with the principle of gravitation. "Just so," he observes, "the same principles which at first view lead to *scepticism,* pursued to a certain point, bring men back to common sense."[42]

The common-sense view that Philonous had in mind was not any *new notion.* He thought of it as an endeavor "only to unite and place in a clearer light that truth, which was before shared between the vulgar and the philosophers: the former being of the opinion, that *those things they immediately perceive are the real things;* and the latter, that *the things immediately perceived, are ideas which exist only in the mind.* Which two notions put together, do in effect constitute the substance of what I advance."[43]

Early on in his *Principles of Human Knowledge* Berkeley formulated both the problem and his answer in the following manner:

> The table that I write on, I say, exists, that is, I see and feel it; and if I were out of my study I should say that it existed, meaning thereby that if I was in my study I might perceive it, or that some other spirit actually does perceive it. . . . For as to what is said about the absolute existence of unthinking things without any relation to their being perceived, that seem perfectly unintelligible. Their *esse* is *percipi,* nor is it possible they should have any existence, out of the minds or thinking things which perceive them.[44]

With this statement we are introduced to Berkeley's central doctrine which is summed up in the Latin formula: *esse est aut percipi aut percipere* ("To be is either to be perceived or to perceive").[45] Berkeley came to this doctrine as the result of his analysis of what it means to say that something exists.

But if to exist is either to be perceived in some way (that is, by being seen, heard, touched, smelt or thought), what happens when we are not around to perceive things? Do they cease to exist? Berkeley has already anticipated the question in his example of the table in his study. The

table still exists, when he (or for that matter, another human being) is
not around to see it, because it is seen by some spirit. Ultimately the only
spirit capable of holding the universe in being by perceiving it simultaneously is God. In the *Third Dialogue between Hylas and Philonous* the question is asked and answered in the following way:

HYLAS. Not so fast, Philonous: you say you cannot conceive how
sensible things should exist without mind. Do you not?

PHILONOUS. I do.

HYLAS. Supposing you were annihilated, cannot you conceive it possible, that things perceivable by sense may still exist?

PHILONOUS. I can; but then it must be in another mind. When I
deny sensible things an existence out of mind, I do not mean my mind
in particular, but all minds. Now it is plain they have an existence
exterior to my mind, since I find them by experience to be independent of it. There is then some other mind wherein they exist, during
the intervals between the times of my perceiving them: as likewise
they did before my birth, and would do after my supposed annihilation. And as the same is true, with regard to all other finite created
spirits; it necessarily follows, there is an *omnipresent eternal Mind,*
which knows and comprehends all things, and exhibits them to our
view in such a manner, and according to such rules as he hath himself
ordained, and are by us termed the *Laws of Nature.*[46]

With this single bold master-stroke, Berkeley had redefined the concept
of matter and demonstrated the existence of God. If Berkeley's notion
of matter is accepted, the existence of God necessarily follows. Moreover,
Berkeley's view makes matter dependent upon being perceived by God,
and thus he solves the age-old problem of whether matter is eternal.

Berkeley's argument has been captured in more modern terms by
Ronald Knox in his pair of limericks about a student who was puzzled
by Berkeley's view of matter as dependent upon the perceiver.[47]

There was a young man who said, "God
Must think it exceedingly odd
   If he finds that this tree
   Continues to be
When there's no one about in the Quad."

REPLY

Dear Sir:
    Your astonishment's odd:
I am always about in the Quad.
    And that's why the tree
    Will continue to be,
Since observed by
        Yours faithfully,
    God.

From Berkeley's day to our own, Berkeley's teaching has been seen as
a denial of matter. A decade after his death the issue was the focus of
a memorable incident involving Dr. Samuel Johnson. One day after
visiting a church where they had spent some time in prayer, James
Boswell found himself discussing with Dr. Johnson the Bishop Berkeley's "ingenious sophistry to prove the non-existence of matter, and that
every thing in the universe is merely ideal." Boswell recalls how

> I observed, that though we are satisfied his doctrine is not true, it is
> impossible to refute it. I shall never forget the alacrity with which
> Johnson answered striking his foot with mighty force against a large
> stone, till it rebounded from it, "I refute it *thus*."[48]

In point of fact, Dr. Johnson's action was not a refutation of Berkeley's
claim, for on Berkeley's view the Doctor's act could be construed as an
action perceived by the Doctor's mind. Berkeley had already anticipated
such a move by his claim that "nothing properly but persons i.e. conscious things do exist, all other things are not so much existences as
manners of the existence of persons."[49] Dr. Johnson's response was
more an expression of his conviction that the bishop could not be right.

Today Berkeley is generally recognized as a brilliant philosopher who
proposed some ingenious answers to the questions of his time. Tribute
is given him for his insight into the part played by the perceiving subject
in the way we think of things. The nature of matter continues to be
debated by both scientists and philosophers. Bertrand Russell's definition of matter as "what satisfies the equations of physics"[50] is in some
respects a modification of the position of Berkeley. The continued pro-

duction of learned studies of Berkeley is testimony to the esteem in which his thought is held. Nevertheless, philosophers continue to discuss the possibility of hidden fallacies lurking in Berkeley's teaching. Granted that I with my finite mind can perceive objects, but how do I know that they are the same objects you perceive? How do we know that they are the same objects that God perceives? Berkeley stopped short of the view held by Malebranche that what we perceive are the ideas of God. He preferred to think that God willed that people should have these ideas, but they were not God's eternal perception of them.[51] But if so, do we not end up with something like a Platonic dichotomy between the world of pure ideas (God's) and the world of corporeal ideas (ours)?

To critics of empiricism, like E. L. Mascall, the line of thought begun by Locke and continued by Berkeley makes the objects of our perceptions hollow.[52] On this view, what we perceive with our senses is sense data. But what lies behind sense data? When we talk about reality are we talking about anything more than a series of hypothetical constructions that we place on our sense experience? The representative theory of knowledge seems to put us on a path which leads to solipsism, the view that the only knowledge possible is the knowledge of ourselves and our perceptions. There is no way of getting outside this. For we cannot stand outside ourselves and the data provided by our senses. We have no way of showing that things or people have any existence independent of our minds. On the other hand, however relentless the logic of this line of thought appears to be, no one actually appears to believe it. The solipsist who tries to convince anyone of the truth of his position implicitly denies the truth of what he professes to believe. Although Berkeley put forward his philosophy in the name of common sense, he was in fact repudiating the common sense distinction between the existence of objects and our perception of them.

Berkeley's view collapses objects into sensation. E. L. Mascall suggests that the problems posed by Berkeley's philosophy would have been avoided if sense datum had not been treated as the *direct* object of perception but as the *indirect* object through which the intellect perceives intelligible reality outside itself. Contrasting his own approach with that of the empiricists, Mascall writes:

Now against this assumption I wish to put forward the view, which has

a very reputable ancestry though its existence has been ignored by
most modern philosophers, that the non-sensory or intellectual element in perception does not consist simply of inference, but of apprehension. According to this view, there is (at any rate normally, for
we are not at the moment concerned with mystical experience) no
perception without sensation, but the sensible particular (the sense-
object or sense-datum or, as the scholastics would say, the sensible
species) is not the terminus of perception, not the *objectum quod* [object
which], to use another scholastic phrase, but the *objectum quo* [object
through which], through which the intellect grasps, in a direct but
mediate activity, the intelligible extramental reality, which is the *real
thing.*[53]

What Mascall is advocating here is a Thomistic form of empiricism
which leads to a critical realism that seeks to do justice to ordinary
experience, modern science and religion. It is a philosophy which avoids
the pitfalls of the skeptical empiricism propounded by David Hume.

14. THE SKEPTICAL EMPIRICISM OF HUME

Of all the British philosophers none has been more discussed than David Hume (1711-76).¹ Certainly no British philosopher has been more controversial. Whether he was truly great or whether he was (in the words of A. E. Taylor) merely a "very clever man"² is a question that continues to be argued over. The answers that people give to this question depend on their own philosophical standpoint. In life and in death Hume continued to provide puzzles. The standard view of Hume sees him as pushing empiricism to its logical limits and showing its inherent skeptical consequences. Yet a recent commentator rejects this on the grounds that Hume "hardly seems to have thought *about* the foundations of this view at all."³ Certainly Hume was committed to a form of empiricism, but he also had firsthand knowledge of Continental skepticism. In some respects Hume was an eighteenth-century Epicurean,⁴ who was broadly empirical, skeptical about human knowledge, but determined to enjoy life. His writings give the impression of an author at pains to present himself as a reasonable man. But they leave behind the feeling of arbitrariness. Having opened Pandora's box of skepticism in the interests of attacking religion and rival philosophies, Hume found that he could not close it. In the end, he had to fall back on "nature" and make a virtue out of the necessities of his skepticism.

To us in the twentieth century it may seem strange that one of the ablest philosophers of all times twice failed in his bids to obtain professorships. But this has to be seen against the background of the times. Hume may have been an engaging dinner guest and a convivial companion for an evening of argument. In appointing men of lesser talents to the chairs of philosophy at Edinburgh and Glasgow, the authorities knew well what they were doing. They had no desire to appoint a skeptic and an infidel to a teaching position in universities where Christianity was still the official religion. They were not the only ones who did not appreciate Hume. A contemporary observed that "the Corpulence of his whole Person was far better fitted to communicate the Idea of a Turtle-eating Alderman than of a refined Philosopher."[5] However, the same writer went on to excuse Hume's unphilosophical appearance, consoling himself with the thought that "the Oracles of old were often delivered by a Stick or a Stone." In the brief account of *My Own Life* that Hume compiled shortly before his death, Hume described himself as "a man of mild Dispositions, of Command of Temper, of an open, social, and cheerful Humour, capable of Attachment, but little susceptible of Enmity, and of great Moderation in all my Passions. Even my Love of literary Fame, my ruling Passion, never soured my humour, notwithstanding my frequent Disappointments."[6]

Hume did achieve literary fame, though not in his lifetime, for his philosophical writings. His early career was, to say the least, checkered. He entered the University of Edinburgh at the age of twelve, and left some two or three years later though without taking a degree. He tried studying law, but soon gave up the attempt. He tried his hand in business, but gave up after a few months. He then went to France, where he eventually settled in the small town of La Flèche in Anjou. It was at the Jesuit College at La Flèche that Descartes had received his education over a century earlier. La Flèche was still a center of Cartesianism. The philosophy and the theology of the Jesuit fathers, the ample library of the college and the leisure that Hume enjoyed at La Flèche, provided the stimulus and the occasion for Hume to work on his *Treatise of Human Nature*[7] which he published anonymously in 1739 on his return to England.

It was at La Flèche that Hume first propounded his argument against miracles while in conversation with a learned Jesuit about a miracle said to have happened at the college. The Jesuit replied that Hume's objections would apply equally to the Gospel miracles. To this Hume acknowledged that they did.[8] The argument was not as original as many have supposed.[9] The main points had already been aired in the course of the

Deist controversy. Hume had intended to include his argument on miracles in his *Treatise*. However, he was dissuaded from doing so on the grounds that its controversial character would damage his reputation. He eventually inserted it in his *Philosophical Essays Concerning Human Understanding* (1748) which were republished in 1758 under the title *An Enquiry Concerning Human Understanding.*[10]

In the meantime Hume's *Treatise of Human Nature,* which eventually became a classic work of philosophy, proved to be a disappointment to its author. As Hume observed in later life, "Never literary Attempt was more unfortunate than my Treatise of human nature. It fell *dead-born from the Press;* without reaching such distinction as even to excite a Murmur among the Zealots."[11] For a time Hume earned his living by serving as a tutor to the mentally unstable Marquess of Annandale. This was followed by a term as secretary to General St. Clair on a military expedition to Brittany and a diplomatic mission in Turin. During this period Hume donned the uniform of an officer which did little to enhance his appearance. Attributing the failure of the *Treatise* to its literary form, Hume resolved to recast the argument and publish it in the volume now known as *An Enquiry Concerning Human Understanding.* This time he included the essay on miracles. But Hume's second major work fared little better than the first, and the discussion of miracles, which was designed to attract attention, was overshadowed by Conyers Middleton's work. Hume observed: "On my return from Italy, I had the Mortification to find all England in a Ferment on account of Dr. Middletons Free Enquiry; while my Performance was entirely overlooked and neglected."[12] Hume's *Enquiry Concerning the Principles of Morals* (1751), which anticipated the utilitarianism and the modern subjective, emotive view of ethics, met with scarcely more success.

Hume never held any academic position. His appointment as keeper of the Avocates Library in Edinburgh gave him the leisure and resources to write his multi-volume *History of England* (1752-57) which, according to Bertrand Russell, was devoted to proving the superiority of the Tories to the Whigs and of Scotsmen to the English.[13] It was this work which established Hume's reputation as a man of letters and also helped him to secure financial independence. Hume toyed with the idea of devoting his remaining years to philosophy. Instead, he turned to diplomacy, serving as secretary to the British ambassador in Paris and even for a time as British *chargé d'affaires*. In Paris Hume became a familiar figure in the world of culture. On returning to London he brought with him Jean-Jacques Rousseau. The latter proved to be an unstable friend and put out stories that Hume had designs on his life. Hume's last public office was as undersecretary in the Northern Department. In his lifetime Hume the historian received more attention than Hume the philosophical writer. Hume published only one small philosophical piece in later life, and this was partly historical. Hume entitled it *The Natural History of Religion* (1757).[14] Somewhat earlier (probably before 1752) Hume composed his *Dialogues Concerning Natural Religion*.[15] However, Hume withheld publication and kept on revising them until the year of his death. They were published posthumously by his nephew in 1779.

Knowledge

Toward the end of his *Enquiry Concerning Human Understanding* Hume reviewed the options available in philosophy. He observed that "a Stoic or Epicurean displays principles, which may not only be durable, but which have an effect on conduct and behaviour. But a Pyrrhonian cannot expect, that his philosophy will have any constant influence on his mind: or if it had, that its influence would be beneficial to society."[16] The arguments of the Pyrrhonist might be momentarily impressive, but ultimately they were destructive of all thought and action. Hume himself preferred what he called a *"mitigated* skepticism," which was, in fact, a compromise between the destructive logic of Pyrrhonism and the need to come to terms with nature and everyday living.

Another species of *mitigated* scepticism which may be of advantage to mankind, and which may be the natural result of the Pyrrhonian doubts and scruples, is the limitation of our enquiries to such subjects as are best adapted to the narrow capacity of human understanding. The *imagination* of man is naturally sublime, delighted with whatever is remote and extraordinary, and running, without control, into the most distant parts of space and time in order to avoid the objects, which custom has rendered too familiar to it. A correct *Judgement* observes a contrary method, and avoiding all distant and high enquiries, confines itself to common life, and to such subjects as fall under daily practice and experience; leaving the more sublime topics to the embellishment of poets and orators, or to the arts of priests and politicians. To bring us to so salutary a determination, nothing can be more serviceable, than to be once thoroughly convinced of the force of the Pyrrhonian doubt, and of the impossibility, that anything, but the strong power of natural instinct, could free us from it.[17]

If there was a single uniting theme in Hume's philosophical writings, this was it. To Hume, philosophical decisions were "nothing but the reflections of common life, methodized and corrected." Philosophers, therefore, will "never be tempted to go beyond common life, so long as they consider the imperfection of those faculties which they employ, their narrow reach, and their inaccurate operations."[18] If there were inconsistencies in Hume's thinking, it did not matter. In fact, Hume was able to make a virtue out of them. The presence of inconsistencies might have given other thinkers pause to wonder whether their approach was right. Hume, however, met this problem in his own philosophy by behaving as if the problems that his thought posed merely served to show the limitations of the human mind and the general unwisdom of indulging in metaphysics.

What in fact Hume's approach did show was the inadequacy of the representative theory of knowledge as an account of how we know the world around us, ourselves and God. For Hume human knowledge is a series of constructs placed on sense data. Thus to speak of substance was not to speak of an existing entity, but only of phenomena of sense data.

The idea of a substance as well as that of a mode, is nothing but a collection of simple ideas, that are united by the imagination, and have a particular name assigned to them, by which we are able to recall, either to ourselves or others, that collection.[19]

We perceive the data of our senses, but we cannot know what, if anything, lies beyond them. Hume took this a step further in his celebrated discussion of causation. Hume observed that there is a certain necessity which appears to us when we observe that two and two make four and when we see that the angles of a triangle are equal to two right angles. But this necessity "lies only in the understanding, by which we consider and compare these ideas." In the same way the notion of cause and effect "belongs entirely to the soul, which considers the union of two or

more objects in all past instances." " 'Tis here that the real power of
causes is plac'd along with their connexion and necessity." Hume went
on to observe:

> I am sensible, that of all the paradoxes, which I have had, or shall
> hereafter have occasion to advance in the course of this treatise, the
> present one is the most violent, and that 'tis merely by dint of solid
> proof and reasoning I can ever hope it will have admission, and
> overcome the inveterate prejudices of mankind. Before we are recon-
> cil'd to this doctrine, how often must we repeat to ourselves, *that* the
> simple view of any two objects or actions, however related, can never
> give us any idea of power, or of a connexion betwixt them: *that* this
> idea arises from the repetition of their union: *that* the repetition nei-
> ther discovers nor causes any thing in the objects, but has an influ-
> ence only on the mind, by that customary transition it produces: *that*
> this customary transition is, therefore, the same with the power and
> necessity; which are consequently qualities of perceptions, not of ob-
> jects, and are internally felt by the soul, and not perceiv'd externally
> in bodies?[20]

Hume's discussion of cause and effect has frequently been taken to be
a denial of the whole idea of causation. Hume makes the point that all
that we can observe is objects and sequences. Simply by looking at an
object, we cannot see causes. To speak of one thing causing another
involves an inference that the mind makes from observing constant or
similar conjunctions of events. If Hume were really denying the notion
of causation and attributing it merely to habits of mind, he would indeed
be undermining the basis of science. On the other hand, there is reason
to think that Hume saw his work as the philosophical equivalent of the
experimental method employed by Newtonian physics and that he believed he was providing a philosophical basis for the modern understanding of reality.[21] What he achieved was not a denial of causation (to
which Hume himself freely appealed in dealing with the cosmological
argument and miracles) but an account of how we come to think of
causation. It was an account which shrank from drawing metaphysical
conclusions about the nature of reality by concentrating on what can be
perceived by the senses. In fact, Hume was unwittingly drawing attention
to the inadequacy of the representative theory of perception as an ac-

count of how we see and understand things. Hume chose to retain the theory and lament the limitations of human knowledge. An alternative course of action would have been to replace the theory and press beyond the impasse that it posed.

To Hume the soul or the self was equally elusive. In his *Treatise of Human Nature* Hume makes the following observation which is in effect a *reductio ad absurdum* of the whole idea of the soul or the self.

For my part, when I enter most intimately into what I call *myself*, I always stumble on some particular perception or other, of heat or cold, light or shade, love or hatred, pain or pleasure. I never can catch *myself* at any time without a perception, and never can observe anything but the perception. When my perceptions are remov'd for any time, as by sound sleep; so long am I insensible of *myself*, and may truly be said not to exist. And were all my perceptions remov'd by death, and cou'd I neither think, nor feel, nor see, nor love, nor hate after the dissolution of my body, I shou'd be entirely annihilated, nor do I conceive what is farther requisite to make me a perfect nonentity. If any one upon serious and unprejudic'd reflexion, thinks he has a different notion of *himself*, I must confess I can reason no longer with him. All I can allow him is, that he may be in the right as well as I, and that we are essentially different in this particular. He may, perhaps, perceive something simple and continu'd, which he calls *himself*; tho' I am certain there is no such principle in me.[22]

The argument runs parallel to Hume's discussion of substance and of cause and effect. What is perceived is a series of sense impressions. Since the self is not an item of sense data like a feeling or a sensation of pleasure or pain, Hume rhetorically casts doubt upon its existence. But again it is the viability of Hume's method that is really in question. The fallacious premise is the implicit claim that only sense data and the physical objects which give rise to sense data are real, though even the latter are suspect in view of the fact that the only things that can be known directly are sense data. On the other hand, the number of times which Hume uses the word *I* in the above quotation serve as a warning that all was not well with the theory. It might in fact alert us to some of the logical peculiarities of the self. It suggests that the self is not an object alongside other objects which may be known objectively in the way that physical objects are known. It suggests rather that the self is a *subject*, and that we become aware of the self *subjectively*. But this was not an issue which Hume chose to pursue. It was sufficient for his purposes to cast doubt upon a major tenet of Christian belief.

Miracles

Hume's celebrated discussion of miracles occurs in his *Enquiry Concerning Human Understanding*.[23] To some readers, including the distinguished Victorian editor of Hume's work, it has been a puzzle why Hume should choose to place a study of the miraculous in the context of a book ostensibly devoted to the human understanding.[24] But the issue remains a puzzle only so long as we fail to appreciate the role of miracles in the Christian apologetics of Hume's day. Miracles were seen as credentials of truth-claims. They served as supernatural attestation of the truth of certain claims. Catholics appealed to ongoing miracles in the Catholic church as proof of the truth of Catholic teaching. Protestants appealed to biblical miracles as divine attestation of biblical teaching. If Hume could undermine the credibility of the testimony to miracles, he was in effect undermining the basis for accepting the truth-claims of teaching which could not otherwise be verified.

It was an argument which he believed served equally well against Catholics and Protestants. Hume saw his argument as a defense against the "impertinent solicitations" of the bigots and the superstitious. "I flatter myself," he wrote, "that I have discovered an argument . . . which, if just, will with the wise and learned be an everlasting check to all kinds of superstitious delusion, and consequently, will be useful as long as the world endures. For so long, I presume, will the accounts of miracles and prodigies be found in all history, sacred and profane."[25] Hume believed that the argument could be applied equally well to prophecy which was also a form of miracles used as "proofs of any revelation."[26] Hume's argument was not that miracles were impossible (although at times he behaved as if he had established this point). Rather, his essay was a series of variations on the claim "that no testimony is sufficient to establish a miracle, unless the testimony be of such a kind, that its falsehood would be more miraculous, than the fact, which it endeavours to establish."[27]

Hume's argument fell into two main parts. The first was a general argument about the laws of nature (which, if it proved anything at all, proved the impossibility of miracles). The second consisted of four observations about the nature of testimony and what could be drawn from it. In neither part did Hume talk directly about the Gospel miracles, though his allusions were unmistakable. His argument was more of an attempt to undercut Christian truth claims by means of general reflections about the issues involved.

The first part of the argument contained a definition of miracles which was in effect a denial of their possibility.

A miracle is a violation of the laws of nature; and as a firm and unalterable experience has established these laws, the proof against a miracle, from the very nature of the fact, is as entire any argument from experience can possibly be imagined.[28]

Hume recognized that scientific laws were based on statistics. But in his view the statistics were against miracles. In fact, experience of life and events conforming to the laws of nature were so uniform that no testimony to the miraculous could shake his expectation of continuing conformity. Hume could find no fault in the reasoning of "the Indian prince" who refused to believe in ice, for all his past experience indicated that water could not become solid.[29] For in assessing testimony to events outside our experience we have to be guided by how the reported event bears "analogy" to the events of our "uniform experience."

In the second part of his argument Hume turned to the kind of testimony advanced in favor of the miraculous and asked what it amounted to. He made four main points. First, he described the kind of witness that he would deem credible.[30] Such a person must be of "such unquestioned good-sense, education, and learning, as to secure us against all delusion in themselves." On top of this they must be utterly beyond suspicion, and must have a great deal to lose in the event of their being detected of falsehood. Moreover, the attested facts must be performed "in such a public manner and in so celebrated part of the world, as to render detection unavoidable."

Secondly, Hume drew attention to the human fondness of gossip and exaggeration.[31] He asked half-rhetorically, "Do not the same passions, and others still stronger, incline the generality of mankind to believe and report, with the greatest vehemence and assurance, all religious miracles?"

Thirdly, Hume noted that miracles "are observed chiefly to abound among ignorant and barbarous nations; or if a civilized people has ever given admission to any of them, that people may be found to have received them from ignorant and barbarous ancestors, who transmitted them with that inviolable sanction and authority, which always attend received opinions."[32]

Fourthly, Hume argued that the miracles of rival religions cancel each other out.[33] By appealing to miracles as divine attestation of their truth-claims, different religions undermine themselves. For they cannot all be true. Hume concluded that this not only undermined the truth-claims, but that it cast serious doubt on the veracity of the miracle stories themselves.

This prompted Hume to embark on a series of reflections, all of which were designed to cast doubt on the veracity of the Gospel miracles, though without directly mentioning any particular Gospel story. Hume began by noting Tacitus's account of a healing attributed to the emperor Vespasian, exonerating the latter of all pretensions to dishonesty and inflated claims to divinity and praising the former as a writer "noted for candour and veracity, and withal, the greatest and most penetrating genius, perhaps, of all antiquity."[34] From here Hume proceeded to more recent times, noting the cures performed in Paris at the tomb of the Jansenist François de Pâris.[35] What is more, many of the alleged cures "were immediately proved upon the spot, before judges of unquestioned integrity, attested by witnesses of credit and distinction, in a learned age, and on the most eminent theatre that is now in the world." Moreover, the Jesuit opponents of the Jansenists were unable to refute the stories or detect fraud. In other words, the reports in question actually met the criteria specified by Hume, and were apparently free from the taint of suspicion attending other miracle stories. But in response to all this Hume doggedly refused to believe the accounts. In words which echoed the language of the Epistle to the Hebrews, Hume asked himself:

> And what have we to oppose to such a cloud of witnesses, but the absolute impossibility or miraculous nature of the events, which they relate? And this surely, in the eyes of all reasonable people, will alone be regarded as a sufficient refutation.[36]

Thus Hume asked and answered the question of the credibility of miracle stories in the same breath. He had, in effect, said that no amount of testimony, even though it met his criteria, would suffice to overthrow his conviction that miracles were impossible, because the laws of nature could not be violated. But Hume was not quite through with the subject. His crowning example was a hypothetical one which was designed to discredit the resurrection accounts in the Gospels. It did so by offering a conjectured parallel which was ostensibly better attested.

He supposed that all historians were agreed that Queen Elizabeth I had died and that her death was publicly ascertained and attested. Then after a month's internment, she reappeared, resumed the throne of England and ruled for three years. Even assuming that all this was well attested, Hume would reply that "the knavery and folly of men are such common phenomena, that I should rather believe the most extraordinary events to arise from their concurrence, than admit so signal a violation of the laws of nature."[37]

It remained for Hume to draw the conclusion that "our most holy religion is founded on *Faith*, not on reason; and it is a sure method of exposing it to put it to such a trial as it is, by no means, fitted to endure."[38] If the first half of this sentence sounded like an endorsement of piety, the second half removes any doubt about Hume's heavy irony. Hume went on to add that the same argument applied equally well to prophecy, which was really a form of miracle. He thus removed the other pillar of traditional apologetic argument in support of Christian truth-claims. Hume's parting shot was a further ironic salvo which was aimed at the final destruction of apologetic claims that Christian faith could be established rationally by appealing to history.

> Upon the whole, we may conclude, that the *Christian religion* not only was at first attended with miracles, but even at this day cannot be believed by any reasonable person without one. Mere reason is insufficient to convince us to its veracity. And whoever is moved by *Faith* to assent to it, is conscious of a continued miracle in his own person, which subverts all the principles of his understanding, and gives him a determination to believe what is most contrary to custom and experience.[39]

If Hume's discussion of miracles was temporarily obscured by that of

Conyers Middleton, it eventually established itself as the classic attack.. Even though many of Hume's points had already been aired by Spinoza and the English Deists, Hume's essay came to be seen as fundamental, not least because Hume addressed the underlying issues and criteria rather than particular phenomena. In due course replies to Hume appeared in print. Among the ablest was George Campbell's *Dissertation on Miracles* (1762), which was an expanded version of a sermon preached before the synod of the Presbyterian Church. Campbell was a fellow Scot, and a friend of Thomas Reid and other members of the Scottish Common Sense school of philosophy. John Wesley thought highly of Campbell's work, and Hume himself acknowledged Campbell to be "certainly a very ingenious man, tho a little too zealous for a philosopher."[40]

If we stand back from Hume's essay and ask what he has actually accomplished, it is clear that Hume has not proved that miracles could not happen. His aim was to show that in the light of the modern scientific understanding of the world and common experience, miracle stories were so improbable as to be unworthy of rational credence. As such, they could not serve to establish religious truth-claims. The strength of Hume's argument lies in its plausibility. Miracles are indeed contrary to the experience of most educated Westerners. What Hume says about miracles being testified to by the less educated, about them occurring in obscure places and about human fondness for gossip and exaggeration, applies to a great many miracle stories. And yet, as a total argument, Hume's essay is seriously flawed. A. E. Taylor was surely right when he observed that "on the face of it, there would seem to be something amiss with reasoning which proceeds from the principle that 'a wise man proportions his belief to the evidence' to the conclusion that in a vast, if not too well defined, field, the 'wise man' will simply refuse to 'consider the evidence' at all."[41] Moreover, there is a certain incongruity in Hume's appeal to the laws of nature in order to reject miracles in view of his previous reservations on the subject of cause and effect. On Hume's premises, Taylor notes, "Properly speaking, there are no laws of nature to be violated, but there are habits of expectation which any of us, as a fact, finds himself unable to break."[42]

Close examination of Hume's observations about the nature of testimony shows that none of the points that he makes could be extended to serve as a universal criterion in historical research. His demand that events must be witnessed by educated witnesses who had a great deal to lose in the event of a possible falsehood being detected, coupled with his insistence that the event should occur in "a celebrated part of the world" would rule out much of history prior to the Renaissance outside certain urban centers of culture. Historians cannot confine their interests and researches merely to those of similar education and outlook as themselves. Hume's point fails to distinguish between the education and social standing of a witness and the witness' veracity. The two are not necessarily connected. Hume's second observation about the nature of testimony is also too wholesale. It assumes that witnesses to miracles are all subject to the love of exaggeration and enlarging upon the truth. A more precise historical method would have sought to determine what kind of people the witnesses are. If it could be shown that the witnesses were initially inclined to doubt, their testimony to the alleged event is all the more impressive.

Hume's third point is also too imprecise to be capable of general application. His claim that miracles "are observed chiefly to abound among the ignorant and barbarous nations" and that the civilized people who admit them generally have no direct experience of them is clearly barbed. It can be taken to apply to the educated Christians of Hume's day who, though never having experienced miracles for themselves, gave credence to them on the basis of Christian tradition. The latter could take the form of reports of miracles performed elsewhere in the church (as in Catholic tradition) or of the Gospel stories themselves, which were originally transmitted by the disciples in Galilee who approximated to Hume's description.

The plausibility of Hume's fourth and final point depends upon a number of unstated assumptions. To begin with, it assumes that different religions base their truth-claims on miracles. But in point of fact, many of them do not. Although in traditional Christian apologetics, as practiced by John Locke and others, the Gospel miracles are thought to function in this way, it is far from clear that this is their function in the New Testament.[43] Moreover, for Hume's argument to work, it is not enough to say that different religions have miracles and therefore they cannot all be true. One would have to put forward similar miracles in support of similar, but conflicting, truth-claims in order to reach Hume's desired conclusion. For example, Christianity regards the resurrection of Jesus as a foundational truth. If another religion were to produce a counter example of its messiah being similarly raised after a similar death, Hume's point would have substance. The advocates of the rival religions would then be obligated to examine the veracity of their resurrection beliefs and evaluate the related truth-claims accordingly. But in point of fact, such a conflict has not actually arisen. The most readily accessible evidence about conflicting miracles has to do with healings which are attested among rival religious groups. Even here Hume's argument is less conclusive than it might appear. For it is not part of the Christian message to claim that God's goodness is limited to those who acknowledge him, or that healing can take place only through Christian agents. Just as natural healing may take place outside a specific religious context, it is no less conceivable that supernatural healing could also take place in different religious contexts. As such it might not be related directly to particular truth-claims, but rather may be a manifestation of divine goodness at large.[44]

A further aspect of Hume's discussion is the fact that he confines his attention to verbal testimony and omits other kinds of evidence such as changed behavior and attitudes. He thus neglects an important part of the Christian evidence for the resurrection of Jesus, which turns on the changed attitude of the disciples after the death of Jesus. In view of the condemnation of Jesus, the emergence of the church is difficult to conceive, unless something had happened to cause the first Christians to risk life and limb by proclaiming the resurrection of Jesus in defiance of the religious and civil authorities.

Not the least questionable part of Hume's discussion is his concept of miracle. The idea of miracles as *violations* of the laws of nature seems at first sight to be acceptable. After all, if miracles were not in some sense different from ordinary events, there would be no reason to distinguish them from the latter. For an event to qualify as a miracle there must be grounds for thinking that it had actually happened and that it was different from normal events. Miracles can qualify as miracles only if they stand out from the regularities of normal experience. But the term *violation* suggests an element of randomness and arbitrariness that is misleading. In a footnote Hume himself put forth a second definition when he wrote: "A miracle may be accurately defined, *a transgression of a law of nature by a particular volition of the Deity, or by the interposition of some invisible agent.*"[45] This second definition still has the possible connotation of arbitrariness, but in fact it contains an important new element which is necessary for such an event to take place. The word *transgression* is itself ambiguous. On the one hand, it could imply arbitrary suspension of natural causes. On the other hand, it could also imply that the agent in question overlooked a particular law by invoking some other (known or unknown) law, force or power, to achieve a particular end. What Hume has given here is a definition which is not a *reductio ad absurdum* of the idea of miracles but an indication of the conditions that would apply if a miracle were to happen!

Perhaps the real significance of Hume's discussion lies in the way he draws attention to the importance of the considerations that we bring to the assessment of issues. If we presuppose that our everyday experience is normative and if we reflect on the fact that the source of our knowledge of the Gospel miracles is limited to at most four books, perhaps drawing material from each other, it would be logical to go along with Hume and adopt a skeptical attitude. On the other hand, there are other factors to be taken into consideration which change the dynamics of the argument. If we have reason to think of God as a God of compassion who is concerned not only with the natural order but also with history, the situation is changed. As Richard Swinburne has observed, if such considerations have any weight:

> we would need only slender historical evidence of certain miracles to have reasonable grounds to believe in their occurrence, just as we need only slender historical evidence to have reasonable grounds for belief in the occurrence of events whose occurrence is rendered probable by natural laws. We take natural laws to show the improbability of violations thereof because they are well-established parts of our overall view of how the world works. But if they are relevant for this reason, then so is any other part of our overall view of how the world works. And if from our study of its operation we conclude that we have evidence for the existence of a God of such a character as to be liable to intervene in the natural order under certain circumstances, the

overall world-view gives not a high prior improbability, but a high prior probability to the occurrence of miracles under those circumstances.[46]

Strictly speaking, Hume had not ruled out the possibility of miracles. Rather, he had formulated a series of difficulties which he placed in the path of anyone who appealed to miracles in order to convince someone else of the truth of his religious beliefs. In short, Hume was extending to religion the same skepticism that he applied to other systems of thought. Hume applied this skepticism both to particular forms of religion and to philosophical arguments about God. Toward the end of his *Enquiry Concerning Human Understanding* Hume compared the cosmological and teleological arguments with a scientific hypothesis. They were defective, not least because (unlike a valid scientific hypothesis) they could not yield useful results.

> While we argue from the course of nature, and infer a particular intelligent cause, which first bestowed, and still preserves order in the universe, we embrace a principle, which is both uncertain and useless. It is uncertain; because the subject lies entirely beyond the reach of human experience. It is useless; because our knowledge of this cause being derived entirely from the course of nature, we can never, according to the rules of just reasoning, return back from the cause with any new inference, or making additions to the common and experienced course of nature, establish any new principles of conduct and behaviour.[47]

A few pages later Hume put the matter more succinctly: "I much doubt whether it be possible for a cause to be known only by its effect."[48] Even if we posit a divine, creative mind, nothing more can be said.

The Existence of God

The theme of causes and effects continued to play a part in Hume's reflections on religion in the writings of his later years. Despite his reservations on the subject, Hume still found it useful to appeal to the notion to defend himself against religion. Large parts of Hume's *History of England* were concerned with the moral and political effects of religion. Hume's brief study of *The Natural History of Religion* addressed the question of the causes and effects of religion on a broad canvas. In attacking the view that the original religion of humankind was a rational, moral monotheism, Hume was undermining the foundations of Deism and also a belief that many Christians attributed to the book of Genesis. The work was presented as a kind of study in religious anthropology, although Hume was no more of an anthropologist than his adversaries. What he did was suggest a kind of evolutionary hypothesis. By dint of drawing on his knowledge of the classics, Hume argued that the gods and goddesses of polytheism (who were simply magnified human beings) were progressively credited with different attributes until they were eventually rolled into one and credited with fidelity. Side by side with this process went a growth in fanaticism. The more unique God became, the more bigoted were his devotees (whether Mohammedan or Christian). Religion presented an enigma from which philosophy provided an escape, as Hume's closing remarks suggest.

What so pure as some of the morals, included in some theological systems? What so corrupt as some of the practices, to which these systems give rise?

The comfortable views, exhibited by the belief of futurity, are ravishing and delightful. But how quickly vanish on the appearance of its terrors, which keep a more firm and durable possession of the human mind?

The whole is a riddle, an aenigma, an inexplicable mystery. Doubt, uncertainty, suspence of judgment appear the only result of our most accurate scrutiny, concerning this subject. But such is the frailty of human reason, and such the irresistible contagion of opinion, that even this deliberate doubt could scarcely be upheld; did we not enlarge our view, and opposing one species of superstition to another, set them a quarrelling; while we ourselves, during their fury and contention, happily make our escape into the calm, though obscure, regions of philosophy.[49]

Hume's *Dialogues Concerning Natural Religion* were a kind of modern version of Cicero's dialogues *On the Nature of the Gods*.[50] This is indicated not only by the form of the work, but also by its theme. Like Cicero, Hume professed to be concerned not with the existence of God but with "the *nature* of the divine Being; his attributes, his decrees, his plan of providence."[51] Moreover, Hume gave his protagonists classical names.

Philo was the name of the skeptical founder of the New Academy, the teacher of Cicero and also of Cotta, the skeptic in Cicero's work. Cleanthes was the successor of Zeno as head of the Stoic school, and in Cicero's work he is the teacher of Balbus, the representative of Stoicism. In Hume's work Cleanthes is the representative of accurate philosophy, Philo of "careless scepticism," and Demea of "rigid inflexible orthodoxy."[52]

There has been much discussion as to what the three protagonists represent and who (if any) represents Hume himself. The problem is not settled by the narrator's conclusion "that PHILO'S principles are more probable than DEMA'S; but that those of CLEANTHES approach still nearer the truth."[53] For Hume's urbane style and dramatic necessities regularly disguised his intentions. In the end, the discerning reader is left to judge who gets the best of the argument. Underneath the classical disguises we may detect Demea as the spokesman for the kind of orthodox theology advocated by Samuel Clarke, Cleanthes as a philosophically minded believer in the mold of Bishop Butler and Philo as the reasonable skeptic modelled on Hume himself.[54]

Hume's *Dialogues* elaborated the skeptical views concerning the design argument for the existence of God which Hume had already put forward in his *Enquiry Concerning Human Understanding*. All the partners in the dialogue take it for granted that God exists, but as the conversation proceeds the impression is given that nothing much may be said beyond that. Moreover, such minimal belief makes no practical difference to human conduct. Nor does it help to give human beings any clear ideas about their destiny. Of the three protagonists Demea is presented as having the weakest case and loosest grip on philosophical argument. Cleanthes puts up a good case. But by allowing Cleanthes to lapse into inconsistency and by not putting into his mouth replies to Philo's strongest arguments, Hume gives the impression that Philo's skepticism is in the end unanswerable.[55] As the *Dialogues* wend their way to their conclusion, Cleanthes is made to say that Philo:

> from the beginning, has been amusing himself at both our expence; and it must be confessed, that the injudicious reasoning of our vulgar theology has given him but too just a handle of ridicule. The total infirmity of human reason, the absolute incomprehensibility of the

divine nature, the great and universal misery and still greater wickedness of men; these are strange topics surely to be so fondly cherished
by orthodox divines and doctors.[56]
This admission represents a retreat from Cleanthes' earlier position
which compared the world with "one great machine, subdivided into an
infinite number of lesser machines."

All these various machines, and even their most minute parts, are
adjusted to each other with an accuracy, which ravishes into admiration all men, who have ever contemplated them. The curious adapting
of means to ends, throughout all nature, resembles exactly, though it
much exceeds, the productions of human contrivance; of human design, thought, wisdom, and intelligence. Since therefore the effects
resemble each other, we are led to infer, by all the rules of analogy,
that the causes also resemble; and that the Author of nature is somewhat similar to the mind of man; though possessed of much larger
faculties, proportioned to the grandeur of the work, which he has
executed. By this argument *a posteriori*, and by this argument alone,
we do prove at once the existence of a Deity, and his similarity to
human mind and intelligence.[57]

Between these two statements Hume gives a number of objections which
anticipate the debates of modern times. The argument is said to be at
best an imperfect *analogy*.[58] Even so, Philo is quick to show the limitations of the analogy. "A great number of men join in building a house
or ship, in raising a city, in framing a commonwealth: Why may not
several Deities combine in contriving and framing a world?"[59] However,
the world looks less like something designed and finished, like a machine or a house, than something living like an animal or vegetable.
Philo draws the distinction between things which proceed from nature
and things which "arise from reason and contrivance."

A tree bestows order and organization on that tree which springs from
it, without knowing the order: an animal, in the same manner, on its
offspring: a bird, on its nest: And instances of this kind are even more
frequent in the world, than those of order, which arise from reason
and contrivance. To say that all this order in animals and vegetables
proceeds ultimately from design is begging the question; nor can that
great point be ascertained otherwise than by proving *a priori*, both

that order is, from its nature, inseparably attached to thought, and that
it can never, of itself, or from original unknown principles, belong to
matter.[60]

Hume anticipated evolution by suggesting that the world could have
attained its present form through "innumerable revolutions" which produced "at last some forms, whose parts and organs are so adjusted as to
support the forms amidst a continued succession of matter."[61] The design argument (claims Philo) contains a flawed *anthropomorphism*.

> In all instances which we have ever seen, ideas are copied from real
> objects, and are ectypal, not archetypal, to express myself in learned
> terms: You reverse this order, and give thought the precedence. In all
> instances which we have ever seen, thought has no influence upon
> matter, except where that matter is so conjoined with it, as to have an
> equal reciprocal influence upon it.[62]

We may note in passing that for Hume ideas are constructs which the
human mind places on experience. Hume did not deny that there were
analogies between the works of nature and human artifacts. His point
was that the analogies were too weak and remote to be pressed. He went
on to insist that "necessary existence" is a concept which has no meaning, and to suggest the absurdity of inquiring for "a general cause or first
Author" in tracing "an eternal succession of objects."[63] The problem is
further compounded by the existence of evil. Philo maintains that the
old questions of Epicurus about God remain unanswered: "Is he willing
to prevent evil, but not able? then he is impotent. Is he able, but not
willing? then is malevolent. Is he both able and willing? whence then
is evil?"[64]

In the *Dialogues* Philo is given the last word. Once more he allows that
natural theology may point us in the direction of a cause or causes of
the universe which may bear some remote analogy to human intelligence, but he denies that we can press further and that this conclusion
yields any useful truth.

> If the whole of natural theology, as some people seem to maintain,
> resolves itself into one simple, though somewhat ambiguous, at least
> undefined proposition, *that the cause or causes of order in the universe*
> *probably bear some remote analogy to human intelligence:* If this proposi-
> tion be not capable of extension, variation, or more particular expli-

cation: If it afford no inference that affects human life, or can be the source of any action or forbearance: And if the analogy, imperfect as it is, can be carried no farther than to the human intelligence; and cannot be transferred, with any appearance of probability, to the other qualities of the mind: If this really be the case, what can the most inquisitive, contemplative, and religious man do more than give a plain, philosophical assent to the proposition, as often as it occurs; and believe that the arguments, on which it is established, exceed the objections which lie against it?[65]

Such thoughts may be entertained as items of dogmatic belief, but it is impossible to "erect a complete system of theology by the mere help of philosophy." Indeed, "to be a philosophical sceptic is, in a man of letters, the first and most essential step towards being a sound, believing Christian."[66] This concluding advice can only be understood ironically. For having (at least to his own satisfaction) demolished natural theology and having elsewhere undermined the pillars of the traditional apologetic argument for the truth claims of revelation, Hume was confident that theology could safely be relegated to an intellectual limbo.

Taken together, Hume's various arguments and observations on religion combine to form a strategic defense against certainty and dogmatism in religion. They do not rule out the feasibility of belief, but raise a series of questions about the status and logic of belief and commitment. Hume's discussion of miracles came to be regarded as the landmark critique of their plausibility. His treatment of teleology highlighted the difficulties of attempting a demonstrative proof of God on the basis of observation of the world (though it did not rule out the kind of approach we noted in discussing Thomas Aquinas[67]). Hume's discussion of natural religion raised serious questions against the eighteenth-century idea of the noble savage. Religion in general did not arise from a lofty quest for truth, beauty and goodness. Rather, it was the reverse.

Those who undertake the most criminal and most dangerous enterprizes are commonly the most superstitious; as an ancient historian remarks. . . . To which we may add, that, after the commission of crimes, there arise remorses and secret horrors, which give no rest to the mind, but make it have recourse to religious rites and ceremonies, as expiations of its offences.[68]

During Hume's lifetime and in the years that followed his death, there has been no lack of those who have offered replies. In the next chapter we shall look at the important criticism of Hume's contemporary Thomas Reid, who challenged Hume's basic approach to knowledge. In the second volume of this book we shall note further replies and attempts to establish foundations for belief by erecting a comprehensive world view on the basis of an indubitable foundation. But as we shall see in the discussion of Thomas Reid and in the concluding chapter of the present book, foundationalism presents serious difficulties.[69] Moreover, these problems do not belong exclusively to the realm of religious belief; they also apply to schemes of thought and world views generally. If there is anything that can be learned from the study of Hume, it is the difficulty of trying to develop a philosophy by starting with some item of alleged empirical evidence. For what we call *evidence* is rarely some self-evident fact, but something which is interpreted within a web of beliefs. This point raises the issue of the appropriate methods and approach in philosophy and theology. It is a question to which we shall return when we review modern trends in philosophy and theology in the second volume of this study.

Hume's Achievement

What had Hume achieved? J. C. A. Gaskin thinks it inaccurate to apply to Hume such conventional ascriptions as "atheist," "agnostic," "materialist" and even "skeptic," for none of these catch the complexity and range of his thought.[70] Instead, Gaskin prefers to speak of Hume's "attenuated deism." Perhaps it would be no less accurate to call Hume an eighteenth-century Epicurean.[71] Not only did Hume speak of Epicurus in admiring terms. Like Epicurus, he conceded (at least hypothetically) the existence of a god or gods, but insisted that popular conceptions were mistaken. The gods did not interfere with the affairs of this world, and death was the end of human existence. In a conversation with James Boswell—Dr. Johnson's famous biographer[72]—shortly before his death, Hume professed that he "never had entertained any belief in Religion since he began to read Locke and Clarke." If there was such a thing as immortality, it must be "general." But the idea of living forever was "a most unreasonable fancy." Hume himself expected "Annihilation."

Earlier on in his career Hume found refuge from pessimism and skepticism in a manner not unlike the ancient Epicureans.

> Most fortunately it happens, that since reason is incapable of dispelling these clouds, nature herself suffices to that purpose, and cures me of this philosophical melancholy and delirium, either by relaxing this bent of mind, or by some avocation, and lively impression of my senses, which obliterate all these chimeras. I dine, I play a game of back-gammon, I converse, and am merry with my friends; and when after three or four hours' amusement, I wou'd return to these speculations, they appear so cold, and strain'd, and ridiculous, that I cannot find in my heart to enter into them any farther.[73]

To his dying day Hume did not radically depart from this *credo*, which permitted religious and philosophical skepticism to be mitigated by the activities and pleasures of everyday living. Over the years Hume's tone mellowed. Although the suave irony of the *Dialogues* replaced the caustic rhetoric of the *Enquiry*, the message remained the same. Hume concluded his *Enquiry Concerning Human Understanding* by consigning theology to the realm of faith and revelation and by pronouncing morals to be matters of "taste and sentiment." Real knowledge was limited to mathematics and the experimental sciences.

> When we run over libraries, persuaded of these principles, what havoc must we make? If we take in our hand any volume; of divinity or school metaphysics, for instance; let us ask, *Does it contain any abstract reasoning concerning quantity or number?* No. *Does it contain any experimental reasoning concerning matter of fact and existence?* No. Commit it then to the flames: for it can contain nothing but sophistry and illusion.[74]

In the 1930s the youthful A. J. Ayer saw in this declaration an anticipation of the program of Logical Positivism.[75] Bertrand Russell was less sanguine about Hume's views. "Hume's philosophy," he observed, "whether true or false represents the bankruptcy of eighteenth-century reasonableness."[76] More recently Roger Scruton has suggested that the root trouble lies in Hume's method. "Hume finds himself trapped within the sphere of his own experience without even the assurance of a self to whom that experience belongs. The loss of the object seems to bring the loss of the subject in its train."[77] Hume himself wryly observed that

15. SCOTTISH COMMON SENSE AND EARLY AMERICAN PHILOSOPHY

Scottish Common Sense and early American philosophy are two separate but related themes. Both belong roughly to the same time-frame, the eighteenth century. Both were concerned with issues raised by British empiricism. Although early American philosophy was concerned with more than that, it was in the course of time deeply affected by the thinking of the Scottish Common Sense School of philosophy.

Thomas Reid and the Scottish Common Sense School

Thomas Reid (1710-96) is one of the neglected figures in the history of philosophy.[1] He was perhaps responsible for the tradition which saw the history of eighteenth-century philosophy in terms of Berkeley undermining Locke, and of Hume undermining Berkeley.[2] Reid and his successors were scornfully dismissed by Kant for what Kant perceived to be their failure to understand Hume and their naive faith in common sense.[3] Kant's verdict virtually ensured that Reid and the Scottish Common Sense Philosophy could safely be consigned to oblivion on the continent of Europe. It is only relatively recently that philosophers have come to see Reid as an important thinker in his own right and as a philosopher whose methods were akin to those of modern analysis and who might have something to say to the twentieth-century world.

Thomas Reid was a contemporary of David Hume, whom he outlived by nearly twenty years. Both were born in Scotland, and both served for a time as librarians. But unlike Hume, Reid succeeded in his ambition

to become a professional philosopher. For fourteen years Reid served
as a parish minister, and it was during this period that he was aroused
by his study of Hume's *Treatise of Human Nature*. In 1751 he was elected
to the chair of philosophy at Aberdeen, where he remained until 1764.
In that year he succeeded Adam Smith as professor of moral philosophy
at Glasgow. The same year marked the publication of his first book, *An
Inquiry into the Human Mind on the Principles of Common Sense*. This theme
was further elaborated by Reid's *Essays on the Intellectual Powers of Man*
(1785). The *Essays* were a major critique of the empiricist theory of
knowledge. Reid's last major work was his *Essays on the Active Powers of
Man* (1788). Here the object of his attack was the subjective approach to
ethics advocated by Hutcheson and Hume.

Early on in his career, Reid had been a convinced follower of Berkeley, believing that "all the objects of my knowledge are ideas in my own
mind."[4] But the more he read Hume and the more he thought about the
skeptical consequences of this view, the more he came to question it.
Eventually he came to reject the whole tradition of Locke, Berkeley and
Hume. Their theory of ideas which underlays this tradition was not
supported by evidence, and in fact rested upon a confusion. Moreover,
it did not perform the function for which it was introduced, since it left
the question about the veracity of perception unanswerable in principle.
Hume's *Treatise* had "drowned all in one universal deluge."[5] The root
error was the *hypothesis*

> That nothing is perceived but what is in the mind which perceived
> it: That we do not really perceive things that are external, but only
> certain images and pictures of them imprinted upon the mind, which
> are called *impressions and ideas*.[6]

If this were so one could not "infer the existence of anything else." Reid
therefore devoted his energies to refuting this hypothesis which "over-
turns all philosophy, all religion and virtue, and all common sense."

Reid argued that it was an elementary confusion to mistake the means
of perception for the thing perceived. Moreover, perception is a personal
activity which posits a personal subject. Reid's basic approach and style
of arguing can be seen if we place together two extracts. The first of the
extracts comes from Reid's *Inquiry into the Human Mind*.

In this passage Reid gives an analysis of everyday language, and asks what is the difference between two types of statements, "I feel a pain" and "I see a tree." His answer is that grammatically they look alike; both have a subject, an active verb and an object. But the verb and its object function differently in the two statements. In the first sentence the distinction between the act and the object is not real but grammatical, whereas in the second sentence it is not only grammatical but real. From his analysis of different kinds of sensation and perception Reid concludes that in cases of perception, the mind and its object are not only distinguishable but unlike in their natures. In short, this means that Berkeley's and Hume's analysis of perception is confused and misleading.

The most simple operations of the mind, admit not of a logical definition: all we can do is to describe them, so as to lead those who are conscious of them in themselves, to attend to them, and reflect upon them; and it is often very difficult to describe them so as to answer this intention.

The same mode of expression is used to denote sensation and perception; and, therefore, we are apt to look upon them as things of the same nature. Thus, *I feel a pain; I see a tree:* the first denoteth a sensation, the last a perception. The grammatical analysis of both expressions is the same: for both consist of an active verb and an object. But, if we attend to the things signified by these expressions, we shall find that, in the first, the distinction between the act and the object is not real but grammatical; in the second, the distinction is not only grammatical but real.

The form of the expression, *I feel pain,* might seem to imply that the feeling is something distinct from the pain felt; yet, in reality, there is no distinction. As *thinking a thought* is an expression which could signify no more than thinking, so *feeling a pain* signifies no more than *being pained.* What we have said of pain is applicable to every other mere sensation. It is difficult to give instances, very few of our sensations having names; and, where they have, the name being common to the sensation, and to something else which is associated with it. But, when we attend to the sensation by itself, and separate it from other things which are conjoined with it in the imagination, it appears to be something which can have no existence but in a sentient mind, no distinction from the act of the mind by which it is felt.

Perception, as we here understand it, hath always an object distinct from the act by which it is perceived; an object which may exist whether it be perceived or not. I perceive a tree that grows before my window; there is here an object which is perceived, and an act of the mind by which it is perceived; and these two are not only distinguishable, but they are extremely unlike in their natures.[7]

The second extract comes from Reid's *Essays on the Intellectual Powers of Man*. Here again Reid examines instances of perception, and implies that the empiricists' analysis of the act of perception involves confusing different kinds of actions, which in common experience people habitually distinguish.

Perception must be the act of some being that perceives. The eye is not that which sees; it is only the organ by which we see. The ear is not that which hears, but the organ by which we hear; and so of the rest.

A man cannot see the satellites of Jupiter but by a telescope. Does he conclude from this, that it is the telescope that sees those stars? By no means—such a conclusion would be absurd. It is no less absurd to conclude that it is the eye that sees, or the ear that hears. The telescope is an artificial organ of sight, but it sees not. The eye is a natural organ of sight, by which we see; but the natural organ sees as little as the artificial.

If anything more were necessary to be said on a point so evident, we might observe that, if the faculty of seeing were in the eye, that of hearing in the ear, and so of the other senses, the necessary consequence of this would be, that the thinking principle, which I call myself, is not one, but many. But this is contrary to the irresistible conviction of every man. When I say, I see, I hear, I feel, I remember, this implies that it is one and the same self that performs all these operations; and, as it would be absurd to say that my memory, another man's imagination, and a third man's reason, may make one individual intelligent being, it would be equally absurd to say that one piece of matter seeing, another hearing, and a third feeling, may make one and the same percipient being.[8]

In making this point about perception Reid did not claim to be propounding some new philosophical doctrine. He saw himself as standing in a long line of philosophers, stretching back to Cicero and beyond, who took a similar view.[9] His approach was in a broad sense inductive.[10] But this does not mean that all knowledge was inferential. In fact, there are many instances when knowledge is not inferential. Much of our everyday perception is of this kind. Reid observed: "When I hear a certain sound, I conclude immediately, without reasoning, that a coach passes by. There are no premises from which this conclusion is inferred by any rules of logic. It is the effect of a principle of our nature, common to us with the brutes."[11] Sensations are a mode of sensing. The function of sensation is to "suggest" the reality that has produced it. Sensations are "signs" of things signified.[12]

This should not be taken to mean that Reid was committed to a naive belief that there was a corresponding object to every sensation. In fact, his writings display careful analysis of what constitutes fallacies and pseudo-problems. Nor was Reid an apologist for common sense as a kind of oracle of truth. Reid's philosophy was an alternative to skeptical empiricism which he believed to be fundamentally flawed. In place of the empiricists' representative view of perception, Reid proposed a view which may be called "indirect realism,"[13] which sought to give an account of the function of the senses in suggesting the reality behind sensation.

As Reid saw it, David Hume was an "ingenious author" who, following the principles of Locke, "hath built a system of scepticism which leaves no ground to believe any one thing rather than its contrary."[14] Hume's position was destructive not only of Christian faith, but also of science and of common prudence. Underlying Hume's skepticism was the apparently reasonable and enlightened claim that we are "to admit nothing but what can be proved by reasoning." Reid's immediate response was to retort, that if this be so, "then we must be sceptics indeed, and believe nothing at all."[15] However, he wryly observed that Hume himself could not keep to this principle either in his daily life or in his philosophy. Nor, for that matter, can any skeptic. Over and over again, Reid pointed out that men could not live by skepticism alone. "If a man pretends to be a skeptic with regard to the informations of sense, and yet prudently keeps out of harm's way as other men do, he must excuse my suspicion, that either he acts the hypocrite, or imposes upon himself."[16]

Reid's point is more than a palpable hit in a verbal fencing match. It raises the question of what constitutes *justified belief*, and it is this question which (as Nicholas Wolterstorff has cogently argued) constitutes the central concern in Reid's writings.[17] Since rationality consists in being *intellectually* justified in one's belief, Reid's answer to skepticism consists in analysis of the nature of rationality. Basic here is what Wolterstorff calls *belief dispositions*, by which he means that at any point in our lives we each have a variety of inclinations, propensities or dispositions to believe certain things.[18] Our beliefs are to be accounted for by the triggering off of one or other disposition. Reid himself spoke of "the principles of common sense" and "the first principles of natural philosophy." Such principles are used and presupposed by all normal human beings in their ordinary thinking and living, even though they might be unable to give a reason for them.[19]

Reid compared these principles with the "common principles or axioms" of Sir Isaac Newton, "the greatest of natural philosophers," and contrasted them with the axioms of mathematics.

> It may, however, be observed that the first principles of natural philosophy are of a quite different nature from mathematical axioms: they have not the same kind of evidence, nor are they necessary truths, as mathematical axioms are. They are such as these: That similar effects proceed from the same or similar causes; That we ought to admit of no other causes or natural effects, but such as are true, and sufficient to account for the effects. These are principles which, though they have not the same kind of evidence that mathematical axioms have; yet have such evidence that every man of common understanding readily assents to them, and finds it absolutely necessary to conduct his actions and opinions by them, in the ordinary affairs of life.[20]

Reid believed that certain belief-dispositions, such as the tendency to believe what we are told, were simply endowed by the Creator, "the wise Author of nature."[21] In due course, this disposition becomes more refined, as we learn from experience whom and what to trust or not. Here induction plays a part. Indeed, Reid contended that the *inductive principle* was itself a natural disposition to acquire belief-dispositions.[22]

The question of God does not figure as a major topic in the writings that Reid published during his lifetime. Nevertheless, the notion of God is pervasive, even though it is something of an exaggeration to say with Louise Marcil-Lacoste that "there is hardly one page of his works without a mention of God."[23] Reid's philosophy was one which readily fitted within the framework of an enlightened Christian theism. For Reid "the laws of Nature are the rules by which the Supreme Being governs the world."[24]

One might have expected that Reid's view of dispositions might have led him to endorse Calvin's view that human beings are endowed with a "sense of divinity" which, when triggered by experience, yields the belief that the world was created and is sustained by God. But Reid does not appear to cite any theistic propositions as principles of common sense.[25] Over against Hume, Reid reiterated the design argument for God's existence, which in the light of the advances of knowledge, was even more convincing in his day than in previous centuries.[26] A similar view is presented in the *Lectures on Natural Theology*,[27] where Reid developed a theme which had echoes of Locke, the Cambridge Platonists and enlightened Christianity.

It is no doubt true that Revelation exhibits all the truths of Natural Religion, but it is no less true that reason must be employed to judge of that revelation; whether it comes from God. Both are great lights and we ought not to put out the one in order to use the other. Revelation is of use to enlighten us with regard to the use of Natural Religion, as one Man may enlighten another in things that it was impossible could be discovered by him, it is easy then to conceive that God could enlighten Man. . . . Revelation was given us not to hinder the exercise of our reasoning powers but to aid and assist them. Tis by reason that we must judge whether that Revelation be really so; Tis by reason that we must judge the meaning of what is revealed; and it is by Reason that we must guard against any impious, inconsistent or absurd interpretation of that revelation.[28]

There is, perhaps, something paradoxical in Reid's position here. As Wolterstorff notes, "The 'testing' that Reid, in his attack on the skeptic, disavows as necessary for our native noetic faculties, *is* necessary for our acceptance of revelation."[29] Perhaps the explanation is to be found in

Wolterstorff's suggestion that Reid "was carefully scrutinizing and defending the inference which, in intuitive fashion, leads the ordinary adult person to God, rather than constructing an argument for a belief which is characteristically arrived at immediately."[30] However, in the writings which Reid himself thought fit to publish, the central concern is not with natural theology but with knowledge, and in particular with the justification of beliefs which belong to knowledge-claims. Empiricism had weakened those claims; Reid's philosophy challenged empiricism, and sought to offer a better alternative.

Although he was an ordained Presbyterian minister, Reid's agenda was set not by the need for a philosophical articulation of Reformed theology but by the epistemological issues raised by empiricism. Reid's response was that of a philosopher of the Age of Enlightenment. But Reid was not simply the child of his age. Nor was he an advocate of common sense as the antidote to everything. Although Reid is remembered as the founder of the Common Sense School of philosophy, common sense does not figure quite as much in his writings as that designation might suggest. In some ways Reid anticipates the concerns and techniques of twentieth-century post-positivistic philosophy. His method was to analyze the structure of everyday language with a view to exploring the structures of experience and of human selfhood.

Attention has been drawn to the similarities between Reid and the twentieth-century Cambridge philosopher G. E. Moore.[31] The Oxford philosopher H. H. Price acknowledged that his own position "with regard to the nature and the validity of perceptual consciousness is in essence identical with that maintained by Reid against Hume."[32] However, Price went on to say that Reid did not carry his analysis far enough by failing to distinguish clearly between acceptance and assurance.

More recently, contemporary American philosophers have taken up Reid's ideas and have seen relevance in them to current questions. Roderick M. Chisholm sees in Reid a better approach to the questions of knowledge than in skepticism or empiricism.[33] Alvin Plantinga has paid tribute to Reid's work in drawing attention to different sources of belief or belief-producing mechanisms, such as perception, memory, testimony and reason. Plantinga notes that "the history of philosophy since Hume is littered with the wreckage of attempts to justify the deliverances of sense perception on the basis of self-evidence and introspection. Reid argues—correctly, I believe—that the deliverances of sense perception don't need justification or certification in terms of such other sources of belief as introspection and self-evidence. Suppose sense perception cannot be certified in terms of those sources: there is nothing epistemically defective or improper in accepting its deliverances as basic."[34]

Nicholas Wolterstorff sees certain shortcomings in Reid's work, but these are far outweighed by his achievements.[35] Among the shortcomings are Reid's failure to distinguish clearly between first principles understood as belief-dispositions and first principles understood as beliefs; his omission of discussion of criteria for justified belief; his omission of discussion of how awareness of God fits into his understanding of perception; the inconsistency between his stance on perception in general (where testing by reason is not a necessary precondition) and his stance on revelation (where testing by reason is deemed necessary); and the narrowness of his account of the sources of belief. Here Reid attends to what might be called the *noble* sources of belief. The economic and psychological factors addressed by Marx and Freud do not enter into Reid's discussion. Nor does he discuss the nature and effects of sin. In this Reid remains a child of the Enlightenment.

But these omissions do not diminish Reid's positive achievements. Reid's philosophy presents a radical alternative to the classical foundationalism of the West, which has sought to erect comprehensive systems of philosophy based upon a foundation of certainty.[36] In particular, Reid has presented a theory of situated rationality. Wolterstorff contends that rationality is always situational. He argues: "In general we cannot inquire into the rationality of some belief by asking whether one would be rational in holding that belief. We must ask whether it would be rational for this particular person to hold it, or whether it would be rational for a person of this type in this situation to hold it."[37] In addition to this, Reid, more than any other philosopher in history, set his theory of rationality within the context of a theory of human nature which explored the psychology of being human. Finally, Reid's non-classical foundationalist theory presents a penetrating reply to skepticism. In contrast to Kant's view of knowledge, which claimed that we can know nothing of reality apart from how it appears to us, Reid's account preserves the world by permitting genuine knowledge of reality outside ourselves.

If Reid did not pursue the implications of his views in answer to the questions that we have today, he nevertheless left behind him a fruitful line of approach. It was an approach which was taken up, though perhaps with less originality and distinction, by Reid's immediate contemporaries and successors. Among them were James Oswald, James Beattie and Dugald Stewart. The turning-point in the common sense revolution came in 1785[38] with the publication of Reid's first set of essays and the fourth edition of his *Inquiry*. It marked a transition from the appeal to common sense in polemics to the recognition of its place in scholarly, scientific inquiry. In the same year Dugald Stewart began to popularize Reid's approach in his lectures at Edinburgh. Stewart went on to publish his views in his *Elements of the Philosophy of the Human Mind* (3 vol., 1792-1827) and his *Outlines of Moral Philosophy* (1793). By the 1790s the Reid-Stewart analytical approach to psychology, epistemology and metaphysics which used everyday experience as its starting point gained ascendancy in Scottish intellectual circles. It was a tradition which was carried on by Sir William Hamilton in the nineteenth century. Hamilton's *Lectures on Metaphysics and Logic* (1859-60) drew on Reid, but modified his position in the light of Kant's teaching. In the meantime, Scottish common sense philosophy attracted not a little attention in France and Germany, especially among moderates who were opposed to the radical skepticism of the Enlightenment. In America the kind of philosophy advocated by Reid and his successors provided philosophers and theologians with an arsenal of weapons in their ongoing war with skepticism and Deism.[39]

Early American Thought

One of the great contemporary historians of religion in America, Sydney E. Ahlstrom, has observed that the history of theology in America is marked by three characteristics.[40] The first is its diversity. New England Congregational thinking was chiefly English in derivation. The Presbyterian tradition, which was strongest in the mid-Atlantic region, relied heavily on Scottish thought, supplemented by Continental Reformed

Scholasticism. Lutheran theology was characteristically German. Although these traditions sometimes touched each other, they were frequently autonomous. The second characteristic of American religious thought is its highly derivative character. This was bound up with the fact that the American people are largely an immigrant people who brought their culture and intellectual traditions with them. In the absence of a longstanding intellectual tradition of their own, it was inevitable that those concerned with intellectual issues should turn to Europe for inspiration and help. Ahlstrom's third characteristic is a refinement of his second. It consists in the observation that the first quarter of the nineteenth century marks a watershed in the flow of theological influences. Up till then British influence was the most important. After 1815 German influence became increasingly strong, even though it was sometimes mediated by English and Scottish writers.

Early American Protestant thought was stamped by the Reformed and Puritan outlook. Even those churches like the Anglican and Baptist, which did not recognize the Synod of Dort (1619) and the Westminster Confession (1647), shared a common ethos in which redemption and salvation were major concerns. Seventeenth-century theology was concerned with these themes; but it also felt the need to vindicate the ways of God and demonstrate their rationality. The publication of Newton's *Principia Mathematica* (1687) and Locke's *Essay Concerning Human Understanding* (1690) gave new impetus to the quest for ordered simplicity and demonstrated reasonableness. Just as Newton had explained the universe in terms of rational laws, preachers and religious writers began to move toward an enlightened form of Christianity. Originally at least, this did not mean the kind of attempt that the Deists in England were making to reduce Christianity to a natural, rational religion. This came later, as Deism began to affect American thinking in the second half of the eighteenth century. Rather, it took the form of an endeavor to express Christian beliefs in terms of law and reasonableness. Traditional Calvinism remained the dominant theology, but it was restated with the help of new philosophical thinking that came from Europe.

By common consent the two most notable early American philosophers were Cotton Mather and Samuel Johnson. Cotton Mather (1663-1728) was the eldest son of the Massachusetts Puritan Increase Mather.

He entered Harvard College at the age of twelve and graduated at fifteen. A speech impediment made him feel unequal to the task of preaching, and so he turned to the study of medicine. However, he overcame his stammer and became the assistant to his father at the Second Church of Boston, where he remained for the rest of his life. Having failed in his bid to succeed his father as the president of Harvard, he threw his energies into the founding of Yale College, which he hoped would more truly embody the Calvinistic faith. He was finally offered the presidency of Yale in 1721, but declined on account of his advancing years. Mather published over 450 writings, but his chief philosophical work was *The Christian Philosopher: A Collection of the Best Discoveries in Nature, with Religious Improvements* (1721).[41] His purpose was to show that *"Philosophy* is no *Enemy,* but a mighty and wonderous *Incentive* to *Religion."*[42] It was in fact the first comprehensive treatise on science written in America.[43] Mather's use of the term *philosophy* carries with it the archaic sense of "natural philosophy" (i.e., natural science). At the same time it presents the first comprehensive exposition of natural theology to be written in America.[44] As such, it attempted to show the harmony between Christian belief and the modern scientific understanding of nature.

Mather lived in an age when plagiarism was widely accepted and even acknowledged as a sign of learning. In this respect *The Christian Philosopher* was a product of its times. Although Mather himself was a contributing member of the Royal Society in London, his review of the state of science was drawn largely from the Boyle lecturers and the Newtonian physico-theologians who had gone before him. Everything in nature has its purpose and function—even insects and vermin. Lest even these creatures exceed their function, providence has ordained other creatures to keep them in bounds. The animal world exhibits a "cunning" which is quite beyond the capacity of the animals themselves. In short, "the *Divine Reason runs like a Golden Vein through the whole Leaden Mine of Brutal Nature."*[45] Mather's review of the natural world culminated in an account of human nature in its complex harmonious order. No one who had studied the human eye "could abandon himself to any *speculative Atheism."*[46] Indeed, the study of nature leads to the conclusion:

> *Atheism* is now for ever chased and hissed out of the World, every thing in the World concurs to a Sentence of *Banishment* upon it. . . .

A BEING that must be superior to *Matter,* even the *Creator* and *Governor* of all *Matter,* is every where so conspicuous, that there can be nothing more *monstrous* than *to deny the God that is above.*[47]
But Mather did not stop with this general conclusion. The God that he believed in was not merely a philosopher's God, invoked to provide a rational explanation of the complex order of nature. Reflection on nature was itself a reasonable incentive to faith in the invisible, triune God of Christianity.[48] In developing this theme Mather marked out a path which has been followed by the orthodox, Protestant, evangelical Christians in America down to the present day.

The other early American philosopher of importance was Samuel Johnson (1696-1772)—the namesake and contemporary of the English lexicographer and writer, Samuel Johnson. The American Samuel Johnson was one of the first colonials to read Bacon, Locke and Newton. He abandoned the rigid Calvinism of his upbringing and received Anglican orders. He became a friend and follower of George Berkeley when Berkeley came to Rhode Island. Later he collaborated in the founding of the University of Pennsylvania and of King's College (later called Columbia University), where he was the first president. Johnson's writings include his *Encyclopedia of Philosophy* (1731) and his *Elementa Philosophica* (1752). Johnson argued for the existence of God by reason of the presence of eternal truths in human minds. Since these truths do not depend on the human mind or on existing objects, they must be communications of the mind of God. Human beings know these truths when they are illuminated by the divine mind. Johnson recognized the applicability of Newton's laws to the physical world, but insisted that the human spirit was not so bound. In opposition to his former pupil, Jonathan Edwards, Johnson defended the freedom of the will and rejected the Calvinistic doctrine of individual predestination. If human beings were not free, moral laws, rewards and punishments were meaningless.

Jonathan Edwards

The prime mover in the process of restating traditional Calvinistic theology by means of the new philosophy from Europe was Jonathan Edwards (1703-58).[49] To many Edwards remains the greatest American philosophical theologian. In his own day he was a thinker ahead of his time.

In the words of Perry Miller, "When Edwards stood up among the New England clergy, it was as though a master of relativity spoke to a convention of Newtonians who had not yet heard of Einstein, or as though among nineteenth-century professors of philosophy, all assuming that man is rational and responsible, a strange youth began to refer, without more ado, to the id, ego, and super-ego."[50] What Miller is referring to here is the way in which Edwards absorbed and assimilated the ideas of John Locke and used them to articulate his Calvinistic theology.

Edwards was born in East Windsor, Connecticut. As a boy he wrote precocious essays on the habits of spiders, the rainbow and colors (showing familiarity with Newton's *Opticks)*, and a demonstration of the immateriality of the soul. In 1716 he entered Yale, where his tutor, Samuel Johnson, introduced him to Locke's *Essay Concerning Human Understanding*. In later life he recalled how at the age of fourteen he "had more Satisfaction and Pleasure in studying it, than the most greedy Miser in gathering up handfuls of Silver and Gold from some new discovered Treasure."[51] After graduation in 1720, he spent two further years at Yale studying theology in preparation for the ministry. During this time, he underwent a profound religious experience. Later in his *Personal Narrative* (1739) he told how he received a new awareness of God's absolute sovereignty and omnipresence and of his own complete dependence on God. The experience and consequent outlook indelibly affected Edwards's thought.

After a brief pastorate in New York, Edwards returned to Yale as senior tutor. In 1727 he became assistant minister to his grandfather, the renowned Solomon Stoddard, in Northampton, Massachusetts. On the latter's death in 1729, Edwards took over. For some twenty years Edwards enjoyed a remarkable ministry, playing a vigorous part in the New England Great Awakening whilst continually engaged in theological writing. He jotted down numerous reflections which were intended as a first draft of "A Rational Account of the Main Doctrines of the Christian Religion Attempted." This monumental work was never completed. Edwards attacked Arminianism in a famous sermon preached in Boston on "God Glorified in Man's Dependence" (1731). His preaching against Arminianism was instrumental in the revival. He gave an account of it in his *Narrative of Surprising Conversions* (1736). The Great Awakening of the

1740s produced cases of hysterical enthusiasm. Edwards examined relig-ious experience in *A Treatise Concerning Religious Affections* (1746).

Throughout his ministry, Edwards was embroiled in controversy. As the 1740s drew to a close, opposition mounted. Criticism of the revival combined with parish strife over Edwards's salary and strict disciplinary attitudes led to his removal. In 1751 Edwards accepted a call to Stock-bridge, a town which was then virtually on the frontier of civilization. Here Edwards ministered to a small group of Indians and whites. He now had time and leisure to write his major philosophical treatise on *Freedom of Will* (1754) and its sequels on *The Nature of True Virtue* and *The End for Which God Created the World.* He also began *The History of the Work of Redemption,* but his labors were interrupted by a call to become president of the College of New Jersey (now Princeton University). He had hardly resumed his duties when he died following a smallpox in-jection.

Edwards's training was influenced by Puritan Platonism, which in turn was an offshoot of Cambridge Platonism in England. It was an outlook which proclaimed that the spiritual world is the ultimate reality. But in the case of Edwards, this outlook was modified by the empiricism of Locke and the science of Newton. As one modern writer has put it, "From Locke he took the notion that all our ideas originate in sensation; from Newton, the conception of space as the divine sensorium."[52] The Newtonian, Platonistic, idealist side of Edwards's thought appears in his notes "Of Being," where he argued that Being possesses the attributes of eternity, omnipresence, omniscience and infinity. In other words, Being is God himself. God is, in fact, identical with space. The universe proceeds from God as light proceeds from the sun. The universe is a revelation of the divine to created minds. Although some of Edwards's ideas suggest the influence of Bishop Berkeley, it would seem that Ed-wards reached them without having read the bishop's works.[53] Edwards's notebook on *Images or Shadows of Divine Things* presents nature as a symbol of God. It is a panorama of shadows and images of the divine mind and will. The contemplation of the traces of God in nature is a sublime and delightful activity.

If all this suggests a kind of pantheism or panentheism akin to the rationalism of Spinoza, it may also be said that Edwards's understanding of human freedom was not dissimilar to that of the pantheistic rational-ist.[54] However, the road which Edwards took to reach his destination led him through a different terrain. His goal was not to devise a speculative account of the will for its own sake but to crush the Arminian objections to Calvinism. It was a goal required by the sovereign grace of God in salvation, lest any part of salvation be ascribed to human endeavor. The vehicle for doing this was Locke's empiricism which appeared to Ed-wards to be admirably suited to the defense of Calvinism.[55] Just as in Locke's view of knowledge the mind is essentially passive, receiving all its ideas from outside, so it is in Edwards's view of the will. Human beings are determined by causes outside themselves. Ultimately these are all to be traced back to God who alone is free in the sense of being able to determine his own volitions.

The full title of Edwards's great work on free will is *A Careful and Strict Enquiry into the Modern Prevailing Notions of that Freedom of Will, which is Supposed to be Essential to Moral Agency, Vertue and Vice, Reward and Pun-ishment, Praise and Blame.* At the outset Edwards observed that the whole debate about free will was muddled by misconceptions and inadequate definitions. Edwards declined to think of the will as some kind of semi-metaphysical entity that resides somewhere inside human beings, con-trolling their actions. He insisted that the will

> is plainly, that by which the mind chooses anything. The faculty of the will is that faculty or power or principle of mind by which it is capable of choosing: an act of the will is the same as an act of choos-ing or choice.[56]

Edwards found endorsement in Locke's statement that "the will signifies nothing but a power or ability to prefer or choose."[57] In other words, the will is the person choosing. Freedom or liberty is "that power and op-portunity to do and conduct as he will, or according to his choice."[58] It involves the absence of constraints and restraints which would prevent a person from acting according to his or her will. But for Edwards this is not the same as saying that a person acts without any motive. Indeed, a basic theme of Edwards's argument is the contention that "the will is always determined by the strongest motive."[59]

By the word *motive* Edwards meant "the whole of that which moves, excites or invites the mind to volition, whether that be one thing singly, or many things conjunctly."[60] He explained the way in which such motives work in terms of Locke's theory of knowledge, insisting that " 'tis most evident, that nothing is in the mind, or reaches it, or takes any hold of it, any otherwise than as it is perceived or thought of."[61] He further explained his notion of determination:

If strict propriety of speech be insisted on, it may more properly be said, that the voluntary action which is the immediate consequence and fruit of the mind's volition or choice, is determined by that which appears most agreeable, than the preference or choice itself; but that the act of volition itself is always determined by that in or about the mind's view of the object, which causes it to appear most agreeable. I say, in or about the mind's view of the object, because what has influence to render an object in view agreeable, is not only what appears in the object viewed, but also the manner of the view, and the state and circumstances of the mind that views.[62]

The outcome of Edwards's deliberations was the paradoxical conclusion that human beings were both free and determined. They were free in the sense that their choices and actions were really their own. They were thus truly being themselves. But they were determined in the sense that, "if it be so, that the will is always determined by the strongest motive, then it must always have an inability . . . to act otherwise than it does."[63] Thus Edwards saw freedom not as some kind of indeterminacy, unaffected by circumstances, character, past choices or habits. To him such a notion was a figment of the imagination, out of touch with reality. Human actions were determined by antecedent factors, whether they be circumstances or whether they be the good or bad character of people which affects the way that they view things and act. Human actions are not random events, but the product of whatever motivates them. In the last analysis, the decisive factor is "the strongest motive."

Edwards linked this idea with a form of psychological hedonism which taught that no one ever does or can do anything except to further his or her own pleasure. The alcoholic who cannot pass up another drink does so because it is "most agreeable to him."[64] If, however, the alcoholic manages to avoid taking another drink, it is because the "lesser pleasant pleasure" of getting drunk is outweighed by the more agreeable prospects of avoiding a hangover and of being delivered from alcoholism.

The same basic principles apply to all human actions. Christians are no exception. In their case, "the strongest motive" is the hope of heaven, the fear of hell and the love of God. It is this which enables them to deny the world, the flesh and the devil in order to seek salvation.

A substantial part of Edwards's book on *Freedom of Will* was devoted to answering the arguments of the Arminian preachers and the ideas of the English Deist Thomas Chubb. To explore the ramifications of his reply would take us too far afield. But two points must be noted. The first is Edwards's argument that his view does not undermine human responsibility. Edwards's opponents argued that, if our actions are determined by antecedent causes, we cannot be held responsible for what we do. Edwards stood this objection on its head, and argued that it is precisely because human beings will to do the things that they do, that their actions may be praised or blamed.[65] Motivation does not remove voluntary action. The fact that we act in accordance with what seems most agreeable to us makes us responsible. The other point to be noted has to do with God's sovereignty and human responsibility. Edwards's critics argued that Edwards was teaching a kind of divine determinism which undermined human responsibility. Edwards met this challenge head-on. It was a fixed point in his thinking.

> God orders all events, and the volitions of moral agents amongst others, by such a decisive disposal, that the events are infallibly connected with his disposal. For if God disposes all events, so that the infallible existence of the events is decided by his providence, then he doubtless thus orders and decides things *knowingly,* and *on design.*[66]

This reply was bound up with Edwards's Calvinistic view of God's sovereign grace in salvation. Without God's help from first to last, no human being could be saved.[67] But it was also bound up with Edwards's view of divine immutability and foreknowledge.[68] For if God were to change, it would mean that he was less than perfect. His divine decrees must therefore be immutable. God's foreknowledge rests upon God's knowledge of his own decrees. "Because the connection between the event and certain foreknowledge, is as infallible and indissoluble, as the event and an absolute decree."[69]

The question of free will continues to exercise philosophers and theologians.[70] It remains a point of contention between Calvinists and

Arminians in contemporary debate. But it also figures in the deliberations of the behavioral scientists and in the philosophical questions raised by psychotherapy. There can be no doubt that Edwards's understanding of an act of the will as an act of choosing marks a definite advance on the nebulous view of the will as some kind of autonomous faculty. Similarly, his view of freedom as the power and opportunity to act according to choice is more realistic than the assumption that freedom consists in not having to make choices. Edwards's account is important for its attempt to give recognition to motivational factors. Nevertheless, Edwards's solution to the problem of free will raises a number of acute questions. In its day it was impressive for the way in which it restated Calvinistic theology in terms of the most modern philosophical tools available (i.e., those furnished by John Locke). However, the question cannot be evaded whether the conceptual framework which made it modern two hundred years ago renders it obsolete today. Locke's view of the mind as essentially passive, receiving its knowledge and motivation from outside, readily fitted a theology which stressed humankind's need of grace from first to last. But the price Edwards paid for this harmonization of Calvinism with a world view drawn from Newton and Locke was the adoption of a deterministic, mechanistic view of causation, which traced every single action back to God's immutable decree.

In the last analysis, no action, thought, feeling or event could have been otherwise than what it was because it followed by necessity from the divine decree. The freedom that Edwards ascribes to human beings turns out, on closer inspection, to be their compliance with their own actions which are always determined by "the strongest motive." To put it another way, history is like a long-running soap opera on TV in which all the actors act out parts that are determined for them. The determination is on two levels. On the level of the segment of the story in which they find themselves, their words and actions are determined by the plot to date, which includes the character played by the actor. Whatever the character does is essentially determined. The actor who plays the part has no freedom to change anything. But the whole story is determined on an even higher level by the fact that God wrote the entire script before anything happened at all.

One does not have to think for more than a few moments to realize that the notion of total, absolute freedom for human beings is a figment of the imagination. Human choices and actions are certainly affected by a whole range of factors which severely limit possible courses of action. One cannot change the past. One cannot change one's sex or race. Past choices and actions clearly affect the way one thinks and chooses. And so on. It is this consistency of action which forms habits and characters. But human beings have the incorrigible feeling that not all of their actions are predetermined. In some cases at least, we have a deep-down feeling that we might have acted otherwise than we did.

We can agree with Edwards and say that if we look back at the past, whether it be our own past or the past in general, it seems reasonable to say that all actions were determined by "the strongest motive." It is plausible to think of the past as a web of causes and effects. It is certainly a major activity of the historian to attempt to discern the actual causes and effects from mere guesswork and popular assumptions about them. Indeed, it is legitimate to try to discern what were the strongest causes and motives. But this can be done only because the past is actually *past* and therefore fixed. The present and the future do not appear to share the same necessary, determined character. It is, in fact, a tautology to say that human actions are determined by "the strongest motive." It says no more than the statement: "The strongest motive is the strongest motive." It is impossible to predict in advance which of the various possible motives will turn out to be the strongest. This is not simply because of the vast range of motives and factors, both known and unknown. It is also because choosing, deciding and acting play a part in making any given motive "the strongest motive." In such instances, it would seem that the act of choosing itself transforms what might otherwise have been a weak or medium-powered motive into the motive which turned out to be the strongest and decisive one.

Edwards's hedonism appears to be no less problematic. For to say that our actions are prompted by whatever appears most agreeable does not explain what finally makes some things most agreeable and other things less agreeable. It leaves out of account the variable factor in human make-up which transforms (for better or worse) the intrinsic value of things and reassigns values in a personal, self-referential way. Edwards's scheme of thought treats this factor as just another item in the determined sequence of cause and effect. Since God is the ultimate author of all things, by whose decree everything comes to pass, Edwards's scheme of thought makes God the author of evil. On his premises it is impossible to resist the conclusion that God not only willed moral evil in general, but willed all evil human actions as well as all good actions. In this respect, Edwards's account of reality shares similar features with those of Spinoza and Leibniz. Common to them is a rationalistic determinism which interprets human action in terms of necessary sequence, of a piece with the necessary sequences exemplified by the natural science of the day.

It was the genius of Edwards to combine a high Calvinistic theology (which to him was a celebration of the greatness of God) with the new philosophical thinking that came from Europe. The synthesis that he produced was a form of Calvinism which not only spoke the language of the Age of Enlightenment but sought to justify Calvinism by means of the philosophy of the Enlightenment. This achievement made Edwards the leading orthodox Christian thinker in the Age of Enlightenment in America. But the price he paid for this was to propound a solution to the free-will question which raised more problems than it solved. Perhaps the root of the problem lay in the terms in which it was set. Edwards thought of it in terms of powers and forces comparable with the way powers and forces were thought of in the physical world. By posing the problem in quasi-physical terms Edwards ensured an answer in those terms. But perhaps this is the wrong model. Perhaps the way to a better answer lies in thinking of it in terms of grace, personality and love.[71]

The theological tradition begun by Edwards came to be known as the New England Theology. His immediate successors were his personal friends, Joseph Bellamy (1719-90) and Samuel Hopkins (1721-1803),[72] whose teaching was termed the *New Divinity*. The Calvinistic tradition continued to be strong in the nineteenth century. However, Nathaniel W. Taylor (1786-1858) introduced a reversal at Yale which came to be known as the New Haven Theology. He rejected Edwards's teaching on the will, arguing that human beings have a natural power of free choice. In the meantime other philosophical ideas from Europe had filtered into American thinking. In the last quarter of the eighteenth century Deism gained a firm foothold in American religious and political thought.[73]

Deism in America

Deism provided the inspiration for works like Ethan Allen's *Reason the Only Oracle of Man* (1784),[74] which ridiculed the Bible and blasted the church. The outlook of Thomas Jefferson (1743-1826) and some of the other framers of the American Constitution was thoroughly Deistic. Jefferson compiled a slim volume which came to be known as *The Jefferson Bible*. It was almost as close as one could get to a scissors-and-paste production. Jefferson himself called it *The Life and Morals of Jesus of Nazareth Extracted textually from the Gospels in Greek, Latin, French & English.*[75] What Jefferson did was to take four copies of the Gospels in these languages and cut out the verses he wanted in order to paste together the life and teaching of Jesus. In so doing he discarded all references to the supernatural and miraculous. He included the accounts of Jesus' birth, but cut out all mention of the Holy Spirit. In the same fashion he omitted mention of the Holy Spirit at Jesus' baptism and elsewhere. He kept some of the teaching of Jesus, but omitted the healings and nature miracles. The work concluded with the burial of Jesus, but contained no hint of the resurrection. Jefferson never published the work, though he toyed with the idea of a version for the use of native Indians.

Jefferson was reluctant to state his religious beliefs in public. Would-be writers on the subject were informed: "Say nothing of my Religion: it is known to myself and God alone."[76] But in private it was another matter. He confessed to John Adams that he could never worship Calvin's God. "If ever man worshiped a false God, he did. The being described in his five points, is not the God whom you and I acknowledge and adore, the creator and benevolent governor of the world; but a daemon of a malignant spirit."[77] To another correspondent Jefferson confessed to being an Epicurean. Epicurus was "our master." In his teaching, classical philosophy had reached its zenith. Epicurus had provided the quintessential philosophy. In Jefferson's scheme of things Jesus figured as a reformer of Judaism. He was in no sense divine. His role in history was to supplement the teachings of Epictetus and Epicurus.

But the greatest of all the reformers of the depraved religion of His own country, was Jesus of Nazareth. Abstracting what is really His from the rubbish in which it is buried, easily distinguished by its luster from the dross of His biographers, and as separable from that as the diamond from the dunghill, we have the outlines of a system of the most sublime morality which has ever fallen from the lips of man; outlines which it is lamentable He did not live to fill up. Epictetus and Epicurus give laws for governing ourselves, Jesus a supplement of the duties and charities we owe to others.[78]

In America Deism enjoyed much more widespread popularity than it did in England. Attempts were made to organize Deism into something like a religious denomination through the formation of Deistic societies. This was due to the efforts of men like the former Baptist preacher Elihu Palmer, who had been expelled from his pulpit for preaching against the divinity of Christ. Palmer's book on *Principles of Nature* (c. 1801) came to be regarded as the Bible of American Deism. The most enduring of the Deists in America was Thomas Paine (1737-1809), who was born in England but who emigrated to America and became an American citizen.[79] Following Sir Isaac Newton, he argued that since the laws of mechanics cannot explain the origin of motion, there must have been an external first cause to set the planets in motion. He also believed in eternal rewards and punishments. But on the question of the Bible he was scathingly skeptical. His tract on *The Age of Reason* (2 parts, 1794-95) was a compendious attack on the Bible in the name of reason. As the work wound its way to its conclusion, Paine made the following pronouncement:

> The study of theology, as it stands in Christian churches, is the study of nothing; it is founded on nothing; it rests on no principles; it proceeds by no authorities; it has no data; it can demonstrate nothing; and it admits of no conclusion. Not any thing can be studied as a science, without our being in possession of the principles upon which it is founded; and as this is not the case with Christian theology, it is therefore the study of nothing.
>
> Instead then of studying theology, as is now done out of the Bible and Testament, the meanings of which books are always controverted and the authenticity of which is disproved, it is necessary that we refer to the Bible of the Creation. The principles we discover there are eternal and of divine origin; they are the foundation of all the science

that exists in the world, and must be the foundation of theology.[80]
Deism made an impact at several levels of American life. In the minds
of some it was associated with revolutionary fervor. The revolt against
authority in religion in the name of reason went hand in hand with the
political revolt against alien authority. This, bound together with the
association of Deism with science and what was deemed to be the truth
behind history, succeeded in giving Deism a far wider hearing in America than it received in England. In the political arena men of Deistic
persuasion like Jefferson and Franklin forged an alliance with more
orthodox Christian believers in building the separation of church and
state into the American Constitution.[81] The Deists wanted a minimal
acknowledgement of God and the exclusion of particular religious beliefs. The more orthodox believers likewise did not want foisted on them
the practices and traditions of other churches. They or their ancestors
had come to America in the first place in the search of freedom to
practice their faith and way of life. The Constitution that was hammered
out gave formal recognition to God, but its republican philosophy was
inspired by a combination of ideas drawn from classical antiquity, the
British constitution (minus the monarchy) and more recent political
thinkers. It established a delicate mechanism designed to check by the
rule of law the ills that flow from human passion.

On another level Deism had the effect of mobilizing the opposition
of the churches to Deistic beliefs and Deistic influence in education. In
a letter to the president of Yale written in 1759, Ezra Stiles mused aloud
on the subject of liberty of thought and the progress of Deism.

> It is true with this Liberty Error may be introduced; but turn the
> Tables the propagation of Truth may be extinguished. Deism has got
> such Head in the Age of Licentious Liberty, that it would be in vain
> to try to stop it by hiding the Deistical Writings: and the only Way left
> to conquer & demolish it, is to come forth into the open Field &
> Dispute this matter on even Footing—the Evidences of Revelation in
> my opinion are nearly as demonstrative as Newton's Principia, & these
> are the Weapons to be used. . . . *Truth* & this alone being *our* Aim in
> fact, open, frank & generous we shall avoid the very appearance of
> Evil.[82]

Stiles was not alone in sensing the danger and in turning to the weapons of scholarship to repel the enemy. In 1768 John Witherspoon accepted the call to the presidency of the College of New Jersey (later Princeton College). In theology a high Calvinist and in philosophy a follower of the Scottish Common Sense School, Witherspoon soon dismissed the college's tutors who favored Berkeley's immaterialism. The latter philosophy was no match for Deism. It was "an evil and ridiculous attempt to unsettle the principles of common sense" and "which never produced conviction even in those who pretend to espouse it." Witherspoon's strategy was "to meet the infidels upon their own ground and show from reason itself the fallacy of their principles."[83] When in 1812 the Presbyterian Church founded at Princeton its first seminary for the training of ministers, the Princeton theologians were called upon to show "the right use of reason in religion" and also the need for biblical revelation. The seminary's "plan" provided that every student "must have read and digested the principal arguments and writings relative to what has been called the deistical controversy. Thus he will be qualified to become a defender of the Christian faith."[84] In a curious roundabout way Deism left its mark on evangelicalism and Protestant orthodoxy. From the days of Ezra Stiles onwards, mainstream American evangelical Protestantism was stamped by a conscious need to demonstrate the rationality of its belief and the historical factuality of the contents of the Bible.

16. ENLIGHTENMENT AND SKEPTICISM IN FRANCE

T he Age of Enlightenment grew out of the Age of Rationalism. It came to full flower in the movements that we have been discussing in the last three chapters—Deism, empiricism and the various movements noted in Scotland and America. It is clear that not everyone who lived in this age was hostile to religion. In Britain Locke, Butler and Berkeley were just as truly sons of the Enlightenment as were the Deists. In America Jonathan Edwards is the classic example of an orthodox believer who reinterpreted orthodoxy in terms of enlightened ideas. On the other hand, David Hume provides the classic example of a British enlightened skeptic.

As we bring this book to its close, we shall devote the next two chapters to looking at four leading Continental thinkers who present critical but contrasting attitudes to religion. Two of them belong to the culture of the French-speaking world: Voltaire and Rousseau. Two of them were German: Lessing and Kant. However, before we examine their ideas, it will be helpful to pause and reflect on the idea of the Age of Enlightenment and see how it transcended international frontiers and cultures.

The Age of Enlightenment

In 1784 Immanuel Kant wrote a magazine article in which he asked himself the question "What is Enlightenment?" His reply was:

Enlightenment is man's release from his self-incurred tutelage. Tutelage is man's inability to make use of his understanding without direction from another. Self-incurred is the tutelage when its cause lies not in lack of reason but in lack of resolution and courage to use it without direction from another. *Sapere aude!* "Have courage to use your own reason!"—that is the motto of enlightenment.[1]

Kant pictured human history as a process of growing up. Children have to do what they are told to do because their elders are assumed to know better. In bygone ages whole societies behaved like children. They did what they were told to do by the state and by the church. But so long as a society acts in this way, it remains immature. It needs to grow up, think for itself, and take charge. Kant did not think that the Prussia of his day was already an enlightened age. Censorship was still in force. The lives of many citizens were molded by habit, custom, tradition and unthinking obedience to the dictates of the state and the dogmas of the church. But the age of Frederick the Great was the Age of Enlightenment. The dawn had broken and people were beginning to throw off their erstwhile bondage. Admittedly, Kant did not think that reason could solve everything. Reason had its limitations. Nevertheless, it remained the best guide that human beings had. The resolve to submit everything to the scrutiny of reason was the basic item on the agenda not only for Kant but for the Age of Enlightenment in general.

Kant was not the only one to discuss the nature of enlightenment. *The Berlin Monthly,* the journal that carried Kant's article, also published an article on the same subject from the pen of the leader of the Jewish Enlightenment in Germany, Moses Mendelssohn. Mendelssohn, who was the grandfather of the composer, was a widely respected figure in intellectual and cultural circles. People called him "the Jewish Socrates." Nevertheless, his Jewish background prevented his admission to the Berlin Academy. On the question of enlightenment Mendelssohn believed that enlightenment lay in intellectual cultivation, which he distinguished from the practical. On the question of religion Mendelssohn opted for an enlightened Deism, which he developed into a universal religion of reason which he believed to be identical with the true spirit of Judaism.[2]

Kant and Mendelssohn mark the pinnacle of the German Enlightenment. It was an age which was already beginning to pass when they penned their attempts to define what it was. Kant and Mendelssohn represent two of the many faces of the Enlightenment. What they shared was the view that the rational intellectual could get beyond received opinions, tradition, custom and dogma, and attain a superior understanding through critical reasoning. However, they differed over how far this should affect practice. Mendelssohn's intellectual aestheticism was a world of its own into which the cultivated might enter and enjoy its delights. Kant, on the other hand, took the view long before Karl Marx thought of it that the duty of the philosopher was not simply to understand the world, but to change it. It was a view that was shared by other enlightened thinkers before him.

When Kant declared that the motto of enlightenment was *Sapere aude* (literally "Dare to be wise") he was in fact echoing a slogan that had been around for a long time. In 1736 the Society for the Friends of Truth had adopted it as its motto. Societies like this played an influential part in the German Enlightenment. In one such society members were required to pledge themselves not to accept or reject any belief except for a "sufficient reason."[3] But the motto *Sapere aude* is much older still. It comes from Horace, the Latin poet of the first century B.C.[4] The enlightened challenge to be wise and bring everything subject to the judgment of critical reason led some thinkers to a benign, though condescending, attitude to institutional religion. In the case of Kant it produced a thinly veiled contempt for institutional Christianity. In France especially, dogmatic atheism was extolled and the Catholic Church condemned.

Curiously enough, some of those who denounced the rites of the church found themselves attracted by the ritualism of Freemasonry. Whereas the Christian sacraments were repudiated as the product of priestcraft, the arcane mysteries of Freemasonry were hailed as the symbolic path to virtue and the means of achieving universal brotherhood. The eighteenth-century vogue of Freemasonry found musical expression in Mozart's opera *The Magic Flute* (1791). However, the extravagant, allegorical tale which Mozart set to sublime music did not please everyone. Instead of receiving commendation for his presentation of Freemasonry as the embodiment of the loftiest human ideals, Mozart found himself rebuked for disclosing to the world secrets which were supposed to be reserved for the initiated. Worse still, he had done it in the form of childish, light-hearted entertainment.

The three guiding lights of the Enlightenment were reason, nature and progress. Helvétius's work *Concerning the Mind* (1758) argued that all human beings have roughly equal powers of understanding. Condorcet's *Sketch for a Historical Picture of the Human Mind* (1794) depicted Western society standing on the threshold of entering a wholly reasonable world. The idea had already been outlined by the *philosophe* Turgot in a speech at the Sorbonne "On the Successive Advances of the Human Mind" (1750). The French word *philosophe* acquired a quasi-technical significance in the eighteenth century when it was appropriated by a number of intellectuals who believed in the educational value of philosophy, the general benefits to humanity of natural science, free inquiry into religion, and social and political toleration.

A major project which drew on the energies of the *philosophes* was the great *Encyclopedia* (1751-1765) edited by Denis Diderot and Jean Le Rond D'Alembert.[5] Some of the *philosophes* were Deists like Voltaire. Others were atheists. Their foremost exponent was Baron D'Holbach (1723-1789). D'Holbach's *System of Nature, of Laws of the Physical World and of the Moral World* (1770) presented the most comprehensive defense of materialist atheism. The idea of the soul was a pure illusion. Human beings were the product of nature which was subject to the laws which govern the physical universe. D'Holbach's atheism had already been anticipated by La Mettrie's *L'Homme machine* (1747) which, as its title suggests, presents the human as an organic machine.[6]

Julien Offray de la Mettrie (1709-1751) was a leading physician in his day. His numerous writings included a defense of Epicureanism. His lifestyle and offensive views brought him many enemies, and he was forced into exile. La Mettrie found a protector in the person of Frederick the Great of Prussia. But D'Holbach's atheism was too strong even for that monarch, who composed a personal refutation, as did Voltaire in the form of an article on "God" which he featured in his own *Philosophical Dictionary*.

The Age of Enlightenment was by no means an age of uniformity. Alongside the intellectualism of the *philosophes* existed the anti-intellectualism of Rousseau. Belief in reason and progress was tinged with a certain pessimism. Some twenty years before Kant's famous essay on enlightenment, a correspondent wrote to Voltaire asking, "Is this the century of Enlightenment which you embellish and which you enlighten? Alas, times and men are like each other and will always be like each other."[7] Paradoxically, Voltaire himself managed to combine a Deism based on the divine ordering of the world with a profound pessimism about human nature and natural evil.

Voltaire

François-Marie Arouet (1694-1778) was born in Paris to a well-to-do family. He was given a fine classical education by the Jesuits. His father wanted him to study law, but François-Marie was quickly lured away from this vocation in order to pursue his literary bent and enjoy the pleasures that society had to offer. The ire of his father and the hostility of the authorities (on account of his defamatory poems) led to several banishments from Paris, a brief exile in Holland and eleven months in the Bastille (1717-1718). It was about this time that he adopted the name of Voltaire.[8] Perhaps the best explanation is the suggestion that Voltaire is a rough anagram of Arouet L.J., short for Arouet Le Jeune (i.e., Arouet the Younger). This is possible if the "u" is transformed into a "v" and the "j" into an "i", as they often are in classical texts.

The course of Voltaire's career was only marginally less checkered than that of the hero of his satirical novel *Candide*. At an early age Voltaire was hailed as the best playwright in France, the equal of Corneille and Racine. Although few of his works merit performance today, Voltaire's plays dominated the French stage for fifty years. He enjoyed favor at the royal court, but rapidly acquired a number of deadly enemies, among them the Chevalier de Rohan. Voltaire went into hiding and took fencing lessons in order to challenge the Chevalier to a duel and kill him. When this was discovered Voltaire found himself once more in the Bastille. The imprisonment turned public opinion once more to Voltaire's favor, and the authorities commuted the prison sentence to a period of exile in England.

There is something to be said for the view that Voltaire came to England as a man of letters and returned to France as a philosopher. Voltaire was in England for nearly three years (1726-1729). In his homeland he had absorbed the skepticism and critical spirit of earlier generations of free thinkers, but in England he learned to admire the empiricism of Locke and the science of Newton. Voltaire was in England at the peak of the Deist controversy. He not only got to know at first hand the burning issues, but in the course of time acquired a substantial personal library of Deist literature which he carefully read and annotated.[9] In due course the names of English Deists began to appear in his writings, where he made use of deistic criticism of the Bible. But this was not until 1763. In the meantime he published his *Letters Concerning the English Nation* (1733), which were composed as if Voltaire had written them from England in 1728 in order to acquaint his fellow countrymen about the state of religion, politics, philosophy, science, economics and culture on the other side of the English Channel. The work was retitled the following year as *Philosophical Letters* (1734). The new title was perhaps made necessary by the inclusion of an attack on Pascal's *Pensées*.[10]

The *Philosophical Letters* met with such hostility that Voltaire was obliged once more to flee from Paris in order to avoid arrest. The next fifteen years were spent mostly at Cirey in Lorraine, where Voltaire studied physics, metaphysics and history in the company of his learned mistress Mme. du Châtelet. In 1738 he published his *Elements of the Philosophy of Newton* with the purpose of acquainting the French public with the exciting world of Newtonian physics. The same year both Voltaire and Mme. du Châtelet wrote dissertations on the nature of fire for a prize offered by the Academy of Science. But their efforts did not meet with success. However, Voltaire's endeavors in the field of history were rewarded by his being named Historiographer of France, and in the following year he was elected to the Académie Française.

In 1750 Voltaire went to the court of Frederick the Great of Prussia, serving as a philosopher-poet in the capacity of Chamberlain to the King. After three years, he quarreled with the King and found himself obliged to travel. In 1755 he acquired a chateau in Geneva, which he named Les Délices. Today it is the home of the Voltaire Institute and Museum. Here he wrote his *Essay on Manners* (1756) and *Candide* (1759). In 1759 he acquired an estate over the border in France at Ferney, where he eventually settled for the rest of his life. The situation of the peasants quickened his concern for social reform. By this time Voltaire had acquired vast wealth. At Ferney Voltaire was hailed not only as France's great literary figure but as the champion of humanity. In his eighty-fourth year (1778) Voltaire returned to Paris, where he received numerous ovations.

Prior to his death Voltaire had made a recantation of his attacks on the church in order to secure a Christian burial. But his efforts failed to satisfy the church authorities, and Voltaire was buried in obscurity. Some time after the burial D'Alembert succeeded in arranging an elaborate ceremony in Voltaire's honor at the Masonic lodge. Eventually his body was brought in triumph to the Panthéon, the former Catholic church which had become a secular national shrine in the French Revolution. In due course the mortal remains of Rousseau were also installed in the Panthéon. However, when the caskets were opened some years later, they were both found to have been pillaged.

Estimates of Voltaire vary wildly.[11] Some detractors see his work as nothing but superficial common sense. He has been said to have failed to scale the summit of any art, just as he failed to plumb the depths of anything. In addition to being a playwright, Voltaire was a noted historian. In this respect he was like a French Edward Gibbon and David Hume rolled into one. Whereas Gibbon and Hume between them covered the history of the Roman Empire and Great Britain, Voltaire wrote at enormous length on the whole sweep of European history. Moreover, he did so from a secular, antireligious perspective. Voltaire has also some claim to be regarded as a moralist, but the claim is tarnished by his personal sexual life and the manner in which he accumulated his vast fortune. He went to great lengths to rehabilitate the name of Jean Calas, who had been unjustly condemned and cruelly tortured to death. Voltaire waged a relentless war against fanaticism, and yet the ways in which he pursued his own vendettas were not entirely free from the taint of fanaticism. A. J. Ayer has observed that "it is one of Voltaire's great merits that he was an uncompromising advocate of freedom of speech, but the form of this freedom which he primarily arrogated to himself was the freedom to expose, ridicule and denounce the past and current abuses of organized religion."[12]

Voltaire's claim to fame as a philosopher rests largely on his *Philosophical Dictionary*. But as Professor Ayer has pointed out, the title was something of a misnomer.[13] Few of the articles were philosophical in the modern sense of the term, and their only claim to form a dictionary resided in the fact that they were presented in alphabetical order. As the years went by, Voltaire expanded the original 118 articles to over 600. He ranged widely over the fields of physics, biology, etymology, anthropology, medicine, politics, law, morals and biography. But a recurring theme is religion. Voltaire used every opportunity to attack Jews in general and the Old Testament in particular. He repeatedly professed shock at the wickedness of King David and other Old Testament characters and denigrated the savagery of primitive religion. Voltaire's *Philosophical Dictionary* was really a vast collection of essays which afforded their author the opportunity to air his views on whatever took his fancy.

In the last fifteen years of his life, Voltaire became increasingly obsessed with attacking religion. To that end he devoted scores of miscellaneous pieces and *Dictionary* articles. He adopted the motto *Écrasez l'infâme*. The infamy that was to be eradicated was superstition and fanaticism, especially where they were to be found in the church. Voltaire defined fanaticism as "the effect of a false conscience, which makes religion subservient to the caprices of the imagination, and the excesses of the passions."[14] As such the definition appears to allow a legitimate place to religion, but in Voltaire's account of Scripture and church history there was no age which had not succumbed to fanaticism. For what it was, Voltaire's own religion took the form of an intellectualistic deism which acknowledged the existence of God, but denied to the deity any active part in the world's affairs. Just as the existence of a watch points to a watchmaker, so the existence of order in nature points to a creator.

> If a clock is not made in order to tell the time of day, I will then admit that final causes are nothing but chimeras, and be content to go by the name of a final-cause-finder—in plain language fool—to the end of my life.[15]

However, once the clockmaker has made the clock, his services are no longer needed. On the other hand, atheism, Voltaire protested, was scarcely better than religious fanaticism. It was "a most pernicious monster in those who govern . . . although less to be dreaded than fanaticism, it is almost always fatal to virtue."[16]

Within this deistic framework of belief Voltaire assigned to Jesus a place of honor among the great sages of the world alongside Socrates, Pythagoras and Zoroaster. His message was much the same as theirs: "Love God with all your hearts, and your neighbor as yourselves; for that is all."[17] For the rest, Voltaire averred, "There is not a single dogma of Christianity that was preached by Jesus Christ."[18]

The problem of evil was an issue which dogged Voltaire continually.

Like David Hume, Voltaire stated the problem in the words of Epicurus: God can either take away evil from the world and will not; or being willing to do so, cannot; or He neither can nor will; or, lastly, He is both able and willing. If He is willing to remove evil and cannot, then He is not omnipotent. If He can, but will not remove it, then is He not benevolent; if He is neither able nor willing, then is He neither powerful nor benevolent; lastly, if both able and willing to annihilate evil, how does it exist?[19]

The problem of evil was brought into sharp focus by the great Lisbon earthquake of 1755 which Voltaire celebrated in a poem the following year. Voltaire returned again to the problem in his tale *Candide, Or the Optimist* (1759), where he relentlessly ridicules Leibniz's notion of the world as the best of all possible worlds. In *Candide* the advocate of this view is the pathetic Dr. Pangloss, who refuses to be shaken from his belief. At the end of the tale Pangloss keeps saying to Candide:

All events are linked together in the best of all possible worlds; for after all, if you had not been expelled from a fine castle with great kicks in the backside for love of Mademoiselle Cunegonde, if you had not been subjected to the Inquisition, if you had not traveled about America on foot, if you had not given the Baron a great blow with your sword, if you had not lost all your sheep from the good country of Eldorado, you would not be here eating candied citrons and pistachios.[20]

To this Candide replies that this is well-said, "but we must cultivate our garden."

On this somewhat enigmatic note Voltaire concludes his tale. Many have felt that this was an anticlimax,[21] but in fact the ending fits both the book and Voltaire's attitude to life. For him the problem of evil defies all solutions. God is not affected by evil. Neither does he concern himself with human wretchedness and misery. There is no Garden of Eden or Paradise to be restored. Human beings have no alternative but to enjoy what they can while they can and cultivate their gardens (as Voltaire himself did at Ferney) for their personal enjoyment and the mutual profit of their fellow human beings. In a sense what Voltaire advocated and practiced was his own enlightened brand of Epicureanism. In this respect it was a revival of a philosophy of the ancient past. But it also anticipated the growing secularism of the future. Later generations would find Voltaire's writings to be too inextricably enmeshed in his vendettas against the church and the concerns of his day to have enduring value. To the agnostic, Voltaire's deism seems like an unwarrantable aberration. There is little in Voltaire's thought that cannot be found elsewhere. His writings were characterized by breadth rather than depth. Philosophy made no major new development with Voltaire. But no one in the Age of Enlightenment preached the gospel of secularism so indefatigably, so clearly, or so engagingly as Voltaire.

Rousseau

Jean-Jacques Rousseau (1712-1778)[22] was a man of many parts. Rousseau was born in Geneva, Switzerland. His mother died shortly after his birth. His erratic father taught him to read through the medium of sentimental novels and Plutarch's *Lives*. Eventually he was befriended by Mme. de Warens, a convert to Roman Catholicism. Rousseau's emotional dependence on her proved to be an abiding influence. He was born a Protestant, became a Catholic and ended up a Deist (after his own style).

In the course of his restless life he offered himself for the Catholic priesthood, but was rejected. He devised a new system of musical notion which failed to find acceptance. He wrote an opera which was performed before Louis XV, but his refusal to be presented before the king deprived him of all chance of procuring favor and financial support. He was in turn an educationist, political theorist, novelist and man of letters. He made and broke numerous friendships with the famous and not-so-famous. To many he was and is an enigma. His educational theories continue to influence paedogogical thinking to the present day, though Rousseau himself never received any formal education.

He was one of the most eloquent exponents of the dignity of humanity, and yet his personal relationships were pathetically sordid. He deposited his own five illegitimate children, born to him by an illiterate servant girl, Thérèse Levasseur, in a foundling home. He justified the action partly on the grounds that it was in line with the recommendations for bringing up children in Plato's *Republic*. Years later he married Thérèse, but he continued to be tormented by guilt over his actions.

Rousseau's literary career began in 1750 with his *Discourse on the Scien-*

ces and the Arts, a prize essay for the Dijon Academy, in which he argued the thesis that progress corrupts human morals. This theme was amplified and elaborated in various subsequent writings. *Julie, or the New Heloise* (1761) was a novel which attacked the conventions of society which divorced love from marriage. The subtitle and the storyline evoked memories of the affair of Abelard and Heloise in the Middle Ages. The book also afforded Rousseau an opportunity to defend natural religion based upon an allegedly undogmatic reading of the Gospels.

With *The New Heloise* Rousseau reached the pinnacle of his success. His next major work *Émile, or On Education* (1762) brought mixed reactions. It extended his fame among his admirers, but roused such opposition among opponents that the book was banned and burned, and its author obliged to flee from France. The book is a series of lengthy disquisitions on educational theory, tied together by the story of Émile's education. The theory underlying Rousseau's views is announced in the opening words: "God makes all things good; man meddles with them and they become evil."[23] This leads Rousseau into head-on conflict with the traditional educational theory of his day. Instead of forcing children to learn rules and regulations, nature should be allowed to take its course. Children should be allowed to follow their natural instincts, freed as much as possible from external constraints and the corrupting influence of society. The young Émile is to be brought up in a kind of quarantine, where harmful influences are kept well at bay. Among the latter are toy weapons and church bells. Both are symbols of decadent society, through which the evils of war and institutionalized religion might corrupt the young. Food is to be kept natural and simple. Among the works Émile is permitted to read is Defoe's *Robinson Crusoe* with its idealized picture of life on a desert island. Émile himself is to be brought up in the country under the watchful eye of a private tutor who will see to it that his natural instincts are naturally led in the right direction.

The fourth of the five books which make up *Émile* contains a lengthy excursus on religion entitled "The Creed of a Savoyard Priest." The passage purports to be the profession of faith delivered by an elderly priest to a young enquirer as they spend a day together surrounded by the splendor of the Alps. The priest disclaims all pretensions to be a great philosopher. What he has to offer is "a certain amount of common-sense and a constant devotion to truth."[24] If he has made mistakes, they are honest mistakes. His hearer is invited to consult his heart and listen to the voice of reason. The discourse falls into two distinct parts. The first part deals with "natural religion." Here the old priest urges that matter, being inert, requires an extraneous cause (God) to set it in motion. The laws of the physical world point to God as supreme Intelligence. Evil is the result of the dualism of body and soul. Freedom is the basis of happiness and immortality. Conscience is the ultimate principle of the moral life and the source of true happiness and virtue.

Having laid the foundations of this positive deism in the first part of the discourse, the priest uses the second part to deploy his deistic arguments against revealed religion. Claims to revelation produce irrational intolerance. It is impossible for any single revealed religion to establish its claims to truth. Although the priest professes admiration for the Gospels, the Christ that he believes in is essentially "the teacher and pattern" of "pure and lofty morality." Jesus is certainly no fiction of the imagination. His actions are better attested than those of Socrates. "If the life and death of Socrates are those of a philosopher, the life and death of Christ are those of a God."[25] But the priest clearly does not intend this to be understood in any traditional, orthodox sense. Human salvation cannot be made dependent upon anything so particular as faith in another historical human being, and the claims of Christianity should not be pressed upon Jews and Mohammedans. Dogmas should be judged by their moral relevance. The young hearer is exhorted to love God, to be honest and humble, and to "learn to be ignorant." "Dare to confess God before the philosophers; dare to preach humanity before the intolerant."[26]

What Rousseau was urging upon his readers was his own version of a deistic undogmatic dogmatism. The reader is exhorted to "seek honestly after truth" and to bring all that he has ever been taught "to the bar of conscience and of reason."[27] At the same time no doubt is left as to what the desired result will be. To place any reliance upon miracles and events in the past is to plunge everything into uncertainty.[28] God, in the last analysis, is not a fit subject for argument and debate. He is known already in the depths of our being. It is dangerous to speculate; it is much better to repose in God.

If I have succeeded in discerning these attributes of which I have no absolute idea, it is in the form of unavoidable deductions, and by the right use of my reason; but I affirm them without understanding them, and at bottom that is no affirmation at all. In vain do I say, God is thus, I feel it, I experience it, none the more do I understand how God can be thus.

In a word: the more I strive to envisage his infinite essence the less do I comprehend it; but it is, and that is enough for me; the less I understand, the more I adore. I abase myself, saying, "Being of beings, I am because thou art; to fix my thoughts on thee is to ascend to the source of my being. The best use I can make of my reason is to resign it before thee; my mind delights, my weakness rejoices, to feel myself overwhelmed by thy greatness.[29]

In the same year that Rousseau published *Émile*, he also published *The Social Contract* which set out his theory of the state and society. The laws of a state are not a matter of divine appointment. They are not to be based upon divine law but upon the will of the people. Church and state should be kept separate.[30] The only valid basis for a society is for its members to agree to a social pact which will combine freedom with just government in the interests of the majority. Rousseau's essay was a seminal work of modern, secular democratic thinking and played no small part in paving the way for the French Revolution.

The outcry provoked by *Émile* caused Rousseau to flee from France, partly for his own safety and partly to avoid embarrassing his patrons. A warrant was issued for his arrest. The book was condemned by the archbishop of Paris, Christophe de Beaumont, in a Pastoral Letter. Later on *Émile* was also condemned in Geneva. In due course Rousseau wrote a reply in the form of an open letter to the archbishop (1762). Together with his *Letters written from the Mountain* (1764), which replied to the Genevan authorities, the letter served to complement the Confession of Faith in *Émile*.

During this period Rousseau found himself not only in conflict with both Catholics and Protestants; he found his relations with the Encyclopedists also increasingly strained. To the former he was too irreligious, to the latter he was too religious. For a time he lived under the protection of Frederick the Great of Prussia. But alarmed by the mounting hostility, Rousseau decided to accept the invitation of David Hume to make his home in England. In England Rousseau's behavior became increasingly erratic. He became convinced that Hume was plotting his downfall, and after a violent quarrel he fled in panic back to France. He continued to be haunted by the fear of persecution. The principal works of his last years were his *Confessions* (1772) and *The Reveries of the Solitary Stroller* (1778). In a sense, the two were complementary. The former is a massive, introspective piece of autobiography, a striking secular counterpart to Augustine's work of the same title. The latter was Rousseau's spiritual testament.

To Immanuel Kant, Rousseau was one of the great philosophical liberators of the modern age. He ranked him alongside Newton. What Newton had done in the sphere of natural science Rousseau had done in the field of the study of humanity.

Newton was the first to discern order and regularity in combination with great simplicity, where before him men had encountered disorder and unrelated diversity. Since Newton the comets follow geometric orbits. Rousseau was the first to discover beneath the varying forms human nature assumes, the deeply concealed essence of man and the hidden law in accordance with which Providence is justified by his observations.[31]

Rousseau stands with Voltaire as the foremost French thinkers of their age. Although the latter might qualify as a kind of universal genius, the thought of Rousseau was more seminal. The two were in fact archenemies, though they attacked each other at long range. Ironically, their (now empty) tombs stand together in the Panthéon. But the two rivals never met, and their teaching pulled in opposite directions.

Like other representatives of the Age of Enlightenment, Voltaire could be described as an eighteenth-century Epicurean. At heart he was an optimistic materialist who prided himself on his open-minded rationality, who cherished enlightenment, and who prized the value of empirical observation.

Rousseau was both a child and a foe of enlightenment. He had profound misgivings about the onward march of civilization and the contribution of science. With his stress on feeling, the heart and his pleading for a return to nature, Rousseau anticipated the Romantic Movement and its criticism of the Enlightenment. But Rousseau's writings contain more than an echo of classical Stoicism.[32] He not only drew on Stoic literature, but developed a post-Christian form of Stoicism for his times. It was a Stoicism which grappled with the problem of evil. It allowed for belief in the divine, but sought to remedy the ills of society by cultivating the inner self. It extended the cultivation of the individual self to society at large by means of the modern myth of the social contract. Kant thought of Rousseau's achievement as a kind of counterpart in the field of educational and social theory to the scientific discoveries of Sir Isaac Newton. But the two were not quite on a par. Rousseau's work could hardly claim the scientific rigor that Newton had brought to his investigations. Rousseau's post-Christian philosophy was no more scientific than was pre-Christian philosophy. In any case, to have his work hailed as a scientific achievement would hardly have been gratifying for Rousseau. But it had one thing in common with the scientific thinking of his day. It marked a significant further step in the continued secularization of modern life.

17. ENLIGHTENMENT AND SKEPTICISM IN GERMANY

F*rom the standpoint of the history of Christianity and Western thought the* German Enlightenment reached its climax in the final quarter of the eighteenth century. It had two focal points. One of them was Lessing's publication of the anonymous writings of Reimarus which launched the quest of the historical Jesus in Germany. The other was the philosophy of Immanuel Kant.

Lessing, Reimarus and the Quest of the Historical Jesus
The name of Gotthold Ephraim Lessing (1729-1781)[1] is one which figures more often in the annals of German literature than in histories of philosophy. Lessing played a leading part in founding the modern German theater with plays like *Emilia Galotti* (1772), *Minna von Barnhelm* (1767) and *Nathan the Wise* (1779). He helped to free German drama from slavish imitation of French classical tragedy and introduced the novel practice of writing plays about the middle class instead of kings, the nobility and characters from the world of antiquity. But Lessing's contribution to the rising tide of skepticism was no smaller than, even though somewhat different from, that of Voltaire and Rousseau. His forays into the theological world proved to be a major turning point in the history of theology.

The son of a pastor, Lessing was brought up in an atmosphere of orthodox piety. In his student days at Leipzig he had studied theology before turning to philosophy and literature. The theological writings of his later years reveal an acute mind that was able to take on the professional theologians on their own terms. In 1767 Lessing came to Hamburg as consultant and resident critic of the short-lived National Theater. It was here that he got to know the family of Hermann Samuel Reimarus (1694-1768). The Reimarus home was a center of culture and enlightenment in the city of Hamburg. This tradition was maintained by the daughter, Elise, and the son, Johann, who was Lessing's physician. It was Lessing's contact with the Reimarus family that led to a series of events which changed the course of theology.

Hermann Samuel Reimarus was widely known as a respected, if somewhat rationalistic, religious writer. In his younger days he had spent some time in Holland and England during the period when the Deistic controversy was approaching its climax. Reimarus spent the last forty years of his life as a teacher of oriental languages in Hamburg. The formidable list of his learned, though now unread, publications indicates his respect for reason and for Christianity as a rational religion. Reimarus combatted the materialistic atheism of La Mettrie and the pantheism of Spinoza. However, Reimarus's published works give little hint of the doubts that he had long been nursing about revealed religion, the historical worth of the Bible, and the origins of Christianity. These doubts were reserved for his *magnum opus*, written to express his personal doubts but deliberately withheld from publication on account of its contents. Reimarus entitled his manuscript *Apology, Or Defence of the Rational Worshippers of God.*

Lessing was admitted to the intimate circle of those who were permitted to see the text, and succeeded in obtaining a copy. On leaving Hamburg he assumed the post of librarian to the duke of Brunswick at the ducal library in Wolfenbüttel. In this capacity Lessing proceeded to publish a series of works *On History and Literature from the Treasures of the Ducal Library at Wolfenbüttel.* The series afforded Lessing the opportunity to begin publication of Reimarus's *Apology.* At that point in time religious censorship was in force, and German authors did not enjoy the same freedom of speech as their English counterparts. This was doubtless a major factor in the decision to withhold the manuscript from publication. Lessing surmounted this obstacle by making two significant moves. First, he obtained exemption from censorship for his series on the grounds of its intrinsic historical interest (though this freedom was eventually forfeited on account of the ensuing controversy). Secondly, he published Reimarus's work, *Fragments of an Unnamed Author*,[2] which he released in the form of extracts spread out over a period of time. To throw heresy hunters still further off the scent, Lessing suggested that the author might have been the well-known Deist Johann Lorenz Schmidt, who had spent the last years of his life at the court in Wolfenbüttel.

Lessing published seven *Fragments* between 1774 and 1778. The topics ranged widely from a piece advocating toleration for the Deists to critical attacks on the veracity of the Old Testament and the resurrection narratives in the Gospels. It was, however, the seventh and last *Fragment* which provoked the greatest controversy. It was an account of Jesus entitled *On the Intentions of Jesus and the Evangelists*.

It presented Jesus as a sincere but misguided religious reformer. In a manner evocative of the English Deists, Reimarus denied that there were any mysteries in Jesus' preaching. Jesus did not intend to introduce any new teaching or novel ceremonies into the Jewish religion. Rather, he sought to purify Judaism and call it back to true Jewish piety. Unfortunately, Jesus made a number of moves which were to prove fatal. He allowed himself to be sidetracked into embracing political messianism. He came to think of the kingdom of God as a political entity which was just around the corner. At first Jesus thought that it would come about through his preaching and calls to repentance and holiness. But then he became desperate, and he decided to force the issue at all costs. Jesus chose the Passover time to display his hand and force a decision. Unfortunately he had miscalculated the strength of popular support. The crowds welcomed him as he rode into Jerusalem, but Jesus had already alienated the authorities. The disturbance that he created in the Temple simply confirmed the authorities in their decision to liquidate him. At the crucial moment all his followers deserted him. Jesus died a broken man. His last words express his disillusionment with God who had failed him.

The entire Christian religion might well have ended then and there but for the imagination and duplicity of Jesus' disciples. At first they were terrified and went into hiding. But when it became clear that the authorities did not intend to persecute them, they hit on a bold master plan. They put out the story that Jesus had risen from the dead and had appeared to them in private. The story was further embellished by the claim that the kingdom of God which Jesus had talked about would materialize when Jesus returned to earth. Such were the disciples' powers of persuasion that they built up a following. The church managed to weather the trials and tribulation which came its way. The Second Coming of Jesus kept on being postponed. The church has flourished for nearly eighteen hundred years, but few have noticed that the whole edifice of Christianity was built upon fraud.

Following the lead of Albert Schweitzer some eighty years ago, generations of scholars have assumed that the publication of Reimarus's Fragment *On the Intentions of Jesus and his Disciples* marked the beginning of the quest of the historical Jesus. The idea that the real Jesus of history was different from the Jesus depicted in the New Testament and the desire to get at the facts have been the central issue in theology from that day to this. Schweitzer went so far as to hail Reimarus's work as "perhaps the most splendid achievement in the whole course of the historical investigation of the life of Jesus, for he was the first to grasp the fact that the world of thought in which Jesus moved was essentially eschatological."[3] What Schweitzer had in mind here was Reimarus's contention that Jesus believed that he was living in the endtimes, and that Jesus cannot be understood apart from this notion of the kingdom of God.

To Schweitzer, Reimarus appeared like a bolt from the blue with no predecessors and no successors. Today it is clear that this verdict cannot stand. Reimarus himself was in England while the Deistic controversy was raging. His personal library contained copies of important Deistic writings, and close study of his work shows his indebtedness to the Deism that emanated from England. Not only was Reimarus familiar with the corpus of Deistic literature, but so too was the intellectual reading public for many years prior to the publication of the *Fragments*. Sundry works had already been translated into German, and those who had not read the books themselves had been kept abreast of developments abroad by journals which informed their readers about what was going on outside the German-speaking world. Nevertheless, Reimarus's work marked a turning point, partly because of the controversy that it unleashed and partly because it was a work evidently written by a German author which cast grave doubts about the historical foundations of the Christian faith.

The opening shots in the pamphlet war were fired as early as 1777. In that year J. D. Schumann restated the traditional arguments from miracles and prophecy for the truth of Christianity. J. H. Ress defended the authenticity of the resurrection narratives against the criticism of the Fragmentist. Lessing himself joined the fray by publishing a series of *Counter Theses* in his capacity as editor and by responding to the writings of Schumann and Ress in pamphlets of his own. The main target of Lessing's writings was the pastor of the Lutheran Church of St. Catherine in Hamburg, J. M. Goeze. The weightiest work in the entire controversy came from the pen of J. S. Semler (1725-1791), who is now widely credited with being the founder of the historical study of the New Testament. In 1779 Semler published a massive *Answer to the Fragments of an Unknown Author*, which analyzed the *Fragments* almost line by line, exploiting the faulty logic, the self-contradictions, and the inadequacies of the historical interpretation of the Fragmentist. Semler's work has never been translated into English. It is a far more substantial and impressive work than Albert Schweitzer's summary of it might suggest. With its publication the immediate controversy began to subside. Within two years Lessing himself died, and other things began to occupy the public's attention.

Throughout the controversy, Lessing behaved like a German Voltaire. He disowned the views of the unnamed Fragmentist, but asserted the author's right to state them. He professed to think that the unnamed author was too extreme, but what if he were right? What difference would it make? The main thrust of Lessing's own contributions to the debate was directed at fundamental questions which the *Fragments* posed. Can the truth of a religion be established by appealing to history? Can any religion show from history that it is uniquely true? In 1777 Lessing published a reply to J. D. Schumann's argument from prophecy and miracles for the truth of Christianity. Lessing entitled his own pamphlet *On the Proof of the Spirit and of Power*. The title deliberately echoes the words of the apostle Paul in 1 Corinthians 2:4. Lessing's strategy was to try to outflank the question of history by denying its relevance. If Lessing had lived at the time of Christ and had seen prophecy fulfilled and miracles performed before his own eyes, then of course they would have weighed with him. But now we have only *reports* of such fulfillments

and such phenomena. Reports do not have the same compelling powers
as the events themselves. Lessing crowned his argument with the celebrated axiom:

> If no historical truth can be demonstrated, then nothing can be dem-
> onstrated by means of historical truths.
>
> That is: *accidental truths of history can never become the proof of necessary*
> *truths of reason.*[4]

Evidently Lessing felt that he had made a real score here. In fact, he was
not saying anything particularly new. Moreover, his argument begged the
question. To say that historical statements are not of the same order as,
say, the proposition that *two plus two make four*, is simply to state an
obvious truism. *Two plus two make four* is self-evident. Once we understand
the meaning of the words in this proposition we can see its truth. No
further observation or historical inquiry is necessary. On the other hand,
the truth of historical statements depends upon the credibility of the
supporting testimony. In propounding his axiom Lessing was restating a
basic dogma of rationalism that had been around since the days of Descartes, that only clear and distinct, self-evident ideas may serve as the basis
for a system of thought. The ideal form of knowledge was geometry with
its self-evident definitions, axioms and logically necessary deductions.
This ideal was exemplified in Spinoza's *Ethics* (1677). Leibniz had explained the point underlying Lessing's distinction in numerous places,
including his essay on "Necessary and Contingent Truths" (c. 1686) and
his *Monadology* (1714).[5] Lessing's distinction between "accidental truths"
and "necessary truths" corresponds to the distinction that Kant made
between "synthetic" and "analytic judgments" in his *Critique of Pure Reason*
(1781), which was published in the year of Lessing's death.[6]

On the basis of this distinction Lessing urged that historical claims
belong to a different category from metaphysical and moral ideas. There
was an "ugly, broad ditch" between the two categories over which Lessing could not jump, however much he might wish to.[7] Despite his protestations of desire to jump over the ditch, Lessing saw no need to jump.
For the basis of religion did not lie in history at all. The value of any
religion (Christian or otherwise) depends upon its capacity to transform
life through love. Lessing gave dramatic expression to this last point in
his play *Nathan the Wise* (1779). By the time that he wrote it, Lessing had

been forbidden to publish anything more on religion. He resolved to get around this by returning to what he called "his former pulpit," that is, the stage. The play was set in the time of the Crusades, but the characters in the play bore marked resemblance to several of the persons involved in the *Fragments* controversy, including Pastor Goeze. The hero, Nathan, was modelled on Moses Mendelssohn. The three great religions are represented by three main characters: Nathan the Jew, Saladin the Moslem and the Knight Templar.

At the heart of the play, in the middle of the third act, Lessing drew upon a tale found in Boccaccio's *Decameron*. Saladin asks Nathan which of the three religions is true. Nathan replies with the allegory of the three rings: There was once an ancient ring which had the power of bestowing on its owner the gift of being loved by God and man. The ring was passed on to successive generations, continually bestowing its wondrous power. At last it came into the possession of a man who had three sons, each equally dear to him. To resolve the problem of who should get the ring, the old man had two replicas made. Each son got a ring, and no one could tell the rings apart. As with religion, the original could not be traced. Each claimed to have the truth. At last the sons appealed to a judge who suggested in exasperation that none of the rings might be genuine. Perhaps the father wanted to destroy the tyranny of the ring. It was clear that none of the brothers was loved by all. Perhaps none of them had the true ring. In the circumstances the judge advised the brothers each to behave as if he possessed the true ring and thereby prove the truth of his claims. The play ends with the discovery of mutual kinship and joyful reconciliation.

Nathan the Wise was not quite Lessing's last word on religion. In his essay *On the Education of the Human Race* (1780) Lessing spelled out the message that was implicit in the play. The world's religions represent merely phases in the progress toward a universal religion of love in which humankind will be perfected.[8] The Old Testament is seen as an "elementary primer" in the education process. Jesus is hailed as "the first reliable, practical teacher of the immortality of the soul." For Lessing history was at best a series of occasions for grasping truths which belonged to a different order from historical truths. As he said elsewhere, "Religion is not true because the evangelists and apostles taught it; on the contrary, they taught it because it was true. The written traditions must be interpreted by their inward truth and no written traditions can give religion any inward truth if it has none."[9] Lessing's theme has a lofty ring about it. It echoes a refrain that can be found in the English Deist Matthew Tindal.[10] But it must be asked whether it is as true as it must appear at first sight. Lessing's overall position makes the gratuitous assumption that religions are more or less all about the same thing, and are merely passing phases in the world's onward progress. It assumes that history cannot have decisive importance for religion, because no human being or event in time can affect the central questions of religion.

Lessing's position makes certain assumptions which an Enlightened thinker like himself would accept without question, but which many would challenge today. He assumes that demonstrable, necessary propositions not only belong to a higher order than other sorts of propositions, but that such propositions can serve as a basis for a belief system. But it may be questioned whether the views that Lessing himself was advocating had been so demonstrated, or indeed whether any belief-system or world view could be demonstrated as being established by "necessary truths of reason."

There is, of course, a profound sense in which it can be said that the evangelists and apostles taught religion because it was true. They bore witness to the action of God in history, as they encountered it in Jesus Christ. The fact that such an encounter is not reducible to a rationally self-evident proposition does not make it any less compelling. At the heart of Lessing's complaint against orthodox Christians was the charge that they were making category mistakes by confusing different kinds of truth. But in fact it was Lessing himself who was making the category mistake by allowing only two types of truth—accidental truths of history and necessary truths of reason—and by failing to see that history can provide the means of apprehending a reality which transcends these categories.[11]

About the time that he wrote his essay *On the Education of the Human Race,* Lessing made some remarks about Spinoza which were taken to mean that he himself had embraced Spinozism. This action gave grave offense to Moses Mendelssohn and resulted in what came to be known as the Pantheism Controversy. Whether Lessing was actually a pantheist is still being debated. There are certain passages in his writings which suggest that he was.[12] What is beyond dispute is the fact that from this time onwards an increasing number of writers professed admiration for Spinoza. Among them are names celebrated in the history of German literature, philosophy and theology—Herder, Goethe, Schleiermacher, Hegel and Schelling. As the Age of Enlightenment was succeeded by the Age of Idealism, the Deism of the Enlightenment came to be replaced by a pantheism which viewed God as the pervasive, divine spirit of the world. Inevitably this affected the way that people thought about Christianity. At the same time the historical skepticism of the Enlightenment continued to thrive. But the story of this belongs elsewhere.[13]

Kant

Immanuel Kant (1724-1804)[14] was one of the most acute and influential philosophers of modern times. The course of his life was outwardly uneventful, but his writing and teaching changed the course of Western thought. It marked the climax of two-hundred years of European philosophy and shaped the course of what was to follow. Kant was born and died at Königsberg, the capital city of East Prussia (now annexed to the U.S.S.R and renamed Kaliningrad). He was the son of a poor harness-maker of Scottish ancestry and had a pietistic upbringing. He was small in physique—evidently never growing taller than five feet two inches or weighing more than one hundred pounds. In his youth it was taken for granted that he would study theology and become a Lutheran pastor. But Kant fell in love with Latin, and was captivated by Lucretius's poem *On the Nature of Things*. Even late in life Kant could recite long sections of it from memory. Lucretius helped to turn Kant's thoughts away from religion toward a naturalistic view of the world. Kant was a student at the University of Königsberg and, apart from a period as a private tutor, spent the rest of his life there. In 1755 he became an unsalaried lecturer and continued in that capacity for the next fifteen years. In 1770 he was appointed to the chair of logic and metaphysics, and despite his weak constitution he continued to be active in that post until 1796, when his faculties had begun to show signs of decline.

Kant's life presents a paradoxical picture. Today Kant is known as a major philosopher, but he owed his early reputation to his views on the nature of the universe. His position at the university required him to lecture on a wide range of subjects, and his earliest publications were mainly in the field of science and natural philosophy.[15] The most important of these early works was Kant's *Universal Natural History and Theory of the Heavens*,[16] which contains the first correct explanation of the appearance of the Milky Way. Kant went on to picture the universe as an infinite, hierarchically ordered system of galaxies which he linked with a theory of the evolution of planetary systems and a theory of atoms. In his preface he acknowledged similarities between his views and those of Lucretius, Epicurus, Leucippus, Democritus and Sir Isaac Newton. But he defended himself against charges of reviving ancient paganism and naturalism, protesting that his conviction of "the infallibility of Divine truth" was so potent that he would hold everything that contradicted it "as sufficiently refuted by that truth." At this stage in his career, Kant professed to value the proofs from the beauty and perfect arrangement of the universe for a supremely wise Creator. At the same time he expressed the wish that the defenders of religion would not use those proofs "in a bad way" so as to perpetuate the conflict with the advocates of naturalism.[17]

Kant also lectured on anthropology and geography. He was fond of books on travel, but never travelled far. He enjoyed company and frequently entertained guests at his midday meal (his sole meal of the day). He liked female company (so long as his lady guests did not pretend that they understood his *Critique of Pure Reason*). He twice contemplated marriage, but put off making a decision until it was too late. The pattern of his daily life was strictly regulated. His servant awoke him at five. He worked at his desk in nightcap and robe until seven. After his morning lectures he returned to his study, donning once more the nightcap and robe. After his midday meal he took a solitary walk. The poet Heinrich Heine put out the story that the housewives of Königsberg could set their clocks by the regularity of Kant's afternoon walk. Kant had no ear for music, and had an intense dislike of noise. On one occasion he urged the police authorities to stop the inmates of a nearby prison from consoling themselves by singing hymns. His own highly regulated personal life was shaped by considerations of practical utility and well-being and by a profound awareness of the dictates of duty.

Any adequate understanding of Kant's thought must grapple with his great *Critiques,* especially the *Critique of Pure Reason.* But there are two relatively minor writings which help to put Kant's philosophy in perspective. We have already noted one of these writings—Kant's journal article of 1784 which addressed the question "What is Enlightenment?"[18] Kant's answer was that enlightenment was the determination to think for oneself and not accept anything on authority. If the world was not yet an enlightened world, Kant had already given proof of his determination to be an enlightened philosopher with the publication in 1781 of his *Critique of Pure Reason* (2nd edition, 1787). It was a work which reappraised the process and scope of human knowledge. The other writing which puts Kant's thought into perspective came a dozen years after the journal article. It was a letter which Kant wrote to C. F. Stäudlin, who was a professor of theology at the University of Göttingen. In this letter Kant writes of his great plan for an enlightened reappraisal of the main areas of human activity.

> My longstanding plan for the reappraisal, incumbent upon me in the field of pure philosophy centered on dealing with three tasks: (1) What can I know? (Metaphysics) (2) What should I do? (Ethics) (3) What may I hope? (Religion); whereupon the fourth should follow: What is man? (Anthropology; on which I have annually delivered a course for more than 20 years). With the accompanying book *Religion within the Limits* etc. I have sought to complete the third division of my plan. In this work conscientiousness and true respect for the Christian religion, but also the proper principle of freedom of thought, have led me to conceal nothing. On the contrary, I have presented everything openly, as I believe I see the possible union of the latter with the purest practical reason.[19]

The work that Kant referred to in this letter was *Religion within the Limits of Reason Alone* (1793). The work did in the sphere of religion what Kant's other great *Critiques* had done in other spheres. His great work on ethics, the *Critique of Practical Reason,* had been published in 1788. It was followed by a major study of aesthetics, the *Critique of Judgment* (1790). The long-awaited enquiry into *Anthropology* finally appeared in 1798. Kant supplemented these major treatises with a number of shorter writings.

Among them are his *Prolegomena to Any Future Metaphysics* (1783) and *Foundations of the Metaphysics of Morals* (1785).

In a wide-ranging historical survey like the present book, it is impossible to give more than the barest outline of a thinker's ideas. The difficulties are infinitely compounded in the case of a philosopher of the stature of Kant. We shall confine our attention to four aspects of his thought: (1) Kant's view of knowledge; (2) his rejection of the traditional proofs of the existence of God; (3) his moral approach to God; and (4) his reappraisal of Christianity.

1. Kant's View of Knowledge. Kant's view of knowledge was a mixture of rationalism and empiricism. He had been educated in the rationalist tradition, but fairly early on he had read David Hume who (in his own phrase) had interrupted his "dogmatic slumber."[20] Hume's discussion of cause and effect and his views on the limited scope of reason shook Kant's faith in rationalism. But Hume's discussion of reason proved to be unsatisfactory, and over the years Kant worked out his own critical philosophy which sought to determine the role and scope of reason in the acquisition of human knowledge. Kant agreed with the empiricists in saying that "all our knowledge begins with experience," but differed from them in insisting that "it does not follow that it all arises out of experience."[21] The "raw material" of knowledge comes from outside us, but the mind also plays a part in processing that material by means of its own built-in concepts and ways of thinking. Kant's aim in the *Critique of Pure Reason* was to examine this process and determine the scope of human knowledge.

Kant formulated the central question of the *Critique of Pure Reason* in the following words: "How are *a priori* synthetic judgments possible?"[22] To grasp what Kant means we need to grasp the basic meaning of two sets of terms. The first is the distinction between *synthetic* and *analytic*. In his introduction to the *Critique* Kant provides the following explanation:

> In all judgments in which the relation of a subject to the predicate is thought . . . this relation is possible in two different ways. Either the predicate B belongs to the subject A, as something which is (covertly) contained in this concept A; or B lies outside the concept A, although it does indeed stand in connection with it. In the one case I entitle

the judgment analytic, in the other synthetic.[23]
If we try to translate this abstract terminology into everyday language, we could say that the statement "A rainy day is a wet day" is an example of an *analytic* statement. The notion of "wet day" is already contained in that of "rainy day." Such a statement is also said to be *necessary*. It is necessarily true. To deny it would involve a contradiction in terms. There cannot be a rainy day which is not also a wet day. However, to make a statement of this kind is merely to offer a definition of terms. Definitions of this kind merely unpack whatever is contained in the terms. They do not refer to any particular state of affairs. On the other hand, if we say that "Tuesday was a wet day," we are making a different sort of statement. It belongs to the class of statements which Kant terms *synthetic*. Such statements are not necessarily true. For Tuesday could have been a dry day or any other kind of day. In *synthetic* statements the predicate says something about the subject which was not already contained in the notion of the subject. To deny it is not to involve oneself in a contradiction of terms. The truth or falsity of the statement depends on whether what is said corresponds with observable facts. In other words, to test whether a *synthetic* statement like "Tuesday was a wet day" is true, you have to check on what people remember about Tuesday.

The other set of terms which require definition is *a priori* and *a posteriori*.[24] Kant defined *a priori* knowledge as knowledge that is "absolutely independent of all experience." He contrasted it with *a posteriori* knowledge which denotes empirical knowledge of the world gained through the senses. Such knowledge is gained "solely from experience." To some extent, the two pairs of concepts that we have noted overlap. *Synthetic* knowledge is also *a posteriori* knowledge, for it involves observation and experience through the senses. Kant believed that knowledge of the world was also both *synthetic* and *a priori*. Hence the central question of his book. His aim was to examine the factors involved in this kind of knowledge. It affected both metaphysical and physical knowledge. For before one could safely embark on these enterprises, it was necessary to embark on a preliminary critique of *pure reason*. By this term Kant meant "the faculty of reason in general" viewed *"independently of all experience."* *"A priori* modes of knowledge are entitled pure when there is no admixture of anything empirical."

Thus Kant's *Critique of Pure Reason* was devoted to examining the scope and limitations of human thought by means of a prior examination of human reason. Kant ventured to claim that his inquiry had been so complete that "there is not a single metaphysical problem which has not been solved, or for the solution of which the key at least has not been supplied."[25] As we shall see shortly, this boast was not intended to open the door to a new age of metaphysical speculation. Quite the reverse. Kant believed that traditional metaphysics involved self-contradictory speculation about illusory entities which (if they existed at all) lay beyond the scope of the human mind.

Kant's view of knowledge may be summed up by saying that its raw material consists of sensible impressions which is processed by the human mind. In processing this raw material the mind employs the *Forms of Intuition* of space and time.[26] Neither space nor time represent properties of things in themselves. Space is nothing but the form of all appearances of outer sense, whereas time is the form of inner sense. Time and space belong to our intuition of objects. But Kant believed that they belong to our a priori intuition. As such "they apply to objects only insofar as objects are viewed as appearances, and do not present things as they are in themselves. This is the sole field of their validity; should we pass beyond it, no objective use can be made of them."[27]

In addition to the forms of intuition Kant argued that the mind employs *Categories* or *Pure Concepts of the Understanding*.[28] Kant identified twelve such categories of understanding which he groups into four groups of three: *Quantity* (Unity, Plurality, Totality); *Quality* (Reality, Negation, Limitation); *Relation* (Inherence and Subsistence, Causality and Dependence, Community) and *Modality* (Possibility-Impossibility, Existence-Non-existence, Necessity-Contingency). The categories of understanding enable the human mind to classify and interpret the objects of experience. They make human understanding possible. However, the mind does not actually perceive things as they are in themselves. As Kant remarked with regard to the forms of intuition, "While much can be said *a priori* as regards the form of appearances, nothing whatsoever can be asserted of the thing itself, which may underlie these appearances."[29] In other words, the Thing-in-Itself (German, *Ding-an-sich*) is unknowable.

If Kant was skeptical about the possibility of knowing material things as they are in themselves, he was doubly so about realities which alleged-ly transcend the material. Use of the forms of intuition was "valid only for objects of possible experience."[30] As soon as the human mind tries to press beyond the material world, it lands itself in *Antinomies* or irrec-oncilable self-contradictions.[31] For the concepts that the mind seeks to apply to the metaphysical realm are concepts which are applicable to the physical realm. And even here the human mind has to live with contra-dictions. A case in point is the belief in free will. Kant believed that the laws of nature preclude human freedom, for science posits an explana-tion of all events in terms of causal sequence. Thus the idea of human freedom is illusory. On the other hand, Kant maintained that it was rational to believe in "absolute spontaneity," for without it no series of causes could ever begin. Moreover, freedom was necessary to morality. For if human beings were not free to respond to moral imperatives, the whole basis of morality would be undermined. As we shall see shortly, Kant could *postulate* freedom as a prerequisite for moral thought and action because ethics required it. But he insisted that the human mind could not attain any understanding of the reality of such postulates. In short, the realm of metaphysical inquiry was off-limits because the hu-man mind is not equipped to penetrate beyond the physical world.

In a sense Kant's view of the human mind is like someone looking at a black-and-white TV set. The TV set can pick up signals sent out by different stations. But what the screen shows is a two-dimensional pic-ture in various shades of gray. The set decodes the signals, but the picture on the screen is not identical with the reality that it represents. Moreover, the viewer cannot get behind the TV screen and see what really lies behind the picture.

Ever since Kant's own day the merits of his views have been hotly disputed. One of Kant's contemporaries was the fellow citizen of Königsberg, J. G. Hamann (1730-1788). Hamann admired Kant's abili-ties, but rejected his views. In a letter to the poet and theologian Herder (who had been a student of Kant), Hamann remarked that Kant "cer-tainly deserves the title of a Prussian Hume. . . . Our countryman keeps on chewing the cud of Hume's fury against causality, without taking this matter of belief into account."[32] At the same time Hamann wryly ob-served that "without knowing it, his [Kant's] enthusiasm for the intellectual world beyond space and time is worse than Plato's." Hamann had read the proofs of Kant's great *Critique* even before Kant himself had done so. He was the first of many who thought that Hume had given to Kant the problem of knowledge, and Kant had given it back as if it were the solution. On this view Kant vainly draws on the rationalist view of innate ideas which reappear in his philosophy under the guise of the forms of intuition and the categories of understanding. But in the end what we call knowledge is really a construct that we place on our sense experience. What lies behind that sense experience is unknowable.

Echoes of this discussion continue to be heard today. On the one side stand admirers of Kant like Roger Scruton and Lewis White Beck who defend his epistemology against modern versions of the charges that Hamann levelled against it. On the other side stand critics like Stanley L. Jaki who sees Kant's work as a monumental failure. Scruton exonerates Kant of being a kind of cryptic Humean. Nor was he, for that matter, a throwback to Leibniz. Kant, he believes, must be understood on his own terms. Scruton does not accept the view that Kant thought of transcendental objects as real things. His final summation makes Kant sound curiously modern and innocuous. Kant's theory of knowledge boils down to the claim that "there is no description of the world that can free itself from experience. Although the world that we know is not our creation, nor merely a synopsis of our perspective, it cannot be known except from the point of view which is ours. All attempts to break through the limits imposed by experience end in self-contradiction, and although we may have intimations of a 'transcendental' knowledge, that knowledge can never be ours. . . . Philosophy, which describes the limits of knowledge, is always tempted to transcend them. But Kant's final advice to it is that given in the last sentence of Wittgenstein's *Tractatus Logico-Philosophicus:* that whereof we cannot speak, we must consign to silence."[33] In similar vein Lewis White Beck downplays the skeptical implications of Kant's epistemology. "Hume's skeptical doubt as to our knowledge of nature is thereby removed, while it is found to be justified as to metaphysical speculation."[34]

Alongside of these positive affirmations of Kant may be placed a series of negative verdicts. Kant's distinction between *analytic* and *synthetic* statements, which has been accepted without question by so many succeeding philosophers, is increasingly being called into question. On the face of it the distinction appears to be plausible. But examination of alleged examples of the two types of statements, like the ones given above (*analytic:* "A rainy day is a wet day"; *synthetic:* "Tuesday was a wet day"), shows how difficult it is to draw a sharp dividing line between the purely logical and the purely factual components. For the examples contain both components. Contemporary American philosopher Willard van Orman Quine sees the distinction as one of the "dogmas of empiricism." He concludes that: "for all its a priori reasonableness, a boundary between analytic and synthetic statements has not been drawn. That there is such a distinction at all is an unempirical dogma of empiricists, a metaphysical article of faith."[35] If this distinction, which is basic to Kant's theory of knowledge, is questionable, serious doubts are inevitably raised about the theory built on it.

Contemporary American philosopher of science Stanley L. Jaki is even more scathing in his comments on Kant's work. Jaki sees little merit in Kant's ventures into the realm of science and rejects Kant's claim to fame as the inaugurator of a Copernican revolution in philosophy and as the philosophical interpreter of Newtonian physics. To Jaki there is something profoundly un-Newtonian and un-Copernican about Kant's work. Whereas Newton's scientific writings present a series of interlocking proofs of the validity of the initial presuppositions, Kant's *Critique* is a work of a very different character. The heart of the book is Kant's argument for the validity of *a priori* synthetic statements. But this covers only a page or two; the rest is amplification and deduction, but not further corroboration. At best Jaki sees Kant as an "amateurish Newtonian" who failed to see beneath the surface of Newton's work. Kant's comparison of himself with Copernicus was, if anything, even less apt. Copernicus's heliocentric theory of the universe involved a shift in humankind's cosmic position, but it did not imply a shift in epistemological perspective. Jaki maintains:

> That shift was grafted on Copernicus's perspective by Kant, the high priest of epistemological geocentrism, an error far more destructive for science than physical geocentrism could ever be. For if the imagined structure of the mind determines the structure of things that are outside the mind, then the raison d'être for experimenting and ob-

servation will hardly ever become a compelling reason. . . . The Kantian knowledge of things was a construction by the mind of the sem-
blance of things and not a natural grasp of intelligibility embodied in
them. As a result, whatever Kant's longing for an intellectual touch
with things other than his own mind, the Kantian impossibility of
being in touch with the Ding an sich meant being trapped within
one's own mind.[36]

2. Kant's Rejection of the Traditional Proofs of the Existence of God. Having
examined the scope of reason in the earlier part of his *Critique of Pure
Reason,* Kant turned his attention to the question of whether God's existence can be proved. He maintained that there were basically only
three such proofs: the *ontological,* the *cosmological* and the *teleological* (or,
as he called it, the *physico-theological*) proof.[37] Of the three it is the *ontological* proof that is not only pivotal but fatally flawed.

In dealing with the ontological argument, Kant pointed out that it just
will not do to assume (as he thought Descartes did) that the mere definition of a necessary being implies its existence in the same way that
the definition of a triangle implies that it has three angles. The argument
only works if we assume the existence of the being in question in the
first place.[38] For the purposes of his exposition of the argument Kant
defined God as the *ens realissimum* (i.e., a being that possesses "all reality"). The question which Kant addresses is the question whether such
a being could be denied without self-contradiction. For "all reality" is
presumed to include existence, and "existence is therefore contained in
the concept of the thing."

Kant's strategy is to unmask the argument as "a mere tautology." If we
speak of God as the most real being, the *ens realissimum,* and then claim
that God's existence is entailed in this definition, we must ask whether
we are making an *analytic* or a *synthetic* statement. Here Kant drew on
his earlier distinction, which held that true *analytic* statements were true
by definition only, whereas the truth of *synthetic* statements depended on
empirical confirmation. By trying to show that the ontological argument
was essentially *analytic* in character, Kant thought that he had shown it
to be no more than an abstract definition which had no basis in reality.

We must ask: Is the proposition that *this or that thing* (which, whatever
it may be is allowed as possible) *exists,* an analytic or a synthetic

proposition? If it is analytic, the assertion of the existence of the thing adds nothing to the thought of the thing; but in that case either the thought, which is in us, is the thing itself, or we have presupposed an existence as belonging to the realm of the possible, and have then, on that pretext, inferred its existence from its internal possibility— which is nothing but a miserable tautology. . . . But if, on the other hand, we admit, as every reasonable person must, that all existential propositions are synthetic, how can we profess to maintain that the predicate of existence cannot be rejected without contradiction? That is a feature which is found only in analytic propositions, and is indeed precisely what constitutes their analytic character.[39]

The point of this line of argument was to show:

"Being" is obviously not a real predicate; that is, it is not a concept of something which could be added to the concept of a thing, or of certain determinations, as existing in themselves. Logically, it is merely the copula of a judgment.[40]

We do not add to a thing by asserting that it exists. Whether a thing exists or not is not determined by definition but by the discovery of grounds from which its existence may be inferred. In short, the argument no more proves the existence of God than the thought of having a hundred dollars in the bank implies that one must actually have such an amount. "We can no more extend our stock of theoretical insight by mere ideas, than a merchant can better his position by adding a few noughts to his cash account."[41]

Turning to the cosmological argument, Kant formulated it like this: "If anything exists, an absolutely necessary being must also exist. Now I, at least, exist. Therefore an absolutely necessary being exists. The minor premise contains an experience, the major premise the inference from there being any experience at all to the existence of a necessary being."[42] Kant noted that the argument had a certain plausibility. He saw it as a form of Leibniz's argument from the contingency of the world. But he pronounced it to be fraught with many "pseudo-rational principles."[43] In particular it had to make tacit use of the worthless ontological argument in order to convert the mere notion of a necessary being into an actual necessary being.[44] Moreover, "the principle of causality has no meaning and no criterion for its application save only in the sensible world."[45] Nor is it possible to conceive what such a being would be like. There are many forces in nature which "manifest their existence through certain effects, [but which] remain for us inscrutable; for we cannot track them sufficiently far by observation."[46]

The teleological argument, which Kant had professed to admire in his early work, still commanded respect. It gives purpose and meaning to life and to scientific investigation. In the world we find clear signs of order and purpose. They are such that the things in this world could not have devised for themselves. They seem to point beyond themselves to a wise, intelligent and free being that ordered them. In view of the reciprocal relations that exist between different parts of the world, it may be inferred that there is only one such being and not several.[47] But in Kant's analysis the teleological proof was really only another form of the cosmological proof, and the latter "is only a disguised ontological proof."[48] The arguments therefore do not afford rational, compelling proof of the existence of God.

But if the objective reality of God cannot be proved, it "also cannot be disproved by merely speculative reason."[49] Although Kant pronounced the use of speculative reason in the area of theology to be "null and void,"[50] he did not close the door altogether on God. He saw his work as a solemn reminder "that all those conclusions of ours which profess to lead us beyond the field of possible experience are deceptive and without foundation; it likewise teaches us this further lesson, that human reason has a natural tendency to transgress these limits."[51] Basic to Kant's philosophy was his conviction that "reason is never in immediate relation to an object, but only to the understanding; and it is only through the understanding that it has its own [specific] empirical employment. It does not therefore, *create* concepts (of objects) but only *orders* them, and gives them that unity which they can have only if they be employed in their widest possible application, that is, with a view to obtaining totality in the various series."[52] Thus, ideas like God, freedom, and immortality are not constitutive for the nature of reality. Rather, Kant saw them as regulative ideas which human beings use in order to organize their thinking.

Kant insisted that if we ask "whether there is anything distinct from the world, which contains the ground of the order of the world and its connection in accordance with universal laws, the answer is that there *undoubtedly* is. For the world is a sum of appearances; and there must therefore be some transcendental ground of the appearances, that is, a ground which is thinkable by the pure understanding."[53] But if we go on to ask "whether this being is substance, of the greatest reality, necessary, etc., we reply that *this question is entirely without meaning*. For all categories through which we can attempt to form a concept of such an object only allow of empirical employment, and have no meaning whatsoever when not applied to objects of possible experience, that is, to the world of sense."[54] If we further ask "whether we may not at least think this being, which is distinct from the world, in *analogy* with the objects of experience, the answer is: certainly, but only as an object in *idea* not in reality, namely, only as being a substratum, to us unknown, of the systematic unity, order, and purposiveness of the arrangement of the world—an idea which reason is constrained to form as the regulative principle of its investigation of nature."[55]

Thus the idea of God is a useful and even necessary concept for organizing our thoughts about the world. Such a notion is a presupposition formed by analogy with our experience of human intelligence. Kant summed up his view in the following way:

> But the question may still be pressed: Can we, on such ground, assume a wise and omnipotent Author of the world?
>
> *Undoubtedly* we may; and we not only may, but must, do so. But do we then extend our knowledge beyond the field of possible experience? *By no means*. All that we have done is merely to presuppose a something, a merely transcendental object, of which, as it is in itself, we have no concept whatsoever. It is only in relation to the systematic and purposive ordering of the world, which, if we are to study nature, we are constrained to presuppose, that we have thought this unknown being *by analogy* with an intelligence (an empirical concept); that is have endowed it, in respect of the ends and perfection which are to be grounded upon it, with just those properties which, in conformity with the conditions of our reason, can be regarded as containing the ground of such systematic unity. This idea is thus valid only in respect of the *employment* of our reason *in reference to the world*. If we ascribed to it a validity that is absolute and objective, we should be forgetting

that what we are thinking is a being in idea only; and in thus taking our start from a ground which is not determinable through observation of the world, we should no longer be in a position to apply the principle in a manner suited to the empirical employment of reason.[56] Kant's criticism of the traditional proofs of the existence of God has been widely followed, especially in Protestant circles. Although the ontological argument continues to be discussed by philosophers, the main line of criticism has tended to follow Kant. In general, thinkers after Kant have been cautious about using the cosmological and teleological arguments. But there is disagreement over whether Kant was correct in saying that the latter proofs were dependent upon the flawed ontological proof. Among those who detect a fallacy in Kant's argument is Frederick Copleston, who observes that Kant's argument "is convincing only on one assumption, namely that the argument based on experience brings us, not to an affirmation of the existence of a necessary being, but only to the vague *idea* of a necessary being. . . . If, however, the argument based on experience brings us to the affirmation of the *existence* of a necessary being, the attempt to determine *a priori* the necessary attributes of this being have nothing to do with the ontological argument, which is primarily concerned with deducing existence from the idea of a being as possible, and not with deducing attributes from the idea of a being the existence of which has already been affirmed on other grounds than possibility."[57] Despite assumptions to the contrary, Kant had not said the last word on the question of arguments for the existence of God.

3. Kant's Moral Approach to God. Kant subjected ethics to the same enlightened, rational scrutiny that we have seen him bringing to the question of knowledge and to philosophical theology. If modern people are to live as if they have come of age, they must throw away all external and pseudo authorities. They must do what reason tells them is right. People have no need of God in the capacity of either a heavenly adviser or of a provider of incentives. They must realize that ethics is like science. The latter is concerned with the laws of nature; the former is concerned with the laws which govern behavior. In neither case does God directly enter into it. This is the theme of the opening words of Kant's *Religion within the Limits of Reason Alone.*

So far as morality is based upon the conception of man as a free agent who, just because he is free, binds himself through his reason to unconditioned laws, it stands in need neither of the idea of another Being over him, for him to apprehend his duty, nor of an incentive other than the law itself, for him to do his duty.[58]

Nevertheless, Kant believed that his conception of ethics pointed toward God. Before we ask how Kant was pointed in this direction, we need to step back and take a look at Kant's view of ethics. Even though few people today would take Kant's ethics in the form in which Kant propounded them, the kind of secularist ethics that Kant proposed has been absorbed in the bloodstream of modern humanism. Kant sought a basis for morality which was independent of religion, custom and social pressures. A right action was not one which was prompted by expectation of personal gain or the desire to avoid trouble or pain.[59] The real test of an action was to see whether it conformed to an "objective principle." In the moral sphere such "objective principles" take the form of *imperatives*.

> The conception of an objective principle, so far as it constrains a will, is a command (of reason), and the formula of this command is called an *imperative*.

> All imperatives are expressed by an "ought" and thereby indicate the relation of an objective law of reason to a will which is not in its subjective constitution necessarily determined by this law. This relation is that of constraint. Imperatives say that it would be good to do or to refrain from doing something, but they say it to a will which does not always do something simply because it is presented as a good thing to do.[60]

In short, if I ought, I can. Kant went on to distinguish two kinds of imperatives: the *hypothetical* and the *categorical*.

> All imperatives command either hypothetically or categorically. The former present the practical necessity of a possible action as a means to achieving something else which one desires (or which one may possibly desire). The categorical imperative would be one which presented an action as of itself objectively necessary, without regard to any other end.[61]

In other words (though they are not Kant's), the *hypothetical imperative* takes the form of a recommendation like the following: "If you want to practice karate, get a good teacher."

Characteristic of this type of imperative is the fact that not everybody wants it. Nor does everybody have to do it. It is not binding upon all. It is relative to individual desires, needs and circumstances. The *categorical imperative* is very different. Kant believed that it embodied a rational moral principle that was valid under all circumstances and was universally binding. He formulated it in two ways:

Act only according to that maxim by which you can at the same time will that it should become a universal law. . . .

Act as though the maxim of your action were by your will to become a universal law of nature.[62]

This was not simply a case of acting according to conscience. For the pain that we feel which we call conscience may be conditioned by habits and circumstances. It was rather a matter of coldly and deliberately following a rational principle. The categorical imperative has with Kant that same status that clear and distinct ideas have for Descartes and the rationalists. Kant accepted it as self-evidently true and valid.

As instances of how it works out, Kant mentions suicide, laziness and self-seeking. In practice the *categorical imperative* means: "Act so that you treat humanity, whether in your own person or in that of another, always as an end and never as a means only."[63] On these grounds Kant concludes that it is wrong to mutilate, corrupt or kill anyone. This includes oneself. Therefore suicide is wrong. The same principle extends to the other actions that we have just mentioned.

It is clear that actions like committing suicide, lying, being lazy and self-seeking cannot be universalized. If everyone did them, life would be impossible. But whether Kant's views provide a really adequate basis for ethics is another matter. At best they seem to provide general rules for moral action. Even so, they do not seem to cater for all contingencies. Both supporters and opponents of abortion and euthanasia could justifiably appeal to Kant's principles to legitimize their case. For both could claim that what they deem proper for themselves would be proper for others. As Hegel pointed out, the categorical imperative "in itself contains no principle beyond abstract identity and the 'absence of contradiction.' "[64] In other words, it instructs us to "act so as not to contradict ourselves." But in that case, we could end up doing nothing!

Kant's position has the merit of making the virtue of an action not dependent upon its consequences. For an action can be well meant and yet misfire. It recognizes the sense of obligation that people feel that it is right to treat others as they would want to be treated themselves. This obligation does not depend upon circumstances and personal likes or dislikes. But in the last analysis it does not say *why* we should act in this way. It appears to take it for granted. For Kant it is something that is just given. It is bound up with his notion of "the autonomy of the will as the supreme principle of morality." By this Kant meant that

> Autonomy of the will is that property of it by which it is a law to itself independently of any property of objects of volition. Hence the principle of autonomy is: Never choose except in such a way that the maxims of the choice are comprehended in the same volition as a universal law.[65]

But this still leaves us with the question of *why* we should act in this way.

If the reply to this question is that we should obey the *categorical* imperative because society needs law and order in order to function, then it must be said that the *categorical* imperative is only a disguised form of the *hypothetical* imperative. The only difference is that it operates on a grander scale. It is desirable that society should function, and obedience to the imperative is the way to secure it. If this is the case, it is not something that is intrinsically universally binding, but simply an expression of what the speaker happens to think desirable. But if it be said that we should obey the *categorical* imperative for its own sake, then we are guilty of oversimplification. For it is not enough simply to ask what we should do. The imperative also raises the question of what kind of authority it is that stands over and above me which demands that I should behave like this.

Kant's description of it as an *autonomous* principle of the will further confuses the issue.[66] For he makes it appear as if the imperative is the result of the individual's resolve to act in accordance with a principle that the individual has evolved. If this is the case, we are back again with a disguised form of the hypothetical imperative. In that case the imperative would be the outcome of a value judgment on the part of the individual who has decided that acting in this way is a good thing. If, however, the imperative is the expression of the recognition of a moral obligation which comes from outside us, we are no longer autonomous in the sense of being self-legislating. Although Kant strenuously resisted the idea of *heteronomy*—subjection of oneself to an authority or law from outside ourselves—it would seem that the *categorical* imperative has to be heteronomous, if it is to avoid relapsing into a form of the hypothetical imperative.

It is worthwhile to compare Kant and Jesus at this point. At first sight they may appear to be saying the same thing, but there are fundamental differences. Jesus taught that the second great commandment was to love one's neighbor as oneself.[67] In saying this, Jesus was not formulating an autonomous rational principle, but summarizing the teaching of the Old Testament.[68] At the same time he was giving expression to an awareness of obligation which people feel generally, whether they are religious or not. But Jesus reminded his hearers of an even higher obligation—to love God with their whole being.[69] This too was the basis and theme of the Old Testament Law.[70] As Calvin, Cicero and many others have observed, people generally have an awareness of God and of their obligation toward him.[71] This is true not only of Christianity but of other religions. It is true whether people take this obligation seriously or not. It is something which is there at the back of their minds, and it is something that Kant discreetly ignored in developing his philosophical system.

Nevertheless, Kant did not rule out God entirely from his philosophical scheme. In his *Critique of Practical Reason* Kant explained how God fitted into the picture. God is given (together with the notions of freedom and immortality) the status of a postulate of pure practical reason.[72] In Kantian terminology "practical reason" is reason as it "deals with the grounds determining the will." As such, it is distinct from the theoretical use of reason which is concerned with "the objects of the merely cognitive faculty."

Freedom, immortality and God are not for Kant "objects of the cognitive faculty." The freedom of the will is not something that can be demonstrated objectively. From a scientific standpoint human actions are subject to the laws of causality which affect all physical entities. But obligation introduces a new factor. Obligation implies freedom to obey or disobey the moral law. *Ought* implies *can*. In this sense we transcend our spatio-temporal existence. But the notion of freedom, Kant believed, does not entitle us to erect a complete metaphysical system upon it. Freedom is a presupposition of ethics. As such, it is a postulate of pure practical reason.

Kant discussed God and immortality in the context of what he termed the *summum bonum*, the highest good. It is the ideal state of affairs where virtue and happiness coincide. However, it is all too painfully obvious that the two do not coincide in this life. Moreover, human attainment of it is conceivable only if humanity is granted an infinite existence.[73] In order to unite happiness and virtue "the existence is postulated of a cause of the whole of nature, itself distinct from nature, which contains the ground of the exact coincidence of happiness with morality. . . . The postulate of the possibility of a highest derived good (the best world) is at the same time the postulate of a highest original good, namely, the existence of God."[74]

What Kant offered was a duty-based theory of personal ethics, which separated morality from religion by making ethics autonomous, ostensibly based on self-evident rational truths. If religion had any public function at all, it was (as Kant would explain later in *Religion within the Limits of Reason Alone*) subservient to ethics. The role of religion was to inculcate ethics. In this respect, Kant's ethics was both an expression of the Age of Enlightenment in which it was conceived and also a portent of things to come in the modern world.

4. Kant's Reappraisal of Christianity. Kant's earlier view of God is re-echoed in *Religion within the Limits of Reason Alone*. Morality does not need religion, but it points to it. It leads to the idea of "a highest good in the world for whose possibility we must postulate a higher, moral, most holy, and omnipotent Being which alone can unite the two elements of the highest good" (i.e., duty and happiness).[75] This is the starting-point for Kant's reappraisal of Christianity. As his title suggests, his aim is to strip Christianity of such extras as faith and belief in a supernatural God who personally intervenes in human affairs. In its place he puts a sober religion, ready for use by the modern enlightened person. The result is a full-blown Deism, adapted for the German culture of his day.

The traditional Christian view of revelation—of God revealing himself

in history and personal experience through events and his Word—is
replaced by reason. Bible stories are all right for the ignorant masses.
They represent a graphic way of teaching them morality. But in the last
analysis it is "universal human reason" which is "the supremely com-
manding principle."[76] The Christian view of grace and salvation—that
God has done for human beings what they could not do for themselves
by blotting out their sins and restoring them to fellowship with himself—
is replaced by an unbending religion of self-help.

> True religion is to consist not in the knowing or considering what God
> does or has done for our salvation but in what we must do to become
> worthy of it . . . and of its necessity every man can become wholly
> certain without any Scriptural learning whatsoever.[77]
>
> Man *himself* must make or have made himself into whatever, in a
> moral sense, whether good or evil, he is or is to become.[78]

In Kant's version of religion Jesus is "the personified idea of the good
principle," the incarnation of moral good who "has come down to us
from heaven."[79] In Kant's hermeneutic of the New Testament this is the
true meaning of such passages as John 1:1-13; 3:16; Hebrews 1:3; Philippians 2:6. Curiously enough, neither here nor elsewhere in his writings does Kant seem to have been able to bring himself to pronounce
the name of Jesus. Instead, he talked abstractly about one who represents "the ideal of a humanity pleasing to God" and "the archetype of
the moral disposition in all its purity."[80] Occasionally, Kant could speak
of "the Master" and "the wise Teacher."[81] He could reprove the author
of the Wolfenbüttel Fragments for imputing unworthy motives to the
Master.[82] At the same time he could insist that we need "no empirical
example to make the idea of a person morally well pleasing to God our
archetype; this idea as an archetype is already present in our reason."[83]

If Kant's discussion was replete with biblical allusions, his account of
Christ and Christianity was secularized, rationalized and demythologized
in all but name. Kant's own term for this process was to describe it as
divesting the vivid, popular mode of representation of its "mystical veil."
When this was duly done, Kant claimed that it is "easy to see that, for
practical purposes, its spirit and meaning have been valid and binding
for the whole world and for all time, since to each man it lies so near
at hand that he knows his duty towards it. Its meaning is this: that there

exists absolutely no salvation for man apart from the sincerest adoption of genuinely moral principles into his disposition."[84] As Kant brought his work to its conclusion, he returned to the theme of "The Christian Religion as a Natural Religion."[85] He concluded with an attack on clericalism. Although Kant made no express references to the Deists, his own critique of institutional Christianity and his restatement of what he considered to be the essence of religion was thoroughly Deistic in spirit.

Postscript

By the time of his death in 1804 Kant had come to enjoy enormous prestige in Germany. In the century that followed, the impact of his thought was felt throughout Europe and the New World. No serious thinker could afford to neglect Kant or remain neutral. At the same time Kant's philosophy was felt to be profoundly unsatisfying. Despite Kant's massive attempt to develop a rational philosophy, there were those who thought that Kant's work was a monumental failure. Among them was the leading philosopher of the next generation, Georg Wilhelm Friedrich Hegel, who complained that "Kantian criticism" was "only a philosophy of subjectivity, a subjective Idealism." It differed from empiricism only with respect to the question of what constituted experience. However, it was in basic agreement with empiricism in its contention that "reason apprehends nothing beyond sensation, nothing rational and divine. It remains in the finite and untrue, namely in an apprehension that has only subjectively an externality and a Thing-in-itself as its condition, which is the abstraction of the formless, an empty beyond."[86]

Hegel's alternative to Kant was his version of absolute idealism. It was a philosophy which proved to be no less influential and no less controversial than Kant's. Nor was it any nearer to orthodox Christianity. But these are matters for discussion in the second volume of this work. One does not have to be a Hegelian to feel the force of Hegel's objection to Kant's procedure of demanding "a criticism of the faculty of cognition as preliminary to its exercise." To Hegel this was like "the error of refusing to enter the water until you have learnt to swim."[87] Kant believed that he had solved the basic problems of metaphysics by proclaiming that the whole subject was off-limits. What Kant bequeathed to posterity was not the solution to the problem but a double agenda. On the one hand, there is the question of *how* do we know. On the other hand, there is the question of *what* do we know. These questions were being asked centuries before Kant, and they are still being asked today.[88]

In Europe the Age of Enlightenment came to its end with the death of Kant. The proliferation of alternative philosophies in the nineteenth century is eloquent testimony both to its shortcomings and to the fact of its demise. But the legacy of the Enlightenment lives on in continued separation of the sacred from the secular. Where the sacred was admitted at all, the modern mind tried to relegate it to the realm of private beliefs and to keep all the important aspects of daily life and thought firmly in the realm of the secular. In the period following World War 2 considerable excitement was generated in religious and academic circles by Dietrich Bonhoeffer's remarks about the world coming of age. The notion was greeted as a brilliant new insight that Bonhoeffer had attained while pondering on the state of the world as he languished in a Nazi prison.[89]

Bonhoeffer himself was under no illusions either about the origin of the term or about its significance. As he jotted down his random thoughts, which were eventually collected and posthumously published as *Letters and Papers from Prison,* Bonhoeffer was well aware of the fact (as any German theological student of his generation would have been) that it was Immanuel Kant who had first spoken of the world coming of age in his article on "What is Enlightenment?" But what to Kant was the dawning of a new age in which people were learning to live independently of external authorities had become a grim reality during the dark days of World War 2. It was not that the world had become mature and responsible. Far from it. Humankind had become a law unto itself and was reaping the bitter harvest. To Bonhoeffer the solution did not lie in trying to put back the clock and live as if the events of the past two hundred years had not happened. It was rather to wrestle with how we should think about God, Christ, the world and religion. That was the question for Bonhoeffer in the post-Enlightenment world. It remains the question for us today.

18. RETROSPECT
AND PROSPECT

As human beings we need many things—food, shelter, companionship, love, a sense of belonging, purpose and fulfillment—to name but a few. But we also need what perhaps, for want of a better word, is called a world view. The term *world view* is apt to suggest rather more than what it often really is. For few people have highly sophisticated and integrated views of the world which take into account all the major academic disciplines. It is doubtful whether there is such a thing as a single world view which is broad enough to embrace everything that is important in a *single* perspective. Perhaps the term *world view* indicates no more than the habitual outlook that people bring to things. On the other hand, people cannot help having views about the way things are. Moreover, human beings have a deep need for deepening and refining their views of the world and reality. Christian philosopher Arthur F. Holmes sees this need as fourfold: "the need to unify thought and life; the need to define the good life and find hope and meaning in life; the need to guide thought; the need to guide action."[1]

The preceeding chapters have taken us on a conducted tour of the history of the way various thinkers from pre-Socratic times down to the Age of Enlightenment have sought to meet this need. Like all conducted tours this particular one has been selective. It has focused on religious questions, especially those which affect the Christian faith. It has been an intellectual history rather than a social history. By this I mean that attention has deliberately been given to challenges and issues, as seen by both skeptics and believers. I have not tried to assess the social impact of their ideas on the church or on society at large. Still less have I sought to assess what rank-and-file members of the church thought about things down the ages. My account is therefore vulnerable to the charge of being elitist. It is a charge to which I am content to plead guilty. I freely confess my belief that there is a need to examine the history of thought from a social point of view, and explore the question of what people on different levels of society believed at different periods in different cultures. But this has not been the purpose of the present book. My aim has rather been to try to listen to what the great thinkers of the past have had to say about questions of belief. What is striking in all this is how deeply questions of belief are intertwined in the history of Western thought.

In his book *The Closing of the American Mind*,[2] Professor Allan Bloom of the University of Chicago accuses the American universities of a reprehensible failure to introduce students to the great thinkers of the past. He finds alarming evidence of closed minds in the higher levels of education, which he attributes to this neglect of the past. As a remedy, he calls for renewed engagement with the major thinkers of the Western intellectual tradition. Professor Bloom's book has sent ripples through American academia. But whether it will have any lasting or beneficial effect is too early to say. His own analysis is certainly different from the present writer's. His preference is for a return to the teaching of Rousseau and the thinkers of the American Enlightenment. My recommendations also urge renewed study of the intellectual history of the West. For without such a study we can hardly expect to understand the questions of the present, or even what various competing truth-claims mean or how they might be tested.

There are two main reasons why we should study the great thinkers of the past. The first is that such a study helps us to understand how and why people think as they do. The study of the intellectual traditions of the past helps us to appreciate better the way people thought not only in ages that are more or less remote from ours but also how their thought has contributed to the shaping of the way people think in the present. This in itself would make the study of the past worthwhile. But the second reason is even more important. It consists in the fact that each generation is confronted by the challenge to think through its basic beliefs, assumptions and attitudes. It is the mark of the closed mind to ignore this challenge. But in the end, nothing is more important than the basic beliefs—whether religious or not—that human beings embrace. For beliefs shape attitudes and ultimately affect the way that we think and the way that we lead our lives. Whether our basic beliefs are religious or irreligious, the great thinkers of the past challenge us to join with them in examining our beliefs and ideas. It is a challenge posed not only by those with whom we might disagree but also by those with whom we might agree. If our thoughts and ideas are wrong and mistaken, we are better off by discarding them. If our thinking is on the right lines, we cannot but be enriched by listening to those who have thought more profoundly and widely than ourselves.

The Sociology of Knowledge
My account of the history of Christianity and Western thought has not been a social history; I have not attempted to identify and analyze the social factors which accompanied the many changes in Western thought since the time of the pre-Socratics. Nevertheless, the foregoing pages bear testimony to the sociology of knowledge.[3] No philosophy was ever worked out in a vacuum. The assumptions and concerns of different ages shaped the questions that people asked and the answers that were given. The post-Socratic philosophers thought differently from the pre-Socratic philosophers. The great Christian thinkers of the Middle Ages thought yet differently. Western thought in the seventeenth and eighteenth centuries, influenced as it was by the Reformation, the rediscovery of pagan antiquity that we call the Renaissance, the rise of modern science, and the attendant political and social changes, turned to new questions and saw old questions in a new light. In all this, changes in Western thought were related to changes in society.

The history of science reveals a progress of knowledge in which later thought supersedes earlier thought. But theology and philosophy—in common with other liberal arts—is not like science. It is not a case that the discoveries of the present make obsolete the views of the previous generation. The latest play on Broadway or the West End of London does not make the plays of Shakespeare obsolete. Modern verse does not supplant the poetry of Wordsworth or Milton. The music of Bach, Mozart and Brahms is not surpassed by twentieth-century compositions. We cannot successfully imitate the past. The present should have its own integrity. But that integrity requires us to listen to what the past has to offer.

One of the things that this study has shown is the remarkable endur-ing power of ideas and ways of thinking. Ideas which may long lie dormant have a way of coming to life again centuries later. We can see this in the way that forms of Platonism affected early Christian thought. Aristotelianism enjoyed a revival in the Middle Ages, affecting Islam and Judaism, as well as Christianity. Later ages witnessed a renewed interest in Epicureanism and classical skepticism. In each case it was not a matter simply of returning to the past but of seeing some value in the way people thought in the past and in adapting past thought to present needs.

This is not the place to attempt some kind of adjudication which would rank the various thinkers and movements in order of merit. I have offered my comments on what I see as the strengths and weaknesses of different ideas and arguments as I went along. To go beyond that would be an exercise in folly and futility. Nor do I wish to anticipate what I want to say in the book on philosophy and theology in the nineteenth and twentieth centuries which I plan as a sequel to the present book. Nev-ertheless, it is not inappropriate to offer some concluding observations that arise from our survey as it has brought us to the end of the eight-eenth century.

One of the things that strikes me is the perennial presence of plural-ism. Today we are often reminded of the fact that we live in a pluralistic society. It is society characterized by instability produced by conflicting cultures, values, beliefs and social change. Sometimes people look back wistfully to some previous golden age that was free from such turbulence. But in reality all the periods that we have been examining have been characterized by change, conflict and competing world views.

The conflicting philosophies that we have looked at are themselves products of cultural change. Inevitably, every important philosopher and every new philosophical movement drew on previous thought. Plato drew upon Pythagorean and pre-Socratic thought, and Aristotle modified Plato. Aquinas drew on Aristotle, Plotinus and the church fathers, not to mention Jewish and Islamic philosophy. Descartes was indebted to medieval thought as well as the skepticism and scientific thought of his own day. Empiricism was essentially a response to rationalism. Although it rejected the rationalist view of innate ideas, there were many things that empiricism held in common with rationalism. The fact is that philosophies do not exist in isolation from each other. There is much overlapping and mutual borrowing. Moreover, philosophies interact not only with each other but with the culture, science and religion of their times.

Philosophy and Philosophizing

It is arguable that philosophy does not exist as an autonomous entity. It is not a subject like physics, astronomy, medieval history or American literature, each of which have a subject matter of their own. Philosophy as such does not have its own subject matter. In a sense, philosophy is always the "philosophy of" something else. It is *the something else* which provides the subject matter for philosophy. We can speak of a philosophy of knowledge (epistemology), a philosophy of morals (ethics), a philosophy of science, a philosophy of religion and so on. In each case philosophy is not some kind of short cut which will enable those who master the appropriate techniques to avoid the arduous labors of the practitioners in the field in question. Rather, philosophy is a kind of para-discipline which asks questions about questions. It is concerned with testing ideas and the validity of the way questions are asked and answered. As such, philosophy performs a valuable service to those engaged in the discipline in question. But as such philosophy can be a good servant but a bad master.

Over two hundred years ago Immanuel Kant remarked that nothing had caused so much damage in philosophy as the imitation by philosophers of the methods of geometry.[4] What he had in mind was the assumption that one academic discipline enjoyed the prerogative of having the right methodology, and the further assumption that all other disciplines should stand in line behind it and model their methods on its methods. By the time that Kant made this observation the weaknesses of rationalism were becoming apparent. Early on in the seventeenth century Descartes had been fascinated by the logical rigor of geometry and had held up geometry as a model for philosophy to follow. Spinoza had gone a step further and had set out his philosophy like a series of geometrical theorems. But the British empiricists had shown that deductive logic alone was an inadequate guide to our knowledge of the world around us. Kant realized that knowledge had an empirical component as well as a rational component. But whether Kant's own proposals were more adequate than those of his predecessors is doubtful. Kant himself has been faulted for substituting his own version of Newtonian physics for geometry as the paradigmatic role model for philosophy. The result has been described as an act of jumping from the frying pan into the fire, where philosophy could only burn to ashes.[5]

Foundations and Methods

The history of Western thought can be read as a story of the relentless conflict between belief and skepticism. But it can also be read as a history of a quest for right methods and right foundations. Immanuel Kant believed that he had succeeded in combining skepticism with the right methods and philosophical foundation in a book which he published in 1793, *Religion within the Limits of Reason Alone.* In it he asserted the right of reason to be the judge of religion. The picture of religion that Kant painted was that of a Christianity pressed into the service of inculcating ethics. It was a thinly disguised form of Deism teaching enlightened morality.

The result was inevitable, given Kant's view of reason. But nearly two centuries later Kant's title and ideas have been turned around by Nicholas Wolterstorff in his book *Reason within the Bounds of Religion* (1976). In this programmatic essay Wolterstorff throws down two major challenges. The first of these challenges is a challenge to foundationalism. As Wolterstorff sees it, a great deal of Western philosophy has been devoted to foundationalism in one form or another. The goal of the foundationalist, says Wolterstorff, is "to form a body of theories from which all prejudice, bias, and unjustified conjecture have been eliminated. To attain this, we must begin with a firm foundation of certitude and build the house of theory on it by methods of whose reliability we are equally certain."[6] The idea has proved to be seductively attractive to a long line of Western thinkers from Aristotle in the ancient world to the logical positivists in the twentieth century. Among its devotees Wolterstorff names Aquinas, Descartes, Leibniz and Berkeley. It would not be difficult to extend the list by adding non-Christian philosophers like Spinoza who were seeking to erect their systems on indubitable rational premises and skeptics like Hume and Kant who devoted their energies to undermining the foundations of Christian theistic systems. In a sense Kant was a foundationalist of a new breed in that he endeavored to base his philosophy on the critical rational powers of the enlightened individual.

Despite its attractions, Wolterstorff pronounces foundationalism to be an illusion and a failure. For in reality human knowledge and human theorizing are not based on a foundation of indubitables.[7] This is not to say that there is no objective reality independent of our conceptions and beliefs. Nor is it to say that we cannot attain to true beliefs concerning objective reality. Rather it is to admit that our knowledge of entities outside ourselves is not based on a rational scheme of a kind imagined by the foundationalist. To quote Wolterstorff as he reflects on the way knowledge is gained in the world of science:

> The conclusion is this: even if there is a set of foundational propositions, no one has yet succeeded in stating what relation the theories that we are warranted in accepting or rejecting bear to the members of that set. Even if there is a set of foundational propositions, we are without a general logic of the sciences, and hence without a general rule for warranted theory acceptance and rejection.[8]

What then is the alternative to foundationalism? Wolterstorff maintains that in weighing a theory we need to distinguish between *data beliefs*, *data-background beliefs* and *control beliefs*. It is not a case that any one of these sets of beliefs provides the foundation. Rather, they function in a way that is relative to a given person's weighing a given theory on a given occasion.

What functions as a data-background belief, or as a control belief, in a given person's weighing of a given theory on one occasion may on another occasion be the theory under consideration. On a given occasion Newton's laws of motion may be the theory which is being weighed and certain beliefs about the optical features of telescopes may remain as a background to the data. On another occasion— perhaps because of the observation of some anomaly within astronomy—the Newtonian theory may be moved into the background as unproblematic and various assumptions about the optics of the telescope may be moved into the foreground for weighing and testing. What also happens sometimes is that a belief which on a given occasion functions as a data belief against which a theory is weighed is on another occasion itself weighed by taking the theory as unproblematic.[9]

On this view it could be said that theories, beliefs, world views and outlooks are tested not by appeal to single observable facts or by a failure to refer them to some indubitable foundation but by what has been called "a death of a thousand qualifications."[10] Such qualifications occur when the tension between *data beliefs, data-background beliefs* and *control beliefs* becomes intolerable. Something somewhere has to give, and it can be any of those three sets of beliefs. Conversely a theory, belief, world view or outlook may be said to be well formed when there is a coherence between these three sets of beliefs.

In assessing the philosophies of the past and the present we need, therefore, to examine the data that they appeal to, the background beliefs against which the data is seen and the control beliefs which underlie the general approach of any given thinker. The shifts of emphasis and approach which have characterized the history of Western philosophy have come about through a shift in one or more of these factors. Perhaps the most important of these factors is that of controlling belief, for it is the underlying beliefs which affect the questions people ask, the data that they think to be significant, and how they view that data. In the ancient world belief in the gods and the nature of the elements profoundly shaped the questions that people asked. In the early centuries of the Christian era, control beliefs were supplied by the Christian faith as it struggled with the challenges of the Hellenistic world. In medieval philosophy the Christian faith again supplied the control beliefs, though this time the major challenges came from Judaism, Islam, and the philosophy of the ancient world which was itself preserved within the Christian tradition. In the seventeenth and eighteenth centuries the control beliefs of Christianity received their major challenge from a skepticism which had its roots in the ancient world. It was a challenge not only about belief in the existence of God but about the way the data of modern science should be viewed.

Earlier we noted that Professor Wolterstorff's book on *Reason within the Bounds of Religion* contained two major challenges. The first was his challenge to foundationalism and its right to determine the agenda for philosophy. Although we may disagree over whether some of the philosophers that Wolterstorff identifies as foundationalists were quite as dedicated to that view as he thinks,[11] his general point is well taken. His other challenge is a challenge to the Christian scholar. It is a challenge to allow *religious beliefs* to function as *control beliefs* within the Christian scholar's devising and weighing of theories.[12] In one sense this is not a new challenge. In my view this is what Augustine, Anselm, Aquinas, Calvin and even Descartes were doing, not to mention Locke, Berkeley, Butler and Jonathan Edwards. This is not the place to assess whether they were all equally successful in this enterprise. In any case I have offered my views on that score in the course of my discussion. What needs to be stressed here is the fact that the underlying conflict, as we bring to a close our account of philosophy at the end of the Age of Enlightenment, is ultimately a conflict over control beliefs. It is a conflict that we shall see renewed and deepened in the sequel to this book in which we shall look at philosophy and theology in the nineteenth and twentieth centuries.

Notes

Introduction

[1]C. S. Lewis, *God in the Dock: Essays on Theology and Ethics,* ed. Walter Hooper (Grand Rapids: Eerdmans, 1970), pp. 24-25.

[2]Thomas S. Kuhn, *The Structure of Scientific Revolutions* (Chicago: Chicago University Press, 2nd ed. 1970), p. 4.

[3]Kuhn, *Structure,* p. 10. The term *paradigm* indicates an example or pattern. In grammar it denotes an example of a conjugation or declension showing a word in all its inflections. Knowledge of the paradigm shows how similar words behave in their various grammatical forms. For a discussion of Kuhn and other contemporary thinkers in the area of the philosophy of science, see W. H. Newton-Smith, *The Rationality of Science* (London-Boston: Routledge & Kegan Paul, 1981). In the light of Kuhn's view of paradigm shifts I myself would question the correctness of Lewis's argument about the modern materialist. I would think that the sensation of being hurled into the Lake of Fire would be sufficient to initiate some kind of paradigm shift!

Chapter 1: Socrates and Pre-Socratic Philosophy

[1]Students pursuing Greek philosophy should consult W. K. C. Guthrie, *A History of Greek Philosophy,* 6 vols. (Cambridge: Cambridge University Press, 1962-81). Guthrie's account goes as far as Aristotle. It is supplemented by A. H. Armstrong, ed., *The Cambridge History of Later Greek and Early Medieval Philosophy* (Cambridge: Cambridge University Press, 1967). On the classical world generally, an important reference work is N. G. L. Hammond and H. H. Scullard, eds., *The Oxford Classical Dictionary* (Oxford: Clarendon Press, 2nd ed. 1960). Among the shorter works is: W. K. C. Guthrie, *The Greek Philosophers from Thales to Aristotle* (New York: Harper & Row, Harper Torchbook, 1960). Other studies include *Essays in Ancient Greek Philosophy,* one edited by John P. Anton and George L. Kustas, two edited by John P. Anton and Anthony Preus (Albany, NY: State University of New York Press, 1971, 1983); Giovanni Reale, *A History of*

Ancient Philosophy. From the Origins to Socrates, ed. and trans. John R. Catan (Albany, NY: State University of New York Press, 1987); A. H. Armstrong, *An Introduction to Ancient Philosophy* (Totowa, NJ: Rowman & Allanheld, 3rd ed. 1981); Werner Jaeger, *The Theology of the Early Greek Philosophers,* Gifford Lectures 1936 (Oxford: Clarendon Press, 1947); A. H. Armstrong and R. A. Markus, *Christian Faith and Greek Philosophy* (London: Darton, Longman and Todd, 1960); Robert S. Brumbaugh, *The Philosophers of Greece* (Albany, NY: State University of New York Press, 1981). Texts of classical writers in Greek or Latin with English translation on the facing page may be found in the volumes of the Loeb Classical Library, which is published jointly in Cambridge, Massachusetts, by Harvard University Press and in London by William Heinemann. Hans Urs von Balthasar has traced the development of metaphysics from early Greek poetry through Plato, Neoplatonism down to Thomas Aquinas in *The Glory of the Lord: A Theological Aesthetics,* 4: *The Realm of Metaphysics in Antiquity,* trans. John Riches (Edinburgh: T. & T. Clark, 1989).

[2]Diogenes Laertius, *Lives and Opinions of Eminent Philosophers* 1.12 (Loeb edition trans. R. D. Hicks, 1:13).

[3]In earlier Greek *Sophia* meant "cleverness" or "skill," and *sophos* "skilled."

[4]From the fifth century B.C. onwards, the word *sophist* was used to denote a wise man or someone who was skilled at some activity. It then came to be applied to people who made a job of being wise and was used to denote professional itinerant teachers who went from place to place giving instruction for fees. Some taught "virtue" which was the ancient Greek equivalent of "how to succeed" teaching which finds such a ready market in America. Others taught memory training and rhetoric. In view of the emphasis placed on success, the sophists acquired a reputation for winning arguments and succeeding at any price, regardless of the truth.

[5]*Lives* 1.16 (Loeb edition, 1:17).

[6]In the twentieth century Martin Heidegger has urged a return to a pre-Socratic notion of being and truth (see Heidegger's *An Introduction to Metaphysics,* trans. Ralph Manheim [Yale University Press, 1959]). The physicist Werner Heisenberg has discussed the importance of early Greek thinking in *Physics and Philosophy: The Revolution in Modern Science* (New York: Harper & Brothers, 1958).

[7]A selection of the most important texts is given in G. S. Kirk and J. E. Raven, eds., *The Presocratic Philosophers: A Critical History with a Selection of Texts* (Cambridge: Cambridge University Press, 1957). A major critical discussion is given by Jonathan Barnes, *The Presocratic Philosophers,* 2 vols. (London: Routledge & Kegan Paul, The Arguments of the Philosophers, 1979). In view of the fragmentary character of the texts Catherine Osborne urges an alternative methodology in the study of pre-Socratic philosophy in her book *Rethinking Early Greek Philosophy: Hippolytus of Rome and the Presocratics* (Ithaca: Cornell University Press, 1987).

[8]See the account of his teaching in Aristotle, *Metaphysics* 1.3.983b20-27 (*Works* 2:1556).

[9]W. P. D. Wightman, *The Growth of Scientific Ideas* (New Haven: Yale University Press, 1953), p. 10.

[10]Aristotle *De Anima* 1.2.405a20 (*Works* 1:646).

[11]Aristotle *De Anima* 1.5.411a9-10 (*Works* 1:655). Plato expresses a similar view to that of Thales in *Laws* 10.899b (*Dialogues*, p. 1455).

[12]See Guthrie, *History* 1:65-66; Guthrie, *The Greek Philosophers*, pp. 10-11. An important study of the relationship between philosophy and religion in the ancient world is F. W. Cornford, *Principium Sapientiae: The Origins of Greek Philosophical Thought* (Cambridge: Cambridge University Press, 1952). See also W. K. C. Guthrie, *The Greeks and their Gods* (Boston: Beacon Press, 1961).

[13]Fragment 4; cited from Guthrie, *History* 1:129.

[14]*Lives and Opinions of Eminent Philosophers* 1.13 (Loeb edition 1:15).

[15]Diogenes Laertius citing Aristotle's lost work *On the Pythagoreans* (*Lives and Opinions* 8, 34 [Loeb edition 2:349]); see also Guthrie, *History* 1:183-95.

[16]*Republic* 7.525d; cited from Edith Hamilton and Huntington Cairns, eds., *The Collected Dialogues of Plato* (Princeton: Princeton University Press, Bollingen Series 71, 1985 reprint), p. 758. See also the discussion in Plato's *Timaeus* 34ff. (*Dialogues*, pp. 1165ff.).

[17]*Republic* 7.527b (*Dialogues*, p. 759). These observations come in the course of a discussion of the ideal curriculum of higher education for the philosopher ruler.

[18]Fragment 53; cf. Guthrie, *History* 1:446.

[19]The saying is widely attributed to Heraclitus by several ancient authors. Although its authenticity has been questioned, its genuineness seems well established (Guthrie, *History* 1:488-92).

[20]Fragment 30; cf. Guthrie, *History* 1:454. Fragments relating to his logos doctrine are given in C. K. Barrett, *The New Testament Background; Selected Documents* (Revised edition, London: S.P.C.K. 1987, San Francisco: Harper & Row, 1989), pp. 59-60. Barrett does not think that Heraclitus's logos doctrine had anything to do with John's logos doctrine or any other New Testament doctrine.

[21]See especially Fragments 7 and 8; Kirk and Raven, *The Presocratic Philosophers*, pp. 271-75.

[22]Guthrie, *The Greek Philosophers*, p. 49.

[23]*Parmenides* is one of Plato's later dialogues (text in *Dialogues*, pp. 920-56).

[24]*Sophist* 237e (*Dialogues*, p. 981).

[25]*Timaeus* 27d (*Dialogues*, p. 1161).

[26]*Fragment* 17; see discussion in Guthrie, *History* 2:138-47.

[27]For brief surveys and literature see A. G. M. van Melderen, "Atomism," *Encyclopedia of Philosophy* 1: 193-198; and G. E. R. Lloyd, "Leucippus and Democritus," *Encyclopedia of Philosophy* 4: 446-451. Leucippus is known largely through

references to him in other sources, and only fragments of Democritus have survived. Democritus was the first to develop a naturalistic system of ethics, as opposed to supernaturalistic ethics. Karl Marx received his doctorate from the University of Jena in 1841 for a treatise on Democritus.

[28]Plato, *Hippias Minor* 368b-d (*Dialogues*, p. 206); cf. Guthrie, *History* 3:283.

[29]He is the central figure in Plato's dialogue *Protagoras* (Dialogues, pp. 308-52). For his social contract theory see Guthrie, *History* 3:136-38.

[30]The words occur in Socrates' summary of his views in Plato's *Theaetetus* 167c (*Dialogues*, p. 873).

[31]The dictum is preserved in Fragment 1. It apparently formed the opening of Protagoras's work on *Truth* (Plato, *Theaetetus* 161c [*Dialogues*, p. 867]). See further Guthrie, *History* 3:183-92.

[32]Plato gives an account of Socrates' defense at his trial in his *Apology* (*Dialogues*, pp. 3-26). Plato's *Crito* (*Dialogues*, pp. 27-39) discusses the options open to Socrates. The *Phaedo* (*Dialogues*, pp. 40-98) purports to review Socrates' last days and gives his thoughts on the immortality of the soul. On Athens see J. W. Roberts, *City of Sokrates: An Introduction to Classical Athens* (London: Routledge & Kegan Paul, 1984).

[33]For accounts of Socrates and his teaching in classical and early Christian writers, see John Ferguson, *Socrates: A Source Book* (London: Macmillan for the Open University Press, 1970). Recent discussions of Socrates' teaching include Gregory Vlastos, ed., *The Philosophy of Socrates: A Collection of Critical Essays* (reprint Notre Dame: University of Notre Dame Press, Modern Studies in Philosophy, 1980); Gersimos Xenophon Santas, *Socrates: Philosophy in Plato's Early Dialogues* (London: Routledge & Kegan Paul, *The Arguments of the Philosophers*, 1979); James Beckman, *The Religious Dimension of Socrates' Thought* (Waterloo, Ontario: Wilfred Laurier University Press, 1979); and Kenneth Seeskin, *Dialogue and Discovery: A Study in Socratic Method* (Albany, NY: State University of New York Press, 1986).

[34]Plato *Theaetetus* 149-161 (*Dialogues*, pp. 853-67).

Chapter 2: Plato's Vision of Reality

[1]Benjamin Jowett's translation of Plato has now been superseded by *The Collected Dialogues of Plato including the Letters,* edited by Edith Hamilton and Huntington Cairns (Princeton: Princeton University Press, Bollingen Series 71, 1985 reprint). It may be noted, however, that this edition includes some of Jowett's translations. A new translation with analysis of *The Dialogues of Plato* is being made by R. E. Allen (vol. 1, New Haven: Yale University Press, 1984). Recent surveys of Plato's thought include: I. M. Crombie, *An Examination of Plato's Doctrines,* 2 vols. (London: Routledge & Kegan Paul, 1962-63); G. C. Field, *The Philosophy of Plato* (London: Oxford University Press, 2nd ed. 1969); R. M. Hare, *Plato* (Oxford: Oxford University Press, 1982); Gilbert Ryle, *Plato's Progress*

(Cambridge: Cambridge University Press, 1966); Gregory Vlastos, *Platonic Studies* (Princeton: Princeton University Press, 2nd ed. 1981); Gregory Vlastos, ed., *Plato: A Collection of Critical Essays*, 2 vols. (New York: Doubleday Anchor Books, 1971); Julia Annas, *An Introduction to Plato's Republic* (New York: Oxford University Press, 1981); Charles L. Griswold, Jr., ed., *Platonic Writing, Platonic Reading* (London and New York: Routledge, 1988). Studies of the religious aspect of Plato's thought include: Paul Elmer More, *The Religion of Plato* (1921, reprint New York: Kraus Reprint Co., 1970); James K. Feibleman, *Religious Platonism: The Influence of Religion on Plato and the Influence of Plato on Religion* (1959; reprint Westport, CT: Greenwood Press, 1971); and John E. Rexine, *Religion in Plato and Cicero* (1959, reprint Westport, CT: Greenwood Press, 1968).

[2]See Letters 7 and 8; widely, though not universally, held to be authentic (*Dialogues*, pp. 1574-1603).

[3]*Republic* 1. 341-42 (*Dialogues*, pp. 590-93).

[4]Education and the possession of property are discussed in Book 4 (*Dialogues*, pp. 661-88). Slaves existed, but do not come into the reckoning as citizens. Of the citizens, only the Third Class (those engaged in economic activities) were allowed to have private property. The Guardians were to ensure that there was neither excessive wealth nor poverty. They also controlled the educational curriculum. The Guardians themselves were to have neither property nor normal family life, which were presumed to be distractions. In Book 5 (*Dialogues*, pp. 688-720) Plato discusses women and the family. Women may perform the same jobs as men. In order to satisfy sexual instincts and produce good citizens, Plato proposed mating festivals. The Guardians were to arrange appropriate mates so that only the best breeds should survive. Weaker strains should be allowed to perish. Children should be brought up in state nurseries.

[5]Plato's views have been subjected to devastating criticism by Karl Popper in *The Open Society and Its Enemies*, 2 vols. (Princeton: Princeton University Press, 5th ed. 1961). Vol. 1 examines Plato's teaching and vol 2. compares it with that of Karl Marx.

[6]*Republic* 6.509ab (*Dialogues*, p. 744).

[7]*Republic* 6.509-11 (*Dialogues*, pp. 744-47).

[8]*Republic* 7.514-17 (*Dialogues*, pp. 747-50).

[9]*Republic* 7.517bc (*Dialogues*, pp. 749-50).

[10]*Meno* 86b (*Dialogues*, p. 371). Earlier Greek thought had distinguished two types of soul. The free soul was identified with the individual, but lacked psychological attributes. It was active outside the body in dreams, semi-conscious states and after death. The body soul endowed human beings with life and consciousness. Gradually, the two kinds of souls were replaced by the idea of a single soul. On this see Jan Bremmer, *The Early Greek Concept of the Soul* (Princeton: Princeton University Press, 1987).

[11]*Phaedo* 106e (*Dialogues*, p. 88).

[12]*Phaedo* 107cd (*Dialogues*, p. 89).

[13]*Republic* 10.614-20 (*Dialogues*, pp. 839-44).

[14]*Timaeus* 27-30 (*Dialogues*, pp. 1161-63). For further discussion of Plato's views of God, see William Lane Craig, *The Cosmological Argument from Plato to Leibniz* (New York: Barnes and Noble; London: Macmillan, 1980), pp. 1-19.

[15]*Timaeus* 30bc (*Dialogues*, pp. 1162-63).

[16]*Laws* 10.884-889e (*Dialogues*, pp. 1440-55).

[17]*Laws* 10.1455b (*Dialogues*, p. 1455). The view that all things are "full of gods" derives from Thales. For discussion see above, p. 21.

[18]*Parmenides* 134bc (*Dialogues*, p. 928).

[19]For brief comparison see Leslie Stevenson, *Seven Theories of Human Nature* (New York and Oxford: Oxford University Press, 2nd ed. 1980), pp. 27-52; and Arthur F. Holmes, *Ethics: Approaching Moral Decisions* (Downers Grove, Illinois, and Leicester, England: InterVarsity Press, 1984), pp. 69-78.

[20]*Ethics*, pp.69-70.

[21]*Euthyphro* 15b (*Dialogues*, p. 184). The work is an inconclusive attempt to define piety, and takes the form of a discussion outside the law courts between Socrates, who is on his way to be tried, and Euthyphro, who is on his way to prosecute his own father for murder.

[22]*Laws* 10.885-888 (*Dialogues*, pp. 1440-44).

[23]For a recent discussion of the problem, see Richard Swinburne, *The Evolution of the Soul* (Oxford: Clarendon Press, 1986). Swinburne rejects the dualism of Plato and Descartes which teaches that the soul has a nature such that it will survive "under its own steam" whatever happens to the body. He believes that there cannot be any justified general account of the nature of the soul. Under normal conditions the soul requires the functioning of the body. However, Swinburne does not reject the notion of the soul. He argues for what he calls a "soft dualism" in which souls exist in an embodied form (p. 10). "The soul is like a light bulb and the brain is like an electric light socket. If you plug the bulb into the socket and turn the current on, the light will shine. If the socket is damaged or the current turned off, the light will not shine. So, too, the soul will function (have a mental life) if it is plugged into a functioning brain" (p. 310). Swinburne believes that his view is compatible with Christian orthodox teaching on the resurrection body, but that it is incompatible with Plato's view of the natural immortality of the soul and views of disembodied existence (pp. 311-12).

[24]See the discussions of reincarnation in John Hick, *Death and Eternal Life* (San Francisco: Harper & Row, paperback reprint, 1980), especially pp. 297-396, 412-19; Hans Küng, *Eternal Life? Life after Death as a Medical, Philosophical, and Theological Problem* (New York: Doubleday, 1984), pp. 59-66. Counterparts to Plato's teaching may be found in various Eastern religions. It would seem that Plato's teaching represents just one form of a very widespread belief which

Plato incorporated into his teaching.

A modern form of belief in reincarnation is held by Scientology, which purports to provide therapy to treat inhibiting unconscious memories acquired in previous existences. For example, L. Ron Hubbard, *Dianetics: The Modern Science of Mental Health. A Handbook of Dianetic Procedures* (Los Angeles: Publications Organization, 1950); *Have You Life Before This Life? A Scientific Survey. A Study of Death and Evidence of Past Lives* (Los Angeles: Publications Organization, 1950). For a critical examination of Scientology, see Roy Wallis, *The Road to Total Freedom: A Sociological Analysis of Scientology* (New York: Columbia University Press, 1977).

Chapter 3: Aristotle and the Physical World
[1]The standard English translation of Aristotle was published by the Oxford University Press in 12 volumes between 1912 and 1954. It has now been reissued in revised form under the title *The Complete Works of Aristotle: The Revised Oxford Translation*, ed. Jonathan Barnes, 2 vols. (Princeton: Princeton University Press, Bollingen Series 71.2, 1984). Barnes has also written a brief introduction, *Aristotle* (Oxford: Oxford University Press, 1982). Modern studies of Aristotle include Werner Jaeger, *Aristotle: Fundamentals of the History of His Development* (Oxford: Clarendon Press, 2nd ed. 1948); Marjorie Grene, *A Portrait of Aristotle* (Chicago: University of Chicago Press, 1963); Abraham Edel, *Aristotle and his Philosophy* (Chapel Hill: University of North Carolina Press, 1982); Anthony Kenny, *The Aristotelian Ethics: A Study of the Relationship between the Eudemian and Nicomachean Ethics of Aristotle* (Oxford: Clarendon Press, 1978); Stephen R. L. Clark, *Aristotle's Man: Speculation upon Aristotelian Anthropology* (Oxford: Clarendon Press, 1975); Felix Grayeff, *Aristotle and his School: An Inquiry into the History of the Peripatos with a Commentary on the Metaphysics Z, H, L and TH* (London: Duckworth, 1974); Franz Brentano, *Aristotle and his World View*, ed. and trans. Rolf George and Roderick M. Chisholm (Berkeley, Los Angeles, London: University of California Press, 1978); Jonathan Barnes, Malcolm Scofield, Richard Sorabji, eds., *Articles on Aristotle*, 4 vols. (New York: St. Martin's Press, 1975-78); Giovanni Reale, *The Concept of the First Philosophy and the Unity of the Metaphysics of Aristotle*, ed. and trans. John R. Catan (Albany, NY: State University of New York Press, 1980).

[2]*Topics* 6.6.145a15 (*Works* 1:244).

[3]*Prior Analytics* 1.1.24b19-22 (*Works* 1:40).

[4]*Posterior Analytics* 1.7.75a38 (*Works* 1:122).

[5]*Metaphysics* 5.12.1019a; 12.5.1071a4-15; and the discussion in Book 9 (Theta) (*Works* 2:1609, 1692, 1651-1661).

[6]*Metaphysics* 1.6-9.987a29-993a10 (*Works* 2:1561-69).

[7]*Metaphysics* 5.2.1013a24-101a25 (*Works* 2:1600-1).

[8]*Metaphysics* 12.1-10.1069a18-1076a4 (*Works* 2:1688-1700). For further discussion

see Craig, *The Cosmological Argument,* pp. 20-47, where attention is drawn to Aristotle's thoughts on the motion of the heavens; and D. W. Hamlyn, "Aristotle's God," in Gerard J. Hughes, ed., *The Philosophical Assessment of Theology: Essays in Honor of Frederick C. Copleston* (London: Search Press; Washington, D.C.: Georgetown University Press, 1987), pp. 15-34.

[9]*Metaphysics* 12.7.1072a23-26 (*Works* 2:1694).

[10]*Metaphysics* 12.7.1072a 25 (*Works* 2:1694).

[11]*Physics* 8.10.267b 24-27 (*Works* 1:446).

[12]*Metaphysics* 12.7.1072a21-29 (*Works* 2:1694).

[13]*Metaphysics* 12.7.1072b 11 (*Works* 2:1694).

[14]*Metaphysics* 12.7.1072b20-31 (*Works* 2:1695).

[15]*Nicomachean Ethics* 10.9.1179b24-32 (*Works* 2:1863-1864).

[16]See, e.g., Psalms 1; 119; Proverbs 8. For further references and literature, see the article on "Wisdom, Folly, Philosophy" in Colin Brown, ed., *The New International Dictionary of New Testament Theology* (Grand Rapids: Zondervan; Exeter: Paternoster Press, 1978), 3: 1023-37. In the New Testament Jesus is presented as the personal embodiment of wisdom (e.g., Matthew 1:18-19; 11:28-30 [cf. Sirach 51:23-27]; 12:41-42; 23:34-37). For further discussion see M. Jack Suggs, *Wisdom, Christology and Law in Matthew's Gospel* (Cambridge, Massachusetts: Harvard University Press, 1971); R. G. Hamerton-Kelly, *Pre-existence, Wisdom, and the Son of Man: A Study of the Idea of Pre-existence in the New Testament* (Cambridge: Cambridge University Press, 1973). Paul presents Christ as the wisdom of God (1 Corinthians 1:24, 30; 8:6; Colossians 1:15-20). For an account of Paul as a teacher of Christian wisdom, see Peter Stuhlmacher, "The Hermeneutical Significance of 1 Corinthians 2:6-16," in Gerald F. Hawthorne and Otto Betz, eds., *Tradition and Interpretation in the New Testament: Essays in Honor of E. Earle Ellis* (Grand Rapids: Eerdmans, 1987), pp. 328-47.

[17]*On the Soul* 1.1.402a7 (*Works* 1:641).

[18]*On the Soul* 3.3.427a19 (*Works* 1:679).

[19]*Politics* 1.2.1253a4 (*Works* 2:1987).

[20]*Politics* 1.2.1253a15-18 (*Works* 2:1988).

[21]The *Nicomachean Ethics* was so called because it was issued by Aristotle's son, Nicomachus. It was long regarded as the definitive statement of Aristotle's ethics, in preference to the version compiled by his pupil Eudemus the mathematician. However, recent scholarship has somewhat revised this view (see Kenny, *The Aristotelian Ethics*). The *Magna Moralia* is widely thought to be a later Peripatetic compilation.

[22]*Nicomachean Ethics* 3.1.1109b30 (*Works* 2:1752).

[23]*Nicomachean Ethics* 10.8.1179a30 (*Works* 2:1863).

[24]*Eudemian Ethics* 3.1-7.1228a23-1234b13 (*Works* 2:1945-55). See also Guthrie, *History* 6:352-76.

[25]The idea of the Golden Mean appears in Horace who wrote: "Whoso cherishes

the golden mean [*auream mediocritatem*], safely avoids the foulness of an ill-kept house and discreetly, too, avoids exciting envy" (*Odes* 2.10.5-8, Loeb Classical Library, 1952, p. 131).

[26]*Nicomachean Ethics* 1.1094a1 (*Works* 2:1728).

[27]*Nicomachean Ethics* 2.1103a16-17 (*Works* 2:1742).

[28]Stanley Hauerwas, *Vision and Virtue: Essays in Christian Ethical Reflection* (Notre Dame: Fides Publishers, 1974); Hauerwas, *Character and the Christian Life: A Study in Theological Ethics* (San Antonio: Trinity University Press, 1975).

[29]Alasdair MacIntyre, *After Virtue: A Study in Moral Theory* (Notre Dame: University of Notre Dame Press, 1980); MacIntyre, *Whose Justice? Whose Rationality?* (Notre Dame: University of Notre Dame Press, 1988).

[30]For a recent discussion see Robert B. Kruschwitz and Robert C. Roberts, eds., *The Virtues: Contemporary Essays on Moral Character* (Belmont, CA: Wadsworth, 1987).

Chapter 4: Epicureans, Stoics, Skeptics and Cynics

[1]The writings of Epicurus have not survived apart from fragments and letters. Diogenes Laertius gives an account of his teaching in book ten of his *Lives of Eminent Philosophers*, which is the chief authority for his teaching. Diogenes Laertius is also a primary source for the Stoics, Skeptics, and Cynics. Epicurus's extant writings are included in *The Stoic and Epicurean Philosophers: The Complete Extant Writings of Epicurus, Epictetus, Lucretius, Marcus Aurelius*, ed. Whitney J. Oates (New York: Random House, 1940). Another sourcebook is Gordon H. Clark, *Selections from Hellenistic Philosophy* (New York: Appleton-Century-Crofts, 1960). A more recent critical edition of texts is A. A. Long and D. N. Sedley, eds., *The Hellenistic Philosophers*, 1 *Translations of the Principal Sources with Philosophical Commentary*, 2 *An Annotated Collection of the Greek and Latin Texts* (Cambridge: Cambridge University Press, 1987, 1988). A primary source for Epicurean teaching is the didactic poem of Lucretius, *On the Nature of Things*. For a modern prose translation see Lucretius, *The Nature of the Universe*, trans. R. E. Latham (Harmondsworth: Penguin Books, 1951). For brief extracts of Stoic and Epicurean teaching, see C. K. Barrett, *The New Testament Background: Selected Documents* (Revised edition, London: SPCK, 1987; San Francisco: Harper & Row, 1989), pp. 65-81. For overviews, see Giovanni Reale, *A History of Ancient Philosophy*, vol. 3 *The Systems of the Hellenistic Age*, ed. and trans. John R. Catan (Albany, NY: State University of New York Press, 1985); A. A. Long, *Hellenistic Philosophy*, 2nd ed. (London: Duckworth, 1987). For specialist studies of religion into the Christian era, see R. van den Broek, T. Baarda, J. Mansfield, eds., *Knowledge of God in the Graeco-Roman World* (Leiden: E. J. Brill, 1988).

An important collection of authoritative articles dealing with various aspects of philosophy in the Roman world, both before and during the Christian era, may be found in the relevant parts and volumes of *Aufstieg und Niedergang der römischen Welt* (= The Rise and Fall of the Roman World), ed. Wolfgang Haase, pt. 2, vol. 36 (Berlin and New York: Walter de Gruyter, 1987 onwards). Many of them are in English. *ANRW* 2.36.1 deals with Platonism. *ANRW* 2.36.2 concludes Platonism, and goes on to discuss Aristotelianism. *ANRW* 2.36.3 reviews Stoicism. *ANRW* 2.36.4 embraces Epicureanism, Skepticism, Cynicism and other themes.

A major attempt to correct traditional misunderstandings about Epicurus has been made by Norman Wentworth DeWitt in his *Epicurus and his Philosophy* (Minneapolis: University of Minnesota Press, 1954; paperback, Cleveland: Meridian Books, 1967). However, some scholars think that DeWitt's account is somewhat extravagant in its enthusiasm. Other studies include R. D. Hicks, *Stoic and Epicurean* (New York: Russell & Russell, 1962); A. A. Long, *Hellenistic Philosophy: Stoics, Epicureans, Sceptics* (Berkeley and Los Angeles: University of California Press, 2nd ed. 1986); A. J. Festiguière, *Epicurus and his Gods* (New York: Russell & Russell, reprint 1969); J. M. Rist, *Epicurus: An Introduction* (Cambridge: Cambridge University Press, 1972); On the impact of Hellenism see Martin Hengel, *Judaism and Hellenism: Studies in their Encounters in Palestine during the Early Hellenistic Period*, 2 vols. (London: S.C.M. Press; Philadephia: Fortress Press, 1974); Helmut Koester, *Introduction to the New Testament*, vol. 1, *History, Culture, and Religion of the Hellenistic Age* (Berlin, New York: Walter de Gruyter, paperback reprint 1987).

[2]Diogenes Laertius *Lives* 10.9 (Loeb edition, 2:539).

[3]*Lives* 10.33 (Loeb edition, 2:563); cf. Lucretius, *The Nature of the Universe*, 1.6-1036, trans. Latham, pp. 130-62.

[4]*Lives* 10.55 (Loeb edition, 2:585); cf. Lucretius, *The Nature of the Universe*, 1.146-634; 2.1-1174, trans. Latham, pp. 31-45, 60-95.

[5]*Lives* 10.123 (Loeb edition, 2:649); cf. Lucretius, *The Nature of the Universe*, 5.91-415, trans. Latham, pp. 172-75.

[6]*Lives* 10.124-126 (Loeb edition, 2:651-53); cf. Lucretius, *The Nature of the Universe*, 3.1-1094, trans. Latham, pp. 96-129.

[7]*Lives* 10.129 (Loeb edition, 2:655).

[8]*Lives* 10.131 (Loeb edition, 2:657).

[9]For texts and works which deal with both Stoicism and Epicureanism, see above n. 1. English translations include Epictetus, *Discourses and Enchiridion*, trans. T. W. Higginson with introduction by I. Edman (New York: Walter J. Black, 1944); *Marcus Aurelius and his Times: The Transition from Paganism to Christianity*, with introduction by I. Edman (New York: Walter J. Black, 1945). Important studies include Edward Vernon Arnold, *Roman Stoicism, Being Lectures on the History of the Stoic Philosophy with Special Reference to its Development within the Roman Empire* (1911, reprint Freeport, NY: Books for Libraries Press, 1971), which despite its title is very valuable for Greek Stoicism; David E. Hahm, *The Origins of Stoic Cosmology* (Columbus: Ohio State University Press, 1977); Benson

Mates, *Stoic Logic* (Berkeley and Los Angeles: University of California Press, 1961); J. M. Rist, *Stoic Philosophy* (Cambridge: Cambridge University Press, 1969); Brad Inwood, *Ethics and Human Action in Early Stoicism* (Oxford: Clarendon Press, 1985); Marcia L. Colish, *The Stoic Tradition from Antiquity to the Early Middle Ages*, 2 vols. Studies in the History of Christian Thought 24-25 (Leiden: E. J. Brill, 1985).

[10]Diogenes Laertius *Lives* 7.5 (Loeb edition, 2:115).

[11]Translation in Oates, *The Stoic and Epicurean Philosophers*, pp. 591-92. The Hymn opens:

> O God most glorious, called by many a name,
>
> Nature's great King, through endless years the same;
>
> Omnipotence, who by thy just decree Controllest all,
>
> hail, Zeus, for unto thee Behooves thy creatures in all lands to call.
>
> We are thy children, we alone, of all.
>
> On earth's broad ways that wander to and fro,
>
> Bearing thine image whereso'er we go.

It goes on to celebrate the ordering of all things by the divine Word:

> Nay, but thou knowest to make crooked straight:
>
> Chaos to thee is order: in thine eyes
>
> The unloved is lovely, who didst harmonize
>
> Things evil with things good, that there should be
>
> One Word through all things everlastingly.

It ends with a call to adore:

> The universal law for evermore.

[12]Diogenes Laertius *Lives* 7.180 (Loeb edition, 2:289).

[13]Diogenes Laertius *Lives* 7.184 (Loeb edition, 2:293 slightly emended).

[14]Text edited by A. Kurfess in E. Hennecke and W. Schneemelcher, *New Testament Apocrypha* (London: Lutterworth Press, 1965), 2:133-41. See further J. N. Sevenster, *Paul and Seneca*, Supplements to Novum Testamentum 4 (Leiden: E. J. Brill, 1961).

[15]*Meditations* 3.5; 5.10; 12.1-36; cf. Epictetus *Discourses* 1.14 (Oates, *The Stoic and Epicurean Philosophers*, pp. 504, 522, 579-85; cf. 250-251). See further Arnold, *Roman Stoicism*, pp. 238-72, especially pp. 242-43.

[16]*Meditations* 12.14 (Oates, p. 581).

[17]P. Merlan in A. H. Armstrong, ed., *The Cambridge History of Later Greek and Early Medieval Philosophy*, p. 124.

[18]Diogenes Laertius *Lives* 7.134 (Loeb edition, 2:239).

[19]Diogenes Laertius *Lives* 7.135 (Loeb edition, 2:241).

[20]Diogenes Laertius *Lives* 7.137-38 (Loeb edition, 2:241-42).

[21]Cicero *On the Nature of the Gods* 2.4.12 (*De Natura Deorum, Academica*, Loeb Classical Library, trans. H. Rackham, 1933, p. 135). Cicero goes on to say, however, that there are various opinions about the nature of the gods. He notes

that "our master Cleanthes" spoke of four causes that account for the formation of the notion of the gods: (1) foreknowledge of future events; (2) the benefits of the earth; (3) the awe inspired by natural phenomena; (4) the uniform motion and revolution of the heavens which compel one "to infer that these mighty-world motions are regulated by some Mind" (2.5.13-15, pp. 137-38). Cicero himself was an eclectic thinker who compiled the opinions of Greek thinkers for the benefit of his Roman readers. He rejected Epicureanism and leaned toward the skeptical Academy. But here, as in other places, he was impressed by the Stoics (cf. 2.59.147-2.77.168, pp. 265-85). Seneca argued that there was no race that had departed so far from the laws and customs that it did not believe in some kind of gods (Letter 117.6). See further Arnold, *Roman Stoicism*, pp. 223-33.

[22]Diogenes Laertius *Lives* 9.69 (Loeb edition, 2:483). The chief source of knowledge of Pyrrho is Book 9 of the *Lives* and the writings of Sextus Empiricus (trans. R. B. Bury, Loeb Classical Library, 4 vols., 1933-49). A modern translation by Sanford G. Etheridge has been published under the title *Scepticism, Man, and God: Selections from the Major Writings of Sextus Empiricus,* ed. Philip P. Hallie (Middletown, Connecticut: Wesleyan University Press, 1964). References below are to this edition. Studies include Edwyn Bevan, *Stoics and Sceptics* (1913, reprint New York: Barnes & Noble, 1959); Mary Mills Patrick, *The Greek Sceptics* (New York: Columbia University Press, 1929); Charlotte L. Stough, *Greek Skepticism: A Study in Epistemology* (Berkeley and Los Angeles: University of California Press, 1969). On the influence of skepticism on later European thought, see Richard H. Popkin, *The History of Skepticism from Erasmus to Spinoza* (Berkeley, Los Angeles: University of California Press, 1979).

[23]Diogenes Laertius *Lives* 9.70 (Loeb edition, 2:483).

[24]Diogenes Laertius *Lives* 9.68 (Loeb edition, 2:481).

[25]"For if a person is worthy of credence when he makes an assumption, then we shall in each case also not be less worthy of credence if we make the opposite assumption. And if the person making the assumption assumes something which is true, he renders it suspicious by taking it on assumption. But if what he assumes is false, the foundation of what he is trying to prove will be unsound. Moreover, if assumption conduces at all towards proof, let the thing in question itself be assumed and not something else by means of which he will then prove the thing under discussion. But if it is absurd to assume the thing in question, it will also be absurd to assume what transcends it" (*Outlines* 1.15; *Scepticism*, pp. 74-75).

[26]*Against the Dogmatists*, vol. 3 (= *Against the Physicists* 1.192; *Scepticism*, p. 215).

[27]*Outlines* 1.28 (*Scepticism*, p. 86).

[28]Diogenes Laertius *Lives* 6.53-54 (Loeb edition, 2:55).

[29]Diogenes Laertius *Lives* 6.60 (Loeb edition, 2:53).

[30]Diogenes Laertius *Lives* 6.51 (Loeb edition, 2:53).

[31]Diogenes Laertius *Lives* 6.41 (Loeb edition, 2:43).

[32]Diogenes Laertius *Lives* 6.72 (Loeb edition, 2:75).

[33]Some writers use the expression "Stoic-Cynic" as if to denote some kind of compounded conception. More recently, however, warnings have been given against the use of the hyphen which suggests something which did not actually exist (cf. Abraham J. Malherbe, *The Cynic Epistles: A Study Edition*, SBL Sources for Biblical Study 12, Missoula, Montana: Scholars Press, 1977, p. 2). Although they valued inner freedom, hardiness, and asceticism, the Stoics frowned upon the Cynic mendicant way of life, and the squalid appearance and insulting manners of some of the Cynics (Long, *Hellenistic Philosophy*, p. 234).

[34]A number of scholars have detected similarities between Jesus and the wandering Cynic teacher. Burton L. Mack observes: "Jesus' wisdom incorporated the pungent invitation to insight and the daring to be different that characterized the Cynic approach to life. . . . Using metaphors such as king, overseer, physician, gadfly, and teacher, Cynics understood themselves to be 'sent' by God to preside over the human situation. Epictetus even refers to the Cynics' vocation as a reign (*basileia*, "kingdom") in order to catch up the challenging aspects of representing publicly a way of life grounded in the divine laws of nature. . . . [Jesus'] themes and topics are much closer to Cynic idiom than to those characteristic for public Jewish piety" (Burton L. Mack, *A Myth of Innocence: Mark and Christian Origins*, Philadelphia: Fortress Press, 1988, pp. 69-73). However, other scholars think that this view utterly fails to do justice to the Jewishness of Jesus and the demonstrable similarities between Jesus' teaching methods and other Jewish teachers. An important study, yet to be translated into English, which deals with Jesus' teaching methods in their Jewish context is Rainer Riesner, *Jesus als Lehrer. Eine Untersuchung zum Ursprung der Evangelien-Überlieferung*, Wissenschaftliche Untersuchungen zum Neuen Testament 2. Reihe 7 (Tübingen: J.C.B. Mohr [Paul Siebeck], 1981).

For a compilation of source material see F. Gerald Downing, *Christ and the Cynics: Jesus and Other Radical Preachers in First-Century Tradition*, JSOT Manuals 4 (Sheffield: Sheffield Academic Press, 1988). Whereas some Christian teaching and practices bear some resemblance to the Cynic lifestyle, Downing's collection reveals profound differences. For criticism of the hypothesis that the Jesus movement was a form of Cynic philosophy and lifestyle, see Richard J. Horsley, *Sociology and the Jesus Movement* (New York: Crossroad, 1989), pp. 43-64, 116-19. Horsley notes that the Cynics and Jesus' disciples had very different "callings." The former sought to be individual paradigms of virtue; the latter were charged as catalysts of a broader movement based in local communities. The Cynics lived without home and possessions as an intentional "way of life"; the leaving of home and possessions by Jesus' envoys was necessitated by their mission. The Cynics were vagabond beggars moving from house to house; the disciples were instructed to stay in local houses and receive what was provided for them. The Cynics prized individual self-sufficiency; the Jesus movement led to the formation of communities in the form of churches dependent on the grace of God and bearing witness to Christ's atoning death and resurrection life.

In the social and religious context of Palestinian Judaism Jesus appeared much closer to the tradition of the prophets, apocalyptic teachers and charismatic leaders. To his enemies Jesus appeared, not as a Cynic philosopher, but as a false charismatic prophet who performed signs and wonders in order to lead the people astray. As such he was put to death for blasphemy so that the land might be purged of his evil (see Colin Brown, *Miracles and the Critical Mind* [Grand Rapids: Eerdmans; Exeter: Paternoster Press, 1984], pp. 293-325; Brown, *That You May Believe: Miracles and Faith—Then and Now* [Grand Rapids: Eerdmans; Exeter: Paternoster Press, 1985], pp. 95-175; Brown, "Synoptic Miracle Stories: A Jewish Religious and Social Setting," *Foundations and Facets Forum* 2 [1986]: 55-76; Brown, *History and Faith: A Personal Exploration* [Grand Rapids: Zondervan; Leicester: InterVarsity Press, 1987], pp. 78-85).

Chapter 5: From Greeks to Gospel

[1]For an example of thinking which sees radical differences between Greek and Jewish thought, see Thorleif Boman, *Hebrew Thought Compared with Greek* (London: S.C.M. Press, 1960). For a critique of this line of approach, see James Barr, *The Semantics of Biblical Language* (Oxford: Oxford University Press, 1961).

[2]Martin Hengel, *Judaism and Hellenism: Studies in their Encounter in Palestine during the early Hellenistic Period*, 2 vols. (London: S.C.M. Press; Philadelphia: Fortress Press, 1974).

[3]Basic surveys of Christianity in relation to the ancient world include A. D. Nock, *Early Gentile Christianity and its Hellenistic Background* (New York: Harper Torchbook, 1964); Frederick C. Grant, *Roman Hellenism and the New Testament* (New York: Charles Scribner's Sons, 1962); Ronald H. Nash, *Christianity and the Hellenistic World* (Grand Rapids: Zondervan; Dallas: Probe, 1984); Ramsey MacMullen, *Paganism in the Roman Empire* (New Haven: Yale University Press, 1981); Calvin J. Roetzel, *The World that Shaped the New Testament* (Atlanta: John Knox Press, 1985); Helmut Koester, *Introduction to the New Testament*, vol. 1, *History, Culture, and Religion of the Hellenistic Age;* vol. 2, *History and Literature of Early Christianity* (Berlin, New York: Walter de Gruyter, Paperback reprint 1987). A major series which explores the Jewish and Graeco-Roman contexts of Christianity is The Library of Early Christianity, general editor Wayne A. Meeks (Philadelphia: Westminster Press, 8 vols.). Among the volumes in this series which are particularly relevant to our present concern are: Robert M. Grant, *Gods and the One God* (1986); James L. Kugel and Rowan A. Greer, *Early Biblical Interpretation* (1986); Abraham J. Malherbe, *Moral Exhortation, a Greco-Roman Sourcebook* (1986); Wayne A. Meeks, *The Moral World of the First Christians* (1986);

David E. Aune, *The New Testament in its Literary Environment* (1987); Stanley K. Stowers, *Letter Writing in Greco-Roman Antiquity* (1987). For documents relevant to the world of the New Testament, see C. K. Barrett, *The New Testament Background: Selected Documents* (Revised edition, London: S.P.C.K., 1987; San Francisco: Harper & Row, 1989).

⁴Henry Chadwick in *The Cambridge History of Later Greek and Early Medieval Philosophy*, p. 137. Chadwick's account of Philo (pp. 137-57) is concise but very well documented.

⁵The Loeb Classical Library edition of Philo runs to twelve volumes. Selections from his writings are given in Nahum H. Glatzer, ed., *The Essential Philo* (reprint New York: Schocken Books, 1971); and the more up-to-date critical *Philo of Alexandria: The Contemplative Life, The Giants, and Selections*, trans. with introduction by David Winston (New York: Paulist Press, The Classics of Western Spirituality, 1981). The foundational studies by H. A. Wolfson, *Philo: Foundations of Religious Philosophy in Judaism, Christianity and Islam*, 2 vols. (Cambridge, Mass.: Harvard University Press, 3rd ed. 1962), and *Religious Philosophy: A Group of Essays* (Cambridge, Mass.: Harvard University Press, 1961) need to be supplemented by more recent work. These include Samuel Sandmel, *Philo of Alexandria: An Introduction* (New York: Oxford University Press, 1979); John Dillon, *The Middle Platonists, 80 B.C. to A.D. 220* (Ithaca, NY: Cornell University Press, 1977), pp. 139-83; the work of Winston and the literature that he notes above; and the *Studia Philonica* published by the Philo Institute (1972-).

⁶Winston, *Philo of Alexandria*, p. 3.

⁷Roetzel, *The World that Shaped the New Testament*, p. 81.

⁸*On the Nature of the Gods* 2.24.63-25.64 (Loeb edition, p. 185).

⁹Winston, *Philo of Alexandria*, pp. 6-7.

¹⁰*On Dreams* 2.247 (Loeb edition, 5:553).

¹¹*Every Good Man is Free* 1.2.13 (Loeb edition, 9:11, 13).

¹²*On the Creation of the World* 1.20 (Loeb edition, 1:17).

¹³ Winston, *Philo of Alexandria*, p. 26.

¹⁴See Grant, *Gods and the One God*, 19-28, 49-51; F. F. Bruce, *The Acts of the Apostles, The Greek Text* (London: Tyndale Press, 2nd ed. 1952), pp. 330-41; Bruce, *The Book of Acts*, Revised Edition, New International Commentary on the New Testament (Grand Rapids: Eerdmans, 1988), pp. 328-44; Ernst Haenchen, *The Acts of the Apostles* (Oxford: Basil Blackwell, 1971), pp. 514-41; Bruce, "The Speeches in Acts—Thirty Years After," in Robert Banks, ed., *Reconciliation and Hope: Essays Presented to L. L. Morris* (Exeter: Paternoster Press, 1974), pp. 53-68; D. W. Kemmler, *Faith and Human Reason: A Study of Paul's Method of Preaching as Illustrated by 1-2 Thessalonians and Acts 17, 2-4*, Supplements to Novum Testamentum 40 (Leiden: E. J. Brill, 1975); and the literature noted in these works.

¹⁵The first may come from a lost work attributed to Epimenides the Cretan (c. 600 B.C.) which, however, was written at a late date, and which appears to be

quoted in Titus 1:12 as that of a Cretan prophet. The second is taken from Aratus (b. 310 B.C.), *Phainomena* 5, which in turn may have drawn on Cleanthes, *Hymn to Zeus* (see above, ch. 4, n. 11).

[16]For a discussion of the themes of preaching in the early church, noting the differences between preaching to Jewish and Gentile audiences, see Colin Brown, "The Structure and Content of the Early Kerygma," in Colin Brown, ed., *The New International Dictionary of New Testament Theology* (Grand Rapids: Zondervan; Exeter: Paternoster Press, 1978) 3:57-67.

[17]Acts 18:1; 20:2-3; cf. Romans 15:25. For discussion see (e.g.) W. G. Kümmel, *Introduction to the New Testament* (Nashville: Abingdon, 1975), pp. 311-320; Ralph P. Martin, *New Testament Foundations* (Grand Rapids: Eerdmans, 1978) 2:190.

[18]Günther Bornkamm, *Early Christian Experience* (London: SCM Press, 1969), pp. 47-70, 105-111; Sevenster, *Paul and Seneca*, passim. For discussion of Paul's literary techniques and his possible links with the Stoic diatribe, see Stanley Kent Stowers, *The Diatribe and Paul's Letter to the Romans*, Society of Biblical Literature Dissertation Series 57 (Chico, CA: Scholars Press, 1981); Stowers, *Letter Writing in Greco-Roman Antiquity;* Aune, *The New Testament in its Literary Environment.*

In a striking recent study of *Paul and the Thessalonians: The Philosophic Tradition of Pastoral Care* (Philadelphia: Fortress Press, 1987), Abraham J. Malherbe has argued that Paul's missionary strategy was influenced by the Hellenistic philosophical schools with which his converts were familiar. Malherbe sees a direct link between Paul's model of pastoral care and philosophical practices. Like Seneca, Paul offered himself as a paradigm for the community. Like the Stoics, Platonists and Epicureans, Paul encouraged mutual concern. Paul's emphasis on the quiet life has links with those of the philosophers, as does his moral exhortation. But unlike the philosophers, Paul encouraged his readers to be "taught by God" rather than be "self-taught." Moreover, in encouraging the Thessalonians to "work with your hands," Paul was distancing himself from the Epicurean contemptuous disengagement from society and from the Cynic way of life.

In *Paul and the Popular Philosophers* (Minneapolis: Fortress Press, 1989) Malherbe explores other letters by Paul and notes numerous allusions to different forms of popular philosophy. He sees Paul as a Christian apostle who knew contemporary philosophy firsthand. Paul did not openly discuss the philosophical traditions in his letters, but he addressed the issues that they raised. Paul frequently used philosophical language, but shrank from the Cynics' preoccupation with the individual. Unlike the Cynics, who had no communities, Paul was concerned to found Christian communities in the form of the churches that he established and nurtured. In his communal concern Paul was closer to the Epicureans. In his pastoral care Paul had absorbed the traditions that he had met and could even behave like a philosopher in the fulfillment of his apostolic vocation.

[19]For further discussion see J. D. G. Dunn, *Romans 1-8*, Word Biblical Commentary (Dallas: Word Books, 1988), pp. 51-76. Dunn observes that the argument "is obviously the deliberate echo of the Adam narratives (Gen 2-3) in vv 19-25. . . . The use of more widely known Stoic categories, particularly in vv 19-20, 23, and 28 . . . would increase the universal appeal of the argument. Equally significant, however, is the fact that in v 21 and overwhelmingly from v 23 onward Paul speaks as a Jew and makes use of the standard Hellenistic Jewish polemic against idolatry; the influence of Wisd Sol 11-15 is particularly noticeable," p. 53. Commenting on Romans 1:20, Dunn observes: "Paul is trading upon, without necessarily committing himself to, the Greek (particularly Stoic) understanding of an invisible realm of reality, invisible to sense perception, which can be known only through the rational power of the mind. With Philo he presumably would not want to say that the rational mind is able to reach or grasp God. And he ensures that his language, however indebted to Stoic thought, should not be understood in terms of Stoicism by giving prominence to the thought of *creation* ('from the act of creation . . . the things which have been made'; 'Paul speaks not of Ideas, but of things and events which manifest God's power' [Schlatter; cf. Acts 14:17]), and by setting it within an apocalyptic framework (the revelation of divine wrath from heaven)," p. 58.

[20]For reviews of the possibilities, see R. P. Martin, *Colossians and Philemon*, New Century Bible (Greenwood, SC: Attic Press, 1974), pp. 9-19, 79; Eduard Lohse, *Colossians and Philemon*, Hermeneia (Philadephia: Fortress Press, 1971), pp. 94-99. On the question of whether there really was a Colossian heresy, see Morna D. Hooker, "Were there False Teachers at Colossae?" in Barnabas Lindars and Stephen D. Smalley, eds. *Christ and Spirit in the New Testament*, Studies in Honour of C. F. D. Moule (Cambridge: Cambridge University Press, 1973), pp. 315-31.

It may be noted that the Jewish historian Josephus said that the Jews had from ancient times "three philosophies pertaining to their traditions": the Essenes, the Sadducees, and the Pharisees (*Jewish Antiquities* 18.11; see also 13.171-173; and Josephus, *The Jewish War* 2.119-166). He may, of course, be using the term *philosophy* to make the three sects more intelligible to non-Jewish readers. However, elsewhere he compared the Essenes with the Pythagoreans (*The Jewish War* 15.371) and the Pharisees with the Stoics (*Life* 12). Hellenistic philosophy was concerned not only with theoretical ideas but with ways of living. Josephus's description of the practices of the sects brings out the connection between beliefs and lifestyle. Josephus also mentions a more recent fourth "school of philosophy" begun by Judas the Galilean and Saddok (*Antiquities* 18.9 and 23-25).

In an impressive recent study Eduard Schweizer has argued that the term translated as "elemental spirits of the universe" (Greek, *ta stoicheia tou kosmou;*

literally, "the elements of the world") refers to the traditional elements which made up the world (earth, water, air and fire). This is the meaning that the term had in the literature of the day. Thus the passage is addressing fear of the elements, and pagan and Jewish ways of trying to control the elements and avert disaster through sundry rites and practices (both pagan and Jewish). The passage contrasts the futility of such practices with the power of the crucified and risen Christ. (See Eduard Schweizer, "Slaves of the Elements and Worshipers of Angels: Gal 4:3, 9 and Col 2:8, 18, 20," *Journal of Biblical Literature* 107 [1988]: 455-68.)

[21]George Holley Gilbert, *Greek Thought in the New Testament* (New York: Macmillan, 1928), p. 85. For other literature and a critique of this view, see Ronald Nash, *Christianity and the Hellenistic World* (Grand Rapids: Zondervan, 1984), pp. 56-64.

[22]See (e.g.) the comment of Ralph P. Martin on 2 Corinthians 4:16: "Yet his 'inmost self' (Rom 7:22, RSV) is undergoing renewal—not by absorption, as in hellenistic and gnostic thought, but by the hope of resurrection which entails a future for the outward person in his bodily existence. This is an important observation, marking off Pauline anthropology from Plato, *Rep.* IX 589A, Epictetus, *Diss.* II 7.3, 8.14, and even Philo, *Quod Det. Pot.* 22f., all of whom make the human person a composite of a material shell and a precious kernel, the soul, which aspires to be immortal. No such dichotomy is really to be found in Paul who, in this passage, comes closest to making the human being a hybrid of body and soul" (*2 Corinthians*, Word Biblical Commentary, Waco, Texas, 1986, p. 91). Similarly, J. D. G. Dunn sees no traces of Platonism in Romans 7:24 and 8:23, but understands these passages in terms of Christ and Adam, and the Christian believer's hope of ultimate deliverance through resurrection (*Romans*, pp. 396-97, 489-91). For a detailed discussion of Paul's teaching about the body, see Robert H. Gundry, *SOMA in Biblical Theology with Emphasis on Pauline Anthropology*, Society of New Testament Studies Monograph Series 29 (Cambridge: Cambridge University Press, 1976).

[23]See (e.g.) F.F. Bruce, *Paul: Apostle of the Free Spirit* (Exeter: Paternoster Press; Grand Rapids: Eerdmans, 1977); E.P. Sanders, *Paul and Palestinian Judaism* (Philadelphia: Fortress Press; London: SCM Press, 1977); Gerd Theissen, *Psychological Aspects of Pauline Theology* (Philadelphia: Fortress Press, 1987).

[24]See the discussion of *logos* in C. H. Dodd, *The Interpretation of the Fourth Gospel* (Cambridge: Cambridge University Press, 1955), pp. 263-85; Leon Morris, *The Gospel According to John*, New International Commentary on the New Testament (Grand Rapids: Eerdmans, 1971), pp. 71-126; James D. G. Dunn, *Christology in the Making: A New Testament Inquiry into the Origins of the Doctrine of the Incarnation* (Philadelphia: Westminster Press, 1980), pp. 213-50; Nash, *Christianity and the Hellenistic World*, pp. 81-88.

[25]John Herman Randall, Jr., *Hellenistic Ways of Deliverance and the Making of the*

Christian Synthesis (New York: Columbia University Press, 1970), p. 157.

[26]For an important reappraisal of the Fourth Gospel, which stresses the closeness of John to Jesus and his times, see J. A. T. Robinson, *The Priority of John*, ed. J. F. Coakley (London: SCM Press; Bloomington: Meyerstone, 1985).

[27]J. D. G. Dunn concludes his detailed examination of Philo with the observation: "The language of philosophy, Stoicism in particular, agreed at this point with the language of Jewish prophecy in providing the most useful term for talk of this experience of revelation and 'right reason'—*logos*—and by means of allegorical interpretation this divine Logos could be shown to have a wide-ranging symbolical expression within the Torah. But in the end of the day *the Logos seems to be nothing more for Philo than God himself in his approach to man, God himself insofar as he may be known by man*" (*Christology in the Making*, p. 228). Other Old Testament passages in which creation is attributed to the Word of God include Ps 33:6; 107:20; 147:15, 18. In the Jewish Wisdom tradition, creation is attributed to God's wisdom, where wisdom is patently a variation of the word theme (Prov 8:22-31; Wisdom of Solomon 9:1-2, 17). For examples of Logos-teaching in Heraclitus, the Stoics and Philo, see C. K. Barrett, *The New Testament Background: Selected Documents* (Revised edition, London: SPCK, 1987; San Francisco: Harper & Row, 1989), pp. 59-60, 66-67, 70, 72, 254, 262-65.

[28]F. F. Bruce, *The Epistle to the Hebrews*, New International Commentary on the New Testament (Grand Rapids: Eerdmans, 1964), p. lvi.

[29]Bruce, *Hebrews*, pp. l-li; see also Nash, *Christianity and the Hellenistic World*, pp. 89-112. Similar reserve concerning possible links between Hebrews and Philo is shown by S. G. Sowers in *The Hermeneutics of Philo and the Hebrews* (Richmond: John Knox Press, 1965) and by Ronald Williamson in his massive study of *Philo and the Epistle to the Hebrews* (Leiden: E. J. Brill, 1970). On New Testament interpretation generally, see Richard N. Longenecker, *Biblical Exegesis in the Apostolic Period* (Grand Rapids: Eerdmans, 1975).

[30]Harold W. Attridge, *The Epistle to the Hebrews*, ed. Helmut Koester, Hermeneia (Philadelphia: Fortress Press, 1989), pp. 29-30. I have omitted from the quotation the numerous scholarly references cited by Attridge in support of his view, and also his allusions to the significance of the Dead Sea Scrolls and earlier Jewish traditions.

Chapter 6: Philosophy and the Church Fathers

[1]Recent accounts of the thought-world of the Roman Empire include Ramsey MacMullen, *Paganism in the Roman Empire* (New Haven: Yale University Press, 1981); MacMullen, *Christianizing the Roman Empire* (New Haven: Yale University Press, 1984); and Robert L. Wilken, *The Christians as the Romans Saw Them* (New Haven: Yale University Press, 1984). On the rise and fall of the Roman world, see the massive encyclopedia *Aufstieg und Niedergang der römischen Welt*, in which many of the articles are in English. On Christianity and pagan religion in the

Roman Empire before Constantine, see volume 2.23.2, ed. Wolfgang Haase (Berlin and New York: Walter de Gruyter, 1980).

[2]For an account of Christianity and the mysteries, see Devon H. Wiens, "Mystery Concepts in Primitive Christianity and in its Environment," *Aufstieg und Niedergang der römischen Welt*, 2.23.2:1248-1284. For texts see Marvin W. Meyer, ed., *The Ancient Mysteries, A Sourcebook: Sacred Texts of the Mystery Religions of the Ancient Mediterranean World* (San Francisco, Harper & Row: 1987); and more briefly C. K. Barrett, *The New Testament Background: Selected Documents* (Revised edition, London: SPCK, 1987; San Francisco: Harper & Row, 1989), pp. 120-34.

[3]For sources see Werner Foerster, ed., *Gnosis: A Selection of Gnostic Texts*, I, *Patristic Evidence; 2, Coptic and Mandean Sources* (Oxford: Clarendon Press, 1972, 1974); the volumes of the *Nag Hammadi Studies* published in Leiden by Brill; James M. Robinson, ed., *The Nag Hammadi Library* in English (San Francisco: Harper & Row, 3rd ed., 1988); and more briefly C. K. Barrett, *The New Testament Background* pp. 92-119. For an authoritative discussion and details of other works, see Kurt Rudolph, *Gnosis: The Nature and History of Gnosticism* (Edinburgh: T. & T. Clark, 1984; paperback edition, San Francisco: Harper & Row, 1987).

[4]Adolf von Harnack, *History of Dogma* (paperback reprint, New York: Dover Publications, 1961), 1:223-66.

[5]Rudolph, *Gnosis*, p. 2.

[6]On Bultmann, see Colin Brown, "Bultmann Revisited," *The Churchman* 88 (1974): 167-87. On the question of Gnosticism and the New Testament, see Edwin M. Yamauchi, *Pre-Christian Gnosticism: A Survey of the Proposed Evidence* (Grand Rapids: Baker Book House, 2nd ed. 1983) and the literature noted by him.

[7]Rudolph, *Gnosis*, p. 276.

[8]Wilken, *The Christians as the Romans Saw Them*, p. 74.

[9]*Lucian*, ed. and tr. A. M. Harmon (Loeb Classical Library, Cambridge, Mass.: Harvard University Press; London: Heinemann, 1915), 2:449-511. See also Lucian's *Hermotimus* (Loeb edition 6:260-415).

[10]*Lucian* 2:507-508. The slave's name is Pyrrhias, a pun on a common slave name and the name of Pyrrho, the founder of skepticism.

[11]*De ordine librorum suorum* 1; cited from R. Walzer, *Galen on Jews and Christians* (London: Oxford University Press, 1949), pp. 19-20.

[12]Walzer, *Galen on Jews and Christians*, p. 43.

[13]Walzer, *Galen on Jews and Christians*, p. 15, citing fragments dealing with the philosophy of Aristotle and Plato which have survived only in Arabic translation.

[14]See John Dillon, *The Middle Platonists, 80 B.C.-A.D. 20* (Ithaca, NY: Cornell University Press, 1977); Robert M. Berchman, *From Philo to Origen: Middle Platonism in Transition*, Brown Judaic Studies 69 (Chico, CA: Scholars Press, 1984).

[15]For a translation of Origen's work, see *Origen: Contra Celsum*, trans. Henry Chadwick (Cambridge: Cambridge University Press, 1953). R. Joseph Hoffmann has attempted to reconstruct Celsus's work in *Celsus: On the True Doctrine, A Discourse against Christians* (New York: Oxford University Press, 1987). For discussion of Celsus see R.L. Wilken, *The Christians as the Romans Saw Them*, pp. 94-125.

[16]Wilken, *The Christians as the Romans Saw Them*, p. 95.

[17]*Against Celsus* 7.58 (trans. Chadwick, pp. 444-45); cf. Wilken, *The Christians as the Romans Saw Them*, pp. 121-22.

[18]*Against Celsus* 1.14 (trans. Chadwick, p. 17).

[19]*Against Celsus* 5.35 (trans. Chadwick, p. 292).

[20]*Against Celsus* 8.68 (trans. Chadwick, p. 504).

[21]There are several complete and edited versions of Plotinus. Among them is the Loeb Classical Library edition, edited by A. H. Armstrong in 7 vols. (1966-88). Armstrong has also edited Plotinus, *Selections* (London: Allen & Unwin; New York: Humanities Press, 1953). Other selections include: Grace H. Turnbull, *The Essence of Plotinus* (reprint Westport: Greenwood Press, 1976); Joseph Katz, *The Philosophy of Plotinus* (New York: Appleton-Century-Crofts, 1950). Studies include: Émile Bréhier, *The Philosophy of Plotinus* (Chicago: University of Chicago Press, 1958); J. M. Rist, *Plotinus: The Road to Reality* (Cambridge: Cambridge University Press, 1967); A. H. Armstrong, *Plotinian and Christian Studies* (London: Variorum Reprints, 1979); J. O'Meara, ed., *Neoplatonism and Christian Thought* (Norfolk, VA: International Society for Neoplatonic Studies, 1982); David T. Runia, ed., *Plotinus amid Gnostics and Christians* (Amsterdam: Free University Press, 1984); Stephen Gersh, *Middle Platonism and Neoplatonism: The Latin Tradition*, 2 vols., Publications in Medieval Studies 23/1-2 (Notre Dame: University of Notre Dame Press, 1986). For an account of Porphyry's criticism of Christianity, see Robert L. Wilken, *The Christians as the Romans Saw Them*, pp. 126-63.

[22]*Enneads* 6.9.6.

[23]See Rist, *Plotinus*, pp. 213-30.

[24]See John Hick, *Evil and the God of Love* (London: Macmillan, 1966), pp. 46-49.

[25]On Porphyry see Anthony Meredith, "Porphyry and Julian against the Christians," *ANRW* 2.23.2: 1120-1149; R.L. Wilken, *The Christians as the Romans Saw Them*, pp. 126-163; Kathleen O'Brien Wicker, tr., *Porphyry the Philosopher: To Marcella* (Atlanta: Scholars Press, 1987).

[26]Quoted from a fragment preserved by Eusebius in his *Ecclesiastical History* 6.19, trans. H. J. Lawlor and J. E. L. Oulton (London: SPCK, 1927), p. 192.

[27]*The Christians as the Romans Saw Them*, p. 151.

[28]Augustine replied to Porphyry's monotheistic claims by pointing out that the Romans had often served evil demons. But the God whom Christians serve is not only the God of the Scriptures which prophesied of Christ. He is also "the

very God whom Varro, most learned of the Romans, thought to be Jupiter, albeit knowing now what he said. . . . Finally, he is the very God whom Porphyry, the most learned of philosophers, though the most bitter foe of the Christians, confesses to be a mighty god, even in accordance with the oracles of those whom he takes to be gods" (*The City of God against the Pagans* 19.22, trans. W.C. Greene, Loeb Classsical Library, [Cambridge, Massachusetts; London: Heinemann, 1960], 7:215).

In the following chapter Augustine went on to discuss Porphyry's use of pagan oracles in order to condemn Christianity. In answer to the question of whether Christ were God, the oracle of Hecate had replied: "You know that the immortal soul advances after it leaves the body; but when it is sundered from wisdom it wanders for ever. The soul in question [i.e., that of Jesus] is that of a man preeminent in piety; they [i.e., the Christians] worship it because they are estranged from the truth" (*The City of God* 19.23; Loeb edition 7:219). Augustine dismissed this with the comment: "Who is so foolish as not to understand that these oracles either were invented by a shrewd man, and one most hostile to the Christians, or were the responses of impure demons of like design? Of course by praising Christ they hope to convince men that their vituperation of Christians is reliable, and so, if possible, to shut off the way of everlasting salvation, whereby the individual becomes a Christian. . . . We, for our part, can approve neither Apollo's vituperation of Christ nor Hecate's praise." (7:221-223).

[29]An older but still important study is Charles Bigg, *Christian Platonists of Alexandria* (Oxford: Oxford University Press, 2nd ed. 1913). A recent study of early Christian relationships with the Hellenistic world is R. M. Grant, *Greek Apologetics of the Second Century* (Philadelphia: Westminster Press, 1988). On early Christian teaching generally, see J. N. D. Kelly, *Early Christian Doctrines* (San Francisco: Harper & Row, revised paperback edition, 1978); Berthold Altaner, *Patrology* (Freiburg: Herder; Edinburgh, London: Nelson, 1960); Johannes Quasten et al., *Patrology*, 4 vols. (Utrecht, Antwerp: Spectrum; Westminster, Maryland: Newman Press, Christian Classics, Inc., 1966-1986). For accounts of Christology, see Aloys Grillmeier, *Christ in Christian Tradition*, 1, *From the Apostolic Age to Chalcedon* (451) (London: Mowbrays, 2nd ed. 1975); Frances Young, *From Nicea to Chalcedon: A Guide to the Literature and its Background* (Philadelphia: Fortress Press, 1983).

[30]Justin gives an account of his pilgrimage in his *Dialogue with Trypho* 1-8.

[31]*Dialogue* 8.

[32]*First Apology* 5, 46; *Second Apology* 8, 13. Justin's thought seems to bear the marks of Stoic influence. He clearly did not teach universalism. He repeatedly pointed out that it was one thing to be given enlightenment, but another to respond to it.

[33]*Dialogue* 61.

[34]*First Apology* 5.

[35]R. P. C. Hanson, *Allegory and Event: A Study of the Sources and Significance of Origen's Interpretation of Scripture* (London: SCM Press, 1959); C. Kannengiesser and W. L. Peterson, eds., *Origen of Alexandria: His World and His Legacy* (Notre Dame: University of Notre Dame Press, 1988); Henri Crouzel, *Origen* (San Francisco: Harper & Row, 1989), pp. 61-84.

[36]Origen, *Commentary on Matthew* 16.9-11; see Hanson, *Allegory and Event*, pp. 235-36.

[37]See Kelly, *Early Christian Doctrines*, pp. 128-37, 153-58.

[38]*On the Proscription of Heretics* 7 (The Ante-Nicene Fathers 3:246). See also Tertullian's discussion of Plato and philosophical ideas in his treatise *On the Soul*. His tract *On the Pallium* justified the Christian wearing of the garment, however.

[39]Quasten, *Patrology* 2:321.

[40]*On the Soul* 2, 3, 20 (The Ante-Nicene Fathers 3:182-84, 200-1).

[41]Timothy David Barnes, *Tertullian: A Historical and Literary Study* (Oxford: Clarendon Press, 1971), p. 231.

[42]*Against Praxeas* 29, 30 (Ernest Evans, ed., *Tertullian's Treatise against Praxeas*, London: SPCK, 1948, pp. 176-79).

[43]Quasten, *Patrology* 2:325; Evans, pp. 38-75, for general discussion of Tertullian's trinitarian terminology, much of which is to be found in *Against Praxeas*.

[44]Kelly, *Early Christian Doctrines*, p. 114. On the history and validity of the term, see Christopher Stead, *Divine Substance* (Oxford: Clarendon Press, 1977).

[45]*Against Praxeas* 2, 3 (Evans, pp. 131-3).

[46]*Against Praxeas* 27 (Evans, p. 174).

[47]There are numerous translations of Augustine's main writings, including nineteenth-century translations in *A Select Library of the Nicene and Post-Nicene Fathers* and a modern version in *The Fathers of the Church*. Selections of his works may be found in *The Library of Christian Classics* and in Whitney J. Oates, ed., *Basic Writings of Saint Augustine*, 2 vols. (New York: Random House, 1948). An old but still valuable account is Eugene Portalié, *A Guide to the Thought of St. Augustine* (London: Burns & Oates, 1960); Gerald Bonner, *St. Augustine of Hippo: Life and Controversies* (London: SCM Press, 1963); Étienne Gilson, *The Christian Philosophy of Saint Augustine* (New York: Random House, 1960); Peter Brown, *Augustine of Hippo: A Biography* (Berkeley, Los Angeles: University of California Press, 1967); R. A. Markus, ed., *Augustine: A Collection of Critical Essays* (Garden City: Doubleday, 1972); Henri Marrou, *Saint Augustine and his Influence through the Ages* (New York: Harper Torchbooks; London: Longmans, 1957); Eugene TeSelle, *Augustine the Theologian* (New York: Herder and Herder, 1970); Henry Chadwick, *Augustine* (Oxford: Oxford University Press, 1986).

[48]*Confessions* 5.10.18.

[49]*Against the Academicians* is a reply to the skepticism of the Academy. It is among the first surviving works of Augustine as well as being among the few works

of Augustine that are strictly philosophical.

[50]*Confessions* 8.2.3.

[51]Copleston, *A History of Medieval Philosophy* (New York: Harper & Row, 1972), p. 28.

[52]For discussions of Augustine's position, see Hick, *Evil and the God of Love,* pp. 43-95; G. R. Evans, *Augustine on Evil* (Cambridge: Cambridge University Press, 1982).

[53]*Confessions* 8.12.29.

[54]Sometime round about A.D. 410 Augustine learned that the scholarly British monk Pelagius had been attacking Augustine's prayer (which, in the context of his *Confessions,* is a prayer for continence): "Give what You order, and order what You will" (*Confessions* 10.29 [40]). Pelagius objected that Augustine was undermining the fabric of morality, because Augustine seemed to be cutting out human responsibility. Pelagius was supported by Julian of Eclanum, who saw Augustine's view of human depravity as Manichaean. Augustine devoted a number of writings to the controversy, including his last major work, *Six Books against Julian* (428-430) and their incomplete sequel.

Augustine's teaching was profoundly influenced by his own experience of sin and grace. He taught that Adam was created with certain supernatural gifts, which were lost by the Fall. Metaphysically, sin is a defect of being, a failure to cleave to God. Ethically, it is culpable, because Adam chose to disobey God by his own free will. Although sin does not deprive human beings of free will, it deprives them of the ability to do the will of God. They are under a "cruel necessity to sin." They are thus guilty before God and unable to save themselves. They can be saved only by the grace of God. Humankind without God's saving grace is a mass of the damned. Yet, in his inscrutable wisdom and irresistible mercy, God has predestined some to salvation. God's will with regard to the elect, who have done nothing to deserve salvation, is active. With regard to the rest, God's will is passive. God permits them to pursue the way they have chosen. Inevitably, this means that they are predestined to perdition.

By contrast Pelagius denied the reality of original sin, maintaining that the Fall affected only Adam, that sin and death were not connected, that Christ came to set a good example and that grace is given to those who merit it. Pelagianism was condemned as a heresy at the Council of Ephesus (431), and again at the Second Council of Orange (529). It disappeared in the second half of the sixth century, though forms of semi-Pelagianism have emerged from time to time. For works dealing with Augustine's thought, see above, n. 47. On Pelagius see John Ferguson, *Pelagius* (Cambridge: Heffer, 1956); Robert F. Evans, *Pelagius: Inquiries and Reappraisals* (London: A. & C. Black; New York: Seabury Press, 1968); Evans, ed., *Four Letters of Pelagius* (London: A. & C. Black; New York: Seabury Press, 1968).

[55]Bertrand Russell, *History of Western Philosophy* (London: Allen and Unwin, 1946),

p. 374, commenting on Augustine's discussion of time in *Confessions* 11.

[56]Ludwig Wittgenstein, *Philosophical Investigations* (Oxford: Blackwell, 2nd ed., 1958) I #1, p. 2; cf. *Confessions* 1.8.13. Wittgenstein comments that "Augustine does not speak of there being any difference between kinds of words." The implication is that each word has a meaning which corresponds to an object. Such an oversimplification pays no attention to rules and conventions which govern the use of words. However, Copleston points out that in the *Confessions* Augustine was merely describing how as a child he learned to speak (*History*, p. 41). In other works he put forward a more complex view of language. In *On the Master* Augustine had already pointed out that we cannot point to objects signified by prepositions like *ex* ("out of," "from"). In his *Principles of Dialectic* Augustine distinguished between the spoken word, its meaning as grasped by the mind, its use as a sign for itself, its use as signifying objects and its effects on the hearer.

[57]Augustine put forward an argument which anticipated Descartes's *cogito ergo sum* in response to the skeptics of the Academy (cf. Cicero *Academica Priora* 2.13.40-42). The skeptics had questioned whether we can trust our senses or even know that we exist. Augustine replied: "Where these truths are concerned I need not quail before the Academicians when they say: 'What if you should be mistaken?' Well, if I am mistaken, I exist. For a man who does not exist can surely not be mistaken either, and if I am mistaken, therefore I exist. So, since I am if I am mistaken, how can I be mistaken in believing that I am when it is certain that if I am mistaken I am" (*The City of God* 11.26, Loeb Classical Library 3, trans. David S. Wiesen, Cambridge, Mass.: Harvard University Press; London: Heinemann, 1968, p. 533). The argument is not used as the foundation for a metaphysic of being. Rather, it draws attention to the absurdity of extreme skepticism. For other statements of the argument, see Augustine, *On Free Will* 2.3.7; *On True Religion* 73; *Against the Academicians* 3.11.25-26; *Soliloquies* 2.1.1; *On the Blessed Life* 2.2.7; *On the Trinity* 10.10.16; 15.12.21. For discussion of Descartes's use of the argument, see pp. 180-84 .

[58]In his work *On Christian Doctrine* 1.7.7, Augustine argued that even those who believe in more than one god still attempt to conceive "the one God of gods" as "something than which nothing more excellent or more sublime exists [*ut aliquid quo nihil melius sit atque sublimius illa cogitatio conetur attingere*]." F. C. Copleston comments: "No doubt St. Anselm was influenced by these words of Augustine when he took as the universal idea of God in the 'ontological argument' 'that than which no greater can be conceived' " (*A History of Philosophy* 2:70; cf. also Étienne Gilson, *The Christian Philosophy of Saint Augustine*, New York: Random House, 1960, p. 326).

[59]*Sermon* 43.7.

[60]*Letter* 120.3 (Augustine, *Letters* Volume 2 [83-130], trans. Sister Wilfrid Parsons, New York: Fathers of the Church, Inc., 1953, p. 302).

[61]Aquinas, *Summa Theologiae* 1. Q. 84 art. 5 (Blackfriars edition 12:31). This view is endorsed by Gilson, *Christian Philosophy*, p. 70.

[62]*City of God* 8.1. In this book Augustine says why he prefers Platonism to other philosophies, but he also notes the warnings of Col 2:8; Rom 1:19-23; Acts 17:28 (8.9).

[63]*Confessions* 1.1.

[64]The ultimate goal of human life is the vision of God, which Augustine discussed in numerous places including a lengthy letter to the noble Christian lady Paulina. He summed up his understanding of the vision of God at the conclusion of the letter. " 'But the only-begotten Son who is in the bosom of the Father' [John 1:18] without sound of words declares the nature and substance of the Godhead, and therefore to eyes that are worthy and fit for such appearance He shows it visibly. Those are the eyes of which the Apostle says: 'the eyes of your heart enlightened' [Ephesians 1:18] and of which it is said: 'Enlighten my eyes that I never sleep in death' [Psalms 12:4]. For the Lord is a spirit [2 Corinthians 3:17; John 4:24]; therefore, 'he who is joined to the Lord is one spirit' [1 Corinthians 6:17]. Consequently, he who can see God invisibly can be joined to the Lord incorporeally" (*Letter* 147.37; Augustine, *Letters* Volume 3 [131-164, trans. Sister Wilfrid Parsons, Fathers of the Church, New York: Fathers of the Church, Inc., 1953, p. 205). For an account of Augustine's view of the vision of God in the context of his spiritual pilgrimage, see K. E. Kirk, *The Vision of God: The Christian Doctrine of the Summum Bonum*, The Bampton Lectures for 1928 (London: Longman, 2nd ed., 1932), pp. 319-416.

[65]*The Christians as the Romans Saw Them*, pp. 200-201.

Chapter 7: Early Medieval Philosophy

[1]Surveys of medieval philosophy include: Étienne Gilson, *History of Christian Philosophy in the Middle Ages* (New York: Random House, 1955); Gordon Leff, *Medieval Thought: St. Augustine to Ockham* (Harmondsworth: Penguin Books, 1958); Maurice de Wulf, *History of Mediaeval Philosophy*, vol. 1, *From the Beginnings to the End of the Twelfth Century* (New York: Dover Publications, 1952); Armand A. Maurer, *Medieval Philosophy* (New York: Random House, 1962; 2nd ed. Toronto: Pontifical Institute of Mediaeval Studies, 1982); Joseph Pieper, *Scholasticism: Personalities and Problems of Medieval Philosophy* (London: Faber and Faber, 1961); David Knowles, *The Evolution of Medieval Thought* (London: Longmans, 1962); F. C. Copleston, *A History of Medieval Philosophy* (New York: Harper & Row, 1972); John Marenbon, *Early Medieval Philosophy (480-1150): An Introduction* (London: Routledge, 1983, paperback 1988); A. H. Armstrong, ed., *The Cambridge History of Later Greek and Early Medieval Philosophy* (Cambridge: Cambridge University Press, 1967); Steven Ozment, *The Age of Reform: An Intellectual and Religious History of Late Medieval and Reformation Europe* (New Haven: Yale University Press, 1980); Norman Kretzmann, Anthony Kenny, Jan

Pinborg, eds., *The Cambridge History of Later Medieval Philosophy from the Rediscovery of Aristotle to the Disintegration of Scholasticism* (Cambridge: Cambridge University Press, 1982); Peter Dronke, ed., *A History of Twelfth-Century Philosophy* (Cambridge: Cambridge University Press, 1988). A comprehensive anthology of writings is given by Arthur Hyman and James J. Walsh, eds., *Philosophy in the Middle Ages: The Christian, Islamic, and Jewish Traditions* (Indianapolis: Hackett Publishing Company, 2nd ed., 1984).

²The Latin *schola* (Greek *scholē*) meant leisure from work, and hence learned leisure, learned conversation, debate, dispute and thus a place where learned disputations were carried on.

³*On the Predestination of the Saints* 5 (*A Select Library of the Nicene and Post-Nicene Fathers* 5:499).

⁴Anselm *Proslogion* 1. See pp. 112-18.

⁵See the stress on the priority of faith as the precondition of understanding in (e.g.) Augustine, *Sermon* 43, 7; *Letter* 120, 3; *On the Trinity* 1.1.1. Augustine's first work after his conversion, *Against the Academicians,* was a rebuttal of skepticism. His treatise *On Christian Learning* urged the need for dialectics and secular study in the articulation of Christian doctrine. His late work *On the Predestination of the Saints* outlined the program adopted by Scholasticism.

⁶For an account of the universities, see Hastings Rashdall, *The Universities of Europe in the Middle Ages,* 3 vols., ed. F. M. Powicke and A. B. Emden (Oxford: Oxford University Press, 1936). On religion and the universities in Britain, see V. H. H. Green, *Religion at Oxford and Cambridge* (London: SCM Press, 1964). On the emergence of theology as an academic discipline, see G. R. Evans, *Old Arts and New Theology: The Beginnings of Theology as an Academic Discipline* (Oxford: Clarendon Press, 1980).

⁷Editions of Boethius's works may be found in the Loeb Classical Library. Modern studies include Howard Rollin Patch, *The Tradition of Boethius: A Study of his Importance in Medieval Culture* (New York: Oxford University Press, 1935); Henry Chadwick, *Boethius: The Consolations of Music, Logic, Theology, and Philosophy* (Oxford: Clarendon Press, 1981); Eleonore Stump, *Boethius's De topiciis differentiis,* translated, with notes and essays on the text (Ithaca: Cornell University Press, 1978); Eleanore Stump, *Boethius's "In Ciceronis Topica": An Annotated Translation of a Medieval Dialectical Text* (Ithaca: Cornell University Press, 1988); Margaret Gibson, ed., *Boethius: His Life, Thought and Influence* (Oxford: Basil Blackwell, 1981); Edmund Reiss, *Boethius* (Boston: Twayne, 1982).

⁸Chadwick, *Boethius,* p. 249.

⁹For literature and a translation of one of his major works, see Dionysius the Pseudo-Areopagite, *The Ecclesiastical Hierarchy,* trans. and annotated by Thomas L. Campbell (Lanham: University Press of America, 1981).

¹⁰Christian Wildberg has attempted to reconstruct Philoponus's lost treatise in *Philoponus: Against Aristotle, On the Eternity of the World* (Ithaca: Cornell Univer-

sity Press, 1987). For recent research see Richard Sorabji, ed., *Philoponus and the Rejection of Aristotelian Science* (Ithaca: Cornell University Press, 1987).

[11]See Meyrick H. Carré, *Realists and Nominalists* (Oxford: Oxford University Press, 1966). The question of universals continues to excite scholarly interest. D. F. Pears has argued that any attempted comprehensive explanation of naming is necessarily circular ("Universals" in Antony Flew, ed., *Logic and Language*, Second Series, Oxford: Blackwell, 1953, pp. 51-64). Nicholas Wolterstorff includes a theological assessment of the question in *On Universals: An Essay in Ontology* (Chicago: Chicago University Press, 1970). For a review of the question and details of other literature, see A. D. Woozley, "Universals," *Encyclopedia of Philosophy* 8:194-206.

[12]See Martin M. Tweedale, *Abailard on Universals* (Amsterdam: North Holland Publishing Company, 1976). A brief work which contains many of Abelard's ideas is his *Dialogue of a Philosopher with a Jew, and a Christian*, trans. P. J. Payer (Toronto: Pontifical Institute of Medieval Studies, 1979).

[13]On Islamic philosophy see Majid Fakhry, *A History of Islamic Philosophy* (New York: Columbia University Press; London: Longman, 2nd ed., 1983); F. E. Peters, *Aristotle and the Arabs: The Aristotelian Tradition in Islam* (New York: New York University Press; London: University of London Press, 1968); Dimitri Gutas, *Avicenna and the Aristotelian Tradition: Introduction to Reading Avicenna's Philosophical Works* (Leiden: E. J. Brill, 1988). For discussion of Islamic philosophical arguments for the existence of God, see William Lane Craig, *The Cosmological Argument*, pp. 48-126; Herbert Davidson, *Proofs for Eternity, Creation, and the Existence of God in Medieval Islamic and Jewish Philosophy* (New York: Oxford University Press, 1987).

[14]*Alfarabi's Philosophy of Plato and Aristotle*, trans. Mushin Mahdi (Ithaca: Cornell University Press, revised paperback edition, 1969).

[15]James A. Weisheipl, *Friar Thomas D'Aquino: His Life, Thought, and Works* (Washington: Catholic University of America Press, new edition, 1983), p. 276. For a recent study see Oliver Leaman, *Averroës and His Philosophy* (Oxford: Oxford University Press, 1988).

[16]Surveys of Jewish philosophy include Joseph L. Blau, *The Story of Jewish Philosophy* (New York: Random House, 1962); Julius Guttmann, *Philosophies of Judaism: The History of Jewish Philosophy from Biblical Times to Franz Rosenzweig* (New York: Holt, Rinehart and Winston, 1962); Colette Sirat, *A History of Jewish Philosophy in the Middle Ages* (Cambridge: Cambridge University Press, 1985). On arguments for the existence of God, see Craig, *The Cosmological Argument*, pp. 127-57; Davidson, *Proofs for Eternity, Creation and the Existence of God*. The most extensive account of the Kabbalah is Gershom Scholem, *Origins of the Kabbalah* (Princeton: Princeton University Press, 1987); but see also Moshe Idel, *Kabbalah: New Perspectives* (New Haven: Yale University Press, 1988).

[17]On his life see Abraham Joshua Heschel, *Maimonides: A Biography* (New York:

Farrer, Straus, Giroux, 1982). Translations of his works include: *The Guide to the Perplexed*, trans. with introduction and notes by Shlomo Pines and an introductory essay by Leo Strauss (Chicago: University of Chicago Press, 1963); and *Rambam: Readings in the Philosophy of Moses Maimonides*, trans. with introduction and commentary by Lenn Evan Goodman (New York: Viking Press, 1976). A modern reassessment containing papers read at a conference commemorating the 850th anniversary of his birth is Eric L. Ormsby, ed., *Moses Maimonides and his Time*, Studies in Philosophy and the History of Philosophy 19 (Washington, D.C.: Catholic University of America Press, 1989).

[18] *The Guide to the Perplexed*, pp. 235-317.

[19] Craig, *The Cosmological Argument*, p. 152. See also Idit Dobbs-Weinstein, "Medieval Biblical Commentary and Philosophical Inquiry as Exemplified in the Thought of Moses Maimonides and St. Thomas Aquinas," in E. L. Ormsby, ed., *Moses Maimonides and His Time*, pp. 101-20.

[20] The term "Ontological Argument" seems to date from the time of Kant who spoke of "The Impossibility of an Ontological Proof of the Existence of God" (*Critique of Pure Reason*, 2nd ed., 1787, Transcendental Dialectic, Book 2, chapter 3.4). The term *ontology* is derived from the Greek word *ōn* which means "being." Ontology is the theory of being. The ontological argument is an argument about the being of God as distinct from the mere idea of God. It may be noted that Kant's discussion does not refer directly to Anselm, but examines later forms of the argument.

The text of Anselm's argument may be found in many anthologies of philosophical theology. Two sources especially may be noted for statements of Anselm's argument and subsequent discussion. They are Alvin Plantinga, ed., *The Ontological Argument from St. Anselm to Contemporary Philosophers* (London: Macmillan, 1968); and John Hick and Arthur McGill, eds., *The Many-Faced Argument: Recent Studies on the Ontological Argument for the Existence of God* (London: Macmillan, 1968). Hick and McGill set out the argument in its various steps. A critical edition is given by M. J. Charlesworth, ed., *St. Anselm's Proslogion with A Reply on Behalf of the Fool by Gaunilo and The Author's Reply to Gaunilo* (Oxford: Clarendon Press, 1965). Other important studies include: Alvin Plantinga, *God and Other Minds: A Study of the Rational Justification of Belief in God* (Ithaca: Cornell University Press, 1967); Plantinga, *The Nature of Necessity* (Oxford: Clarendon Press, 1974), pp. 196-221; and in a more popular form *God, Freedom, and Evil* (Grand Rapids: Eerdmans, 1974), pp. 85-112; Charles Hartshorne, *The Logic of Perfection, and Other Essays in Neoclassical Metaphysics* (LaSalle, Ill.: Open Court Press, 1962); Hartshorne, *Anselm's Discovery: A Re-examination of the Ontological Proof of God's Existence* (LaSalle, Ill.: Open Court Press, 1965); Karl Barth, *Anselm: Fides Quaerens Intellectum; Anselm's Proof of the Existence of God in the Context of his Theological Scheme* (London: SCM Press; Atlanta: John Knox Press, 1960); Jonathan Barnes, *The Ontological Argument* (London: Macmillan, 1972); R. A. Harrera, *Anselm's Proslogion: An Introduction* (Washington, D.C.: University Press of America, 1979); Richard Campbell, *From Belief to Understanding: A Study of Anselm's Proslogion on the Existence of God* (Canberra: Australian National University, 1976); E. L. Mascall, *The Openness of Being: Natural Theology Today,* Gifford Lectures, 1970-71 (London: Darton, Longman and Todd, 1971), pp. 36-58; Gillian R. Evans, *Anselm and Talking about God* (Oxford: Clarendon Press, 1978); Evans, *Anselm and a New Generation* (Oxford: Clarendon Press, 1980); T. Morris, *Anselmian Explorations* (Notre Dame: University of Notre Dame Press, 1987).

The present discussion draws on the translation in Jasper Hopkins and Herbert Richardson, editors and translators, *Anselm of Canterbury,* 4 vols. (London: SCM Press; Toronto and New York: The Edwin Mellen Press, 1974-76). An account of his life was written by his chaplain Eadmer, *The Life of St. Anselm: Archbishop of Canterbury,* edited and translated by R. W. Southern (Oxford: Clarendon Press, reprint ed., 1979). On his contribution to logic, see Desmond Paul Henry, *The Logic of Saint Anselm* (Oxford: Clarendon Press, 1967).

[21]The title is generally translated *Why God Became Man.* But other alternatives include *Why the God Man* and *Why God Became a Man.* For discussion see *Anselm of Canterbury* 3:253-54. There is a similarity of method here with that of the ontological argument. It consists in discovering the reasons for belief on the basis of what is given and believed.

[22]Eadmer, *Life,* p. 142.

[23]*Anselm of Canterbury* 1:1-86.

[24]*Proslogion* vol. 1 (*Anselm of Canterbury* 1:93). Both the *credo ut intelligam* and the ontological argument were derived from Augustine, see above, pp. 96-97.

[25]Hick and McGill, eds., *The Many-Faced Argument,* p. 23.

[26]*Meditations* 3 and other writings (see Plantinga, *The Ontological Argument,* pp. 31-49).

[27]*Monadology* 45 states briefly what Leibniz argued more fully elsewhere (see Plantinga, *The Ontological Argument,* pp. 54-56).

[28]*Summa Theologiae* 1, Q. 2 art. 1 (Plantinga, *The Ontological Argument,* pp. 28-30).

[29]See above n. 20 and Plantinga, *The Ontological Argument,* pp. 57-64. For further discussion see below, pp. 123-24, 181, 186, 190, 318-22.

[30]G. E. Moore, "Is Existence a Predicate?" *Proceedings of the Aristotelian Society* 15 (1936), reprinted in Plantinga, *The Ontological Argument,* pp. 71-85. Kant had earlier rejected the idea that existence is a predicate.

[31]So J. N. Findlay, "Can God's Existence be Disproved?" Numerous objections have been made to Findlay's argument, pointing out that logical necessity is not the only kind of necessity, and Findlay himself later modified his stance. For Findlay's argument and rejoinders see Antony Flew and Alasdair MacIntyre, eds., *New Essays in Philosophical Theology* (London: SCM Press, 1955), pp. 47-75. See also Mascall, *The Openness of Being,* p. 53.

[32]See above, n. 20. On process theology see volume 2.

[33]*The Openness of Being*, p. 54.

[34]Barth, *Anselm: Fides Quaerens Intellectum*, p. 168.

[35]Barth, *Anselm*, p. 171.

[36]Thus Plantinga observes: "We have no reason to believe . . . either that existence in reality cannot be predicated of a being presupposed to exist in the understanding, or that Anselm's argument necessarily involves predicating real existence of such a being. I think the conclusion to be drawn is that we do not yet have a general refutation of Anselm's ontological argument" (*God and Other Minds*, p. 63).

[37]Norman Malcolm, "Anselm's Ontological Arguments" (*The Philosophical Review* 69 [1960]:41-62; reprinted in Plantinga, *The Ontological Argument*, pp. 136-59; and Hick and McGill, *The Many-Faced Argument*, pp. 301-20).

[38]*The Ontological Argument*, pp. 145-46.

[39]*The Ontological Argument*, p. 147.

[40]*The Ontological Argument*, p. 159.

[41]*God and Other Minds*, p. 94; cf. *The Ontological Argument*, pp. 160-71; John Hick in *The Many-Faced Argument*, pp. 341-56; Mascall, *The Openness of Being*, pp. 57-58.

[42]Campbell, *From Belief to Understanding*, p. 221.

Chapter 8: Aquinas and Later Medieval Philosophy

[1]James Denney, *The Christian Doctrine of Reconciliation* (London: James Clarke, reprint ed., 1959), p. 84.

[2]Francis Schaeffer, *Escape from Reason* (Downers Grove, Ill.: InterVarsity Press, 1968), pp. 11-12.

[3]*In libros de coelo et mundo expositio*, lecture 22; cited from Chenu, *Toward Understanding Saint Thomas*, p. 28. See below, n. 4.

[4]The standard English edition of Thomas's *Summa Theologiae* with Latin text and English translation on facing pages is the Blackfriars edition in 60 vols. (London: Eyre & Spottiswoode; New York: McGraw-Hill, 1964-). The *Summa Contra Gentiles* appears in a 5-volume translation (reprint Notre Dame: University of Notre Dame Press, 1975). Selections from his writings are given by Anton C. Pegis, *Basic Writings of St. Thomas Aquinas*, 2 vols. (New York: Random House, 1945); and more briefly in *Introduction to St. Thomas Aquinas* (New York: Modern Library, 1965); Thomas Gilby, ed., *St. Thomas Aquinas: Philosophical Texts* and *St. Thomas Aquinas: Theological Texts* (reprint ed., Durham, N.C.: Labyrinth Press, 1982); Christopher Martin, ed., *The Philosophy of Thomas Aquinas: Introductory Readings* (London: Routledge, 1988). Gilby's work draws widely from his many writings and arranges Thomas's thought thematically under subject headings. Also valuable is *Albert and Thomas: Selected Writings*, translated, edited and introduced by Simon Tugwell, The Classics of Western Spirituality (New York:

Paulist Press, 1988). Details of other writings are given in the following general introductions: Étienne Gilson, *The Christian Philosophy of St. Thomas Aquinas* (New York: Random House, 1956); M.-D. Chenu, *Toward Understanding Saint Thomas* (Chicago: Henry Regnery, 1964); Josef Pieper, *Guide to Thomas Aquinas* (reprint ed., Notre Dame: University of Notre Dame Press, 1987); F. C. Copleston, *Aquinas* (Harmondsworth: Penguin Books, 1955); Ralph McInerny, *St. Thomas Aquinas* (Notre Dame: University of Notre Dame Press, 1982). The standard biography is James A. Weisheipl, *Friar Thomas D'Aquino: His Life, Thought, and Works* (updated reprint, Washington, D.C.: Catholic University of America Press, 1983). A brief but important study from the standpoint of reassessing Thomas's significance for Protestant thought is Arvin Vos, *Aquinas, Calvin, and Contemporary Protestant Thought: A Critique of Protestant Views on the Thought of Thomas Aquinas* (Grand Rapids: Eerdmans for Christian University Press, 1985). Specialist essays on aspects of Thomas's thought are given in Anthony Kenny, ed., *Aquinas: A Collection of Critical Essays* (reprint ed., Notre Dame: University of Notre Dame Press, 1976). Other specialist studies on the five ways and analogy are noted below.

[5]Peter Lombard (c. 1100-60) taught at the cathedral school in Paris, where he became bishop shortly before his death. The four books of the *Sentences* contain an account of Christian doctrine illustrated from Latin and Greek fathers. Despite early rejection, it became the standard theological textbook of the Middle Ages, though eventually it was superseded by the *Summa Theologiae*. On Thomas and Peter Lombard see W. J. Hankey, *God in Himself: Aquinas' Doctrine of God as Expounded in the "Summa Theologiae"* (Oxford: Oxford University Press, 1987). Hankey also stresses the continuing importance of Neoplatonism in Thomas's teaching about God.

[6]See Chenu, *Toward Understanding Saint Thomas*, pp. 298-301. *Summa Theologiae* means "Compend of Theology." This title is thought to be more authentic than the later commonly used title *Summa Theologica* ("Theological Compend").

[7]Weisheipl, *Friar Thomas D'Aquino*, pp. 333-44.

[8]Weisheipl, *Friar Thomas D'Aquino*, pp. 320-23; Josef Pieper, *The Silence of St. Thomas* (New York: Pantheon, 1953).

[9]From the account given at the beginning of each volume of the Blackfriars edition of the *Summa Theologiae*.

[10]For the text see *Summa Theologiae*, Blackfriars edition, 2:13-17. An earlier version is given in the *Summa Contra Gentiles* 1, 13 (1:86-96). For classical discussions of the issues, see Donald R. Burrell, ed., *The Cosmological Arguments: A Spectrum of Opinion* (Garden City, N.Y.: Doubleday Anchor Books, 1967). Modern discussions are given in E. L. Mascall, *He Who Is: A Study in Traditional Theism* (London: Longman, 1943); Mascall, *The Openness of Being;* Anthony Kenny, *The Five Ways: St. Thomas Aquinas' Proofs of God's Existence* (London: Routledge & Kegan Paul, 1969); Richard Swinburne, *The Existence of God* (Ox-

ford: Clarendon Press, 1979); Norman L. Geisler, *Philosophy of Religion* (Grand Rapids: Zondervan, 1974); William Lane Craig, *The Cosmological Argument from Plato to Leibniz;* A. G. N. Flew, *God and Philosophy* (London: Hutchinson, 1966); J. L. Mackie, *The Miracle of Theism: Arguments for and against the Existence of God* (Oxford: Clarendon Press, 1982).

[11]*Summa Theologiae* 1, Q. 2, art. 2 (Blackfriars edition, 2:9-11).

[12]See above, pp. 42-48.

[13]Modern discussions of the teleological argument are given in F. R. Tennant, *Philosophical Theology,* 2, The World, the Soul and God (Cambridge: Cambridge University Press, 1930); Thomas McPherson, *The Argument from Design* (London: Macmillan, 1972); and the general works dealing with the existence of God noted above in ch. 7, nn. 13 and 20.

[14]Cf. Geisler, *Philosophical Theology,* pp. 87-102.

[15]Craig, *The Cosmological Argument,* pp. 195-96.

[16]Victor Preller, *Divine Science and the Science of God: A Reformulation of Thomas Aquinas* (Princeton: Princeton University Press, 1967), p. 24.

[17]Cf. David Hume, *Enquiry Concerning Human Understanding,* Section 11, #110. See above, p. 250.

[18]David Hume, *Dialogues Concerning Natural Religion,* Part 5, ed. Norman Kemp Smith (reprint ed., Indianapolis: Bobbs-Merrill, n.d.), p. 167.

[19]*Summa Theologiae* 1, Q. 32, art. 1 (Blackfriars edition 6:103).

[20]*Summa Theologiae* 1, Q. 45, art. 2 (Blackfriars edition 8:79).

[21]Hume, *Enquiry,* Section 11, #113; cf. *Dialogues,* Parts 8, 12.

[22]Stanley L. Jaki, *The Road of Science and the Ways to God,* The Gifford Lectures 1974-75 and 1975-76 (Chicago: University of Chicago Press, 1978), p. 297.

[23]*Summa Theologiae* 1, Q. 44, art. 2 (Blackfriars edition 8:9-15).

[24]*The Openness of Being,* p. 61; cf. also Mascall, *Existence and Analogy: A Sequel to "He Who Is"* (London: Longmans, 1949), pp. 78-79.

[25]*Summa Contra Gentiles* 1. 30 (Notre Dame edition 1:141). Compare this with the Neoplatonist element in Aquinas's thought stressed by W. J. Hankey, *God in Himself,* pp. 36-86, 136-42, 143-61.

[26]Thomas's views of analogy are given in *Summa Contra Gentiles* 1. 28-34 (Notre Dame edition 1:135-48); *Summa Theologiae* vol. 1. Q. 13 (Blackfriars edition 3:46-97); and in sundry other passages given in Latin in an appendix to George P. Klubertanz, *St. Thomas Aquinas on Analogy: A Textual Analysis and Systematic Synthesis* (Chicago: Loyola University Press, 1960). Discussions are given by Frederick Ferré, *Language, Logic, and God* (London: Eyre & Spottiswoode, 1962), pp. 67-77; E. L. Mascall, *Existence and Analogy,* pp. 92-122; Wolfhart Pannenberg, "Analogy and Doxology," in *Basic Questions in Theology* (London: SCM Press, 1970), 1:212-38; Humphrey Palmer, *Analogy: A Study of Qualification and Argument in Theology* (London: Macmillan, 1973); Ralph McInerny, *The Logic of Analogy* (The Hague: Martinus Nijhoff, 1961); McInerny, "Analogy and Foun-

dationalism in Thomas Aquinas," in Robert Audi and William J. Wainwright, eds., *Rationality, Religious Belief, and Moral Commitment: New Essays in the Philosophy of Religion* (Ithaca: Cornell University Press, 1986), pp. 271-88; Colin Brown, *Karl Barth and the Christian Message* (London: Tyndale Press, 1967), pp. 47-54; David Burrell, *Analogy and Philosophical Language* (New Haven: Yale University Press, 1973); Gerard J. Hughes, "Aquinas and the Limits of Agnosticism," Richard Swinburne, "Analogy and Metaphor," and Janice Thomas, "Univocity and Understanding God's Nature," in Gerard J. Hughes, ed., *The Philosophical Assessment of Theology: Essays in Honor of Frederick C. Copleston* (London: Search Press; Washington, D.C.: Georgetown University Press, 1987), pp. 35-64, 65-84, 85-100.

[27]*Summa Theologiae* 1. Q. 13, art. 3 (Blackfriars edition, 3:57-59).

[28]*Summa Theologiae* 1. Q. 13, art. 5 (Blackfriars edition, 3:65).

[29]The idea of "eschatological verification" was mooted by I.M. Crombie in a paper on "Theology and Falsification" in Antony Flew and Alasdair MacIntyre, eds., *New Essays in Philosophical Theology* (London: SCM Press, 1955), p. 126; and developed by John Hick in *Faith and Knowledge* (London: Macmillan, 2nd ed. 1967), pp. 176-199; and in "Theology and Verification," in John Hick, ed., *The Existence of God* (New York: Macmillan; London: Collier-Macmillan, 1964), pp. 253-274. The idea has provoked considerable discussion among philosophers and theologians. Hick lists numerous responses and replies to criticism in "Eschatological Verification Reconsidered," *Religious Studies* 13 (1977): 189-202.

[30]*Summa Theologiae* 1. Q. 13. art. 5 (Blackfriars edition, 3:67); cf 1. Q. 4. art. 3.

[31]Romans 1:20, cited in *Summa Theologiae* 1. Q. 13, art. 5 (Blackfriars edition 3:65).

[32]*Opuscula* 16, Exposition, *On the Trinity* 2.3 (cited from Gilby, ed., *Aquinas: Philosophical Texts*, p. 30).

[33]*Summa Theologiae* 1. Q. 46, art. 2 (Blackfriars edition, 8:81).

[34]For writings in translation see *The Works of Bonaventure, Cardinal, Seraphic Doctor and Saint*, 5 vols. (Patterson, NJ: St. Anthony Guild Press, 1960-70). On his thought see Étienne Gilson, *The Philosophy of St. Bonaventure* (Patterson, NJ: St. Anthony Guild Press, 1965); J. Guy Bougerol, *Introduction to the Works of Bonaventure* (Patterson, NJ: St. Anthony Guild Press, 1964); Robert W. Shahan and Francis J. Kovach, eds., *Bonaventure and Aquinas: Enduring Philosophers* (Norman: University of Oklahoma Press, 1976).

[35]Recent studies include James E. McEvoy, *The Philosophy of Robert Grosseteste* (Oxford: Clarendon Press, 1982); R. W. Southern, *Robert Grosseteste: The Growth of an English Mind in Medieval Europe* (Oxford: Clarendon Press, 1986).

[36]His characteristic thought is contained in *The Opus Majus of Roger Bacon*, Eng. trans. Robert Belle Burke, 2 vols. (New York: Russell and Russell, reprint ed., 1962). For a general survey of Bacon's thought, see Stewart C. Easton, *Roger Bacon and his Search for a Universal Science: A Reconsideration of the Life and Work of Roger Bacon in the Light of his own Stated Purposes* (reprint ed., Westport, Conn.:

Greenwood Press, 1970).

[37]For extracts from his writings dealing with God and the soul, see John Duns Scotus, *Philosophical Writings: A Selection*, trans. with an introduction by Allan Wolter (Indianapolis: Bobbs-Merrill, reprint ed., 1980). On his thought see Efrem Bettoni, *Duns Scotus: The Basic Principles of his Philosophy* (Washington, D.C.: Catholic University of America Press, 1961); John K. Ryan and Bernardin M. Bonansea, *John Duns Scotus, 1265-1965,* Studies in Philosophy and the History of Philosophy 3 (Washington, D.C.: Catholic University of America Press, 1965).

[38]For discussion and literature see Craig, *The Cosmological Argument,* pp. 205-35.

[39]See Nathaniel Micklem, *Reason and Revelation: A Question from Duns Scotus* (Edinburgh: Thomas Nelson, 1953).

[40]See Allan Wolter in *Encyclopedia of Philosophy* 2:436.

[41]Recent discussions include Gordon Leff, *William of Ockham: The Metamorphosis of Scholastic Doctrine* (Manchester: Manchester University Press; Totowa, NJ: Rowman and Littlefield, 1975); Marilyn McCord Adams, *William Ockham,* 2 vols., Publications in Medieval Studies 26 (Notre Dame: University of Notre Dame Press, 1987); Anne Hudson and Michael Wilks, eds., *From Ockham to Wyclif,* Studies in Church History: Subsidia 5 (Oxford: Blackwell, 1985). See also William Ockham, *Predestination, God's Knowledge and Future Contingents,* translated, with Notes and Appendices by Marilyn McCord Adams and Norman Kretzmann (Indianapolis: Hackett Publishing Company, 2nd ed. 1983).

[42]See Heiko Augustinus Oberman, *The Harvest of Medieval Philosophy: Gabriel Biel and Late Medieval Nominalism* (Durham, NC: The Labyrinth Press, 3rd ed. 1983); John L. Farthing, *Thomas Aquinas and Gabriel Biel: Interpretations of St. Thomas Aquinas in German Nominalism on the Eve of the Reformation,* Duke Monographs in Medieval and Renaissance Studies 9 (Durham, NC: Duke University Press, 1988). On the transition from the Middle Ages to the Reformation, see Oberman, *The Dawn of the Reformation: Essays in Late Medieval and Early Reformation Thought* (Edinburgh: T. & T. Clark, 1986); A. H. T. Levi, "The Breakdown of Scholasticism and the Significance of Evangelical Humanism," in Gerard J. Hughes, ed., *The Philosophical Assessment of Theology,* pp. 101-28.

[43]*A History of Philosophy* 3:11.

[44]See above, n. 42 and also E. J. D. Douglass, *Justification in Late Medieval Preaching: A Study of John Geiler of Strassburg* (Leiden: E. J. Brill, 1966); H. A. Oberman, *Forerunners of the Reformation: The Shape of Late Medieval Thought, Illustrated by Key Documents* (New York: Holt, Rinehart and Winston, 1966); Oberman, *Masters of the Reformation: The Emergence of the New Intellectual Climate in Europe* (Cambridge: Cambridge University Press, 1980); Alister E. McGrath, *Iustitia Dei: A History of the Doctrine of Justification,* 1, *From the Beginnings to 1500* (Cambridge: Cambridge University Press, 1986); Alister E. McGrath, *The Intellectual Origins of the European Reformation* (Oxford: Blackwell, 1987).

[45]Quoted by Adams, *William Ockham* 1:13.

[46]For an extensive account of his theology, see Adams, *William Ockham* 2: 903-1347.

[47]Leff, *William of Ockham,* p. 35.

Chapter 9: Philosophy and the Reformers

[1]See above, pp. 101-102. Classic studies include Jacob Burckhart, *The Civilization of the Renaissance in Italy* (London: Phaidon; New York: Oxford University Press, reprint ed., 1944); and Jan Huizinga, *The Waning of the Middle Ages: A Study of the Forms of Life, Thought and Art in France and the Netherlands in the XIVth and XVth Centuries* (reprint ed., New York: St. Martin's Press, 1967). More recent accounts include Wallace K. Ferguson, *The Renaissance* (reprint ed., New York: Holt, Rinehart and Winston, 1961); Ferguson, *Renaissance Studies* (London, Ontario: University of Western Ontario, 1963); Ferguson, *The Renaissance in Historical Thought: Five Centuries of Interpretation* (Cambridge, Massachusetts: Houghton Mifflin, 1948); G. R. Potter, ed., *The New Cambridge Modern History,* 1 *The Renaissance, 1493-1520* (Cambridge: Cambridge University Press, 1957). For other literature and a concise overview, see Neal W. Gilbert, "Renaissance," *Encyclopedia of Philosophy* 7: 174-178. On Renaissance humanism see *The Renaissance Philosophy of Man,* ed. Ernst Cassirer, Paul Oskar Kristeller, and John Herman Randall, Jr. (Chicago: Chicago University Press, 1948).

[2]See above, pp. 52, 170.

[3]See above, p. 80.

[4]General accounts of the Reformation include J. S. Whale, *The Protestant Tradition: Essays in Interpretation* (Cambridge: Cambridge University Press, 1955); G. R. Elton, ed., *The New Cambridge Modern History,* 2 *The Reformation, 1520-1559* (Cambridge: Cambridge University Press, 1958); Wilhelm Pauck, *The Heritage of the Reformation* (Glencoe, Ill: Beacon Press, 2nd ed., 1961); G. R. Elton, *Reformation Europe, 1517-1559* (London: Collins, 1963); Owen Chadwick, *The Reformation* (Harmondsworth: Pelican Books, 1964); Franz Lau and Ernst Bizer, *A History of the Reformation in Germany to 1555* (London: A. & C. Black, 1969); Steven Ozment, ed., *The Reformation in Medieval Perspective* (Chicago: Quadrangle Books, 1971); Steven Ozment, *The Age of Reform, 1250-1550; An Intellectual and Religious History of Late Medieval and Reformation Europe* (New Haven: Yale University Press, 1980); B. M. G. Reardon, *Religious Thought in the Reformation* (London: Longman, 1981); Wilhelm Pauck, *From Luther to Tillich: Reformers and Their Heirs,* ed. Marion Pauck (San Francisco: Harper & Row, 1984); J. Pelikan, *Reformation of Church and Dogma, 1300-1700* (Chicago: Chicago University Press, 1984); Lewis W. Spitz, *The Protestant Reformation, 1517-1559* (New York: Harper & Row, 1985); A. G. Dickens and John Tomlin with Kenneth Powell, *The Reformation in Historical Thought* (Cambridge, MA: Harvard University Press, 1985); Timothy George, *Theology of the Reformers* (Nashville: Broadman, 1988). On the

Radical Reformation see Walter Klaassen, ed., *Anabaptism in Outline: Selected Primary Sources* (Kitchener, Ontario, and Scottdale, PA: Herald Press, 1981); E. G. Rupp, *Patterns of Reformation* (Philadelphia: Fortress Press, 1969). G. H. Williams, *The Radical Reformation* (Philadelphia: Westminster Press; London: Weidenfeld and Nicolson, 1972).

[5]*Melanchthon and Bucer*, Library of Christian Classics 19, ed. Wilhelm Pauck (Philadelphia: Westminster Press; London: SCM Press, 1969), pp. 21-22.

[6]For source documents see Hans J. Hillerbrand, *The Reformation in its Own Words* (New York: Harper & Row; London: SCM Press, 1964). On Luther's career and thought, see James Atkinson, *Martin Luther and the Birth of Protestantism* (Harmondsworth: Pelican Books, 1968); Heinrich Bornkamm, *Luther in Mid-Career, 1521-1530* (Philadelphia: Fortress Press, 1983); David C. Steinmetz, *Luther in Context* (Bloomington: Indiana University Press, 1986); Paul Althaus, *The Theology of Martin Luther* (Philadelphia: Fortress Press, 1966); Heiko A. Oberman, *Luther: Man between God and the Devil* (New Haven: Yale University Press, 1990).

[7]For an account of Luther's teaching on justification in its historical setting and the subsequent debates, see Alister E. McGrath, *Iustitia Dei: A History of the Christian Doctrine of Justification, 2 From 1500 to the Present Day* (Cambridge: Cambridge University Press, 1986).

[8]The first edition (1536) of Calvin's *Institutes of the Christian Religion* has been translated by Ford Lewis Battles (Grand Rapids: Eerdmans, 1986). For an English translation of the final Latin (1559) edition with critical notes, see *Calvin: Institutes of the Christian Religion*, edited by John T. McNeill, translated by Ford Lewis Battles, 2 vols., Library of Christian Classics 20-21 (Philadelphia: Westminster Press; London: SCM Press, 1961).

[9]The articles are to be found in *The Book of Common Prayer*. The date given above is that of their Elizabethan form, but their substance goes back to earlier English versions which were in part indebted to continental statements of faith. On the teaching of the English Reformers generally, see Philip Edgcumbe Hughes, *Theology of the English Reformers* (London: Hodder & Stoughton, 1965).

[10]The most comprehensive collection of Christian creeds is still Philip Schaff, *The Creeds of Christendom*, 3 vols. (1877, reprint ed., Grand Rapids: Baker Book House, 1977). See also Arthur C. Cochrane, *Reformed Confessions of the 16th Century*, edited with historical introductions (Philadelphia: Westminster Press; London: SCM Press, 1966); Wilhelm Niesel, *Reformed Symbolics: A Comparison of Catholicism, Orthodoxy, and Protestantism* (Edinburgh: Oliver and Boyd, 1962); Eric Routley, *Creeds and Confessions: The Reformation and its Modern Implications* (London: Duckworth, 1962). For Christian and non-Christian creeds in America, see J. Gordon Melton, ed., *The Encyclopedia of American Religions: Religious Creeds* (Detroit: Gale Research Company, 1988).

[11]On post-Reformation theology see Heinrich Heppe, ed., *Reformed Dogmatics, Set Out and Illustrated from the Sources* (London: Allen and Unwin, 1950); Heinrich

Schmid, *The Doctrinal Theology of the Evangelical Lutheran Church* (Minneapolis: Augsburg, 3rd ed. reprint n.d.); Richard A. Muller, *Post-Reformation Reformed Dogmatics*, 1 *Prolegomena to Theology* (Grand Rapids: Baker Book House, 1987). Muller's *Dictionary of Latin and Greek Theological Terms, Drawn Principally from Protestant Scholastic Theology* (Grand Rapids: Baker Book House, 1985) not only gives clear definitions of terms but also illustrates the continuity of Reformed thought with earlier theology and philosophy.

[12]*Luther's Works* (Philadelphia: Muhlenberg Press, 1959), 51:371-80.

[13]See B. A. Gerrish, *Grace and Reason: A Study in the Theology of Luther* (Oxford: Clarendon Press, 1962), 1-2.

[14]Gerrish, *Grace and Reason*, p. 36, citing Luther's table talk.

[15]*The Bondage of the Will* (1525), Eng. trans. J. I. Packer and O. R. Johnson (London: James Clarke, 1957), p. 317; see also *Luther and Erasmus: Free Will and Salvation*, Eng. trans. E. Gordon Rupp, Philip S. Watson et al., The Library of Christian Classics 17 (London: SCM Press; Philadelphia: Westminster Press, 1969), pp. 331-32; Gerrish, *Grace and Reason*, p. 171.

[16]*First Disputation against the Antinomians* (1537), quoted from Philip S. Watson, *Let God Be God! An Interpretation of the Theology of Martin Luther* (London: Epworth Press, 1947), p. 95.

[17]Steinmetz, *Luther in Context*, pp. 47-58; Denis R. Janz, *Luther and Late Medieval Thomism: A Study in Theological Anthropology* (Waterloo, Ontario: Wilfred Laurier University Press, 1983); John L. Farthing, *Thomas Aquinas and Gabriel Biel: Interpretation of St. Thomas Aquinas in German Nominalism on the Eve of the Reformation*, Duke Monographs in Medieval and Renaissance Studies 9 (Durham and London: Duke University Press, 1988).

[18]Arvin Vos, *Aquinas, Calvin, and Contemporary Protestant Thought: A Critique of Protestant Views on the Thought of Thomas Aquinas* (Grand Rapids: Eerdmans, 1985).

[19]See above, pp. 64-66, 90.

[20]*Luther's Works* (Saint Louis: Concordia, 1963), 26:440.

[21]For Luther on Scripture see Paul Althaus, *The Theology of Martin Luther*, pp. 72-102. On his exegetical methods see the discussion of Wilhelm Pauck in the introduction to his edition of *Luther: Lectures on Romans*, Library of Christian Classics 15 (London: SCM Press; Philadelphia: Westminster Press, 1971), pp. xvii-lxvi.

[22]On the continued interest in classical philosophy and especially on the ongoing influence of Aristotle, see Paul Oskar Kristeller, *Renaissance Thought: The Classic, Scholastic, and Humanist Strains* (New York: Harper & Row, 1961); Charles B. Schmitt, *Aristotle and the Renaissance* (Cambridge, Mass.: Harvard University Press, 1983); William T. Costello, *The Scholastic Curriculum at Early Seventeenth-Century Cambridge* (Cambridge, Mass.: Harvard University Press, 1958).

[23]*Institutes* (1559) 1.2.1. On Calvin's approach see Edward A. Dowey, Jr., *The Knowledge of God in Calvin's Theology* (New York: Columbia University Press, 1952); T. H. L. Parker, *The Doctrine of the Knowledge of God: A Study in the Theology of John Calvin* (Edinburgh: Oliver and Boyd, 1952); B. B. Warfield, "Calvin's Doctrine of the Knowledge of God," in *Calvin and Augustine*, ed. by S. G. Craig (Philadelphia: Presbyterian and Reformed Publishing Company, 1956), pp. 29-130. On Luther's views see Watson, *Let God be God!*, pp. 73-101; Althaus, *The Theology of Martin Luther*, pp. 15-102. For a general overview see Jack B. Rogers and Donald K. McKim, *The Authority and Interpretation of the Bible: An Historical Approach* (San Francisco: Harper & Row, 1979).

[24]*Institutes* 1.3.

[25]*Institutes* 1.5.

[26]*Institutes* 1.4.

[27]*Institutes* 1.2.1; cf. 1.6-14 for further discussion of Scripture, and Book 2 for Calvin's account of the knowledge of God the redeemer in Christ.

[28]*Institutes* 1.14.1.

[29]*Commentary* on 2 Tim. 3:16 quoted from Calvin's *Commentaries on the Epistles to Timothy, Titus, and Philemon*, Eng. trans. William Pringle (Grand Rapids: Eerdmans, reprint ed., 1948), p. 249.

[30]*Institutes* 1.3.1, alluding to Cicero, *On the Nature of the Gods* 1.16.43, where Cicero is discussing the views of Epicurus and his follower, Velleius (see above, p. 57). Calvin's knowledge of Epicurus seems to have come via the writings of Cicero.

[31]See Charles Partee, *Calvin and Classical Philosophy*, Studies in the History of Christian Thought 14 (Leiden: E. J. Brill, 1977). For a discussion of Calvin in the context of the thought-world of sixteenth-century culture and religion, see William J. Bouwsma, *John Calvin: A Sixteenth-Century Portrait* (New York: Oxford University Press, 1988).

[32]Commentary on Titus 1:12, quoted from *Commentaries on the Epistles to Timothy, Titus, and Philemon*, pp. 300-1.

[33]See Richard A. Muller, *Christ and the Decree: Christology and Predestination in Reformed Theology from Calvin to Perkins*, Studies in Historical Theology 2 (Durham, NC: The Labyrinth Press, 1986), pp. 17-38.

[34]Calvin, *The Epistles of Paul the Apostle to the Galatians, Ephesians, Philippians and Colossians*, Eng. trans. T. H. L. Parker (Grand Rapids: Eerdmans, 1965), p. 126.

[35]*The Epistles*, p. 128.

[36]*The Epistles*, p. 127.

[37]Partee, *Calvin and Classical Philosophy*, pp. 105-25.

[38]See Arvin Vos, *Aquinas, Calvin, and Contemporary Protestant Thought: A Critique of Protestant Views on the Thought of Thomas Aquinas* (Grand Rapids: Eerdmans, 1985). Vos examines such issues as faith, the existence of God, and nature and grace. He concludes that Protestants have frequently misunderstood Aquinas,

and that the differences between Aquinas and Calvin on certain basic questions were not as great as have been frequently imagined.

[39]Luther observed that "there are people like the Epicureans, Pliny, and others who deny it with their mouths [that there is a God]. But they must force themselves to do so; and by trying to extinguish the light in their hearts they act like men who plug their ears and close their eyes so that they may neither see nor hear. This does not solve their problem, however, for their conscience tells them something else" (*WA* 19, 206). In this connection, Luther was familiar with Cicero, claiming that the pagans "know from experience that there has never been a man of great deeds or any extraordinary man who had not been specially inspired by *[sine afflatu]* God" (*WA* 51, 222). These passages are cited from Althaus, *The Theology of Martin Luther*, pp. 15, 442.

[40]Reijer Hookyaas, *Philosophia Libera: Christian Faith and the Freedom of Science* (London: Tyndale Press, 1957). On the course of the relationship between science and religion, see Colin A. Russell, ed., *Science and Religious Belief: A Selection of Recent Historical Studies* (London: University of London Press, 1973).

[41]Karl Barth, *Protestant Theology in the Nineteenth Century: Its History and Background* (London: SCM Press, 1972), pp. 49-50.

Chapter 10: Old Questions and New Crises

[1]See above, pp. 54, 362-63.

[2]See above, pp. 149-50, 376.

[3]See above, pp. 153-54, 377.

[4]Thomas de Vio (1469-1534) was known as Gaetano ('Cajetan'), from the Latinized form of the name of his birthplace, Gaeta. He taught philosophy and theology at Padua, Pavia and Rome. He was general of the Dominican Order (1508-18), cardinal (1517) and bishop of Gaeta (1519). He sought to dissuade Luther in a momentous confrontation (1518) and played a major part in political and religious events. His commentary on the *Summa Theologiae* of Thomas Aquinas (1507-1522), which contains a restatement of the doctrine of analogy, remains a classic of Scholasticism. In his later career he turned to biblical interpretation in response to the interpretations of the humanists and the reformers.

[5]*Summa Theologiae* 1. Q 23, art. 2, citing Augustine, *On the Gift of Perseverance* 14 (Blackfriars edition, 5:113). For discussion of Aquinas's view in the context of his times, see Tamar Rudavsky, ed., *Divine Omniscience and Omnipotence in Medieval Philosophy: Islamic, Jewish and Christian Perspectives* (Dordrecht, Boston, Lancaster: D. Reidel Publishing Company, 1985).

[6]*Scientia media* is thought of as a form of divine knowledge which lies in between God's natural knowledge of everything that can be and his simple, direct vision of what will be. The term was coined by Pietro de Fonseca, the Jesuit theologian and teacher of Molina. It is explained by R. Garrigou-Lagrange as follows:

This knowledge is called middle by reason of its proper object, which is the conditional future or the conditionally free act of the future. It is intermediate between the purely possible which is the object of God's knowledge of simple intelligence, and the contingent future which is the object of God's knowledge of vision. By this middle knowledge, according to Molina, God knows previous to any determining decree, how a free will would act if placed in certain circumstances, and how in certain other cases it would decide otherwise. After that God decides, according to His benevolent designs, to render this free will effective by placing it in those circumstances more or less favorable or unfavorable to it (*God, His Existence and His Nature: A Thomistic Solution of Certain Agnostic Antinomies,* St. Louis and London: B. Herder Book Co., 1947, 2:82).

[7]Anton Pegis, "Molina and Human Liberty," in Gerard Smith, ed., *Jesuit Thinkers of the Renaissance: Essays Presented to John F. McCormick* (Milwaukee: Marquette University Press, 1939), p. 99. See also Gerard Smith, *Natural Theology: Metaphysics II* (New York: Macmillan, 1951), pp. 273-77.

[8]Suárez taught at several Spanish colleges of the Jesuit Order, the Roman College and the University of Coimbra. His style was influenced by the Renaissance, but the substance of his teaching was a modification of Aristotle and Aquinas. His departure from Thomism is so radical that some scholars regard "Suarism" as a separate system. See further Jorge J. E. Gracia and Douglas Davis, *The Metaphysics of Good and Evil According to Suárez: Metaphysical Disputations X and XI and Selected Passages from Disputation XXIII and Other Works,* Translation, with Introduction, Notes and Glossary (Munich, Hamden, Vienna: Philosophia Verlag, 1989).

[9]According to Thomism, God's knowledge is the cause of all future events (See Smith, *Natural Theology,* pp. 193-208).

[10]F. Copleston, *A History of Philosophy* 3:344.

[11]The incomplete nineteenth-century translation by James and William Nichols of *The Works of Arminius* has been reissued with an introduction by Carl Bangs, 3 vols. (Grand Rapids: Baker Book House, 1986). Carl Bangs has also written *Arminius: A Study in the Dutch Reformation,* 2nd ed. (Grand Rapids: Francis Asbury Press, 1985). The traditional picture of Arminius has been substantially modified by the researches of Richard A. Muller, who has drawn attention to the links between Arminius and Molina and Suárez in "Arminius and the Scholastic Tradition," *Calvin Theological Journal* 24 (1989): 263-77, and in a forthcoming monograph, *God, Creation and Providence in the Thought of Jakob Arminius.* Muller has shown that Arminius not only possessed major works by Molina and Suárez, but that passages in his own writings are clearly indebted to them. The continuity between Arminius and previous Scholasticism is much closer than has been suspected. On the subsequent history of Arminianism, see A. W. Harrison, *The Beginnings of Arminianism to the Synod of Dort,* 2 vols. (Lon-

don: University of London Press, 1926); Harrison, *Arminianism* (London: Duckworth, 1937); and Howard A. Slatte, *The Arminian Arm of Theology: The Theologies of John Fletcher, first Methodist Theologian, and his Precursor, James Arminius* (Washington, D.C.: University Press of America, 1979).

[12]Text in Schaff, *Creeds of Christendom* 3:545-49.

[13]Text in Schaff, *Creeds of Christendom* 3:550-97.

[14]See Charles Hartshorne, *Omnipotence and Other Theological Mistakes* (Albany, NY: State University of New York Press, 1984); John C. Moskop, *Divine Omniscience and Human Freedom: Thomas Aquinas and Charles Hartshorne,* with a foreword by Charles Hartshorne (Macon: Mercer University Press, 1984). A critique of process thought will be given in volume two. For recent discussion of divine attributes, see Richard Swinburne, *The Coherence of Theism* (Oxford: Clarendon Press, 1977); Alfred Freddoso, ed., *The Existence and Nature of God,* University of Notre Dame Studies in the Philosophy of Religion 3 (Notre Dame: University of Notre Dame Press, 1983); Ronald H. Nash, *The Concept of God* (Grand Rapids: Zondervan, 1983); James E. Tomberlin and Peter Van Inwagen, eds., *Alvin Plantinga,* Profiles 5 (Dordrecht, Boston, Lancaster: D. Reidel Publishing Company, 1985).

[15]See William Lane Craig, *The Only Wise God: The Compatibility of Divine Foreknowledge with Human Freedom* (Grand Rapids: Baker Book House, 1987); William Lane Craig, *The Problems of Divine Foreknowledge and Future Contingents: From Aristotle to Suárez,* Brill's Studies in Intellectual History (Leiden: E. J. Brill, 1988). For a brief overview of different viewpoints, see Ronald Nash, *The Concept of God,* pp. 51-66.

[16]R. Garrigou-Lagrange, *God: His Existence and Nature* 2:82-83; see also the discussion in Brian Davies, *Thinking about God,* Introducing Catholic Theology (London: Geoffrey Chapman, 1985), pp. 173-199. Davies observes that "it seems that the whole notion of *scientia media* rests on a misguided premise, viz. that there can be knowledge of what people would do if created, and that this knowledge can be had without knowledge of what people do as created" (p. 189).

[17]J. R. Lucas, *The Freedom of the Will* (Oxford: Clarendon Press, 1970), p. 76.

[18]Peter Geach, *Providence and Evil,* The Stanton Lectures 1971-72 (Cambridge: Cambridge University Press, 1977), p. 58.

[19]For modern statements of the Arminian position, see Clark H. Pinnock, ed., *Grace Unlimited* (Minneapolis: Bethany Fellowship, 1975); Pinnock, ed., *The Grace of God and the Will of Man* (Grand Rapids: Zondervan, 1989). For statements of the Reformed position, see J. I. Packer, "Arminianisms," in Robert W. Godfrey and Jesse L. Boyd III, eds., *Through Christ's Word: A Festschrift for Dr. Philip E. Hughes* (Phillipsburg, NJ: Presbyterian and Reformed Publishing Co., 1985), pp. 121-48; Paul K. Jewett, *Election and Predestination* (Grand Rapids: Eerdmans, 1985).

[20]Cases in point are the ways in which theologians have argued that Paul's teaching in Romans 8—11 must be understood as referring to the election of individuals to salvation rather than to God's overall purposes for humankind (cf. K. Grayston, "The Doctrine of Election in Romans 8, 28-30," in F. L. Cross, ed., *Studia Evangelica* [Berlin: Akademie-Verlag, 1964] 2:574-83). For details of the vast literature on the subject, see J. D. G. Dunn, *Romans*, Word Biblical Commentary, 2 vols. (Dallas: Word Books, 1988). Likewise, the many references to election in the letter to the Ephesians are commonly read as if they refer to the election of individuals. But close examination of the text shows that the "we" that Paul is talking about are Jew and Gentile, and that the mystery hidden for generations but revealed is "how the Gentiles are fellow heirs, members of the same body, and partakers of the same promise in Christ Jesus through the gospel" (Eph 3:6). For the argument that models of physical power instead of love and personality have been wrongly used in the discussions of the past, see John Oman, *Grace and Personality* (Cambridge: Cambridge University Press, 1917).

[21]Erasmus made the observation in his *Diatribe on Free Will* (1524) which provoked Luther's answer in *The Bondage of the Will* (1525). For the above quotations see *Luther and Erasmus: Free Will and Salvation*, trans. and ed. E. Gordon Rupp, Philip S. Watson, in collaboration with A. N. Marlow and B. Drewery, Library of Christian Classics 17 (Philadelphia: Westminster Press; London: SCM Press, 1969), pp. 37 and 109. It would seem that the Latin word *scepticus* which gave rise to the English word *skeptic* first appeared in the fourteenth century in Latin translations of Diogenes Laertius.

[22]*Institutes* 1.7.4.

[23]Karl Barth, *Church Dogmatics* 1/2 (Edinburgh: T. & T. Clark, 1956), p. 535.

[24]For an account of Pyrrhonian skepticism and literature on the subject, see Richard H. Popkin, *The History of Skepticism from Erasmus to Spinoza* (Berkeley and Los Angeles: University of California Press, 1979). For another aspect of skepticism, see Lucien Febvre, *The Problem of Unbelief in the Sixteenth Century: The Religion of Rabelais* (Cambridge, Mass.: Harvard University Press, 1982). On the atheistic implications of the thought of seminal thinkers of this period, see Michael J. Buckley, *At the Origins of Modern Atheism* (New Haven: Yale University Press, 1987).

[25]Popkin, *The History of Skepticism*, p. 19, alluding to Bayle's article on Pyrrho in his *Historical and Critical Dictionary*. On Pyrrho and Sextus Empiricus, see above pp. 57-60.

[26]For an account of his thought, see Robert R. Orr, *Reason and Authority: The Thought of William Chillingworth* (Oxford: Clarendon Press, 1967).

[27]Popkin, *The History of Skepticism*, p. 46, citing Montaigne's "Apology for Raimond Sebond." This piece is sometimes omitted from editions of Montaigne's *Essays* (e.g., the translation of J. M. Cohen, Harmondsworth: Penguin Books,

1958). See further I. D. McFarlane and Ian Maclean, eds., *Montaigne: Essays in Memory of Richard Sayce* (Oxford: Clarendon Press, 1982); Montaigne, *In Defense of Raymond Sebond*, trans. Arthur H. Beattie (New York: Frederick Ungar, 1959).

[28]Popkin, *The History of Skepticism*, p. 47.

[29]On this issue see Peter Stuhlmacher, "The Hermeneutical Significance of 1 Cor. 2:6-16," trans. Colin Brown in Gerald F. Hawthorne and Otto Betz, eds., *Tradition and Interpretation in the New Testament: Essays in Honor of E. Earle Ellis* (Grand Rapids: Eerdmans, 1987), pp. 328-47.

[30]Similar questions could be asked about François Rabelais (c. 1494-1533), the former monk, admirer of Erasmus, Renaissance author. His colorful tales about giants satirized both the papacy and Protestantism. They contain professions of belief in Christ, as well as elements of Stoicism and Platonism. See A. J. Krailsheimer, *Rabelais and the Franciscans* (Oxford: Oxford University Press, 1963); Lucien Febvre, *The Problem of Unbelief in the Sixteenth-Century Religion of Rabelais*, trans. Beatrice Gottlieb (Cambridge, Massachusetts: Harvard University Press, 1982).

[31]See Pierre Bayle, *Historical and Critical Dictionary: Selections*, trans. with introduction and notes by Richard H. Popkin, with the assistance of Craig Bush (Indianapolis: Bobbs-Merrill Company, 1965).

Chapter 11: The Age of Rationalism

[1]On Copernicus and his background see Hans Blumberg, *The Genesis of the Copernican World* (Cambridge, Massachusetts: MIT Press, 1987). On the general background of scientific ideas, see Charles Singer, *A Short History of Scientific Ideas to 1900* (London: Oxford University Press [1959] paperback reprint, 1963); Amos Funkenstein, *Theology and the Scientific Imagination from the Middle Ages to the Seventeenth Century* (Princeton: Princeton University Press, 1986); Imre Lakatos with Elie Zahar, "Why did Copernicus's Research Programme Supersede Ptolemy's?" in Imre Lakatos, *The Methodology of Scientific Research Programmes: Philosophical Papers*, ed. John Worrall and Gregory Currie (Cambridge: Cambridge University Press, 1978) 1:168-92.

[2]English translations of Galileo include his *Dialogue on the Great World Systems*, in the Salusbury Translation, revised, annotated and with an introduction by Giorgio De Santillana (Chicago: Chicago University Press, 1953); and *Two New Sciences, Including Centers of Gravity and Force of Percussion*, trans. with introduction and notes by Stillman Drake (Madison: University of Wisconsin Press, 1974). On Galileo's thought and historical significance, see Stillman Drake, *Galileo at Work: His Scientific Biography* (Chicago: University of Chicago Press, 1978); Drake, *Galileo* (Oxford: Oxford University Press; New York: Hill and Wang, 1980); William A. Wallace, *Prelude to Galileo: Essays on Medieval and Sixteenth-Century Sources of Galileo's Thought*, Boston Studies in the Philosophy of Science 62 (Dordrecht, Boston, London: D. Reidel Publishing Company,

1981); Wallace, *Galileo and his Sources: The Heritage of the Collegio Romano in Galileo's Science* (Princeton: Princeton University Press, 1984); Wallace, *Reinterpreting Galileo* (Washington, D.C., University Press of America, 1986); Pietro Redondi, *Galileo Heretic* (Princeton: Princeton University Press, 1987); Paul Cardinal Poupard, ed., *Galileo Galilei: Toward a Resolution of 350 Years of Debate, 1633-1983*, with an epilogue by John Paul II (Pittsburgh: Duquesne University Press, 1987); Maurice A. Finocchiaro, ed., *The Galileo Affair: A Documentary History* (Berkeley, Los Angeles, London: University of California Press, 1989).

³Quoted by Pope John Paul II in Poupard, *Galileo Galilei*, p. 198; see also Stillman Drake, *Galileo*, pp. 90-91.

⁴On November 10, 1979, in an address to the Pontifical Academy of Science marking the centenary of Einstein's birth, Pope John Paul II spoke on the theme of "Faith, Science and the Galileo Case" (see above, n. 3). In it the pope paid tribute to Einstein and to Galileo and put forward arguments in his defense. The pope said that the Catholic Church had no desire to violate the autonomy of science in research matters and called for a re-examination of the Galileo case. On May 9, 1983, Pope John Paul II delivered an address on the church and science, marking the 350th anniversary of Galileo's *Dialogue Concerning the Two Chief World Systems* (trans. in *Origins* 13/3 [1983]: 50-52). In it he acknowledged that Galileo had "suffered from departments of the church." He spoke of "the indispensable need for a frank and open dialogue between theologians, scientific specialists and those who exercise leadership in the church," and noted the encouraging process in the study of the Galileo question. In the fall of 1989 *The Christian Century* reported that the pope, speaking in Pisa, said, "Galileo Galilei's scientific work was imprudently opposed at the beginning, but now it is recognized by all as an essential stage in the methodology of research . . . and in the path toward understanding the world of nature" (*The Christian Century*, October 25, 1989, p. 952).

⁵The doctrine of transubstantiation received classical formulation by Thomas Aquinas, who drew on Aristotelian categories for its formulation in the *Summa Theologiae* 3, Questions 73-78 (Blackfriars edition, vol. 58). The doctrine was made an article of the Catholic faith at the Lateran Council (1215) and was reaffirmed by the Council of Trent in its Decree Concerning the Most Holy Eucharist, Session 13, October 11, 1551 (text in Schaff, *Creeds of Christendom* 2:126-139). Although there is a tendency among contemporary Catholic theologians to seek alternative terminology, the term *transubstantiation* continues to represent the official Catholic position (*Eucharisticum Mysterium*, May 25, 1967, see Austin Flannery, ed., *Vatican Council II: The Conciliar and Postconciliar Documents*, Grand Rapids: Eerdmans, 1975 and reprints, p. 104). For Redondi's argument see above, n. 2. Redondi notes that the corpuscular theories of Descartes and Gassendi eventually came under the same condemnation (pp. 307, 320).

[6]Stillman Drake, *Galileo*, pp. 86-87; cf. also *Encyclopedia of Philosophy* 3:266.

[7]Lakatos, *The Methodology of Scientific Research Programmes*, 1:188-89.

[8]For an overview of rationalism see John Cottingham, *The Rationalists* (Oxford: Oxford University Press, 1988). The new standard translation of Descartes is *The Philosophical Writings of Descartes*, translated by John Cottingham, Robert Stoothoff and Dugald Murdoch, 2 vols. (Cambridge: Cambridge University Press, 1984-85); also in separate editions Descartes, *Meditations on First Philosophy with Selections from the Objections and Replies*, trans. John Cottingham, with an introduction by Bernard Williams (Cambridge: Cambridge University Press, 1986); and Descartes, *Selected Philosophical Writings*, trans. John Cottingham, Robert Stoothoff and Dugald Murdock with an introduction by John Cottingham (Cambridge: Cambridge University Press, 1988). Among the shorter selections, mention may be made of *Descartes: Philosophical Writings*, trans. and ed. Elizabeth Anscombe and Peter Thomas Geach, with an introduction by Alexandre Koyré (Edinburgh: Thomas Nelson, 1954). Studies include Jacques Maritain, *The Dream of Descartes* (London: Editions Poetry, 1946); Albert G. A. Balz, *Descartes and the Modern Mind* (New Haven: Yale University Press, 1952); Norman Kemp Smith, *New Studies in the Philosophy of Descartes* (London: Macmillan, 1952); Willis Doney, ed., *Descartes: A Collection of Critical Essays* (reprint ed., Notre Dame: University of Notre Dame Press, 1968); Tom Sorrell, *Descartes* (Oxford: Oxford University Press, 1987).

[9]*History of Western Philosophy*, p. 582.

[10]*Discourse*, Part 2 (*Philosophical Writings* 1:116). The event is thought to have taken place on November 10, 1619 in a village near Ulm in southern Germany. The "stove" is often taken to mean a stove-heated room. It was probably a large stove with a built-in seat.

[11]*Discourse*, Part 2 (*Philosophical Writings* 1:120).

[12]*Discourse*, Part 3 (*Philosophical Writings* 1:122-26).

[13]*Discourse*, Part 4 (*Philosophical Writings* 1:127).

[14]*Discourse*, Part 4 (*Philosophical Writings* 1:129). See also the longer discussion of the existence of God in *Meditations* 3 (*Philosophical Writings* 2:24-36).

In *Meditations* 5 Descartes returned again to the argument: "Since I have been accustomed to distinguish between existence and essence in everything else, I find it easy to persuade myself that existence can also be separated from the essence of God, and hence that God can be thought of as not existing. But when I concentrate more carefully, it is quite evident that existence can no more be separated from the essence of God than the fact its three angles equal two right angles can be separated from the essence of a triangle, or than that the idea of a mountain can be separated from the idea of a valley. Hence it is just as much of a contradiction to think of God (that is, a supremely perfect being) lacking existence (that is, lacking a perfection), as it is to think of a mountain without a valley" (*Philosophical Writings* 2:46). Elsewhere, he explained that "a mountain without a valley" meant an uphill slope without a downhill slope.

Clement Dore has defended Descartes's argument against its critics, claiming that the argument turns on *conceptual* truth rather than on *logical* truth. It is a *conceptual* truth that God exists. *Conceptual truths* (unlike mere *logical truths*) depend for their truth on the peculiar properties of their material, nonlogical terms. See Clement Dore, "Descartes's Meditation V Proof of God's Existence," in Alfred J. Freddoso, ed., *The Existence and Nature of God*, University of Notre Dame Studies in the Philosophy of Religion 3 (Notre Dame: University of Notre Dame Press, 1983), pp. 143-160; Dore, *Theism*, Philosophical Studies Series in Philosophy 30 (Dordrecht, Boston, Lancaster: D. Reidel Publishing Company, 1984), pp. 82-103.

[15]*Discourse*, Part 4 (*Philosophical Writings* 1:130).

[16]"By *substance* we can understand nothing other than a thing which exists in such a way as to depend on no other thing for its existence. And there is only one substance which can be understood to depend on no other thing whatsoever, namely God. In the case of all other substances, we perceive that they can exist only with the help of God's concurrence" (*Principles of Philosophy* 1.51; [*Philosophical Writings* 1:210]).

[17]*Principles of Philosophy* 1.53 (*Philosophical Writings* 1:210-11).

[18]Letter to Princess Elisabeth of Bohemia, May 21, 1643 (Anscombe and Geach, eds., *Descartes: Philosophical Writings*, p. 276).

[19]*The Passions of the Soul* (1649) 1.34 (*Philosophical Writings* 1:341). The work grew out of the correspondence with Princess Elisabeth.

[20]See Gilbert Ryle, *The Concept of Mind* (London: Hutchinson, 1949; reprint ed., Peregrine Books, 1963). For different views from Descartes onwards, see G. N. A. Vesey, ed., *Body and Mind: Readings in Philosophy* (London: Allen and Unwin, 1964); Vesey, *The Embodied Mind: Readings in Philosophy* (London: Allen and Unwin, 1965). For views from classical philosophy to the present, see Antony Flew, ed., *Body, Mind, and Death* (New York: Macmillan; London: Collier Macmillan, 1964). Contemporary studies include C. C. Chappell, ed., *The Philosophy of Mind* (Englewood Cliffs, NJ: Prentice-Hall, 1962); Peter Geach, *God and the Soul* (London: Routledge and Kegan Paul, 1969); C. V. Borst, ed., *The Mind-Brain Identity Theory* (London: Macmillan, 1970); Antony Flew, *A Rational Animal and Other Essays on the Nature of Man* (Oxford: Clarendon Press, 1978); Richard Swinburne, *The Evolution of the Soul* (Oxford: Clarendon Press, 1986); William Barrett, *Death of the Soul: From Descartes to the Computer* (New York: Doubleday, 1987).

[21]Letter dated November 1640 commenting on Augustine's use of the argument in *On the Trinity* 10.10 and 12 (*Descartes: Philosophical Writings*, ed. Anscombe and Geach, pp. 263-64). In a letter to the Marquis of Newcastle, dating from March or April 1648, Descartes described it as "a proof of our soul's capacity

for receiving from God an intuitive kind of knowledge" (p. 301). Other instances of Augustine's use of the idea are *On Free Will* 2.3.7; *On True Religion* 73; *Against the Academicians* 3.11.25-26; *Soliloquies* 2.1.2; *On the Blessed Life* 2.2.7; *On the Trinity* 10.10.16; 15.12.21. See above, p. 96.

[22]*Objections and Replies*, Third Set (*Philosophical Writings* 2:122).

[23]*History of Western Philosophy*, pp. 589-90.

[24]*The Problem of Knowledge* (Harmondsworth: Pelican, 1956), p. 46.

[25]In *Descartes: Philosophical Writings*, ed. Anscombe and Geach, p. xxxiv.

[26]*Nature, Man and God*, Gifford Lectures 1932-34 (London: Macmillan, 1934), p. 57, in a chapter on "The Cartesian Faux-Pas."

[27]Popkin, *The History of Skepticism*, pp. 193-213.

[28]The old translation by R. H. M. Elwes of *The Chief Works of Spinoza*, 2 vols. (London, 1883) is published in paperback (New York: Dover Publications, 1951, 1955 and reprints). A new translation of *The Collected Works of Spinoza* based on critical editions of the text is in process of translation by Edwin Curley in 2 vols. (Princeton: Princeton University Press, vol. 1, 1985). Studies include H. A. Wolfson, *The Philosophy of Spinoza*, 2 vols. (Cambridge, Mass.: Harvard University Press, 1954-58); Richard McKeon, *The Philosophy of Spinoza: The Unity of his Thought* ([1928] reprint ed., Woodbridge, CT: Oxbow Press, 1987); Stuart Hampshire, *Spinoza* (Harmondsworth: Pelican Books, 1951); Leo Strauss, *Spinoza's Critique of Religion* (New York: Schocken Books, 1965); Marjorie Glicksmann Grene, ed., *Spinoza: A Collection of Critical Essays* (Garden City, NY: Doubleday, 1973; reprint ed., Notre Dame: University of Notre Dame Press, 1979); J. G. van der Bend, ed., *Spinoza on Knowing, Being and Freedom* (Assen: Van Gorcum, 1974); James Collins, *Spinoza on Nature* (Carbondale and Edwardsville: Southern Illinois University Press, 1984); Roger Scruton, *Spinoza* (Oxford: Oxford University Press, 1987); Y. Yovel, *Spinoza and Other Heretics*, 2 vols. (Princeton: Princeton University Press, 1989).

[29]Letter 54 (48) dated March 30, 1673 (*Chief Works* 2:374-75).

[30]Spinoza was influenced by Isaac La Peyère (Popkin, *The Rise of Skepticism*, 214-48). He questioned the authorship of the Pentateuch and claimed that Jewish belief in election and the law was a political rather than a religious issue (*Tractatus Theologico-Politicus*, 8). He went on to advocate a historical-critical approach to Scripture generally. See further Emil G. Kraeling, *The Old Testament since the Reformation* (London: Lutterworth Press, 1955, pp. 45-46).

[31]Pierre Bayle treated Spinoza as an atheist (*Historical and Critical Dictionary*, pp. 288-338). Hume referred to the "hideous hypothesis" of his atheism (*Treatise of Human Nature* 1.4.5). Hegel discussed the question in his *History of Philosophy* 3.2. But the Romantic poet Novalis described Spinoza as "a man intoxicated by God" (Miscellaneous Fragment 15, in *Novalis: Hymns to the Night and Other Selected Writings* [New York: Liberal Arts Press, 1960] p. 72).

[32]*Ethics* 1, Definition 3 (*Collected Works* 1:408).

[33]*Ethics* 1, Definition 8, Scholium 2 (*Collected Works* 1:414).

[34]*Ethics* 1, Definition 14 (*Collected Works* 1:420).

[35]*Ethics* 1, Definition 15 (*Collected Works* 1:420).

[36]*Ethics* 1, Definition 18 (*Collected Works* 1:428).

[37]*Ethics* 5, Definition 6 (*Collected Works* 1:599-600).

[38]*Ethics* 5, Definition 17: "Strictly speaking, God loves no one, and hates no one. For God . . . is not affected with any affect of Joy or Sadness. Consequently . . . he also loves no one and hates no one" (*Collected Works* 1:604).

[39]*Ethics* 5, Definition 36 (*Collected Works* 1:612).

[40]Popkin, *The Rise of Scepticism*, pp. 229-48.

[41]*Tractatus* 15 (*Chief Works* 1:194).

[42]*Tractatus* 6 (*Chief Works* 1:81-97). For discussion see Colin Brown, *Miracles and The Critical Mind*, pp. 30-34. In speaking of divine decrees, Spinoza was using the language of Calvinism to argue for his scientific pantheistic determinism.

[43]Cf. Copleston, *History of Philosophy* 4:209-10, with Julius Guttmann, *Philosophies of Judaism*, pp. 265-85; and Joseph L. Blau, *The Story of Jewish Philosophy*, pp. 255-60.

[44]For details see Colin Brown, *Jesus in European Protestant Thought, 1778-1860*, pp. 23, 33, 37, 68.

[45]Hegel discussed Spinoza at numerous points in his writings. He gave him a prominent place in his *Lectures on the History of Philosophy* 3. 2, Eng. trans. E. S. Haldane and Frances H. Simson (reprint ed., London: Routledge and Kegan Paul; New York: Humanities Press, 1968), 3:252-90.

[46]Extracts from Leibniz's writings may be found in Philip P. Wiener, ed., *Leibniz: Selections*, The Modern Student's Library (New York: Charles Scribner's Sons, 1951); *Leibniz: Philosophical Writings*, ed. G. H. R. Parkinson, trans. Mary Morris and G. H. R. Parkinson, Everyman Library (London: J. M. Dent, revised edition, 1973); Leibniz, *Monadology and Other Philosophical Essays*, trans. Paul Schrecker and Anne Martin Schrecker, Library of Liberal Arts (Indianapolis: Bobbs-Merrill, 1967). For the *Theodicy* see *Theodicy: Essays, on the Goodness of God, the Freedom of Man, and the Origin of Evil*, ed. Austin Farrar, trans. E. M. Huggard (London: Routledge and Kegan Paul, 1951). Other works include *New Essays Concerning Human Understanding*, ed. A. G. Langley (La Salle: Open Court, 3rd ed. 1949); *Philosophical Papers and Letters*, trans. and ed. Leroy E. Doemker (Dordrecht: D. Reidel, 2nd ed. 1976); *Discourse on the Natural Theology of the Chinese*, Monographs of the Society for Asian and Comparative Philosophy 4, trans. with introduction, notes and commentary by Henry Rose-Mont, Jr. and Daniel J. Cook (Honolulu: University Press of Hawaii, 1977); H. G. Alexander, ed., *The Leibniz-Clarke Correspondence, Together with Extracts from Newton's Principia and Opticks* (New York: Philosophical Library, 1956).

Recent studies include R. W. Mayer, *Leibniz and the Seventeenth-Century Revolution* ([1952] reprint New York: Garland Publishing, 1985); Ruth Lydia Saw,

Leibniz (Harmondsworth: Pelican Books, 1954); Nicholas Rescher, *The Philosophy of Leibniz* (Englewood Cliffs, NJ: Prentice-Hall, 1967); C. A. van Peursen, *Leibniz* (New York: Dutton, 1970); Leroy E. Loemker, *Struggle for Synthesis: The Seventeenth Century Background of Leibniz's Synthesis of Order and Freedom* (Cambridge, Mass: Harvard University Press, 1972); Ivor Leclerc, ed., *The Philosophy of Leibniz and the Modern World* (Nashville: Vanderbilt University Press, 1973); John Hostler, *Leibniz's Moral Philosophy* (New York: Barnes and Noble, 1975); C. D. Broad, *Leibniz: An Introduction,* ed. C. Levy (Cambridge: Cambridge University Press, 1975); Harry G. Frankfurt, ed., *Leibniz: A Collection of Critical Essays* (New York: Doubleday, 1972; reprint ed., Notre Dame: University of Notre Dame Press, 1976); David E. Mungello, *Leibniz and Confucianism: The Search for Accord* (Honolulu: University Press of Hawaii, 1977); Stuart Brown, *Leibniz* (Minneapolis: University of Minnesota Press, 1984); G. MacDonald Ross, *Leibniz* (Oxford: Oxford University Press, 1984); Benson Mates, *The Philosophy of Leibniz: Metaphysics and Language* (New York: Oxford University Press, 1986).

[47]Paul Schrecker in Leibniz, *Monadology,* p. xxiv.

[48]*Monadology* 31, 32 (trans. Schrecker, p. 153).

[49]*Monadology* 33 (trans. Schrecker, p. 153). Leibniz made the point in various other works, e.g., his study of "Necessary and Contingent Truths" (c. 1686) (*Philosophical Writings,* ed. Parkinson, pp. 96-105). In this piece Leibniz applied the distinction to our knowledge of God and God's decrees.

[50]*Monadology* 38 (trans. Schrecker, p. 1, 54).

[51]Cf. the chapter on "The Knowledge that we have of God" in *New Essays Concerning Human Understanding* with *Monadology* 39-45 (trans. Schrecker, pp. 154-55). For discussion and literature see Craig, *The Cosmological Argument,* pp. 257-81.

[52]*Monadology* 1 (trans. Schrecker, p. 148).

[53]*Monadology* 47 (trans. Schrecker, p. 155).

[54]*Monadology* 87 (trans. Schrecker, p. 162).

[55]*Monadology* 89 (trans. Schrecker, p. 163).

[56]*Theodicy* 224, 225 (trans. Huggard, pp. 267-68).

[57]*Theodicy* 84 (trans. Huggard, p. 168).

[58]On Wolff's place in German philosophy, see Lewis White Beck, *Early German Philosophy: Kant and His Predecessors* (Cambridge, MA: Harvard University Press, 1969). There is a modern German edition of Wolff's voluminous writings, but little is available in English. However, Wolff's approach can be studied from his *Preliminary Discourse on Philosophy in General,* trans. Richard J. Blackwell (Indianapolis: Bobbs-Merrill, 1963).

[59]There are numerous translations of Pascal's writings. Richard H. Popkin, ed., *Pascal Selections* (New York: Macmillan, 1989) contains both scientific and religious writings. A. J. Krailsheimer's translation of the *Pensées* (Harmondsworth: Penguin Books, 1966) is based on modern critical work on the French text.

References below are to this edition. Krailsheimer has also translated Pascal's *Provincial Letters* (Harmondsworth: Penguin Books, 1967) and written a study of Pascal (Oxford: Oxford University Press, 1983). Other studies include J. H. Broome, *Pascal* (London: E. Arnold, 1972); J. Miel, *Pascal and Theology* (Baltimore: Johns Hopkins University Press, 1969); Antoine Adam, *Grandeur and Illusion: French Literature and Society, 1600-1715* (London: Weidenfeld and Nicolson; New York: Basic Books, 1972); John Barker, *Pascal in England during the Age of Reason* (Montreal: McGill-Queen's University Press, 1980); Robert James Nelson, *Pascal: Adversary and Advocate* (Cambridge, Mass: Harvard University Press, 1981); Anthony R. Pugh, *The Composition of Pascal's Apologia* (Toronto: University of Toronto Press, 1984); Sara E. Melzer, *Discourses of the Fall: A Study of Pascal's Pensées* (Berkeley, Los Angeles, London: University of California Press, 1986).

[60]*Pensées*, #913, p. 309.

[61]*Pensées*, #622, p. 235.

[62]*Pensées*, ##77-79, 132-39, pp. 50-51, 66-72.

[63]*Pensées*, p. 355.

[64]*Pensées*, #190, p. 86.

[65]*Pensées*, #131, p. 62.

[66]*Pensées*, #131, p. 64.

[67]*Pensées*, ##423, 424, p. 154.

[68]*Pensées*, ##418-26, pp. 149-55. For discussion of the implications of the "wager," see Nicholas Rescher, *Pascal's Wager: A Study of Practical Reasoning in Philosophical Theology* (Notre Dame: University of Notre Dame Press, 1985).

[69]See (e.g.) *Pensées*, ##189, 832-58, pp. 85-6, 284-94, and the discussion in Colin Brown, *Miracles and the Critical Mind*, pp. 36-40.

[70]*Pensées*, #377, p. 137.

Chapter 12: Rational Religion and the Era of Deism

[1]There are numerous reprints of the *Leviathan*, but not all of them include the discussion of religion and miracles. However, this discussion may be found in the edition of Nelle Fuller in *Great Books of the Western World*, vol. 23 (Chicago: Encyclopedia Britannica, Inc., 1952). General studies on the subject include Richard Peters, *Hobbes* (Harmondsworth: Penguin Books, 1956); Samuel I. Mintz, *The Hunting of Leviathan: Seventeenth-Century Reactions to the Materialism and Moral Philosophy of Thomas Hobbes* (Cambridge: Cambridge University Press, 1962); Ralph Ross, Herbert W. Schneider, Theodore Waldman, eds., *Thomas Hobbes in his Time* (Minneapolis: University of Minnesota Press, 1974); D. D. Raphael, *Hobbes: Morals and Politics* (London: Allen and Unwin, 1977); Tom Sorrell, *Hobbes* (London: Routledge and Kegan Paul, 1986); J. Hampton, *Hobbes and the Social Contract Tradition* (Cambridge: Cambridge University Press, 1986); David Berman, *A History of Atheism in Britain: From Hobbes to Russell* (London:

Croom Helm, 1988), pp. 48-69.

[2]Hobbes's fifteen objections, which dealt with doubt, figure in the "Third Set of Objections with the Author's Reply" (Descartes, *Philosophical Writings* 2: 121—137). Although Descartes described the author of the objections as "a celebrated English philosopher," he curtly dismissed them.

[3]*Leviathan* 1.13, ed. Fuller, p. 85.

[4]*Leviathan* Introduction, ed. Fuller, p. 47; cf. Job 3:8; 41:1; Psalms 74:14; 104:26; Isaiah 27:1.

[5]*Leviathan* 1.14, ed. Fuller, p. 86

[6]*Leviathan* 1.14, ed. Fuller, p. 87.

[7]*Leviathan* 4.46, ed. Fuller, p. 269.

[8]*Leviathan* 4.46, ed. Fuller, p. 270.

[9]Hobbes stated his position succinctly in *Leviathan* 2.21: "Liberty and necessity are consistent: as in the water that hath not only liberty, but a necessity of descending by the channel; so likewise in the actions which men voluntarily do, which, because they proceed from their will, proceed from liberty, and yet because every act of man's will and every desire and inclination proceedeth from some cause, and that from another cause, in a continual chain (whose first link is in the hand of God, the first of all causes), proceed from necessity" (ed. Fuller, p. 113). Hobbes's views brought him into prolonged conflict with Bishop John Bramhall, whom he had met when both were exiled in Paris. Bramhall's *Vindication of True Liberty* (1655) was directed against Hobbes's materialism and determinism. Hobbes replied with his *Questions concerning Liberty, Necessity, and Chance* (1656), which provoked Bramhall's *Castigations of Hobbes' Animadversions* (1658) with its appendix on "The Catching of Leviathan, the Great Whale." See further Ralph Ross, "Some Puzzles in Hobbes," in *Thomas Hobbes in his Time*, pp. 42-60.

[10]A case in point is his rhetorical discussion of transubstantiation. Instead of putting men "in mind of their redemption by the Passion of Christ, whose body was broken and blood shed upon the cross for our transgression," the priest "pretends that by the saying of the words of our Saviour, 'This is my body,' and 'This is my blood,' the nature of bread is no more there, but his very body; notwithstanding there appeareth not to the sight or other sense of the receiver anything that appeared not before the consecration" (*Leviathan* 4.46, ed. Fuller, p. 249).

[11]See Herbert W. Schneider, "The Piety of Hobbes," and Paul J. Johnson, "Hobbes's Anglican Doctrine of Salvation," in *Thomas Hobbes and his Time*, pp. 84-101, 102-125.

[12]*Leviathan* 4.46, ed. Fuller, p. 267.

[13]*Leviathan* 3.37, ed. Fuller, pp. 190-91. For discussion of Hobbes's views on miracles, see Colin Brown, *Miracles and the Critical Mind*, pp. 34-26.

[14]*Leviathan* 3.37, ed. Fuller, p. 191.

[15]For selections from their writings, see Gerald R. Cragg, ed., *The Cambridge Platonists*, A Library of Protestant Thought (New York: Oxford University Press, 1968); C. A. Patrides, *The Cambridge Platonists*, The Stratford-upon-Avon Library 5 (Cambridge, Mass: Harvard University Press, 1970).

[16]On the Arminian connections of Cambridge Platonism, see A. W. Harrison, *Arminianism* (London: Duckworth, 1937), pp. 157-84. The dominant Calvinism at Cambridge began to be challenged in the 1730s by several of the nominees appointed by Archbishop Laud who were opposed to the rigorous positions of Calvinism. In Harrison's judgment kinship between the Remonstrants in Holland and the Cambridge Platonists was not due to the common influence of Arminius upon both schools. "Where the Cambridge men accepted Arminian views they had arrived at them independently" (p. 168). However, the writings of the Remonstrant leader, Simon Episcopius (1583-1643), were a real influence on the Cambridge Platonists. The English Arminian, John Goodwin, dedicated his *Redemption Redeemed* (1651) to Whichcote.

[17]Cragg, *The Cambridge Platonists*, p. 14.

[18]"S.P.," *A Brief Account of the New Sect of the Latitude Men*, p. 9 (Cragg, p. 15).

[19]Cragg, p. 22.

[20]*Aphorism*, #76 (Cragg, p. 18).

[21]Culverwel, *An Elegant and Learned Discourse of the Light of Nature* (1652), ch. 1 (Cragg, p. 60); cf. Whichcote, *Sermons*, p. 449; *Aphorism* # 916 (Patrides, pp. 11-12, 18, 50, 197, 334). The Cambridge Platonists linked Proverbs 20:27 ("the spirit of man is the candle of the Lord") with reason. However, they also compared the limited light given by the candle with the light of the sun.

[22]A number of major Deistic works and replies by opponents noted in the following discussion have been published in facsimile reprint by Garland Publishing, Inc., New York. They include Thomas Woolston, *Six Discourses on the Miracles of our Savior, and Defences of his Discourses, 1727-1730* (1979); Thomas Sherlock, *The Tryal of the Witnesses, 1743, and The Use and Intent of Prophecy, 1728* (1978); and Conyers Middleton, *A Free Inquiry into the Miraculous Powers, 1749* (1976). For selections of extracts from Deistic writers, see Peter Gay, ed., *Deism: An Anthology* (Princeton: Van Nostrand, 1968); E. Graham Waring, ed., *Deism and Natural Religion* (New York: Frederick Ungar, 1967). An old but still useful account of Deism and the eighteenth century in general is Leslie Stephen, *History of English Thought in the Eighteenth Century*, 2 vols. ([1876] paperback reprint of 3rd ed. [1902] with preface by Crane Brinton, New York: Harcourt, Brace & World, Inc.; London: Rupert Hart-Davis, 1962).

While the Deists criticized revealed religion, they all professed some kind of religious belief. However, it may be asked how far these professions were really genuine or whether they were tongue-in-cheek expressions of covert atheism. Like David Hume after them, Collins, Toland, Tindal and Blount were all skilled in inserting protestations of belief in passages whose general tenor favored disbelief. See David Berman, "Deism, Immortality, and the Art of Theological Lying," in J. A. Leo Lemay, ed., *Deism, Masonry, and the Enlightenment: Essays Honoring Alfred Owen Aldridge* (Newark: University of Delaware Press; London and Toronto: Associated University Presses, 1987, pp. 61-78). Other studies in this volume explore the background and ramifications of Deism in Britain and North America.

[23]Henning Graf Reventlow's *The Authority of the Bible and the Rise of the Modern World* (London: SCM Press, 1984; Philadelphia: Fortress Press, 1985) is a massive study of the part played by British writers, especially the Deists, in the beginnings of biblical criticism.

[24]Colin Brown, *Jesus in European Protestant Thought, 1778-1860* (Durham, NC: The Labyrinth Press, 1985), pp. 29-55.

[25]See R. M. Burns, *The Great Debate on Miracles: From Joseph Glanvill to David Hume* (Lewisburg: Bucknell University Press, 1981); Colin Brown, *Miracles and the Critical Mind* (Grand Rapids: Eerdmans; Exeter: Paternoster Press, 1984), pp. 47-100 and William Lane Craig's discursive study of *The Historical Argument for the Resurrection during the Deist Controversy,* Texts and Studies in Religion 23 (Lewiston-Queenston: Edwin Mellon Press, 1985).

[26]This view dates from Thomas Halyburton's *Natural Religion Insufficient, and Revealed Necessary to Man's Happiness in his Present State* (1714) which contains a detailed account of Lord Herbert and his disciple Charles Blount.

[27]Richard Popkin, *The Rise of Skepticism*, p. 151.

[28]An English translation of Lord Herbert's *De Veritate* was made by Meyrick H. Carré from the 1645 edition (University of Bristol Studies 6, Bristol: Arrowsmith, 1937).

[29]*An Essay Concerning Human Understanding* 1.3.19.

[30]See John Ferguson, *The Religion of the Roman Empire* (London: Thames and Hudson, 1970), p. 182. For literature and further discussion of Apollonius of Tyana, see Colin Brown, *Jesus in European Protestant Thought*, pp. 37, 41, 206, 283, 289; Colin Brown, *Miracles and the Critical Mind* (see index). For an assessment of Jesus as a miracle worker in the light of contemporary beliefs, see Colin Brown, *That You May Believe: Miracles and Faith, Then and Now* (Grand Rapids: Eerdmans; Exeter: Paternoster Press, 1985), pp. 81-178.

[31]Recent studies of Toland include Robert E. Sullivan, *John Toland and the Deist Controversy: A Study in Adaptations* (Cambridge, Mass: Harvard University Press, 1982) and Stephen H. Daniel, *John Toland: His Methods, Manners, and Mind* (Kingston and Montreal: McGill-Queen's University Press, 1984). Toland's checkered career brought him to Germany where for a time he served as secretary to the court at Hanover. He was introduced to the court at Berlin. He got to know Leibniz. However, he alienated many friends and patrons and died in poverty, having lost everything in the South Sea Bubble in 1720.

[32]See S. G. Hefelbower, *The Relation of John Locke to English Deism* (Chicago:

University of Chicago Press, 1918) for a comparison of ideas and attitudes. Hefelbower sees Locke and the Deists as "co-ordinate parts of one and the same general movement" which was rationalistic in character (p. 183). For a discussion of Collins which concludes that he was not a Deist but a speculative atheist, see Berman, *A History of Atheism in Britain*, pp. 70-92.

[33]Examination of the passages concerned indicates that traditional apologetics from the patristic period onwards have been too hasty in treating such prophecies as simply predictive. Hosea 11:1 is evidently referring to the nation of Israel as God's son. Isaiah 7:14 refers to the birth of a child from a woman presently a virgin which will be a sign of God's presence. Before the child is weaned the current danger will be a thing of the past. Examination of Matthew's Gospel suggests that Matthew's view of fulfillment is not simply that of a prediction coming about. Rather, it involves multiple or deeper fulfillments, in which an event in the past, present or near future anticipates another event of greater magnitude. In other words, Matthew's notion of fulfillment is typological rather than simply predictive or allegorical in Collin's sense.

[34]The argument about the credibility of ice occurs in John Locke's *Essay Concerning Human Understanding* 4.15.5. It was also taken up by Joseph Butler in *The Analogy of Religion*, Introduction #3; David Hume, *An Enquiry Concerning Human Understanding* 10, #89 and J. S. Mill, *A System of Logic* (edited edition, London: Longmans, 1925), p. 411. For fuller details see Colin Brown, *Miracles and the Critical Mind*, p. 335 and the discussions of these thinkers in that book.

[35]*The Works of Bishop Sherlock*, ed. T. S. Hughes (London: Valpy, 1830), p. 216.

[36]Cited from a letter dated March 13, 1761 in *The Gospel Magazine* 2 (1775) 67-72, reprinted in Robert Manson Myers, *Handel's Messiah: A Touchstone of Taste* (New York: Macmillan, 1948), pp. 120-24.

[37]Part 3 of *Messiah* was based largely on Scripture passages which figure in the Burial Service of the Anglican *Book of Common Prayer*. The work as a whole focuses on the central themes of the Christian Year.

[38]For an account of the background of Handel's *Messiah*, his other oratorios and of public reactions, see Christopher Hogwood, *Handel* (London: Thames and Hudson, 1984), pp. 140-231. Hogwood observes that "the present-day standing of *Messiah* makes it difficult for us to realize that for Handel its composition was an offbeat venture, unsure in its rewards and probably unrepeatable. It is the only truly 'sacred' oratorio he ever wrote, it was the only one performed during his lifetime in a consecrated building, and yet it was intended, in Jennens's words, as 'a fine Entertainment' " (p. 167).

Many devout people, especially Methodists, continued to regard the work with suspicion in view of its performance in places of entertainment. John Wesley, however, became an admirer of the work. After a performance in Bristol Cathedral, at a time when *Messiah* had become widely accepted, Wesley observed: "I doubt if that congregation was ever so serious at a sermon as they were during this performance. In many parts, especially several of the choruses, it exceeded my expectations" (*Journal*, August 17, 1758).

[39]There are numerous reprints of the *Analogy*, including that in the first volume of *The Works of Joseph Butler, D.C.L.*, ed. W. E. Gladstone, 2 vols. (Oxford: Clarendon Press, 1896). Studies include E. C. Mossner, *Bishop Butler and the Age of Reason: A Study in the History of Thought* (New York: Macmillan, 1936); William J. Norton, Jr., *Bishop Butler, Moralist and Divine* (New Brunswick: Rutgers University Press, 1940); Austin Duncan-Jones, *Butler's Moral Philosophy* (Harmondsworth: Pelican Books, 1952); Terence Penelhum, *Butler* (London: Routledge and Kegan Paul, 1985). For Butler's views on miracles and other literature, see Colin Brown, *Miracles and the Critical Mind*, pp. 58-63.

[40]*Works* 1:5. A similar position had already been argued by Berkeley and others (G. R. Cragg, *Reason and Authority in the Eighteenth Century* [Cambridge: Cambridge University Press, 1964], pp. 110, 115).

[41]Cf. Karl Popper, *The Logic of Scientific Discovery* (London: Hutchinson, 6th impression, revised 1972), pp. 59, 423.

[42]*Works* 1:177.

[43]*Works* 1:188.

[44]E. C. Mossner, *Bishop Butler*, pp. 164, 181.

[45]For an account of the episode, see Rupert E. Davies, *Methodism* (Harmondsworth: Pelican Books, 1963), pp. 75-76.

[46]For Butler's beliefs see the sermons in vol. 2 of his *Works*, and also E. C. Mossner, *Bishop Butler*, pp. 165-76; Alexander Whyte, *Bishop Butler: An Appreciation* (Edinburgh: Oliphant, 1903).

[47]See (e.g.) John Wesley's detailed reply to Conyers Middleton, noted below (n. 50).

[48]Ian Ramsey, *Joseph Butler 1692-1752, Some Features of His Life and Thought* (London: Dr. Williams's Trust), p. 21.

[49]For analysis and discussion see Colin Brown, *Miracles and the Critical Mind*, pp. 64-72.

[50]*Journal*, January 28, 1749. Wesley wrote an extensive personal reply to Middleton (*The Letters of the Rev. John Wesley, A.M.*, ed. John Telford [London: Epworth Press, 1931], 2:312-88). Hume's remarks about Middleton's book occur in his account of "My Own Life" (see ch. 14, n. 6).

[51]*History of the Decline and Fall of the Roman Empire* (reprint edition New York: Peter Eckler, 1923), pp. 148-49.

[52]See Colin Brown, *History and Faith: A Personal Explanation* (Grand Rapids: Zondervan; Leicester: Inter-Varsity Press, 1987), pp. 44-50.

[53]On French Deism see Norman L. Torrey, *Voltaire and the English Deists* (New Haven: Yale University Press, 1930; reprint ed., New York: Archon Books, 1967); C. J. Betts, *Early Deism in France: From the so-called 'déistes' of Lyon (1564) to Voltaire's 'Lettres philosophiques' (1734)* (The Hague: Martinus Nijhoff, 1984).

On Reimarus and Deism see Colin Brown, *Jesus in European Protestant Thought*, pp. 36-55.

Chapter 13: The Rise of British Empiricism

[1]Details of works by and on Locke, Berkeley and Hume are given separately below. For a general anthology see A. J. Ayer and Raymond Winch, eds., *British Empirical Philosophers: Locke, Berkeley, Hume, Reid and J. S. Mill* (reprint ed., New York: Simon and Schuster, 1968). For a recent overview see R. S. Woolhouse, *The Empiricists* (Oxford: Oxford University Press, 1988). On the religious background see G. R. Cragg, *From Puritanism to the Age of Reason: A Study of the Changes in Religious Thought within the Church of England 1160-1700* (Cambridge: Cambridge University Press, 1950); Cragg, *Reason and Authority in the Eighteenth Century* (Cambridge: Cambridge University Press, 1964); Roland N. Stromberg, *Religious Liberalism in Eighteenth-Century England* (Oxford: Oxford University Press, 1954); Basil Willey, *The Seventeenth Century Background* (London: Chatto and Windus, 1934); Willey, *The Eighteenth Century Background* (London: Chatto and Windus, 1940); John Redwood, *Reason, Ridicule and Religion: The Age of Enlightenment in England, 1660-1750* (London: Thames and Hudson, 1976). On key philosophical questions see Jonathan Bennett, *Locke, Berkeley, Hume: Central Themes* (Oxford: Clarendon Press, 1971); Anthony Kenny, ed., *Rationalism, Empiricism, and Idealism* (Oxford: Oxford University Press, 1986).

[2]*Critique of Pure Reason*, trans. Norman Kemp Smith (London: Macmillan, 1973), p. 667.

[3]For writings see *Selected Writings of Francis Bacon*, ed. Hugh G. Dick (New York: The Modern Library, 1955). Modern studies include Catherine Drinker Bowen, *Francis Bacon: The Temper of a Man* (Boston: Little, Brown and Co., 1963); Jonathan Marwil, *The Trials of Counsel Francis Bacon in 1621* (Detroit: Wayne State University Press, 1976); Anthony Quinton, *Francis Bacon* (New York: Hill and Wang, 1980); Jerry Weinberg, *Science, Faith, and Politics: Francis Bacon and the Utopian Roots of the Modern Age, A Commentary on Bacon's Advancement of Learning* (Ithaca: Cornell University Press, 1985).

[4]*Essay on Man* (1734) 4.

[5]On science and religion in this period, see R. S. Westfall, *Science and Religion in Seventeenth-Century England* (New Haven: Yale University Press, 1958); Henry G. van Leeuwen, *The Problem of Certainty in English Thought, 1630-1690* (The Hague: Martinus Nijhoff, 1963); Robert E. Schofield, *Mechanism and Materialism: British Natural Philosophy in an Age of Reason* (Princeton: Princeton University Press, 1970); R. M. Burns, *The Great Debate on Miracles: From Joseph Glanvill to David Hume* (Lewisburg: Bucknell University Press, 1981); Margaret J. Osler and Paul Lawrence Farber, eds., *Religion, Science, and Worldview: Essays in Honor of Richard S. Westfall* (Cambridge: Cambridge University Press, 1985).

[6]The motto contracts a line from Horace, "Nullius addictus iurare in verba

magistri" ("Not bound to swear allegiance to any master") (*Epistles* 1.1.14).

[7]Editions of his scientific writings include *Newton's Philosophy of Nature: Selections from his Writings*, ed. H. S. Thayer (New York: Hafner, 1953); *Mathematical Principles of Natural Philosophy and Optics* etc., Great Books of the Western World 34 (Chicago: Encyclopedia Britannica Inc., 1952). Studies include Richard S. Westfall, *Force in Newton's Physics: The Science of Dynamics in the Seventeenth Century* (London: MacDonald, 1971); Westfall, *Never at Rest: A Biography of Isaac Newton* (Cambridge: Cambridge University Press, 1980). On Newton's links with Cambridge Platonism and the developments on Newtonianism, see Arthur Quinn, *The Confidence of British Philosophers: An Essay in Historical Narrative*, Studies in the History of Thought 17 (Leiden: E.J. Brill, 1977), pp. 8-79.

[8]"I. Absolute, true, and mathematical time, of itself and from its own nature, flows equably without relation to anything external, and by another name is called duration: relative, apparent, and common time, is some sensible and external (whether accurate or unequable) measure of duration by means of motion, which is commonly used instead of true time; such as an hour, a day, a month, a year.

"II. Absolute space, in its own nature, without relation to anything external, remains always similar and immovable. Relative space is some movable dimension or measure of the absolute spaces; which our senses determine by its position to bodies; and which is commonly taken for immovable space; such as the dimension of a subterraneous, an aerial, or celestial space, determined by its position in respect of the earth. Absolute and relative space are the same in figure and magnitude; but they do not remain numerically the same. For if the earth, for instance, moves, a space of our air, which relatively and in respect of the earth remains always the same, will at one time be one part of the absolute space into which the air passes; at another time it will be another part of the same, and so, absolutely understood, it will be continually changed" (*Mathematical Principles of Natural Philosophy* [1687], Definitions, cited from Sir Isaac Newton, *Mathematical Principles of Natural Philosophy* and *Optics;* and Christiaan Huygens, *Treatise on Light,* Great Books of the Western World 34, Chicago: Encyclopaedia Britannica, 1952, pp. 8-9).

[9]"And the instinct of brutes and insects can be the effect of nothing else than the wisdom and skill of a powerful, ever-living agent, who being in all places, is more able by His will to move the bodies within His boundless sensorium, and thereby to form and reform parts of the part of the Universe, than we are by our will to move the parts of our own bodies. And yet we ought not to consider the world as the body of God, or the several parts thereof as the parts of God. He is a uniform Being, void of organs, members or parts, and they are his creatures, subordinate to him, and subservient to His will; and He is no more the soul of them than the soul of man is the soul of the species of things carried through the organs of sense into the place of sensation, where it per-

ceives them by means of its immediate presence, without the intervention of any third thing" (*Optics*, Book 3, Part 1, edition quoted, pp. 542-43).

[10] *The Leibniz-Clarke Correspondence, Together with Extracts from Newton's Principia and Opticks*, ed. H. G. Alexander (New York: Philosophical Library, 1956), p. 14. Clarke originally published the exchange in 1717 under the title of *A Collection of papers which passed between the late Learned Mr. Leibniz and Dr. Clarke in the years 1715 and 1716 relating to the Principles of Natural Philosophy and Religion, With an Appendix*.

[11] Sir Isaac Newton, *Theological Manuscripts*, ed. H. McLachlan (Liverpool: Liverpool University Press, 1950). See also Frank E. Manuel, *The Religion of Isaac Newton*, The Freemantle Lectures 1973 (Oxford: Clarendon Press, 1974).

[12] *Theological Manuscripts*, p. 17. See also Newton's "Queries regarding the Word 'Homoousios' " (pp. 44-47).

[13] Editions of Locke's works include *An Essay concerning Human Understanding*, abridged and edited by A. S. Pringle-Pattison (Oxford: Clarendon Press, 1924 and reprints) and the revised edition edited by Peter H. Nidditch (Oxford: Clarendon Press, 1975); *The Reasonableness of Christianity with A Discourse of Miracles and part of A Third Letter concerning Toleration*, edited by I. T. Ramsey (London: A. & C. Black; Stanford, CA: University of Stanford Press, 1958); *The Correspondence of John Locke*, ed. E. S. de Beer, 8 vols. (Oxford: Clarendon Press, 1976-). For an account of his life see Maurice Cranston, *John Locke: A Biography* (London: Longman, 1957; paperback reprint, Oxford: Oxford University Press, 1985). For overviews and details of other studies, see Richard I. Aaron, *John Locke* (Oxford: Oxford University Press, 2nd ed. 1955); J. D. Mabbott, *John Locke* (London: Macmillan, 1973); John Dunn, *Locke* (Oxford: Oxford University Press, 1984). On Leibniz and Locke see Nicholas Jolley, *Leibniz and Locke: A Study of the New Essays on Human Understanding* (Oxford: Oxford University Press, 1984; paperback, 1987).

[14] See John Locke, *Two Treatises of Government, With a Supplement Patriarcha by Robert Filmer*, ed. Thomas I. Cook (New York: Hafner Publishing Company, 1947). Editions of Locke include *The Second Treatise of Government*, ed. Thomas P. Peardon (New York: The Liberal Arts Press, 1952); and *Second Treatise of Civil Government: An Essay Concerning the True Original, Extent, and End of Civil Government; A Contemporary Selection*, abridged and ed. Lester DeKoster (Grand Rapids: Eerdmans, 1978). Filmer's *Patriarcha and Other Political Works* have been edited by Peter Laslett (Oxford: Blackwell, 1949). Studies include John Dunn, *The Political Thought of John Locke* (Cambridge: Cambridge University Press, 1969); Geraint Parry, *Locke* (London: Allen and Unwin, 1978); John Dunn, *Political Obligation in its Historical Context* (Cambridge: Cambridge University Press, 1980); W. von Leyden, *Hobbes and Locke* (London: Macmillan, 1981).

[15] *Essay* 4.19.14.

[16] *Essay* 2.29.1-16.

[17]*Essay* 1.1.5; 4.3.20. See above ch. 16, n. 10. The Cambridge Platonist Benjamin Whichcote was Locke's favorite preacher.

[18]*Essay* 1.1-4.

[19]*Essay* 1.4.9-12; cf. his criticism of Lord Herbert in *Essay* 1.3.19 (see above, p. 153). In *The Reasonableness of Christianity, as Delivered in the Scriptures,* Locke stresses ignorance of God and the moral law, which is aggravated by sin, as reasons why human beings differ so much in their views (*Works* 11th ed., 1812, 7:133-47).

[20]*Essay* 2.1.2.

[21]*Essay* 2.1.3.

[22]*Essay* 2.1.4-5.

[23]*Essay* 4.1.1.

[24]*Essay* 4.1.2.

[25]*Essay* 4.18.2.

[26]*Essay* 4.17.23.

[27]*Essay* 4.19.4. Although Locke's argument is a basic restatement of the traditional apologetic argument from prophecy and miracles, some of Locke's readers accused him of Socinianism. Among them was John Edwards and Edward Stillingfleet (Maurice Cranston, *John Locke,* pp. 409-416; I. T. Ramsey, ed., *A Discourse of Miracles,* pp. 8-19). Socinianism was a popular term for the Unitarian view of God, which denies the divinity of Christ and the Trinity, and is so called after Faustus Socinus (1539-1604). Critics of Locke's position could argue that a miracle might attest the one who wrought it as a bearer of revelation, but it did not necessarily show that such a person was divine. Locke himself rejected the charge of Socinianism.

[28]*A Discourse of Miracles,* ed. Ramsey, p. 82.

[29]*A Discourse of Miracles,* ed. Ramsey, p. 79.

[30]*A Discourse of Miracles,* ed. Ramsey, pp. 84-85.

[31]*Essay* 4.15.5.

[32]*The Reasonableness of Christianity,* #58, ed. Ramsey, p. 37.

[33]*The Reasonableness of Christianity,* #252, ed. Ramsey, p. 75.

[34]The standard edition is *The Works of George Berkeley, Bishop of Cloyne,* ed. A. A. Luce and T. E. Jessop, 9 vols. (London: Thomas Nelson, 1948-57). George Berkeley, *Philosophical Works, Including the Works on Vision,* with introduction and notes by M. R. Ayers (London: Dent; Totowa, NJ: Rowan and Littlefield, 1975) is based on texts from the edition of Luce and Jessop. Modern studies include J. D. Wild, *George Berkeley: A Study of his Life and Philosophy* (New York: Russell and Russell, 1936); A. A. Luce, *The Life of George Berkeley* (London: Nelson, 1949); G. J. Warnock, *Berkeley* (Harmondsworth: Pelican, 1953); George Pitcher, *Berkeley* (London: Routledge and Kegan Paul, 1977); C. B. Martin and D. M. Armstrong, eds., *Locke and Berkeley: A Collection of Critical Essays* (London: Macmillan, 1968); Harry M. Bracken, *Berkeley* (London: Macmillan, 1974); J. O.

Urmson, *Berkeley* (Oxford: Oxford University Press, 1982); Edwin S. Gaustad, *Berkeley in America* (New Haven: Yale University Press, 1979); J. Foster and H. Robinson, eds., *Essays on Berkeley* (Oxford: Oxford University Press, 1985); Jonathan Dancy, *Berkeley: An Introduction* (Oxford: Blackwell, 1987). For other works see T. E. Jessop, *A Bibliography of George Berkeley* (The Hague: Martinus Nijhoff, 1973).

[35]Locke wrote a refutation of Malebranche. His influence on British thinkers is discussed by A. A. Luce, *Berkeley and Malebranche* (Oxford: Clarendon Press, 1934); Charles J. McCracken, *Malebranche and British Philosophy* (Oxford: Clarendon Press, 1983).

[36]"For we have shown the doctrine of matter or corporeal substance to have been the main pillar and support of *scepticism,* so likewise upon the same foundation have been raised all the impious schemes of *atheism* and irreligion. Nay so great a difficulty hath it been thought, to conceive matter out of nothing, that the most celebrated among the ancient philosophers, even of these who maintained the being of God, have thought matter to be uncreated and coeternal with him. How great a friend material substance hath been to *atheists* in all ages, were needless to relate. All their monstrous systems have so visible and necessary dependence on it, that when this corner-stone is once removed, the whole fabric cannot choose but fall to the ground; insomuch that it is no longer worth while, to bestow a particular consideration on the absurdities of every wretched sect of *atheists*" (*Principles of Human Knowledge* 92 *[Works]* 2: 81, where the editors note that the doctrine of the eternity of matter was taught by the pre-Socratics and Aristotle, *On the Heavens* 2.1.283b26 *[Works]* 1: 470). Plato, however, regarded time as "the moving image of eternity," *Timaeus* 38b6 (*Dialogues,* p. 1167), and put the corporeal on the same level. Most physicists of Berkeley's day assumed the eternity of matter.

[37]*Principles of Human Knowledge* 18 (*Works* 2:48).

[38]*Principles of Human Knowledge* 86 (*Works* 2:78).

[39]*Philosophical Commentaries* 567 (*Philosophical Works,* ed. Ayers, p. 306).

[40]*Principles of Human Knowledge* 3 (*Works* 2:42).

[41]*Philosophical Commentaries* 751 (*Philosophical Works,* ed. Ayers, p. 324).

[42]*Third Dialogue* (*Works* 2:263).

[43]*Third Dialogue* (*Works* 2:262).

[44]*Principles of Human Knowledge* 3 (*Works* 2: 42).

[45]In his notebooks Berkeley expressed it as "Existence is percipi or percipere" (*Philosophical Commentaries* 429; *Works,* p. 290).

[46]*Third Dialogue* (*Works* 2:230-31).

[47]Cited from Bertrand Russell, *History of Western Philosophy,* p. 673.

[48]The incident took place in 1763 outside a church in Harwich prior to a voyage to Holland. Boswell went on to note that Johnson's action was "a stout exemplification" of the "first truths" of Claude Buffier or the "original principles"

of Reid and Beattie, "without admitting which, we can no more argue in metaphysicks, that we can argue in mathematicks without axioms" (James Boswell, *Life of Samuel Johnson*, ed. G.B. Hill [New York: Harper and Brothers, 1891], 1:545).

[49]*Philosophical Commentaries* 24 (*Philosophical Works*, ed. Ayers, p. 254).

[50]*History of Western Philosophy*, p. 684.

[51]Cf. Urmson, *Berkeley*, p. 63; Pitcher, *Berkeley*, pp. 163-79.

[52]E. L. Mascall, *Words and Images: A Study in Theological Discourse* (London: Longman, 1957), pp. 30-33.

[53]*Words and Images*, p. 34.

Chapter 14: The Skeptical Empiricism of Hume

[1]The standard biography is Ernest Campbell Mossner, *The Life of David Hume* (Oxford: Clarendon Press, 2nd ed. 1980). Studies include H. H. Price, *Hume's Theory of the External World* (Oxford: Oxford University Press, 1940); Norman Kemp Smith, *The Philosophy of David Hume* (London: Macmillan, 1941); J. A. Passmore, *Hume's Intentions* (Cambridge: Cambridge University Press, 1952); Antony Flew, *Hume's Philosophy of Belief: A Study of his First Inquiry* (New York: Humanities Press, 1961); V. C. Chapell, ed., *Hume* (London: Macmillan, 1968; reprint ed., Notre Dame, n.d.); D. C. Stove, *Probability and Hume's Inductive Scepticism* (Oxford: Clarendon Press, 1973); Nicholas Capaldi, *David Hume: The Newtonian Philosopher* (Boston: Twayne, 1975); James Noxon, *Hume's Philosophical Development* (Oxford: Clarendon Press, 2nd ed. 1975); Terence Penelhum, *Hume* (London: Macmillan, 1975); Jonathan Harrison, *Hume's Moral Epistemology* (Oxford: Clarendon Press, 1976); Donald W. Livingston and James T. King, eds., *Hume: A Re-evaluation* (New York: Fordham University Press, 1976); Barry Stroud, *Hume* (London: Routledge & Kegan Paul, 1977); J. C. A. Gaskin, *Hume's Philosophy of Religion* (2nd ed., Atlantic Highlands, N.J.: Humanities Press, 1988); A. J. Ayer, *Hume* (Oxford: Oxford University Press, 1980); J. L. Mackie, *Hume's Moral Theory* (London, Boston and Henley: Routledge & Kegan Paul, 1980); John Bricke, *Hume's Philosophy of Mind* (Princeton: Princeton University Press, 1980); Tom L. Beauchamp and Alexander Rosenberg, *Hume and the Problem of Causation* (Oxford: Oxford University Press, 1981); Robert J. Fogelin, *Hume's Skepticism in the Treatise of Human Nature* (London, Boston and Henley: Routledge & Kegan Paul, 1985); M. A. Stewart, ed., *Studies in the Philosophy of the Scottish Enlightenment* (Oxford: Oxford University Press, 1989).

[2]A. E. Taylor, "David Hume and the Miraculous," *Philosophical Studies* (London: Macmillan, 1934), p. 365.

[3]Robert J. Fogelin, *Hume's Skepticism*, p. 3. See also A. J. Ayer's criticism of the standard view which he dates from Thomas Reid's *Inquiry into the Human Mind on the Principles of Common Sense* (1764) (*Hume*, pp. 15-34).

[4]Hume put forward a defense of Epicureanism in his *Enquiry Concerning Human*

Understanding, Section 11. On Epicureanism see above, pp. 50-54.

[5]The future Earl of Charlemont describing Hume when he was attached to the British embassy in Turin in 1748 (Mossner, *Life,* pp. 213-14).

[6]Mossner, *Life,* p. 615. The complete text of *My Own Life* is given on pp. 611-15.

[7]References are to Hume, *A Treatise of Human Nature,* ed. L. A. Selby-Bigge, 2nd ed. revised by P. H. Nidditch (Oxford: Clarendon Press, 1978).

[8]Mossner, *Life,* p. 101.

[9]See the discussion of R. M. Burns, *The Great Debate on Miracles: From Joseph Glanvill to David Hume* (Lewisburg: Bucknell University Press, 1981), and the conclusion on p. 141.

[10]References below are to Hume, *Enquiries Concerning Human Understanding and Concerning the Principles of Morals,* ed. L. A. Selby-Bigge, 3rd ed. revised by P. H. Nidditch (Oxford: Clarendon Press, 1975).

[11]Mossner, *Life,* p. 612.

[12]Mossner, *Life,* p. 612.

[13]*History of Western Philosophy,* p. 686.

[14]References below are to Hume, *The Natural History of Religion,* ed. H. E. Root (London: A. & C. Black, 1956).

[15]References below are to Hume, *Dialogues Concerning Natural Religion,* ed. Norman Kemp Smith (Indianapolis: Bobbs-Merrill reprint n.d.). This edition includes a modernized version of *My Own Life.*

[16]*Enquiry* #128, p. 160.

[17]*Enquiry* #130, p. 162.

[18]*Enquiry* #130, p. 162.

[19]*Treatise* 1.1.6, p. 16.

[20]*Treatise* 1.3.14, p. 166.

[21]*Treatise,* introduction, pp. xii-xix; *Enquiry,* # 9, p. 14; cf. Capaldi, *David Hume,* pp. 49-70.

[22]*Treatise* 1.4.6, p. 252.

[23]*Enquiry,* Section 10, ##86-101, pp. 109-31. For detailed discussion and literature, see Colin Brown, *Miracles and the Critical Mind,* pp. 79-100, 340-42.

[24]L. A. Selby-Bigge, ed., *Enquiries,* p. viii.

[25]*Enquiry* #86, p. 110.

[26]*Enquiry* #101, pp. 130-31.

[27]*Enquiry* #91, pp. 115-16; cf. #98, p. 127.

[28]*Enquiry* #90, p. 114.

[29]*Enquiry* #89, pp. 113-14. See above, pp. 208 and 226, for the views of Locke and Sherlock on this point.

[30]*Enquiry* #92, pp. 116-17.

[31]*Enquiry* #93, pp. 117-19.

[32]*Enquiry* #94, p. 119.

[33]*Enquiry* #95, p. 121.

[34]*Enquiry* #96, p. 123; cf. Tacitus *Histories* 4.81.

[35]*Enquiry* #96, p. 124. Following the death of François de Pâris (1690-1727), his tomb became a place of pilgrimage, and numerous cures were reported (see C. Brown, *Miracles and the Critical Mind*, pp. 63-64). For literature and discussion of events, see B. Robert Kreiser, *Miracles, Convulsions, and Ecclesiastical Politics in Early Eighteenth-Century Paris* (Princeton: Princeton University Press, 1978).

[36]*Enquiry* #96, p. 125; cf. Heb 12:1.

[37]*Enquiry* #99, p. 128.

[38]*Enquiry* #100, p. 130.

[39]*Enquiry* #101, p. 131.

[40]Mossner, *Life*, p. 292, quoting a letter to the Rev. Hugh Blair.

[41]*Philosophical Studies*, p. 332; cf. *Enquiry* #87, p. 110.

[42]*Philosophical Studies*, p. 349.

[43]Apologists sometimes make the mistake of confusing evidence with the report of evidence. The two do not have the same compelling force. It is one thing to witness an event and to be convinced that it actually happened; it is another thing to receive a report of the event. In the latter case one may or may not be in a position to examine its credibility. In the New Testament the miracles of Jesus are sometimes described as signs (e.g., Jn 2:11; 20:30-31; Acts 2:22). But there is a difference between a sign and a proof. Signs indicate something, but they do not conclusively demonstrate the truth of what they point to. The New Testament presents the miracles and other actions of Jesus as prophetic signs which illustrate and embody the message, work, and person of Jesus. See further Colin Brown, *Miracles and the Critical Mind*, pp. 281-325; Brown, *That You May Believe*, pp. 95-175; Brown, "Miracle," *ISBE* 3 (1986): 371-81.

[44]Just as God gives his sun and rain to the just and the unjust (Mt 5:45), he also sends health and healing. Acts 14:8-20 tells of a case of healing which was attributed to pagan deities. The exorcism of demons was not limited to Jesus and his own disciples (Mt 12:27; Lk 11:19; cf. Mt 7:22-23; Mk 9:38; Acts 19:13-19).

[45]*Enquiry* #90, p. 115.

[46]*The Concept of Miracle* (London: Macmillan, 1970), pp. 68-69.

[47]*Enquiry* #110, p. 142.

[48]*Enquiry* #115, p. 148.

[49]*The Natural History of Religion*, p. 76.

[50]Norman Kemp Smith, ed., *Dialogues*, pp. 60-63; J. V. Prince, "Sceptics in Cicero and Hume," *Journal of the History of Ideas* 25 (1964): 97-106.

[51]*Dialogues*, p. 128; cf. Cicero, *On the Nature of the Gods*, 1.1.

[52]*Dialogues*, p. 128.

[53]*Dialogues*, p. 228.

[54]Cf. the interpretation of Norman Kemp Smith (*Dialogues*, pp. 57-75) with the

review of the more recent interpretations by J. C. A. Gaskin (*Hume's Philosophy of Religion*, pp. 209-218). Gaskin concludes that he finds it difficult to see that Kemp Smith's position has been seriously disturbed. "Hume is still Philo except when Cleanthes refutes Demea. Not every single sentence fits this formula, but most of the *Dialogues* do, and that is sufficient identification for the sympathies of their author in a Ciceronian dialogue" (p. 218). Hume lifted material for Cleanthes' speeches from the works of the Scottish Newtonians, George Cheyne and Colin Maclaurin.

[55]See Norman Kemp Smith, *Dialogues*, pp. 62-63, 120-23.

[56]*Dialogues*, Part 11, p. 213.

[57]*Dialogues*, Part 2, p. 143.

[58]*Dialogues*, Part 2, p. 144.

[59]*Dialogues*, Part 5, p. 167.

[60]*Dialogues*, Part 7, p. 179.

[61]*Dialogues*, Part 8, p. 184.

[62]*Dialogues*, Part 9, p. 186.

[63]*Dialogues*, Part 10, p. 190.

[64]*Dialogues*, Part 10, p. 198. The Christian writer Lactantius gives a longer version of this saying of Epicurus in *On the Anger of God*, 13.

[65]*Dialogues*, Part 13, p. 227.

[66]*Dialogues*, Part 13, p. 228.

[67]See above, pp. 125-29.

[68]*The Natural History of Religion*, pp. 72-73, alluding to Diodorus Siculus's *Library of History* 20.43.

[69]See below, pp. 259-68 and 336-39.

[70]*Hume's Philosophy of Religion*, p. 229.

[71]On Epicurus see above, pp. 51-54.

[72]Boswell's Journal, March 3, 1777, reproduced in an appendix by Kemp Smith, *Dialogues*, pp. 76-79.

[73]*Treatise*, 1.4.7, p. 269. The remarks come at the conclusion of Book 1, following Hume's discussion of skepticism with regard to reason, the senses of ancient and modern philosophy, of the soul and personal identity.

[74]*Enquiry* #132, p. 165.

[75]*Language, Truth and Logic* (London: Gollancz, 2nd ed. 1946), p. 54.

[76]*History of Western Philosophy*, p. 698.

[77]*From Descartes to Wittgenstein*, pp. 132-33.

[78]*Enquiry* #128, p. 160.

Chapter 15: Scottish Common Sense and Early American Philosophy

[1]References below are to *The Works of Thomas Reid, D.D.*, ed. Sir William Hamilton with an account of Reid's life and writings by Dugald Stewart, 2 vols. (Edinburgh: MacLachlan and Stewart, 7th ed. 1872).

Reid's *Inquiry and Essays* are available in a paperback edition, ed. Ronald E. Beanblossom and Keith Lehrer (Indianapolis: Hackett, 1983). This edition contains an updated bibliography. Other editions include *An Inquiry into the Human Mind*, ed. Timothy Duggan (Chicago: University of Chicago Press, 1970) and the facsimile reprint of Reid's *Essays on the Active Powers of Man* (New York: Garland Publishing, 1977). Reid's *Lectures on Natural Theology (1780)* have been transcribed and edited by Elmer H. Duncan with a new essay by William R. Eakin on "Reid: First Principles and Reason in the Lectures on Natural Theology" (Washington, D.C.: University Press of America, 1981). Studies include S. A. Grave, *The Scottish Philosophy of Common Sense* (Oxford: Clarendon Press, 1960); S. F. Barker and T. L. Beauchamp, eds., *Thomas Reid: Critical Interpretations* (Philadelphia: Philosophical Monographs 3, 1976); William J. Ellos, *Thomas Reid's Newtonian Realism* (Washington: University Press of America, 1981); Louise Marcil-Lacoste, *Claude Buffier and Thomas Reid* (Kingston and Montreal: McGill-Queen's University Press, 1982); Nicholas Wolterstorff, "Thomas Reid on Rationality," in Hendrik Hart, Johan van der Hoeven, Nicholas Wolterstorff, eds., *Rationality in the Calvinian Tradition* (Washington, D.C.: University Press of America, 1983), pp.43-70; Paul Helm, "Thomas Reid, Common Sense and Calvinism," in *Rationality and the Calvinian Tradition*, pp. 71-89; M. Jamie Ferreira, *Skepticism and Reasonable Doubt: The British Naturalist Tradition in Wilkins, Hume, Reid, and Newman* (Oxford: Oxford University Press, 1987); Marvin Dalgarno and Eric Matthews, eds., *The Philosophy of Thomas Reid* (Hingham, MA: Kluwer Academic Publishers, 1989).

[2]A. J. Ayer, *Hume* (Oxford: Oxford University Press, 1980, p. 17). The discussion of Locke, Berkeley and Hume is a recurrent theme in Reid. See, for example, the introduction to his *Inquiry (Works)* 1:97-104) where he traces their ideas through to Pyrrho, "the father of this philosophy."

[3]Immanuel Kant, *Prolegomena to Any Future Metaphysics* (1783), introduction, trans. ed. Lewis White Beck (Indianapolis: Bobbs-Merrill, 1950), p. 6. It is widely assumed that Kant had never actually read Reid. However, there is reason to think that he had at least read a French translation of Reid's *Inquiry*. Moreover, a strong case has been made out for thinking that Reid and Scottish Common Sense Philosophy provided a positive stimulus to Kant and German philosophy in the last third of the eighteenth century (see Manfred Kuehn, *Scottish Common Sense in Germany, 1768-1800: A Contribution to the History of Critical Philosophy* (Kingston and Montreal: McGill-Queen's University Press, 1987).

[4]*Works* 1:7.

[5]*Inquiry* 1.7 (*Works* 1:103).

[6]*Inquiry* Dedication (*Works* 1:96); cf. Hume, *A Treatise of Human Nature 1.1*.

[7]*Inquiry* 6.20 (*Works* 1:182-83).

[8]*Essays* 2.2 (*Works* 1:246-47).

[9]*Essays* 2.2; cf. Cicero, *Tusculan Disputations* 1.20 (*Works* 1:247).

[10]Louise Marcil-Lacoste, *Claude Buffier and Thomas Reid*, p. 145.

[11]*Inquiry* 4.1 (*Works* 1:117).

[12]*Essays* 2.21 (*Works* 1:332).

[13]A. D. Woozley, *Encyclopaedia Britannica* 19:77.

[14]*Inquiry*, Dedication (*Works* 1:95).

[15]*Inquiry* 5.7 (*Works* 1:126).

[16]*Inquiry* 6.20 (*Works* 1:184); cf. also p. 183; *Inquiry* 7.4 (*Works* 1:209); *Essays* 2.5 (*Works* 2:259).

[17]*Rationality in the Calvinian Tradition*, p. 45.

[18]*Rationality in the Calvinian Tradition*, p. 47.

[19]"If there are certain principles, as I think there are, which the constitution of our nature leads us to believe, and which we are under a necessity to take for granted in the common concerns of life, without being able to give a reason for them—these are what we call the principles of common sense; and what is manifestly contrary to them, is what we call absurd" (*Inquiry* 2.6 [*Works* 1:108]).

[20]*Essays on the Intellectual Powers of Man* 1.2 (*Works* 1:231).

[21]*Essays* 6.5 (*Works* 1:450).

[22]Wolterstorff, *Rationality in the Calvinian Tradition*, pp. 48-49, citing Reid's example: "When I hear a certain sound, I conclude immediately, without reasoning, that a coach passes by. There are no premises from which this conclusion is inferred by any rules of logic. It is the effect of a principle of our nature, common to us with the brutes" (*Inquiry* 4.1 [*Works* 1:117]).

Reid agreed with Hume that "our belief of the continuance of nature's laws is not derived from reason." He explained the belief by referring to "an instinctive prescience of the operations of nature, very like to that prescience of human actions which makes us rely upon the testimony of our fellow-creatures; and as, without the latter, we should be incapable of receiving information from men by language, so, without the former, we should be incapable of receiving information of nature by means of experience." Similarly, he appealed to *the inductive principle* in response to Hume's doubts about causation:

It is from the force of this principle that we immediately assent to that axiom upon which all our knowledge of nature is built, That effects of the same kind must have the same cause; for *effects* and *causes*, in the operations of nature, mean nothing but signs and the things signified by them. We perceive no proper causality or efficiency in any natural cause; but only a connection established by the course of nature between it and what is called its effect. Antecedently to all reasoning, we have, by our constitutions, an anticipation that there is a fixed and steady course of nature: and we have an eager desire to discover this course of nature. We attend to every conjunction of things which presents itself, and expect the continuance of that conjunction. And, when such a conjunction has often been observed, we conceive the things to be naturally connected, and the appearance of the one, without any reasoning or reflection, carries along with it the belief of the other (*Inquiry* 6. 24 [*Works* 1:199]).

[23]Marcil-Lacoste, *Claude Buffier and Thomas Reid,* p. 145.

[24]*Essays* 7.3 (*Works* 1: 484; cf. also pp. 209, 330, 416).

[25]Wolterstorff, *Rationality in the Calvinian Tradition,* p. 60. On Calvin see above, pp. 152-53; and also Charles Partee, "Calvin, Calvinism, and Rationality," and Dewey J. Hoitenga, Jr., "Faith and Reason in Calvin's Doctrine of the Knowledge of God," in *Rationality in the Calvinian Tradition,* pp. 1-15 and 17-39.

[26]*Essay* 6.6 (*Works* 1:460). "The argument from final causes, when reduced to a syllogism, has these two premises:—*First,* That design and intelligence in the cause, may, with certainty, be inferred from marks or signs of it in the effect. This is the principle we have been considering, and we may call it the *major* proposition of the argument. The *second,* which we call the *minor* proposition, is, That there are in fact the clearest marks of design and wisdom in the works of nature; and the *conclusion* is, That the works of nature are the effects of a wise and intelligent Cause. One must assent to the conclusion, or deny one or other of the premises" (pp. 460-461).

[27]*Lectures on Natural Theology,* p. 51.

[28]*Lectures on Natural Theology,* pp. 1-2.

[29]*Rationality in the Calvinian Tradition,* p. 64.

[30]*Rationality in the Calvinian Tradition,* p. 63.

[31]Cf. Ronald E. Beanblossom's introduction to Reid's *Inquiry and Essays,* pp. xliii-xlvii.

[32]H. H. Price, *Perception* (reprint ed., London: Methuen, 1961), p. 203.

[33]Roderick M. Chisholm, *Theory of Knowledge* (Englewood Cliffs, NJ: Prentice-Hall, 2nd ed. 1977, pp. 131-132; Chisholm, *The Foundations of Knowing* (Minneapolis: University of Minnesota Press, 1982), pp. 68-69.

[34]Cited from Plantinga's "Self-Profile" in James E. Tomberlin and Peter van Inwagen, eds., *Alvin Plantinga* (Dordrecht, Boston, Lancaster: D. Reidel Publishing Company, 1985), p. 63.

[35]*Rationality in the Calvinian Tradition,* pp. 52-64.

[36]*Rationality in the Calvinian Tradition,* p. 64. For further discussion of foundationalism and Wolterstorff's critique of it, see pp. 336-39.

[37]*Rationality in the Calvinian Tradition,* p. 65.

[38]Richard B. Sher, *Church and University in the Scottish Enlightenment: The Moderate Literati of Edinburgh* (Princeton: Princeton University Press, 1985), p. 318.

[39]On Reid's influence and its eventual decline, see George Marsden, "The Collapse of Evangelical Academia," in Alvin Plantinga and Nicholas Wolterstorff, eds., *Faith and Rationality: Reason and Belief in God* (Notre Dame: University of Notre Dame Press, 1983, pp. 219-64).

[40]Sydney E. Ahlstrom, "Theology in America: A Historical Survey," in James

Ward Smith and A. Leland Jamison, eds., *Religion in America*, I, *The Shaping of American Religion* (Princeton: Princeton University Press, 1961 [pp. 232-321], pp. 234-35). Ahlstrom's account is supplemented by the anthology he edited, *Theology in America: The Major Protestant Voices from Puritanism to Neo-Orthodoxy* (Indianapolis: Bobbs-Merrill, 1967); his magisterial survey, *A Religious History of the American People* (New Haven: Yale University Press, 1972); Winthrop S. Hudson, *Religion in America: An Historical Account of the Development of American Religious Life* (New York: Scribner, 2nd ed. 1973); and the older but still valuable work by Frank Hugh Foster, *A Genetic History of New England Theology* (1907; reprint ed., New York: Russell and Russell, 1963). For a survey of American philosophy see Elizabeth Flower and Murray G. Murphey, *A History of Philosophy in America*, 2 vols. (New York: Capricorn Books, 1977). For extracts from a variety of writers, see Paul Kurtz, ed., *American Thought before 1900: A Sourcebook from Puritanism to Darwinism* (New York: Macmillan, 1966). An important series of reprints of major works is American Religious Thought in the Eighteenth and Nineteenth Centuries, edited by Bruce Kuklick and published by Garland Publishing, New York.

[41]The work was actually first published in London in 1720, though it bears a 1721 imprint. Facsimile reproduction with an introduction by Josephine K. Piercy (Gainesville, Florida: Scholars' Facsimiles and Reprints, 1968). For an appraisal see Winton U. Solberg, "Science and Religion in Early America: Cotton Mather's *Christian Philosopher*," *Church History* 56 (1987): 73-92.

[42]*The Christian Philosopher*, p. 1.

[43]Winton U. Solberg, *Church History* 56 (1987): 75.

[44]The first book to have "Natural Theology" as a title was that of the Spanish philosopher Raymond of Sebonde, *Theologia Naturalis* (1484). The book argued that it was possible to discover the contents of the Christian revelation in nature alone. The work achieved posthumous fame in the sixteenth century through the translation by Montaigne, who championed its ideas. Although some Catholic writers esteemed it, the work was placed on the Index of Prohibited Books in 1559. See above, p. 169.

[45]*The Christian Philosopher*, p. 161.

[46]*The Christian Philosopher*, p. 245.

[47]*The Christian Philosopher*, p. 294.

[48]*The Christian Philosopher*, pp. 296-304.

[49]There are numerous editions of the writings of Jonathan Edwards, including *Jonathan Edwards: Representative Selections*, ed. Clarence H. Faust and Thomas H. Johnson (New York: Hill and Wang, 1935 and paperback reprints); and a paperback edition of *Freedom of the Will*, ed. Arnold S. Kaufman and William J. Frankena (Indianapolis: Bobb-Merrill, 1969). The new standard edition of *The Works of Jonathan Edwards* is published under the general editorship of Perry Miller and John E. Smith (New Haven: Yale University Press, 1957-). The

many studies of Edwards's thought include Perry Miller, *Jonathan Edwards* (1949; reprint Westport, Connecticut: Greenwood Press, 1973); Douglas J. Elwood, *The Philosophical Theology of Jonathan Edwards* (New York: Columbia University Press, 1960); Alfred Owen Aldridge, *Jonathan Edwards* (New York: Washington Square Press, 1964); Conrad Cherry, *The Theology of Jonathan Edwards: A Reappraisal* (Garden City: Doubleday, 1966); William J. Scheick, ed., *Critical Essays on Jonathan Edwards* (Boston: G. K. Hall, 1980); Norman Fiering, *Jonathan Edwards's Moral Thought and its British Context* (Chapel Hill: University of North Carolina Press, 1981); Robert W. Jenson, *America's Theologian: A Recommendation of Jonathan Edwards* (New York: Oxford University Press, 1987); R. C. DeProspo, *Theism in the Discourses of Jonathan Edwards* (Newark: University of Delaware Press, 1985); Nathan O. Hatch and Harry S. Stout, eds., *Jonathan Edwards and the American Experience* (New York: Oxford University Press, 1988); San Hyun Lee, *The Philosophical Theology of Jonathan Edwards: A Dispositional Interpretation* (Princeton: Princeton University Press, 1988); Allen C. Guelzo, *Edwards on the Will: A Century of American Theological Debate* (Middletown, CT: Wesleyan University Press, 1989).

[50]Miller, *Jonathan Edwards,* pp. 63-64.

[51]Quoted from the anonymous *The Life and Character of the Late Reverend Mr. Jonathan Edwards* (Boston: S. Kneeland, 1765), p. 4.

[52]Armand Maurer, "Edwards, Jonathan," *Encyclopedia of Philosophy* 2:460. See above, p. 219.

[53]Miller, *Jonathan Edwards,* p. 61; cf. Fiering, *Jonathan Edwards's Moral Thought,* p. 35.

[54]Paul Ramsey in his introduction to *Freedom of the Will* (*Works* 1:13); cf. Scheick, ed., *Critical Essays,* pp. 73, 79, 114, 115, 199. The term *panentheism* was coined by the German idealist philosopher Karl Christian Friedrich Krause (1781-1832) to describe his own view that God or the Absolute Being was one with the world, though he is not exhausted by it. Douglas J. Elwood detects a panentheistic tendency in Edwards's thought which he finds illustrated in Edwards's conclusion:

> The whole universe, including all creatures, animate and inanimate, in all its actings, proceedings, revolutions, and entire series of events, should proceed from a regard and with a view, to God, as the supreme and last end of all; that every wheel, both great and small, in all its rotations, should move with a constant, invariable regard to Him as the ultimate end of all; as perfectly and uniformly, as if the whole system were animated and directed by one common soul; or, as if one possessed of perfect wisdom and rectitude, became the *common soul of the universe,* and actuated and governed it in all its motions (Edwards, *God's End in Creation,* in *Works* [New York edition] 2: 202-3; cited by Elwood, *The Philosophical Theology,* p. 59).

[55]In his *Freedom of the Will* Edwards protested that "the term 'Calvinist' is in these

days, among most, a term of greater reproach than the term 'Arminian'; yet I should not take it at all amiss, to be called a Calvinist, for distinction's sake: though I utterly disclaim a dependence on Calvin, or believing the doctrines which I hold, because he believed and taught them; and cannot justly be charged with believing in everything just as he taught" (Preface, *Works* 1: 131). See above, pp. 151-54. 163-66.

[56]*Freedom of Will* 1.1 (*Works* 1:137).

[57]*Freedom of Will* 1.1 (*Works* 1:138; cf. Locke, *An Essay Concerning Human Understanding* 2.21.17).

[58]*Freedom of Will* 1.4; cf. 1.2 (*Works* 1:160, cf. 1:142).

[59]*Freedom of Will* 1.4; cf. 1.2 (*Works* 1:160, cf. 1:142).

[60]*Freedom of Will* 1.2 (*Works* 1:141).

[61]*Freedom of Will* 1.2 (*Works* 1:142).

[62]*Freedom of Will* 1.2 (*Works* 1:144).

[63]*Freedom of Will* 1.4 (*Works* 1:160).

[64]*Freedom of Will* 1.1 (*Works* 1:143).

[65]*Freedom of Will* 3.1-7 (*Works* 1:275-333).

[66]*Freedom of Will* Conclusion (*Works* 1:434).

[67]*Freedom of Will* 2.12 (*Works* 1:269).

[68]*Freedom of Will* 2.11-12; cf. 3.7 (*Works* 1:239-69; cf. 333).

[69]*Freedom of Will* 2.12 (*Works* 1:261).

[70]For a critique of Edwards's view from a modern Arminian standpoint, see James D. Strauss, "A Puritan in a Post-Puritan World," in Clark H. Pinnock, ed., *Grace Unlimited* (Minneapolis: Bethany Fellowship, 1975, pp. 243-64). An important philosophical and theological study is Austin Farrer, *The Freedom of the Will*, Gifford Lectures 1957 (London: A. & C. Black, 1958). Modern philosophical discussions include Donald M. Mackay, *Freedom of Action in a Mechanistic Universe*, Eddington Memorial Lecture, 1967 (Cambridge: Cambridge University Press, 1967); J. R. Lucas, *The Freedom of the Will* (Oxford: Clarendon Press, 1970); Brian O'Shaughnessy, *The Will: A Dual Aspect Theory*, 2 vols. (Cambridge: Cambridge University Press, 1980); Gary Watson, ed., *Free Will* (Oxford: Oxford University Press, 1982); Peter van Inwagen, *An Essay on Free Will* (Oxford: Clarendon Press, 1983).

[71]See the argument of John Oman in *Grace and Personality* (Cambridge: Cambridge University Press, 1917; reprint ed., London: Collins, Fontana, 1960). This is not to endorse all that Oman says. However, his plea for thinking about personality in terms of love rather than physical forces presents an alternative model which has not yet been adequately pursued.

[72]A recent important study is Joseph A. Conforti, *Samuel Hopkins and the New Divinity Movement: Calvinism, the Congregational Ministry and Reform in New England between the Great Awakenings* (Grand Rapids: Eerdmans for the Christian University Press, 1981).

[73]See Herbert M. Morais, *Deism in Eighteenth Century America* (New York: Columbia University Press, 1934; reprint ed., New York: Russell & Russell, 1960); G. Adolf Koch, *Religion of the American Enlightenment* (New York: Thomas Y. Crowell Company, 1968; originally published in 1933 under the title *Republican Religion*).

[74]Reprint ed., New York: Kraus Reprint Co., 1970.

[75]For critical edition see *Extracts from the Gospels, The Papers of Thomas Jefferson*, Second Series, ed. Dickinson W. Adams (Princeton: Princeton University Press, 1983).

[76]Robert M. Healey, *Jefferson on Religion in Public Education*, Yale Publications in Religion 3 (New Haven: Yale University Press, 1962, p. 25). For an account of Jefferson's religion see Charles B. Sanford, *The Religious Life of Thomas Jefferson* (Charlottesville: University Press of Virginia, 1984).

[77]Letter to John Adams (April 11, 1823), *The Writings of Thomas Jefferson*, ed. A. Bergh (Washington, D.C.: Thomas Jefferson Memorial Association, [1903] 4:363). For extracts of Jefferson's correspondence dealing with philosophy and religion, see Kurtz, *American Thought before 1900*, pp. 150-59. The five points to which Jefferson alludes were not formulated as such by Calvin. They refer to the doctrines of total depravity, unconditional election, limited atonement, irresistible grace and the preservation of the saints. These doctrines were formulated by the Synod of Dort (1618-19) in response to the Remonstrance presented by the followers of Arminius (1610). For the text of both documents see P. Schaff, *The Creeds of Christendom* 3:545-97. See above, pp. 163-66.

[78]Letter to William Short (October 31, 1819), *The Writings of Thomas Jefferson*, ed. P. L. Ford (New York: G.P. Putnam [1892-99] 10:143-46).

[79]For writings see *The Complete Writings of Thomas Paine*, ed. Philip S. Foner, 2 vols. (New York: Citadel Press, 1947). For discussion see Alfred Owen Aldridge, *Man of Reason: The Life of Thomas Paine* (Philadelphia: Lippincott, 1959).

[80]*Complete Writings* 1:601.

[81]The secular character of the Constitution is illustrated by the three-volume work by John Adams, a signer of the Declaration of Independence and the second President of the United States, *A Defence of the Constitutions of Government of the United States of America, against the attack of M. Turgot, in his letter to D. Prince, 22 March, 1778* (1787-1788). See the discussion of Andrew J. Reck, "The Philosophical Background of the American Constitution(s)," in Marcus G. Singer, ed., *American Philosophy*, Royal Institute of Philosophy Lecture Series 19 (Cambridge: Cambridge University Press, 1985, pp. 272-293). On the relationship of church and state, see Thomas J. Curry, *The First Freedoms: Church and State in America to the Passage of the First Amendment* (New York: Oxford University Press, 1986).

[82]Quoted from Koch, *Religion of the American Enlightenment*, p. 239.

[83]Rogers and McKim, *The Authority and Interpretation of the Bible*, pp. 245 and 246.

[84]Mark A. Noll, ed., *The Princeton Theology, 1812-1921: Scripture, Science, and Theological Method from Archibald Alexander to Benjamin Breckinridge Warfield* (Grand Rapids: Baker Book House, 1983, p. 57). See also Rogers and McKim, *The Authority and Interpretation of the Bible*, p. 269.

Chapter 16: Enlightenment and Skepticism in France

[1]Quoted from the translation of Lewis White Beck in his edition of Kant's *Foundations of the Metaphysics of Morals and What is Enlightenment?* (Indianapolis: Bobbs-Merrill, 1959), p. 85. Studies of the Enlightenment include: J. M. Robertson, *A History of Freethought, Ancient and Modern to the Period of the French Revolution* 2 vols. (4th ed. reprint London: Dawsons, 1969); J. H. Brumfitt, *The French Enlightenment* (London: Macmillan, 1972); Ernst Cassirer, *The Philosophy of the Enlightenment* (reprint ed., Boston: Beacon Press, 1960); Carl L. Becker, *The Heavenly City of the Eighteenth-Century Philosophers* (New Haven: Yale University Press, 1932 and numerous reprints); Paul Hazard, *The European Mind, 1680-1715* (Harmondsworth: Pelican, 1964); Hazard, *European Thought in the Eighteenth Century: From Montesquieu to Lessing* (London: Hollis and Carter, 1954); R. O. Rockwood, ed., *Carl Becker's Heavenly City Revisited* (Ithaca: Cornell University Press, 1958); J. S. Spink, *French Free-Thought from Gassendi to Voltaire* (London: University of London, The Athlone Press, 1960); Peter Gay, *The Enlightenment: An Interpretation*, 1 *The Rise of Paganism*, 2 *The Science of Freedom* (London: Weidenfeld and Nicolson, 1967-1970) (containing extensive bibliographies); Robert C. Solomon, *Continental Philosophy since 1750: The Rise and Fall of the Self* (Oxford: Oxford University Press, 1988). For an insightful study of the eighteenth century as background to later theology see Karl Barth, *Protestant Theology in the Nineteenth Century* (London: SCM Press, 1972), pp. 33-421. Selections of texts may be found in Crane Brinton, ed., *The Portable Age of Reason Reader* (New York: Viking Press, 1956) and J. F. Lively, ed., *The Enlightenment* (London: Longmans, 1966).

[2]Mendelssohn, *Jerusalem, Or on Religious Power and Judaism*, 2 vols. (Berlin: 1783). A major modern study is Alexander Altmann, *Moses Mendelssohn: A Biographical Study* (London: Routledge and Kegan Paul, 1973).

[3]Lewis White Beck, *Early German Philosophy: Kant and his Predecessors* (Cambridge, MA: The Belknap Press of the Harvard University Press, 1969), p. 260.

[4]Horace, *Epistles* 1.2.40.

[5]The work was perhaps the most famous but only one of many such works in this period (see William Gerber, "Philosophical Dictionaries and Encyclopedias," *The Encyclopedia of Philosophy* 6:170-99).

[6]French text and English translation together with the eulogy of Frederick the Great read before the Berlin Academy at his death in La Mettrie, *Man A Machine* (LaSalle: Open Court, 1974).

[7]A. Owen Aldridge, *Voltaire and the Century of Light* (Princeton: Princeton Uni-

versity Press, 1975), p. 302.

[8]There are a number of translations of Voltaire's more popular works like *Candide* and *Zadig*. The most complete edition of his writings remains the edition of Tobias Smollett and others, *The Works of Voltaire*, 42 vols. (Paris, London, New York, Chicago: E. R. Du Mont, 1901). This is supplemented by Theodore Besterman, ed., *Voltaire's Correspondence*, 107 vols. (Geneva: Musée de Voltaire, 1953-1965). Selections include Ben Ray Redman, ed., *The Portable Voltaire* (New York: Viking Press, 1957); Theodore Bestermann, ed., *Select Letters of Voltaire* (London: Nelson, 1963); Norman L. Torrey, *Voltaire and the Enlightenment: Selections from Voltaire* (New York: Appleton-Century-Crofts, 1931); Paul Edwards, ed., *Voltaire Selections* (New York: Macmillan, 1989). Modern editions of his more philosophical writings include *Philosophical Dictionary*, trans. and ed. Peter Gay, 2 vols. (New York: Basic Books, 1962) and *Philosophical Letters*, trans. and ed. Ernest Dilworth (Indianapolis: Bobbs-Merrill, 1961). Studies include A. Owen Aldridge, *Voltaire and the Century of Light* (Princeton: Princeton University Press, 1975); A. J. Ayer, *Voltaire* (London: Weidenfeld and Nicolson, 1986); C. J. Betts, *Early Deism in France: From the so-called 'déistes' of Lyon (1564) to Voltaire's 'Lettres philosophiques' (1734)* (The Hague: Martinus Nijhoff, 1984); William F. Bottiglia, ed., *Voltaire: A collection of Critical Essays* (Englewood Cliffs, NJ: Prentice-Hall, 1968); Henry N. Brailsford, *Voltaire* ([1935] reprint Oxford: Oxford University Press, 1963); John H. Brumfitt, *Voltaire Historian* (Oxford: Oxford University Press, 1958); Peter Gay, *Voltaire's Politics* (Princeton: Princeton University Press, 1959); Bernard N. Schilling, *Conservative England and the Case Against Voltaire* ([1950] reprint ed., New York: Octagon Books, 1976); Norman L. Torrey, *Voltaire and the English Deists* ([1930] reprint ed., New York: Archon Books, 1967); Torrey, *The Spirit of Voltaire* ([1938] reprint ed., Oxford: The Marston Press, 1962); Mina Waterman, *Voltaire, Pascal and Human Destiny* (New York: King's Crown Press, 1942).

[9]Voltaire's library was acquired by Catherine the Great of Russia and transferred to St. Petersburg. His use of the English Deists and the writings of Conyers Middleton forms the basis of Torrey's study of *Voltaire and the English Deists*.

[10]Voltaire selected for discussion sixty-five of Pascal's *Pensées* in the 1734 edition of his *Philosophical Letters* and added eight more in a note dated 1738. For a comparative analysis of some of the main points at issue, see Ayer, *Voltaire*, pp. 64-81. It may be noted that Ayer's outlook makes him more sympathetic to Voltaire, though he is not uncritical of him.

[11]See Bottiglia, ed., *Voltaire*, pp. 130-31.

[12]Ayer, *Voltaire*, p. 172.

[13]Ayer, *Voltaire*, p. 108.

[14]Article on "Fanaticism," *Philosophical Dictionary* (*Works* 9:5).

[15]Article on "Final Causes," *Philosophical Dictionary* (*Works* 9:82). For similar arguments see the articles on "Atheism" (*Works* 6:105-28); "Atheist" (*Works* 6: 128-

40); and "God-Gods" (*Works* 9:212-52); Paper "On the Existence of God" (*Works* 38:238-44).

[16]Article on "Atheism" (*Works* 6:126).

[17]Article on "Religion," *Philosophical Dictionary* (*Works* 13:71).

[18]Article on "Miracles," *Philosophical Dictionary* (*Works* 11:297). The article is an ironical discussion of the notion of miracles as violations of the laws of nature in the interests of a favored few. Voltaire used the occasion to review the work of Thomas Woolston, and note the fate of such critics as Jean Meslier and Nicholas Anthony.

[19]Article on "Optimism," *Philosophical Dictionary* (*Works* 12:82-83). The article on "Good" (*Works* 9: 259-68) adopts the same basic standpoint.

[20]Cited from Voltaire, *Candide, Zadig, and Selected Stories,* trans. Donald M. Frame, (New York: The New American Library, 1961, p. 101). On Leibniz see above p. 191.

[21]For discussion see William F. Bottiglia, "Candide's Garden" in Bottiglia, ed., *Voltaire,* pp. 112-130.

[22]There is no standard complete critical edition of Rousseau's writings in English. There are, however, numerous translations of his best-known works. They include the somewhat flawed translation by Barbara Foxley of *Émile,* with a brief introduction by A. B. de Monvel (London: J. M. Dent; New York: E. P Dutton, 1911 and numerous reprints); *The Social Contract and Discourses,* trans. G. D. H. Cole (London: J. M. Dent; New York: E. P. Dutton, 1913 and reprints); *The Social Contract,* trans. M. Cranston (Harmondsworth: Penguin Books, 1968); *Confessions,* trans. J. M. Cohen (Harmondsworth: Penguin Books, 1953) and Maurice Cranston, ed., *Rousseau Selections* (New York: Macmillan, 1988). Rousseau's various writings on religion have been brought together in the original French with an English introduction by Ronald Grimsley in his edition of Rousseau, *Religious Writings* (Oxford: Clarendon Press, 1970). The standard biography is Jean Guéhenno, *Jean-Jacques Rousseau,* 2 vols. (London: Routledge and Kegan Paul; New York: Columbia University Press, 1966). Studies include Ernst Cassirer, *Rousseau, Kant, and Goethe* (reprint ed., New York: Harper & Row, 1963); John Charvet, *The Social Problem in the Philosophy of Rousseau* (Cambridge: Cambridge University Press, 1974); Sir Gavin De Beer, *Jean-Jacques Rousseau and his World* (London: Thames and Hudson, 1972); Ronald Grimsley, *Rousseau and the Religious Quest* (Oxford: Clarendon Press, 1968); Grimsley, *The Philosophy of Rousseau* (Oxford: Oxford University Press, 1973); J. C. Hall, *Rousseau: An Introduction to his Political Philosophy* (London: Macmillan, 1973); Ann Hartle, *The Modern Self in Rousseau's Confessions: A Reply to St. Augustine* (Notre Dame: University of Notre Dame Press, 1983); Asher Horowitz, *Rousseau, Nature, and History* (Toronto: University of Toronto Press, 1987); Ramon M. Lemos, *Rousseau's Political Philosophy: An Exposition and Interpretation* (Athens, GA: University of Georgia Press, 1977); Vincent A. McCarthy, *Quest for a Philosophical*

Jesus: Christianity and Philosophy in Rousseau, Kant, Hegel, and Schelling (Macon, GA: Mercer University Press, 1986); Kennedy F. Roche, *Rousseau: Stoic and Romantic* (London: Macmillan, 1973); Robert Wokler, *Rousseau* (Oxford: Oxford University Press, 1988); Wokler, *Social Thought of J.-J. Rousseau* (New York: Garland Publishing, 1987).

[23]*Émile*, trans. Foxley, p. 5.

[24]*Émile*, p. 272.

[25]*Émile*, p. 272.

[26]*Émile*, p. 277.

[27]*Émile*, p. 261.

[28]*Émile*, p. 261.

[29]*Émile*, pp. 248-49.

[30]Rousseau's view of Jesus here bears some formal resemblance to that of traditional Christianity, but the resemblance is superficial. "Jesus came to establish a spiritual kingdom on earth; this kingdom, by separating the theological system from the political, meant that the state ceased to be a unity, and it caused those intestine divisions which have never ceased to disturb Christian peoples" (*The Social Contract*, trans. Cranston, p. 178). Jesus is here the same exemplary teacher of spiritual values that he is in *Émile*.

[31]*Fragments* 8:630; cited from Cassirer, *Rousseau, Kant, and Goethe*, p. 18.

[32]Roche, *Rousseau: Stoic and Romantic*, pp. x, 1-21.

Chapter 17: Enlightenment and Skepticism in Germany

[1]The more important theological pieces by Lessing may be found in Henry Chadwick, ed., *Lessing's Theological Writings: Selections in Translation with an Introduction* (London: A. & C. Black; Stanford, CA: Stanford University Press, 1956). A recent study of some of the issues raised by Lessing is Gordon E. Michalson, *Lessing's "Ugly Ditch": A Study of Theology and History* (University Park: Pennsylvania State University Press, 1985). For a critical discussion of Lessing and the controversies he provoked, see Colin Brown, *Jesus in European Protestant Thought, 1778-1860* (Durham, North Carolina: The Labyrinth Press, 1985; reprint ed., Grand Rapids: Baker Book House, 1988), pp. 1-55.

[2]Two modern translations of the final *Fragment* have been made: George Wesley Buchanan, trans., *The Goal of Jesus and His Disciples* (Leiden: E. J. Brill, 1970); and Ralph S. Fraser, trans., *Reimarus: Fragments*, ed. Charles H. Talbert (Philadelphia: Fortress Press, 1970; London: SCM Press, 1971). Major German editions of Lessing's works include all the *Fragments*. Reimarus's work was published in its entirety only relatively recently by Gerhard Alexander, eds., *Apologie oder Schutzschrift für die vernünftigen Verehrer Gottes*, 2 vols. (Frankfort: Suhrkamp Verlag, 1972). Although at the time of publication a few people correctly guessed the identity of the author of the *Fragments*, the issue was not finally settled until Dr. J. A. H. Reimarus donated copies of the manuscript to the state

library in Hamburg and the university library in Göttingen in 1814. The version used by Lessing does not appear to have survived.

[3]Albert Schweitzer, *The Quest of the Historical Jesus: A Critical Study of its Progress from Reimarus to Wrede*, with an introduction by James M. Robinson ([1910]; reprint ed., New York: Macmillan, 1968), pp. 22-23.

[4]*Lessing's Theological Writings*, p. 53.

[5]See above, p. 190.

[6]See above, pp. 312-13.

[7]*Lessing's Theological Writings*, p. 55.

[8]*Lessing's Theological Writings*, pp. 82-98, see especially pp. 92, 96.

[9]Lessing's "Counter Propositions" in *Lessing's Theological Writings*, p. 18.

[10]"Christian Deists . . . believe not the Doctrines because contain'd in Scripture; but the Scripture, on Account of the Doctrines" (Matthew Tindal, *Christianity as the Creation* ([1730]; reprint ed., New York: Garland Publishing, 1978), p. 371. The remark comes in the context of a discussion of different kinds of doctrines, some of which are "in their own Nature, *necessarily, and demonstrably"* whereas others are "in their own Nature, *indifferent,* or *possible,* or perhaps, *probable* to be true" (p. 370). Tindal's use of *necessity* in relation to doctrine suggests that he was working with a different concept of *necessity* from Lessing's. However, it may be noted that Tindal's work was translated into German by J. L. Schmidt (1741) who lived in Hamburg and finally settled in Wolfenbüttel. Schmidt also produced a German translation of Spinoza's *Ethics*.

[11]For discussion of this see Colin Brown, *History and Faith: A Personal Exploration* (Grand Rapids: Zondervan, 1987).

[12]*Lessing's Theological Writings*, pp. 94, 99-101. On the Pantheistic Controversy see Colin Brown, *Jesus in European Protestant Thought*, pp. 22, 33, 283.

[13]See Colin Brown, *Jesus in European Protestant Thought* for discussion of later developments.

[14]Although Kant's major works have been translated into English, many of his writings remain untranslated. The standard edition of Kant's *Critique of Pure Reason* is that of Norman Kemp Smith ([1929] reprint ed., London: Macmillan, 1973 and often). An older translation of Kant's ethical works is that of T. K. Abbott, *Kant's Critique of Practical Reason and Other Works on the Theory of Ethics* (London: Longmans, 1879 and reprints). More recently Lewis White Beck has translated the following: *Critique of Practical Reason* (Indianapolis: Bobbs-Merrill, 1956); *Foundations of the Metaphysics of Morals and What Is Enlightenment?* (Indianapolis: Bobbs-Merrill, 1959); *Prolegomena to Any Future Metaphysics* (Indianapolis: Bobbs-Merrill, 1950). Lewis White Beck has also edited *Kant Selections* (New York: Macmillan, 1988). Kant's *Critique of Judgment* has been translated by J. C. Meredith (Oxford: Oxford University Press, 1928). Kant's *Religion within the Limits of Reason Alone* has been translated with introduction and notes by Theodore M. Greene and Hoyt H. Hudson ([1934] paperback reprint ed.,

New York: Harper & Brothers, 1960). Kant's *Lectures on Philosophical Theology* have been translated by Allen W. Wood and Gertrude M. Clark (Ithaca: Cornell University Press, 1978).

Studies of Kant include: Lewis White Beck, *A Commentary on Kant's Critique of Practical Reason* (Chicago: Chicago University Press, 1960); Beck, *Early German Philosophy: Kant and his Predecessors* (Cambridge, MA: The Belknap Press of Harvard University Press, 1969); Beck, ed., *Kant Studies Today* (La Salle: Open Court, 1969); Frederick C. Beiser, *The Fate of Reason: German Philosophy from Kant to Fichte* (Cambridge, MA: Harvard University Press, 1987); J. F. Bennett, *Kant's Analytic* (Cambridge: Cambridge University Press, 1966); Bennett, *Kant's Dialectic* (Cambridge: Cambridge University Press, 1974); Ermanno Bencivenga, *Kant's Copernican Revolution* (Oxford: Oxford University Press, 1987); Ernst Cassirer, *Kant's Life and Thought*, with introduction by Stephan Körner (New Haven: Yale University Press, 1981); Donald W. Crawford, *Kant's Aesthetic Theory* (Madison: University of Wisconsin Press, 1974); A. C. Ewing, *A Short Commentary on Kant's Critique of Pure Reason* (London: Methuen, 1938); Stephan Körner, *Kant* (Harmondsworth: Pelican Books, 1955); H. J. Paton, *The Categorical Imperative* (London: Hutchinson, 1946); Roger Scruton, *Kant* (Oxford: Oxford University Press, 1982); P. F. Strawson, *The Bounds of Sense* (London: Methuen, 1966); Ralph C. S. Walker, *Kant, The Arguments of the Philosophers* (London: Routledge and Kegan Paul, 1978); Keith Ward, *The Development of Kant's View of Ethics* (New York: Humanities Press, 1972); W. H. Werkmeister, *Kant: The Architectonic and Development of his Philosophy* (La Salle: Open Court: 1980); Robert Paul Wolff, ed., *Kant: A Collection of Critical Essays* (London: Macmillan, 1968); Allen W. Wood, *Kant's Rational Theology* (Ithaca: Cornell University Press, 1978); Ping Cheung Lo, *Treating Persons as Ends: An Essay on Kant's Moral Philosophy* (Langham, MD: University Press of America, 1987).

I have discussed aspects of Kant's religious thought more fully in Colin Brown, *Miracles and the Critical Mind* (Grand Rapids: Eerdmans, 1984), pp. 103-107 and *Jesus in European Protestant Thought, 1778-1860* (reprint ed., Grand Rapids: Baker Book House, 1988), pp. 58-67.

[15]See *Kant's Inaugural Dissertation and Early Writings on Space*, trans. John Handyside (Chicago: Open Court, 1929).

[16]The first two parts are contained in *Kant's Cosmogony, As in his Essay on the Retardation of the Rotation of the Earth and his Natural History and Theory of the Heavens*, trans. W. Hastie, revised and edited by Willy Ley (New York: Greenwood Publishing Company, 1968). The third part of the *Universal Natural History* has been translated by Stanley L. Jaki in A.D. Breck and W. Yourgrau, eds., *Cosmology, History of Science, and Theology* (New York: Plenum Press, 1977), pp. 387-403. Jaki gives a critique of the work in *The Road of Science and the Ways to God*, Gifford Lectures 1974-75 and 1975-76 (Chicago: University of Chicago Press, 1978), pp. 112-24.

[17]*Kant's Cosmogony,* p. 7.

[18]See above, p. 284-85.

[19]Author's translation of Kant's letter dated May 4, 1793 (*Gesammelte Schriften* 11:429, Letter # 574).

[20]*Prolegomena to Any Future Metaphysic,* introduction and trans. Beck, p. 8; cf. also p. xi.

[21]*Critique of Pure Reason,* introduction, trans. Norman Kemp Smith, p. 41.

[22]*Critique of Pure Reason,* Introduction, p. 55.

[23]*Critique of Pure Reason,* Introduction, p. 48.

[24]*Critique of Pure Reason,* Introduction, pp. 42-43.

[25]*Critique of Pure Reason,* preface to first ed., p. 10.

[26]*Critique of Pure Reason,* "Transcendental Aesthetic," pp. 67-91. In this context Kant used the word *transcendental* to refer to "all knowledge which is occupied not so much with objects as with the mode of our knowledge in so far as this mode of knowledge is to be possible *a priori*" (introduction, p. 59).

[27]*Critique of Pure Reason,* "Transcendental Aesthetic," p. 80.

[28]*Critique of Pure Reason,* "Transcendental Aesthetic," pp. 111-19.

[29]*Critique of Pure Reason,* "Transcendental Aesthetic," p. 87.

[30]*Critique of Pure Reason,* "Transcendental Aesthetic," p. 91.

[31]Kant expounded four main Antinomies (corresponding to the four types of categories): that the world was both finite and infinite; that every substance is made up of simple parts and that nothing is made up of simple parts; that we must posit freedom and that the laws of nature preclude freedom; that the world posits a necessary being and that an absolutely necessary being does not exist (*Critique of Pure Reason,* "Transcendental Aesthetic," pp. 396-421).

[32]Letter to Herder dated May 10, 1781 cited from Ronald Gregor Smith, *J. G. Hamann, 1730-1788: A Study in Christian Existence with Selections from his Writings* (London: Collins, 1960), p. 244.

[33]Roger Scruton, *Kant,* p. 94.

[34]Lewis White Beck's introduction to Kant's *Prolegomena to Any Future Metaphysic,* p. xviii.

[35]Willard van Orman Quine, *From a Logical Point of View: Nine Logico-Philosophical Essays* (New York: Harper & Row, 2nd ed., 1963), p. 37, from the reprint of Quine's 1951 article on "Two Dogmas of Empiricism" (pp. 20-46).

[36]Stanley L. Jaki, *The Road of Science and the Ways to God,* pp. 118-19.

[37]*Critique of Pure Reason,* "Transcendental Dialectic," p. 500.

[38]*Critique of Pure Reason,* pp. 501-02: "The absolute necessity of the judgment is only a conditioned necessity of the thing, or of the predicate in the judgment. The above proposition does not declare that three angles are absolutely necessary, but that under the condition that there is a triangle (that is, that a triangle is given), three angles will necessarily be found in it. So great, indeed, is the deluding influence exercised by this logical necessity that, by the simple

device of forming an *a priori* concept of the thing in such a manner as to include existence within the scope of its meaning, we have supposed ourselves to have justified the conclusion that because existence necessarily belongs to the object of this concept . . . we are also of necessity . . . required to posit the existence of its object."

[39]*Critique of Pure Reason,* p. 504.

[40]*Critique of Pure Reason,* p. 504.

[41]*Critique of Pure Reason,* p. 507.

[42]*Critique of Pure Reason,* p. 508.

[43]*Critique of Pure Reason,* p. 509.

[44]*Critique of Pure Reason,* p. 511.

[45]*Critique of Pure Reason,* p. 511.

[46]*Critique of Pure Reason,* p. 514.

[47]*Critique of Pure Reason,* p. 521.

[48]*Critique of Pure Reason,* p. 524.

[49]*Critique of Pure Reason,* p. 531.

[50]*Critique of Pure Reason,* p. 528.

[51]*Critique of Pure Reason,* p. 532.

[52]*Critique of Pure Reason,* p. 532-33.

[53]*Critique of Pure Reason,* p. 565.

[54]*Critique of Pure Reason,* p. 565-66.

[55]*Critique of Pure Reason,* p. 566.

[56]*Critique of Pure Reason,* p. 566-67.

[57]Frederick Copleston, *A History of Philosophy,* 6:298.

[58]*Religion within the Limits of Reason Alone,* preface to first ed., p. 3.

[59]*Foundations of the Metaphysics of Morals,* p. 19.

[60]*Foundations,* p. 30.

[61]*Foundations,* p. 31.

[62]*Foundations,* p. 39. In Kant's terminology a *maxim* is a moral principle that one adopts for oneself as distinct from the underlying *law* which is valid for everyone.

[63]*Foundations,* p. 47.

[64]Hegel, *Philosophy of Right,* Part 2, 3, 135, trans. T. M. Knox (reprint ed., Chicago: Encyclopedia Britannica, 1952), p. 47.

[65]*Foundations,* p. 59.

[66]"The concept of each rational being as a being that must regard itself as giving universal law through all the maxims of its will, so that it may judge itself and its actions from this standpoint, leads to a very fruitful concept, namely, that of a *realm of ends.* . . . We can think of a whole of all ends in systematic connection, a whole of rational beings as ends in themselves as well as of the particular ends which each may set for himself" (*Foundations,* p. 51).

[67]Matthew 22:39; cf. 19:19; Mark 12:31; Luke 10:27. For Kant's own discussion of this see *Critique of Practical Reason*, pp. 85-86 and *Religion within the Limits of Reason Alone*, p. 148.

[68]Leviticus 19:18; cf. the last six of the Ten Commandments (Ex 20:12-17; Deut 5:16-21).

[69]Matthew 22:37-38; Mark 12:29-30; Luke 10:27.

[70]Deuteronomy 6:4-9; cf. the first four of the Ten Commandments (Ex 20:1-11; Deut 5:6-15).

[71]See above, pp. 57, 152-53 and ch. 11 n. 21.

[72]*Critique of Practical Reason*, pp. 117-39.

[73]*Critique of Practical Reason*, pp. 126-28.

[74]*Critique of Practical Reason*, pp. 129-30.

[75]*Religion within the Limits of Reason Alone*, pp. 4-5. I have given more extended discussions of this book in *Miracles and the Critical Mind*, pp. 103-07; and *Jesus in European Protestant Thought, 1778-1860*, pp. 60-67.

[76]*Religion*, p. 152.

[77]*Religion*, p. 123; cf. p. 110.

[78]*Religion*, p. 40.

[79]*Religion*, p. 54.

[80]*Religion*, p. 55.

[81]*Religion*, pp. 54 and 55.

[82]*Religion*, p. 76.

[83]*Religion*, p. 56.

[84]*Religion*, p. 78.

[85]*Religion*, p. 145.

[86]G. W. F. Hegel, *Encyclopedia of the Philosophical Sciences in Outline* (1817), # 33 (author's translation from *Sämtliche Werke*, Jubiläumsausgabe, reprint Stuttgart: Fr. Frommanns Verlag, 1956, 6:46). For a comprehensive account of the whole range of Hegel's criticism, see Stephen Priest, ed., *Hegel's Critique of Kant* (Oxford: Oxford University Press, 1987).

[87]*The Logic of Hegel*, translated from *The Encyclopaedia of the Philosophical Sciences*, by W. Wallace (Oxford: Clarendon Press, 2nd ed. 1892), # 42, p. 84.

[88]For an alternative critical epistemology see Bernard Lonergan, *Insight: A Study of Human Understanding* (New York: Philosophical Library, 3rd ed. 1958). See pp. 339-42 for Lonergan's comparison of his own position with Kantian analysis.

[89]See (e.g.) Ronald Gregor Smith, ed., *World Come of Age: A Symposium on Dietrich Bonhoeffer* (London: Collins, 1967), p. 9, where the editor identifies the phrase as belonging to "the best known of his coinages." For Bonhoeffer's own thought on the subject, see his *Letters and Papers from Prison*, ed. E. Bethge (Enlarged edition, London: SCM Press, 1971), pp. 341, 360-61, 380-84 and passim. On Kant's view see above, pp. 284-85.

Chapter 18: Retrospect and Prospect

[1]Arthur F. Holmes, *Contours of a World View* (Grand Rapids: Eerdmans, 1983), p. 5.

[2]Allan David Bloom, *The Closing of the American Mind* (New York: Simon and Schuster, 1987).

[3]On the problems of writing a history of philosophy, see the reflections of Fred Copleston, the doyen of contemporary historians of philosophy in *On the History of Philosophy and Other Essays* (London: Search Press; New York: Barnes and Noble, 1979), pp. 3-39.

[4]Immanuel Kant, "Enquiry concerning the Clarity and Principles of Natural Theology and Ethics" (1763), in *Kant: Selected Pre-Critical Writings and Correspondence with Beck*, translated and introduced by G. B. Kerferd and D. E. Walford, with a contribution by P. G. Lucas (Manchester: University of Manchester Press, 1968), pp. 5-35; discussed by Stanley L. Jaki, *The Road of Science and the Ways to God*, pp. 116-117.

[5]Jaki, *The Road of Science*, p. 117.

[6]Nicholas Wolterstorff, *Reason within the Bounds of Religion* (Grand Rapids: Eerdmans, [1976] 2nd ed. 1984), p. 28.

[7]*Reason within the Bounds*, p. 56.

[8]*Reason within the Bounds*, p. 45.

[9]*Reason within the Bounds*, pp. 69-70. I do not think that Wolterstorff falls into the trap which Jaki sees Kant and others falling into, i.e., of assimilating philosophical method to one particular discipline like geometry. Rather, he is reflecting on the way knowledge is acquired generally. Philosophical method should not be determined a priori by making it conform to some arbitrary method. On the other hand, it is appropriate to ask how knowledge is acquired in various fields and to reflect on what is involved in the procedure. I have attempted to offer a similar approach to Wolterstorff's in the area of historical knowledge in my study of *History and Faith: A Personal Exploration* (Grand Rapids: Zondervan, 1987).

[10]Antony Flew in Antony Flew and Alasdair MacIntyre, eds., *New Essays in Philosophical Theology* (London: SCM Press, 1955), p. 97.

[11]My account of (e.g.) Aquinas and Descartes raises the question of whether they were as committed to foundationalism as they are commonly assumed to be. See above, pp. 128-29, 183.

[12]Wolterstorff, *Reason within the Bounds*, p. 70. The point is developed in the ensuing discussion.

A Note on Books

The purpose of this note is to draw attention to various reference works and histories of philosophy which I have generally not referred to in the course of my account. The reason for this omission was simply to avoid repetition. Details of studies of individual thinkers, philosophical movements and particular questions will be found in the endnotes. A review of books on particular issues will be included in the sequel to this volume.

Reference Works

A major authoritative source of information is *The Encyclopedia of Philosophy*, ed. Paul Edwards, originally published in 8 volumes but reprinted unabridged in 4 combined volumes (New York: Macmillan and Free Press; London: Collier Macmillan [1967] 1972). On a much smaller scale, but indispensable for the student of philosophy, is Antony Flew, ed., *A Dictionary of Philosophy*, rev. 2nd ed. (New York: St. Martin's Press, 1984). Also useful are William L. Reese, *Dictionary of Philosophy and Religion: Eastern and Western Thought* (New Jersey: Humanities Press; Sussex, Harvester Press, 1980); and Geddes MacGregor, *Dictionary of Religion and Philosophy* (New York: Paragon House, 1989). For an up-to-date annotated bibliography see William L. Reese, ed., *The Reader's Adviser: A Layman's Guide to Literature*, vol. 4, *The Best in the Literature of Philosophy and World Religions*, 13th ed. (New York and London: R.R. Bowker Company, 1988). On philosophy and religion in the ancient world and the early centuries of the Christian era, see the massive multivolume encyclopedic treatment of the rise and fall of the Roman world *Aufstieg und Niedergang der römischen Welt*, ed. Wolfgang Haase et al. (Berlin and New York: Walter de Gruyter) which is currently in process of publication. Many of the articles are in English.

A number of theological dictionaries give information on matters of philosophical and general interest. The most comprehensive of these is *The Oxford Dictionary of the Christian Church*, ed. F. L. Cross and A. E. Livingstone (London and New York: Oxford University Press, 2nd ed. 1974, reprinted with corrections and some revisions, 1983). Other dictionaries which are directed more to the general reader, but which also contain material not included in *The Oxford Dictionary of the Christian Church*, are Richard A. Muller, *Dictionary of Latin and Greek Theological Terms, Drawn Principally from Protestant Scholastic Theology* (Grand Rapids: Baker Book House, 1985); Alan Richardson and John Bowden, eds., *The Westminster Dictionary of Christian Theology* (Philadelphia: Westminster Press, 1983) which is published in England as *A New Dictionary of Christian Theology* (London: SCM Press, 1983); Walter A. Elwell, ed., *Evangelical Dictionary of Theology* (Grand Rapids: Baker Book House, 1984); and Sinclair B. Ferguson and David F. Wright, eds., *New Dictionary of Theology* (Downers Grove and London: Inter-Varsity Press, 1988). *The Oxford Companion to the Mind*, ed. Richard L. Gregory with the assistance of O.L. Zangwill (Oxford and New York: Oxford University Press, 1987) contains numerous short articles of topical and biographical interest. For terms and scholars connected with biblical interpretation, see Richard N. Soulen, *Handbook of Biblical Criticism*, Second Edition (Revised and Augmented) (Atlanta: John Knox Press, 1981).

General Histories and Source Books

The most comprehensive history by a single author is Frederick Copleston's *A History of Philosophy*, 9 volumes (London: Burns and Oates; Search Press; Westminster, Md.: Newman Bookshop, 1946-74; paperback reprint Garden City, NY: Image Books, 1962). Other modern multivolume histories include Émile Bréhier, *The History of Philosophy*, 7 volumes (Chicago: University of Chicago Press, 1963-69); Ralph M. McInerny and A. Robert Caponigri, *A History of Western Philosophy*, 5 volumes (Notre Dame: University of Notre Dame Press, 1963-71); Anders Wedberg, *A History of Philosophy*, 3 volumes (Oxford: Clarendon Press, 1982-84); and *A History of Western Philosophy*, a paperback series designed for general readers currently in process of publication by Oxford University Press in 8 projected volumes.

The one-volume history which is generally judged to be the most entertaining, though somewhat idiosyncratic, is Bertrand Russell's *A History of Western Philosophy* (London: Allen and Unwin; New York: Simon and Schuster, [1946], 2nd ed. 1961). An authoritative work which brings together the contributions of a variety of distinguished philosophers is D. J. O'Connor, ed., *A Critical History of Western Philosophy* (Glencoe: The Free Press; London: Collier-Macmillan, 1964); paperback, Basingstoke: Macmillan, 1985). For a narrative history up to the Middle Ages, see James N. Jordan, *Western Philosophy: From Antiquity to the Middle Ages* (New York: Macmillan, 1989). Other overviews include Julian Marias, *History of Philosophy* (New York: Dover Publications, 1967); Diogenes Allen, *Philosophy for Understanding Theology* (Atlanta: John Knox Press, 1985); D. W. Hamlyn, *A History of Western Philosophy* (New York: Viking, 1987; Harmondsworth: Penguin Books, 1988); Wallace I. Matson, *A New History of Philosophy*, 2 vols. (San Diego,

York: Harcourt Brace Jovanovich, 1987); Bryan Magee, *The Great Philosophers: An Introduction to Western Philosophy* (Oxford: Oxford University Press, 1988); Ben-Ami Scharfstein, *The Philosophers: Their Lives and the Nature of their Thought* (Oxford: Oxford University Press, paperback edition, 1989).

Standard works which combine historical, critical introduction with a wide selection of texts arranged under topics are Paul Edwards and Arthur Pap, eds., *A Modern Introduction to Philosophy: Readings from Classical and Contemporary Sources* (New York: Free Press; London: Collier-Macmillan, [1965] 3rd ed. 1973); L. Russ Bush, *Classical Readings in Christian Apologetics A.D. 100-1800* (Grand Rapids: Zondervan, 1983); and David Stewart and H. Gene Blocher, eds., *Fundamentals of Philosophy* (New York: Macmillan, 2nd ed. 1987). Albert B. Hakins, ed., *Historical Introduction to Philosophy* (New York: Macmillan, 1987) provides an extensive anthology arranged chronologically. A more personal history which is liberally laced with shorter extracts from a great number of philosophers is Antony Flew, *An Introduction to Western Philosophy: Ideas and Arguments from Plato to Sartre* (London: Thames and Hudson, 1971). A recent general introduction is John Perry and Michael Bratman, *Introduction to Philosophy: Classical and Contemporary Readings* (Oxford: Oxford University Press, 1986). For anthologies dealing specifically with religious questions, see John Hick, *Classical and Contemporary Readings in the Philosophy of Religion* (Englewood Cliffs, NJ: Prentice-Hall, [1964] 2nd ed. 1970); Baruch A. Brody, *Readings in the Philosophy of Religion: An Analytic Approach* (Englewood Cliffs, NJ: Prentice-Hall, 1974 and reprints).

On the role of women in the history of Western thought, see Ethel M. Kersey and Calvin O. Schrag, consulting editors, *Women Philosophers: A Bio-Critical Source Book* (New York; Westport, CT; London: Greenwood Press, 1989); Mary Ellen Waithe, ed., *A History of Women Philosophers*, 1 *Ancient Women Philosophers, 600 B.C.-500 A.D.;* 2 *Medieval, Renaissance and Enlightenment Women Philosophers A.D. 500-1600* (Dordrecht, Boston, London: Kluwer Academic Publishers, 1987, 1989). Further projected volumes are vol. 3 *Modern Women Philosophers, 1600-1900* and vol. 4 *Contemporary Women Philosophers, 1900-Today.* On women in the history of the church, see Ruth A. Tucker and Walter Liefeld, *Daughters of the Church: Women and Ministry from New Testament Times to the Present* (Grand Rapids: Zondervan Academie Books, 1987).

A Note on the Role of Women
in the History of Western Thought

Accounts of the history of philosophy and theology tend to be male-oriented. This is bound up with the fact that most of them have been written by men from a male point of view. But it is also bound up with the domestic role assigned to women in society and with the fact that the intellectual agenda has largely been set by men. The purpose of this note is to offer some observations and to draw attention to some relevant literature.[1]

The Ancient World

In general women lacked the educational opportunities that were open to men, and were not treated as intellectual equals. This was particularly true of the ancient world.[2] However, there were exceptions. Women were admitted to the Pythagorean society on an equal basis. Fragments of their thought have survived. Plato's mother, Perictione, may have been a Pythagorean. Diogenes Laertius mentions a number of women in his *Lives and Opinions of Eminent Philosophers,* and devoted a whole chapter to Hipparchia the Cynic (c. 300 B.C.),[3] who dressed and behaved like the male Cynics.

The priestess and teacher Diotima of Mantinea appears in Plato's *Symposium,*[4] where Socrates declares that she taught him "the philosophy of Love." Her method was to proceed by question and answer. Love *(eros)* is "neither beautiful nor good." It is a powerful spirit halfway between the mortal and the immortal, which drives humans to generate and conceive the beautiful. There is a debate among scholars, whether the figure of Diotima in the *Symposium* is a mere literary device, or whether (as was usual in Plato's dialogues) it was based on a real person. In his *Republic*[5] Plato advocated equal status and educational opportunities, and approved of women as Guardians. But this has to be set alongside his disapproval of the family. In the *Republic* Plato recommended its abolition, but backtracked in his *Laws,* where he observed that "the native disposition" of women was "inferior to man's."[6]

Aristotle also thought that "the male is superior to the female."[7] He observed that in common with other animals "the female is softer in character, is sooner tamed, admits more readily to caressing, is more apt in the way of learning."[8] The female "is, as it were, a mutilated male, and the menstrual fluids are semen, only not pure; for there is only one thing they have not in them, the principle of soul."[9] In human beings the female provides the matter, the body; the male provides the principle, the soul.[10] Although Aristotle advocated education for women, it was for the pragmatic reason that women needed some education in order to run their households and bring up their offspring.[11]

The New Testament and the World of the Early Church

The prevailing male dominance in the Graeco-Roman world coexisted with devotion to female deities and the cult of the feminine divine.[12] By contrast the Jewish tradition was patriarchal and monotheistic.[13] The Christian church presents both continuity and discontinuity with the culture, religion, and traditions of Judaism and the Hellenistic world.[14] Although women were not numbered among Jesus' twelve disciples, they figured prominently in his ministry and in the accounts of the resurrection.[15]

The apostle Paul profoundly influenced the attitude of the church, and the subsequent course of Western thought. Frequently he is represented as the archetypal misogynist and retarder of the cause of women. 1 Timothy 2:11-12 states: "Let a woman learn in silence with all submissiveness. I permit no woman to teach or to have authority over men; she is to keep silent" (RSV). The reason given for this prohibition recalls the story of Genesis 2 and 3. Adam was formed first, though it was actually Eve who was deceived by the serpent and Adam foolishly followed Eve.[16] Paul takes it as a salutary warning. The practice stated here is in line with what he recommended elsewhere (1 Cor 14:34-35; but see also 11:5; Acts 21:9). In this respect Paul was consistent with his declared policy of being a Jew to Jews and under the law to those under the law, though he himself was not under the law (1 Cor 9:19).

Elsewhere Paul stands out ahead of his time as a pioneer of women's rights. In conversing with Lydia (Acts 16:13-14) he did what few rabbis would have done. He warmly acknowledged the work of a number of women, including Phoebe, the deacon of Cenchreae, to whom he evidently entrusted the carrying of his letter to the church in Rome (Rom 16:1). He named Priscilla and Aquila as outstanding "fellow workers in Christ Jesus" (Rom 16:3). This couple are also mentioned in Acts 18:26 as teachers of the learned Apollos. Another woman named by Paul as a prominent Christian was Junia (Rom 16:7).[17]

As in other matters, like faith and works, gospel and law, bondage and freedom, Paul's teaching presents a subtle dynamic. Paul speaks of the male as the head (1 Cor 11:3), but in the context of the marriage relationship each partner is ruled by the other (1 Cor 7:4). This dynamic is present even in those passages where Paul urges wives to submit to their husbands (Col 3:18; Eph 5:22). His teaching is to be seen in the overall context of mutual submission out of reverence for Christ (Eph 5:21; Col 3:12-13). The exhortation to wives is counterbalanced by an exhortation to husbands to love their wives. When Paul describes the headship of the husband, it is a primacy of self-giving modelled on the self-giving of Christ (Eph 5:22). In Paul's gospel the divisions of race, society, and sex are transcended: "There is neither Jew nor Greek, there is neither slave nor free, there is neither male nor female; for you are all one in Christ Jesus" (Gal 3:28 RSV; cf. Col 3:11)

There were many outstanding women in the church of the early centuries, but the church fathers did not favor women bishops or women theologians. Women enjoyed prominence as teachers in Gnosticism,[18] certain fringe groups, and in Montanism, but not among the orthodox.[19] There are a number of possible explanations.[20] It may have been that female leadership was so closely associated with heresy that the church could not countenance it within its ranks. It has also been suggested that, as the church became upwardly mobile, it accepted the social roles assigned to women by the middle-class culture of the day. Such social factors would be reinforced by theological considerations. When isolated pronouncements by Paul were wrenched from the wider context of his thought, and coupled with statements from Plato[21] (and later from Aristotle) about male superiority, the case for female subordination seemed unassailable.

Women intellectuals were not unknown in the early centuries of the Christian era. However, they tended to belong to the upper strata of society. Among them was the empress Julia Domna (170-217), second wife of Septimius Severus, the soldier emperor who forbade the church to make conversions, and mother of the tyrant Caracalla. Julia Domna was the daughter of a Syrian pagan high priest. She assembled a circle of intellectuals and sophists which included Galen and Diogenes Laertius, who may have dedicated his *Lives and Opinions of Eminent Philosophers* to her. Hailed as "the philosopher Julia" by Philostratus, she commissioned the latter to write *The Life of Apollonius of Tyana*,[22] which may have been a form of anti-Christian propaganda. In the fifth century the empress Eudocia enjoyed a reputation for learning. She was taught by her father, a sophist, and later converted to Christianity, changing her name from Athenais ("Maid of Athens").

A number of women were attracted to Neoplatonism. Porphyry records that Plotinus lived in the house of a certain Gemina and that she and others "had a great devotion to philosophy."[23] The leading woman philosopher of the early centuries was Hypatia (c. 370-415), who succeeded her father as head of the Neoplatonic school at Alexandria. The form of Neoplatonism espoused by Hypatia stressed science, mathematics and philosophy, and does not appear to have been openly hostile to Christianity.[24] Hypatia enjoyed a great reputation, attracting students from far and wide. Letters addressed her as "the Muse" and "the Philosopher." Her disciple and convert, Synesius of Cyrene, considered her to be the greatest living exponent of Platonic, Aristotelian and Neoplatonic philosophy. Even after he became a convert to Christianity and was made a bishop, Synesius continued in his devotion to Hypatia's Neoplatonism.[25] Hypatia's philosophical writings have been lost, but two of her mathematical treatises have survived.[26] Hypatia was involved in a political power struggle with Cyril, bishop of Alexandria, who was jealous of her influence over the prefect of police. The church historian Socrates records how Cyril had her brutally murdered, bringing the greatest opprobrium not only upon himself but also upon the church in Alexandria.[27]

The Middle Ages

Thomas Aquinas followed Aristotle in seeing the female as a defective male.[28] His explanation reflected the current state of biological knowledge, and did little to change existing attitudes. Thomas explained that the defect did not apply to "the species as a whole." However, he conjectured that the active seed of the male which produced a female might be defective or damaged in some way. Thomas saw life as hierarchically ordered, with man placed above all other creatures, having been given the "nobler function . . . of understanding things." Woman had been created to help man, not by doing work which a man could do, but by helping him in procreation. The woman had originally been formed from man's rib as a symbol of companionship.[29] If she had been taken from his head, she would have had authority over man; if she had been taken from his feet, she would have been his slave.

In the Middle Ages women found themselves marginalized in the affairs of church and society.[30] The options open to them were severely limited. In the early and central Middle Ages especially, their acquaintance with the world of learning came through the religious life of the cloister. A number of women emerged as spiritual writers and mystics. Some of their writings indicate a profound grasp of philosophical issues. However, this grasp appears not in the form of treatises of the kind written by the theologians of the church, but in contemplative works which approached the great questions of life in a spiritual key. The cloistered life was a way open to the daughters of the aristocracy, some of whom found it a welcome alternative to a loveless marriage and a life of childbearing. To middle-class women medieval society offered no recognized role except marriage. However, widows and spinsters from the middle class found outlet in the late Middle Ages in the form of marginal movements like the Beguines.[31] Some Beguines lived with their families, while others lived as wandering mendicants. Most of them formed unofficial religious communities, sharing a passionate desire for intense mystical experience.

Among the early medieval nuns who were philosophers are the dramatist Hrotsvith of Gandersheim (c. 935-1001), the mystic Hildegard of Bingen (1098-1179), and the abbess Heloise (c. 1101-1164).[32] The writings of the English mystic

Julian of Norwich (c. 1342-c. 1413) suggest that she was familiar with the thought of Aquinas. Her mysticism is, however, closer to Neoplatonism, Scotus and Occam. Julian lived at the time of the Black Death, when waves of the bubonic plague swept across Europe. She lived a contemplative life, dwelling in a small cell built into the wall of St. Julian's Church in Norwich. She taught that Divine love, which transcends human reason, provides the key to the problems of human existence. Her references to God as "our Mother" anticipate feminist theology by five hundred years. Little is known about her life. Her reputation as a spiritual teacher rests on her *Sixteen Revelations of Divine Love* or *Showings*, as she preferred to call them.[33] The description that she gives of herself as "a woman, lewd, feeble and frail" is seen by scholars as an attempt, perhaps ironical, to parry criticism by the male clergy.[34] In justification of her writing she asked whether, because she was a woman, she should not tell of the love of God. When people see God's goodness, they will forget her and contemplate Jesus, who is everyone's teacher.

The Age of the Renaissance and of the Reformation

Although traditional notions of the subordinate role of women continued, the status and lot of women slowly began to change in the Renaissance.[35] In Italy daughters of the aristocracy and the upper middle class were encouraged to acquire learning. Girls in such families received the same education as their brothers, but marriage or the cloister remained the main options for the educated woman. Some thirty women intellectuals have been identified in Renaissance Italy, among them Dorotea Bocchi (fl. 1390-1430), the daughter of a professor of medicine and moral philosophy, who succeeded her father at the University of Bologna.[36] At this time women were not allowed to attend classes in the university, but on rare occasions were granted doctorates and allowed to teach. Giovanni d'Andrea, the famous professor of canon law at Bologna, had several well-educated daughters. According to an anecdotal but well-attested story, his daughter Novella lectured in his absence, but behind a curtain lest the students be distracted.[37] In Spain Beatrix Galindo (1474-1534) taught philosophy, rhetoric and medicine at the University of Salamanca. Oliva de Nantes Barrera Sabuco (1562-1625) wrote a treatise on *New Philosophy* (1587) which was destroyed by the Inquisition but later republished.

The Reformation era saw women play prominent parts on both the Protestant and Catholic sides.[38] Through accident of birth several women found themselves as monarchs shaping the destiny of nations. A number of women were martyred for their outspoken testimony. The education of women continued to be a low priority except where Renaissance ideals and privilege enabled the daughters of the titled and wealthy to be tutored alongside their brothers. The topics studied brought the writings of classical antiquity once more to the fore. In England Sir Thomas More (1478-1535), who was Lord Chancellor under King Henry VIII, advocated a classical education for daughters of the aristocracy. His own daughters received the same education as their brothers. His eldest daughter, Margaret Roper (1505-1544), is reputed to have been the first learned woman in England. Two of the wives of Henry VIII were noted for their learning, Catherine of Aragon and Catherine Parr. His daughter Elizabeth I (1533-1603) was the most learned of the English queens. She spoke fluent Latin, and translated numerous works from Greek, Latin and French, including *The Consolation of Philosophy* by Boethius. She also wrote a commentary on Plato.[39]

In the year that Elizabeth I assumed the English throne the Scottish Reformer John Knox delivered *The First Blast of the Trumpet Against the Monstrous Regiment of Women* (1558). The blast was directed against Mary of Guise, but it was felt equally by her daughter Mary Stuart, who assumed the Scottish throne in 1561, and by Elizabeth I. Knox's opening words leave no doubt as to where he stood: "To promote a Woman to beare rule, superioritie, dominion, or empire above any Realme, Nation, or Citie, is repugnant to Nature; contumlie to God, a thing most contrarious to his reveled will and approved ordinance; and finallie, it is the subversion of good Order, of all equitie and justice."[40] Despite this, Knox was not the anti-feminist that he has been made out to be. His correspondence with numerous women, especially Mrs. Anna Lock of London, shows his respect for their wisdom and spiritual counsel, and deep pastoral concern.[41]

Women, including Luther's wife, the former nun Katherine von Bora, played a significant part in the Lutheran and other churches.[42] There were also female "preachers" in the Catholic Reformation,[43] though they did not receive much encouragement. The papal nuncio Sega described the Carmelite nun and mystic Teresa of Avila as "a restless, gadabout, disobedient, contumacious woman who promulgates pernicious doctrine under pretense of devotion. . . . She is ambitious and teaches theology as if she were a doctor of the Church in spite of St. Paul's prohibition."[44] Evidently he took 1 Timothy 2:12 to be a blanket prohibition, as many have done before and after him.[45] In this respect the papal nuncio might have found himself in agreement with Calvin, who believed that teaching (apart from family instruction) was an office committed only to men.[46] With regard to the status of women in general Calvin was ambivalent.[47] On the one hand, he defended the subordination of women as part of the divinely constituted order of creation. On the other hand, he believed that with the passing of the present order women like men would be renewed in the image of God.

Rationalism, Empiricism and the Age of Enlightenment

The year following the death of Calvin saw the birth of Marie le Jars de Gournay (1565-1645).[48] While still in her teens she was struck by Montaigne's *Essays,* and became obsessed by a desire to know their author. During the last four years of Montaigne's life (1588-1592) she became his "spiritual daughter." She devoted the rest of her life to editing his works and defending his views.

In the seventeenth century female participation in intellectual affairs was confined to a relatively small number of royalty, aristocracy and the privileged. University education remained beyond reach. Queen Christina of Sweden (1626-1689) carried on a philosophical correspondence with Descartes. She not only studied his writings, but required her advisors to do so as well. The queen brought Descartes to her court for personal instruction. But the 5 a.m. lessons (held at that hour because the queen's mind was then at its freshest and she was less likely to be disturbed) and the rigors of the Scandinavian winter brought about the philosopher's premature death. Princess Elisabeth of Bohemia (1618-1680) was a German disciple of Descartes with whom she had a lifelong correspondence. Descartes dedicated his *Principles of Philosophy* (1644) to her.[49] In later life she became the abbess of Hervorden Convent.

An acquaintance and contemporary of Descartes was the Dutch scholar Anna Maria van Schurman (1607-1678), who in the course of her career made a pilgrimage from feminism to pietism.[50] She had been tutored with her brothers, and was taught Greek and Hebrew by Voetius, the professor of oriental languages and theology at Utrecht where she spent most of her life. Known as "the star of Utrecht" and "the Minerva of Holland," she had a phenomenal command of languages and was probably the most erudite woman of the age. Her Latin *Dissertation on the Natural Capacity of Women for the Sciences* (1638) defended the Bible from the charge of anti-feminism.[51] She joined issue with Lecretia Marinella's *The Nobility and Excellence of Woman* (1600), which had argued for the superiority of women over men, and the more moderate essay of Marie le Jars de Gournay on *The Equality of Men and Women* (1622). Anna Maria van Schurman preferred not to address the question of equality, being content to argue the issue of education. She had a firsthand knowledge of Descartes and his thought. But her mistrust fostered by Voetius was intensified when Descartes published his *Discourse on Method* (1637). The break became final when Descartes suggested that there were no "clear and distinct ideas" in the Bible. In later years she came to think that Tertullian was right when he said that Christianity has nothing to do with philosophy. She joined an extreme pietistic sect, and found refuge from persecution with her friend, Elisabeth of Bohemia.

In France women disciples of Descartes became known as "femmes philosophes." Among them was Mme. Grignan, daughter of the celebrated letter writer Mme. de Sévigné.[52] Molière's comedy *Les Femmes Savantes* (1672) addressed the contemporary debate about equality and education, poking fun at the pretensions of would-be learned women. When women were not made fun of on account of their pretensions, they were apt to be treated as unique prodigies and ornaments to be admired. They owed their education to the good fortune of being born into families of title and wealth, or to having scholars as fathers. Denied the opportunity of university education and membership of elite bodies like the Académie Française and the Royal Society, educated society women surmounted the problem through their patronage of the salon where the titled, the brilliant and the not-so-brilliant could converse. In eighteenth-century England cultured women were given the nickname of "blue stocking," though the term originally included men, indicating eccentricities of dress and behavior. French government decrees of 1609 and 1724 required the appointment of male and female teachers in all parishes, and education up to the age of fourteen became in theory compulsory for all. But the decrees were never fully enforced, and it was not until the nineteenth century that women were admitted in France and elsewhere to universities and centers of higher learning.

In England university education was confined to the privileged. Graduates of the two universities of Oxford and Cambridge had to be male members of the Church of England. The majority of the fellows of their constituent colleges had to be ordained clergymen. Women who were fortunate enough to receive a good education acquired it through tutors. Inevitably this was a privilege of the relatively affluent. A number of titled women were deeply interested in philosophy and science.[53] Among them was Margaret Cavendish (1623-1673), wife of the Marquis and later Duke of Newcastle. Along with Thomas Hobbes, the couple belonged to a group of English royalist émigrés known as "the Newcastle circle" which resided in Paris during the 1640s. During this period they got to know Descartes and Gassendi. With the restoration of Charles II to the English throne, the Cavendishes returned to England. Lady Margaret's eccentricities earned her the nickname of "Mad Madge." She sought to popularize atomism in crude verse which she published under the title of *Poems and Fancies* (1653), and later advocated a mechanistic view of the world in *Grounds of Natural Philosophy* (1668).

A woman scholar who is taken more seriously is Anne Viscountess Conway (1631-1679). Like Margaret Cavendish, she was privately tutored and self-educated. Her posthumous work on *The Principles of the Most Ancient and Modern Philosophy* (1690)[54] influenced Leibniz and anticipated some of Wittgenstein's ideas. She was well acquainted with ancient philosophy as well as with the thought of Descartes, Hobbes and Spinoza. She was a personal friend of the Cambridge Platonist Henry More. Her own philosophy was a form of vitalism, arguing that nature was a unity of spirit and matter, with Christ an intermediary between God and nature.

Another learned English woman was Lady Damaris Masham (1658-1708). She was educated in the classical tradition by her father, the Cambridge Platonist Ralph Cudworth. However, she became a disciple of John Locke, whom she first met in 1682. After an initial romantic involvement, the relationship became a lifelong friendship, and Locke spent the last thirteen years of his life as a paying guest in the home of Lord and Lady Masham. She defended Locke's Christian empiricism against the attacks of the Platonist and feminist Mary Astell,[55] and wrote a biography of Locke. Lady Masham was one of several women disciples of Locke. Others were Catherine Trotter Cockburn (1679-1749), Lady Mary

Chudleigh (1656-1710), Lady Mary Wortley Montagu (1689-1762), and Hannah More (1745-1833).[56]

The first woman to receive a doctorate in philosophy was Elena Lucrezia Cornaro Pisciopia (1640-1684) who received her degree from the University of Padua after giving a public defense of two theses from Aristotle dealing with logic and science.[57] In the eighteenth century a number of notable women made significant contributions to science and philosophy. Laura Maria Caterna Bassi (1711-1778) was awarded a doctorate by the University of Bologna for a dissertation on Cartesian thought and an oral defense of propositions from Aristotle. She taught philosophy and physics at the university until her death. Maria Gaetana Agnesi (1718-1799) was a saintly scholar who held the chair of philosophy at Bologna for some years, after which she retired in order to devote her life to the care of the sick and poor. Her *Analytical Institutions* (1748), which treated the thought of Newton and Leibniz, was translated into French and English.

In Germany Sophie (1630-1714), the younger sister of Elisabeth of Bohemia who became Electress of Hanover and mother of George I of England, was interested in philosophy and theology. She was an admirer of Leibniz who was her teacher and adviser. Her daughter, Queen Sophie Charlotte of Prussia (1668-1705), for whom the Berlin district of Charlottenburg was named, was also a patron and disciple of Leibniz. She encouraged her husband to create the Berlin Academy of Sciences (1700) with Leibniz as perpetual president. In Russia, Catherine the Great (1729-1796), who came from German stock, was a philosophical disciple of the French Encyclopedists. She sought to foster French culture in her adopted country, and had a profound admiration for Voltaire with whom she carried on a lengthy correspondence. On his death she acquired the philosopher's library which was brought to St. Petersburg.

In eighteenth-century France especially women began to play a major part in the worlds of art, learning, science and politics.[58] Perhaps the most accomplished woman scientist and philosopher was Mme. du Châtelet (1706-1749) who married the Marquis du Châtelet at the age of twenty and after seven years of marriage entered a liaison with Voltaire which endured for the rest of her life.[59] Her major work, *Institutions of Physics* (1740), rejected Locke's empiricism in favor of Leibniz's metaphysics as a better basis for Newtonian physics. Mme. Roland (1754-1793)[60] was a woman intellectual who was thoroughly conversant with contemporary philosophy. She was attracted to atheism, but came to believe in a form of natural religion. Rousseau's writings turned her thoughts to revolutionary politics. She was one of the women guillotined in the French Revolution, and is remembered for her cry : "O Liberty, what crimes are committed in thy name!" Her younger contemporary, Mme. de Staël (1766-1817), was also a political activist, achieving fame in the salons of revolutionary France. Her father was a Swiss banker and finance minister to King Louis XVI. She was tutored by her mother along the lines of Rousseau's *Émile*. She wrote a number of novels and treatises, including *Germany* (1810), in which she reviewed the current state of literature and philosophy. Mme. de Staël was exiled by Napoleon who clamped down on the political activities of women. In so doing he was consolidating a move which had begun already during the Revolution, and which in fact coincided with the outlook of Rousseau. The latter had exalted women, but for their wifely and maternal roles, but excluded them from the civil, political and economic activities that he championed for men. In so doing, the advocate of enlightenment reverted to a form of patriarchalism in which women were qualitatively different but still subordinate to men.[61]

Retrospect

This brief survey has tried to take note of the roles that women have played (and been denied) in this history of Western thought. One does not have to be a militant feminist to recognize the ways in which women have been marginalized in intellectual life. The exceptional achievements of a number of women serve to highlight the fact that they were exceptions rather than the rule. Here as in other matters the church reflected society at large. Over the centuries the church has been confronted by countless issues and numerous philosophies, and has had to work through them in order to articulate its faith and its mission. The apostle Paul wrote to the Galatian church that there is neither Jew nor Greek, slave nor free person, male nor female, for all are one in Christ Jesus. The church is still working on the implications of this agenda.

Notes

[1]On women philosophers see Ethel M. Kersey and Calvin O. Schrag, Consulting Editors, *Women Philosophers: A Bio-Critical Source Book* (New York; Westport, Conn.; London: Greenwood Press, 1989); Mary Ellen Waithe, ed., *A History of Women Philosophers*, 1 *Ancient Women Philosophers 600 B.C.-500 A.D.*, 2 *Medieval, Renaissance and Enlightenment Philosophers, A.D. 500-1600* (Dordrecht, Boston, London: Kluwer Academic Publishers, 1987, 1989). For excerpts from philosophers giving their views on women see Mary Briody Mahowald, *Philosophy of Woman: Classical to Current Concepts* (Indianapolis: Hackett Publishing, 1978). On the role of women in the church see Ruth A. Tucker and Walter Liefeld, *Daughters of the Church: Women and Ministry from New Testament Times to the Present* (Grand Rapids: Zondervan Academie Books, 1987). Gilles Ménage (Aegidius Menagius), *Historia Mulierum Philosopharum* (1690) has been translated by Beatrice H. Zedler with the title *The History of Women Philosophers* (Lanham, Md: University Press of America, 1984).

[2]On education in the Greek world see Werner Jaeger, *Paideia: The Ideals of Greek Culture*, 3 vols. (New York: Oxford University Press, 2nd ed. 1945). On the role of women see John Peradotto and J. P. Sullivan, eds., *Women in the Ancient World: The Arethusa Papers* (Albany: State University of New York Press, 1984); Helene

P. Foley, ed., *Reflections of Women in Antiquity* (New York, London, Paris: Gordon and Breach Science Publishers, 1981); Sarah B. Pomeroy, *Goddesses, Whores, Wives and Slaves: Women in Classical Antiquity* (New York: Schocken Books, 1975), and *Women in Hellenistic Egypt: From Alexander to Cleopatra* (New York: Schocken Books, 1984); Judith P. Hallett, *Fathers and Daughters in Roman Society* (Princeton: Princeton University Press, 1984).

³Diogenes Laertius, *Lives and Opinions of Eminent Philosophers* 6.7 (Loeb edition, 2:99-103).

⁴*Symposium* 201d-212b (*Dialogues,* pp. 553-63).

⁵*Republic* 5. (*Dialogues,* pp. 688-720), see above, chapter 2, n. 4. Women were theoretically allowed to perform the same work as men, including service in the army. They could also exercise in the gymnasium and compete in games.

⁶*Laws* 6.781b (*Dialogues,* p. 1356). See further Dorothea Wender, "Plato: Misogynist, Paedophile, and Feminist" in Peradotto and Sullivan, eds., *Women in the Ancient World,* pp. 213-28; Susan Moller Okin, *Women in Western Political Thought,* pp. 15-70.

⁷*Parts of Animals* 2.648a14 (*Works* 1:1008).

⁸*History of Animals* 9.1.608a22-24 (*Works* 1:948).

⁹*Generation of Animals* 2.3.737a27-30 (*Works* 1:1144).

¹⁰*Generation of Animals* 2.4.738b20-27 (*Works* 1:1146).

¹¹See Aristotle's discussion of education in *Politics* 7.17-8.1-7.1336a3-1342b34 (*Works* 2:2119-2129); cf. Okin, *Women in Western Political Thought,* pp. 73-96.

¹²See Joan Chamberlain Engelsman, *The Feminine Dimension of the Divine* (Philadelphia: Westminster Press, 1979); Christine Downing, *The Goddess: Mythological Images of the Feminine* (New York: Crossroad, 1981); Judith Ochshorn, *The Female Experience and the Nature of the Divine* (Bloomington: Indiana University Press, 1981); Carl Olson, ed., *The Book of the Goddess: Past and Present* (New York: Crossroad, 1983); Pamela Berger, *The Goddess Obscured: Transformation of the Grain Protectress from Goddess to Saint* (Boston: Beacon Press, 1985); P. E. Easterling and J. V. Muir, eds., *Greek Religion and Society* (Cambridge: Cambridge University Press, 1985); R. M. Grant, *Gods and the One God,* Library of Early Christianity (Philadelphia: Westminster Press, 1986); David Kinsley, *The Goddesses' Mirror: Visions of the Divine from East and West* (Albany: State University of New York Press, 1989); Richard Caldwell, *The Origin of the Gods: A Psychoanalytic Study of Greek Theogonic Myth* (New York, Oxford: Oxford University Press, 1989).

¹³The God of the Old Testament is the God of Abraham, Isaac and Jacob, who has bound Israel to himself through covenants made with the patriarchs which were renewed on successive occasions. Only men could be priests, and only men could receive the covenant sign of circumcision. However, a number of exceptional women figure in the story of Israel. Three outstanding prophets are mentioned: Miriam (Ex 15:20-21); Deborah (Judg 4:4-6); and Huldah (2 Kgs

22:14-20). Other prominent women include Ruth and Esther who are the central figures in the books that bear their name. Occasionally, God is depicted in female imagery (Num 11:12; Deut 32:18; Is 42:14; 46:3-4; Jer 31:22; Hos 11:1-4). Wisdom is depicted as a woman (Prov 3:13-18; 4:5-13; 8:22-31). See further Barbara J. MacHaffie, *Her Story: Women in Christian Tradition* (Philadelphia: Fortress Press, 1986); Rosemary Ruether and Eleanor McLaughlin, eds., *Women of Spirit: Female Leadership in the Jewish and Christian Traditions* (New York: Simon and Schuster, 1979).

[14]On women in the New Testament see Ben Witherington, *Women in the Ministry of Jesus: A Study of Jesus' Attitudes to Women and Their Roles as Reflected in His Earthly Life*, Society for New Testament Studies Monograph Series 51 (Cambridge: Cambridge University Press, 1984); Witherington, *Women in the Earliest Churches*, Society for New Testament Studies Monograph Series 59 (Cambridge: Cambridge University Press, 1988).

[15]See (e.g.) Matthew 27:55-56, 61; 28:1-10; Mark 15:40-41; 16:1-8; Luke 8:1-3; 23:55—24:11, 24; John 20:1-18. The Gospels represent them as the first witnesses to Jesus' resurrection. Jewish tradition would not accept the testimony of women as witnesses, which may account for Paul's omission of the women in his reference to the appearances of the risen Christ (1 Cor 15:4-7).

[16]On the influence of Genesis 3 on thought see Elaine Pagels, *Adam, Eve, and the Serpent* (New York: Random House, 1988).

[17]Junia(s) was almost certainly the wife of Andronicus who is mentioned with her. Although it has often been assumed that Junias was male, there are no other instances of Junias as a male name (J. D. G. Dunn, *Romans 9-16*, p. 894).

[18]See above, p. 100; Elaine Pagels, *The Gnostic Gospels* (New York: Random House, 1979), pp. 48-69; Jorunn Jacobsen Buckley, *Female Fault and Fulfilment in Gnosticism* (Chapel Hill, London: University of North Carolina Press, 1986).

[19]For accounts of women in the patristic church see G. H. Tavard, *Woman in Christian Tradition* (Notre Dame: University of Notre Dame Press, 1973); Jean Laporte, *The Role of Women in Early Christianity* (New York, Toronto: Edwin Mellon Press, 1982); Elisabeth Schüssler Fiorenza, *In Memory of Her: A Feminist Theological Reconstruction of Christian Origins* (New York: Crossroad, 1983). In the late patristic period women figure prominently in asceticism (Rosemary Ruether, "Mothers of the Church: Ascetic Women in the Late Patristic Age" in *Women of Spirit*, pp. 71-98).

[20]See Tucker and Liefeld, *Daughters of the Church*, p. 100.

[21]Augustine even had to argue against those who appealed to Ephesians 4:13 and Romans 8:29 in support of the contention that women would lose their sexual identity in the resurrection (*City of God* 22.17). He replied that God who made us male and female would raise us up male and female. Augustine's own views reflect the influence of Plato as mediated by Plotinus. For extracts from Augustine, *The Trinity* 12 and other discussions of women and marriage see Ma-

howald, ed., *Philosophy of Woman*, pp. 71-77.

[22]Philostratus, *The Life of Apollonius of Tyana*, Greek text with English translation by F. C. Conybeare, 2 vols. Loeb Classical Library (Cambridge, Massachusetts: Harvard University Press; London: Heinemann, 1912). On the role of this work in anti-Christian polemics see above, p. 205.

[23]Porphyry, *The Life of Plotinus* 9 (cited from *Plotinus* [Loeb Classical Library] 1:31).

[24]Jay Bregman, *Synesius of Cyrene: Philosopher-Bishop* (Berkeley, Los Angeles, London: University of California Press, 1982), pp. 20, 22, 36-39.

[25]Bregman, *Synesius*, p. 156, citing *Epistle* 105.

[26]Extracts in Waithe, *A History of Women Philosophers* 1: 169-95.

[27]*Historia Ecclesiastica* 7.15.

[28]*Summa Theologiae* 1 Q. 92 art. 1 (Blackfriars edition 13:35); alluding to Aristotle, *Generation of Animals* 2.3 737a27 (*Works* 1:1144).

[29]*Summa Theologiae* 1 Q. 92, art. 3 (Blackfriars edition 13:43); cf. Genesis 2: 22).

[30]See Joan Morris, *The Lady Was a Bishop: The Hidden History of Women with Clerical Ordination and the Jurisdiction of Bishops* (New York: Macmillan; London: Collier-Macmillan, 1973); reprint under the title *Against Nature and God: The History of Women with Clerical Ordination and the Jurisdiction of Bishops* (London, Oxford: Mowbrays, 1974); Rosmarie Thee Morewedge, ed., *The Role of Women in the Middle Ages* (Albany: State University of New York Press, 1975); Eileen Power, ed., *Medieval Women* (Cambridge: Cambridge University Press, 1975); Susan Mosher Stuard, ed., *Women in Medieval Society* (University of Pennsylvania Press, 1976); Katharina M. Wilson, ed., *Medieval Women Writers* (Athens, Ga: University of Georgia Press, 1984); Patricia H. Labalme, ed., *Beyond Their Sex: Learned Women of the European Past* (New York: New York University Press, 1980).

[31]See Norman Cohn, *The Pursuit of the Millennium* (London: Secker & Warburg, 1957), pp. 166-68.

[32]Heloise was seduced by her tutor, Peter Abelard, who was castrated by her uncle's servants. Heloise took the veil, and Abelard became a monk. They met some ten years later, and Abelard helped her to establish a convent. Her correspondence with Abelard shows her to have been a woman of considerable learning. Abelard observed that she was a woman "wholly dedicated to philosophy in the true sense," but that she had "left logic for the Gospel, Plato for Christ and the academy for the cloister" (*Letters of Abelard and Heloise* [Harmondsworth: Penguin Books, 1974], p. 278).

[33]Julian of Norwich, *Showings*, The Classics of Western Spirituality (New York, Ramsey, Toronto: Paulist Press, 1978).

[34]Waithe, *A History of Women Philosophers* 2:192; cf. short text in *Showings* 6 (p. 135) from which the following quotation is taken.

[35]See Ian Maclean, *The Renaissance Notion of Woman: A Study in the Fortunes of Scholasticism and Medical Science in European Intellectual Life* (Cambridge: Cam-

bridge University Press, 1980); Labalme, ed., *Beyond Their Sex,* passim; Retha M. Warnicke, *Women of the English Renaissance and Reformation,* Contributions in Women's Studies 38 (Westport, Conn.; London: Greenwood Press, 1983).

[36]Kersey, *Women Philosophers,* p. 8.

[37]Oskar Kristeller, "Learned Women of Early Modern Italy: Humanists and University Scholars," in Labalme, ed., *Beyond Their Sex* (pp. 91-116), p. 102.

[38]See Roland H. Bainton, *Women of the Reformation in Germany and Italy* (Minneapolis: Augsburg Publishing House, 1971); Bainton, *Women of the Reformation in France and England* (Minneapolis: Augsburg Publishing House, 1973); Bainton, *Women of the Reformation from France to Scandinavia* (Minneapolis: Augsburg Publishing House, 1977); Joyce L. Irwin, *Womanhood in Radical Protestantism, 1525-1675* (New York, Toronto: Edwin Mellon Press, 1979); Warnicke, *Women of the English Renaissance and Reformation,* passim.

[39]Hersey, *Women Philosophers,* p. 10; Paul Johnson, *Elizabeth I: A Biography* (New York: Holt, Rinehart and Winston, 1974), pp.16-20. Elizabeth's tutors included Dr. Richard Cox, Provost of Eton, and several Cambridge scholars, including Sir John Cheke, Regius Professor of Greek and later Master of St. John's College, who was a key figure in the English Reformation and Renaissance.

The ill-fated Lady Jane Grey (1537-1554), who, along with her husband, Guildford Dudley, was beheaded following an abortive plan to make her Queen of England, was reputed to have been an accomplished scholar.

[40]Knox, *The Monstrous Regiment of Women* (*The Works of John Knox,* 6 vols., ed. David Laing [Edinburgh: James Thin, 1845] 4:374).

[41]See *Works* vol 6 for Knox's letters, including more temperate, solicitous correspondence with Queen Elizabeth I. Vol. 3 contains correspondence with Knox's mother-in-law and her daughter, Elizabeth, and Marjory Bowes, revealing his deep pastoral concern.

[42]Bainton, *Women of the Reformation in Germany and Italy,* pp. 19-164; Tucker and Liefeld, *Daughters of the Church,* pp. 171-200.

[43]Tucker and Liefeld, *Daughters of the Church,* pp. 200-206.

[44]Quotation from Bainton, *Women of the Reformation from Spain to Scandinavia,* p. 56. As a spiritual writer, Teresa was the first to draw attention to different states of prayer, and to give a careful description of the life of prayer from meditation to so-called mystic marriage. Recent editions of her writings include *The Interior Castle,* introduction by Kieran Kavannaugh, *The Classics of Western Spirituality* (New York, Ramsey, Toronto: Paulist Press, 1979); and *A Life of Prayer,* ed. James M. Houston, introduction by Clayton L. Berg (Portland, Oregon: Multnomah Press, 1983).

[45]For discussion of theological issues see Paul K. Jewett, *Man as Male and Female: A Study of Sexual Relationships from a Theological Point of View* (Grand Rapids: Eerdmans, 1975); Jewett, *The Ordination of Women: An Essay on the Office of Christian Ministry* (Grand Rapids: Eerdmans, 1980); Willard M. Swartley, *Slavery,*

Sabbath, War and Women: Case Issues in Biblical Interpretation (Scottdale, PA, and Kitchener, Ontario: Herald Press, 1983).

[46]*Commentaries on the Epistles to Timothy, Titus, and Philemon* (reprint ed., Grand Rapids: Eerdmans, 1948), p. 67.

[47]For Calvin's views see Jane Dempsey Douglass, *Women, Freedom and Calvin* (Philadelphia: Westminster Press, 1985); John L. Thompson, *"Creata ad Imaginem Dei, Licet Secundo Gradu:* Woman as the Image of God according to John Calvin," *Harvard Theological Review* 81 (1988): 125-43.

[48]Marjorie H. Isley, *A Daughter of the Renaissance: Marie le Jars de Gournay, Her Life and Works* (The Hague: Mouton, 1963).

[49]Descartes, *Philosophical Writings* (ed. Cottingham et al.) 1: 177-291; Dedicatory Letter, pp. 190-92. For the exchange of letters dealing with the relation of soul and body, and with conditions for good judgment see *Philosophical Writings,* ed. Anscombe and Geach, pp. 274-86.

[50]See Kersey, *Women Philosophers,* p. 188; J. Irwin, "Anna Marie van Schurman: From Feminism to Pietism," *Church History* 46 (1977): 48-62.

[51]The work appeared in English under the title of *The Learned Maid, or Whether a Maid May Be a Scholar* (1659). She wrote an autobiography, *Eukleria* (1673), and published her correspondence.

[52]*Letters from Madame la Marquise de Sévigné,* trans. and ed. Violet Hammersley (New York: Harcourt, Brace, 1956). A number of the letters discuss Cartesianism.

[53]See Gerald D. Meyer, *The Scientific Lady in England, 1650-1760* (Berkeley, Los Angeles, London: University of California Press, 1955); Robert Hugh Kargon, *Atomism in England from Hariot to Newton* (Oxford: Clarendon Press, 1966); Hilda Smith, *Reason's Disciples: Seventeenth-Century English Feminists* (Urbana: University of Illinois Press, 1982). For details of writings see Hilda L. Smith and Susan Cardinale, *Woman and the Literature of the Seventeenth Century: An Annotated Bibliography Based on Wing's Short-title Catalogue* (New York: Westport, CT, London: Greenwood Press, 1990).

[54]Latin text and English translation with an introduction by Peter Lopston (The Hague: Martinus Nijhoff, 1982).

[55]On Mary Astell (1666-1731) see Ruth Perry, *The Celebrated Mary Astell: An Early English Feminist* (Chicago: Chicago University Press, 1987). For a brief account of the controversy see Kersey, *Women Philosophers,* pp. 47-49, 154-56.

[56]Sheryl O'Donnell, "Mr. Locke and the Ladies: The Indelible Words on the Tabula Rasa," *Studies in Eighteenth Century Culture* 8 (1979): 151-64; Kersey, *Women Philosophers,* pp. 78, 79-81.

[57]Kersey, *Women Philosophers,* p. 85; Paul Oskar Kristeller, "Learned Women of Early Modern Italy: Humanists and University Scholars;" and Patricia Labalme, "Women's Roles in Early Modern Venice: An Exceptional Case," in Labalme, ed., *Beyond Their Sex,* pp. 91-116; 129-52.

[58]See Samia I. Spencer, ed., *French Women and the Age of Enlightenment* (Bloomington: Indiana University Press, 1984).

[59]Ira Owen Wade, *Voltaire and Mme. du Châtelet: An Essay on the Intellectual Activity at Cirey* (Princeton: Princeton University Press, 1941); Wade, *Studies on Voltaire with Some Unpublished Papers of Mme. du Châtelet* (Princeton: Princeton University Press, 1947); Linda Gardner, "Women in Science," in Spencer, ed., *French Women and the Age of Enlightenment*, pp. 181-93.

[60]Gita May, *Madame Roland and the Age of Revolution* (New York: Columbia University Press, 1970).

[61]Claire G. Moses in *French Women and the Age of Enlightenment*, p. 409; cf. Gita May, "Rousseau's 'Antifeminism' Reconsidered," pp. 309-17; Susan Moller Okin, *Women in Western Political Thought*, pp. 99-194.

Select Index

Knit Something
SPECIAL

Knit Something SPECIAL

A Gift for Every Occasion

Polly Pyne

Photography: Janet C. Patricoski
Sketches: Katherine Pyne

CROWN PUBLISHERS, INC.
NEW YORK

Published by Crown Publishers, Inc., One Park Avenue, New York, New
York 10016, and simultaneously in Canada by General Publishing
Company Limited

Manufactured in the United States of America

LIBRARY OF CONGRESS CATALOGING IN PUBLICATION DATA

Pyne, Polly.
  Knit something special.

  1. Knitting.   I. Title.
TT820.P95 1984   746.43'2   83-15286
ISBN 0-517-55258-2
ISBN 0-517-55259-0 (pbk.)

10 9 8 7 6 5 4 3 2 1

First Edition

CONTENTS

Author's Note

Knitting is a year-round avocation. It need not be
restricted solely to preparation for warmth during the
cold months. Knitters who live in areas where snug
mittens and scarves are rarely required should have
projects too. You will find that the majority of the
patterns in this book are for gifts not limited to
cold-weather use. I want you to benefit from the pas-
time of knitting, to learn the satisfaction of creativity,
the pleasure in giving something you made yourself.

INTRODUCTION AND GENERAL INFORMATION

1

Hello! Welcome to the happy world of knitted-gift giving. How nice it would be if you and I were together to exchange our thoughts, ideas, and ambitions in knitting.

So that I may declare myself an authority, so that you may judge whether to take what I say as gospel, let me tell you about myself. I was born into a family of needleworkers. My mother, both grandmothers, an aunt, great-aunts, and some uncles were capable handworkers. My father hooked many a rug. I married into a family of knitters. I had a yarn shop in our home, with the aid of an outstanding crew, until our older children entered their teens. I then began selling patterns to hand-knitting-yarn companies and craft magazines. When our younger children were no longer babies, I taught knitting and crochet classes, and the other teachers for a chain of department stores. I have developed and copyrighted some needlecraft courses and am currently teaching adult education classes.

There may be much here that you already know about knitting, or more than you think you care to know, but I do hope that you will garner some bits of information that will give you more pleasure in your creative work.

If you are learning to knit, I am so glad you have asked for my help. There are many projects included for you. As you progress and gain courage and try more advanced projects, you will learn new techniques. I cannot avoid my

desire to teach, so there are presented not only a range of projects, but a variety of methods. For instance, there are sweaters made in pieces to be sewn together and sweaters made all in one from the top or from the back ribbing, requiring only that side or sleeve seams be sewn. There are mittens made on two needles, mittens made on four needles, and even mittens made sideways.

In the gift chapters, except the one for holidays, projects are in increasing order of ability or knowledge. Because it is easier to learn when it is pertinent, many of the hints are given where they apply.

The yarn-required amounts are generous. It is better to have extra yarn than not enough.

Make notes in your book by each project you knit. Include for whom it was made, the size, how it fit, the brand name and amount of yarn used, and your own ideas for possible variations. I also urge you to read through each pattern and the hints before you start, to gain a perspective on what you are making.

I give you my knitting time on some of the patterns. Since I have been knitting for 137 years, my speed is good and I already know the patterns. If you have not done much knitting, you may want to double the hours in estimating your time. But remember, your knitting time is often that otherwise used to rest your body or to occupy your mind. You are making double use of your leisure by keeping your fingers busy.

Do you know that doctors often recommend knitting to calm nerves? There are many of us who can attest to how well it works.

Gift Giving

When you present someone with a gift you have made, you are giving of yourself, your time and your thoughts. You want your gift to be suitable. If it is apparel, it must fit and be in a color that blends into the wardrobe of the recipient. Remember use and care. A sweater to keep someone warm should be made of wool. A toy for a baby should be made with a synthetic yarn that can withstand frequent washing. A house gift should be in accord with the decor.

It is especially thoughtful to include the yarn label, or that part of it which contains the fiber content and washing instructions. You also prove how very considerate you are when you include a yard or so of the yarn, in case a repair becomes necessary. With a garment that buttons, sew an extra button inside, on the left seam a few inches above the bottom.

Yarn

There are so many different manufacturers producing so many varieties of yarn that it has become difficult to write directions that will work all the time. Therefore, I give you the traditional names and the standard yardages per weight.

Baby yarn	1 ounce = 200 yards
3-ply fingering yarn	1 ounce = 180 yards
Sport weight yarn	2 ounces = 210 yards
4-ply worsted weight yarn	4 ounces = 270 to 280 yards
Average bulky yarn	2 ounces = 270 to 280 yards

Look for yardages on yarn labels. When you want to repeat a project, if your gauge is the same, total yardage can be helpful in figuring the amount of yarn required, especially if you substitute a different yarn.

There are many interesting imported yarns. On most of them the information on the labels is in the metric system. There are 28 grams in an ounce. One hundred grams is 3.53 ounces. One meter is 39.4 inches, and 100 meters is about 110 yards. An inch is equal to 2.54 centimeters.

Wool that has been well spun is the easiest yarn to use in knitting. It has a good spring, which enables you to knit more evenly and to slide the stitches more easily on your needles. It is rare, but should you find a yarn spun from reused wool, avoid it. (I am not advising you not to reuse yarn. Wool items many years old, if they have been well cared for, can be ripped, and the yarn washed in hanks and reknit with quite satisfactory results.)

Synthetic yarns are available in a wide variety of weights and twists. The quality varies. The best for knitting are those that closely resemble wool. Some are so good that it is hard to tell the difference. Before you purchase any synthetic, check the spring. Synthetic yarn should have built into it the crimp that occurs naturally in wool, so try pulling on a little bit of the yarn. You can do so without disturbing the skein or ball. It should have nice elasticity.

There are many very interesting blends of synthetic and natural fibers. Mixing wool or mohair with a synthetic adds warmth, and the mohair gives a fuzzy texture. Specialty yarns with loops or slubs often are more effective in reverse stockinette stitch.

Pilling, the formation of tiny balls on knitwear, is annoying. Pilling is more likely to occur with synthetics or very soft wools. To completely avoid pilling you have to use a sturdy worsted yarn. It is a trade-off. If you want a soft material, you must endure some pilling and learn the habit of pulling off the pills regularly.

Needles

Three styles of knitting needles are generally available in the United States. Straight single-point needles are made in plastic or aluminum. They come in 10" and 14" lengths, and the sizes run from 0, the smallest, to 19. There are larger specialty needles, such as broomstick-lace pins. Single-point needles are used in pairs except for broomstick pins, which are used singly with a crochet hook.

Double-point needles come in sets of 4 or occasionally 5. They are made in plastic or aluminum and are available in 7" and 10" lengths. The size range is 0 to 15.

Circular needles are made in plastic or aluminum with plastic cables. The sizes are from 0 to 15, and the lengths from 16″ to 36″. Circular needles are used for circular work, such as skirts and V necks, or projects for which you have too many stitches for 14″ needles, such as a one-piece afghan.

The size and length combinations are not complete. The smallest sizes are not always made in the longest lengths, nor are the largest sizes made in the shortest lengths.

Knitting-needle kits are available, consisting of a range of point sizes that can be fastened to various circular cable lengths or to cables with stops.

KNITTING NEEDLE CONVERSION CHART*

American	English	Metric (mm)
#0	#14	2
1	13	2¼
2	12	2¾
–	11	3
3	10	3¼
4	–	3½
5	9	3¾
–	8	4
6	–	4¼
7	7	4½
8	6	5
–	–	5¼
9	5	5½
–	–	5¾
10	4	6
10½	3	6½
–	2	7
–	1	7½
11	0	8
13	00	9
15	000	10

(mm measurements are diameters)

Abbreviations

Knitting
k—knit.
p—purl.
inc—increase.
dec—decrease.

*Courtesy C. J. Bates & Son.

tog—together.
yo—yarn over.
beg—beginning.
sl—slip.
st, sts—stitch, stitches.
sl st—slip stitch.
st st—stockinette stitch.
S (M, L)—Small (Medium, Large).
psso—pass slip stitch over.
SKP—slip, knit, pass.
sp—single-point needle or needles.
dp—double-point needle or needles.
MC—main color.
CC—contrast color.
AC—accent color.
CN—cable needle.
⊥—perpendicular.
#, no.—number.
″—inches.
′—feet
oz—ounce, ounces.

Crochet
ch—chain.
sl st—slip stitch.
sc—single crochet.
dc—double crochet.

Definitions

shape—increase or decrease.
ply—number of filaments twisted together to form a strand of yarn.
twist, Z or S—direction of the twist of the ply, which is in the same direction as the center of Z or S.
strand—full piece of yarn.
(right side), (wrong side)—given for information, not a direction.
row—in flat knitting, working from one edge to the other.
edge—beginning or end of row.
ridge—horizontal elevation formed by interlocking loops in knitting. Alternate sides in garter stitch, same side in stockinette stitch.
round—in circular knitting, once around.
around—repeat the direction for 1 round.
ring marker—a small ring kept on the needle to indicate a particular place.
side—front or back of work.

dye lot—yarn is dyed in batches. Dye lots are noted on the label, usually by number. Dye lots differ, so buy enough yarn to complete your project. In fact, it is often a good idea to buy more yarn than suggested. Most stores will allow you to return full skeins for cash or credit if you have saved the sales slip.

split stitch—by accident, to send the needle between the plies of the yarn instead of catching the full strand.

Procedures

garter stitch—in flat work, knit every row; in circular work, knit 1 round, purl 1 round.

stockinette stitch—in flat work, alternately knit 1 row and purl 1 row; in circular work, knit every round. When you are to begin working in stockinette, your first row is knit unless otherwise directed.

ribbing—alternating knit and purl stitches to make vertical rows in stockinette and reverse stockinette.

reverse stockinette—the side of stockinette with the ridges.

front (in front, to the front)—the side of your knitting facing you.

back (in back, to the back)—the side of your knitting away from you.

with yarn to front, to back—take the yarn between the points of the needles to the front, to the back.

*—the directions beginning after * to the word "repeat" are to be repeated as directed.

——the directions between the asterisks will be returned to later.

( ) 2 times—repeat the directions within the parentheses the number of times indicated, in this example twice.

S (M, L)—when the directions read "5 (6, 7) times," follow the directions 5 times when you are making the small size, 6 times for the medium size, and 7 times for the large size.

yo—when you are knitting, wrap the yarn around the right-hand needle the same as in working a stitch—between the needles, then over the right-hand needle.

⊥—Measure knitting vertically (length) at a right angle to the rows or rounds.

slip stitch—a stitch is slipped from one needle to the other without being worked. Slip as if to knit when the stitch is to be used again in the same row, such as SKP; slip as if to purl if the stitch is not to be used until the next row.

work even—continue without decreasing or increasing.

short row—to allow one part of your knitting to "grow" more than another, you sometimes use short rows. Work the row partway across, turn the knitting around, slip 1 stitch, and work back.

stitches that look like k or p—when a stitch is smooth and you can see a V, the stitch looks like knit; when you see an inverted U, the stitch looks like purl. This may or may not be how the stitch was made.

measuring—uncurl the edges and lay the work on a flat surface. Allow time for a synthetic yarn to rest and return to its normal shape.

how to alter pattern measurements—when you want to make a size larger or smaller than those given, measure your gauge. To find out how many stitches you need for the back, multiply the gauge by half the total desired chest or bust measurement. For example, 5 stitches per inch × ½ 40" (chest or bust) = 100 stitches. Note the increments given in the pattern. If the directions are "cast on 76 (84, 92)" and you want a larger size, increase by 8s until you are closest to the desired number. If the underarm bind-off is "3 (4, 5)," add 1 for each 8 added to the beginning. Add the same to the underarm decreases. For each 8 you have compensated 4. For the other 4, add 1 to each shoulder and 2 to the back of the neck. Remember to note the increments and add to the armhole depth. Whenever you increase the size, don't forget to purchase extra yarn of the same dye lot.

slip as if to knit—send the right-hand needle through the stitch on the left needle as if you were going to knit.

slip as if to purl—send the right-hand needle

KNOTS

slip

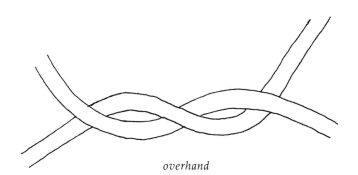

overhand

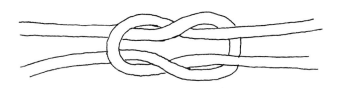

square

through the stitch on the left needle as if you were going to purl. Slip as if to purl when you are transferring stitches from one needle to another.

AT THE SAME TIME—directions written in small capital letters are an alert sign.

bind off, bind off loosely, bind off LOOSELY—increasingly important.

evenly spaced—spread evenly across the row or round.

mult (2), (4) + 1—Multiple of 2 must be an even number, (4) + 1, you must be able to divide the number by 4 and have a remainder of 1. When enlarging or reducing, do so in increments of the multiple.

HOW TO . . . .

Gauge

"I knit a sweater for my husband but it fit the Ford." This was the reason once given by a student for joining my knitting class. Disregard of the importance of gauge is a major factor in discouraging many knitters. To have spent time, money, and energy in making a garment, then find that it does not fit, is sad indeed. A half hour spent checking your gauge before you start on a knitted project can make the difference between success and failure. So do it!

At the beginning of all good directions you will see the word "gauge," often in bold print. With the yarn you will be using and the needle size suggested for the major part of the garment (usually the larger of two sizes), make a swatch: Cast on enough stitches for 4". Knit in the pattern used in the major part of the garment (unless otherwise directed)* and knit for at least 2". Count the stitches in 2 horizontal inches in the center of your swatch (because the stitches on the edge are distorted). Divide by 2 for your stitches per inch.

For example, if you are using worsted-weight yarn and your gauge is supposed to be 4½ stitches per inch in stockinette stitch (knit 1 row, purl 1 row), on size 8 needles, cast on 18 stitches (4½ stitches per inch × 4 inches = 18 stitches). Work in stockinette for at least 2".

*With some fisherman knits, if you are lucky the designer gives the gauge based on stockinette.

GAUGE   Do you know why this photograph is titled gauge? You can see that both cardigans have the same design. What you may not be able to see but might have guessed is that they have exactly the same number of stitches and exactly the same number of rows. Get the point?

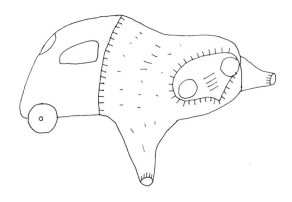

When you look at the swatch on the right side—the knit side—each stitch is a V. Do you see a series of Vs in a vertical row? Using a ruler or stitch gauge, count the number of stitches in 2" on a horizontal row. Divide by 2 to get your stitch gauge.

When you are using bulky or uneven yarn, make a larger swatch and count the stitches in a larger measure.

Should you not get the gauge specified, change your needle size. Unless you knit so tightly that sliding the stitches on the needle is difficult, or so loosely that your needles often fall out, I urge you not to try to change the way you knit. Knitting should be relaxing and a pleasure. If you are getting more stitches per inch than the gauge suggests, make another swatch with larger needles. If you are getting fewer stitches per inch, try smaller needles. When it is necessary to change the larger needles by more than one size, also change the smaller needles.

The experienced knitter both makes a gauge swatch before starting and continues to check the gauge on any project in progress. If you are knitting a sweater, measure the width a few inches above the ribbing and after you have completed the increases if any. To do so, work halfway across a row. You can then spread out your work and take a true measurement.

Do not trust all four-ply worsted weight to be exactly the same. Check your gauge before every project.

I recently bought some yarn imported from a European country. The number of stitches per inch suggested on the label was entirely unreasonable. I finally realized that some translator,

knowing that inches are used in the United States, changed the word "centimeter" to "inch" without changing the number. In a case such as this, you have to calculate the correct gauge. To do so, divide the number of stitches on the back below the underarm by half of the bust or chest measurement in inches. Or use a centimeter tape.

This gives me the opportunity to mention mistakes in directions. The directions may have been written abroad, translated to American (which can be different from English) for a hand-knitting-yarn manufacturer, then sent to a grocery-store-magazine publisher. I often get the feeling that some of the intermediary people do not know how to knit. When you come upon directions that are terribly strange, they may very well have a mistake. There may, Heaven forbid, even be a mistake in this book.

Cast On

Flip loop is the quick and easy method of casting on stitches to begin knitting. Hold a needle and the yarn end together in one hand, the yarn coming from the ball in the other hand. Send your finger under the yarn, toward you; then flip up your finger to point in the same direction as the needle. Run the needle up your finger to get the stitch. Whether you use the right- or left-hand method does not especially relate to your right- or left-handedness. Right-hand flip loop is easier to knit from. Left-hand gives a firmer base but works against the twist of the ply, making the yarn easier to split. Flip loop is useful for a minimal foundation, but control of tension is difficult.

Single-strand cast-on begins with a slip knot. Start to knit a stitch. Bring out the new stitch, but do not discard the old. Enlarge the new stitch and put it on the left needle at the correct angle—not twisted. This is done with the needles side by side, not nose to nose. Pull your yarn to reduce the size of the new stitch, then start another. Beginners may find that removing, then reinserting the right-hand needle helps clarify how to cast on. Later, by correctly positioning the left needle over the right, this step can be eliminated.

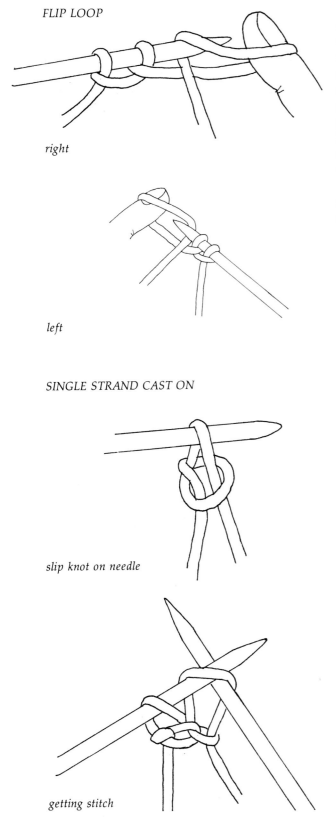

FLIP LOOP

right

left

SINGLE STRAND CAST ON

slip knot on needle

getting stitch

If you must know only one cast-on, this is the one to learn. There are occasions—for example, when casting on stitches for the front neck when knitting a raglan sweater from the neck down—when a single-strand cast-on is necessary. Also, except for the first and last stitches, should a stitch slip from your needle, it is not gone and can be retrieved. Finally, when you have a large number of stitches to cast on, you eliminate the chance of running out of yarn, which can happen with double-strand cast-on.

Double-strand cast-on, stockinette and garter stitch: How much yarn to allow for how many stitches is learned with experience, and even one knitter I know well, with 137 years experience, sometimes guesses wrong. Roughly, allowing 1" per stitch of worsted-weight yarn on #8 needles should give you ample length. Make a slip knot the distance from the end of the yarn that you think you should allow. Slide the slip knot onto the needle and hold it in one hand. Catch both strands of yarn with the little finger of your other hand for tension control. Send the thumb and forefinger of your yarn hand down between the two strands of yarn, then apart and up.

Stockinette cast-on: The needle is in your left hand, the two strands of yarn are in position on your right hand. Run the needle up your right thumb and through the loop. Send the needle under (to the right of) the strand in front from your forefinger, then back over to catch the stitch. Bring the stitch back down through the thumb loop. Slide your thumb out of the loop and back to position to pull in the loop. This last step should not be too tight, because that would make your cast-on tight. Ideally, both strands of yarn should be used at the same rate.

You are looking at the right side of the stockinette cast-on, which means that when you are casting on for ribbing you should work an even number of rows of ribbing. If you are casting on for stockinette stitch, your first row is knit.

Garter cast-on: The needle is in your right hand, the two strands of yarn are in position on your left hand. Run the needle up your left thumb and through the loop. Send the needle over (to the right of) the strand to the front from your forefinger, then under to catch the stitch. Bring the stitch back down through the thumb

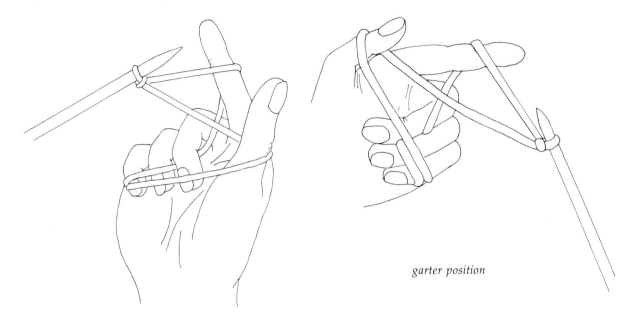

garter position

stockinette position

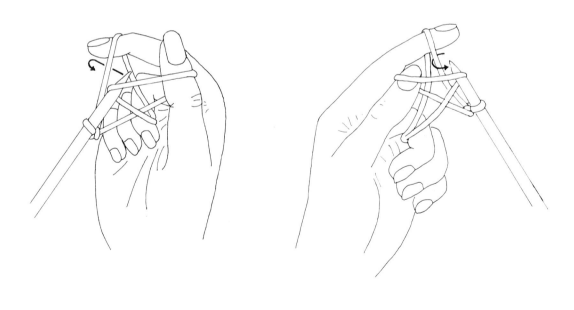

stockinette stitch   *garter stitch*

loop. Slide your thumb out of the loop and back to position to pull in the loop. Again, this last step should not be too tight. You want to use up the yarn in both strands equally.

Garter cast-on is used when you are going to work in garter stitch (knit every row)—you will have already formed one ridge.

Knit

The word "knit" is both generic and specific. The generic "knit" means a system of forming fabric by interlocking loops of a strand of yarn or thread. The specific "knit" means interlocking so that a ridge is formed on the side away from you.

There are two methods of generic hand knitting, English and Continental. The superficial difference is which hand holds the yarn— English, right hand; Continental, left hand— but the end product is the same. If you are a right-handed beginner, I suggest you try the English method. If you are a left-handed beginning knitter, I recommend the Continental method, since your left hand is more agile. If you are a crocheter, you may prefer Continental, but be alert to the direction in which the yarn is sent around your needle.

Most of the directions written in America are by English-method knitters and tend to require a firmer gauge, so Continental knitters may need to use smaller needles. Most European designers are Continental knitters, which will require English knitters to use larger needles. Check your gauge.

A special word to those of you who are left-handed: When I say, "Send the needle through the stitch," bring the stitch over the needle. And a warning to left-handed knitters: Do not knit mirror-opposite, because you would be working against the twist of the yarn and inviting split stitches.

Knit English: Hold the needle with the cast-on stitches in your left hand. Your hand is over the needle, which is held in your curled fingers. If you are an absolute beginner, hold the yarn in your right hand between your thumb and forefinger. The yarn is coming from the rest of your curled fingers, which also hold the other needle. The yarn coming from the work when you are knitting is always to the back, away

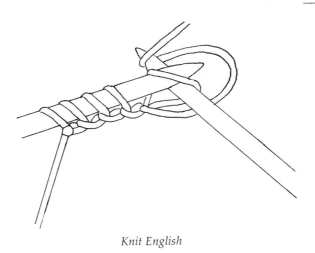

Knit English

from you. If you have some experience, wrap the yarn once around your little finger, for tension control, then over your forefinger. When you are very experienced and if your fingers are long enough, the yarn is held the same, but the needle rests over your hand on the crotch of your thumb and you shove the yarn around the needle. Slide the cast-on stitches toward the point of the needle, so that the first stitch is near the start of the point taper. Send the point of your right needle, left to right, behind the front strand of the first stitch. Remember, Lefty, you bring the stitch over the needle. Dear beginner, you should be working at a table so that you can read about what you are doing, and to rest the ends of your needles to prevent them from slipping out of your work, because you will release your hold on the right needle when you are wrapping the yarn around your needle. Send the yarn under and over the point of your right needle. This forms your new stitch. Bring your new stitch back through the front strand of the old stitch. The new stitch stays on your right needle as you slide the old stitch off your left needle. What you have done is bring a loop through a loop.

Knit Continental: The needle with the cast-on stitches is held in the curled fingers of your left hand. The yarn is around the little finger of your left hand for tension control and over your forefinger for direction. Send the point of the right needle behind the front strand of the first stitch, left to right. The yarn is always in back,

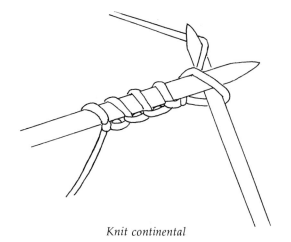

Knit continental

away from you, when you are knitting. Send the point of the right needle over the yarn, then under, to form your new stitch. Bring the new stitch back through the front strand of the old stitch. The new stitch stays on your right needle as you slide the old stitch off your left needle.

Continue to knit across the row, working stitches off the left needle and forming the new stitches on the right needle. Trade the needles in each hand. The yarn should come down in front from the first stitch to avoid a problem for some new knitters, extra stitches. (Take the yarn over to the back to see what I am talking about.) Below the first stitch you may see a large loop. This will be pulled up when you start to knit; another will be formed as you begin the next row.

Knitting every row on two needles forms ridges on both sides of your work; this is called **garter stitch**.

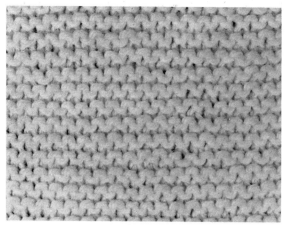

Garter stitch

Purl

Purl English: The needle with the stitches is in your left hand. The yarn for purling is always in front, toward you. Send the right needle behind the front strand of the first stitch, right to left. The point of your right needle is to the front. Send the yarn over and under the point of your right needle for the new stitch. Your new stitch is taken back through the old stitch, which is slid off the left needle.

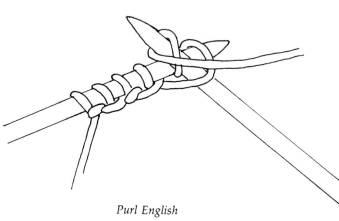

Purl English

Purl Continental: The needle with the stitches is in your left hand. The yarn for purling is always held in front of the left needle, toward you. Send your right needle behind the front strand of the first stitch, right to left. Your right needle is in front of the left needle, but behind the yarn and the strand of the first stitch. Swing the point of the right needle to the

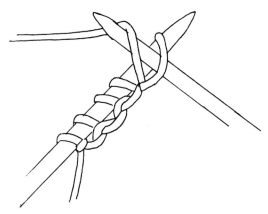

Purl continental

front of the yarn, around on the right and behind the yarn to form a new stitch. Take the new stitch back through the old, which is slid off the left needle.

Alternating knit and purl rows on two needles puts all the ridges on the same side; this is called **stockinette stitch.** The smooth side is considered the right side. You would be wise to learn early to recognize that when the right side is toward you, you knit, and when the wrong side is toward you, you purl.

When you are working in stockinette stitch, do not be alarmed by the fabric's rolling and curling. The cast-on edge will roll up toward the right side, and the side edges will curl toward the wrong side. In practically all cases, the edges will be finished to eliminate the curl.

Now, everyone pay attention. Whether you are working in the English or Contnental method, knitting or purling, right- or left-handed, as you look face on at the point of the right needle, the yarn must go around counterclockwise. Hand-knitting yarn should always have an S twist. If the yarn goes around the needle the wrong way, you are more likely to split stitches. Also, sending the yarn around wrong can result in crossed stitches, which will cause difficulty with your gauge.

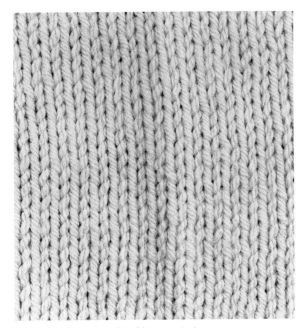

Stockinette stitch

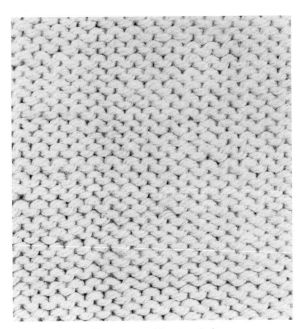

Reverse stockinette stitch

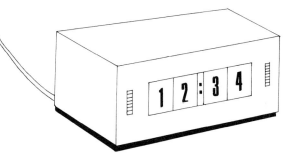

What do you mean, counterclockwise?

Knit and purl in the same row: You now know that when you knit, the yarn is in back; when you purl, the yarn is in front. When you change from knit to purl within a row, bring the yarn between the points of the needles to the front. Likewise, when you change from purl to knit, take the yarn between the points of the needles to the back. Failure to switch the position of your yarn will give you an extra stitch and throw off your pattern.

Knit and purl in the same row

Decrease

Decreasing is one way of shaping. There are several ways to do it.

K2 tog: Knit 2 stitches together. This means send your right needle through two stitches as if they were one and knit them. When your directions read "decrease 1 stitch" without further specification, and you are on a knit row, k2 tog. This decrease slants to the right.

P2 tog: Purl 2 stitches together. On a purl row, send your right needle through two stitches as if they were one and purl them.

Sl 1, k1, psso: Slip 1 stitch, knit 1 stitch, pass the slipped stitch over (over the knit stitch). Slip a stitch as if to knit, which means send your right needle through the stitch as if you were going to knit it, but just slip it onto your right needle. Knit the next stitch. With the point of your left needle, lift the slipped stitch over the knit stitch and off the point of your right needle. This decrease slants to the left— the opposite of k2 tog.

Should you find that the slipped stitch becomes enlarged and you would like to avoid that, you can. On a knit row, slip 2 stitches as if to knit, one at a time. Send the yarn around your right needle. With the point of your left needle, pass the two slipped stitches together over the yarn on your right needle.

SKP: Slip, knit, pass, which is merely a different way of writing sl 1, k1, psso.

Let me tell you a third way this decrease may be made. When I am decreasing 1 stitch at each edge at regular intervals, I like to balance the direction of the slant, so I k2 tog at the beginning of the row and SKP at the end. I find, however, that I can forget the decrease at the end of the row. So to assist my memory, at the beginning of the purl row preceding the decrease row I wrap the yarn around the needle the wrong way when purling the 2 stitches on which I will decrease. On the decrease row, when I come upon the stitches with a wrong slant I remember and knit those 2 stitches together through the back. This is the best that can be done in balancing decreases. There is a slight difference in appearance, because of the twist of the ply in the yarn.

Yaw, p2 tog: Yarn around wrong, purl 2 together. When you purl 2 together on the wrong side, the slant on the right side is to the right. To slant a purl decrease to the left, on the row preceding the decrease, wrap the yarn around wrong on the stitches that are to be decreased. This I find I am capable of forgetting, so on the decrease row these 2 stitches can be turned before working. Purl them together through the back. To do so, send the right needle, left to right, catching the back strands of the stitches.

Double decrease: This means reduce 3 stitches to 1 in one step. You can purl 3 together, or knit 3 together, which is more easily done through the back. There are two other ways you may encounter. To complete the top of a diamond in a lace pattern you often read "sl 1, k2 tog, psso." Slip 1 stitch as to knit, knit 2 stitches together, and pass the slipped stitch over. This is a relatively flat double decrease. For a raised double decrease, slip as if to knit 2 stitches together. The right needle is sent through both stitches together as if you were decreasing, so their order is reversed on your right needle. Knit the next stitch. With the point of your left needle, lift the 2 slipped stitches over the knit stitch and off the needle. A vertical series of this decrease forms a raised stitch with stitches on each side disappearing under it.

Increase

Increasing is another way of shaping. There are several ways to do it.

Knit in front and back: When your directions read "increase in the next stitch" and you are on a knit row, this is the increase you normally will use. To do so, start to knit the stitch. Bring out the new stitch, but do not discard the old. Instead, send the point of your right needle around to the back and knit a second stitch in the back strand of the same stitch. Look at this increase. Notice that the stitch knit from the back has formed a little nub. When your directions read "increase 1 stitch at each edge," balance the appearance: If you increase in the first stitch of a row, increase in the next to last stitch. If you increase in the second stitch at the beginning, increase in the third stitch from the end of the row.

Purl in front and front: When you are to increase on a purl row, it is unreasonable to purl in the front and the back of a stitch. This is how you do it: Start to purl. Bring the new stitch out. Remove the point of your left needle from the old stitch and reinsert it from the back. You now have a front strand in the old stitch in which to purl again. This also forms a nub, so to balance the appearance at the edges, work the same as for the knit increases.

Yo: Yarn over. The yarn is sent around the right needle the same as in working a stitch. When the stitches on either side of the yo are knit, yo by bringing the yarn between the points of the needles, then over the right needle. When the stitches on either side of the yo are purl, take the yarn over the right needle, then between the points of the needles. When a yo is between unlike stitches, you have to think. Remember, the result you want is an extra stitch, because yo is an increase. When your directions read "k1, yo, p1," after the knit stitch, bring the yarn between the needles, over the right needle, and between the needles again. When you see "p1, yo, k1," leave your yarn in front after the purl stitch. Knitting the next stitch will take the yarn over the needle, thus forming your yo. You may have made this yo when you were learning to rib. If you have trouble remembering how to yo between unlike stitches, try this: First put your yarn in position for the next stitch, then yo.

Hidden increase: This somewhat resembles an upside-down decrease. It can be used when you are working in stockinette stitch. On a knit row, knit through the top of the stitch in the row below the first stitch on the left needle, then knit the stitch on the needle. I find it a good idea to first pull out the top of the lower stitch from the back, using the point of the right needle. When you are to increase on the first stitch, the stitch in the row below is the one that often enlarges. Send your right needle, front to back, through the lower stitch and knit it; then knit the stitch above, the one on the needle. When you are to increase on an inside stitch, look for the bar centered between your needles. The bar runs between 2 stitches. The stitch on the left is the one you are looking for; you want to knit through the top of it. Use your right needle to slightly lift it from the back, then enter through the front to knit. Knitting the stitch above, on the needle, completes the increase; it is *not* included when you are given a number of stitches to knit *following* the increase. This can also be done on a purl row— purl the lower, then the upper stitch.

Make 1 (M1): Sometimes you read this in British directions. It is an increase, and usually means cast on one stitch by the flip-loop method. I find this increase useful when the increase row (the row on which I want to increase) is the first row of a new color. Using the M1 increase keeps the line between the colors clean.

Pick up bar: Here is another form of increase you may find in British directions. It means pick up the horizontal bar between the points of your needles with your left needle, then work it. Whether you are on a knit row or a purl row, the bar is picked up the same way. Send the point of the left needle, front to back, under the bar.

Bind Off

Many beginning knitters learn to bind off by

knitting every stitch and continue doing so, unaware that there are other ways.

Bind-off in knit: At the beginning of the row, loosely knit 2 stitches onto the right needle. Use the point of your left needle to lift the first stitch you knit, the one away from the point, over the second stitch, and let it drop off the point of your right needle. Knit another stitch onto the right needle and again lift the preceding stitch up, over, and off. Continue to knit one stitch at a time, binding off each. Each stitch is interlocked with the next. When you have 1 stitch remaining at the end of the row, cut the yarn and send the end through the last stitch. But before you cut, think. If there is a seam to be sewn, leave a length of yarn with which to sew it. If there is no seam, cut the yarn at 2" or 3" and run in the end along the edge. Do not cut your bind-off tail short, and do not tie it in a knot.

Bind-off in purl: Left-handed and Continental knitters will have fewer problems binding off on a purl row. Lefty and Continental, hold your yarn in front and send your left needle behind it to reach for the stitch to lift it over and off. English, you will have to lower your yarn in front so that your left needle can come in over it to reach the stitch to lift it over and off. Or you can learn to reach the back stitch from the back.

Bind-off in pattern: Knit or purl each stitch as though you were working across the row. The ribbed neck of a sweater bound off in all knit is very unattractive. The character of the ribbing is lost.

It is important to bind off loosely. The best way to be sure you do so is to use a larger needle.

Should your directions read "bind off on row 4," complete row 3, then bind off. When you are working in stockinette stitch and your directions read "bind off on a knit row," complete a purl row, then bind off in knit.

I want to talk some more about binding off on stockinette stitch. Your bound-off edge will roll, just as the cast-on edge does. If the bind-off is not to be joined to something, such as a neckband or collar, it should be finished with a row or more of single crochet, or turned under and hemmed. If that is not what you plan, you can lessen the roll by binding off in k1, p1.

Should you have need to bind off VERY LOOSELY, avoid a sloppy bind-off by chaining 1 stitch between each bind-off stitch.

One more thing about binding off. Let's say you have 10 stitches. Your directions say "bind off 5, k5." You bind off 5 stitches—but there are only 4 left to knit. The stitch on your right needle is included in that "k5," and you have already knit it.

Join Yarn

Perusing my collection of old knitting manuals, I find a charming variety of methods for joining a new ball of yarn. These books were written before the innovation of the pull skein. In the old days, yarn usually was available in skeins that had to be wound into balls. Do you remember having to hold out your arms while Grandmother wound the ball? When you grew tired and let the yarn go slack, it caused a terrible mess. Some very clever grandmothers would wind a ball while holding on to the beginning end, so that the yarn could be pulled from the inside and the ball would stay put instead of jumping or rolling around. Some yarn was sold already in balls, but if you wanted to work from the center you often had to pull out nearly half the inside before you found the end. Come to think of it, some things never change.

I have digressed. Some of my old manuals suggested that to join a new ball of yarn you should knit a half dozen stitches with the two strands of yarn held together. Some had you tie each end around the other strand and then pull until the knots met. I suppose you were to ignore the lumps in your sweaters or socks. One elaborate method was to split the plies and cut 3" from two of the plies from each end (when working with four-ply yarn). Then, with a darning needle, you were to weave the remaining two plies into the other end, for each end.

I suspect that all of the elaborate methods of joining new yarn were an economy effort, perhaps inherited from the woman who did her own spinning.

Some of my students tie a nice firm square knot and knit merrily along. This is a better method than any of the above. However, the knot may slip through to the right side, or you may have uneven knitting, because when you work back across the row the yarn in the stitches shifts slightly. This will give you some loose stitches next to a tight stitch or two.

In flat knitting, it is better to join a new skein at the edge and use an overhand knot, the first half of a granny or square knot. This may loosen, so give it a little tug the next time you knit by. When there is a long end, use it for sewing. To keep a long end from getting in the way, if you are working in stockinette stitch, tuck it in the natural curl of the edge.

When you encounter a knot in the skein, treat it the same way. (Did you ever, especially when working with a dark color, untie a knot in the skein and find that the dye had not penetrated completely?) If you have already started the row, take out the stitches back to the beginning, remove the knot, and join the yarn. However, when there is a knot in just one of the plies, I am inclined to overlook it and work on.

Sometimes you find a section in the yarn in which the spinning is bad. Cut it out and return to the edge.

There will be times, for instance, when you are knitting a raglan cardigan from the neck down and have a great number of stitches that you really do not want to go all the way back to the edge. You can join a new skein in the row. You can go back to an increase seam line or if there is a knit pattern such as a cable, join next to that. Join by using an overhand knot, and tighten it when you work back. When you are sewing up your project, cut the ends off at an angle to about 2". Again tighten the knot, if necessary, and run the ends in, in opposite directions, up and down. To do this, with a tapestry needle and on the wrong side, catch a strand in every other row in almost a straight line. On the reverse of stockinette, zigzag slightly. On a line between knit and purl, alternate between each. An end sewn in a straight line is more likely to show through. When you are making a seamless skirt or sweater on a circular needle, this is the way you will finish your ends. The natural crimp in wool or the manufactured crimp in good synthetic yarns will

lock and hold the ends. Trust me.

When you are working in colors, be sure to bury each end in its own color. Tie the overhand knot to send each color end in the correct direction. If your color bands are narrow, finish your ends diagonally or even horizontally. In Argyle the best place to work in the ends is along the line where you changed colors.

Pick Up Dropped Stitches

There are two meanings to the term "pick up stitches." To the new knitter it means retrieving a stitch that has dropped off the needle and laddered down. Shortly we will discuss picking up stitches along an edge of your work for further knitting.

A dropped stitch that has gone down the work a few rows can send a new knitter into a panic. Take a deep breath. Then take up a crochet hook. If you are working with four-ply worsted-weight yarn, #00 steel is an appropriate size hook. It is easiest to pick up a ladder or runner in stockinette stitch. From the right side, the smooth side, send the hook, barb up, through the stitch below the bottom "rung" of the ladder. Catch the rung with the hook. Twist the hook slightly to one side and press the hook slightly in the other direction so as to be able to bring the center of the rung through the stitch on the hook. Repeat to work the dropped stitch up to the current row, and put the stitch on the left needle so that the yarn coming from the right is in front, toward you. That wasn't so hard, was it?

If you were purling when the stitch was dropped, turn your knitting around to work on the knit side; when you get your stitch up to the current row, put it, yarn from the right in front, on the right-hand needle.

OK, you were working in garter stitch and a stitch dropped. Let's call the garter rows ridges and valleys. When the stitch is in a valley, ready to be worked into a ridge, send the hook down from above, behind the rung in the ridge row, out toward you through the stitch. With barb toward you, take the stitch above the rung, turn the barb to the opposite direction, catch the rung, and draw it through. Now catch the rung from the valley and draw it through as you would for stockinette. To continue, hold on to the stitch with your fingers, remove the hook to send it behind the ridge rung next in line in the ladder, and work your stitch up to the current row.

When you have mastered these two methods and you are working on a more advanced pattern, you should be able to recognize the knit and purl stitches and be able to duplicate the pattern while retrieving the stitch. Now that you know all this, you will see that it is possible to drop a stitch down deliberately to correct a mistake, then work it back up.

Here is one more dropped-stitch problem: You find a stitch that was missed a few rows down. You can work it back up by pulling a little from each of the adjacent stitches, so that you have rungs. It will show as a tighter place in your knitting, but if you don't tell, I won't.

Pick Up New Stitches

The first encounter you are likely to have with picking up new stitches will be for the neck of a sweater. There may be bound-off edges, side edges, stitches on holders, and sometimes cast-on edges. Your directions may tell you specifically how many stitches to get from each area, or you may be given just the total number of stitches.

To pick up new stitches you need the correct size needle, the yarn, and a crochet hook. You work from the right side, and whether you are right- or left-handed, your needle points to the left. Picking up stitches is easier for Lefty, but come on, Righty, you usually have the advantage, so you can walk in the other's shoes for a few steps—can't you?

Bound-off edge: Send the hook under the top two strands of the bound-off stitch, catch the yarn from the ball, and draw it through. Put the stitch on the needle so that the yarn coming from the ball is on the back side. On a bound-off edge you will usually pick up 1 stitch from each bound-off stitch. Should you need to decrease, your hook is sent under the front strand of each of 2 stitches; the order in which these two strands are used depends on which is in front of the other, which depends on the direction in

which you bound off. You go under the front strand first. Should you want to increase while picking up stitches on a bound-off edge, the extra stitches can be gained as for a decrease, and you also get stitches from each of the 2 stitches.

Side edge: Look at a side edge closely; you may need to uncurl it. There are nubs and bars, little bumps with straight strands between them. When picking up stitches on a side edge, you want to work on the very edge, to minimize the welt that forms on the wrong side. Now pay attention! This means that you must look carefully. Send the crochet hook through the nub to catch the yarn for your new stitch. When you are picking up 1 stitch for each nub (it takes 2 rows to form a nub), send the hook under two strands in the nub to catch the yarn. You are using half of a stitch on the edge. Approach all nubs uniformly. Whether you approach the nub on the right or the left depends on whether you are working up or down the direction in which the edge was knit.

When you have kept a 1-stitch border—slip as if to knit the first stitch of every row, knit the last stitch of every row—send the crochet hook under the single strand of the nub that is on the very edge.

Let's say that you need extra stitches from a side edge. You try going through the same place twice. It doesn't work. You try going under the bar between the nubs. That leaves a hole. You try going deeper into the work. That looks messy, because the line of stitches along the edge is broken. When there are decreases on the side edge of a neck, you can easily find two different areas in the nub at the decrease through which to send your hook. On a plain edge an extra stitch can be derived by sending your hook under one strand from the nub and the bar. Which you do first, the extra stitch or the nub stitch, depends on which is easier and which looks better. To reduce the number of stitches on a side edge, send the hook under 2 nubs to form your 1 stitch.

Cast-on edge: There are such a variety of ways to cast on stitches that I cannot be specific as to how to pick up new stitches. Aren't you glad? I will say only that your aim usually is to get 1 new stitch for each cast-on stitch. There-

Cardigan sweater for him

Hat and hunter mittens for him

Cardigan, pullover, vest, mittens, scarf, hat, and gloves for her

Cardigan, hat, scarf, and mittens for her

Jacket with mandarin collar for a child

Hat for a child

Dishcloth and potholders for the house

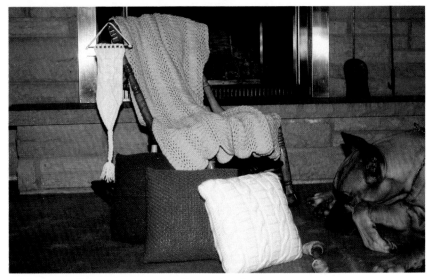

Afghan, wall hanging, and pillows for the house

Party favor, newborn hat, and lace and basket weave sacque and bonnet sets for a baby

Ball and boot booties for a baby

Find the pairs afghan for a patient

Decorated Christmas stockings for the fireplace

fore, find a uniform method of entering cast-on stitches (preferably under two strands) that gives you the neatest appearance.

Here is something important: There are corners between side edges and bound-off or cast-on edges, in which there inevitably will be a hole. To cure this, send your crochet hook under one strand from each side of the corner to get a new stitch. If this gives you an unneeded extra stitch, you can decrease at that spot on your first row.

Sometimes you can pick up stitches in whatever way gives a neat appearance and avoids making holes, then on your first row increase or decrease evenly to obtain the desired number of stitches.

Let me now give you a couple of exceptions to all of the above. To pick up the stitches for a collar that is to fold down, work on the wrong side (the inside) of the neck. To make a sham pocket flap, knit the desired number of stitches on the purl row where you want to locate the flap. Then pick up stitches by sending the hook through the ridge in your knitting.

Sew

There are nearly as many ways to sew knitted pieces together as there are people telling you how to sew. Listen to them all, then select the method you like best. Now I will tell you my method.

First, I do not block pieces before sewing; I prefer to match rows. For instance, in a sweater, I have the same number of rows in the ribbing in the back and in the front, the same number of rows (or within one) between the ribbing and the underarm back and front, and the same number of rows in back and front from underarm to shoulder. Also, I use the yarn ends from the cast-on and bind-off, and anyplace where a new ball has been joined on the edge, for sewing.

Finally, knots are rarely necessary, because the natural crimp in wool or the constructed crimp in synthetic yarn locks to hold the ends. I want to explain further: The outer layer of wool fiber, called the cuticle, consists of overlapping scales. Humidity and temperature cause these scales to open and close and interlock with adjacent fibers. This action will permanently hold the ends in place.

Sewing needles: There are needles packaged to be used for sewing knitting. Generally, they are on the large side and are suitable for bulky or multiple-strand work. Tapestry needles usually work well. With four-ply worsted weight yarn, #16 is a good size. For sport-weight yarn use #18, and for three-ply fingering or baby yarn, #20. What is important is to use sewing needles with blunt points. With a sharp point, it is too easy to catch a part of a strand of yarn.

To thread the needle, fold the yarn over the needle near the point and pinch the yarn as close to the needle as you can. Slide the needle out, put the eye to the fold, and roll open your fingers as you encourage the yarn through the eye.

Side edge to side edge: Look carefully at the edge of your knitting. You will have to uncurl stockinette. There are nubs with bars between them. With right sides together, go through one strand in the top of a nub from each side, then back under the bars next to the nubs. Continue snaking back and forth. You very likely will need to uncurl the edges as you sew. Count ahead. If there are more nubs on one side than the other, you have to cheat—sew a nub to a bar. If you have to cheat more than once, space it out evenly. Be sure all joints match, such as where you change from the ribbing to the stockinette, from the body to the sleeve. If your project has color bands, leave an end for sewing when you start a new color, and see that the colors match at the seams.

The reasons I use the **nub-and-bar** method of sewing are several. Knitting directions use the gauge to calculate the exact measure of a garment, so you do not want to lose any width due to the seam. Sewing on the very edge keeps your full measurement. Nub-and-bar produces a flat seam, and because you snake back and forth, your seam has give, as does the knitting. Of course, for your seams to look their best, the edges of your knitting must be neat.

When sewing seams in nub-and-bar, when the yarn end from the top meets the yarn end from the bottom, send each through the other's nubs for a couple of inches. Remember, no knots.

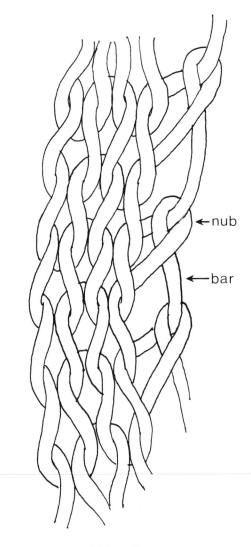

←nub

←bar

Nub and bar

Bind-off to bind-off: Your bound-off-edge seam is better-looking when you take care to avoid letting the line formed in binding off show on the right side. Sew two bound-off edges right sides together, using the yarn ends left from binding off. Send the needle under the top two strands of one edge, then under the top two strands of the other. Bring the needle back to send it through the next 2 stitches in the same direction. Continue in whip stitch. If there is a pattern below the edges that should match, check. When you are joining shoulders that have steps (the jogs can be minimized by slipping the first stitch in pattern in each level) you will need to take care to avoid holes. Skipping a pair of stitches, then coming back to them may help. When the end from one direction meets the end from the other, send each into the other's seam for a couple of inches.

Should you have a shoulder seam that needs to be firm, use a crochet hook to slip stitch it together. As each front shoulder is completed, before cutting the yarn, join it to the back, right sides together. Send the hook under the two strands of each of the first 2 stitches, catch the yarn, and draw out a loop. Send the hook through the next 2 stitches, catch the yarn, draw it out, then through the loop on your hook. Continue across the seam. Check for any pattern that should match. Although you are crocheting to form a firm seam, you may need to take care not to crochet too tightly.

Bind-off to side edge: This seam you most often find when setting in sleeves. When you are sewing a fabric garment you are told to first sew the seams, then set in the capped sleeve. This makes sense. Some finishing directions for knitted garments suggest you do the same. This does not make sense. Sewing the cap of a sleeve into an armhole is the more difficult seam to do, so you should have the other seams open so that you can see what you are doing. In fabric sewing, the cap of the sleeve is slightly larger than the armhole. In fact, you often will have ease across the top of the sleeve. In knitting, unless you are making a puff sleeve, the cap should be slightly smaller than the armhole. Find the center of the top of the sleeve by folding the bound-off edge in half. Pin this to the shoulder seam, right sides together. Match the underarm bound-off stitches on the sleeve to those on the body and pin. Match the nubs on the armhole of the body to the nubs along the side of the cap of the sleeve and pin the top—the end of the top bind-off—to the body. If there is no distortion, this will be how it is sewn. If it does look distorted, move the side pins to a better position and cheat in the nub-and-bar sewing. Sew the underarm bind-offs together, skip and return as for shoulder steps at the corner between bound-off and side edge—there is always a hole there—sew nub-and-bar to the bind-off at the top of the sleeve, then whip stitch across the top. Count ahead on the top of the sleeve—how many bound-off stitches, how many nubs to match them with. Take care to send the needle under both strands of every stitch on the bind-off, so that the line will not be seen on the right side. Distribute the number of stitches sewn to the nubs.

There is a poncho pattern consisting of two rectangles in which the bound-off edges are sewn to side edges. I remind you again to bind off loosely in pattern. Mark with a pin the end of the area on the side edge that the natural width of the bound-off edge fits. Count the bound-off stitches and the side nubs and sew with a whip stitch. Ease in extra bound-off stitches by sewing 2 stitches to 1 nub.

Bind-off to cast-on: There are a variety of ways of casting on, so I give you a general direction. Find a repeat in your cast on that occurs in every stitch where you can send the needle under two strands without interfering with the first row. Sewing bind-off to cast-on is usually done stitch to stitch, as for the two toys in the new-baby chapter in this book. Sew with a whip stitch. If you are easing one edge to the other, count ahead, then as often as necessary sew a new stitch to one just used rather than skipping stitches.

Cast-on to side edge: The previously mentioned two-rectangle poncho can also be sewn cast-on to side edge with whip stitch. Otherwise, why didn't you pick up the stitches along the side edge instead?

As with all hand sewing, it is necessary from time to time to drop or hang your yarn needle to permit the yarn to unwind. Better yet is learning to twist the needle every few stitches to counteract the twist caused by sewing. Also, do I need to remind you to sew with the yarn used for knitting? There are exceptions. When you have knit with multiple strands, sometimes just one strand will suffice for sewing. Some bouclés are absolutely impossible to use for sewing; look for a plain yarn of the same color and fiber. When your project is knit with an unspun yarn such as Icelandic wool, you will need to determine the grain. Think of shingles laid on a roof. This is how the strand is spun, or constructed when unspun. In running your fingers along a strand of yarn you will find it smoother in one

direction than the other. Sew in the direction that will not ruff up the yarn. Better yet, find a regular yarn of the same color and fiber to use for sewing. Persian needlepoint yarn comes in a wide range of colors and is strong.

Wash and Block

Good wool can and should be hand washed. Cheap wool must be sent to a dry cleaner. Does that really make it inexpensive? You especially should hand wash natural water-resistant wool, because dry cleaning removes the lanolin.

There are some things to worry about. One is colorfastness. When you have knit a sweater using more than one color, take a few inches of each color yarn, and if none of the colors is white, add a piece of white. Wet the pieces of yarn thoroughly, twist them around each other, and let them dry completely, then inspect. In fact, you might be wise to make this test *before* you knit with the yarn. If any of the colors fails the test, return the yarn and explain why. But there is something else that can be done. The final process the yarn dyer must perform is rinsing out all excess dye. There is an occasional dyer who may skimp on this. (Can you imagine an American manufacturer taking a shortcut!) Your yarn should be in a hank. You will probably have to wind yourself. Wind it into a large circle and tie pieces of yarn or string around in at least three places. Swish the hank around in a tub of lukewarm water, which you may want to change once. If the yarn continues to bleed, you are in trouble. If all is well, squeeze out as much water as possible, then straighten out the hank and allow it to dry on a towel that is not part of your best set. When the yarn is completely dry, wind it loosely (so as not to stretch it) into a ball. Remember to examine the towel for dye.

Another thing to worry about is buttons or decorative trim. I once washed a sweater with some beaded trim and the silly beads dissolved.

Do not be afraid to wash good wool. First, check the water temperature. It should be body temperature, because the oil from our skin holds soil, and warmth is needed to soften it. If you have hot and cold water coming from the same tap, put your wrist under the running water. Adjust the temperature until you can feel your wrist throbbing warm and cool. Then you have the correct temperature.

You can use a mild soap, but be sure to rinse the wool well. Do you know that moths like soap? Or you can use a mild detergent, one without bleach. If you are using flakes or granules, dissolve them before you submerge the sweater or whatever you are washing. But do you know what I often recommend? Liquid hand dishwashing detergent, the mild variety. Look over your laundry for spots, wet them, then gently massage in a small amount of detergent. If the spot does not come out, it is better to leave it there than to continue working on it, because you could mat the area. Pour a little detergent into the water and knead your inside-out laundry by squeezing water through and through.

Rinse in water of the same temperature. When you transfer the laundry from wash to rinse, support it. Wool can hold a great amount of water, which is heavy. If you pull a wool garment from the water, the weight of the water can stretch it out of shape. After you have rinsed your laundry, remove as much water as possible. You can use the spin cycle on a top-loading washing machine. Bunch your garment so that it will not be flung out and stretched. For the machine's sake, use a balance—it can be a towel. Better yet, wash more than one item. I remember a relative in the days when washing machines had wringers, who was a swinger. She had a net bag in which she put her delicate things. She took this out to the back yard and swung it around above her head.

Some no-nos in washing wool are: agitation—it shrinks wool; hot water—that shrinks wool too; strong soaps—the free alkali harms the wool fiber.

Some never-nevers in drying wool are: direct sunlight—some colors, especially blues, are vulnerable when wet and can fade; direct heat, such as that of a radiator—it can shrink wool; and hanging on a line—that will stretch wool out of shape.

To dry, lay your garment on a towel. An area with good air circulation is best. It is a good idea with a multicolored sweater to insert another towel inside. Push or pull your garment

into shape. This is usually all the blocking that is needed.

For more serious blocking I have a 3' × 4' piece of fiberboard covered with unbleached muslin. I use rustproof T pins. When the sweater, skirt, jacket, or whatever has been washed and is thoroughly dry—still inside out—I pin it on the board. With a sweater or jacket, I measure and pin the bust or chest first, at the underarm and partway down the edges. Exaggerate any alteration. That is, to enlarge 2", pin out 2½"; to reduce 1", push in 1½". Next, pin the shoulders, checking the armhole depth. Measure the underarm length and pin that, but pin above any ribbing. Pin the sleeves, but again, not the ribbing. If you are blocking a cardigan, close the buttons and pin the front so that there are no gaps.

When you block a skirt, both the waist and the bottom edge should have an arc. Measure and pin the length in fanning radii.

Use a piece of smooth, undyed cotton. Gauze diapers are ideal. Dear young mothers, in the olden days diapers were cotton cloth. Douse the cloth in water and squeeze, leaving it still drippy. Spread the cloth over the garment and pat with an iron on the wool setting. Do not block the ribbing. You will have to rewet the cloth as you move to new areas. Allow your garment to dry completely. The next day remove the pins and aim the steam from a steam iron at the pinholes. I then use a sleeve board to steam out the side creases. Lay your garment again on a dry towel and let the moisture of the steam dry.

Synthetic yarns: Machine wash if you must, but be sure to turn your garments inside out. The agitation in a machine causes pilling, and it is better to have that on the inside. Follow all the other rules for washing wool. I hand wash knitted items made with synthetic yarn the same way I do wool, and they look better longer.

My blocking instructions for synthetic yarns are easy—don't. Synthetic yarns are manufactured to keep their shape. With well-made yarn, blocking is ineffective. Not-so-well-made yarns may melt. I don't mean melt into a puddle, but heat can form a crust.

Rip

This is a book about knitting. Unfortunately, knitting often involves ripping. So you might just as well learn how to rip and get the stitches back on the needles correctly. Incidentally, often an indication of who is going to be a good knitter, in my beginning classes, is who is willing to rip.

We have already talked about dropping a single stitch down to correct an error, then working it back up. When you have worked too far or have a serious mistake, you have to rip. When you only need to back up a few stitches or even a row or two, you are safer picking each stitch. To do this, have your yarn coming from the left needle. Wrap the yarn around a finger so that you can pull up. With two other fingers, pull your work down in order to see clearly.

Insert the right needle, toward you, through the stitch below the first left-needle stitch, then slide the upper one off. By doing this, you pick up a stitch before you rip it.

Sometimes you must rip out too much for picking. Pull out the needle and rip. But rip one row less than you need to. On the last row, pick each stitch. Have the yarn coming from the left. Insert the needle, toward you, through each stitch in the row below before you pull out the upper stitch. Are the stitches on your needle correctly? Whether a stitch is knit or purl, the front strand of the stitch should come from the right. When a stitch is twisted on your needle, the angle is noticeably different and you can see that the ply is unwound.

Do you know that ravel and unravel mean the same? I knew you would be fascinated by this tidbit of information.

FYI

3

Kitchener Weaving

This is a knitting procedure rarely mentioned, but how valuable it is when you really need it. The English term is grafting. In the days when we knitted socks—remember Argyles made with three-ply fingering yarn on #2 needles?—we wove the toe stitches on the top of the foot to those on the bottom. You could not see where the socks were finished because there was no seam. And socks are more comfortable without a seam, which is why you weave the toe. Sometimes mittens are woven at the top. The shaping (decreasing) is done at both edges instead of all around. This lets you avoid interfering with a pattern. Knowledge of kitchener weaving can also be a lifesaver should you want to shorten or lengthen something internally. The scary part is cutting a strand to take out a row. You can then rip out or add rows, then weave your work back together. I cannot say that it is as easy to do as it is to tell, and you do need to be careful with the tension to make the operation invisible.

Stockinette to stockinette: Have your stitches divided equally on two needles, both needle points at the right, and wrong sides together. The yarn, if attached, should be coming from the back. The piece of yarn should be at least three times the length of the row you are weaving. A little more for good measure would not hurt. Use a tapestry needle. To start, send the yarn through the first stitch on the front needle as if to purl, then through the first stitch on the back needle as if to knit. **Now,** send the yarn through the first stitch on the front needle as if to knit and slide the stitch off the needle, through the next stitch on the front as if to purl and leave it on, through the first stitch on the back needle as if to purl and slide it off, through the next stitch on the back as if to knit and leave it on. Repeat from *Now* until all the stitches are used. You will end through the front as if to knit and off, through the back as if to purl and off. If any of the stitches on the needle were twisted, I hope you straightened them. The hardest part for me in kitchener weaving is tension. What I usually do is weave loosely, then every half dozen or so stitches I work the yarn forward. I bet you will be better than I.

Garter to garter: You really have to comprehend kitchener weaving to get this right—to have a true garter result. We talked about ridges and valleys in garter in picking up dropped stitches. Look at each needle from the outside when you are holding them together. On one needle you must have just completed a ridge, on the other a valley. Look at both needles, from the same direction. Each should have the same immediately under the needle, both ridges or both valleys. I will explain both ridges first. Send the yarn through the first stitch on the front needle as if to purl, through the first stitch on the back needle as if to purl. **Now,** through the first stitch on the front needle as if to knit and slide off, through the next stitch on the front needle as if to purl and leave on, through the first stitch on the back needle as if to knit and slide off, through the next stitch on the back needle as if to purl and leave on. Repeat from *Now*. When you have valleys under both needles, start through the first stitch on the front needle as if to knit, through the first stitch on the back needle as if to knit. **Now,** through the first stitch on the front needle as if to purl and slide off, through the next stitch on the front needle as if to knit and leave on, through the first stitch on the back needle as if to purl and slide off, through the next stitch on the back needle as if to knit and leave on. Repeat from *Now*.

You think that you are adding only one row, and really you are, but there are two interlacings, thus two new ridges. The object is to get one ridge on each side of your knitting in the correct order.

Ribbing to ribbing—almost: Here we get down to the hard part. Do you understand in garter to garter that when you want the interlacing or stitch above the front needle to be knit—a valley—it is entered first as if to purl, then as if to knit? But between these two steps you do what you do on the back needle. Should you want a stitch above a stitch on the back needle to be purl as you see it—knit on the right side—it is first entered as if to knit, then as if to purl. These two steps are interrupted to do whatever on the front needle. Let's go over that again.

You are weaving together k1, p1 ribbing that was separated. The direction of the knitting is continuous. The first stitch on each needle is knit on the right side, although the back one looks purl from your angle. Send the yarn through the first front stitch as if to purl, through the first back stitch as if to knit. **Now,** through the first front stitch as if to knit and slide off, through the next front stitch as if to knit and leave on, through the first back stitch as if to purl and slide off, through the next back stitch as if to purl and leave on, through the first front stitch as if to purl and slide off, through the next front stitch as if to purl and leave on, through the first back stitch as if to knit and slide off, through the next back stitch as if to knit and leave on. Whew! Repeat from *Now*.

A more common use of weaving ribbing to ribbing is when you have been knitting from opposite directions, your pieces meet, and you prefer weaving to a seam. You cannot weave ribbing to ribbing perfectly when the approach is opposite. Believe me. If you have understood the weaving instructions thus far, try it. If not—well—bind off and sew.

Is There Enough Yarn for One More Row?

Now I will talk about something more comprehensible. When you are working across a row and reach the end of the yarn before you reach the end of the row, you wish you had had a way of knowing ahead whether there was enough yarn. When you are working in stockinette or garter, if your yarn will reach generously three times across the row you should be able to make it. But, better yet, two rows ahead, tie a slip knot at the halfway point in the remaining yarn. If you reach the end of the row before you arrive at the knot, you can work one more row.

Working Equal Sections

When you have two sections that are equal or mirror equal, there are times when you would be wise to knit them simultaneously. Specifically, I am talking about the shoulders around the neck of a sweater. You will be more certain to have done the shaping the same and to have the number of rows the same on both sides. I do urge you, should it be necessary to put your knitting down, complete a two-part row. That is, have all the stitches on the same needle. When you have one shoulder on each needle, will you remember which direction you were working? You will use two balls of yarn or both ends of a skein.

Some knitters like to work the sleeves of a sweater or the fronts of a cardigan together. In doing so, any counting, such as the number of rows between increases, need be done only once.

Colors

For your information, I would like to give you my theory on blending colors so as to have a pleasing, harmonious result.

First, I want to mention the rules I was taught a century or so ago in art class. We were given the color wheel. Yellow, red, and blue are spaced clockwise around it. Between these colors are orange, violet, and green. Between all these colors are yellow-orange, orange-red, red-violet, and so on. Get the picture? You must have seen one. We were given three methods of combining colors harmoniously:

Complementary—two colors opposite each other across the color wheel.
Triad—three colors at the points of an equilateral triangle in the wheel.
Contiguous—three colors in a row around the wheel.

This system of putting colors together made me uncomfortable then, and it does now.

Observe what knowledgeable artists do. Look at paintings in a museum. Notice how color is used in better wallpaper or printed fabric. I found the clue in fine china.

There are several major classes of colors. Rainbow colors are true red, orange, yellow, green, blue, and violet. Pastels are paler tints—those let down with white. The earth tones include tans and browns, off-white, gold, olive, and burnt orange. Ivory, burgundy, bottle green, and plum can be classified as formal shades. I call them Rembrandt colors. House-paint companies have a line of gray-softened colors they call colonial.

When you are combining colors, stay within a class. You can then use any two or more colors that please you and find you have good harmony.

One more system is monochromatic—various strengths of the same color. This can be very effective when well done, but I often see mistakes, usually in blues, so be careful.

International Care Labeling System

FIVE BASIC SYMBOLS*
Each figure symbolizes one method of textile care.

means WASHING

means BLEACHING

means DRYING

means PRESSING or IRONING

means DRY CLEANING

WASHING INSTRUCTIONS
These symbols tell you either not to, or how to, wash articles.

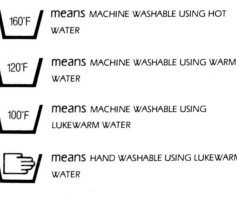

160°F means MACHINE WASHABLE USING HOT WATER

120°F means MACHINE WASHABLE USING WARM WATER

100°F means MACHINE WASHABLE USING LUKEWARM WATER

means HAND WASHABLE USING LUKEWARM WATER

means DO NOT WASH

*Symbols and care instruction reproduced with permission of Ministers of Supply and Services, Canada, "Care Labeling for Textiles," Catalog No. RG 23-872.

Reproduced by permission of American Wool Council.

BLEACHING INSTRUCTIONS

These symbols tell you when to, and when not to, use bleach.

 means USE CHLORINE BLEACH AS DIRECTED ON THE CONTAINER LABEL

 means DO NOT USE CHLORINE BLEACH

DRYING INSTRUCTIONS

These symbols tell you how an article should be dried.

 means IT MAY BE DRIED IN A TUMBLE DRYER

means IT SHOULD BE HUNG TO DRY

 means IT SHOULD BE HUNG SOAKING WET TO DRIP DRY

means IT SHOULD BE DRIED ON A FLAT SURFACE

PRESSING OR IRONING INSTRUCTIONS

These symbols tell you what may, or may not, be ironed and at what heat.

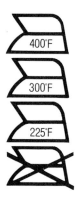

means THAT A SETTING UP TO COTTON AND LINEN MAY BE USED

means THAT A SETTING OF MEDIUM SHOULD BE USED

means THAT A SETTING OF LOW SHOULD BE USED

means DO NOT PRESS OR IRON

DRY CLEANING INSTRUCTIONS

These symbols tell you what may, or may not, be dry cleaned.

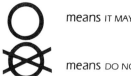 **means** IT MAY BE DRY CLEANED

means DO NOT DRY CLEAN

Hints I Don't Know Where to Put

Do you have trouble with uneven knit and purl? Use a pair of needles made of two sizes. Check your gauge using this pair.

Not all needles bearing the same size number are exactly the same size. Check with a needle gauge or poke a hole with one in paper, then see how the other fits.

No yarn bobbin? Use a book of matches.

No stitch holder? Use a double-point needle and rubber bands.

No cable needle? Use a toothpick, a bobby pin, straighten a paper clip.

Trouble knitting from a cable needle? Slide the stitches from the cable needle back onto the left needle. Keep the held stitches in the same order.

Do not knit after reading newspapers or magazines. Newsprint ink is very hard to remove. Some hand lotions can leave a permanent stain.

Wash dirty yarn before knitting with it.

Gauge is individual. Shared knitting will probably show.

Do not hang knitted garments on hooks or hangers.

For a too-tight armhole, insert a gusset made as follows: Cast on 2 stitches. Increase 1 stitch at the beginning of every third row to the desired width, then decrease 1 stitch at the beginning of every third row. Open the underarm sleeve and side seam and sew in the gusset. The cast-on and bind-off are in the seams.

FOR HIM

4

When he is someone special to you, why not do something special for him? Knit a gift for him. As a beginning knitter, your very-first-ever project can be a garter stitch scarf. True, there is not much excitement in knitting a garter stitch scarf, unless it is your first venture into knitting. Then the adventure may be in maintaining the right number of stitches.

I suspect that you may have bought some inexpensive synthetic yarn to see if you like knitting. But do you know what? For a couple of reasons, a better first yarn is good wool. Knitting is easier with wool, because it has better spring and will cooperate with you. It takes a very experienced knitter to make an item of inelastic, inexpensive synthetic yarn look good. Second, when you invest a little more money in a project, you are more inclined to stay with it.

Garter Stitch Scarf

Supplies: For his garter stitch scarf you will need about 3 ounces of four-ply worsted-weight yarn and a pair of #10 needles. This will make a scarf 9″ by 48″.

Let me give you a few suggestions about selecting your needles. Ten-inch single-point needles will be easier than longer needles to handle. You may prefer plastic to metal, as they are lighter in weight. And try to find needles with a slightly concave point that ends in a bulb, rather than those that look as though they were shaped in a pencil sharpener.

Gauge: Your gauge should be about 3½ stitches per inch. I dislike starting you out breaking a golden rule of knitting, but gauge is not vital when making a scarf, so long as you are pleased with its texture.

Begin by casting on 30 stitches. Work in garter stitch—knit every row—until you have used all but 1 yard of the yarn. Bind off loosely.

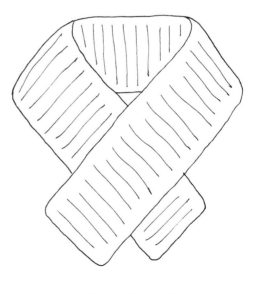

Garter stitch scarf

A final hint: Do not cut your cast-on and bind-off tails short. Leave about 2″, which should be cut at an angle. Use a tapestry needle to run the ends up the edge through the nubs.

Now you are finished. Aren't you proud? You have opened the door to the world of knitting.

Ribbed Scarf

You are not an absolute novice at knitting and you want to make him a scarf. The tweed one shown in the photograph took me five hours to knit. A Continental knitter could have made it in less time, because less time is used taking the yarn back and forth between the needles.

Supplies: 4 ounces of four-ply worsted-weight yarn will be ample. You will need a pair of #10 needles. I also used a pair of #8 needles, for working the first and the last inch, to prevent the ends of the scarf from flaring out.

Gauge: The gauge when you are working in ribbing is difficult to determine, because it depends on the elasticity of the yarn. The wool I used has good spring, so my gauge in k1, p1 ribbing is almost 7 stitches per inch, which makes the scarf only 6″ wide. Of course, it will stretch out. Yarn with less spring will give you fewer stitches per inch.

Scarf: Cast on 40 stitches. Work in k1, p1 ribbing until you have used all but 1 yard of your yarn, or until the scarf is 48″. Every row will begin with k1 and end with p1. Bind off loosely in pattern—knit each stitch you would have knit and purl each stitch you would have purled were you working the row. The use of a larger size needle helps to keep the bind-off loose. I think this ribbing is a good pattern for a tailored scarf, and I feel fringe is superfluous.

Vest

You would like to make a vest for him, but you have never followed directions all by yourself. I will try to tell you how, very clearly. It is best to go over the directions before starting. Circle all the numbers that you will be using, all those intended for the size you are making. First, do you know how to read the sizes written with parentheses (☐)? S (M, L) means Small (Medium, Large), so 5 (6, 7) means that you do the stitch or patterns 5 times when you are making the small size, 6 times for the medium size, and 7 times for the large size. When you are given only one number, it applies to all sizes.

The knitting knowledge you will need for this vest is: cast on, knit, purl, decrease, bind off. To make the decrease, knit through two stitches as if they were one. The directions will read "k2 tog"—knit 2 together.

Supplies: The sizes S (M, L) are for a chest measurement of the garment of 37″ (41″, 45″). The yarn is four-ply worsted weight, wool or synthetic. You will need 12 (14, 16) ounces. Remember to check the dye-lot numbers when buying your yarn. The suggested needle sizes are 5 and 8.

Gauge: 4½ stitches per inch in stockinette stitch on #8 needles.

Check your gauge. With the yarn you are using for the vest and #8 needles, work in stockinette stitch (knit 1 row, purl 1 row). Read the section on gauge in Chapter 2. If you must, change the needle size to get the correct gauge, then change the smaller needle accordingly.

Ready to start?

Back: On #5 needles, cast on 84 (94, 102) stitches. Work in garter stitch (knit every row) until there are 8 ridges on the right side. Change to #8 needles. (Just knit off the left needle with an 8.) Work in stockinette stitch for about 3″ above the garter stitch. To check the width, work to the center of a row and spread out the work. Edges in stockinette will curl under; be sure to uncurl them in order to get a true measurement. You should have 18″–19″ (20″–21″, 22″–23″). Continue in stockinette stitch until the back of the vest measures 12″ (12½″, 13″) from the beginning (the stitches you cast on). End having just completed a knit row.

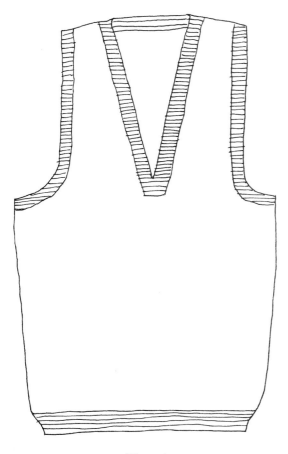

His vest

Armhole edging:

Row 1: K8 (10, 11), p68 (74, 80), k8 (10, 11).
Row 2: Knit all stitches.
Repeat these two rows twice more. (This means in total you work rows 1, 2, 1, 2, 1, 2.) There should be three garter ridges each edge on the right side.

Armholes:

Row 1: Bind off 4 (6, 7) stitches, k4 (you really knit only 3 more stitches, because there is a stitch on your right needle remaining from binding off, which you have already knit, but this is the way directions must be written so that the numbers will add up correctly), p68 (74, 80), k8 (10, 11).
Row 2: Bind off 4 (6, 7) stitches and knit across. (This means knit to the end of the row.)
Row 3: K4, purl to the last 4, k4.
Row 4: (Decrease row) K3, k2 tog, knit to the last 5 stitches, k2 tog, k3.

Repeat rows 3 and 4, 3 (4, 5) times more. These decreases are somewhat hidden. You can see them when you hold your work up to a light. But realize, if you have lost count of the decreases, that there is a decrease at each edge following a garter ridge on the right side, so you can count the ridges. And, of course, you can check the decreases by counting the stitches remaining on your needle. This is why you are given the total number of stitches.

Work even (no decreasing) on 68 (72, 76) stitches as follows:

Purl side: K4, purl to the last 4, k4.
Knit side: Knit.

Repeat these two rows until the armhole is the required depth. To get this measurement, draw an imaginary line across the back of the vest from bind-off to bind-off. Pin a safety pin along this line. Measure from the pin. When you are in doubt about measuring armhole depth, be generous. Many new knitters err in measuring armholes. Do you remember symbol ⊥ from high school geometry? It means perpendicular. Measurements are almost always made ⊥, especially armholes. A too-tight armhole is very uncomfortable. When the armhole measures ⊥ 8½″ (9″, 9½″), ending with an all-knit row, change to #5 needles and knit 6 rows. There should be three garter ridges on the right side. Using a #8 needle, bind off loosely. Your bind-off forms a fourth garter ridge on the right side.

Take a look at the vest back you have just made. Check again to be sure the chest measurement is good. The width across between the armholes should be 15" (16", 17"). When you have completed the vest back, you should have used about half of the yarn.

Front: On #5 needles, cast on 84 (94, 102) stitches. Work the same as for the back to the start of the armhole edging.

Armhole and neck edging:

Row 1: K8 (10, 11), p30 (33, 36), k8, p30 (33, 36), k8 (10, 11).

Row 2: Knit.

Repeat these two rows twice more. You will have three garter ridges at each edge and in the center on the right side.

Armholes and V neck: Bind off 4 (6, 7), k4, p30 (33, 36), k8, p30 (33, 36), k8 (10, 11). Bind off 4 (6, 7), k38 (41, 44). Join a second ball or the other end of your skein. To do so, tie the new yarn with a single knot around the current yarn. Leave a tail about 4". Using two balls of yarn permits the separation for the V neck. With the new yarn, knit the remaining 38 (41, 44) stitches. From now on I advise you to complete every two-part row—that is, when you put your knitting down, have all the stitches on the same needle. Should you stop with a shoulder on each needle, you will need to count the garter ridges to know in which direction you are to work. Start back on the two-part row with the second ball to the V, k4, purl to the last 4, k4. With the original ball, give a little tug to avoid a loop, k4, purl to the last 4, k4. You are to decrease 1 stitch at each arm edge every knit row 4 (5, 6) times AND AT THE SAME TIME decrease 1 stitch at each neck edge every other knit row 14 (15, 16) times. You would be wise to make a chart to keep track of the decreasing.

Row 1: K3, k2 tog, knit to the last 5 stitches, k2 tog, k3. Repeat for the second shoulder.

Row 2: K4, purl to the last 4, k4. Repeat for the second shoulder.

Row 3: K3, k2 tog, knit to the V neck. Knit to the last 5, k2 tog, k3.

Row 4: Repeat row 2.

Repeat these 4 rows until you have completed 4 (5, 6) armhole decreases. You really need the chart, don't you? Continue decreasing every other knit row at each neck edge by knitting together the fourth and fifth stitches from the neck edges until you have completed 14 (15, 16) decreases. Each shoulder will have 20 (21, 22) stitches. Work even—no more decreases—until the fronts are the same as the back above the underarm bind-off. Count the garter ridges. On the fronts the stockinette-and-garter pattern is worked to the top on #8 needles. This will make the front measure slightly longer than the back, so it is necessary to count. Bind-off the shoulder stitches loosely in pattern on wrong-side rows. Cut the yarn, leaving ends long enough to sew the shoulder seams.

Finishing: Sew the left shoulder in whip stitch, taking care to include both lines of the bind-off. Match the bound-off stitches on the right shoulder to the back so that you will know where to begin. Sew the right shoulder. Run the sewing ends and the end from the back bind-off into the shoulder seams for about 2". Using any ends from knitting plus yarn from the skein, sew the side seams in nub-and-bar. (See Side Edge to Side Edge in Chapter 2.) Be

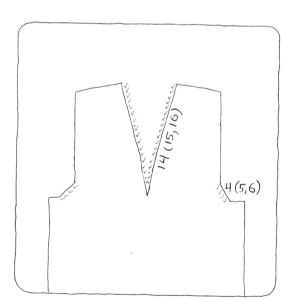

Decrease chart

sure the garter and stockinette areas match. Use the end at the V to close the space, if any, then work it in. If you have joined a new skein on the edge in the armhole, run one yarn end up and the other down about 2″ to hide them in the edge.

You would be wise to make a note of the amount and brand of yarn you have used and for which size, for future reference. Why not use this book to keep your record?

Hat

How about making a hat for him to match his ribbed scarf? Can you work with a set of four double-point (dp) needles? This hat, called a watch cap, really looks better without a seam. It takes me four hours to make one.

Supplies: 3 ounces of four-ply worsted-weight yarn should be ample.

Gauge: If you work with average tension, you probably will find #7 needles the right size, and you may feel safer with a set of 10″ needles. Again, it is difficult to give a gauge for k1, p1 ribbing. The needles on which you get 5 stitches per inch in stockinette are a good size to use.

Hat: On a #7 needle, cast on 96 stitches. (You may want to use a single-point needle for this.) Work k1, p1 ribbing for 32 stitches on each of 3 dp needles. Bring the knitting ends together to form a triangle. Check that the work is not twisted. Join and work around in ribbing. Your cap will look small, but it will stretch out. To verify this, when you have about 3″, work to the center of one of the needles. Spread the stitches out on the needles as far as you dare and try it on your head. Continue in ribbing until you have 9″ or the desired length from the cast-on. It will take 3″ more to complete the crown decreasing.

The decrease used in this cap is a special double decrease (d dec). This is how it is made: Slip 2 together, k1, p2sso. What this means is send the right needle as if to knit through 2 stitches together on the left needle and slip them to the right needle, knit the next stitch, then pass the 2 slipped stitches back over the knit stitch, as in binding off. Read over how to do it again. It is a little tricky, but I like the result, a predominant knit stitch with ribbing dissolving under it. Start the decrease rounds above the cast-on tail. Pin a safety pin at the top of the work at that point to remind you where the rounds begin.

Round 1: (Rib 11, d dec, rib 10) 4 times.
I know knitting directions sometimes are confusing. What this direction means is that there are 4 double decreases, separated by 21 stitches in which the rib pattern is maintained. And it also means that you start the round at the mid-point, between two decreases, so that the beginning of each round will always be maintained with a knit stitch. Now you can see the advantage of knitting-directions shorthand.

Round 2: (Rib 11, k1, rib 10) 4 times. (This means that for four times there will be 3 knit stitches together.)
Round 3: (Rib 10, d dec, rib 9) 4 times.
Round 4: Rib around.
Round 5: (Rib 9, d dec, rib 8) 4 times.
Round 6: (Rib 9, k1, rib 8) 4 times.
Round 7: (Rib 8, d dec, rib 7) 4 times.
Round 8: Rib around.
Round 9: (Rib 7, d dec, rib 6) 4 times.
Round 10: (Rib 7, k1, rib 6) 4 times.
Round 11: (Rib 6, d dec, rib 5) 4 times.

Round 12: Rib around.
Round 13: (Rib 5, d dec, rib 4) 4 times.
Round 14: (Rib 5, kl, rib 4) 4 times.
Round 15: (Rib 4, d dec, rib 3) 4 times.
Round 16: Rib around.
Round 17: (Rib 3, d dec, rib 2) 4 times.
Round 18: (Rib 3, k1, rib 2) 4 times.
Round 19: (Rib 2, d dec, p1) 4 times.

As you are decreasing you will need to shift some stitches forward to accommodate the d dec. Keep the beginning stitch on each needle a knit stitch, and remember not to disturb the beginning of the rounds. When the total number of stitches is small enough, without disturbing the starting place of the rounds, shift the stitches so that the first needle after the start of the round has half the total number of stitches, and each of the other two has a fourth of the total. At the end of round 19, cut the yarn at about 6". With a tapestry needle, send the yarn through each of the remaining 16 stitches, in the same direction you have been knitting, and close. I like to go around again through all the stitches. Run the yarn down through the center of the little star you have made and hide the end for a couple of inches behind one of the decrease lines. Use the starting tail to close the space that you always get on the bottom edge, then run the tail up on the outside, because a cuff will be turned up.

Let me talk about watch caps in general. The size — the width around — can be varied by changing the needle size. For those who have full hair that they do not want crushed, the warmth lost in the cap by working on larger needles is compensated for by the individual's hair. For a youngster, reduce the needle size and the length before decreasing. A still smaller cap can be made with #4 needles and sport-weight yarn.

The magic number for watch caps is 96, because you can use a variety of ribbings: 1/1, 2/2, 3/3, 4/4, 6/6, or 6/2.

The basic adult watch cap pattern is as follows: On #7 needles cast on 96 stitches. K2, p2 ribbing, having 32 stitches on each of three needles, for 8". Change to stockinette (in circular work, all knit) for 2" or desired length. It will take 2" more for the crown decreasing.
Round 1: (K14, k2 tog) 6 times.

Round 2: (K13, k2 tog) 6 times.
Round 3: (K12, k2 tog) 6 times.
Round 4: (K11, k2 tog) 6 times.

Continue decreasing 6 stitches every round until 12 stitches remain. Send the yarn twice around through the remaining stitches, close, and send it inside and secure. Notice the design your decreasing has made.

In knitting a cap, be creative. Add a contrast stripe. Keep in mind where you put the ends of yarn, because of the turned-up cuff. In finishing, work the ends into their own color. Add another 3" for a double roll cuff. Sew on a pompon or tassel. See how you can play around when you understand what you are doing? You can even stray from the magic number by adding or subtracting in multiples of 12 when you work in 2/2 ribbing, or in multiples of 6 when you work in 1/1 or 3/3 ribbing. When you add a contrast, remember not to mix fibers. Make your project of all the same material, because different fibers wear differently and you care for them differently. Treat part wool as if it were all wool.

Cardigan

Think how pleased he will be with a cardigan in his favorite color that you have knit especially for him.

The directions for the green cardigan are for S (M, L) with chest measurements for the garment of 37" (41", 45").

Supplies: This sweater requires 18 (20, 22) ounces of four-ply worsted-weight yarn. The needles are #4 and #8, or the size you require to get the correct gauge.

Gauge: The gauge is 4½ stitches per inch in stockinette stitch.

Back: On #4, cast on 84 (92, 100) stitches. Work in k2, p2 ribbing for 2½". Change to #8 needles and stockinette stitch. When you have a few inches above the ribbing, work to the center of a row and measure across. The width should be 18"–19" (20"–21", 22"–23"). Work until the back measures 15" (15½", 16") from the cast-on.

Armhole: Bind off 3 (4, 5) stitches at the beginning of the next 2 rows. Decrease 1 stitch at each edge every knit row 3 (4, 5) times. Work even on 72 (76, 80) stitches until the armhole measures ⊥ 8½" (9", 10"). End with a purl row.

Shoulder: At the beginning of each of the next 2 rows bind off 11 (12, 12) stitches in pattern. Slipping the first stitch in pattern, bind off 11 (11, 12) stitches at the beginning of the next 2 rows. (When you shape a shoulder like this you build steps. When you slip as if to knit or purl the first stitch, you smooth over the steps.) Bind off the remaining 28 (30, 32) stitches for the back of the neck.

Right front: On #4 cast on 52 (56, 60) stitches.

Row 1: K10, p2, *k2, p2. Repeat from * across. (Right side.)

Row 2: K2, *p2, k2. Repeat from * to the last 10 sts, p5, k5.

Repeat these two rows until the ribbing is the same length as that for the back. End having just completed row 2. Change to #8 needles AND decrease 2 stitches evenly spaced in the first row of stockinette stitch. (Decrease 1 stitch at about a third of the way across and another at two thirds of the way across.) To make the decreases subtle, knit together a second purl and a first knit. The pattern above the ribbing is:

Row 1: Knit.

Row 2: Purl to the last 5 stitches, k5.

Repeat these 2 rows on 50 (54, 58) stitches. If you have trouble remembering to knit the last 5 stitches on the purl row, keep a small ring marker on the needle between the garter and the stockinette. The 5 garter stitches at the center front are a facing. Notice two things about the facing—how willing it is to fold back and how well it draws up. Cardigans have a tendency to droop in front, some so badly that the lower corners swing around to the sides. The garter facing helps to prevent this. The 2 purl stitches in the ribbing next to the 5 stockinette stitches define the section in which the buttons will be sewn on. Continue until the length of the front is the same as that of the back to the armhole.

Armhole and V neck: Bind off in purl 3 (4, 5) stitches at the beginning of a purl row at the arm edge. Decrease 1 stitch at the arm edge every knit row 3 (4, 5) times AND, starting on the same row, decrease 1 stitch for the V neck every other knit row 12 (13, 14) times. To make the V-neck decrease, knit the first 9 stitches, slip 1 stitch as if to knit, k1, psso. You may need a decrease chart for a while, yet do learn to look at your work in counting the decreases. The slip, knit, and pass decrease is not as neat as the k2 tog decrease because of the direction in which the ply in hand-knitting yarn is twisted. It is used on the right side of the V neck because it better defines the 5 stockinette stitches at the neck edge. The fact that this decrease is not as neat makes it more easily recognized. When you have made some neck decreases, look carefully at them so you can learn what they look like, then understand when it is time to decrease again. If you lose track of how many times you have decreased, try to count your decreases. To check, add the number of stitches you are to bind off for the shoulder to 10 (for the back of the neck edging). Subtract this from the stitches on your needle. The difference is the number row you have yet to decrease.

The shoulder shaping may begin before you have completed the V-neck decreases. If you have made the armhole too shallow, you must increase the frequency of the V-neck decreases to get them all in.

Shoulder: When the armhole depth is the same as that of the back, starting at the arm edge, bind off in purl 11 (12, 12) stitches, complete the row, then knit back. Bind off 11 (11, 12) stitches at the beginning of the next arm edge row. Remember to slip the first stitch. Work on the remaining 10 stitches, keeping the garter-and-stockinette pattern, until the piece is half the width of the back of the neck. Be a little stingy in this measurement. If you wish, you can try kitchener weaving, as described in Chapter 3, or bind off on a knit-and-purl row. If you are going to weave, put the 10 stitches on a holder and leave a length of yarn.

Mark with safety pins the location of the buttons on the right front. The tradition is an uneven number. The bottom button is placed ½" above the cast-on stitches, the top button immediately below the start of the V-neck shaping. Space the rest of the pins evenly, about 3" apart. As you work the left front you will make buttonholes to correspond with the safety pins on the right front.

Buttonholes: On the knit side in the 10 border stitches, k2 tog, cast on 2 stitches (flip loop), k2 tog, k2, k2 tog, cast on 2, k2 tog.

Left front: On #4 needles, cast on 50 (54, 58) stitches.
Row 1: *K2, p2. Repeat from * to the last 10 sts, k10.
Row 2: K5, p5, *k2, p2. Repeat from * to the end.
Repeat these two rows, remembering the buttonholes, until the ribbing is the same length as that of the other front. Change to #8 needles and stockinette stitch, keeping the 5-stitch garter facing. There are no decreases on the left front at the end of the ribbing.

Armhole and V neck: When the front is the same length as the back to the armhole, bind off 3 (4, 5) stitches at the arm edge at the beginning of a knit row. The top buttonhole should be made no later than this row. Work a purl row. Decrease 1 stitch at the arm edge every knit row 3 (4, 5) times AND decrease 1 stitch for the V neck every other knit row 12 (13, 14) times, by knitting together the eleventh and tenth stitches from the front edge. When the left front armhole is the same depth as that of the back, bind off 11 (12, 12) stitches at the beginning of the arm edge, complete the row, work back, then bind off 11 (11, 12) stitches. Work on the remaining 10 stitches, keeping the garter-and-stockinette pattern, until the piece is half the width of the back of the neck. If you are going to weave the halves of the neck border together, put the remaining stitches on a holder and cut the yarn at least 4 times the width of the 10 stitches. If you are going to sew the ends together, bind off on a knit-and-purl row and leave an end long enough for sewing.

Sleeves: On #4 needles, cast on 40 (44, 48) stitches. Work in k2, p2 ribbing for 3". Change to #8 needles AND in the first row of stockinette increase 4 stitches evenly spaced—(knit 7, inc in 1) 4 times. Continue in stockinette, increasing 1 stitch at each edge every third knit row 12 times. When you are using the "knit in the front and the back of the same stitch" increase, the edges will be neater if the increases are made in the first stitch and the next to last stitch. Work even on 68 (72, 76) stitches until the sleeve measures 19" (19½", 20") from the cast-on.

Cap of sleeve: Starting on the knit side, bind off 3 (4, 5) stitches at the beginning of the next 2 rows. Decrease 1 stitch at the beginning of every row—k2 tog at the beginning of the knit row, p2 tog at the beginning of the purl row—until the cap measures ⊥ 4½″ (4½″, 5″). Bind off the remaining stitches. You can round the corners by decreasing 1 stitch at the beginning and at the end of the bind-off row.

Finishing: Join the back of the neck border by weaving, or sewing bind-off to bind-off. Join the shoulders. Watch that the neck border is straight. Set in the sleeve cap. Pin the center of the bind-off at the top of the sleeve to the shoulder seam. Match the underarm bind-offs and nub to nub along the sides of the cap of the sleeve. Sew the side edges in nub-and-bar, sending the needle under two strands when the nub is a decrease. The top of the sleeve is sewn side edge to bind-off. Count so that you can sew bound-off stitches to bars evenly spaced. Sew the border to the back of the neck in the same way. Sew the side and sleeve seams, matching all junctures. Sew the facing in place without tension, so that a line is not obvious on the right side. Be sure that the pairs of buttonholes are together. Close the opening at the bottom or not, as you choose. Send the needle under one strand in a garter nub, then under the top of a stitch opposite the next nub. You are catching every other nub and 1 stitch every fourth row. The stitches you are using on the back of the stockinette should be in a straight vertical line up to the V. When you run out of yarn sewing back the facing, duplicate the path of the last 2″ or 3″ with the new strand. No knots. As I have told you, wool and wool-like synthetics are self-locking. At the back of the neck, sew the garter facing to the seam. Sew the pairs of buttonholes together. These buttonholes are easy to make but they are small. They can stretch, and you want to avoid losing the stretch. Run some yarn on a tapestry needle on the inside of the facing, entering an inch or two from the buttonhole and catching what garter ridges you can. Come out at the buttonhole. Whip the pair of buttonholes together, being careful not to pull in, then run the end into the facing. It is better not to use a continuous strand. I would sew the buttonholes first, then take the sweater to the store for buttons that fit. If possible, use yarn to sew on the buttons.

Hunter Mittens

Supplies: To make a pair of hunter mittens, 4 ounces of four-ply worsted-weight yarn is ample. You will need 4 small stitch holders.

Gauge: You will probably need #4 needles to get a gauge of 5½ stitches per inch. Use a set of double-point needles.

These directions are sufficient for a palm girth to 9″ or 9½″. I give you generous lengths. Always a good idea when making mittens is drawing an outline of the hand on a piece of paper, for reference.

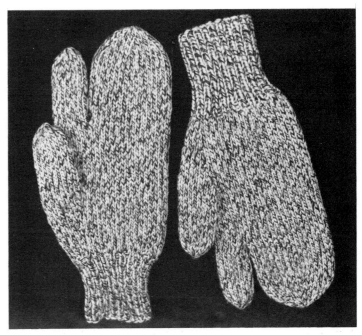

Hunter mittens: Cast on 40 stitches. Work in k1, p1 ribbing for 12 stitches on the first needle, 14 each on the second and third. Each needle will start with k1 and end with p1. Join, being careful not to twist. Rib for 3″. End above the cast-on tail.

Increase round: Use the "knit in the front and the back" increase. Increase in each of the first 2 stitches, k1, p1—this begins the thumb gusset —(k3, inc in 1) 8 times, k3, p1. Work 3 rounds even, keeping the purls as follows: needle #1, k5, p1, k10; needle #2, k17; needle #3, k16, p1.

Outline

Be aware that the needle number refers not actually to the needle itself, but to the position. Needle #1 is the needle beginning above the starting tail. For the second thumb gusset increase, on needle #1, increase in the first stitch, k2, inc in 1, k1, p1, knit the remainder of the round to the very last stitch, which is purled. Work 3 rounds even, keeping the purls. Continue increasing every fourth round in the first stitch on needle #1 and the second stitch before the purl until there are 13 stitches between purl stitches. Keep the purls on the even rounds. I like the purl outline of the gusset not only as an aid for the increasing, but also for the neater fit it gives the thumb base. Notice how nicely the purls continue from the ribbing.

There are a number of ways to keep track of the rounds when the directions say, as in this thumb gusset, to do something every such and such round. Usually one first thinks of making marks on a piece of paper. For these mittens you can also count the ridges on the inside above the ribbing. After each multiple of 4 you are ready for the next increase. It is very useful to learn to count what you see. Look at your work after the increase, then when you have knit 1 plain round, then 2 plain rounds, then 3 plain rounds. In the "knit in the front and the back increase" you can see the nub of the increase and count above it. Can you also understand why this increase is made in the first stitch after the first purl and in the second stitch before the second purl? Look at the increase nub on each side of the gusset and see how far it is from the purl.

One other way to count every fourth round is to have an odd-color needle in your set of four or to mark one with a dab of nail polish. Use the odd or marked needle for the first increase. It will return to the same position every fourth round.

Back to your hunter mittens. After your final gusset increase, work 2 rounds even. Start the third round k13, p1, then put the last worked 15 stitches on a holder. This includes both purls. Your stitches on the holder will be safer, should the holder become undone, if you slide the stitches on around to the other side. Complete the third round. Cast on 5 stitches on needle #3. Slip 7 stitches from needle #3 to the spare

needle and complete needle #1. Knit around for 4 or 5 rounds on 48 stitches. Knit and shift 3 stitches from needle #1 back to needle #3. This puts the beginning of your round back where it belongs. It was off center for a while, to avoid a hole at the base of the thumb. Work until 2″ above the cast-on, or the length from the crotch of the thumb to the crotch of the first finger on your outline.

For the left hand, knit 11 stitches (for the right hand, knit 6 stitches) on needle #1. Put the last worked 14 stitches on a stitch holder. Complete the round. Cast on 2 stitches. For the left hand, slip 4 stitches to the spare needle (for the right hand, knit 2 stitches from needle #1 and put them on needle #3) and complete needle #1. Work 4 or 5 rounds. Shift your stitches so that there is a change of needles directly above and between the 2 cast-on stitches. Keeping this beginning split, shift so that there are 12 stitches on each needle. Knit until 2½″ above the 2 stitches cast on, or allow 1″ for the shaping, measuring on his outline.

Round 1: (K4, k2 tog) 6 times.
Round 2: Knit.
Round 3: (K3, k2 tog) 6 times.
Round 4: Knit.
Round 5: (K2, k2 tog) 6 times.
Round 6: Knit.
Round 7: (K1, k2 tog) 6 times.
Round 8: Knit.
Round 9: (K2 tog) 6 times.

Cut the yarn at 4″ and with a tapestry needle pass it through the remaining 6 stitches twice, then send it to the inside and secure.

Finger: Slip 14 stitches from the holder to a needle. Join the yarn and knit 7 stitches onto

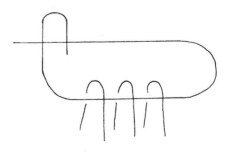

Stitches on holder

each of 2 needles. With a crochet hook—#00 steel is a handy size—and yarn, pick up 3 or 4 stitches from the cast-on 2. I will explain how to pick up stitches for mittens. Do you see a bar between a stitch under the last stitch knit and the stitch to the left? Send your hook in on the right and then out on the left, duplicating the path of the bar. I sometimes send the hook under a third strand on the left on the edge of the cast-on. Catch the yarn, draw it through, and put this stitch on a third needle so that the yarn from the skein is to the back. Pick up 1 or 2 stitches from the cast-on, sending the hook under two strands for each. For the last stitch, send the hook under a strand on the edge of the cast-on, then in and out, duplicating the path of the bar in the space before the next needle. Do you see how you have eliminated the holes that can be so discouraging for mitten or glove knitters? Shift 1 stitch from each of the other two needles to the crotch needle, needle #3. If necessary, in the first round decrease in the center of the crotch needle to 5 stitches. Knit around even on 17 stitches until the finger measures 2½", or allow ⅓" for the shaping, measuring on the outline.

Round 1: (K1, k2 tog) 5 times, k2.
Round 2: Knit.
Round 3: (K2 tog) 6 times.
Cut the yarn and pass it through the remaining 6 stitches twice, then to the inside.

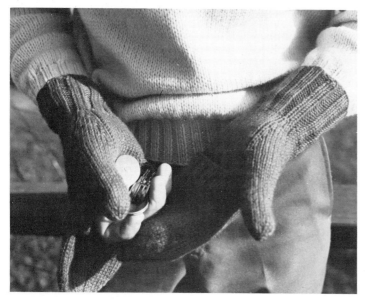

Thumb: Slip 15 stitches from the holder to a needle. Join the yarn and knit 8 stitches onto the first needle, 7 stitches onto the second. Pick up 6 or 7 stitches from the cast-on 5 as for the finger, except when getting the first stitch, send the hook toward you through the top of the purl stitch. Shift 2 stitches from needle #1 and 1 stitch from needle #2 to the crotch needle. Decrease 2 stitches on the first round on needle #3 and 1 or 2 stitches on the second round, so that each needle will have 6 stitches. Knit around even on 18 stitches until the thumb measures 2¼", or allow ⅓" for shaping using the outline.
Round 1: (K1, k2 tog) 6 times.
Round 2: Knit.
Round 3: (K2 tog) 6 times.
Finish as for the finger.

Finishing: Turn the mitten inside out. Work in the ends in areas that will receive wear, for reinforcement. Use the starting tail to close the gap, then work it in on the inside.

Access Mittens

Does he have to take off his mittens when he works outside in cold weather because he needs to use his fingers? He can wear his mittens and have the use of his fingers too. I made a pair of access mittens for our mailman several years ago, and they enable him easily to sort the mail and still have warm hands. I think he is ready for another pair this year.

Supplies: You will need 4 ounces of four-ply worsted-weight yarn and a set of #4 double-point needles. You also will need two small stitch holders.

Gauge: Your gauge should be 5½ stitches per inch in stockinette stitch.

Cast on 40 stitches. Divide them 12, 12, and 16 on three needles. Work in k2, p2 ribbing for 3".

Increase round and start of gusset: Use the "knit in the front and the back" increase. On needle #1—starting above the cast-on tail—increase in the first stitch, k1, p1, (k3, inc in 1) 8 times, k4, p1. You have now made the first increase in the thumb gusset plus increased to 48 stitches for the palm. Work 3 rounds even—no increasing—keeping the 2 purl stitches. For the second gusset increase, increase in each of the first 2 stitches, k1, p1, knit to the very last stitch, p1. Work 3 rounds even, keeping the purls. Continue the gusset, increasing every fourth round by increasing in the first stitch and in the second stitch before the purl. (See the methods for counting rows by 4s in the hunter mitten directions.) When there are 11 stitches between the purls, work 2 rounds even, keeping the purls. On needle #1, k11, p1. Put the last worked 13 stitches on a holder for the thumb. Complete the round.

Access flap: Cast on 4 stitches on needle #3. The single-strand cast-on in Chapter 2 is the safest. (For the right-hand mitten, slide the 4 cast-on stitches to the spare needle, then knit 18 stitches from needles #1 and #2 to the spare needle.) For both left and right mittens—I suggest you do the left mitten first—start working in the opposite direction.

Row 1: On 22 stitches, p2, *k2, p2. Repeat from *.

Row 2: Turn. K2, *p2, k2. Repeat from *.

Work 2″ of ribbing on 22 stitches. Bind off LOOSELY in pattern on row 1. Cut the yarn, leaving a 6″ end for sewing.

Palm: Join the yarn at the left of the flap, leaving a 6″ end for sewing, and knit the remaining stitches. Cast on 22 stitches. You will have to turn your work for single-strand cast-on. Tuck the flap inside so that it will not be in the way. Shift some stitches so that they are on three of your needles. Join the knitting, being careful not to twist, and knit around to where you cast on the 22 stitches. K2, *p2, k2. Repeat from * across the cast-on stitches and knit the remainder. It is easier to start a needle with k2 than p2. Keep the cast-on stitches in ribbing for 1″, then knit all the stitches. Shift the stitches again, if necessary, so that there is a needle split centered above the thumb, and 16 stitches on each of the needles. Needle #1 begins above the thumb. Knit around until you have 4″ above the access cast-on, or allow 1½″ for decreasing the tip.

Tip: Start on needle #1.

Round 1: (K6, k2 tog) 6 times.

Round 2: Knit.

Round 3: (K5, k2 tog) 6 times.

Round 4: Knit.

Round 5: (K4, k2 tog) 6 times.

Round 6: Knit.

Round 7: (K3, k2 tog) 6 times.

Continue decreasing every other round until 6 stitches remain. Do not work a plain round. Cut the yarn, leaving 4″. With a tapestry needle, send the yarn in the same direction as you have been knitting, through the remaining 6 stitches twice, then to the inside.

Thumb: Slip the stitches from the holder to a needle. Join the yarn and knit the stitches onto two needles: 7 stitches on one, 6 stitches on the other. For the inside of the thumb, pick up 1 stitch in the corner, to prevent a hole (see the direction for the hunter mittens), 4 or 5 stitches from the 4 stitches you cast on for the inner flap, and a stitch in the other corner to prevent a hole. Knit 1 stitch from the 7 to the crotch needle. Knit around, decreasing 1 stitch in the center of the crotch needle each round until there are 6 stitches on each needle. Complete the thumb following the directions for the hunter mittens.

Finishing: Turn the mittens inside out. Look at the lower corners of the flap. You probably will see loose areas. It is next to impossible to avoid this. As you sew the sides of the inner flap toward the tip with the tails you have left, close the holes. Work in all the ends for a couple of inches in areas that will benefit by being reinforced. Use the beginning tail to close the gap in the cast-on, then run it up on the inside.

Plain Mittens

Would you prefer a pair of plain mittens? Follow the directions for access mittens through the end of the thumb gusset. Cast on 4 stitches at the crotch of the thumb. Knit around on all stitches to the desired length, then decrease the tip as for the access mittens. The thumb is made the same. There is no difference between the right and left mittens unless you put a pattern on the back. There are a few things to keep in mind in varying the size. The number of stitches cast on for the cuff should be a multiple of 4 for k2, p2 ribbing. The stitches for the hand should be a multiple of 6. The thumb gusset comes from the first k2 on needle #1 and has a purl stitch on either side. The thumb crotch cast-on is 4 stitches, because you are replacing the k2 and the 2 purls that have gone into the thumb.

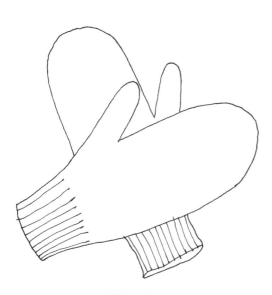

Plain mitten

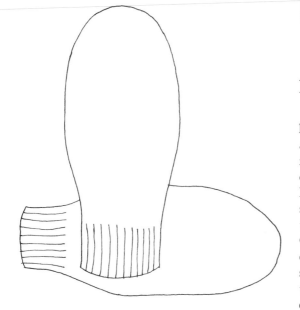

Jogger mitten

Jogger Mittens

I have recently learned from joggers that on a cold early-morning run, even with mittens, a thumb gets cold and so is taken in with the fingers to keep warm. Why not make a pair of mittens sans thumbs for a jogger? And wouldn't it be wise to make them in a bright color?

Fair Isle Pullover Sweater

Isn't this a good-looking sweater? Would you like to make one like this for him? If so, there are a number of things we should talk about first. Notice the shoulder line, which is dropped. This is called a Continental shoulder. I want to tell you the way I prefer making sleeves, which is to pick up the stitches from the armhole and work down to the wrist. The Continental shoulder is best for a first try, because the sleeve has no cap. By picking up stitches for the sleeve, you avoid having to sew the sleeve into the armhole. Also, you can try on the sweater to determine the best sleeve length. Then, if you work the cuff on four needles, there is no seam, whether the cuff remains down or is turned up. The wrist ribbing worked on four double-point needles also seems to hold better.

Next, let's talk about the color design in the yoke. I have already talked about colorfastness in the wash-and-block section. I have obeyed my rules in blending the colors oyster, sage, and cranberry, which are earth tones. This pattern has been designed to be easy to follow. You never are to carry more than two colors, and you never carry any color behind more than 3 stitches. When you knit across a row, twisting two colors by taking the new color over the old, your yarn is in a tangle. When you purl back, and the new color is taken over the old, you untwist the tangle. If you feel you cannot tolerate the tangled yarn, there are things to do about it. You can put pins or rubber bands on the skeins of yarn and hold your knitting high to allow the skeins to unwind, or put point guards on your knitting needles and hold the knitting up by the yarn so that it can spin. You can also purchase large yarn bobbins on which to wind the yarn.

Problem number one in Scandinavian or Fair Isle knitting is avoiding having your pattern buckle because the yarn of the color being carried is pulled too tightly. Keep the stitches on the right needle pulled out—expanded—so that the carried color must reach when it is brought into use.

Problem number two is preventing your design from going askew vertically. Read the chart across AND up and down. On the chart for his sweater yoke, in patterns I and III every 3 of a kind is centered above or below a 1 of a kind, and every 1 of a kind is centered above or below a 3 of a kind.

Supplies: For sizes S (M, L), having a chest measurement of the garment of 37" (41", 45"), you will need 18 (20, 22) ounces of four-ply worsted-weight yarn for the main color, 1 ounce of four-ply worsted-weight yarn for the contrast color, and 1 ounce of four-ply worsted-weight yarn for the accent color. You will need two stitch holders. Use a pair of #4 needles and a set of #4 dp or a 16" circular #4, and #8 needles or the size you require to obtain the gauge.

Gauge: 4½ stitches per inch in stockinette stitch.

Back: On #4 needles, cast on 84 (92, 100) stitches. Work in k2, p2 ribbing for 3". Now let me tell you an interesting way to work the ribbing.

Row 1: P1, k2, *p2, k2. Repeat from * to the last stitch, p1.

Row 2: K1, p2, *k2, p2. Repeat from * to the last stitch, k1.

Row 1 is the right side. The edges have purl stitches which will be joined to the purl stitches on the front. When sewn in nub-and-bar, this makes a very neat detail. There is something I want you to realize. In many directions you will see "k2, p2 ribbing." This takes the least space, but the pattern I have given you above can be used when the number of stitches is a multiple of 4. Do not use this ribbing for his cardigan in this chapter, because I have made another compensation. After the ribbing, change to #8 needles and stockinette stitch, increasing 1 stitch in the first row. We need this extra stitch in order to make the design work. Work in stockinette on 85 (93, 101) stitches until you have 14" (14½", 15") from the cast-on. Did you remember to measure the width when you were partway up? See the back directions for his cardigan.

Armhole: Starting on a knit row, bind off 2 stitches at the beginning of each of the next 2 rows. Now you are ready for the design chart. Start in the lower right-hand corner at A. K2 MC (main color). Join CC (contrast color) and k1, take MC over and k3, expand the stitches on the right needle, take CC over, and k1. Continue across—3 MC and 1 CC. End k2 MC. This is a balanced pattern left and right, but read the purl row from the left to establish good habits, because someday you may work with a pattern that is not balanced. When you have completed pattern I, to cut the CC yarn or not to cut it is the question. When and where will you need it again? Pattern II is four rows. That is less than an inch. But on which edge will you be when you next need CC?

Pattern II on the chart begins and ends with half circles. When I am following a chart and find a pattern such as this, which does not have to match a pattern at the seam, I omit the pattern design on the edges. In this case, it involves 2 stitches. This means start the fourth row with p4 MC, p1 AC (accent color), p3 MC.

The row ends with p4 MC. Complete the 25 rows of the chart.

Shoulder: When the armhole measures ⊥ 8½" (9", 10") bind off in pattern 7 (7, 8) stitches at the beginning of each of the next 2 rows. Slipping the first stitches, bind off in pattern 6 (7, 8) stitches at the beginning of each of the next 4 rows, 6 (7, 7) stitches at the beginning of the next 2 rows. Put the remaining 31 (33, 35) stitches on a holder, for the back of the neck. Neck stitches for pullover sweaters are often put on stitch holders because this allows the neck to stretch more, so the sweater is more easily pulled over the head.

Front: Work the same as for the back until 6" (6½", 7½") above the underarm bind-off. On size S, the following may be your last row on the chart. Knit 52 (57, 62) stitches, put the last knit 23 (25, 27) stitches on a holder for the neck front, and knit the remaining 29 (32, 35) stitches. You may want to work both shoulders at the same time. It makes counting easier. Purl the stitches on the right shoulder. Join a second ball of MC and purl the stitches for the left shoulder. See Working Equal Sections in Chapter 3. Decrease 1 stitch at each neck edge every knit row 4 times. Hint: When the decrease is at the end of a row, use a SKP decrease; at the beginning, k2 tog. When the armhole is the same depth as the back—you can count the rows above the pattern—bind off as for the back. You have not necessarily made a mistake when the shoulder bind-off begins before the neck decreasing is complete. Do you know why you bind off shoulders in levels? It is to slant the line from the arm up to the neck. When you have bound off all the shoulder stitches, cut the yarn, leaving ends for sewing, then join the shoulders.

Sleeves: Use your larger needles and MC. With a crochet hook, pick up 64 (68, 72) stitches. Read the section on picking up stitches in Chapter 2. Count the 2 bound-off stitches, an extra stitch in the corner to prevent a hole, and the nubs to the shoulder seam. Figure half the number of stitches required for the sleeve. Extra stitches will be necessary. If your count were 20 and half the stitch requirement for the sleeve were 30, you would pick up an extra stitch after every second nub. Your ratio will probably not be so even. Extra fullness is more desirable near the underarm than near the top. When you have picked up half the required number of stitches for the sleeve and are at the shoulder seam, put a marker on your needle. When you are picking up the stitches for the second half you need count only the stitches for that half. When you have all the sleeve stitches on the needle, work in stockinette stitch for 6". Then decrease 1 stitch at each edge every third knit row. I like to decrease at the beginning by knitting together the second and third stitches and at the end by SKP the third and second. This keeps the edges neater, so the seam will be neater. Another hint: I find the decreases at the beginning of a row much easier to remember than those at the end. So at the beginning of the purl row preceding the decrease row I wrap the yarn around the needle in the wrong direction when purling the second and third stitches. When I come upon these stitches at the end of the decrease row, I will note that they are wrong and remember to decrease. Not only that, but I can knit these two stitches together through the back and the result is the same as SKP, but better because the slip stitch does not become enlarged.

Continue decreasing every third knit row. Do not get fewer than 44 (48, 52) stitches. Stop decreasing when you have reduced your number of stitches to this number, but continue working if necessary until the sleeve measures 16" (16½", 17"). The wrist ribbing is worked on #4 needles, preferably double-point. Decrease, evenly spaced, to 40 (44, 48) stitches in the first row of ribbing. The decreases will show less when done on the first knit of a k2. The cuff ribbing can be worked the same as the bottom of the sweater if you are using single-point needles. K2, p2 ribbing for 3". Bind off LOOSELY in pattern. Use your larger needle for binding off.

Neck: With either your #4 double-point needles or a 16" #4 circular needle, a crochet hook, and MC yarn, start at the left shoulder seam. Pick up 3 stitches per 2 nubs and a stitch in the corner to close the hole, knit across the stitches on the front holder, pick up a stitch in the corner, 3 stitches per 2 nubs, a stitch in the

Knit row
 Work right to left
 Repeat A to B, end C

Purl row
 Work left to right
 Repeat C to D, end A

□ = Main Color
X = Contrast Color
O = Accent Color

		C	B						D	A		K
		C	B						D	A		
			X					X				K
I	P	X	X	X			X	X	X			
			X					X				K
	P	O			O	O	O			O		
			O	O		O	O					K
III	P		O	O				O	O			
		O	O			O			O	O		K
	P	X				X			X			
			X		X		X		X			K
II	P		X		X		X		X			
		X				X		X				K
	P		O				O					
I			O	O	O		O	O	O			K
	P		O				O					
		X			X	X	X		X			K
	P		X	X		X	X					
III			X	X			X	X				K
	P	X	X			X		X	X			
		O			O		O			O		K
	P		O		O		O		O			
II			O		O		O		O			K
	P	O				O			O			
			X				X					K
I	P	X	X	X			X	X	X			← start
			X				X					K
		C	B						D	A		

corner, knit across the back neck stitches, and finally pick up a stitch in the corner. Try to get the same number of stitches on each neck edge. Count your total number of stitches. It must be a multiple of 4. Between 92 and 108 is a good area. If necessary, you can increase or decrease on the first round while you are setting the k2, p2 pattern. Should you need to increase, do so with the knit in the front and the back increase on the second knit of a k2 and pretend that the increased stitch is a purl. Rib for 2". Bind off LOOSELY in pattern, using a larger needle.

Finishing: Fold the neck ribbing in half to the inside and sew it down, avoiding any tension in the yarn. Work in the color ends for a couple of inches in their own color. Sew the long side and sleeve seams in nub-and-bar with the ends available and with yarn from the skein.

Now haven't you knit a beautiful sweater!

I want to tell you a few things about Scandinavian knitting that were not mentioned earlier. In patterns in which you carry colors

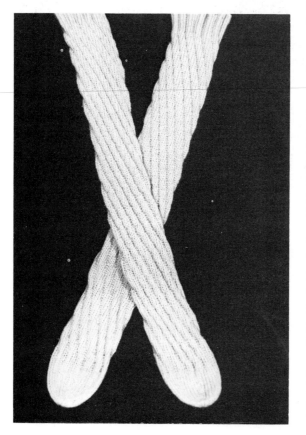

behind more than 3 stitches, catch the carried color with a twist around the color in use, and you might as well twist the opposite direction from your color change, to lessen the yarn entanglement. Actually, which way you twist is not important; consistency is. Whether you take the new color yarn over or under the old in bringing it into use, the stitches will slant one way or the other. Your eye accepts an overall direction of the stitches. Taking the new over the old is a little faster. You will be wise always to twist in the same direction for Scandinavian knitting. This also applies to Argyle knitting and figure knitting, such as a horse or bowling pin on the back of a sweater. A clever ambidextrous knitter can hold a color in each hand and work in both English and Continental. Your work certainly goes faster this way, but alas, there is a catch: The row does not stay in line, the design becomes distorted. Now here is an exception for the perfectionist. In pattern II, the circle in his pullover sweater, in the middle two rows, the MC and AC yarns were twisted so as to slant the AC stitches in the direction of the circle.

Tube Socks

When he has all the sweaters, mittens, and hats that he needs, you may want to knit him a pair of spiral tube socks. They take a long time, but that gives you the chance to dream about your next project. The advantages of a pair of tube socks are that the length of the foot is not a problem and a spot on the heel does not wear through, because they can be rotated.

S (M, L) are for skinny (muscular, lard legs). These socks will measure 24" from top to toe. The largest measurement around a foot is the heel-ankle-instep. Take this measurement, and when you have a few inches on his sock, see if it will stretch to that width. Do not be afraid to pull hard, because you want the sock to cling to the leg.

Supplies: You will need 4 (5, 6) ounces of sport-weight yarn. When selecting a yarn for his tube socks, you want to consider warmth and wear. Wool is warmer than synthetic fiber, but synthetic yarn can withstand hard wear and machine washing. A blend of the two is really the best choice. And hand washing will keep his socks looking good for a long time.

Gauge: You will need a set of #4 double-point needles, or the size you require to get a gauge of 6½ stitches per inch. You will find that an odd-colored needle in your set of four, or one you have marked with a dab of nail polish, is truly a help, since the pattern shifts every fourth round. (See the directions for his hunter mittens.)

Tube socks: Loosely cast on 48 (52, 60) stitches. Try a larger needle for casting on. Divide the stitches as evenly as you can on three needles so that each holds a multiple of 4. Each needle should begin with k2 and end with p2. Work in k2, p2 ribbing for at least 2½". To start the spiral pattern, shift 1 stitch from each needle to the needle before it. Calling the needle that begins above the starting tail #1—keep in mind it is the position, not the actual needle— shift 1 stitch to needle #3, 1 stitch from #3 to #2, and 1 stitch from #2 to #1. Begin by using the odd or marked needle as the spare to work the stitches at position #1, and k2, p2 for 4 rounds. You have completed 4 rounds when the odd needle is the spare one, with which you are ready to work on needle #1. Now that you understand that, I will give you a hint to make your work easier: When the odd needle is in position #3, work across needle #1 following the existing pattern. Knit the first stitch from the following needle and shift it back to the needle just completed. Do the same twice more. Now you are ready for your shift round, but the shifting has been done.

You will be able to use the starting tail for a while to indicate where the rounds begin, but eventually there will have been too many shifted stitches. A help in locating the start of a round is a safety pin below the needle split, which you will need to move periodically as your tube sock grows.

When his sock is 22", or when you begin to panic over whether or not you will have enough yarn, start the toe decreasing. The toe is about 2". I like to use smaller needles for the toes, because that makes them wear better, but if you haven't any, it is hardly worthwhile buying a set of needles to knit just 2". The toe is worked

in stockinette—all knit when you are working around.

Toe:

For M: (K15, k2 tog, k7, k2 tog) 2 times.
Knit 3 rounds plain.

For L: (K8, k2 tog) 6 times.
Knit 3 rounds plain.
(K7, k2 tog) 6 times.
Knit 3 rounds plain.

For all sizes
(K6, k2 tog) 6 times.
Knit 3 rounds plain.
(K5, k2 tog) 6 times.
Knit 3 rounds plain.
(K4, k2 tog) 6 times.
Knit 3 rounds plain.
(K3, k2 tog) 6 times.
Knit 1 round plain.
(K2, k2 tog) 6 times.
Knit 1 round plain.
(K1, k2 tog) 6 times.
Knit 1 round plain.
(K2 tog) 6 times.
Cut the yarn and with a tapestry needle send it through the remaining 6 stitches, then to the inside, and secure.

When you have ends, tie a simple overhand knot; it may loosen, but you can tighten it again. You don't want him to have lumps in his socks. Later, work in the yarn ends in opposite directions up and down on the inside for a couple of inches.

Should his socks not stay up as well as he would like, use some elastic thread. You may need to shop for it. Try a store that carries machine-sewing notions. It is manufactured to be used for machine shirring. With a needle, run several separate lines of elastic thread around the top of his socks on the inside. Tie each line with a firm tiny knot.

If you want to play around with the directions, go up or down by 4s. When it comes time for the toe decreasing, if your total number of stitches is not also a multiple of 6, you have to adjust it first, as we did for M. Now, if you are a true masochist, you can knit him a pair of tube socks with three-ply fingering yarn—4 (4, 5) ounces should be enough. Use a set of #2 dp needles and cast on 60 (68, 76) stitches. For the toe decreasing, decrease 6 stitches every fourth round until after (k5, k2 tog) 6 times or 36 stitches, then decrease every other round.

Make a note for yourself of the brand of yarn, the amount required for the length, and the size.

Useless, unfascinating fact: One spiraling rib is a tad larger than the rest because every fourth round it has 3 knit stitches.

FOR HER

Slippers

You would like to let her know how much she means to you. You can show your love by knitting a gift for her. If you are just learning to knit, make her a pair of slippers. To make them requires knowing how to cast on, to knit, to knit and purl in the same row, to decrease, and to bind off. One nice thing about making a pair of something, when you are a beginning knitter, is seeing how your knitting has improved when you have completed the second of the pair. It takes me a little over two hours to make a pair of the medium-sized slippers.

Supplies: For her slippers S (M, L) for hose size 8½ (10, 11½) you will need 2 (2½, 3) ounces of four-ply worsted-weight yarn. It may be wool, a synthetic, or a blend of the two. I urge you, if you plan to use a synthetic yarn, make certain that it has good spring or elasticity. This is important so that the slippers will stay on. You can easily test for spring in the yarn shop without damaging the ball or skein of yarn. Separate one strand and tug lightly. Try this on a few different kinds of yarn. You will feel the elasticity I am talking about. This test does not work for cotton or linen yarns. Plant-fiber yarns do not have any give.

Gauge: You should have a pair of #8 needles or the size you require to get 4⅓ stitches per inch in garter stitch (knit every row).

Slippers: Cast on 28 (32, 36) stitches. You are

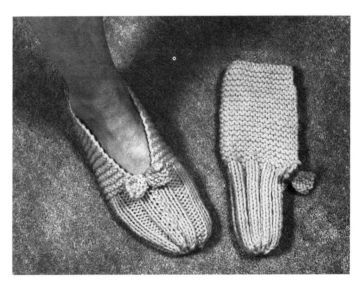

starting at the back of the heel, and you will be grateful later if you have left a cast-on tail of at least 6″ for sewing. Work in garter stitch until you have 4″ (5″, 6″) from your cast-on.

Toe: K2, p2 ribbing for 3½″ (4″, 4½″). To work ribbing, you start k2, then p2, and continue alternating k2 and p2 across the row. Because you have a number of stitches that is a multiple of 4, every row will start with k2 and end with p2. Beginning knitters sometimes unintentionally increase stitches by neglecting to take the yarn between the needles between knit and purl or purl and knit. This will make a hole, jog the ribbing out of line, and add a stitch.

When you have the required length of ribbing, work a decrease row: Knit together each k2 and purl together each p2 across. Slip all of the remaining stitches as if to purl to the other needle. I do this because the stitches will not become telescoped by the finishing. Cut the yarn at about 12″. Using a tapestry needle, send the yarn through all the stitches as you slide them from the knitting needle. Gather in the stitches, and to prevent an open toe, send the yarn through again.

When you make the second slipper, count the number of garter ridges on the first so that they will be the same size.

Finishing: Using the same strand of yarn used for closing the toe, sew the ribbed section in nub-and-bar. (See the sewing section in Chapter 2.) End going through 2 nubs, send the needle again through the last used 2 bars and again through the 2 nubs, to prevent the seam from becoming loose. Do not work in the end yet. Sew the heel seam.

Bow: Cast on 10 stitches. Work in garter stitch until there are three ridges on each side. Bind off. This makes a fourth ridge. Use the side with four ridges for the right side. With a tapestry needle, work in the cast-on and bind-off ends about 1½″ on the wrong side. With the strand used for sewing the toe, run the tapestry needle in and out through the center of the bow to keep it from sliding off center. Then send the yarn through the slipper and around the bow two or three times to secure it, and finish by running the end down the seam on the inside.

Have you noticed that the slippers are knitted 1″ less in length than the hose size? We do so because we want her slippers to stay on her feet. Garter stitch has give, but you must use a good yarn to help it do its job. To make larger or smaller slippers, adjust the number of stitches you cast on by multiples of 4 (4, 8, etc.) and knit the garter and ribbing sections relatively shorter or longer. The ratio of garter rows to ribbing rows is 2 to 1. To make the top of the toe area symmetrical, use the variation of ribbing in the directions for his Fair Isle sweater. Start the ribbing on row 2. This will make the ribbing row 1 the right side. Look carefully at the line between the garter and the ribbing to see why I say one side looks better.

Vest

Do you think she would like a vest? Not only will she be warm when she wears it, but she will have warm thoughts of you because you made it for her. This vest can be worn as a sleeveless shirt, over a blouse, or under a jacket. It requires knowing how to cast on, knit, purl, bind off, and knit and purl in the same row. The small size takes me about eight hours to make.

Supplies: For sizes S (M, L) having bust measurements of the garment of 32″ (35″, 38″) you will need 7 (8, 10) ounces of four-ply worsted-weight yarn.

Gauge: For the main part of the vest use #8 needles or the size you require to get a gauge of 4½ stitches per inch in stockinette stitch (knit 1 row, purl 1 row). Use #4 needles for the garter stitch at the bottom.

Back: On #4 needles, cast on 72 (80, 86) stitches. Work in garter stitch (knit every row) until there are nine ridges. Change to #8 needles and work in stockinette stitch until your knitting measures 9″ (10″, 11″) from the cast-on. The width of the stockinette area should be 16″ (17½″, 19″). Be sure to uncurl the edges when you measure across.

Armhole: Starting at the beginning of a knit row, bind off 7 (9, 10) stitches. At the beginning of the next purl row bind off 7 (9, 10) stitches, purling each stitch. To bind off in purl you must keep the yarn out of the way. Either take it back to the knit position or lower it so that you can reach the stitch to be pulled over and off. Not purling when you bind off on a purl side puts an unwanted ridge on the right side. Finish the purl row.

Row 1: (K1, p1) 3 times, k46 (50, 54), (p1, k1) 3 times.

Row 2: (P1, k1) 3 times, p46 (50, 54), (k1, p1) 3 times.

Repeat these two rows alternately until the armhole measures ⊥ 6½″ (7″, 8″). To measure armhole depth, draw an imaginary line across between the two bind-offs. Pin a safety pin along this line near the center. Measure from the pin up to the needle. It is necessary to measure in the center because the edges are elongated by the ribbing. End having completed a knit row.

Row 1: (P1, k1) 3 times, p1, k44 (48, 52), p1, (k1, p1) 3 times.

Row 2: (K1, p1) 3 times, k46 (50, 54), (p1, k1) 3 times.

Repeat these two rows 3 times more. This means you will work 8 rows altogether, have four ridges on the right side, and end having completed a right-side row—row 2. Bind off all the stitches in pattern for row 1. Your bind-off gives you a fifth ridge on the right side. When you are binding off, do so loosely. The ribbing on the arm edges and the garter stitch at the neck are designed to make the neck round, but you have to help by binding off loosely. Cut the yarn, leaving an 8″ end for sewing the shoulder.

Front: Make the front the same as the back. To be sure to have the same length as the back, count the rows. This is easier to do on the purl side. Below the armhole remember that one ridge is formed when binding off. Above the armhole bind-off, start counting the ridges alongside the ribbing.

Finishing: Sew the vest with the right sides together. With the yarn ends you have saved, join the 7 ribbing stitches of each edge at the top of the shoulders in Bind-Off to Bind-Off. (see Chapter 2). Bury the ends in the seam. Start sewing the side edges together in nub-and-bar, using the tail from the cast-on. Vests or sweaters look ever so much better when there is no bunch of yarn at the bottom edge of the side seam. When the cast-on tail is used for sewing, this is avoided. Sew with the tail as far as you can. Use any lengths of yarn on the edges for sewing. Close the seam from the bottom to the underarm bind-off. If there are ends on the armhole edge, run one up and the other down for about 2″ each, hiding them in the ribbing.

Scarf

How pretty she will look wearing a lovely mohair-blend scarf.

Supplies: For the one pictured I used a very lightweight yarn, a blend of acrylic, wool, and mohair. This comes in 50-gram balls, and the label states that each ball contains 220 meters, or 240 yards. One ball is ample. The scarf took me about five hours to knit. The first and last 1″

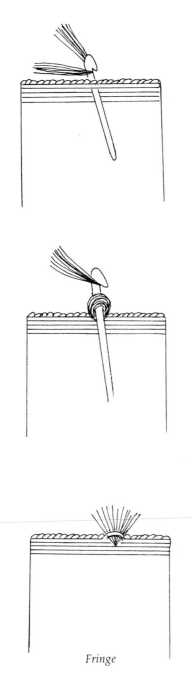

Fringe

the end of the row you find there are only enough stitches to end P1. That's it. I have always suspected that is the reason this pattern is called "mistake stitch." Work for 48". Bind off loosely in pattern, using the larger needle.

Fringe: For a 4½" fringe, cut 80 pieces of yarn, 9" long. To make this easy to do, find a book that measures 10" around. (When you are winding the yarn, it will stretch.) Wind the yarn around the book 80 times, then cut through all the strands. Use two pieces of yarn in every other stitch at each end. To do this, align the two pieces and fold them in half. Send a crochet hook through the scarf, two strands from the edge, catch the pieces in the fold, and draw them through. Then draw the four ends through the loop made of the fold and pull the ends to tighten. Cut the cast-on tail and the bind-off end to 4½" and include them in the fringe. I don't know that there is a right or wrong side of fringe, but there is a difference, so always work on the same side. Notice that in mistake stitch every fourth stitch is stockinette, and centered between them is a reverse stockinette stitch. Put your fringe in each of these stitches and you will come out even. My hint is, cut the fringe before completing the scarf. This eliminates the worry of whether or not you will have sufficient yarn for it.

of the scarf are made on #8 needles, to stop the edges from flaring. The major part of the scarf is knit on #10 needles. The pattern is mistake stitch, which is my favorite scarf pattern, because it accordions in to narrow around the neck, but spreads out nicely to keep a chest warm.

Gauge: The gauge is 3½ stitches per inch in pattern on #10.

Scarf: Cast on 39 stitches. Every row starts: *K2, p2. Repeat from * across. When you reach

Hat

Here is a hat made with the same fine acrylic-wool-mohair-blend yarn used for her scarf. The scarf, this hat, and the mittens following all are made with the same yarn, so you can knit a set if you like. A fine yarn is used so that her scarf will be lacy. To make the hat and mittens warm, use two strands of yarn. How to work with a double strand is something every knitter should know, and doing so with a part-mohair yarn is the best way to learn, because the strands tend to cling together.

Supplies: One 50-gram ball of the yarn described in the scarf directions is sufficient for the hat. Also, 1 ball will be enough for the mittens, so if you plan to make both hat and mittens buy 2 balls, which will make double-strand knitting easier. For the hat alone use both ends of a ball.

Gauge: Use #11 needles or the size you require to get a gauge of 3 stitches per inch.

Hat: The hat is worked with two strands throughout. Cast on 67 stitches. Work in mistake stitch. Every row begins: *K2, p2. Repeat from *, ending the last repeat p1. Continue in mistake stitch until you have 10″ from the cast-on.

Shape top:

Row 1: *K1, k2 tog, p1. Repeat from * across, ending the last repeat k1, k2 tog. This is the right side.

Row 2: *K1, p2. Repeat from * across, ending the last repeat k1, p1.

Row 3: *K1, p2 tog. Repeat from * across, ending the last repeat k1, p1.

Row 4: *K1, p1. Repeat from * across.

Row 5: K1, *k2 tog. Repeat from * across, ending k1.

Cut the yarn to about 12″. Slip all 18 stitches to the other needle. Using a large tapestry needle, send the yarn through each stitch as you slide it from the knitting needle. Draw up the stitches to close. I like to send the yarn through a second time. Use the cast-on tail to sew the seam in nub-and-bar as far as you can. Use the end from the top to sew down the seam. Run each end into the other's seam, remembering that the lower 3″ or 4″ will be rolled up, making the inside the outside.

Cable Mittens

Have you seen cable-stitch knitting and been afraid to try it? I will do my best to make it clear.

Supplies: For these mittens you will need one 50-gram ball of fine acrylic-wool-mohair-blend yarn. Please read the first paragraphs, describing the yarn, in the preceding scarf and hat directions. You will also need two stitch holders and a cable needle. I prefer the cable needle shaped like a letter J.

Gauge: Use #8 needles or the size you require with two strands of yarn to get a gauge of 4½ stitches per inch in stockinette stitch.

Left mitten: On #8 needles, using double-strand yarn, cast on 35 stitches. Work 3″ in mistake stitch. Every row begins: *K2, p2. Repeat from *, ending the last repeat p1.

Thumb gusset: Use the "knit in the front and the back" increase.

Row 1: K13, p1, inc in 1, k1, p1, k4, inc in 1, p1, k5, inc in 1, p1, k5.

Row 2: P5, k2, p6, k2, p5, k1, p3, k1, p13.

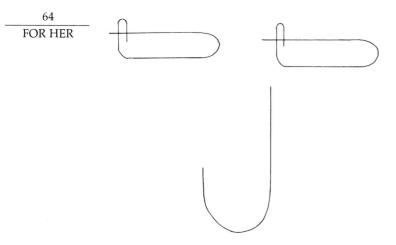

2 stitch holders and cable needle

Row 3: K13, p1, k3, p1, k5, p2, k6, p2, k5.
Row 4: Repeat row 2.
Row 5: K13, p1, inc in 2, k1, p1, k5, p2, slip as if to purl 3 stitches onto the *short* end of the cable needle (CN) to the curve, put the CN with 3 stitches to the back of your work with the points down, knit the next 3 stitches from your left needle, slide the 3 CN stitches to the *long* end and knit them, p2, k5.
Row 6: P5, k2, p6, k2, p5, k1, p5, k1, p13.
Row 7: K13, p1, k5, p1, k5, p2, k6, p2, k5.
Row 8: Repeat row 6.
Row 9: K13, p1, inc in 1, k2, inc in 1, k1, p1, k5, p2, k6, p2, k5.
Row 10: P5, k2, p6, k2, p5, k1, p7, k1, p13.
Row 11: K13, p1, k7, p1, k5, p2, k6, p2, k5.
Row 12: Repeat row 10.
Row 13: K13, p1, inc in 1, k4, inc in 1, k1, p1, k5, p2, slip 3 stitches onto the CN and hold to the back, k3 from your left needle, k3 from the long end of the CN, p2, k5.
Row 14: P5, k2, p6, k2, p5, k1, p9, k1, p13.
Row 15: K13, p1, k9, p1, k5, p2, k6, p2, k5.
Row 16: Repeat row 14.
Row 17: K13 and slide these 13 stitches onto a stitch holder. (They will be safer, should the holder become opened, if you slide the stitches on around to the other side.) Knit 11 and put the remaining 20 stitches on a stitch holder.
Thumb: At the beginning of the 11 stitches

remaining on the needle, cast on 2 stitches. Use flip-loop or single-strand method (described in Chapter 2). Purl 13. Cast on 2 stitches. Work 10 rows in stockinette stitch on 15 stitches, ending with a purl row. *K1, k2 tog and repeat from * across. Purl back on 10 stitches. K2 tog across. Slide the remaining 5 stitches to the other needle. Cut the yarn at 8". With a tapestry needle, send the yarn through the 5 stitches as you slide them from the needle. Pull to close, and send the yarn through again. Sew the thumb seam. Slide the 20 stitches with the cable pattern from the holder to a needle. Pick up 5 stitches at the crotch of the thumb as follows: Look at the area between the thumb and the stitches still on a holder. Send a crochet hook in through the center of the stitch below the end stitch on the holder, out through the center of the stitch to the left, then under a strand on the edge of the cast-on stitches. Catch the yarn about 2" or 3" from the end and draw it through. Put this stitch on the spare needle so that the yarn from the ball is to the back. Send the hook under two strands on the edge of the cast-on, catch the yarn, draw through, and put this stitch on the spare needle in the same manner. Pick up a third stitch, sending the crochet hook under one strand from each side of the sewn seam. Pick up a forth stitch as you did the second. For the fifth stitch, send the hook down through the top of the last purl stitch below, around and out through the center of the stitch to the left, catch the yarn, draw through, and put it on the spare needle. Complete row 17 as follows: K5, p2, k6, p2, k5.
Row 18: P5, k2, p6, k2, p10, slide 13 stitches from the holder to the spare needle and p13.
Row 19: K23, p2, k6, p2, k5.
Row 20: P5, k2, p6, k2, p23.
Row 21: K23, p2, put 3 on CN to back, k3, k3 from CN, p2, k5.
Rows 22-28: Keep the knits and purls as in rows 19 and 20. You can tell the right side from the wrong. The clue is: Is the row number odd or even?
Row 29: Repeat row 21.
Rows 30–36: Keep the knits and purls.
Row 37: Slip 1 stitch as if to knit, k1, psso (pass slipped stitch over), k14, k2 tog, sl 1,

k1, psso, k3, p2, put 3 on CN to back, k3, k3 from CN, p2, k3, k2 tog.

Row 38: P4, k2, p6, k2, p20.

Row 39: Sl 1, k1, psso, k12, k2 tog, sl 1, k1, psso, k2, p2, k6, p2, k2, k2 tog.

Row 40: P3, k2, p6, k2, p17.

Row 41: Sl 1, k1, psso, k10, k2 tog, sl 1, k1, psso, k1, k2 tog, k6, k2 tog, k1, k2 tog.

Row 42: P24.

Row 43: Sl 1, k1, psso, k8, k2 tog, sl 1, k1, psso, k8, k2 tog.

Purl 10 stitches. Cut the yarn at 18″. Hold the needles together, both pointing to the right, with the right side of the mitten out. With a tapestry needle, send the yarn through the top of the stitch below the first stitch on the back needle. Now you are ready to weave. Turn to Chapter 3 to review kitchener-weaving stockinette to stockinette. BUT before you leave this page: To round the corners, weave the first 2 pairs of stitches firmly, the center 6 pairs to gauge, and the last 2 pairs firmly. Now turn.

Finishing: Use the yarn remaining from weaving to sew down the seam. Sew up the seam with the cast-on tail. Use the two ends at the crotch of the thumb to close any holes—you should have none if you have picked up the 5 stitches as I described—and then run them up each side of the thumb seam for reinforcement, because thumbs often show wear first.

Right mitten: Work 3″ of mistake stitch as for the left mitten. To count the rows, count the stitches adjacent to the predominant stockinette stitch.

Thumb gusset:

Row 1: K4, inc in 1, p1, k5, inc in 1, p1, k5, p1, inc in 1, k1, p1, k13.

Row 2: P13, k1, p3, k1, p5, k2, p6, k2, p5.

Rows 3–4: Keep the knits and purls.

Row 5: K5, p2, put 3 on CN to back, k3, k3 from CN, p2, k5, p1, inc in 2, k1, p1, k13.

Rows 6-8: Keep the knits and purls.

Row 9: K5, p2, k6, p2, k5, p1, inc in 1, k2, inc in 1, k1, p1, k13.

Can you continue by yourself? Cross the cable every eighth row. Increase for the thumb gusset every fourth row in the first stitch after the first p1, and in the second stitch before the second p1.

Row 17: K5, p2, k6, p2, k5. Put these 20 stitches on a stitch holder. K11. Put the remaining 13 stitches on a holder.

Complete the right thumb as for the left. Slide the 13 palm stitches to a needle. Pick up 5 stitches and put them on the spare needle. Complete row 17 by knitting 13 stitches.

Row 18: P18, slide 20 stitches from the holder to the spare needle, p5, k2, p6, k2, p5.

Row 19: K5, p2, k6, p2, k23.

Row 20: P23, k2, p6, k2, p5.

Row 21: K5, p2, put 3 on CN to back, k3, k3 from CN, p2, k23.

Work through row 36. Read the left mitten directions right to left, crossing the cable as you have been doing.

Row 37: Sl 1, k1, psso, k3, p2, cross cable on 6 stitches, p2, k3, k2 tog, sl 1, k1, psso, k14, k2 tog.

Row 38: P20, k2, p6, k2, p4.

Row 39: Sl 1, k1, psso, k2, p2, k6, p2, k2, k2 tog, sl 1, k1, psso, k12, k2 tog.

Row 40: P17, k2, p6, k2, p3.

Row 41: Sl 1, k1, psso, k1, k2 tog, k6, k2 tog, k1, k2 tog, sl 1, k1, psso, k10, k2 tog.

Row 42: P24.

Row 43: Sl 1, k1, psso, k8, k2 tog, sl 1, k1, psso, k8, k2 tog.

Purl 10 stitches. Cut the yarn at 18″. Complete as for the left mitten.

Pullover

You want her to look pretty and keep warm. In this pullover she will be cute and cozy.

Supplies: For sizes S (M, L) with a bust measurement of the garment of 34″ (37″, 40″) you will need 12 (14, 16) ounces of four-ply worsted-weight yarn in the main color (MC) and 1 ounce in a contrasting color (CC) of the same yarn. Use a pair of #8 needles or the size you require to get the gauge. You also will use a pair of #4 needles, a circular 16″ #4 needle, and two stitch holders.

Gauge: The gauge is 4½ stitches per inch in stockinette stitch.

Back: On #4 needles, cast on 76 (84, 92) stitches with MC.

Right-side row: P1, *k2, p2. Repeat from *, ending k2, p1.
Wrong-side row: K1, *p2, k2. Repeat from *, ending p2, k1.
Repeat these 2 rows alternately until the ribbing measures 2½". End ready to work on the right side. Without changing needles or cutting MC, join CC and knit 2 rows. The third CC row is the eyelet row and is worked as follows: K2, *yo, k2 tog. Repeat from * to the end. Knit one more row in CC, then cut it, leaving an end for sewing. Bring up the MC yarn loosely and use the #8 needles to continue in stockinette until the piece measures 12" (13", 13½") from the cast-on. End with a purl row. The width of the stockinette should be 17" (18½", 20").

Armhole: Bind off 3 (4, 5) stitches at the beginning of the next 2 rows. Decrease 1 stitch at each edge every knit row 3 (4, 5) times. Draw an imaginary line between the bind-offs and pin a safety pin along this line. Work on 64 (68, 72) stitches until the armhole measures ⊥ 6½" (7", 7½") from the pin. End ready for a knit row. Read Working Equal Sections in Chapter 3. K18 (19, 20), slide the next 28 (30, 32) stitches to a stitch holder. (Your stitches will be safer, should the stitch holder become undone, if you slide the stitches around to the other side.) Join a new ball of yarn and knit the remaining 18 (19,

20) stitches. Decrease 1 stitch at each neck edge EVERY row 4 times. To do so, purl to the last 2 stitches, p2 tog. With the original yarn, on the right shoulder as worn, p2 tog, purl the remaining stitches. Knit to the last 2 stitches, k2 tog. On the left shoulder, k2 tog, knit the remaining stitches. Repeat the last 2 two-part rows once more. Purl back on 14 (15, 16) stitches on each shoulder. Bind off each shoulder.

Front: Work as for the back until the armhole measures ⊥ 4" (4½", 5"). You should have 64 (68, 72) stitches. End ready for a knit row. K20 (21, 22), slide the next 24 (26, 28) to a stitch holder for the front neck, join a new ball and knit the remaining 20 (21, 22) stitches. Purl back across each shoulder with each shoulder's own ball of yarn. Decrease 1 stitch at each neck edge every KNIT row 6 times. Work even on 14 (15, 16) stitches on each shoulder until you have the same armhole depth as the back. I prefer counting nubs to measuring. Bind off both shoulders and cut the yarn, leaving ends for sewing.

Sleeves: On #4 needles, with MC cast on 36 (40, 44) stitches. Work in k2, p2 ribbing as you did at the bottom of the sweater for 2½". Work 4 rows of eyelet pattern in CC. Loosely bring up MC, change to #8 needles, and knit 1 row. Purl back, increasing 4 stitches evenly spaced, using "purl in front and front" increase. Pretend that you have increased in the previous knit row. You did not because that would have made little contrast-color dots with each increase. Notice that you have clean lines between the colors on the right side, faulty on the wrong side. There are times when you may want the unclean lines between colors on the right side, but this is not one of them. Increase 1 stitch at each edge in the first and the next to last stitch every fourth knit row. This means every eighth row. There will be 3 plain knit rows and 4 purl rows between increases. Do not get more than 60 (64, 68) stitches. Continue until the sleeve measures 17" (17½", 18") from the cast-on. To make the sleeve cap, starting on a knit row, bind off 3 (4, 5) stitches at the beginning of the next 2 rows. Decrease 1 stitch at the beginning of every row—k2 together or p2 together—until the cap measures ⊥ 4" (4¼", 4½"). Bind off the remaining stitches, decreasing 1 stitch at the beginning and the end to round the corners.

Neck: Sew the shoulders together. Starting at the left shoulder seam with MC, a #4 circular needle, and a crochet hook, pick up a stitch through each nub and an extra stitch to close the corner. Slide the front neck stitches from the stitch holder to the other end of the circular needle, then knit them. Pick up a stitch in the corner, a stitch per nub along the neck side, a stitch in the corner, slide the back neck stitches to the other end of the needle, then knit them, pick up a stitch in the corner, and a stitch per nub to the left shoulder seam. Knit 1 round, increasing or decreasing, if necessary, to 96 (104, 112) stitches. You must have a multiple of 4. Increase along the sides of the neck or decrease at the back or front of the neck. The left shoulder seam is the beginning of the round. Join CC. Knit 1 round, purl 1 round. Work an eyelet round, starting: Yo, k2 tog. Purl 1 round. Cut the CC yarn. Bring up MC and knit 1 round. This is necessary for a clean line between the colors. On the first round of the k2, p2 ribbing, decrease 4 stitches, 2 near each front neck corner, by knitting together 2 stitches to be the first stitch of a k2. Work in k2, p2 ribbing for 1″. Bind off loosely in pattern. It is important to bind off loosely so she will be able to pull the sweater over her head. It is also important to make the bound-off edge of ribbing behave, so you must knit the knit stitches and purl the purl stitches when binding off.

Finishing: Sew the set-in sleeves as described in the cardigan directions in Chapter 4. Sew the underarm and sleeve seams in nub-and-bar with the matching yarn pieces you have saved on the edges. Hide all ends in their own color.

I hope you are reading through the directions before starting each project. I told you to in the introduction. If you have read ahead, your reward is alternate methods for the neck and the sleeves.

The neck can be made on straight #4 needles. Join only the right shoulder seam. Pick up the stitches as described. Purl back in MC, decreasing or increasing stitches if necessary. Work the 4 rows of eyelet pattern in CC, as you did at the waist. Knit 1 row in MC. Decrease 4 stitches in the first row of ribbing, 2 at each front neck corner, by purling together 2 stitches that are to be the second stitch in a p2.

After the shoulders have been joined, the sleeve stitches can be picked up and the sleeves worked from the top down. You can follow the sleeve directions given for her cardigan, which follows. Allow ½″ for the eyelet pattern, so work ½″ less on the sleeve on the #8 needles. On the last row, a purl row, make the decreases, evenly spaced, by purling 2 tog. Join CC and on #4 needles work the four eyelet rows. This can be done on a set of #4 double-point needles as described for the circular needle in the neck directions. Work the ribbing on the dp needles. Cuffs made this way hold their shape better and look better when folded up.

I think this is a very pretty sweater, don't you?

Cardigan

Is there anyone who would not be pleased to receive a hand-knit cardigan? This sweater is made all in one piece. You knit up the back, over the shoulders, and down the front. The stitches for the sleeves are picked up from the armholes and the sleeve is knit down to the cuff.

Supplies: For sizes S (M, L) with a bust measurement of the garment of 34″ (37″, 40″) you should have 14 (16, 18) ounces of four-ply worsted-weight yarn. You will need a stitch holder.

Gauge: The suggested needle size is #8 or the size you require to get a gauge of 4½ stitches per inch in stockinette stitch. #4 needles are used for the ribbing and the garter stitch shoulder.

Back: On #4 needles, cast on 76 (84, 92) stitches. Work in k2, p2 ribbing for 2½″ as follows:

Right side: P1, *k2, p2. Repeat from *, ending k2, p1.

Wrong side: K1, *p2, k2. Repeat from *, ending p2, k1.

With #8 needles, work in stockinette until you have 12″ (13″, 13½″) from the cast-on. The width across the stockinette should be 17″ (18½″, 20″).

Armhole: Starting on a knit row, bind off 3 (4, 5) stitches at the beginning of the next 2 rows. Decrease 1 stitch at each edge every knit row 3 (4, 5) times. Continue on 64 (68, 72) stitches until the armhole measures ⊥ 7″ (7½″, 8″). When in doubt, be generous. End with a purl row.

Shoulder: Knit 18 (19, 20) stitches, bind off 28 (30, 32) stitches for the back of the neck, knit the remaining 18 (19, 20) stitches. Stitches at the back of the neck for a cardigan are usually bound off to better hold the shape of the shoulder. For pullovers the back neck stitches are often put on stitch holders; knitting them up as part of the neckband allows more ease in pulling over a head. With #4 needles, knit the last worked 18 (19, 20) stitches. Slide the right shoulder stitches from the #8 needle to a stitch holder.

Left front: Work in garter stitch on #4 needles until there are six ridges on the right side. With #8 needles work 4 (6, 8) rows in stockinette stitch. Increase 1 stitch at the neck edge in the first stitch of every knit row 5 times. End with a purl row. Using single-strand or flip-loop method, cast on 17 (18, 19) stitches for the front neck.

Right-side row: Knit.

Wrong-side row: Purl to the last 5 stitches, k5.

If you think you will have trouble remembering the 5 garter stitches for the front facing, put a small ring marker on the needle between the 5 garter stitches and the stockinette stitches.

Armhole: Count the nubs on the back from the end of the decreasing to the shoulder garter stitch. Hints: It takes 2 rows of knitting to form a nub. In stockinette the nubs are more easily seen on the wrong side. If you are not confident in locating the end of the decreasing, realize that you have decreased 3 (4, 5) times after the bind-off, so there are that number of nubs which you do not count. Make a note in the book of the number. The garter stitch section is the top center of the shoulder. When you have the same number of nubs following the garter stitch section, increase 1 stitch at the arm edge in the next to last stitch every knit row 3 (4, 5) times. After your final increase, purl 1 row and knit 1 row. Cast on 3 (4, 5) stitches at the underarm edge. Work on 46 (50, 54) stitches, keeping 5 stitches in garter at the center front edge, until the front is the same as the back between the underarm and the ribbing. Notice two things: how willing the garter facing is to fold back and how well it draws up to prevent a drooping front.

To accommodate the ribbing pattern in the front, you will need to increase 1 stitch. To do so, on the first row of the ribbing, increase near the underarm edge in the second of a k2, because the increased stitch looks like a purl and is counted as the first of the p2. On #4 needles work the front ribbing on 47 (51, 55) stitches.

Right-side row: K10, *p2, k2. Repeat from *, ending p1.

Wrong-side row: K1, *p2, k2. Repeat from * to the last 10 stitches, p5, k5.

When the front ribbing is the same length as the back ribbing, bind off loosely IN PATTERN. Using the larger needle for binding off is a good idea.

Pin safety pins on the left front where the buttons will be. The bottom button should be between the second and third ridges. Remember that the top button will be in the neckband between the second and third ridges. You will make pairs of buttonholes, because you are making facings, but locate the buttons in the garter stitch area. Space the button sites 2½" to 3" apart. An uneven number of buttons is traditional.

Do you want to count rather than measure? If her sweater is to have 7 buttons, there are 6 spaces between them. The bottom buttonhole is made above the second ridge. The top buttonhole is made above the second ridge in the neckband. Count the number of ridges on the left front facing. Divide by the number of spaces. Chances are you will not come out evenly. If you have 1 or 2 left over, that can be allowed between the bottom two buttonholes, because the rows at the bottom have been worked on smaller needles. If the remainder after dividing is larger, add 1 ridge in each of the upper spaces between buttonholes, then make the bottom two buttonholes closer together.

Buttonholes: On the 10 stitches at the front edge, on a knit row, k2 tog, cast on 2 stitches (flip loop), k2 tog, k2, k2 tog, cast on 2, k2 tog.

Right front: Slide the 18 (19, 20) stitches from the stitch holder to a #4 needle. Work in garter stitch until you have 6 ridges on the right side. With #8 needles, work 4 (6, 8) rows in stockinette stitch. Increase 1 stitch at the neck edge in the second from last stitch every knit row 5 times. End with a knit row. Cast on 17 (18, 19) stitches for the front neck.

Wrong-side row: K5, purl to the end.
Right-side row: Knit.

Armhole: Repeat the above two rows until you have 1 fewer nub following the shoulder garter stitch than the number you noted in the book for the left. Starting the knit row forms the final nub. At the same time remember to make the buttonholes when the right front is opposite a safety pin on the left front. When there are the correct number of nubs on the armhole edge, increase 1 stitch at the arm edge in the first stitch of every knit row 3 (4, 5) times. Purl back after the last increase row. Cast on 3 (4, 5) stitches at the arm edge. Continue on 46 (50, 54) stitches, remembering to make the buttonholes, until the right front is the same as the left front to the ribbing. On #4 needles, on the first row of ribbing, increase 1 stitch near the underarm edge in the second stitch of a k2.

Right-side row: P1, *k2, p2. Repeat from * to the last 10 stitches, k10.
Wrong-side row: K5, p5, *k2, p2. Repeat from *, ending k1.

Work the same number of rows and bind off as for the left front.

Sleeves: If you are not familiar with picking up new stitches with yarn and a crochet hook, read that section in Chapter 2. You should pick up 60 (64, 68) stitches on #8 needles. You will pick up 1 stitch from each bound-off and each cast-on stitch at the underarms, and 1 stitch in each corner. You also can get a stitch from every nub. Total up your count to see how close you are to the required number of stitches for the sleeve. If you need to decrease some, that should be done near the top of the shoulder. For instance, you can decrease by sending the hook under 2 nubs in the garter stitch section, drawing out the yarn for 1 stitch. If you need to get extra stitches, that should be done near the underarm. When picking up stitches on an edge where there is increasing, be careful. The stitch must come from the nub to avoid a hole. Pick up the sleeve stitches with the right side of the sweater facing you and start on the right at the top of the underarm seam. When you have picked up half the total number of stitches for the sleeve and are at the midpoint in the garter section on the shoulder, put a marker on your needle. This way, you need count only the stitches from the marker for the second half. When you reach the top of the seam on the left, cut the yarn. Slide 15 (17, 19) stitches to the spare needle. Join the yarn and purl 30 stitches. There should be 15 (17, 19) left unworked. Work short rows for the cap of the sleeve:

Turn, slip 1 stitch as if to knit, k30.
Turn, slip 1 stitch as if to purl, p31.
Turn, slip 1 stitch as if to knit, k32.
Turn, slip 1 stitch as if to purl, p33.

Notice that you are working 1 stitch beyond the break formed by turning around the previous time. The number of unworked stitches at each end should be the same or within 1 of each other. Continue working back and forth one more stitch until 4 (5, 6) stitches remain unworked at each end. Work to both ends. Continue in stockinette stitch on 60 (64, 68) stitches for 4″. Decrease by knitting together the second and third stitches from each edge every fourth knit row. (This means every eighth row.) There are 3 plain knit rows between decrease rows. Do not decrease to fewer than 40 (44, 48) stitches. When the sleeve measures 14½″ (15″, 15½″) from the underarm, start the wrist ribbing on #4 needles, decreasing evenly spaced to 36 (40, 44) stitches. Decreases made as the first of a k2 show least. Work the ribbing in the same pattern as for the beginning of the back. Or if you wish, make the wrist ribbing on a set of #4 dp needles. Bind off loosely in pattern.

Neck: With the right side of the sweater facing you, start at the top corner of the right front edge to pick up the stitches for the neck, on #4 needles. Get a stitch from the corner and 4 more in the garter area. Because you are to work in the opposite direction from that in which the front facing was knit, you will be ½ stitch off. Pick up a sixth stitch above the line between the garter and stockinette. Continue picking up stitch per stitch on the cast-on and bound-off edges, an extra stitch in each of the four inner corners, a stitch per nub on the sides of the neck, and 1 in the final top left front corner. Do not cut the yarn. You want 94 (98, 102) stitches for the neck. The number must be a multiple of 4 plus 2. If necessary, you can increase or decrease in the first row while establishing the pattern. Increases should be made on the neck sides, decreases in the back.

Wrong-side row: K5, p5, k2, *p2, k2. Repeat from * to the last 10 stitches, p5, k5.
Right-side row: K10, p2, *k2, p2. Repeat from * to the last 10 stitches, k10.
Make a pair of buttonholes on the fourth row on the first 10 stitches. Bind off in pattern on the seventh row.

Finishing: Sew the underarm seams in nub-and-bar, being sure to match all junctures. Sew the front facings as invisibly as you can, avoiding any pull. Work the pairs of buttonholes together with yarn, taking care not to reduce the size. Run the yarn ends into the facing. I would not use a continuous piece of yarn for the buttonholes. Work in other ends behind the

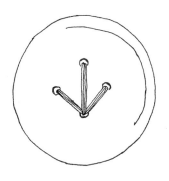

nearest seam line. Take the finished sweater to the store to select the buttons. Sew on the buttons with yarn, if the holes in the buttons are large enough.

If you are adept at machine sewing, you can create a costume. Sew a dress. If you have used a print fabric, pick up one of the colors for the yarn for the cardigan. Line the fronts of the cardigan from the shoulders to the top of the ribbing with the dress fabric. Or if the print has a motif, appliqué one or more on the sweater. Sew a skirt. Replace the ribbing around the cardigan neck with a row or two of single crochet to hold it in, and sew on a collar made with skirt fabric. Or how about a couple of sham pocket flaps? They can be fabric on the sweater or knit on the skirt. Dream.

Gloves

You know that in each chapter of projects I have put the most difficult last. If you love her deeply, show it by knitting her a pair of gloves.

Supplies: Use sport-weight yarn. Wool is warm, synthetic yarn is strong. A blend of wool and synthetic yarn would be nice. I used a 50-gram ball for the gloves pictured, so 2 ounces will be ample. You will need a stitch holder, a J-shaped cable needle, and two point guards or rubber bands.

Gauge: Use a set of #4 double-point needles or the size you require to get a gauge of 7 stitches per inch in stockinette stitch.

Hem: On one #4 needle, cast on 48 stitches. You may want to use the point guards or rubber bands wound around the other ends of the needles while you are working back and forth.

Right-side row: Knit, increasing in the first and the next to last stitches.

Wrong-side row: Purl.

Repeat these 2 rows 3 times more. Knit 1 row —56 stitches.

Picot row: K2, *yo, k2 tog. Repeat from * across. Knit 1 row.

Wrong-side row: Purl.

Right-side row: Knit, decreasing at each edge by knitting together the second and third stitches at the beginning and SKP on the third and second stitches from the end.

Repeat these 2 rows 3 times more. Divide the 48 stitches on three needles: 16, 16, and 16. Knit around for 1". Needle #1 is the first beginning above the split.

Thumb gusset: Knit needle #1. On needle #2, for the left glove k3 (for the right glove k9), p1, inc in 1, k1, p1, k9 (k3). Knit needle #3. Work 3 rounds even, keeping the purls. Work through the first purl stitch, inc in 2, k1, p1, complete the round.

Work 3 rounds even, keeping the purls.

Increase round: Inc in the first stitch after the first purl and in the second stitch before the second purl.

Repeat these 4 rounds until there are 11 stitches between the purls. Work 2 rounds even, keeping the purls. Work a third round, keeping the purls through the second purl. Slide the last worked 13 stitches to a stitch holder. Complete the round. Knit the next round, casting on (single strand or flip loop) 4 stitches above the stitches on the holder. Knit around on 48 stitches for 1½" or to the crotch between the forefinger and the middle finger. Count the rounds above the thumb crotch cast-on and make a note in the book for the second glove.

Pinky: Knit 5 stitches on needle #1. Put a point guard or rubber band on the short end of the cable needle. Slide onto the long end of the cable needle the rest of the stitches on needle #1, the stitches on needle #2, and the stitches on needle #3 to the last 5. Secure the long end with a point guard or rubber band. Cast on 2 stitches on needle #1, then slide the 2 cast-on

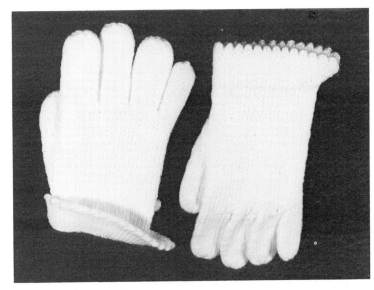

stitches plus 1 more to a spare needle to be #2. Knit 1 stitch from needle #3 and add it to #2. Knit around on 12 stitches until pinky is 2". Count the rounds and make a note. K2 tog around. Cut the yarn and with a tapestry needle send it through the remaining 6 stitches and close. Send the yarn down through the center to the inside.

Ring finger: See the directions for picking up stitches for fingers and thumbs in Chapter 4 under the hunter mitten directions. Should you find it necessary to pick up more than the suggested number of stitches to prevent holes, reduce by decreasing 1 stitch each round above the picked-up stitches.

Knit 6 stitches from the short end of the cable needle, cast on 2 stitches, slide 6 stitches from the long end of the cable needle to a spare needle, then knit them. Rearrange the stitches on the needles as necessary. Pick up 3 stitches from the cast-on 2 of pinky. Knit around on 17 stitches for 2⅓" or 4 rounds more than pinky. K2 tog around, ending k1. Send the yarn through the remaining 9 stitches and close.

Middle finger: Knit 6 stitches from the short end of the cable needle, cast on 2, slide 6 stitches from the long end of the cable needle to a spare needle, then knit them. Pick up 3 stitches from the cast-on 2 of ring finger. Knit around on 17 stitches for 2½" or 2 rounds more than ring finger. Finish as for ring finger.

Forefinger: Knit the 14 stitches from the short end of the cable needle onto two needles, pick up 3 stitches from the cast-on 2 of middle finger. Knit around on 17 stitches for 2⅓" or the same number of rounds as for ring finger. Finish as for ring finger.

Thumb: Knit the 13 stitches from the stitch holder onto two needles, pick up 5 stitches from the cast-on 4. Knit around on 18 stitches for 2". K2 tog around. Send the yarn through the remaining 9 stitches and close.

When you are making the second glove, to start the thumb gusset at the same place, count the rows. This is most easily done on the inside. Count the ridges on the first glove from the top of the picot to the beginning of the 2 gusset outline stitches.

Finishing: Turn up the hem on the outside and sew the seams on each side of the gauntlet cuff split so that the eyelet row will be on the fold to form the picot edge. The cast-on tail can be used for sewing one side. Turn right side out and push out the corners. Turn the gloves inside out. There are a lot of ends, aren't there? Work in each end for about 2" where it will give benefit by reinforcing areas most likely to wear—that is, on the palm side of the fingers and thumb. Work the ends in loosely, catching every second or third row and not in a straight line, because this will make them less likely to show through. Sew the hem loosely to avoid a pucker, so that it is folded to form the picot edge.

These gloves also can be made with ribbing cuffs and worn as gloves or used for liners when extra warmth or absorption is important.

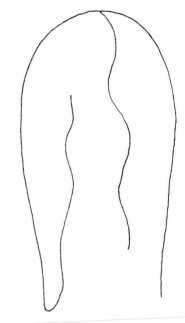

Work in ends on glove

FOR A CHILD

Mittens

I call these super-easy mittens and they really are, but you do need to know how to read knitting directions. Once you understand the pattern, you can easily make a small pair of mittens in an evening. The hand section is garter stitch, which is thicker and therefore warmer than stockinette stitch. When you use a yarn with good spring, garter stitch is accommodating, and the mittens will stretch and fit a growing child a second year.

Supplies: S (M, L) corresponds to child sizes 2 (6, 10). Two (2, 3) ounces of four-ply worsted-weight yarn will be ample.

Gauge: Use a pair of #4 needles or the size you require to get a gauge of 5 stitches per inch in garter stitch. One smaller needle, say a #1 if you have it, will come in handy for gathering the ribbing stitches.

Mitten: Garter cast-on 18 (24, 30) stitches, leaving a 12″ tail for sewing. Slip the first stitch of every garter row except after a cast-on. This will make sewing the top and gathering the stitches for the ribbing much easier. Knit 3 rows. Hold your knitting with the skein yarn and the needle point to the left, the cast-on tail to the right. There should be two garter ridges.

Work short rows: *Knit to the last 2 stitches, turn, slip 1 stitch, knit to the end. Knit 4 full rows. Repeat from * except end the last repeat: Knit 3 full rows. When the longer edge meas-

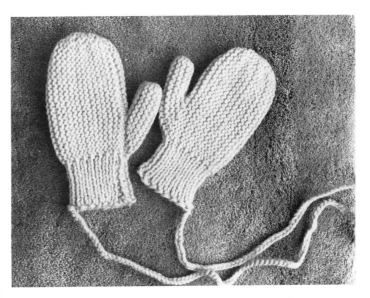

ures 5″ (6″, 7″), start the thumb. Do you understand how this pattern works? The length measurement is around the hand. The stitches left unknit by the short rows are on the edge that is to be the top of the mitten.

Thumb and gusset: You are going to bind off 12 (16, 20) stitches BUT bind off until there are 6 (8, 10) stitches on your left needle, 1 still on the right. Slip 1 stitch and bind off the final stitch. This helps to prevent a hole in the crotch of the thumb. Return the slipped stitch to the left needle. Single-strand cast-on 6 (8, 10) stitches. You now have 12 (16, 20) stitches for the thumb.

Short rows:

K8 (10, 12), turn, sl 1, knit to the end.
K9 (12, 14), turn, sl 1, knit to the end.
K10 (13, 16), turn, sl 1, knit to the end.
K0 (14, 17), turn, sl 1, knit to the end.
K0 (0, 18), turn, sl 1, knit to the end.
When your direction reads ''knit 0,'' that means

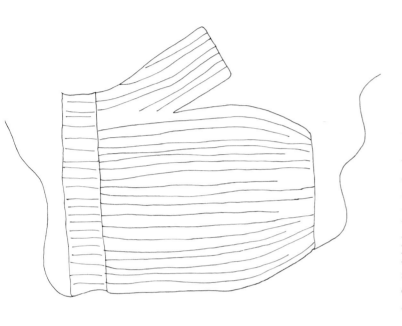

Super easy mitten

Finishing: Use the cast-on tail to sew the top. Start at the other end of the top edge. With a tapestry needle, send the yarn under one strand of each nub. Draw in. Send the yarn through again in the same direction to close the hole fully. Sew the seam bind-off to cast-on to the crotch of the thumb. With the end of yarn left from binding off the ribbing, sew the ribbing, thumb gusset seam, and thumb seam. Close the top of the thumb as you did the top of the mitten. Bury the thumb end of yarn in the thumb seam. Use the end of the cast-on tail yarn to close any thumb crotch hole, then bury it in the palm seam.

Cord: A cord is to prevent lost mittens. The mittens, joined by a cord, are inserted through the sleeves of the coat from the inside and stay with the coat. Ideally, each coat should have its own pair of mittens. To make the cord, use double-strand yarn (hold together and work two strands as if they were one). You can use both ends of a skein. With a crochet hook and leaving ends for sewing, chain 32'' (36'', 40''). I like to make the chain a little longer and tie a slip knot in the center. You may have trouble convincing someone beyond second grade that a cord is a good idea.

ONLY, knit through the back of the stitches and purl normally to work the row in k1, p1 ribbing. it does not apply to the size you are making. Knit 4 full rows. Repeat the short rows in reverse order. Bind off the thumb stitches starting from the top and ending at the wrist, but save the final stitch. Do not cut the yarn.

Wrist ribbing: Use a spare needle—a small one will work more easily. Starting from the cast-on, slide the needle under one strand for each ridge. This forms stitches for the wrist ribbing. Add the stitch remaining from the bind-off. If you have an uneven number of stitches, decrease once in the middle of the first row. Slip the first stitch (because you have already knit it) and purl 1. To continue the first row Rib for 1½'' (1¾'', 2''). Bind off LOOSELY in pattern. Cut the yarn, leaving an end for sewing. Right and left mittens are made the same.

Stripes: On the row preceding the first short row, work 2 stitches in MC (main color), join CC (contrast color), and knit to the end. Work short row: Knit to the next to last CC stitch, with yarn to front, slip the last CC stitch, turn, with MC knit to the end. CC waits and is brought up when needed.

Should you want to make adult mittens this way, you will need a higher percentage of short rows, because the hole at the top becomes difficult to close with additional length on the edge. Your repeat is: 2 full rows, short rows leaving 2 stitches, 2 full rows, short rows leaving 4 stitches.

Hat

Here is a nice little hat for a young child, with ties to keep it in place. There are earflaps to keep little ears warm, and a cuff that can be turned down for even more protection from the wind. The sizes S (M, L) correspond to child sizes 1 (2, 4).

Supplies: Use four-ply worsted-weight yarn. One 4-ounce skein is ample.

Gauge: You will need a set of #7 double-point needles or the size you require to get a gauge of 5 stitches per inch in stockinette stitch. You will need a pair of #4 dp needles for the earflaps. You also will use some regular sewing thread in a contrasting color.

Hat: On #7—you may find it safer to use a single-point needle—cast on 80 (88, 92) stitches. With a dp #7 work 24 (28, 28) stitches in k2, p2 ribbing, with a second dp, work 28 (28, 32) stitches in ribbing, with a third, work 28 (32, 32) stitches in ribbing. Join, being careful not to twist. This means to form a triangle of the three needles having stitches, so that all work is on the lower side of the needles. Use the fourth needle to rib across the stitches on the first needle, then the spare needle to rib the stitches on the next needle, then the spare needle to rib across the next needle. Now is your last chance to make sure that the work is not twisted, that it is all located in the same direction. The cast-on tail is below the beginning of the rounds and the needle starting above the tail is needle #1. Understand that needle #1 means the position,

not the actual needle. Continue working around in ribbing until you have 2″ from the cast-on. Starting on needle #1, rib 8 (10, 11) stitches. Working with your yarn and a piece of thread in a contrasting color held together, KNIT 14 stitches. Cut the thread. You want about 2″ of thread hanging from each end of the 14 knit stitches to eliminate any chance of the thread's slipping out. Rib in the established pattern the next 36 (40, 42) stitches. With yarn and thread together, knit 14 stitches. Cut the thread. Rib the remaining 8 (10, 11) stitches on needle #3. You have marked and prepared the site for the earflaps. Work in ribbing for 1″, reestablishing the rib pattern over the 14 knit stitches. Work in stockinette (all knit when working around) for 2″ (2½″, 3″).

Crown: Starting on needle #1:
S: (K38, k2 tog) 2 times.
M: (K27, k2 tog, k13, k2 tog) 2 times.
(K12, k2 tog) 6 times.
L: (K44, k2 tog) 2 times.
(K13, k2 tog) 6 times.
(K12, k2 tog) 6 times.

All sizes: You should have a total of 78 stitches. Keeping the beginning of your round where it is, adjust by shifting stitches, if necessary, so that you have 26 stitches on each needle.

(K11, k2 tog) 6 times.
(K10, k2 tog) 6 times.
(K9, k2 tog) 6 times.
(K8, k2 tog) 6 times.

Continue decreasing 6 stitches every round in this manner until 12 stitches remain. Cut the yarn at 6″. With a tapestry needle, send the yarn through each of the 12 stitches, continuing in the direction in which you have been working. I like to close the hole, then send the yarn through the stitches a second time. Send the end down through the center to the inside. Did you notice the pinwheel formed by your decreases?

Earflaps: These directions require careful reading, but this is certainly preferable to sewing on the earflaps. Turn the hat inside out, crown up, ribbing down. Start on the right-hand side of one of the groups of marked 14 stitches. Look for this . Send a #4 dp needle down under the upper strand, catching it for the first stitch. Repeat until you have 14 stitches. Without turning the work, join the yarn, starting in the first stitch you caught:

Right-side row: K14.
Wrong-side row: P2, k10, p2.
Repeat these two rows until you have 1″.
Right-side row: K1, SKP, knit to the last 3, k2 tog, k1.
Wrong-side row: P2, knit to the last 2, p2.

Repeat these two rows until you complete a wrong-side row of p4.

Tie: On the right side, k1, SKP, k1. Do not turn your work, but change each needle to the other hand and slide the 3 stitches up to the working position. Bring the yarn firmly around from the back and knit the 3 stitches again on the right side. Continue knitting without turning until the tie is 10″. Cut the yarn. With a tapestry needle, send it through the 3 stitches, then to the inside. I knit in the English method and have no trouble knitting a tie this way. However, I do have trouble trying to work it in the Continental method. If you are a Continental knitter and cannot do any better than I, you may want to chain a tie. Use a crochet hook, about size F, and a double strand of yarn.

Finishing: Work in the final end of yarn under one of the decrease lines and the earflap starting ends along the base of the earflaps. Remove the contrasting thread. Use the starting tail to close the gap that always occurs in circular work, then run it up on the outside.

To make a larger hat, lengthen the amount of stockinette before the crown.

Pullover

For many reasons, raglan sweaters are the best style for children. The difference between a child's shoulder and chest measurement is not great enough, as a rule, to design a set-in sleeve and have room for an adequate sleeve cap. Raglans, without a shoulder line, eliminate concern about fitting a shoulder. And best of all, when a raglan has been made from the neck down, it can be lengthened as the child's arms and torso grow longer.

For this pattern S (M, L) correspond to child sizes 4 (7, 10) having a chest measurement of the garment of 25″ (28″, 31″). The upper arm circumference is 8″ (9″, 10″).

Supplies: Four-ply worsted-weight yarn is used, and you will need 6 (8, 11) ounces. You should have four small ring markers to keep on the needles to help you remember the increases. You also will need three buttons; I think shank buttons are easier for little fingers to manipulate.

Shank buttons

Gauge: The needle sizes are #8, or the size you require to get a gauge of 4½ stitches per inch in stockinette stitch, and #4. You need a 24" circular needle in each size, plus a pair of #8 needles for the sleeves.

Neck: Cast on 64 (72, 80) stitches on the #4 circular needle. You will be working back and forth. If you happen to have a pair of #4 needles, using them will be more convenient, but I did not mention them in the required supplies because you can work on the circular needle and the supply list was beginning to look too long for one little sweater. So: On the #4 needle work in k2, p2 ribbing for 1". Change to the pair of #8 needles. Use the "knit in front and back" increase. *Increase in the first stitch, knit 4 (4, 6), inc in 1, slip a ring marker to the right needle, inc in 1, knit 24 (28, 30), inc in 1, slip on a marker. Repeat from * for now omitting the final marker. You now should have 72 (80, 88) stitches. You have added 8 stitches, 1 on each side of each marker and 1 each at the beginning and the end. You have started, looking at the right side, the left sleeve, the back, the right sleeve, and the front.

Wrong-side row: P6, take the yarn to the back and slip 1 stitch as if to purl. *K1, slip 1 as if to purl. Repeat from * until 7 stitches remain before the first ring marker. Bring the yarn to the front and complete the row in purl. Slide the markers from the left to the right needle as they appear.

Right-side row: Knit, increasing in the first stitch, on each side of each marker, and in the last stitch —8 additional stitches.

Repeat these two rows 3 times more.

Wrong-side row: P8, yarn to back, sl 1 as if to purl, knit and slip as established until 9 stitches before the next marker, purl to the end.

Right-side row: Knit, increasing as above.

Wrong-side row: P10, yarn back, sl 1 as if to purl, knit and slip until 11 stitches before the next marker, purl to the end.

Right-side row: Knit, increasing as above.

Wrong-side row: P12, yarn back, sl 1 as if to purl, knit and slip until 13 stitches before the next marker, purl to the end.

Right-side row: Knit, increasing as above. If you have been working on straight needles, use the circular #8 for this row.

When you switch from working rows back and forth to working rounds (knitting around), if you were to maintain the increasing as established, one pair of marker increases would not be together. This not only would be difficult to remember, but one of the raglan seam lines would look funny. So, to correct for this, one of the increases is postponed once. Slide on the fourth marker. Join and knit 1 round without increasing, to a few stitches beyond the just-inserted marker. The placket is at the left front, you are in the left sleeve, and you have made the correction. Your rounds begin in this area. If you think you will need a reminder, put a safety pin in the sweater here. You will now increase every OTHER round on each side of each marker — 8 additional stitches. You are ready for an increase round. Knit around until each sleeve has 36 (40, 46) stitches and the front and back each has 56 (64, 70) stitches. Knit a non-increase round to the marker at the back end of the left sleeve.

Left sleeve: Turn and purl the sleeve stitches. You will now be working back and forth on the sleeve. This can be done for about 1" on the circular needle, but then start using the straight #8 needles. Remove these two sleeve markers. Work even in stockinette until 3" from the underarm. Decrease at each edge: Knit together the second and third stitches from the beginning and SKP the third and second from the end every third knit row. (This means every sixth row.) Do not decrease below 28 (32, 36) stitches. When the sleeve measures 13" (15", 17") or desired length from the beginning of the stockinette after the neck ribbing, change to #4 needles and decrease if necessary to 28 (32, 36) stitches while establishing the k2, p2 ribbing. When the ribbing is 2", bind off LOOSELY in pattern. You probably will not be lucky enough to come to the end of the first skein of yarn at a convenient spot, such as the end of a row in a sleeve. Read in Chapter 2 how to handle ends when they occur where you have no edges.

Right sleeve: Leaving an end for sewing, join the yarn at the left underarm and knit across the back and the sleeve to the second marker. Complete this sleeve as you did the first.

Torso: Leaving an end for sewing, join the yarn at the right underarm and knit around, uniting the front and the back, until you have 11" (13", 16") or desired length from the beginning of the stockinette at the back of the neck. Directly below—above as you are knitting—the left underarm is a good place to start the ribbing. Your total number of stitches must be a multiple of 4. Working from the #8 circular needle onto the #4 circular needle, begin the k2, p2 ribbing. When the ribbing is 2", bind off LOOSELY in pattern, starting below the left underarm.

Finishing: Using the ends left for sewing and a tapestry needle, close the holes that always occur in raglan underarms. Sew the sleeve seams in nub-and-bar. Mark with safety pins the sites of the three placket buttons. For a girl the buttons are on the sleeve, for a boy on the front. Use a steel crochet hook about size #1. Right-handed crocheters start at the top of the sleeve, lefties at the top of the front, so that you are working on the right side. Work 1 row of single crochet down to the joining point, then up. Make the button loops opposite the buttons as you are crocheting. The button loops are made by chaining 2 or 3 stitches. You will have to make a test loop to decide on the correct size to fit your buttons. When the crochet is completed, sew on the buttons.

The length of the sleeves in these directions is a little long, so that the cuffs can be turned up for wearing now. When you become familiar with knitting neck-down raglan sweaters, you can learn to make adjustments. For skinny arms, when casting on, subtract 2 stitches from each sleeve—you must keep a multiple of 4 for the neck ribbing. For a fat tummy, add 2

stitches each to the front and the back. To make a sweater proportionally a little smaller or larger, work fewer or more increase rows. Have you figured out what the pattern at the front neck is for? You earn a gold star if you have. People are built with the base of their necks lower in front than in back. Children are people too. The slip stitch pattern lowers the front neck.

If you have read through top-down sleeve directions elsewhere in this book, you know that I prefer working cuffs, where possible, on a set of dp needles. This raglan sweater is a where-possible. Working the cuffs on dp needles makes it easy later to undo the binding off and lengthen the sleeve.

Make a note in the book if you used other than the suggested needle sizes. Also note any variations you try. Have you thought about putting in a stripe? It is a piece of cake if done above (before) the underarm. Or what about a contrasting-color yoke?

Jacket

Do you have a young friend who would be pleased with a knit jacket? This one is worked with three strands of yarn, together, on very large needles. I must admit that I do not find knitting on such large needles relaxing, but the work goes fast.

Small (Medium, Large) are sizes 4 (6, 8). The chest measurements of the garment are 26" (28", 30"), and the upper arm circumference is 9" (10", 11").

Supplies: You will need 15 (18, 21) ounces of four-ply worsted-weight yarn. You should also have four ring markers large enough to use on #13 needles. You will use a 29" or 36" circular #13, a 14" pair of #10½, and a pair of #13 needles.

Gauge: Use #13 needles or the size you require to get a gauge of 2⅓ stitches per inch with triple-strand yarn in stockinette stitch.

There is a special technique for knitting with three strands of yarn. Pull the yarn from each skein, then run the three strands together through your fingers to make them even. Also, when working with triple-strand yarn, I am in-

knit row until each front has 14 (16, 18) sts, each sleeve 20 (24, 28) sts, and the back 28 (32, 36) sts. End with a purl row.

Sleeves: Knit to the second marker, omitting the increases (but don't take off the markers). Turn and purl the sleeve stitches. It is easier to work a few rows on the circular needle before you start using the #13 straight needles. Work 8 rows, including the row on which you omitted the increases, ending with a purl row. Decrease 1 stitch at each edge on the next knit row and on every fourth knit row. (This means every eighth row.) Continue until the sleeve measures 14″ (16″, 18″) from the neck. Be generous in measuring, because the cuff can be turned up. End with a purl row. You should have 14 (16, 18) sts. On #10½ needles, work in garter stitch (all knit) until there are four ridges on the right side. Knit 1 row. Bind off LOOSELY on the next wrong-side row. This forms a fifth ridge. Cut the yarn long enough to sew the sleeve seam. Join the yarn, leaving a few inches to close the hole that always occurs under the arm in raglan sweaters, and knit across the back and the second sleeve. Complete this sleeve as you did the first.

Torso: Join the yarn, leaving an end to close the hole, and knit across the last front. Purl a

clined not to worry about joining a new skein only at the edge. When one strand ends and another is joined, I do so leaving 3″ ends tied with an overhand knot. Later I hide the ends horizontally on the wrong side. One more thing: I like to use two strands of one color and a third strand almost the same color.

Neck: Starting at the neck, with the #13 circular needle and the triple strand, cast on 18 stitches.

Row 1: K1, inc in 1, marker, inc in 2, marker, inc in 1, k8, inc in 1, marker, inc in 2, marker, inc in 1, k1.

Row 2: Purl (slipping the markers).

Row 3: Knit, increasing 1 st on each side of each marker—8 additional sts.

Row 4: Purl.

Row 5: Knit, increasing in the first st and on each side of each marker, to the last 2 sts; inc in 1, k1.

Row 6: Purl.

Row 7: Cast on 2 and knit, maintaining the 8 raglan increases.

Row 8: Cast on 2 and purl.

You now have 9 sts, marker, 10 sts, marker, 18 sts, marker, 10 sts, marker, 9 sts (for front, sleeve, back, sleeve, front). Continue in stockinette, maintaining the raglan increases every

full row, uniting the front, back, and front. Work in stockinette stitch until the jacket measures 15" (17", 19") from the back of the neck, or allow 1½" for the garter stitch. End with a purl row. On #10½ needles, work in garter stitch until you have three ridges on the right side. Knit 1 row. Bind off loosely on the next wrong-side row.

Front edging: Count the number of nubs on the front edge. Divide by 3 and add the answer to the number of nubs. Subtract 6 for the top and bottom and divide the remainder by the number of spaces between the buttons. Add or subtract any amount left over to 1⅓ the number of nubs. Stay with me—I shall make it clearer. Traditionally the number of buttons is uneven, but that is not a golden rule. Let's say you have 29 nubs on the front edge.

29 divided by 3 is about 10. Allow 3 sts for the top and 3 sts for the bottom.
If you plan 5 buttons, there are 4 spaces between them, so divide by 4. Your answer is 8 with 1 left over. 8 is your space number. Subtract 1 from 39. Pick up 38 sts.

$$
\begin{array}{rl}
29 & \text{number of nubs} \\
+10 & \text{add } \frac{1}{3} \\
\hline
39 & \\
-6 & \text{top and bottom allowance} \\
\hline
33 & \\
\end{array}
$$

$$
\begin{array}{rl}
4/33 & \text{spaces} \\
8 & \text{space number} \\
+1 & \\
\end{array}
$$

$$
\begin{array}{rl}
39 & \\
-1 & \\
\hline
38 & \text{sts to pick up} \\
-29 & \text{nubs} \\
\hline
9 & \text{extra sts to pick up} \\
\end{array}
$$

Another example: You have 22 nubs. One-third is about 7. You plan 4 buttons, which have 3 spaces. 8 is the space number, but you must add 1.
Pick up 30 stitches.

$$
\begin{array}{r}
22 \\
+7 \\
\hline
29 \\
-6 \\
\hline
3/23 \\
8 \\
\quad -1 \\
29 \\
+1 \\
\hline
30 \\
\end{array}
$$

You will pick up 1 extra stitch about every third nub. You want to have the same number on both front edges. Buttonholes for boys are on the left front, for girls on the right front. Using triple strand and #10½ needles, working on the right side, pick up the button side first, as described in Chapter 2. Work in garter stitch and bind off LOOSELY on the seventh row, which is a wrong-side row. Pick up the stitches on the buttonhole side and knit 3 rows. On the fourth row k1, k2 tog, cast on 2 (flip loop), *k2 tog, k4 less than your space number, k2 tog, cast on 2. Repeat from * to the last 3 stitches, k2 tog, k1. Knit 2 more rows and bind off LOOSELY on the seventh row, which is a wrong-side row. If your front edges are just a tad short, good, because they tend to drop. But they should not be short because you did not bind off loosely enough.

Collars: Notched or mandarin. The stitches for the collars are picked up with triple strand and #10½ needles from the outer corner of the stockinette to the other outer corner of the stockinette; no stitches from the garter edgings. Check that you have the same number of stitches in front of the top of the sleeves on each side. Both collars are worked in garter stitch.

Notched collar: On the wrong side of the jacket, pick up about 30 stitches. On your first row, increase in 2 stitches at each neck back corner. This will help the collar to fold and fit better. Work 1" in garter on #10½ needles, then on #13 work 1" (1½", 1½") more. Bind off loosely on the wrong side of the collar.

Mandarin collar: On the right side of the jacket, pick up about 30 stitches. Work in garter stitch and bind off loosely on the fifth row.

Finishing: Using a large blunt-pointed needle, sew the sleeve seams. Close the holes under the arms. Hide all ends. Take the jacket to the button store and select chunky buttons, because your knitting is chunky and little fingers will be able to handle them better.

FOR THE HOUSE

Dishcloth

Have you been invited to a kitchen shower? In this chapter there are several project suggestions for the kitchen. For a beginning knitter, this dishcloth worked in garter stitch is a good choice. It requires an all-cotton yarn for absorption and durability. Wool is not desirable for dishcloths. Acrylic is worse, especially for making potholders, because of the danger of flashing. Acrylic material will sustain a flame; that is, when removed from the source, it will continue to burn. Though cotton will burn when held in flame, when removed it will cease burning. I have complained to yarn manufacturers about the flammability of acrylic. But under current law, they have no responsibility, because we knitters make the garments. They only make the yarn.

Supplies: For the dishcloth and the potholders in this chapter you will need a four-ply cotton yarn that is lighter than rug yarn. The brand I find most widely available is Sugar 'n Cream, made by Lily Craft Products. For a dishcloth, one 125-yard ball is ample.

Gauge: Use #5 needles or the size you require to get a gauge of 4½ stitches per inch in garter stitch (knit every row).

You will find that knitting with cotton or linen is very different from knitting with wool or most synthetic yarns. I rarely suggest that you change your tension, but if you are a very

firm knitter, you may need to loosen up a bit when using cotton.

Dishcloth: Cast on 40 stitches. Work in garter stitch for 9". Should you have a knot in your yarn, remove it and rejoin your yarn on the edge. Bind off loosely. Cut the ends at an angle at 2". Using a large tapestry needle, work in the ends through the nubs along the edges.

This project also can be a washcloth for a baby, since it is soft and washable.

Square Potholder

How about knitting an easy and useful potholder?

Supplies: Please read what is written about using cotton with the dishcloth directions. One 125-yard ball of all-cotton four-ply will be ample.

Gauge: Use #5 needles or the size you require to get a gauge of 4½ stitches per inch in garter stitch.

Square potholder: Cast on 25 stitches. Work in garter stitch for 12″. Bind off loosely. Fold the potholder in half to form a square. Using any ends on the edges first, sew the side seams through the nubs alternately on each edge with a large tapestry needle. Bury the remaining end for 2″ in the seam. Turn right side out and sew the bind-off to the cast-on.

Garter Stitch Pillow

You are a weekend guest and you want to offer a special thank you. A box of candy or a bouquet of flowers can say thank you, but you prefer something more permanent. What about a toss pillow? Remember to match or accent the color scheme in the room for which it is intended. As you gain proficiency in your knitting, there are three pillow covers and an afghan you can make for the house that belongs to someone really special. This pillow cover took me four hours' knitting time.

Supplies: Pillow forms are available in a variety of sizes and shapes; 14″ by 14″ is one you should be able to find easily. You want a knife edge rather than a box form. The pillow cover measures 12″ by 12″, so that it will be firm and there will be less chance of snagging. Six ounces of four-ply worsted-weight yarn are ample.

Gauge: Use #8 needles or the size necessary for you to get a gauge of 4⅓ stitches per inch, or 13 stitches in 3″, in garter stitch (all knit).

Garter stitch pillow: On #8 needles, cast on 52 stitches. Work in garter stitch for 24″. The

width should be 12". After the first row, you can slip as if to knit the first stitch of every row. This often is difficult for a beginning knitter to remember. If you cannot, it is not vital. However, I do want you to know that methods of treating edges in knitting exist, that there are ways to keep them neat. A 1-stitch border is made by slipping as if to knit the first stitch of every row and knitting the last stitch of every row. When done correctly, the nubs on the edges are not lost, but indeed are more definite. Bind off so that the end will be on the opposite edge from the cast-on tail.

Finishing: With a tapestry needle, use the cast-on tail and the bind-off end to sew, or start sewing, the sides in nub-and-bar. If you have not already done so, read the section on sewing in Chapter 2. Complete sewing the side edges and run in the ends a couple of inches along the seams. Turn the pillow cover right side out and insert the form. Encourage the form corners into the cover corners. Cut a piece of yarn twice the length of the remaining seam to be sewn. Start by hiding the end in an inside seam. Sew bind-off to cast-on, encouraging the corners into place. Run in the final end as well as you can down the inside of a side seam.

You are a thoughtful gift giver when you tuck some extra yarn inside the package, to be used should a repair become necessary or to resew a seam if the pillow form is not washable and the cover has to be removed for washing.

Modified Moss Pillow

You might find it helpful to read over what is written about the garter stitch pillow. This pattern, which I call Modified Moss, is a four-row repeat with an interesting textured look. I have advised its use for jackets and coats, and the results have been good. If your memory is as poor as mine, until you can learn to understand the pattern and recognize each row, you will need a row reminder. There are handy little gadgets, called "knit count" or "knit tally," that you slide to the back end of your knitting needle. They have dials you turn after each row to keep track of what row you are on.

Supplies: Six ounces of four-ply worsted-weight yarn are ample.

Gauge: Use #8 needles or the size you require to get a gauge of $4\frac{1}{2}$ stitches per inch in stockinette stitch.

Modified Moss pattern

Row 1: Knit.
Row 2: *K1, p1. Repeat from * to the end.
Row 3: Knit.
Row 4: *P1, k1. Repeat from * to the end.

Modified Moss pillow: On #8 needles, cast on 54 stitches in flip loop or single-strand. Work in pattern for 24". Do not slip the first stitch or keep a 1-stitch border, because either will interfere with the pattern. The width should be 12". Notice on the right side that the stitches that look like purls alternate. This is what you check, not only to be sure you have not made a mistake, but also to discern which row is next. The stitches that look like purls on the right side were knitted on the wrong side. When you are ready for a wrong-side row, find, close to the beginning of the row, the stitch on

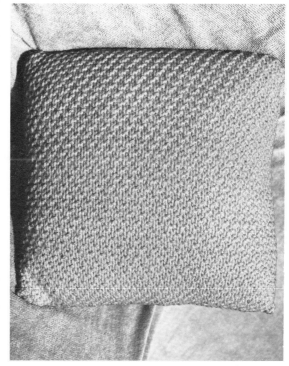

the right side on your needle directly above a "purl." Name the stitches—knit, purl—to the beginning to see which you are to start with. As you work on the wrong-side rows, learn to look at your work. When there are three vertical "purl" stitches below the next stitch, you knit it. When there is just one "purl" stitch below, you purl. Every right-side row is knit. Bind off IN PATTERN on a row 4.

Finishing: Your cast-on tail and bind-off end should be on opposite edges. With the pillow cover wrong side out, use the ends of the work and a tapestry needle to sew, or start sewing, the side edges together in nub-and-bar. After sewing the side seams, hide the ends along the seam. Turn the pillow cover to the right side and insert the 14" by 14" pillow form. Be sure the corners are filled. When sewing the bind-off and cast-on edges, watch the pattern. You bound off on row 4 so that the purls will continue to alternate around this seam.

Daisy Potholder

Pot lids can become as hot and uncomfortable to pick up as the handle. This potholder is designed for the top nob on a lid.

Supplies: First read over the directions for the dishcloth at the beginning of this chapter. Ten yards of four-ply cotton yarn in each of three colors, green, white, and yellow, will be ample.

Gauge: Use a pair of #5 needles or the size you require to get a gauge of 4½ stitches per inch in garter stitch.

Daisy potholder: With green, loosely cast on 59 stitches in stockinette. Do not use single-strand cast-on. Knit 5 rows.

Row 6: K5, *drop 1 stitch all the way down, send the needle under the 7 strands front to back, yo and bring back a stitch, k5. Repeat from * to the end.

Row 7: K5, *p1, k5. Repeat from * to the end. Change to white yarn.

Row 1: Knit. This is the right side.

Row 2: P1, *k1, p1. Repeat from * to the end.

Row 3: K1, *p1, k1. Repeat from * to the end.

Row 4: Repeat row 2.

Row 5: K1, p1, k1, p1, k1, *k2 tog, p1, k1, p1, k1. Repeat from * to the end.

Row 6: P1, *k1, p1, k1, p2. Repeat from *, ending the last repeat p1.

Row 7: P2 tog, k1, p1, *SKP, p1, k1, p1. Repeat from * to the last stitch, k1.

Row 8: *P1, k1. Repeat from * to the end. Change to yellow yarn. K2 tog across. You now have 20 stitches. Work in garter stitch until there are five ridges on the right side. K2 tog across—10 stitches. K2 tog across. Cut the yellow yarn and with a large tapestry needle send it through the remaining 5 stitches and close.

Finishing: Sew the yellow and white seams with their own color, using a large tapestry needle. Take a few stitches in green to match the other leaf divisions.

Occasionally dark dyes in cotton may bleed. The dying process manufacturers must follow to meet current pollution-control requirements may not always result in well-set colors. To check for colorfastness see how to wash and block wool in Chapter 2.

Afghan

For this afghan or sofa throw I have used a pattern with a long history. You can find it in museums on old christening dresses. Called Old Shale, the pattern was worked on tiny needles with fine linen. The dresses were worn by both girl and boy babies. In some of my knitting manuals from the thirties this same pattern, now called Feather and Fan, is used in a bed jacket for a new mother and in a sacque, bonnet, and booties for her baby. Although the pattern is not difficult, it does require that you pay attention, and therefore, I suggest it for an experienced knitter. It takes me a half hour for each four-row pattern repeat.

Supplies: For a throw 36″ by 48″, 28 ounces of four-ply worsted-weight yarn will be ample.

Gauge: Use a 29″ or 36″ circular #8 needle or the size you require to get a gauge of 1 pattern = 3¼″. To measure your gauge, cast on 34 stitches (the pattern is a multiple of 17 stitches) and work in the pattern for 2″.

Row 1: Knit. (Right side.)

Row 2: Purl.

Row 3: (K2 tog) 3 times, yo, (k1, yo) 5 times, *(k2 tog) 6 times, yo, (k1, yo) 5 times. Repeat from * to the last 6 stitches, (k2 tog) 3 times.

Row 4: Knit.

Observe the center stitch in the increase area. Measure between these stitches.

Afghan: Cast on 187 stitches. Work in pattern for 48″. You will be wise to learn to understand the pattern and to check your work vertically. On row 3, decrease repeats begin above a fifth hole and end above a second hole in increase repeats below. For those of you who are more comfortable using ring markers on your needle in lace work, put them in the center of the decreases. This means (k2 tog) 3 times, marker, (k2 tog) 3 times. You will need 10 rings. End having completed a row 2. Bind off, knitting all the stitches. To make the scallop end behave, you should bind off firmly over the decreases and loosely over the increases.

Aran Fisherman Pillow

This is an especially attractive pillow cover. The pattern contains a secret known to knitters of fisherman sweaters. The cable, I am sure you can recognize. The three patterns between the cables are called Jacob's Ladder. I also am giving you a two-stitch border, because I want you to know how to make it, and I needed four more stitches to obtain the width.

Supplies: Please read over the section on the garter stitch pillow earlier in this chapter. Six ounces of four-ply worsted-weight yarn will be ample. You may want ring markers to put on your needles to separate the patterns. You will use eight of them. You will need a cable needle. I prefer one shaped like the letter J.

Gauge: Use #8 needles or the size you require to get a gauge of 4½ stitches per inch in stockinette stitch.

Two stitch border: 2 sts.
At the beginning of every row after the first, slip 1 stitch as if to knit, k1. At the end of every row k2.

Cable stitch: 10 sts.
Row 1: P2, k6, p2. (Right side.)
Row 2: and all even-numbered rows: K2, p6, k2.
Rows 3 and 5: Repeat row 1.
Row 7: P2, slide the next 3 sts onto the short end of the cable needle (CN) to the curve and hold, points down, in back of your work. Knit the next 3 sts, then knit the 3 sts from the long end of the cable needle.
Rows 9 and 11: Repeat row 1.
Row 12: Repeat row 2.
Jacob's Ladder: 6 sts.
Rows 1, 3 and 5: Knit. (Right side.)
Rows 2 and 4: Purl.
Row 6: Knit.

Aran fisherman pillow: On #8 needles, cast on 62 stitches. The first 2 stitches are the 2-stitch border; the next 10, cable; the next 6, Jacob's Ladder; then 10 cable; 6 Jacob's Ladder; 10 cable; 6 Jacob's Ladder; 10 cable; 2 for the 2-stitch border. Did I lose you? Let's go through it together.
Row 1: K2 (this is the first row), p2, *k6, p2. Repeat from * to the last 2 sts, k2.
Row 2: Sl 1 as if to knit, k3, p6, *k2, p6. Repeat from * to the last 4 sts, k4.
Row 3: Slip 1, k1, complete as for row 1.

Repeat rows 2 and 3 once.
Row 6: Sl 1, k3, p6, *k10, p6. Repeat from * to the last 4 sts, k4.
You have now made the first rungs on the ladder.
Row 7: Sl 1, k1, row 7 of cable, *row 1 of Jacob's Ladder, row 7 of cable. Repeat from * to the last 2 sts, k2.
Continue, keeping the border at each edge. Work through row 12 of the cable and row 6 of Jacob's Ladder. Note that you run through the ladder pattern twice for each cable pattern run through. Learn to pay attention to the wrong side of the ladder pattern. A rung is made every sixth row, which is a wrong-side row. You can see, when starting a wrong-side row, whether there have been 1, 3, or 5 rows since the last rung. Look at the ridges above the last rung or valley. Here is the secret: The cable is crossed on the row following every other rung. This eliminates the need for counting rows. That is why in Aran fisherman sweaters you often see Jacob's Ladder with a cable on either side of it. The width of the pillow cover should be 12". Continue in pattern until you have about 24" from the cast-on and are ready for row 12 on the cable pattern and row 6 on Jacob's Ladder. Bind off IN PATTERN on rows 12 and 6.

Finishing: With the wrong side out, using a tapestry needle, sew the side edges in nub-and-bar. If both cast-on tail and bind-off end are on the same corner, use the longer. Turn the pillow cover right side out and insert a 14" by 14" pillow form. Sew the bound-off and cast-on edges, carefully matching the pattern. Be sure that you do not include in the seam the final rungs made when binding off.

Have you noticed that 4½ stitches per inch times 12" does not equal 62 stitches? When there are cables or other crossover patterns in your knitting, you lose width. You must add compensating stitches. For a 6-stitch cable that is crossed 3 and 3, 2 compensating stitches are needed. Multiply 4½ times 12, then add 2 for each of the four cables.

Now I want to talk about keeping borders on the edges of your knitting. To remind you, a 1-stitch border is made by slipping as if to knit the first stitch of every row and knitting the last stitch. A 2-stitch border is made by slipping as if to knit the first stitch, knitting the second, and knitting the last 2 stitches of every row. When done correctly, the nub not only remains, but is better defined and can be worked with more uniformity. When you are sewing two side edges together nub-and-bar, there is no decision to make as to which strand of the nub to use. With a border, it is easier to count rows—1 nub represents 2 rows. When there is a border around an armhole, you pick up the stitches for the sleeve more easily. I have not included a garter border on the side edges of any of the sweater directions because each has other techniques I want to tell you about. However, unless it interferes with a pattern stitch, I always like to make borders on every sweater I knit, for the reasons already mentioned and because a border marks a sweater as hand knit.

Ear of Corn Potholder

Have you ever taken hold of the handle of your cast-iron frying pan and received a surprise? It hurts! This potholder is such a good idea that after you make one for a gift you may want to make one for yourself.

Supplies: I urge you to read over the directions for the dishcloth at the beginning of this chapter, and also the note about colorfastness at the end of the directions for the daisy potholder. Two 125-yard balls of four-ply cotton, one each of yellow and white, plus a few yards of green will be ample to make an ear of corn potholder. Indeed, I used just three balls, one in each color, for the four cotton projects in this chapter.

Gauge: Use a set of double-point #4 needles or the size you require to get a gauge of 14 stitches = 3″ in garter stitch.

Ear of corn: Cast on 36 stitches in stockinette BUT to do so, tie a slip knot using two strands together, one each of yellow and white, and put it on your needle. This is an anchor and you will remove it later. Cast on 4 stitches with yellow in back so that you have 4 yellow stitches. Switch colors on your fingers so that white is in back and cast on 4 white stitches. Repeat until you have 36 stitches, 5 groups of yellow stitches

and 4 groups of white stitches. Slide 12 stitches onto each of two spare needles. Form a triangle of your cast-on so that you are ready to work at the slip knot. The cast-on ridge should be on the outside. Your first round is to be purled, but read carefully. You are going to take both colors with you and work with them alternately. The unused colors are to be carried on the inside, at the back of your work. When you are ready to purl with one of the colors, bring it between the needles to the front. Then, to change colors, take the old color back between the needles and bring the new forward. Take courage, for the knit round will be easier. NOW start the first round. Remove the slip knot. The first 4 cast-on stitches are yellow, so purl them with white. Take the white yarn to the back between the

needles and bring the yellow from back to front. Forget everything you have learned about working with two colors. When you change colors, pull firmly. The rows of kernels are formed by the carried color. Purl the next 4 white stitches with yellow. Complete the round purling each group of stitches in the other color.

Increase round: The first 4 stitches are white, so knit with yellow as follows: K1, inc in 1, k2. The next 4 stitches are yellow, so knit with white: K1, inc in 1, k2. Complete this round knitting each group in the other color and increasing 1 stitch in each group. You now have 45 stitches. Your next round is a purl round. Things to remember: Each group of 5 stitches is purled with the other color; when changing colors, take the old to the back between the needles and bring the new firmly forward. On the knit round, things to remember: Each group of 5 stitches is knit in the other color; when changing colors, bring the new firmly into use. Work in garter stitch (on circular work alternate knit and purl rounds) until you have 5″. End with a purl round. Hint: When you put down your work, you would be wise to do so with a k5 or p5 in process. It is always wise when working with four dp needles to leave them all in your knitting. When making an ear of corn, if you stop with 5 stitches in process, it will be easier to see where you are and to start again.

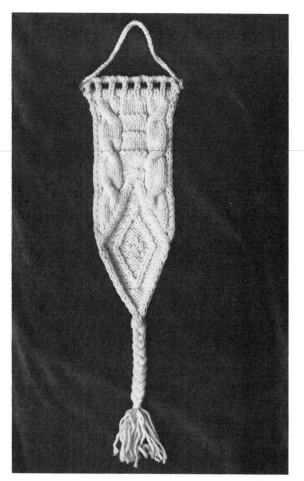

Decreasing:

Knit, decreasing 1 stitch in each color group around.
Purl around.
Knit, decreasing 1 stitch in each group of 4.
Purl around.
Knit, decreasing 1 stitch in each group of 3.
P2 tog around.

Cut both yarns and, using a large tapestry needle, send the ends through the remaining 9 stitches and close. Send the ends to the inside and bury them down the inside of a row of kernels. The ear of corn potholder is virtually impossible to turn inside out. Send the starting ends up a row of kernels.

Leaves: With green, cast on 10 stitches, leaving an end for sewing. Knit 10. Purl back 10. Bind off 8 stitches, then *slip the stitch from the right needle to the left needle. Cast on 8 stitches. Knit 10. Purl 10. Bind off 8. Repeat from * 2 times more, ending the last repeat bind off 10. Cut the yarn, leaving an end for sewing. Gather the center. Sew the four leaves, purl side out, on the closed end of the ear of corn.

Wall Hanging

The directions for the wall hanging appear long and difficult, don't they? But if you are an experienced knitter, I am sure you will have no trouble. There are some interesting principles for you to learn, such as an Italian edge, and how to make the edge on the lower half of the diamond behave. Notice that the cables are crossed in the opposite direction. I have used yarn in the fisherman color to match the Aran pillow, which is always suitable for such pattern work. You may prefer keeping in mind the decor of the room in which your gift is to be hung.

Supplies: Two ounces of four-ply worsted-weight yarn are ample. You will use a cable needle—I prefer one shaped like the letter J—and a 7″ length of ¼″ dowling with slits parallel to each other in the ends.

Gauge: Use #9 needles or the size you require to get a gauge of 4⅓ stitches per inch in stockinette stitch.

Wall hanging: Garter cast-on 30 stitches.

Row 1: Knit. (Right side.)

Row 2: K2, *yo, k2 tog. Repeat from * across. (Eyelet row.)

Row 3: Knit

Rows 4, 5, and 6: *K1, pl. Repeat from * across.

Row 7: K1, yarn forward and sl 1 as if to purl, p2, k6, p2, k6, p2, k6, p2, k1, yarn forward and sl 1 as if to purl.

You have now started an Italian edge—Ie—on the first 2 stitches and the last 2 stitches.

Row 8: Ie on first 2, take the yarn to the back to k2, p6, k2, p6, k2, p6, k2, Ie.

Row 9: Repeat row 7.

Row 10: Repeat row 8.

Row 11: Repeat row 7.

Row 12: Ie, k2, p6, K10, p6, k2, Ie.

Row 13: Ie, p2, slide the next 3 stitches to the short end of the cable needle (CN) to the curve and hold in front, allowing the points to drop, k the next 3 stitches, k the 3 stitches from the long end of the cable needle—cable front cross made—p2, k6, p2, slide the next 3 stitches to the short end of the cable needle to the curve and hold in back, k3, k3 from the long end of the cable needle—cable back cross made—p2, Ie.

Row 14: Repeat row 8.

Row 15: Repeat row 7.

Row 16: Repeat row 8.

Row 17: Repeat row 7.

Row 18: Repeat row 8.

Rows 19 to 30: Repeat rows 7 through 18.

Row 31: Repeat row 7.

Row 32: Repeat row 8.

Row 33: Ie, p2, k6, p2, k1, 2 sts on CN to the back, k2, k2 from CN, k1, p2, k6, p2, Ie.

Row 34: Repeat row 8.

Row 35: Ie, p2, k6, p2, 1 on CN to back, k2, p1 from CN, 2 on CN to front, p1, k2 from CN, p2, k6, p2, Ie.

Row 36: Ie, k2, p6, k2, p2, k2, p2, k2, p6, k2, Ie.

Row 37: Ie, p2, work front cross cable as in row 13, p1, 1 on CN to back, k2, p1 from CN, p2, 2 on CN to front, p1, k2 from CN, p1, work cable back cross, p2, Ie.

Row 38: Ie, k2, p6, k1, p2, k4, p2, k1, p6, k2, Ie.

Row 39: Ie, p2, k6, 1 on CN to back, k2, pl from CN, p4, 2 on CN to front, pl, k2 from CN, k6, p2, Ie.

Row 40: Ie, k2, p8, k6, p8, k2, Ie.

Row 41: Ie, p2, k5, 1 on CN to back, k2, p1 from CN, p6, 2 on CN to front, p1, k2 from CN, k5, p2, Ie.

Row 42: Ie, k2, p7, k3, p2, k3, p7, k2, Ie.

Row 43: Ie, p2, k4, 1 on CN to back, k2, p1 from CN, p3, 1 on CN to back, k1, k1 from CN, p3, 2 on CN to front, p1, k2 from CN, k4, p2, Ie.

Row 44: Ie, k2, p6, k4, p2, k4, p6, k2, Ie.

Row 45: Ie, p2, k3, 1 on CN to back, k2, p1 from CN, p3, 1 on CN to back, k1, p1 from CN, 1 on CN to front, p1, k1 from CN, p3, 2 on CN to front, p1, k2 from CN, k3, p2, Ie.

Row 46: Ie, k2, p5, k4, p1, k2, p1, k4, p5, k2, Ie.

Row 47: Ie, p2, k2, 1 on CN to back, k2, p1 from CN, p3, 1 on CN to back, k1, p1 from CN, p2, 1 on CN to front, p1, k1 from CN, p3, 2 on CN to front, p1, k2 from CN, k2, p2, Ie.

Row 48: Ie, k2, p4, k4, p1, k4, p1, k4, p4, k2, Ie.

Row 49: Ie, p1, k2 tog, 1 on CN to back, k2, p1 from CN, p3, 1 on CN to back, k1, p1 from CN, p4, 1 on CN to front, p1, k1 from CN, p3, 2 on CN to front, p1, k2 from CN, SKP, p1, Ie.

Row 50: Ie, k1, p3, k4, p1, k6, p1, k4, p3, k1, Ie.

Row 51: Ie, 2 on CN to back, k2, p2 tog from CN, p3, 1 on CN to back, k1, p1 from CN, p2, k2, p2, 1 on CN to front, p1, k1 from CN, p3, 2 on CN to front, p2 tog, k2 from CN, Ie.

Row 52: Ie, p2, k4, p1, k3, p2, k3, p1, k4, p2, Ie.

Row 53: 2 on CN to back, k2, p2 tog from CN, p3, 1 on CN to back, k1, p1 from CN, p2, k1, p2, k1, p2, 1 on CN to front, p1, k1 from CN, p3, 2 on CN to front, p2 tog, k2 from CN.

Row 54: Sl 1 as if to purl, p1, k4, p1, k3, p1, k2, p1, k3, p1, k4, p2.

Row 55: Sl 1 as if to knit, SKP, p3, 1 on CN to

front, p1, k1 from CN, p3, k2, p3, 1 on CN to back, k1, p1 from CN, p3, k2 tog, k1.

Row 56: Sl 1 as if to purl, p1, k4, p1, k3, p2, k3, p1, k4, p2.

Row 57: Sl 1 as if to knit, SKP, p3, 1 on CN to front, p1, k1 from CN, p6, 1 on CN to back, k1, p1 from CN, p3, k2 tog, k1.

Row 58: Sl 1 as if to purl, p1, k4, p1, k6, p1, k4, p2.

Row 59: Sl 1 as if to knit, SKP, p3, 1 on CN to front, p1, k1 from CN, p4, 1 on CN to back, k1, p1 from CN, p3, k2 tog, k1.

Row 60: Sl 1 as if to purl, p1, k4, p1, k4, p1, k4, p2.

Row 61: Sl 1 as if to knit, SKP, p3, 1 on CN to front, p1, k1 from CN, p2, 1 on CN to back, k1, p1 from CN, p3, k2 tog, k1.

Row 62: Sl 1 as if to purl, p1, k4, p1, k2, p1, k4, p2.

Row 63: Sl 1 as if to knit, SKP, p3, 1 on CN to front, p1, k1 from CN, 1 on CN to back, k1, p1 from CN, p3, k2 tog, k1.

Row 64: Sl 1 as if to purl, p1, k4, p2, k4, p2.

Row 65: Sl 1 as if to knit, SKP, p3, 1 on CN to back, k1, k1 from CN, p3, k2 tog, k1.

Row 66: Sl 1 as if to purl, p1, k8, p2.

Row 67: Sl 1 as if to knit, SKP, p6, k2 tog, k1.

Row 68: Sl 1 as if to purl, p1, k6, p2.

Row 69: Sl 1 as if to knit, SKP, p4, k2 tog, k1.

Row 70: Sl 1 as if to purl, p1, k4, p2.

Row 71: Sl 1 as if to knit, SKP, p2, k2 tog, k1.

Row 72: Sl 1 as if to purl, p1, k2, p2.

Row 73: Sl 1 as if to knit, SKP, k2 tog, k1.

Row 74: Sl 1 as if to purl, p3.

Row 75: 2 on CN to back, bind off 2, bind off 2 from CN. Cut the yarn at 9".

Braid: Cut 16 pieces of yarn, each 18". With hanging right side up (cast-on edge at the top), send the cut pieces to their midpoint through the space made by the cross in row 75. Include the bind-off end and divide for braiding to three 11-strand sections. Secure the hanging, such as placing it between your knees, so that you can pull firmly. Take the section on the right over the middle section, the section on the left over the now middle section. Continue braiding in this manner to within 3" of the end. Using another piece of yarn, wrap several times around the braid. Tie a firm knot in the back. Cut the wrapping yarn ends at 3" to blend in with the other ends.

Hanger: With double-strand yarn, chain 12". Tie a knot at each end, hiding the yarn ends. Thread the dowling in and out through the eyelet row, then catch the ends of the hanger in the slits.

Braid

FOR THE NEW BABY

Toy Party Favor

This is a nice little toy party favor to give to a baby. It is the right size for little hands to hold and has ends that are good for chewing. It is easy for a beginning knitter to make, and fun when a variegated yarn—one that changes colors every few inches—is used, because of the color patterns that develop. I knit party favors in an hour and a half with another half hour for finishing.

Supplies: You will need about an ounce of four-ply worsted-weight yarn, but you probably will have to buy a 3-ounce skein. Do you know three babies? You will do baby's mother a favor by using washable yarn. You also will need a pair of discarded pantyhose (clean, please) or some polyester fiber fill and a #16 tapestry needle for sewing.

Gauge: Use a pair of #4 needles or the size on which your gauge is 5 stitches per inch in garter stitch (knit every row).

Party favor: Cast on 30 stitches. Work in garter stitch for 6″. Bind off all stitches, ending at the opposite edge from the starting tail. Cut the yarn, leaving an end for sewing. If you have trouble binding off loosely enough, if the top pulls in and is narrower than the rest of your piece, use a larger needle. A #8 needle would be good, if you have one.

Finishing: Sew the bound-off edge to the cast-on edge. Use a tapestry needle to sew knit-

ting, because it has a blunt point so you can avoid catching parts of strands of yarn. See the directions for sewing in Chapter 2. Since you have the same number of stitches at the top and bottom, you should come out even sewing cast-on stitches to bound-off stitches. Use the bind-off end and the starting tail to sew in from both directions. When the sewing ends meet, send each 2″ into the other's seam. No knots please. Knitting yarn, whether wool or synthetic, locks in place because of the natural crimp in wool or the constructed crimp in synthetic yarn.

When the seam is completed, select the better-looking side for the outside. Thread the tapestry needle on the yarn. Run a basting line around, 1½" from one of the edges. Gather in. You now have permission to tie a knot, a tight, firm one such as a square knot. Cut the ends to about 3" each. Wrap the ends around the knitting tightly and tie another knot on the opposite side. With the tapestry needle, run the ends through the tight area to the inside. To make the filling from a pair of punctured pantyhose, cut off the feet. Cut the remainder into 1" strips, discarding all seams and cotton or thick areas. Fill one foot lightly, fold over the top, and push it into the other foot. Insert the filling into the party favor and close the second side as you did the first.

Newborn Hat

Have you been invited to a baby shower for a coming event?

Supplies: One ounce of baby-weight yarn or three-ply fingering yarn, if you cannot find the baby yarn, will be more than enough for a newborn hat. In fact, you may be able to make 2 newborn hats from 1 ounce of baby-weight yarn. If you find that you like making this thoughtful little gift, why not buy several skeins in different colors and make some striped hats? How nice it would be to have several on hand so that when you hear of a new baby, you have a ready gift.

Gauge: Use a pair of #3 needles or the size you require to get a gauge of 7½ stitches per inch in garter stitch (all knit).

Newborn hat: Cast on 80 stitches. Work in k1, p1 ribbing for 3". Work in garter stitch for 2" more. Then decrease every other row on what is to be the right side.

Decrease:
Row 1: (K8, k2 tog) 8 times.
Row 2: Knit.
Row 3: (K7, k2 tog) 8 times.
Row 4: Knit.
Row 5: (K6, k2 tog) 8 times.

Row 6: Knit.
Row 7: (K5, k2 tog).
Continue decreasing 8 stitches every other row until:
Row 17: (K2 tog) 8 times.
Do not knit back. Cut your yarn, leaving an end long enough to sew the seam. "Pass yarn through remaining 8 stitches" is how your directions usually read, but do you know what I like to do? Slip all the stitches to the other needle. A size 20 tapestry needle is good for working with baby yarn. Using the tapestry needle, send the yarn through all the stitches. By doing this you are making a circle with the yarn through the stitches and you will not telescope some of them through others. Do you know what else I do? I run the yarn through again in the same direction, being careful not to go through the sewing yarn that went through the first time. This will close the hole at the top of the hat very nicely.

Finishing: You want to make the seam as flat as possible so that a welt in the hat will not make a line in baby's head. Look under sewing in Chapter 2, Side Edge to Side Edge. Nub-and-bar sewing is easy in the garter area. Be sure that the ridges of garter stitch before the

ribbing match. In sewing the ribbing seam you want to get the very edge, so look at your knitting closely. Use the cast-on tail to sew partway up the seam and the finishing end to sew partway down. Count ahead to see if you have to cheat—you shouldn't on this—and run each end about 2" into the other's seam.

Now I will tell you how to make a newborn hat without a seam. I prefer using four double point needles when I can, not only because it will not need to be sewn, but also because I think it looks better. I prefer the 7" dp needles to the 10".

Four-needle newborn hat: You may want to use a single-point needle to cast on the 80 stitches. With the first dp needle, work k1, p1 ribbing for 26 stitches, with the second dp rib the next 26 stitches, and with the third dp rib the remaining 28 stitches. Each needle begins with a knit stitch and ends with a purl. Join, being careful not to twist. This means that the work you have already done—the little ridge of knitting—should be all on the underside of the needles. Bring the two ends of your work together to form a triangle. With the fourth dp needle, rib across the first needle you have worked. When that is done, you have a spare needle to work across the second needle, then the third. Handle your work gently at this point, because you do not want to have a long strand between the first and last needles. This is your last chance to make sure that your work is not twisted. Now you are ready to work around until you have 3". You can tell where each round begins because it is directly above the starting tail. When I am knitting with four dp needles and must put it aside for a while, I work to the middle of one of the needles, and if I am ribbing I leave my work ready to knit. This keeps all four needles in the work, so you are less likely to lose one.

When you have 3" of ribbing, knit 1 round. Here comes the rub: Garter stitch worked around is knit 1 round, purl 1 round. You may have noticed that under each needle division there is a line of loose stitches. You will learn ultimately to give a little tug at each needle change to prevent that loose line. Avoiding the loose line while purling around requires a special technique. For English knitters—right-hand

yarn holders—take the yarn to the knitting position, send the spare needle behind the yarn, and start to purl, working in back of the needle last completed. Continental knitters—left-hand yarn holders—have your yarn in the purl position, send the spare needle behind the needle last completed, and begin purling. Work 2" in garter, ending with a purl round. Decrease as previously described with a purl round between each decrease round. When a needle starts with a decrease, after you have knit the two stitches together, put your stitch on the previous needle, because that is where you will need it the next time you decrease. Do not purl a round after the final decrease. Cut the yarn at about 3".

Finishing: With a tapestry needle, send the yarn through the remaining 8 stitches in the same direction that you have been working. Go through again, then send the needle and yarn down the center of the little star you have formed to the wrong side. To hide the end, work it under one of the decrease lines. To work in the starting tail, with a tapestry needle go under a strand across the little split at the beginning, then back, catching a strand at the base of the tail. Work the end in on the right side, because there is a cuff.

Ball

In my knitting classes my gift to all mothers-to-be is a little ball made with baby yarn on #1 needles. This makes a ball with a 2-inch diameter. I use the colors blue, pink, white, green, and yellow and then repeat once for the 10 bands. You do not cut each color until you have used it the second time. When you are making the ball with two colors, you pull each up in turn until you have finished. Use any standard yarn and the appropriate needle size to make your knitting firm enough to contain the fill. Polyester fiber may be used for filling, and so can a pair of pantyhose, as described in the directions for the party favor.

With baby yarn or three-ply fingering yarn use #1.

With sport yarn use #3.

notice in working the short rows that each ends 2 stitches short of the previous turn, which you can locate by the space on the needle. Cut the yarn, leaving an end for sewing that is at least three times the length of the bind-off.

Finishing: With a tapestry needle, catch all the ends except the sewing end on the inside of the ball. The right side is the one having clean lines between the color bands. Send the sewing end through every nub on the edge clockwise and pull in, then run through again to close. Whip stitch part of the seam—see Bind-Off to Cast-On in the sewing directions in Chapter 2—fill, then complete the seam and close the other end. Send the sewing end to the inside of the ball.

With four-ply worsted weight use #5.

It is, of course, a good idea to use washable yarn and fill for your ball.

Knit a ball to fit baby's hands. The size is determined by the yarn and needle used. Make a small ball for the baby who is learning to hold and examine, a large ball for the toddler destined for a little league pitcher's mound. Think how pleased baby's mother will be with a washable ball that will not break windows.

Ball: In these directions there are slipped stitches. Do so as if to purl, but keep the yarn in the knit position. Using the flip-loop method, cast on 28 stitches.

*Knit 2 rows.
Short rows:
Knit 26, turn.
Sl 1, k23, turn.
Sl 1, k21, turn.
Sl 1, k19, turn.
Sl 1, k17, turn.
Sl 1, k15 turn.
Sl 1, k13, turn.
Sl 1, k11, turn.
Sl 1, k9, turn.
Sl 1, k7, turn.
Sl 1, knit to the end of the row.
Knit 1 row. Change yarn color.

Repeat from * 9 times more, but on the last repeat bind off on the final full knit row. You will

Boot Booties

I have made these booties in red with white cuffs, which makes them appropriate around Santa Claus time or even Saint Valentine's Day, but they can be made in baby colors in one color or with a contrasting cuff. The directions are given in two sizes: newborn and (Big Foot). I need two hours to knit the smaller pair and three hours for the larger.

Supplies: Use four-ply worsted-weight yarn, 1 ounce in each of two colors or 2 ounces in one color.

Gauge: Use #6 needles or the size on which your gauge is 5½ stitches per inch in stockinette stitch.

Boot booties: Starting at the top with the contrast color cast on 24 (30) stitches, leaving a tail to use in sewing. Work in garter stitch until there are 4 (6) ridges on the right side. Join the main color, leaving an end to sew to the bottom of the heel. Work in stockinette until the bootie measures 2″ (3″) from the cast-on. End with a purl row. Work an eyelet row: (K2 tog, yo, k1) 8 (10) times. Purl 1 row. You should have 8 (10) holes. Knit 1 row. Purl 8 (10) stitches and put them on a holder, purl 8 (10) stitches, and put the remaining 8 (10) stitches on a holder. Work in stockinette on the center 8 (10) stitches for 14 (18) rows. There will be 7 (9) nubs on each edge. End with a purl row. To pick up stitches along the side of the instep, use the yarn attached to your knitting and a crochet hook about size #00 steel or #E aluminum. With the right side facing you, send the hook through each nub, catch the yarn, draw it through, and put your stitch on the needle so that the yarn from the ball is in front. Pick up an 8th (10th) stitch in the corner. This is to prevent a hole. Send the hook under one strand from each side of the corner and draw out the yarn and put the stitch on your needle. Replace the 8 (10) stitches from the holder on the spare needle and purl them. Knit all 24 (30) stitches on the needle. With the right side facing you, pick up a stitch from each nub on the other side of the instep, having the yarn from the ball in the back of each stitch. Pick up an 8th (10th) stitch in the corner. Slip the 8 (10) stitches from the holder to the spare needle and knit them. Did you notice that on each side when you slipped the stitches from the holder onto the spare needle, they were in the correct position to work? Isn't that neat! Knit 1 row on 40 (50) stitches. To increase for the toe—using the "knit in front and back" increase—knit 16 (21) stitches, for both sizes (increase in 1, k1) 4 times, knit to the end of the row. Work in garter on 44 (54) stitches until there are 4 (6) ridges on the right side. The first few rows are difficult, but take heart, it becomes easier.

Shape the sole:

Row 1: K1, k2 tog, k11 (16), k2 tog, k2, k2 tog, k4, k2 tog, k2, k2 tog, k11 (16), k2 tog, k1.

Row 2: K38 (48).

Row 3: K1, k2 tog, k10 (15), k2 tog, k1, k2 tog, k2, k2 tog, k1, k2 tog, k10 (15), k2 tog, k1.

Row 4: K32 (42).

Row 5: K1, k2 tog, k9 (14), k2 tog 4 times, k9 (14), k2 tog, k1.

Bind off 26 (36) stitches. Cut the yarn long enough to sew the sole.

Finishing: Turn the bootie inside out. With a tapestry needle, sew the sole seam. It is important to avoid letting the bind-off lines show. To sew the sole seam, send the needle under the top two strands of the bind-off on one edge, then the top two strands on the other edge. Bring the needle back to go through the next 2 stitches in the same direction. Finish the seam in whip stitch and bury the end inside the seam. Use the cast-on tail to sew the cuff in nub-and-bar. When you have used two colors of yarn, sew each seam in its own color. Be sure the line between the garter and stockinette areas meets. Hide the ends in the seams in their own color.

Ties: Use a #00 steel hook and double-strand yarn. Try one strand of each color if you have made a contrast color cuff. Chain for 16″ (18″). Run the tie through the eyelets by sending the other end of a crochet hook into the hole next to the center front, out the next, in and out a couple more; catch the tie in the barb of the hook and pull through. Send the hook, other end first, in and out of the eyelets back to the front and pull the tie the rest of the way through. Tie little knots at each end of the tie, in which the yarn ends can be hidden. Be sure to run the ties through the eyelets before you tie the knots. If you don't, you'll find out why.

Sacque and Bonnet Sets

You have done quite a bit of knitting, can read patterns easily, and have a good supply of needles. Now there is a special baby in your life. I need about twelve hours of knitting time to make either of the sets. These sacque and bonnet sets are small enough for a first public debut and will fit a baby up to twelve pounds. To make them in a larger version, see the last paragraph at the end of the directions.

Supplies: Each set requires 3 ounces of three-ply fingering yarn. You will need four small ring markers.

Gauge: Use #4 needles or the size required for you to get a gauge of 7 stitches per inch in stockinette stitch. You will also need #7 and #2 needles. A circular #4 or the size necessary for the gauge is easier for working on raglans. If you change the gauge needle, adjust the others also.

Baby sacque: For either pattern, on #4 cast on 44 stitches, using four markers to divide the stitches: 2—6—28—6—2. Work back and forth in stockinette, increasing 1 stitch on each side of each marker every knit row, AND after the second raglan increase—on the fifth row—also increase 1 stitch at each neck edge, in the first stitch at the beginning and the next to last stitch at the end, in every knit row for 5 knit rows. Starting on a knit row, cast on 7 stitches at the beginning of each of the next 2 rows—rows 15 and 16. Your stitches should now be 22—22—44—22—22 for front, sleeve, back, sleeve, front. Continue the raglan increases until you have 33—44—66—44—33 stitches. End with a purl row.

Four-row lace pattern:

Row 1: K1, *yo, sl 1 st as if to knit, k1, psso, k1,

k2 tog, yo, k1. Repeat from * to the end. (Right side.)

Row 2: Purl.

Row 3: K1, *k1, yo, sl 1 st as if to knit, k2 tog, psso, yo, k2. Repeat from * to the end.

Row 4: Purl.

On #4, omitting the raglan increases, knit across the left front and left sleeve. Purl back across the sleeve stitches. Put all but the left sleeve stitches on stitch holders or leave the stitches on the circular needle. You now know why using a circular needle is easier. Point guards or rubber bands on the points of the circular needle will keep the remaining stitches in place. With #7 needles, work row 1 of the pattern, substituting k1 for one of the yo's so that you will have 43 stitches. Work in pattern on #7 needles until you have 4½" of pattern. End with row 4. To prevent the sleeve from rolling, bind off loosely in p1, k1. The bind-off stitches over the yo's and over the center stitch of the 3 knit stitches are the ones that you purl. Cut the yarn long enough for sewing.

Join your yarn, leaving an end to close the hole that always exists under the arm in raglans. With #4, knit across the back and right sleeve stitches. Proceed as for the first sleeve.

Leaving an end for sewing, join your yarn and knit across the right front on #4. On #4, purl back, uniting the front, the back, and the other front. Change to #7 needles. In working row 1 of the pattern, substitute k1 for one of the k2 tog's, so that you will have 133 stitches. Isn't that a neat way to increase 1 stitch? Work in pattern for the same length as that of the sleeves. Bind off as for the sleeves, but do not cut the yarn unless you are a left-handed crocheter.

Finishing: Finish with 1 row of single crochet (sc) up the front, around the neck, and down the front. Go into each nub on the right side with a #1 steel crochet hook. Work 3 sc in each neck outer corner. Also make three button loops, evenly spaced in the yoke on the appropriate side. If the baby is yet to be born, the loops are made on the girl side. To make a button loop, chain 2 or 3, depending on the size of the button, and do not skip any nubs. Using the ends you have saved, sew the underarm seam and close the hole under the arm.

stitch. It should take you 3 go-rounds of the pattern to decrease to 13 stitches. End with row 4. Cut the yarn, leaving an end to sew a back side seam.

Tie: Using #2 needles, cast on 48 stitches in single-strand. With the right side facing you, pick up 2 stitches in the ribbing on the left side as worn, pick up 3 stitches from every 4 nubs along the side, knit the 13 stitches at the back of the neck, pick up stitches on the second side to match the first, and cast on 48 stitches. Knit 1 row. Purl 1 row. Bind off in knit. The tie can be sewn purl side out, but it really isn't necessary, as it rolls well. Sew the two back seams, easing slightly a little extra fullness of the back section toward the top.

Four-row lace bonnet: On #7 needles, cast on 41 stitches.

Row 1: K1, *p1, k1. Repeat from * to the end.
Row 2: P1, *k1, p1. Repeat from * to the end.
Repeat these 2 rows once more. Then substitute for the first row 1 of the lace pattern: K1, *yo, k3, yo, k1. Repeat from * across. Continue with row 2 of the pattern on 61 stitches. Notice how nicely the ribbing merges into the pattern. Work until you have 3½" from the cast-on, ending with row 4. Bind off 18 stitches in knit, work 25 stitches in pattern, knit 18 stitches. Bind off 18 stitches in purl, and purl the remaining stitches. Work in pattern on 25 stitches for about 1¾", ending with row 4. Decrease 1 stitch at each edge every right-side row by omitting a yo. This will require ingenuity to maintain the pattern on the center stitches. To determine your place in the pattern as you decrease, locate the continuous single vertical stockinette stitch. On row 1 it is between 2 yo's and on row 3 it is the center of 3 knit stitches. On both rows it is the last stitch in the repeat. Orient your location in the pattern from the vertical stockinette

Basket weave pattern:
Row 1: Knit. (Right side.)
Row 2: K2, p3, *k7, p3. Repeat from * to the last 2 sts, k2.
Row 3: P2, k3, *p7, k3. Repeat from * to the last 2 sts, p2.
Row 4: Repeat row 2.
Row 5: Knit.
Row 6: K7, *p3, k7. Repeat from * to the end.
Row 7: P7, *k3, p7. Repeat from * to the end.
Row 8: Repeat row 6.

On #4 needles, omitting the raglan increases, knit across 33 stitches of the left front and 44 stitches of the left sleeve. You will work on the left sleeve stitches. Put the remaining stitches on holders, or leave them on your circular needle. Use point guards on the ends of the circular needle. With #7 needles, work row 2 across the sleeve, increasing to 47 stitches. To increase in Basket Weave, on the third stitch of p3, purl in the front of the stitch and knit through the back of the same stitch, which becomes the first of the k7. Continue in pattern on #7 until you have 4½" of pattern. End with row 3 or 7. Bind off in pattern on row 4 or 8. Were you to bind off on an all-knit row, the end of the sleeve would tend to flare out. Cut the yarn, leaving an end for sewing.

Leaving an end to close the inevitable hole under the arm in a raglan, join your yarn and on #4 needles knit across the back and the second sleeve. Work this sleeve to match the first.

Leaving an end, join your yarn and with #4 needles knit across the right front. Change to #7 needles. Work row 2 of the pattern, uniting the front, the back, and the front, AND while doing so increase 5 stitches evenly spaced, as previously described, to 137 stitches. Continue in pattern for the same length as that of the sleeves. Bind off as for the sleeves, but do not cut the yarn unless you are a right-handed crocheter.

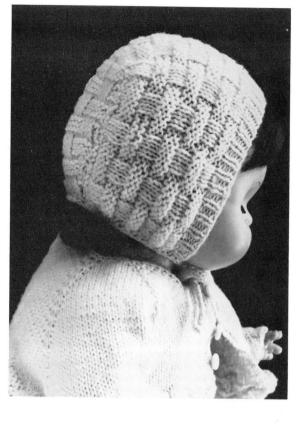

Finishing: Finish with 1 row of single crochet, as described in the four-row lace directions. Sew the underarm seam.

Basket Weave bonnet: With #4 needles, cast on 70 stitches. Work in k1, p1 ribbing for 6 rows. Knit 1 row. Change to #7 needles. Work row 2 of the pattern, increasing at the end of every p3, except the last, to 77 stitches. Continue in pattern until you have 3½" from the cast-on. End with row 4 or 8. Bind off 25 stitches in knit, and knit to the end. Bind off 25 stitches in purl, finish the row in pattern, BUT watch it! You are off 4 rows. Continue in pattern on 27 stitches until about 2" from the bind-offs. Starting on row 1 or 5, decrease 1 stitch at each edge every right-side row, maintaining the pattern as established, until you have 15 stitches in single-strand, pick up 3 stitches in the ribbing left side, 2 stitches from every 3

cut the yarn, leaving an end to sew one of the back seams.

Tie: Use #2 needles for the tie. Cast on 48 stitches in single-strand, pick up 3 stitches in the ribbing left side, 2 stitches from every 3 nubs along the side, knit the 15 stitches at the back of the neck, pick up stitches along the second side to match the first, and cast on 48 stitches. Read the directions given under four-row lace for making the tie and sewing the bonnet.

For a larger set you will need 4 ounces of sport-weight yarn. Use #6 needles or the size you need to get a gauge of 6 stitches per inch in stockinette stitch. This size will fit a baby up to 20 pounds. Use #8 for the larger needles and #3 for the ties. Make the sleeves and body pattern area 6", the bonnet depth 5" before the bind-off. Add about 1" after the bind-off before the back head decreasing.

FOR THE PATIENT

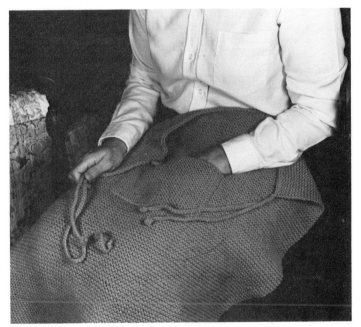

9

Wheelchair Lap Robe

Do you know someone who uses a wheelchair? Is there a nursing home in your area where some lonely souls seem to have no one who cares? A wheelchair lap robe can warm knees and hearts. Garter stitch is used because it is thicker than stockinette stitch and therefore warmer. The knowledge required is cast-on, knit, bind-off, and chain. The lap robe measures 24″ wide by 30″ long. This may seem narrow, but it should be, so as not to become entangled in the wheels. There is a pocket for a handkerchief or a treasure, and you can attach ties to secure it to the chair.

Supplies: You will need 12 ounces of four-ply worsted-weight yarn.

Gauge: Use a pair of #8 needles or the size you require to get a gauge of 4 1/5 stitches per inch in garter stitch (all knit).

Lap robe: Cast on 100 stitches. Work in garter stitch for 30″. Bind off loosely. When you join a new skein or remove a knot, do so on the edge. Tie the yarn ends together with a simple overhand knot. This is not a firm knot and may need to be tightened later, but is preferable to a rigid knot.

Pocket: Cast on 32 stitches. Work in garter stitch for 5″. Bind off loosely. The pocket is wide enough to accommodate hands no longer agile.

Finishing: With a tapestry needle, work the ends in through the nubs on the edge, in oppo-site directions for about 2″ or 3″ each. Work in the starting and binding ends in the same way. If the bind-off on the pocket is not too tight, use that as the open edge, because it is more finished than the cast-on. Center the pocket with the open end about 7″ from the top of the lap robe and sew in place. Use the cast-on tail, the bind-off end, and any long lengths of yarn from the edge for sewing. The cast-on should be sewn to a single ridge and the side edges should follow a single vertical stitch line, ending at the top on the same row.

Ties: Should you feel ties to be necessary, they are made by using about a size #D aluminum or #00 steel crochet hook and double-strand yarn. Chain 12″, slip stitch to an upper corner, chain 12″. Put a tie in each upper corner. Tie a knot in each end of each tie, and include the yarn ends.

Let me suggest some variations so that you can become a creative knitter. You can make a striped lap robe. You must use all the same fiber—for instance, acrylic. Also, all the yarn should be the same weight. When you are an experienced knitter, you will learn that not all four-ply worsted-weight yarn is exactly the same. Sometimes, even in the same brand the weight may vary, but you will be safest staying with a line of yarn you find satisfactory. You can also make the lap robe in strips. If your strips have 34 stitches, 32 stitches, 34 stitches, you can sew the pocket on the seams and you will know that it is centered. You should count the ridges so that all the strips will be the same, and when they are sewn in nub-and-bar, they will be even. When strips are striped, leave ends for sewing on the edge so that the yarn used for sewing will match one of the two edges you are joining.

the size you require to get a gauge of 3½ stitches per inch in garter stitch (knit every row).

Shawl: Cast on 2 stitches. Work in garter stitch, increasing in the first stitch of every row. I want to explain a few things for you. Remember, you are working back and forth. You are using a circular needle for its length. I used the ''knit in front and back'' increase. The first row is: Inc in 1, k1. The second row: Inc in 1, k2, and so on. Join all new skeins on the edges. See Chapter 3, Is There Enough Yarn for One More Row? Also, look ahead at the yarn to watch for knots. If you plan to add a fringe, be sure all the ends—the cast-on tail, yarn joinings, and the bind-off end—are at least as long as you want the fringe, because the fringe is the best place for them. Measuring from the cast-on point, at the end of the first 4-ounce skein I had 14,″ at the end of the second skein 6″ more, and 4″ more after the third skein. Should you feel 24″ is not long enough, purchase more yarn of the same dye lot. It is very important to bind off very LOOSELY. When you are binding off, the front corners will be more alike if you increase on the first stitch.

Finishing: For a shawl sans fringe, use a tapestry needle to hide all ends for 2″ or 3″ along the side edges.

Shawl

This shawl is so simple to knit, has such a great number of variations, and can be given for so many different purposes that I had trouble deciding in which chapter to include it. It is here because chilly shoulders are not limited by gender. A cozy knitted shawl will warm both female and male backs. The knowledge required to make this shawl is cast-on, knit, increase, and bind-off. It took me around twelve hours knitting time.

Supplies: Sixteen ounces of four-ply worsted-weight yarn is ample. Indeed, I used only 12 ounces for the shawl. The fourth skein makes the fringe. I would omit a fringe for a patient, because it tends to become matted.

Gauge: Use a 29″ or 36″ #10 circular needle or

Fringe: Use something firm to wind the yarn around. Try a hard-cover book. I found that the 9″ circumference around my crochet hook case, which is rigid and has a tiny flange to guide the scissors, makes a 3½″ fringe. The lost measurement is partly in the fringe knot and because the yarn is wound tightly and springs back. Cut enough yarn pieces for fringing several inches along an edge. Hold two pieces together and fold in half. Send a crochet hook, about size #00 steel, through a nub on an edge, catch the pieces in the fold, and draw out a loop, then draw the four ends through the loop and tighten. See the sketches for her scarf in Chapter 5. Always work the fringe from the same side of your shawl. Where you have joined a new skein, use only one cut piece, but draw all four ends through the loop. Where there is a single end, use two cut pieces and draw five ends through the loop. Put fringe in every nub along both sides.

Now let me tell you about the variations. Actually, this shawl can be made with any yarn on any appropriate needle size. For a beautiful evening shawl you might use a lightweight mohair-blend yarn, such as that used for the hat, mittens, and scarf in Chapter 5. Or you can stripe it. Be sure to join new colors always on the same edge if you want clean lines between colors.

My final hint is fringe as you go. When you want to make your shawl as large as you can with the yarn you have, but are not certain how much yarn to save, fringe the edges from the cast-on point to just below where you are knitting. Cut sufficient pieces for the remaining nubs.

Broken-Leg Toe Cozy

It's a poultice bag. No. A container for a hanging plant? No. An oat bag for a miniature horse, a portable wastebasket, a hat for a child to tie mittens to? No. No. No. It's a broken-leg toe cozy.

Supplies: One ounce of four-ply worsted-weight yarn will be ample. You probably have yarn remaining from other projects. If you make a striped toe cozy, all the yarn should be the same weight and fiber.

Gauge: You will need a set of #4 double-point needles or the size on which your gauge is 5 stitches per inch in garter stitch.

Toe cozy: On one needle, cast on 60 stitches. Work 20 stitches in k1, p1 ribbing onto each of 3 needles. Join, being careful not to twist, and work the ribbing pattern for 2½″. Work 6 rounds in garter stitch. To do this in circular work, (knit 1 round, purl 1 round) 3 times. You will have three ridges on the outside.

Decreasing:

K8, k2 tog around. Purl 1 round.
K7, k2 tog around. Purl 1 round.
K6, k2 tog around. Purl 1 round.

Continue decreasing 2 stitches on each needle every other round until:

K1, k2 tog around. Purl 1 round.
K2 tog around. Do not purl.

Cut the yarn. With a tapestry needle, send the yarn through each of the remaining 6 stitches in the same direction in which you have been knitting. To insure a firm closing, send the yarn

through again, then through the center to the inside and secure.

Ties: Using double-strand yarn, chain two 30" ties. Sew them to opposite sides of the cast-on. Tie knots in the free ends, hiding the yarn ends.

Should you want to make a toe cozy for Big Foot, the multiple is 6. This means you cast on 66 or 72 stitches. Each needle has 22 or 24 stitches. Add length if necessary. The decreasing begins: K9, k2 tog, or K10, k2 tog.

Bed Socks

One need not be bedridden to suffer cold feet. Many of us would appreciate a warm pair of bed socks on a cold winter night. Someone with unsteady footing should not use these as slippers, as they can be slippery on a bare floor. The bed socks have a ribbed top to hold them on, garter stitch for warmth, and two stockinette stitches in front for fit.

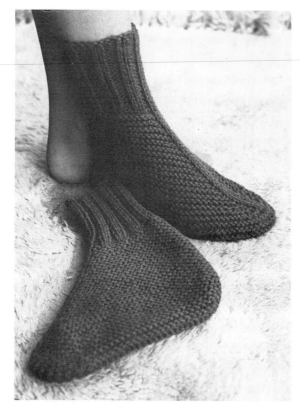

Supplies: Four-ply worsted-weight yarn is used. For a small narrow foot you will need 4 ounces; for a medium foot of medium width, 6 ounces; for a large wide foot, 8 ounces. S (M, L) are for feet measuring 8½" (10", 11½") in length. Width is accounted for later. You also will need to keep a ring marker on the needles.

Gauge: Use a pair of #8 needles or the size you require to get a gauge of 4⅓ stitches per inch in garter stitch.

Bed socks: Loosely cast on 36 (40, 44) stitches.

Row 1: P1, *k2, p2. Repeat from *, ending the last repeat p1.

Row 2: K1, *p2, k2. Repeat from *, ending the last repeat k1.

Repeat these two rows until you have 3" (3½", 4") of ribbing, ending with row 2 (1, 2). If you feel a tie is necessary, work an eyelet row: K2, *yo, k2 tog. Repeat from * to the end. However, if you are using yarn with good spring, this should not be necessary, so knit 1 row instead. For the return row, with or without the eyelet row: K17 (19, 21), p1, put the ring marker on the right needle, p1, K17 (19, 21). Use the "knit in front and back" increase.

Right-side row: Knit to the 2nd stitch before the marker, inc in 1, k1, marker, inc in 1, knit to the end.

Wrong-side row: Knit to the stitch before the marker, p1, marker, p1, knit to the end.

Repeat these two rows, for a total of 10 (14, 18) times. You should have 56 (68, 80) stitches.

Right-side row: Knit to 5 stitches before the marker, inc in each of the next 4 stitches, k1, marker, inc in 4, knit to the end.

Wrong-side row: Knit, keeping 2 purls.

Repeat these two rows once more. Work in garter stitch, eliminating the purls but not the ring marker, on 72 (84, 96) stitches for 1" (1½", 2") for narrow (medium, wide) widths. Measure from the end of the two stockinette stitches. End ready for a right-side row.

Sole:

Row 1: K1, k2 tog, knit to 15 stitches before the marker, (k2 tog, k3) 3 times, marker, (k3, k2 tog) 3 times, knit to the last 3 stitches, k2 tog, k1.

Row 2: Knit.

Row 3: K1, k2 tog, knit to 12 sts before the marker, (k2 tog, k2) 3 times, marker, (k2, k2 tog) 3 times, knit to the last 3 sts, k2 tog, k1.

Row 4: Knit.

Row 5: K1, k2 tog, knit to 9 sts before the marker, (k2 tog, k1) 3 times, marker, (k1, k2 tog) 3 times, knit to the last 3 sts, k2 tog, k1.

Row 6: Knit.

Row 7: K1, k2 tog, knit to 6 sts before the marker, k2 tog 3 times, marker, k2 tog 3 times, knit to the last 3 sts, k2 tog, k1.

Bind off the remaining 40 (52, 64) stitches. Cut the yarn, leaving an end for sewing the sole.

Finishing: Sew the sole seam in bind-off to bind-off and the back seam in nub-and-bar. If you have made eyelet rows, using double-strand yarn, chain the ties for 24″ each.

Surprise Cape

As you can see in the photograph, what you knit is very different from the finished cape. The dropped stitch is one of the several old standard procedures that were, and still are, good, so I have used it in this book of gift suggestions. The knowledge required is cast-on, knit, purl, bind-off, and chain. I would prefer that you also be able to work single crochet (sc) and double crochet (dc), in order to conceal the yarn carried along the neck edge. But I will tell you how to knit the neck finishing, in addition to crochet neck-finishing directions. Many knitters are not enthusiastic crocheters.

Supplies: Four-ply worsted-weight yarn is used. Six ounces of color A and 4 ounces of color B will be ample.

Gauge: Use #9 needles or the size you require to get a gauge of 4⅓ stitches per inch in stockinette stitch.

Surprise cape: Stockinette cast-on 45 stitches with color A. Do not use single-strand cast-on.

Row 1: With color A, knit.

Row 2: A, purl. (Right side.)

Row 3: A, knit.

Row 4: A, purl.

Row 5: A, knit.

Row 6: A, purl.

Row 7: A, knit.

Join color B. Do not break off color A.

Row 8: With color B, knit.

Row 9: B, purl.

Row 10: B, knit.

Row 11: B, purl.

Row 12: B, knit.

Row 13: B, purl.

Row 14: Firmly bring up A, knit.

Repeat these 14 rows, bringing up B for row 8 and A for row 14, until you have 24 stripes in color A. End with row 6. This pattern is called Quaker Stitch. Notice that 7 rows of stockinette alternate with 7 rows of reverse stockinette. Also notice that the right side has clean lines between the colors. Do you understand how this occurs? Count the number of rows worked in each color. If you are an experienced crocheter, do not break off color B after the 23rd B stripe. This is how you bind off on row 7 with A. Loosely bind off 4 stitches, drop the 5th stitch, ch 1, bind off 2, drop the 8th stitch, ch 1, bind off 2, drop the 11th stitch, ch 1. Start the dropped stitches running down a dozen rows or so, so that you can judge the necessary looseness in binding. Continue dropping every third stitch to the last 4, bind off 4. All the dropped

stitches are to be run all the way down to the cast-on. They will not go down as easily as you would think. Bits of fuzz will continually lock the stitches and need to be removed.

Crochet finishing: Use an aluminum hook size #G. With the right side facing you and with color B, work 2 sc in each of the 47 stripes, burying the colors that were brought up. Ch 3, turn, work a dc in every other sc across.

For those of you who are experienced crocheters, here is a challenge. With the still-attached B, work the sc row backward. To do this, with the wrong side facing you, holding the yarn to the front, send the hook through the work from back to front, catch the yarn, draw it through and complete the single crochet. Bury the strands of brought-up colors as you work. Of course, if you are left-handed you will have no trouble working on the right side from left to right. Ch 3, turn, work a dc in every other sc.

Now for the very experienced crocheter here are more specific directions. There are 4 nubs in each color A stripe, 3 nubs in each color B stripe. Sending the hook through each nub, work 3 decrease sc, then 1 sc. This gives you 2 stitches in each stripe. Repeat across. Ch 3, turn, work a dc in every other sc.

Knit finishing: With the right side facing you, using color B and #9 needles, pick up 2 stitches in each of the 47 stripes. Be sure to keep the brought-up colors to the back.
Row 1: Purl.
Row 2: K2, *yo, k2 tog. Repeat from * across. (Eyelet row.)
Row 3: Purl.
Bind off.

Tie: With double-strand yarn—I like to use one of each color—chain 5'. Yarn ends at the start and finish will allow you to tie on pompons. Or tie a knot at each end, hiding the yarn ends. Thread the tie in and out between the dc's or through the eyelet row before completing the ends of the tie.

The number of stitches for the surprise cape is a multiple of three. Should you desire a longer cape, add 3, 6, 9, etc., to the number of stitches you cast on. And of course you can knit it longer. Do remember to allow more yarn if you plan to make a larger cape.

Find-the-Pairs Afghan

How would you like to knit a gift for a youngster that is useful, educational, and fun to make? The afghan illustrated consists of 24 pairs of matching squares worked in bright cheerful colors. From this a very young child can learn colors. Later he can look for lines going sideways, lines going up and down, squares with no lines, and squares with diamonds. Eventually, the child will find the pairs. I have included the afghan in this chapter because it can be used to fill time for a child who must stay quiet.

Supplies: Eight ounces of four-ply worsted-weight yarn in each of five colors will be ample. The colors A, B, C, and D are used for the squares and should be bright rainbow colors, so that you can see the pattern easily. Color E is for the edging and can be dark, so as to outline the squares. A #00 steel crochet hook is used for the edging.

Gauge: Use #8 needles or the size on which you get a gauge of 4½ stitches per inch in stockinette stitch. Each square is to measure 6" by 6".

Patterns:
Garter: Cast on 24 stitches.
Every row: Knit.
When the square measures 6", bind off loosely.
Moss: Cast on 25 stitches.
Every row: K1, *p1, k1. Repeat from * to the end.
At 6", bind off loosely in pattern.
Seed: Cast on 24 stitches.
Rows 1 and 2: *K1, p1. Repeat from * to the end.
Rows 3 and 4: *P1, k1. Repeat from * to the end.
At 6", bind off loosely in pattern.
Mistake Stitch: Cast on 27 stitches.
Every row: *K2, p2. Repeat from * across, ending: K2, p1.
At 6", bind off loosely in pattern.
Quaker Stitch: Cast on 25 stitches.
Row 1: Knit.
Row 2: Purl.
Row 3: Knit.
Row 4: Purl.
Row 5: Purl.

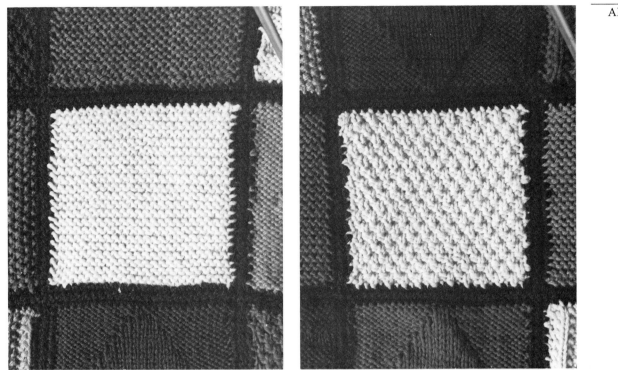

Row 6: Knit.
Row 7: Purl.
Row 8: Knit.
Repeat these 8 rows 3½ times more. Bind off loosely in purl on row 4. The right side has 5 reverse stockinette bands and 4 stockinette bands.

Diamond: Cast on 26 stitches.
Row 1: P12, k2, p12.
Row 2: K12, p2, k12.
Row 3: P11, k4, p11.
Row 4: K11, p4, k11.
Row 5: P10, k6, p10.
Row 6: K10, p6, k10.
Row 7: P9, k8, p9.
Row 8: K9, p8, k9.
Row 9: P8, k10, p8.
Row 10: K8, p10, k8.
Row 11: P7, k12, p7.
Row 12: K7, p12, k7.
Row 13: P6, k14, p6.
Row 14: K6, p14, k6.
Row 15: P5, k16, p5.
Row 16: K5, p16, k5.
Row 17: P4, k18, p4.
Row 18: K4, p18, k4.
Row 19: Repeat row 15.
Row 20: Repeat row 16.
Row 21: Repeat row 13.
Row 22: Repeat row 14.
Row 23: Repeat row 11.

Row 24: Repeat row 12.
Continue reducing the diamond every other row. Bind off loosely in pattern on row 34 as for row 2. The right side has a stockinette diamond with reverse stockinette background.

Afghan: In each of the colors A, B, C, and D make 2 squares in each of the six patterns (48 squares). Join all yarn on the edge. Leave yarn ends about 2" long. These you will bury when you crochet the edging. All your squares may not be exactly 6" wide. This is not a cause for worry, as they will tend to pull each other into shape when they are put together in the afghan.

Edging: One round of single crochet is to be worked around each square. When working sc on the bind-off, send the crochet hook under the top two strands; on the cast-on, send the hook under two strands that will not interfere with the pattern; on the side edges send the hook through the nubs. You often will need to make 2 sc in 1 nub in order to have at least 20 sc on an edge. Crochet on the right side of the Quaker Stitch and Diamond squares. On the garter, Moss, Seed, and Mistake Stitch squares the side on which you crochet becomes the right side.

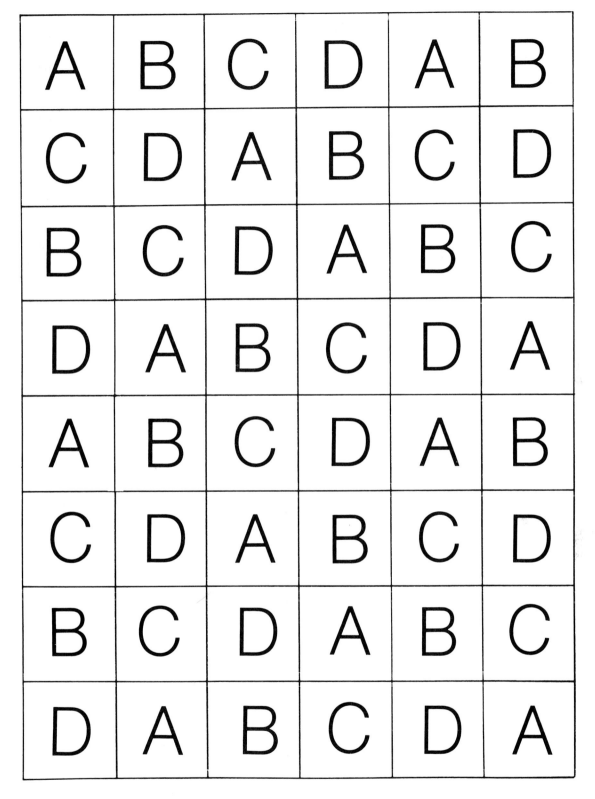

Color array chart

To start edging, begin in a corner having no yarn end. Send the hook through the corner of the square under two strands, catch color E, and draw out a loop, leaving a 2" end of yarn. Chain 1. Lay the end of color E yarn along the edge and work your sc covering or burying it as you proceed to the next corner. Work 3 sc in the same spot in the corner. Have 20 to 25 sc along each side plus 3 sc in each corner. Bury all knitting ends as you pass them. In your final corner work 2 sc—the beginning chain stitch represents the third.

Let me tell you a neat way to finish the crochet around each square. Enlarge the loop on the hook to 2" after the last stitch. Cut it at the top and withdraw the skein end. Using a tapestry needle, follow the top of the starting chain stitch front to back. This will be under the top two strands of the first sc. Returning to the final sc, send the yarn down where the finishing end comes up, and through the little nub directly below. Finish by sending the end within the last worked line of sc. If your tension is right, you will not be able to detect your start-finish spot.

Using the chart, arrange the edged squares by color on a large table or bed. All squares should be right side up and have the up and down of the knitting patterns running in the same direction. You can consider the garter and Quaker patterns as having no up or down. After you have arranged the squares by color, switch by color and scatter the patterns.

When you are satisfied with your arrangement, sew the squares together. To sew, use a tapestry needle and color E yarn and a whip stitch. The whip stitch is worked by sending the needle under the top two strands of a sc on the edge of one square, then under the top two strands of a sc on the other square. The needle is then aimed in the same direction and sent under the top 4 strands of the next 2 sc. Hold 2 squares with the wrong sides together. Start by joining the corner stitches, the center of the 3 sc in the corners. Leave 2" ends of the yarn on the outer edge of the afghan. Continue whipping together a few more stitches, then count the number of sc to the corner stitches at the end of each side you are joining, to see whether one side has more than the other and you will need to ease. To ease, sew through an already used sc on the shorter side and a new sc on the longer side. Sew from the corner stitches of the first 2 squares to the corner stitches of the next 2 squares. When you reach the end of a length of sewing yarn, start a new piece by running it within the seam for a couple of inches. Enclose the remaining end from the previous length in the seam as you continue. When you reach the edge, cut the yarn at 2". The simplest way to join the squares is to sew all the seams in one direction, then all the seams in the other. After joining the squares, work 1 row of sc around the entire afghan, burying all sewing ends. Work 1 sc in each sc, including the sc in each square corner at the seams, and 3 sc in each corner of the afghan.

Should you have sufficient yarn remaining from the afghan, think about making a pillow cover. Have 4 squares, one of each color, for each side of the pillow. In Chapter 7 you can learn how to cover a pillow form.

If you are going to teach someone to knit, consider this afghan. I would start with the garter squares, then Quaker Stitch.

FOR A HOLIDAY

Easter Rabbit

Are you familiar with the Beatrix Potter rabbits? Would you like to knit one? Why? Why, to cover an Easter egg. Or to keep a soft-boiled egg warm. Doesn't everybody need a rabbit?

Supplies: Four-ply worsted-weight yarn is used; ½ ounce is ample.

Gauge: Use #4 needles or the size on which your gauge is 5 stitches per inch in garter stitch (all knit).

Rabbit: Cast on 35 stitches, leaving a 12″ tail for sewing.

Wrong-side row: K1, *p1, k1. Repeat from * to the end.

Right-side row: P1, *k1, p1. Repeat from * to the end.

Repeat these two rows once more. Work in garter stitch until there are 4 ridges on the right side.

K15, k2 tog, k1, k2 tog, k15. Knit back 33.

K11, (k2 tog) 2 times, k3, (k2 tog) 2 times, k11. Knit back 29.

K2 tog, k9, inc in each of next 6 sts, k10, k2 tog. Knit 33.

K2 tog, k12, inc in each of next 4 sts, k13, k2 tog. Knit 35.

K2 tog, k31, k2 tog. Knit 33.

You now have 9 ridges on the right side.

K2 tog and bind off 6 sts, knit to the end. You now have 26 sts.

K2 tog and bind off 6 sts, knit to the end. You now have 19 sts.

Short rows: *K2, turn, sl 1, k1. K3, turn, sl 1, k2. K4, turn, sl 1, k3. Knit 19. Repeat from * once more to lengthen the other edge.

K2 tog, k6, sl 1, k2 tog, psso, k6, k2 tog.

Bind off, decreasing 1 stitch at each edge. Cut the yarn, leaving an end to sew the head.

Ears: Cast on 4 stitches and work in stockinette stitch (knit 1 row, purl 1 row) for 8 rows, ending with a purl row. K1, k2 tog, k1. Purl 3. Sl

1, k2 tog, psso. Cut the yarn and send it through the 1 remaining stitch. Make 2.

Tail: Find something sturdy measuring 4" around. For me, three fingers held together are the answer. Cut and reserve an 8" piece of yarn. Wind the yarn 20 times around the 4" whatever. Remove and use the 8" piece to tie very firmly around the middle of the doubled loop of yarn. Hold the pompon by the ends of the 8" piece, cut each bunch of loops, shake, and trim to a ball.

Finishing: Sew the top of the rabbit's head with the end from the bind-off, taking care not to allow the bind-off lines to show on the right side. Sew the back of the rabbit with the cast-on tail. Sewing through the nubs only, on the side edges, should be adequate for this seam. Sew the bound-off edges as you did the head. Sew the back of the head. Hide the final ends inside the ears and use the cast-on tails to sew the ears in place. Use the ends from the 8" piece to fasten the tail to the seam between the ribbing and the garter, then send them to the outside and trim to match the pompon.

ing the yarn to the back sl 1 stitch as if to purl, k29. Bring up red and purl 1 row. Knit 1 row keeping the folding stitch. Bring up white and work 2 rows as established. Continue until you have 6 stripes, ending with a white. Cut red and white with ends to sew the side seam. Join blue and purl 13, rejoin red and purl to the last 13, join a second blue and purl 13. Knit 1 row, keeping each stitch the same color and slipping the folding stitch. Remember to interlock when changing colors between the stripes and the fields by bringing the new color under and over the old. On the following purl row use the pieces or bobbins of white to make the first 3 stars on each of the blue fields, as indicated on row 3 of the chart. Rejoin white for a white stripe. Alternate 2 rows each of red and white for the stripes, keeping the folding stitch, and follow the chart for the blue fields. On row 5 of the chart you will notice that the white yarn for the stars is not where you need it. Here is the way you take care of this. Insert the right needle as to purl through the stitch to be a star. With-

Fourth of July American Flag

Celebrate the Fourth of July by knitting a flag. Stand it against the saltshaker on the table, or on the mantel, or hang it in a window. You can always find a place for an American flag. There are 13 stars, because 9 rows of stars cannot be aligned and spaced easily with the 7 stripes.

Supplies and gauge: You may use any weight yarn with needles that will give you a firm gauge. For the model, I used four-ply worsted-weight yarn at 5 stitches per inch. You can knit the flag from one ball each of red and white, and of blue yarn to which you have access at both ends. You also will use two 1-yard pieces of white. You may prefer using yarn bobbins. Two white bobbins and two blue bobbins will be helpful.

Flag: With red, cast on 59 stitches stockinette, leaving an end for sewing the bottom seam. Knit 1 row. Join white and purl 1 row. Knit 1 row with a folding stitch as follows: K29, keep-

out pulling, lay the white yarn over the point of the right needle—the bobbin is at the right—and complete the purl stitch. When you reach the location of the next star, insert your right needle, lift the span of white without twisting, put it over the needle point, and complete the purl stitch. Bind off on the knit row of the top red stripe, but pay attention to this note: Knit the last stitch in the blue field with red and knit the last stitch in the red stripe with blue. Cut the yarn, leaving ends for sewing.

Finishing: Adjust any stars annoyingly out of shape by pulling the running white yarn on the back. Carefully bury ends you are not saving for sewing in their own color. With your flag inside out, sew the top and side seams in their own color. Turn the flag right side out and sew the bottom seam.

Stars on blue field

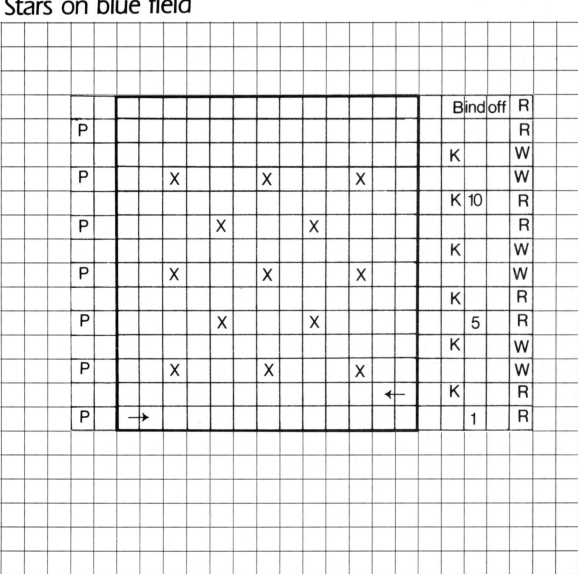

Thanksgiving Pumpkin

What fun it can be to knit a pumpkin for each guest who will share a Thanksgiving feast with you. It can hold candy, nuts, or other goodies. Made with acrylic, it may be washed and re-used many times. Allow about two hours for knitting the second and each subsequent pumpkin.

Supplies: Two shades of orange yarn are used, not so much for the color effect as for facilitating your knitting. It will be easier to bring forward the correct yarn when there is a difference in the shade. Use four-ply worsted-weight yarn. One skein in each shade of orange will be ample for several pumpkins.

Gauge: Use a set of #4 double-point needles or the size on which your gauge is 5½ stitches per inch in stockinette.

Pumpkin: Cast on 30 stitches in stockinette BUT do so in this special way: Holding together a strand of each shade, tie a slip knot and put it on your needle. The slip knot is an anchor and you will remove it later. Cast on 2 stitches. Switch the yarn on your fingers so that the next 2 stitches are the other shade. Continue switching after every second stitch. When you have 30 stitches you will have 15 pairs, 8 in one shade and 7 in the other. Slide 10 stitches to each of

two spare needles and form your work into a triangle, ready to start at the slip knot. The ridge should be on the outside. Remove the slip knot. Knit 1 round working each pair of stitches in the other shade. That is, every stitch is knit in the shade of orange it is not. As you bring up alternate yarns, pull them firmly.

Increasing:
Round 2: In every pair, using the other shade, inc in 1, k1.
Round 3: In every group of 3, using the other shade, inc in 1, k2.
Round 4: In every group of 4, using the other shade, k2, inc in 1, k1.

You now have 75 stitches. Break the rules you have learned about working with two colors. Do not catch the carried color and pull firmly when bringing a new yarn up to use. This is how you form the ribs of the pumpkin. Continue knitting around, working each group of 5 stitches in the other shade until you have 2½". Can you see that using two shades of orange does make the knitting of a pumpkin easier to understand?

Decreasing:
Round 1: In every group of 5, k2, k2 tog, k1.
Round 2: In every group of 4, k1, k2 tog, k1.
Round 3: In every group of 3, k1, k2 tog.
Round 4: In every group of 2, k2 tog.

Cut both yarns and, using a tapestry needle, send them together through the remaining 15 stitches. Close, send the ends to the inside, and bury within a rib. Push your pumpkin down and form it into the round pumpkin shape.

Hanukkah Yarmulke

What could be a better Hanukkah gift than a yarmulke or kipah you have made? You must knit it with wool, because it will hold to the head better and because you can rely on the behavior of wool in blocking.

Supplies: Two ounces of four-ply worsted-weight wool will be ample.

Gauge: You will need one pair of single-point and one set of double-point #4 needles or the size on which your gauge is 5½ stitches per inch in stockinette stitch.

Cut the yarn. With a tapestry needle, send the yarn through the remaining 9 stitches in the same direction you have been knitting. Draw in. For security, send the yarn through the 9 stitches again, then to the inside, and hide it behind one of the decrease seams.

Yarmulke: On sp needles cast on 99 stitches in garter and knit 1 row. Continue in garter stitch (all knit), slipping as if to knit the first stitch of each row until you have 3 ridges on the right side. The slipped stitch allows for a neater seam. Knit 1 row increasing in every 10th stitch to 108. Divide the stitches on three needles, 36—36—36. Join, being careful not to twist.

Knit 3 rounds.
K10, k2 tog around.
Knit 3 rounds.
K9, k2 tog around.
Knit 3 rounds.
K8, k2 tog around.
Knit 2 rounds.
K7, k2 tog around.
Knit 2 rounds.
K6, k2 tog around.
Knit 2 rounds.
K5, k2 tog around.
Knit 1 round.
K4, k2 tog around.
Knit 1 round.
K3, k2 tog around.
Knit 1 round.
K2, k2 tog around.
K1, k2 tog around.
K2 tog around.

Smaller yarmulke: Should you prefer the smaller version, cast on 82 stitches. Knit until you have the three ridges. Knit 1 row increasing in every 9th stitch 8 times to 90 stitches. Divide the stitches on three dp needles, 30—30—30. Join and knit 3 rounds. Starting at "K8, k2 tog around," continue as for the larger yarmulka.

With the contrasting color in the garter stitch I have found the best increase to use is the Make 1, because this keeps the line clean between the colors.

To block the yarmulka, use an iron at wool or medium setting and a very damp cloth. You do not want your iron to touch the wool, but steam from the iron is not sufficient. Press from the inside, rolling the yarmulke around until you obtain the correct shape. Allow it to dry thoroughly, upside down.

Hanukkah Challa Cover

Another Hanukkah gift is a challa cover for the Sabbath meal.

Supplies: Four ounces of four-ply worsted-weight yarn will make a cover 16″ by 20″. You may prefer to use a synthetic yarn, to accommodate frequent washing. You will use a cable needle (CN) for the braid in the center of the cover. If you have read other cable directions in this book, you are aware that I prefer a J-shaped cable needle. The held stitches are slid onto the short end, kept on the bend, and knit off from the long end.

Gauge: You will need #10 needles or the size necessary for you to get a gauge of 4 stitches per inch in stockinette.

Challa cover: Cast on 50 stitches in garter. Increase 1 stitch at each edge in the first and next to last stitch every row as you knit 8 rows. You now have 66 stitches.

Row 9: K28, p2, 2 on CN held in back, inc in 1, k1, on CN sts inc in 1, k1, inc in 1, k1, p2, k28. You now have 69 stitches.

Row 10 and all even-numbered rows: K5, p23, k2, p9, k2, p23, k5.

Row 11: K28, p2, k9, p2, k28.

Row 13: K28, p2, k3, 3 on CN to front, k3, k3 CN, p2, k28.

Row 15: Repeat row 11.

Row 17: K28, p2, 3 on CN to back, k3, k3 CN, k3, p2, k28.

Repeat rows 10–17. At 19″, end having just completed row 12 or 16. As you work row 13 or 17, in the 9 stitches of the braid, decrease 1 stitch in each 3—k1, k2 tog—to correspond with the increases at the beginning of the braid. This shaping is to prevent distortion in the garter stitch border. Knit 1 row on 66 stitches. Decrease by knitting together the second and third stitches from each edge every row as you knit 7 more rows. Bind off the remaining 52 stitches, decreasing 1 stitch at the beginning and 1 stitch at the end.

Christmas Tree Ornaments

Give a friend a Christmas tree ornament that will be a reminder every year of how much you care. And it can be something you have knit. Here are three ornaments. They are given in order of ease of knitting.

Supplies: For each ornament you will use small amounts of worsted-weight yarn. A golf ball size should be ample for each of the first two. For the third, in addition to a white golf ball, you should have a few yards each of red and green. Suggested notions are jingle bells for the bell, toothpicks for the sweater, and five bobbins for the tiny Christmas stocking.

Gauge: Use #5 needles or a size on which your gauge is firm so that the ornaments will hold their shape.

Bell: Cast on 16 stitches.

Right-side row: Knit.

Wrong-side row: P6, k10.

Repeat these two rows until you have 21 ridges on the right side. Bind off in pattern on row 2. Cut the yarn, leaving an end for sewing.

Finishing: With a tapestry needle, send the bind-off end through one strand of the nub for each ridge on the garter stitch edge. Draw up to close. You may need to send the yarn through a second time. Sew the seam, matching the pattern. For the hanger, cut a 12″ piece of yarn. With a tapestry needle, send the piece through the top from the inside to the outside and back

strand cast-on 6 stitches at the beginning of the knit row. Knit 18. Single-strand cast-on 6 stitches at the beginning of the purl row. K2, p20, k2. Knit 24. K2, p20, k2. Knit 24. K2, p6, bind off 8 in knit, p6, k2. To do this, after the first p6, bind off in knit until there are 8 stitches on your left needle, 1 near the point on your right, p1, bind off 1, p5, k2. Next row: K8, single-strand cast-on 8, k8. You will have to turn your work to cast on, then turn back to finish the row. You have now made the neckhole. K2, p6, k8, p6, k2. Knit 24. K2, p20, k2. Knit 24. K2, p20, k2. Bind off 6 stitches, knit to end of row. Bind off 6, knitting 2 and purling 4, purl to end of row. Work 7 rows stockinette on 12 stitches, ending with a knit row. Knit 4 rows. Bind off. This forms the third ridge.

Finishing: Sew the side seams. To make the ball, start by winding the yarn a few times around two fingers. Remove the loop from your fingers, twist to a figure eight, and fold in half. Wind firmly around this until your teeny ball is nearly the size you want. Cut the yarn at 24″. With a tapestry needle, send the yarn through and around the ball until it is secure. Take a few stitches in one side of the neck, allowing the ball to dangle below the bottom of the sweater. Take a few stitches in the other side of the neck, forming the hanger. Insert two toothpicks under a few strands of yarn to look like stitches on knitting needles.

Christmas stocking: Wind 3 bobbins with white yarn, 2 with green. With red, cast on 21 stitches.

Right-side row: P1, *k1, p1. Repeat from * to the end.

Wrong-side row: K1, *p1, k1. Repeat from * to the end.

Repeat these two rows once more. Cut the red, leaving an end for sewing. Leaving an end for sewing, join a white bobbin and k5. When joining each of the bobbins, tie the end with an overhand knot to the previous bobbin yarn, join a green bobbin and k1, join a white bobbin and k9, join a green bobbin and k1, join a white bobbin and k5. Purl 1 row. On all purl rows each stitch stays the same color. On every row, when changing bobbins, the new color is brought under and over the old to interlock. Bobbins are less apt to tangle when kept short.

to the inside. Tie the ends firmly. To add a jingle bell, cut the piece of yarn 16″. When you tie the knot for the hanger, allow 2″ on each end on the inside. Use the 2″ ends to tie on the jingle bell.

Sweater: Cast on 12 stitches in garter. Knit 4 rows. Including the cast-on, there are 3 ridges on the right side. Work 8 rows in stockinette. End with a purl row. For the sleeves, single-

Knit 4W, 3G, 7W, 3G, 4W. Purl back.
Knit 3W, 5G, 5W, 5G, 3W. Purl back.
Knit 2W, 7G, 3W, 7G, 2W. Purl back.
Knit 1W, 9G, 1W, 9G, 1W.
Purl 1W, 3G taking W—to do this, catch by twisting, because you will need white here on the next row—6 more G, 1W, 3G taking W, 6 more G, 1W.
Knit 4W taking G, 1 more W, 1G, 8W taking 2nd G, 1 more W, 1G, 5W. Purl 1 row, keeping colors.
Knit across all the stitches with the first W bobbin, tying the other bobbins with an overhand knot as you pass them. Cut all but the white bobbin in use. Purl 1 row.

Heel: Work short rows. Join red. Taking the white bobbin:

Knit 6R, drop W, turn, slip 1 stitch as if to purl, p5.
K5, turn, slip 1, p4.
K4, turn, sl 1, p3.
K3, turn, sl 1, p2.
K2, turn, sl 1, p1.
Knit 6R, k9W taking R—catch R every 3rd stitch—drop W, k6R.
Short rows:
P5, turn, sl 1 as if to knit, k4.
P4, turn, sl 1, k3.
P3, turn, sl 1, k2.
P2, turn, sl 1, k1.
P6, turn, sl 1, k5 taking W.
Cut red, leaving an end for sewing the heel. Starting with a purl row, work 8 rows W stockinette. End with a knit row. Cut the white bobbin, leaving an end for sewing.

Toe: Join red and purl 1 row.
K3, k2 tog, SKP, k7, k2 tog, SKP, k3. Purl back 17.
K2, k2 tog, SKP, k5, k2 tog, SKP, k2. Purl back 13.
K1, k2 tog, SKP, k3, k2 tog, SKP, k1. Purl back 9.
K2 tog, SKP, k1, k2 tog, SKP.
Cut red, leaving an end for sewing. Slide the remaining 5 stitches to the other needle. You do this so that as you send the yarn with a tapestry needle through the stitches you will not telescope them.

Finishing: Sew down the internal ends, hiding them in their own color areas. Sew the seams with matching color ends on the edges. Be sure your color pattern matches. For the hanger, cut a 12″ piece of red and secure each end to the ribbing seam.

Little Christmas stockings are hung empty on the tree. Christmas morning you will find that Santa Claus has filled them with wrapped candy.

Tree ornaments can be given as gifts. Or use them to decorate a package, or at every place at the dinner table. In a sturdy envelope include one, with a note, as a permanent Christmas card.

Christmas Stocking

There is only one way to make a Christmas stocking, and that is to knit it. No other kind of stocking shows the lumps and bumps of the contents so well. No other stocking can arouse so much anticipation. I recommend this project for an experienced knitter.

Supplies: Four-ply worsted-weight yarn is used. You will need 2 ounces each of red, white, and green, plus bits of other colors. For Santa's beard and the snow on the roof of the house, white 100 percent French angora is a touch of luxury. You will use four ring markers and a collection of yarn bobbins. For decorating you should have sequins, seed beads, and a very fine sewing needle.

Gauge: Use #7 needles or the size you require to get a gauge of 5 stitches per inch in stockinette stitch. You will need both a pair of single-point and a set of double-point needles.

By arranging the five designs knit into each stocking, you enable every child to have a different one. The child's name can be worked in the white band below the ribbing. Plan the designs ahead, because some are limited as to the color of the background band on which they may be knit.

Let me first give you the basic directions. I urge you to read through the general hints and the specific hints for the designs you select before you begin to knit.

Christmas stocking: With red yarn, on single-point needles, loosely cast on 60 stitches.
Right-side row: P1, *k2, p2. Repeat from *, ending the last repeat p1.
Wrong-side row: K1, *p2, k2. Repeat from *, ending the last repeat k1.
Repeat these two rows until you have a total of 8 rows. With white, work 10 rows stockinette. With green, k8, put a ring marker on your needle, k18 for row 1 of a design, ring marker, k8, ring marker, k18 for row 1 of a design, ring marker, k8. Proceed in stockinette, following the charts for the two designs. Decrease 1 stitch at each edge on rows 5 and 19. When you have completed 28 rows, change to white. You now have 56 stitches. The rings are kept in place. Proceed following the charts for the next two

designs. Decrease on rows 5 and 19. When you have completed 28 rows, change to red and change to two ring markers as follows: K17, ring marker, k18 for a design, ring marker, k17. Purl back.

Heel: Work short rows:
K5, turn, sl 1 as if to purl, p4.
K6, turn, sl 1 as if to purl, p5.
K7, turn, sl 1 as if to purl, p6.
Continue adding 1 stitch each short row through:
K12, turn, sl 1, p11.
Knit 1 full row starting the pattern, if necessary.
Work short rows:
P5, turn, sl 1 as if to knit, k4.
P6, turn, sl 1 as if to knit, k5.
Continue through:
P12, turn, sl 1, k11.

Proceed following the chart for the design. Do not consider the short rows when counting rows. Decrease on rows 5 and 19. On row 28 remove the rings.

Toe: Start using green and the dp needles. Knit 16 stitches onto each of three needles. The needle beginning at the split is needle #1. Knit around for a total of 4 rounds.

To decrease:

K6, k2 tog around.

Knit a plain round.

K5, k2 tog around.

Knit a plain round.

K4, k2 tog around.

Knit a plain round.

Continue until "K2 tog around." Do not knit a plain round. Cut the yarn and, using a tapestry needle, send it through the remaining 6 stitches and close.

Lettering: The little people in our family have their name and year of birth on their stockings. Unless the names are short, it will be difficult to knit them in or put them on with duplicate stitch. I have found it to be more satisfactory to use a double running stitch, also called Holbein. Use a tapestry needle and a piece of red yarn. Sew a letter in a running stitch over one strand and under the next, then run back over the strand you have gone under and under the strand you have gone over. The trick on the run back is to send the needle down on one side of the red yarn from the first run and up on the other side. Your tension must be loose when sewing the letters. When you are knitting a Christmas stocking for an unknown, such as one for a bazaar, why not letter-in "GOOD NOEL" or "JOY JOY JOY"?

Finishing: For most projects I tell you to work in all the ends, but with some of these designs there is not enough room. Work in the ends you can. When you have two ends very close to each other and no place to hide them, it is fair to tie a knot. Tie a firm knot, 1½ of a square knot. Be sure that you do not pull too tightly and distort the design. Cut the yarn ½" from the knot. When the ends have been finished, sew on the decorations. Do you know how to sew a sequin? With a fine needle and sewing thread, send the needle through the knitting from the back, through the hole in the sequin, through the tiny seed bead, back through the hole in the sequin and to the wrong side of the knitting. You then reach loosely to the next sequin. Sew the seam using the ends on the edge so that each band is sewn in its own color.

Hanger: Use three strands, one each of red, white, and green, and a crochet hook about size #G to chain 12". Yarn ends may be allowed at 2". Sew the hanger to the seam in the ribbing with yarn the color of the ribbing. Add a jingle bell if you wish.

General hints: Planning ahead is the first suggestion.

When changing colors for the bands, leave ends on the edge for sewing.

Red and green can be switched—that is, green ribbing, the first design band red, green heel, red toe.

To count rows, on the wrong side, the mixed-color ridge is the first row. On the heel band, count in the area without short rows.

The seam will be neater if the decreases are made on the second and third stitches from the edges. To balance the appearance, work the beginning decrease k2 tog and the decrease at the end of the row SKP.

Use the background-color bobbin on the side of the design nearest an edge of your knitting.

When a background bobbin is added, it is done to avoid having to carry the background color behind the design.

On the charts read the knit rows right to left, the purl rows left to right.

When changing from one color bobbin to another, or background color and bobbin, bring the new color under and over the old to interlock.

When you are taking two colors along, as in the center band in the ornament, bring the new color over the old. Also, to prevent puckering when taking two colors, be sure that the stitches on the right needle are expanded, not bunched up.

Never carry an unused color for more than 3 stitches without catching—twisting around the color in use. Try to avoid catching a carried color directly above a catch in the previous row. There are places in which while you are working with one color you will need to carry another along by catching it, in order to have the carried color in place for use in the next row. Plan ahead.

To store a Christmas stocking, wrap it in tissue paper, then enclose it in something airtight—a plastic bag or a cookie tin.

Think about creating a design of your own. When you use graph paper with a square grid, you have to make your designs tall and thin, because a knit stitch is not square. A square in stockinette is close to 2 stitches and 3 rows.

The designs are in order of ease in working and are upside down because that is the way they are knit.

Tree On red or white band

Bobbins:
1 background
1 green
20″ piece of brown

On row 5, a knit row and a decrease row, join the green bobbin on the 9th stitch from the ring. The background bobbin is joined on row 5 or 6, depending on which side is nearer the edge of your knitting. The tree expands one stitch in each direction every knit row. Remember to interlock. The diagonal line between the colors on the wrong side should resemble a mixed-color ridge. On row 22, while purling with green, carry the background color for 7 stitches, because you will need it there on the next row after the trunk stitches. On row 23 join the brown piece for the trunk. On row 25 or 26 discontinue use of the background bobbin and continue with the yarn from the skein. Decorate your tree with sequins.

Tree — on red or white

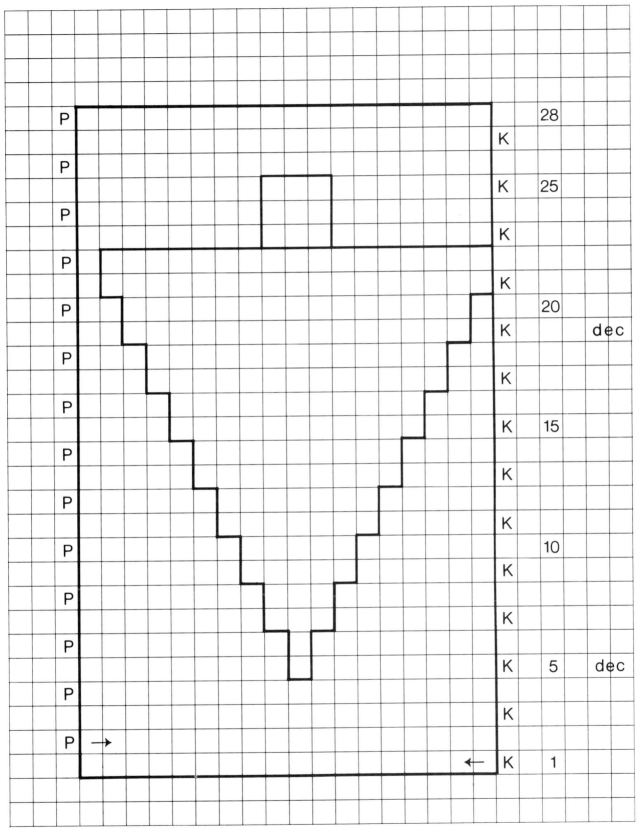

Star On red, white, or green band

Bobbins:
2 background
2 yellow

On row 4 join a yellow bobbin. On row 4 or 5 join a background bobbin, depending on which side is nearer your knitting edge. On row 10 carry the yellow for 7 stitches, in preparation for the next use. This is 1 stitch beyond the ring. Sorry about that. On row 11 carry the second background color 7 stitches for use on this row. On row 20 join the second background bobbin and the second yellow bobbin. When the star is complete, continue with the yarn from the skein.

Star — on red, white, or green

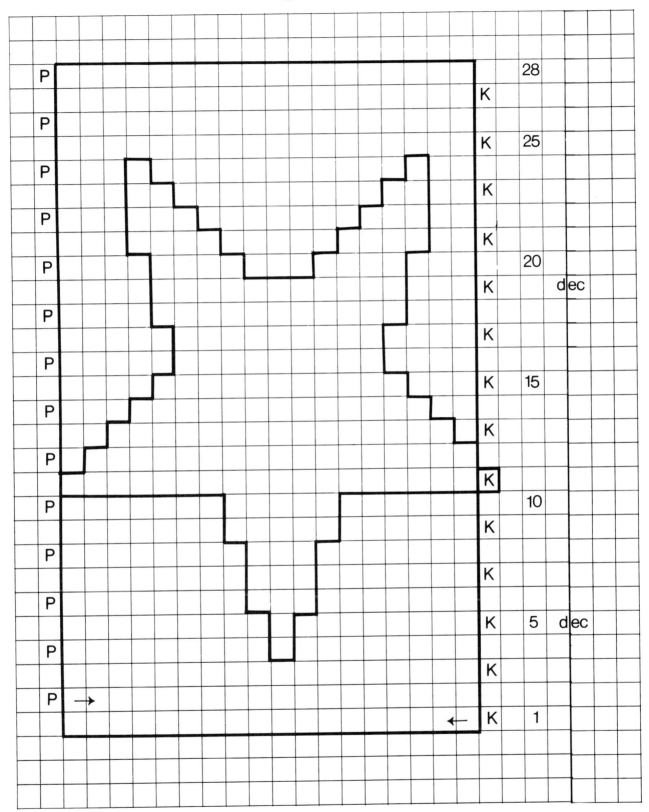

Ornament On red, white, or green band

Bobbins:
1 background
1 ornament color
1 band on ornament
1 band design

The colors in the ornament are your choice. The design is begun on row 5, a decrease row. Join the background bobbin on row 5 or 6, depending on which side is nearer the edge. Do not break off the ornament color after row 12, but bring it up loosely for row 17. On rows 13 through 16 avoid puckering. When the ornament is complete, continue with the yarn from the skein.

Ornament, color of choice — on red, white, or green

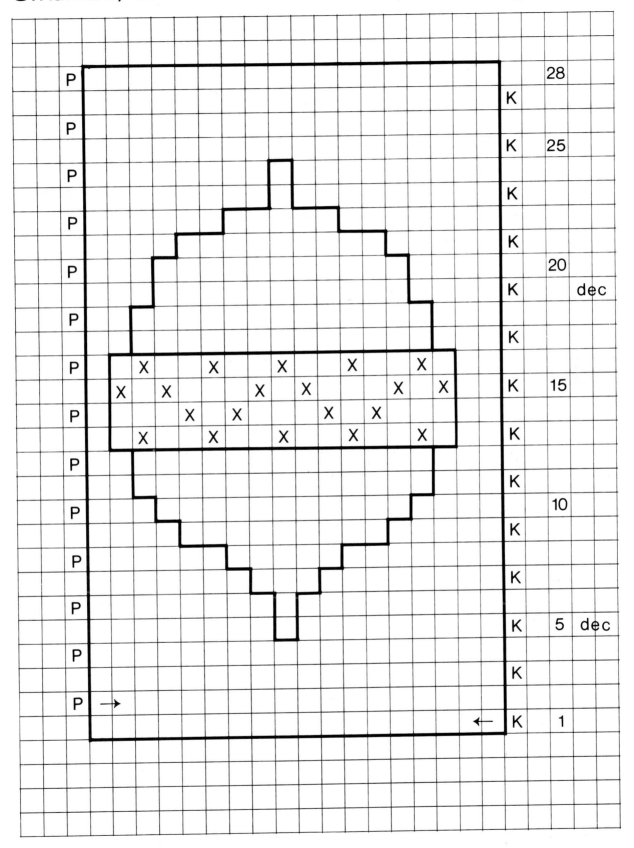

Wreath On white band

Bobbins:
2 green

The first green bobbin is joined on row 7. Carry the white yarn
from the skein loosely, remembering to catch it every second or
third stitch. The second green bobbin is added on row 10. If you
have trouble with puckering, consider adding two white bobbins. Berry and ribbon decorations are sewn on later. The berries may be in clusters of 3 red beads, or embroidery. The red of
the ribbon and the berries should match the red of the yarn.

Wreath — on white

P	28
	K
P	K 25
P	K
P	K
P	K 20
P	K dec
P	K
P	K 15
P	K
P	K
P	K 10
P	K
P	K
P	K 5 dec
P	K
P →	K 1

Candy Cane On green band

Bobbins:
1 red
1 white
12" piece of white

Join the white bobbin for the seventh purl stitch on row 4.
Carry the green yarn from the skein loosely, remembering to
catch it every second or third stitch. On row 6 join the red
bobbin. On row 7 carry the red bobbin when knitting the 4
stitches with green yarn inside the crook of the cane. The white
piece is joined on row 8. The white and red bobbins are
brought up loosely on alternate purl rows.

Candy cane — on green

P	28
	K
P	K 25
P	K
P	K
P	K
P	20
	K dec
P	K
P	K 15
P	K
P	K
P	10
	K
P	K
P	K 5 dec
P	K
P →	K
P	← K 1

Candle On red or green band

Bobbins:
1 background
1 yellow
1 white
1 brass

On row 5 join the yellow bobbin for the flame. On row 5 or 6 join the background bobbin. On row 9 join the white bobbin for the candle. I used yarn of an old gold color for the brass candle holder. Join it on row 16. On row 20 carry the second background color for the last 6 brass stitches.

Candle — on red or green

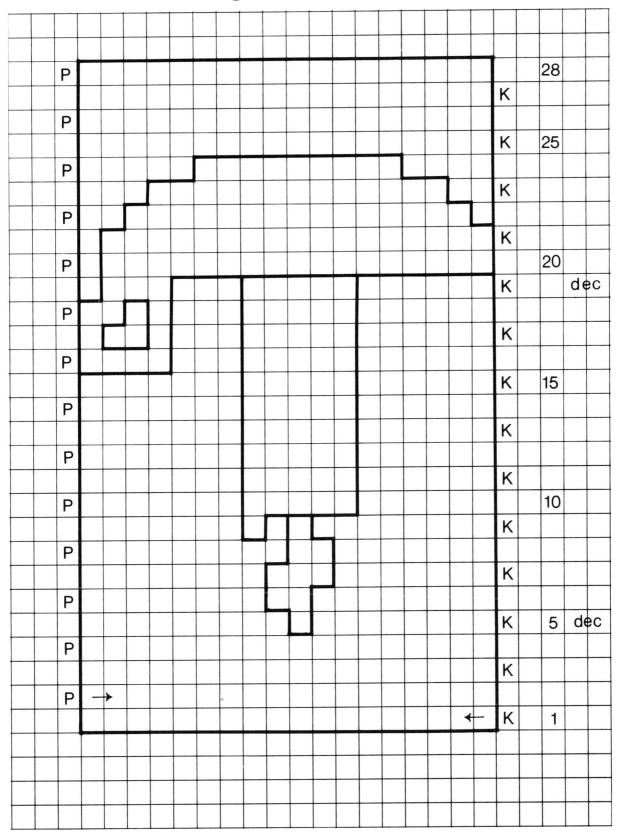

Teapot On red, white, or green

Bobbins:
1 background
1 teapot color
1 pattern color

The colors in the teapot are your choice. Join the teapot color bobbin on row 7. The background bobbin is joined on row 7 or 8, depending on which side is nearer the knitting edge. Join the pattern bobbin on row 10 and cut it after row 11. Reaching from row 11 to row 18, when it is used again, is too far. On row 13, carry the teapot color bobbin for 3 stitches, to have it ready for the spout on the next row.

Teapot, color of choice — on red, white, or green

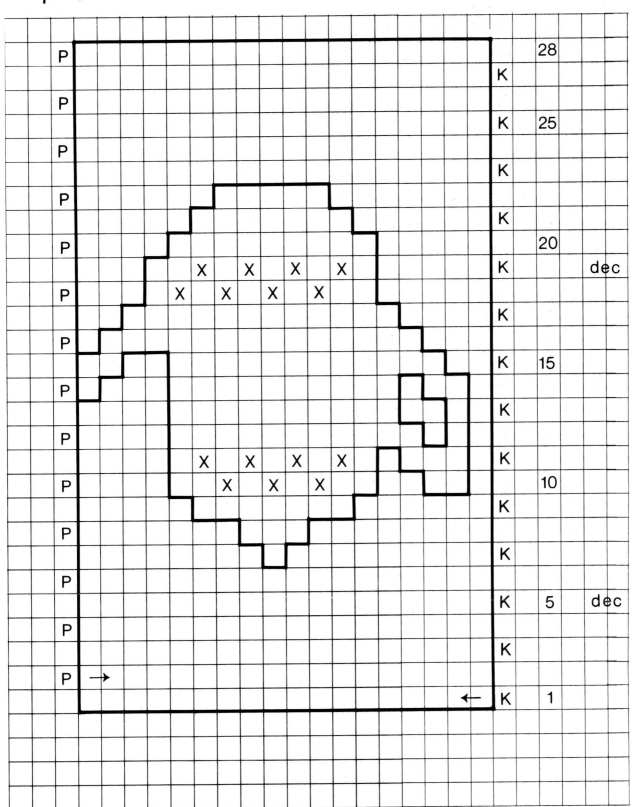

Santa On green band

Bobbins:
1 green
1 red
1 pink
1 white angora
8″ piece of blue
10″ piece of red

Join the red bobbin for Santa's hat on row 5. Remember, row 5 is a decrease row. Join the green bobbin on row 5 or 6, depending on which side is nearer the edge. Join the angora bobbin on row 9. Santa's pink face is started on row 11. Carry the angora when knitting the 5 pink stitches. The eyes are in row 13. They can be knit in with the blue piece or worked later in duplicate stitch. The nose and mouth are made on rows 15 and 17. They also can be knit in with the red piece or worked later. I prefer putting in the features in duplicate stitch when the design is complete, because they keep their shape better.

Santa — on green

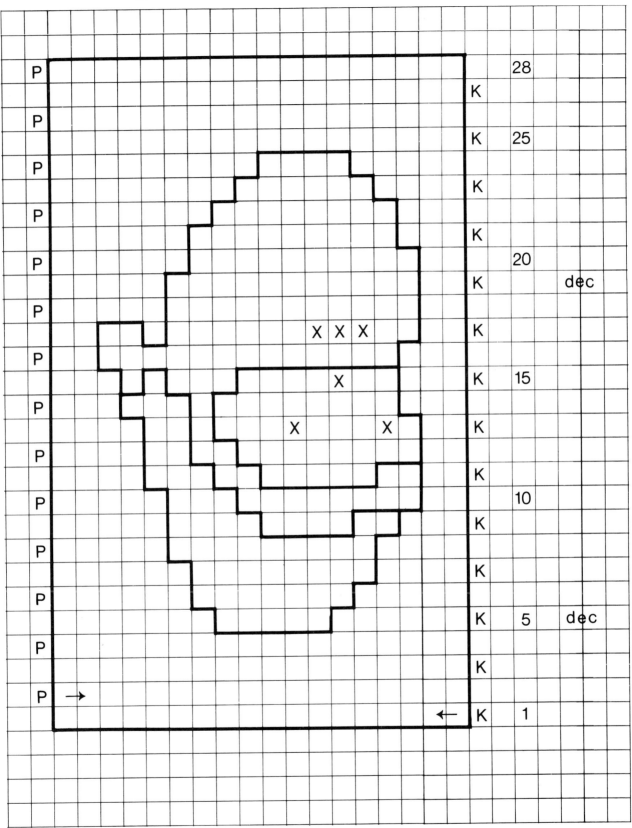

Poinsettia On white or green band

Bobbins:
2 red
1 background
8″ piece of yellow

On row 5 join a red bobbin. Join the background bobbin on row 5 or 6, depending on which side is nearer the knitting edge. The second red bobbin is joined on row 7. Carry the background color back and forth behind this bract. The first red bobbin joined is used for the 3 bracts on the left. The second red bobbin joined is used for the 3 bracts on the right. On row 8 carry the first background for 3 stitches with the red, to be ready for the next row. Carry the first red on row 10 for 5 stitches. On rows 11 and 14 change red bobbins in the center. Join the piece of yellow on row 12. Carry the second background on row 13. As you can see, the poinsettia design requires that you plan ahead. Remember the decreases.

Poinsettia — on white or green

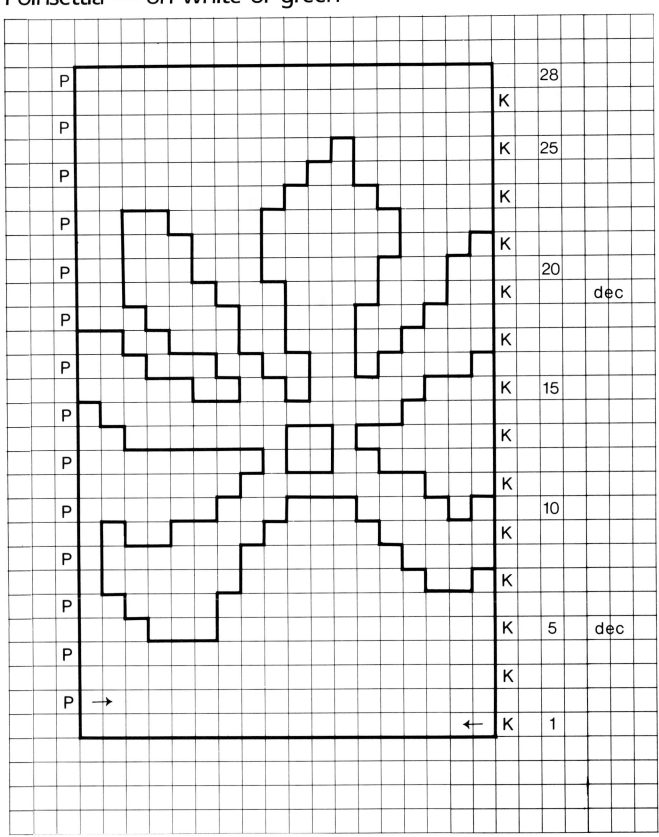

House On green band

Bobbins:
1 green
1 brown
1 white angora
1 red
2 house color
24″ piece of brown
16″ piece of angora

The house color is your choice. For clarity there are letters, A for angora and B for brown, on part of this chart. On row 3 join the angora bobbin for the smoke. Join the green bobbin on row 3 or 4, depending on which side is nearer the edge. On row 4, to purl the 3 smoke stitches, see the directions for the second row of stars in the Fourth of July flag. On row 7 join the piece of angora for the snow on the right side of the roof and the red bobbin for the chimney on the left. On row 8 bring up the angora bobbin for the snow on the left side of the roof. Add the brown piece for the next stitch, in the CENTER of the piece. One half is for the left side of the roof; the other half for the right side. The next stitch is purled with the piece of angora. On row 9 join a house-color bobbin. On row 13 join the brown bobbin for the window, then the second house-color bobbin. On row 19, a decrease row, join the red bobbin again for the door. Row 23 shows the location of the doorknob, a sequin to be sewn on later.

House — on green

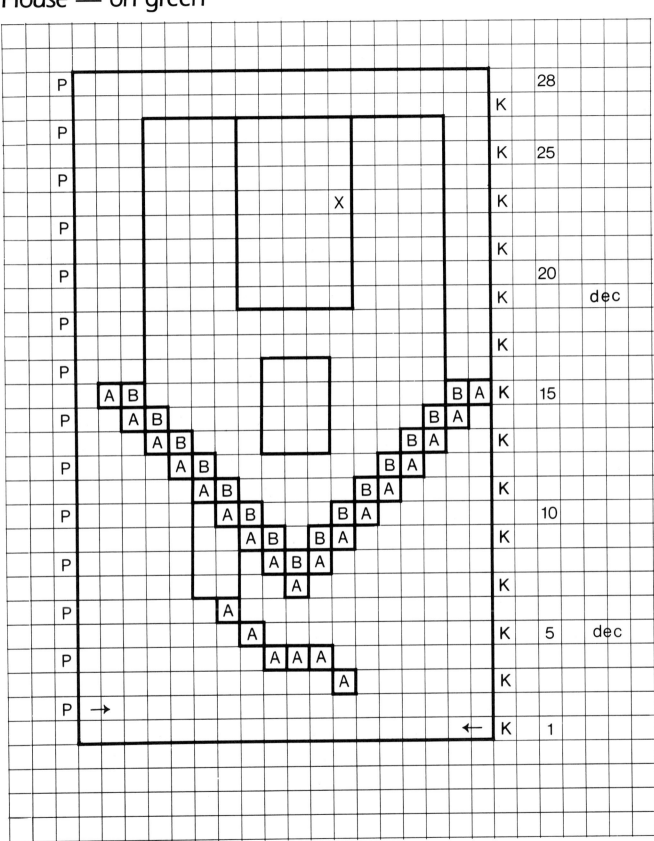